Handbook of Research on Fair Trade

Edited by

Laura T. Raynolds

Co-Director, Center for Fair & Alternative Trade and Professor, Sociology Department, Colorado State University, USA

Elizabeth A. Bennett

Assistant Professor, International Affairs Department, Lewis & Clark College and Research Associate, Center for Fair & Alternative Trade, Colorado State University, USA

EE Edward Elgar PUBLISHING

Cheltenham, UK • Northampton, MA, USA

Published by
Edward Elgar Publishing Limited
The Lypiatts
15 Lansdown Road
Cheltenham
Glos GL50 2JA
UK

Edward Elgar Publishing, Inc.
William Pratt House
9 Dewey Court
Northampton
Massachusetts 01060
USA

A catalogue record for this book
is available from the British Library

Library of Congress Control Number: 2014954945

This book is available electronically in the **Elgar**online
Social and Political Science subject collection
DOI 10.4337/9781783474622

MIX
Paper from responsible sources
FSC www.fsc.org FSC® C013056

ISBN 978 1 78347 460 8 (cased)
ISBN 978 1 78347 462 2 (eBook)

Typeset by Columns Design XML Ltd, Reading
Printed and bound in Great Britain by T.J. International Ltd, Padstow

Contents

PART III THE BUSINESS OF FAIR TRADE

PART IV FAIR TRADE AND INTERNATIONAL DEVELOPMENT

Figures

Tables

Contributors

Christopher M. Bacon is an Assistant Professor in the Department of Environmental Studies and Sciences at Santa Clara University. He has a PhD from UC Santa Cruz and did postdoctoral work at UC Berkeley. His research focuses on environmental and food justice in the Americas and addresses issues of governance, food security and sustainable livelihoods. As an environmental social scientist, he is interested in deepening and diversifying a dialogue about interdependent society–nature relationships. Formal training in environmental studies, the wisdom of practical teachers, insight from marginal communities and student curiosity inform his research and teaching. Bacon often uses a community-based participatory action research approach. He has published a book titled *Confronting the Coffee Crisis: Fair Trade, Sustainable Livelihoods and Ecosystems in Mexico and Central America* (2008) and several recent articles in *Ecology and Society* and the *Journal of Political Ecology*.

Gaëlle Balineau is an Economist and Research Coordinator at the French Agency for Development (*Agence Française de Développement*, AFD). She holds a PhD in Development Economics from the Centre for Studies and Research on International Development (CERDI, Clermont-Ferrand, France). Her research interests include development and agricultural economics (innovation and adoption pathways, certification schemes and aid-for-trade programs), economics of standards, value chains analysis and responsible consumption. Before she joined the AFD in 2014, she worked for the World Bank and international agro-food companies, mainly on agricultural sustainability and impact evaluation programs. Fair trade was the subject of her PhD thesis and she has published on this theme in the *Journal of Business Ethics* and *World Development*. From May 2013 to May 2014, she chaired Fairness Fr, the French-speaking branch of Fairness, an international network bringing together academics working on subjects associated with fair and ethical trade.

Leonardo Becchetti is Full Professor of Economics at the University of Rome Tor Vergata where he is Director of the graduate course in European Economy and Business Law and of the Masters in International Development and Cooperation. Leonardo is also President of the Ethical Committee of Banca Popolare Etica, a blogger and an editorialist. He holds an MSc from the London School of Economics and a PhD from Oxford University. He is author of around 360 works, which include 11 edited books, 90 (published or forthcoming) publications in international journals (among them *Journal of Public Economics*, *Journal of Money Credit and Banking*, *World Development*, *Journal of Banking and Finance*, *Journal of International Money and Finance*, *Journal of Business Ethics*), 53 publications in Italian journals, 73 chapters of books and several working papers. His main fields of research are fair trade, microfinance, economics of happiness, financial economics and ethics and economics.

Elizabeth A. Bennett is an Assistant Professor of International Affairs at Lewis & Clark College in Portland, Oregon, and a Research Associate at the Center for Fair & Alternative Trade at Colorado State University. Her research centers on issues of inequality in sustainable development, global governance, social enterprise, ethical certifications and civic engagement. Her current agenda examines the factors that facilitate or impede North–South power sharing in voluntary standards-setting organizations and focuses on an in-depth historical study of Fairtrade International. Elizabeth is co-author of *The Civic Imagination: Making a Difference in American Political Life*, a political ethnography of civic engagement in America (2014). She has also written chapters for edited volumes on social enterprise and fair trade and published in the peer reviewed journals the *American Journal of Sociology*, *Globalizations* and the *Journal for International Policy Studies.* Elizabeth holds a MALD in political economy and international development at The Fletcher School at Tufts University (2008) and an AM and PhD in Political Science from Brown University (2014).

Valéry Bezençon is Professor of Marketing at the University of Neuchâtel in Switzerland. He focuses his research on social marketing and sustainable products' marketing. He has studied fair trade from a consumer behavior and marketing perspective, and published his work on fair trade in the *Journal of Business Ethics*, *European Journal of Marketing*, *Psychology & Marketing* and *Sustainable Development.* He founded and manages the Fair Trade Institute, a network that promotes information exchange within the scientific community and between researchers and practitioners.

Keith Brown is an Assistant Professor of Sociology at Saint Joseph's University. His research and teaching interests include fair trade, ethical consumption, globalization, culture, identity formation and ethnographic methods. His book is entitled *Buying into Fair Trade: Culture, Morality and Consumption* (2013). The book examines what it means to be an ethical consumer, how individuals became a part of the fair trade movement and how consumers make sense of the contradictions involved in the search for status while shopping for a cause. *Buying into Fair Trade* also discusses the limits and possibilities involved in trying to change the world through shopping. Keith's research and writings have appeared in *Sociological Forum*, *Contexts*, *Qualitative Sociology*, *Sociological Inquiry*, *Social Forces*, *Contemporary Sociology*, the *Journal of Disability Policy Studies* and the *Analyses of Social Issues and Public Policy*.

Sandy Brown's work attempts to bridge some of the many divides between agricultural production, activism and academia. Broadly focused on the political economy and governance of agrifood systems within the United States and Latin America, she has conducted research on fair trade certification in the banana sector, labor regulation in organic agriculture and the politics of pesticide regulation in California's strawberry industry. She received her PhD in Geography at the University of California, Berkeley, and is currently Assistant Professor and Faculty Director of the Public Affairs Program at the University of San Francisco and a Research Associate affiliated with the University of California, Santa Cruz.

Stefano Castriota has a PhD in Economics and Finance from the University of Rome Tor Vergata, an MPhil in Finance from the Stockholm School of Economics and a Masters in Economics from Bocconi University in Milan. He has been a visiting fellow at the IMF in Washington and Pompeu Fabra University in Barcelona. Stefano is an applied academic researcher; his interests range from industrial to labor and development economics.

Pierluigi Conzo is an Assistant Professor at the University of Turin, Department of Economics and Statistics 'Cognetti de Martiis'. He holds a PhD in Economic Theory and Institutions from the University of Rome Tor Vergata. His research focuses on development and experimental economics, social capital, fair trade, microfinance and impact analysis.

Eileen Davenport holds a BA in Sociology (Exeter), and MA and MPhil degrees in Planning (Nottingham Trent). Currently she is an adjunct faculty member at Royal Roads University supervising graduate research projects and fieldwork practicums in the Human Security and Peacebuilding, Conflict Analysis and Management, and Disaster and Emergency Management programs. Eileen chaired the Standards and Monitoring Committee of the International Fair Trade Association (IFAT) from 2004 to 2006 and joined the World Fair Trade Organization (WFTO) taskforce on the relationship between fair trade and the solidarity economy in 2013. She has published a number of articles with William Low relating to the fair trade movement.

Bob Doherty (formerly of Liverpool John Moores University and Liverpool Hope University) is Professor of Marketing and Director of Faculty at The York Management School, University of York. Bob specializes in the marketing aspects of fair trade social enterprises. He is an Honorary Research Fellow in the Third Sector Research Centre at the University of Birmingham. Bob has also been editor in chief for eight years of the *Social Enterprise Journal*. Prior to moving into academia, Bob spent five years as Head of Marketing at the Fairtrade social enterprise, Divine Chocolate. Bob is currently the Chair of the Liverpool Fairtrade Steering Committee. Bob has published on fair trade in the *Journal of Business Ethics*, *Business History Journal* and the *Journal of Strategic Marketing*.

Christy Getz is an Associate Cooperative Extension Specialist in UC Berkeley's Department of Environmental Science, Policy and Management. Trained as a sociologist, she conducts applied research and outreach that promote socially just food systems in California. Currently, her programs focus on: social justice and labor in food systems; challenges and opportunities facing immigrant and refugee farmers; urban agriculture; and community food security. Getz is chair of the California Communities and Food Systems Program Team of the UC Division of Agriculture and Natural Resources.

Michael K. Goodman is a Professor of Geography (Environment and Development) at the University of Reading, UK where he is chair of the Human Environments Research Group. He holds a PhD in Environmental Studies from UC Santa Cruz where he focused on the early discourses and materialities of fair trade's mainstreaming. His work on the corporatization of fair trade has been published in *Geoforum*, *Transactions* and in a co-authored book entitled *Alternative Food Networks* (2012). Other work has engaged with the wider 'celebritization' and shifting cultural politics of consumption, environment and development – of which fair trade plays a key role – in the context of food, climate change and new forms of transnational market and charity-led development. Recent publications include two co-edited books: *Food Transgressions: Making Sense of Contemporary Food Politics* (2014) and *Consuming Space: Placing Consumption in Perspective* (2010). He is also editor of two book series: one on critical food politics and another on contemporary food studies. Forthcoming publications will appear in *Geoforum*, *Food, Culture and Society* and *Environmental Communications*. He is currently working on a textbook on the geographies of food.

Nicholas Greenfield is a Sociology PhD student at Colorado State University working with the Center for Fair & Alternative Trade. He is a UK and South African national with a MA in Critical Global Politics from the University of Exeter. His MA thesis analyzes to what extent the fair trade movement can defetishize the commodity, drawing on the case of gold. Nicholas's current research interests include how reciprocity is formed in global trade through the everyday practices of consumers and producers.

Agatha Herman is a Lecturer in Human Geography and Leverhulme Early Career Fellow at the University of Reading, UK. Her research interests focus on questions of ethics, justice and resilience within food production systems, particularly analyzing their impact on the everyday spaces, practices and livelihoods of producers. Her work on the power relations and tactical discourses of fair trade has been published in *Environment and Planning A*, the *Journal of Environmental Policy and Planning* and *Geoforum*. She is currently working on a Leverhulme Trust funded project that is investigating the power of fair trade to promote resilient and ethical development within and beyond its producer communities.

Alex Hughes is Reader in Economic Geography at Newcastle University in the United Kingdom. Her research interests lie in the fields of ethical and fair trade, corporate responsibility, retailing and global commodity chains. She has published more than 20 journal papers and book chapters on the themes of corporate ethical trading approaches and their impacts on supply networks. She is co-editor (with Suzanne Reimer) of *Geographies of Commodity Chains* (2004) and, with Jane Pollard and Cheryl McEwan, of *Postcolonial Economies* (2011). Her research has been funded by the United Kingdom's Economic and Social Research Council, The Leverhulme Trust, the British Academy and the Nuffield Foundation, including projects on UK–US contrasts in corporate ethical trading approaches, the knowledge economy surrounding practices of ethical auditing in supply chains, the effects of global economic recession on corporate ethical trading, the impacts of labor codes on Kenyan cut flower production, the interplay of social and environmental standards in the case of sustainable wildflower harvesting in South Africa and the introduction of ethical trading standards into the UK's public sector.

Benjamin Huybrechts is an Assistant Professor at HEC Management School, University of Liege (Belgium). He is the holder of the SRIW-Sowecsom Chair in Social Enterprise Management and belongs to several academic networks including the Fairness (FR) research network on fair trade. He holds a PhD in Economics and Management (University of

Liege) and has been on a postdoctoral research stay at the Skoll Centre for Social Entrepreneurship, Saïd Business School (University of Oxford). Besides several book chapters and a book on *Fair Trade Social Enterprises* (2012), he has published articles in several journals such as the *Journal of Business Ethics* (co-editing a special issue on fair trade), the *Annals of Public and Co-operative Economics* and the *Social Enterprise Journal*. His research topics include social enterprise and institutional theory, social innovation, hybrid organizational models, institutional logics, governance, and institutionalization processes. In the context of the Master's program in Social Enterprise Management at HEC Management School, Dr. Huybrechts teaches classes on social innovation and social enterprise governance, as well as a doctoral seminar in social entrepreneurship.

Jennifer Keahey is an Assistant Professor of Sociology at Arizona State University and an Associate of the Center for Fair & Alternative Trade (CFAT). She possesses a professional background in multiple world regions, including West and Southern Africa where she has conducted ethnographic and action-oriented fieldwork with producers. Her research explores agrifood system dimensions within the broader context of alternative globalization and sustainable development. With a focus on applied scholarship, her work seeks to generate practical solutions to social problems via a critical praxis of reconciliation, integration and adaptation.

Ronan Le Velly is Assistant Professor in Economic Sociology in Montpellier SupAgro (France) and member of the Joint Research Unit Innovation and Development in Agriculture and the Agri-Food Sector. His works focus on the organization of the various supply chains that are established between the producers and the consumers of fair trade. He is also interested in local and short food supply chains, especially those that are built to offer quality food to schools. His research aims to better know the functioning and impacts of alternative agrifood systems and to contribute to the sociological understanding of markets. Ronan Le Velly has published numerous articles on these topics, notably in the *Revue Française de Sociologie*, *Sociologie du Travail* and *Sociologia Ruralis*. He is the author of the book *Sociologie du marché* (2012).

April Linton holds a PhD in Sociology from the University of Washington. She is the author of *Fair Trade from the Ground Up: New Markets for Social Justice* (2012) and numerous articles about fair trade from producer, consumer and activist perspectives. She is co-editor of *The Global Governance of Food* (2009). April has served on the National

Steering Committee for Fair Trade Campaigns. In 2012 and 2013 she worked for the Fair Labor Association.

Mary A. Littrell is Professor and Department Head Emerita in Design and Merchandising at Colorado State University. Since 2011 she has been a Research Associate at the Museum of International Folk Art in Santa Fe, New Mexico. Dr. Littrell's research addresses multiple facets of business social responsibility, with special focus on artisan enterprises. In her research she examines models for how textile artisan enterprises achieve viability in the increasingly competitive international market for artisan products. Recent books with co-author Dr. Marsha Dickson include *Social Responsibility in the Global Market: Fair Trade of Cultural Products* and *Artisans and Fair Trade: Crafting Development*. In recognition of their research in India, the co-authors were named Rockefeller Center Scholars in Bellagio, Italy. She is currently conducting research for a new book on models for artisan sustainability, leadership development and control of cultural property in the global market. Dr. Littrell is a Fellow of the International Textile and Apparel Association and the Society for Applied Anthropology. She served as President of the International Textile and Apparel Association and as Board Member of the Textile Society of America. Dr. Littrell received her MA from Michigan State University and her PhD from Purdue University.

William Low holds a BA and MA from the University of British Columbia and a PhD from the London School of Economics. Trained as an Economist, he is currently a Professor teaching sustainable business at Royal Roads University, with a particular interest in sustainable consumption. He has taught in Canada, the United States, the United Kingdom, Australia, Thailand and New Zealand. William also does consulting work for private companies and NGOs, including The Warehouse Group, Oxfam International and UNICEF. His recent research, with Eileen Davenport, has been published in *Social Enterprise Journal*, *Journal of Business Ethics*, *Auckland University Business Review* and *Critical Perspectives on International Business*.

Sarah Lyon is an Associate Professor of anthropology at the University of Kentucky. She is the author of *Coffee and Community: Maya Farmers and Fair Trade Markets* (2011), winner of the Society for Economic Anthropology's Book Prize and the co-editor of *Fair Trade and Social Justice: Global Ethnographies* (2010) and *Global Tourism: Cultural Heritage and Economic Encounters* (2012). She has also published multiple journal articles on fair trade. In addition to her ongoing research on coffee, fair trade certification and the gendered dimensions of economic development in Mexico and Central America, she is currently investigating the fair trade movement and ethical consumption in the United States. At the University of Kentucky, Sarah teaches courses on economic anthropology, ethical consumption and globalization. She is a past editor of the *Anthropology of Work Review* and the current editor of *Human Organization*.

Rie Makita is an Associate Professor in the Graduate School of Social Design Studies at Rikkyo University, Japan. Her policy research and advisory work for Japan International Cooperation Agency (JICA) and other related organizations has focused on rural development and sustainable livelihoods in Asia and Africa. Her first book, titled *Livelihood Diversification and Landlessness in Rural Bangladesh* (2007), was awarded the 12th Okita Memorial Prize for International Development Research in Japan. Makita is interested in how fair trade can(not) work for poverty alleviation and environmental conservation in the global South and how fair trade can be incorporated in the livelihoods of producers and workers. She has published refereed articles on fair trade in *Development in Practice*, *Development Policy Review* and *Geoforum*. Makita holds a Master of Professional Studies (Agriculture) degree from Cornell University and a PhD in Geographical Science from the Australian National University.

Adrienne Martin is Director of Program Development and a Social and Institutional Development and Evaluation Specialist at the Natural Resources Institute, University of Greenwich, UK. She has over 35 years experience in international development and research relating to poverty, livelihoods, agriculture and trade. Adrienne's work has spanned detailed rural and urban studies and policy and program level evaluation, analysis and advice. She has worked in over 33 countries in Africa, Asia and Latin America. Her research expertise includes impact evaluation methodology development, value chain development and poverty reduction, gender and value chains, social impacts of standard systems, participatory research approaches, and local institutional development and capacity building. She has a particular interest in the challenges of impact assessment of sustainability standards and other trade based initiatives directed at alleviating poverty; for example, a four-year poverty impact assessment of sustainability standards and currently the evaluation of the 'Trade and Global Value Chains Initiative', which is supporting social upgrading in global value chains (both funded by DFID UK).

Hannah Maryanski is a double major in English and Environmental Studies at Santa Clara University and is from Ventura, CA. She has studied abroad in Bologna, Italy, and is an active blogger and hiker. Her writing has been published in the *Packinghouse Review*. Hannah has interned with the Community Agroecology Network and hopes to pursue a career in sustainable agriculture after graduation.

Manush McConway is a PhD candidate in fair trade at Durham University, United Kingdom. She is a Durham University MBA graduate with over a decade of experience in managing small and medium-size businesses. Prior to her doctoral research, Manush was a director of a management consultancy specializing in enterprise training and development. She has a particular interest in business enterprises that contribute to the alleviation of poverty and the subject of leadership.

Geoff Moore is Professor of Business Ethics at Durham University Business School, United Kingdom. He is the author of several papers on fair trade, and has had a long-standing practical engagement including being a Non-Executive Director on the Boards of Gateway World Shop, Shared Interest and Traidcraft. He has published extensively on the application of virtue ethics to business organizations.

Tad Mutersbaugh is a Professor of Geography at the University of Kentucky. He has been studying the social, political and gender impacts of certification on fair trade and organic producers in Oaxaca and other areas of Mexico for 15 years. He has published 16 articles and book chapters on the political economy and lived experience of certification. His current research examines the relationship between certified fair trade-organic production and the feminization of farming in Oaxacan indigenous communities.

Valerie Nelson is Reader in Rural Development and a Principal Scientist in the Livelihoods and Institutions Department at the Natural Resources Institute, University of Greenwich, UK. She has worked at the NRI since 1996, with prior experience at the University of the State of Mexico and Oxfam GB. Valerie conducts research and consultancy on sustainability standards and market led development especially studies on their poverty impact and politics. She has worked on impact assessments since the late 1990s focusing on fair trade including coffee, tea, cocoa, cotton, wine, vegetables and flowers in Africa, Latin America and Asia for a number of standard bodies and donors. She completed a four-year poverty impact assessment of sustainability standards for DFID in late 2013. Livelihood and climate change adaptation issues are also a particular focus as is participatory development and governance, including pioneering work in participatory video. She is currently leading a program on Equitable Trade and Responsible Business at the NRI and is a council member of the UK Development Studies Association. She has published in numerous journals. Currently, Valerie is evaluating a DFID programme entitled the 'Trade and Global Value Chains Initiative' and completing a fair trade coffee impact study for Fairtrade International.

Laura T. Raynolds is the Co-founder and Co-director of the Center for Fair & Alternative Trade (CFAT) and Professor of Sociology at Colorado State University. She is co-editor and a lead author of the seminal book, *Fair Trade: The Challenges of Transforming Globalization* (2007). Raynolds is the author of over 37 articles and book chapters as well as numerous reports and popular press pieces on fair trade and related themes. Her fair trade articles in *World Development*, *Sociologia Ruralis*, *Journal of Rural Studies* and *Agriculture and Human Values* are identified as being among the most downloaded and cited articles in these journals. Raynolds has been awarded grants from the National Science Foundation, the Ford Foundation and the John D. and Catherine T. MacArthur Foundation for her path breaking fair trade research in Latin America and the Caribbean. She is an active participant in national and international conferences as an organizer and presenter. Raynolds holds a PhD in Development Sociology from Cornell University.

Darryl Reed teaches in the Business and Society program at York University in Toronto. His research interests include business ethics, development ethics, corporate social responsibility and international regulation. His primary research focus, however, is on the social economy in the context of development, with a special emphasis on cooperatives and fair trade movements. He currently serves as the President of the Canadian Association for Studies in Co-operation.

Marie-Christine Renard is a Sociologist from the University of Louvain in Belgium. She studied a Master degree in Social Anthropology in the Universidad Nacional Autónoma de México and a PhD in Rural Studies (Sociology) at the University of Toulouse le-Mirail in France. She works as Professor and Researcher in the Department of Rural Sociology at Chapingo University, Mexico, and belongs to the Mexican National Researchers System. She has carried out research on peasants and Indian movements in Chiapas, the coffee commodity market, quality certification in agro-food and fair trade. Marie-Christine is currently working on the governance of fair trade and other alternative networks in the agro-food system. She is outgoing President of the Research Committee 40 on Sociology of Agriculture and Food at the International Sociological Association (2010–2014); she is a member of the Editorial Board of the *Journal of Rural Studies* and the *International Journal of Sociology of Food and Agriculture*.

Robert A. Rice has worked at the Smithsonian Migratory Bird Center (SMBC) since 1995, focusing on policy issues related to migratory bird habitat and conservation. His research centers on managed lands' impact upon the environment, including the ways that new technologies transform physical and social landscapes. A central theme of his publications is the management of tropical agroecosystems and their relation to ecological processes, as well as the socio-economic benefits derived from agroforestry systems. He has worked with colleagues to develop scientifically based criteria for shade coffee (the 'Bird Friendly' certification), which identify coffee systems that can serve as viable, quality habitat.

Lone Riisgaard, PhD, is an Associate Professor at the Department of Society and Globalization at Roskilde University, Denmark. She has carried out extensive research on multi-stakeholder initiatives in the cut-flower industry and has for many years been involved in research related to the governance of agricultural value chains, regulation through private sustainability standards and the regulation and agency of labor in agricultural value chains.

Claudia Rosty is an advanced PhD student in Sociology at Colorado State University and a research assistant at the Center for Fair & Alternative Trade. She has been awarded an Inter-American Foundation Fellowship to conduct her dissertation research on 'Fair Trade Certified coffee estates: Can Fair Trade promote workers' empowerment and gender equity in Brazilian coffee plantations?' Claudia's research interests include globalization, development, gender and social movements.

Alastair M. Smith is a Research Fellow at the School of Planning and Geography, Cardiff University, and specializes in international development and planning. His work has focused on the role of international trade in promoting socio-economic development in line with social justice aspirations. Alastair has complemented research and teaching with consultancy projects for national and international NGOs. He is also the Founding Director of a knowledge exchange network focused on fair trade, Fairness UK; is the Chair of the Fair Trade Cardiff steering group (the world's first Fair Trade City); and a member of the Board of Directors of Fair Trade Wales (administering trade justice campaigns in the world's first Fair Trade Country).

Sally Smith is an Independent Research Consultant. Her research centers on trade, development, poverty and gender, with specialist knowledge of fair and ethical trade and the gendered economy. Her research has covered agricultural and industrial sectors across Africa, Asia and Latin

America, with journal publications including *World Development*, *Gender and Development* and the *Journal of Business Ethics*. She has provided research and advisory services to a range of organizations, including Fairtrade International, Ethical Trading Initiative, World Food Programme, Oxfam, Comic Relief, WIEGO, Cadburys plc and Marks and Spencer plc. She is a member of various committees, including Comic Relief's Trade Programme Advisory Group and Women and Girls Advisory Group, and Fairtrade International's Gender Working Group. Sally was a Researcher at the Institute of Development Studies (University of Sussex) from 2002 to 2010 and prior to that spent eight years working as a Project Manager in Guatemala and Cambodia.

Dimitris Stevis is Professor of International Politics at Colorado State University. His research interests revolve around the social regulation of the world political economy, with particular attention to labor and environmental regulation. During the last several years he has published on global environmental politics, socio-environmental justice, socio-technical transitions, union environmentalism, transnational labor politics and on the formation and implementation of global framework agreements. He is co-editor of *Advances in International Environmental Politics*, 2nd edition (2014) and co-author of *Globalization and Labor: Democratizing Global Governance* (2008). He is currently studying union environmentalism and the efforts of unions and environmentalists to find common ground globally and in the United States.

Steven Suranovic received a PhD in Economics from Cornell University. He is currently an Associate Professor of Economics and International Affairs at the George Washington University. He has published in numerous academic journals, including the *Journal of International Economics*, the *Canadian Journal of Economics*, *World Economy* and the *Journal of Health Economics*. His books include: *A Moderate Compromise: Policy Choice in an Era of Globalization* (2011), offering a critique of current methods of policy evaluation and choice and suggesting a simple, principled and moderate alternative, and *International Economics: Theory and Policy* (2010), an international economics textbook. His diverse research interests include international trade policy analysis, fairness in international trade and the behavioral economics of cigarette addiction and dieting. His most recent research evaluates market ethics, including unfair trade policies, and examines the world's addiction to fossil fuels with its implications for global climate change.

Anne Tallontire is a Senior Lecturer in the Sustainability Research Institute at the University of Leeds, United Kingdom, where she teaches on corporate social responsibility and international development. In 1999

Anne completed one of the first PhDs on fair trade in Africa, focusing on the relationship between the 100 per cent fair trade enterprise Cafédirect and one of its producer groups, the Kilimanjaro Native Cooperative Union (KNCU) in Tanzania. Before taking up an academic position, Anne was a Research Fellow at the Natural Resources Institute, University of Greenwich, playing a key role in the Natural Resources and Ethical Trade program. She has undertaken research and consultancy for bilateral and multilateral donors and sustainability standards organizations, including Fairtrade International, particularly in East and Southern Africa. She was Principal Investigator for a DFID–ESRC project on 'The Governance Implications of Private Standards Initiatives in Agri-food Chains', which involved field work in the Kenyan export horticulture sector. She has written widely on fair trade and other standards, publishing in international development and agriculture journals (including *World Development*, *Third World Quarterly*, *Agriculture and Human Values*, *Journal of International Development, Development in Practice*, *Social Enterprise Journal*). She is motivated by enhancing the voice of marginalized producers in standards development and enhancing the impact of trade for those at the bottom of the value chain.

Peter Utting is International Co-ordinator at the Center for Social Economy (CES) in Nicaragua. Until August 2014 he was Deputy Director, United Nations Research Institute for Social Development (UNRISD). He specializes in research on corporate social responsibility, social dimensions of sustainable development and social and solidarity economy. With a doctorate degree in Sociology and working at the interface of various disciplines, he has authored or edited 19 books and more than 40 journal articles and chapters. Recent co-edited books include *Social and Solidarity Economy: Beyond the Fringe* (forthcoming); *Business Regulation and Non-State Actors: Whose Standards? Whose Development?* (2012) and *Corporate Social Responsibility and Regulatory Governance* (2010).

Bradley R. Wilson is an Assistant Professor of Geography at West Virginia University. For the past ten years he has been engaged in ethnographic research on the Fair Trade coffee campaign in the United States and Nicaragua. His work on Fair Trade coffee and certified product networks has appeared in journals such as *Geoforum*, *Antipode*, *Applied Geography* and *Human Organization*. His current research explores changing perspectives on the politics and practice of local and global solidarity among consumers and farmers through a case study of the development of the Fair Trade coffee network in post-revolutionary Nicaragua.

Abbreviations

AGICES	Association of Italian Fair Trade Organizations
AGM	Annual General Meeting
AIACA	All India Artisans and Craftworkers Welfare Association
AJP	Agricultural Justice Project
AMSA	United Agroindustries of Mexico (Agroindustrias Unidas de Mexico S.A.)
ANAPQUI	The National Association of Quinoa Producers
ATC	Alter Trade Corporation
ATFI	Alter Trade Foundation Incorporation
ATO	Alternative Trade/Trading Organization
BAFTS	British Association of Fair Trade Shops
BAMCO	Bon Appétit Management Company
B-BBEE	Broad-Based Black Economic Empowerment
BEE	Black Economic Empowerment
BKCU	Banyankole Kweterana Cooperative Union
BSCA	Brazil Specialty Coffee Association
BTC	Belgian Development Agency
CAFOD	Catholic Agency for Overseas Development
CARP	Comprehensive Agrarian Reform Program
CBA	Collective Bargaining Agreement
CEO	Chief Executive Officer
CEPCO	State Coordinator of Oaxacan Coffee Producers (Coordinador Estatal de Productores de Café de Oaxaca)
CFAT	Center for Fair and Alternative Trade
CHAI	Community Health Advancement Initiative
CIW	Coalition of Immokalee Workers
CLAC	Latin American and Caribbean Network of Small Fair Trade Producers (Coordinadora Latinoamericana y del Caribe de Comercio Justo)
COFTA	Cooperation for Fair Trade in Africa

COP	Communication on Progress
COSA	Committee on Sustainability Assessment
CSPO	Certified Sustainable Palm Oil
CSR	Corporate Social Responsibility
CTM	Cooperazione Terzo Mondo
DFID	Department for International Development
DFTA	Domestic Fair Trade Association
DO	Designation of Origin
DRC	Democratic Republic of Congo
EFI	Equitable Food Initiative
EFTA	European Fair Trade Association
EPA	Environmental Protection Agency
ESG	Environmental, Social and Governance
ESRC	Economic and Social Research Council
EUR	Euro
FairTSA	Fair Trade Sustainability Alliance
FAO	Food and Agriculture Organization of the United Nations
FDI	Foreign Direct Investment
FINE	Acronym of four organizations' names: Fairtrade Labelling Organizations International (now Fairtrade International), the International Fair Trade Association (now the World Fair Trade Organization or WFTO), the Network of European Worldshops (NEWS!) and the European Fair Trade Association (EFTA)
FLA	Fair Labor Association
FLO	Fairtrade Labelling Organizations International (now Fairtrade International)
FLSA	Fairtrade Label South Africa
FSC	Forest Stewardship Council
FSP	Fairtrade Sourcing Program
FTF	Fair Trade Federation OR Fairtrade Foundation
FTO	Fair Trade Organization OR Fairtrade/Organic Certified
FToA	Fair Traders of Australia
FUNAI	National Indian Foundation
FUNDEPPO	Foundation of Organized Small Producers

GBP	Pound Sterling (Great Britain)
GFA	Global Framework Agreement
GHG	Greenhouse Gas
GMCR	Green Mountain Coffee Roasters
GMO	Genetically Modified Organism
GPN	Global Production Network
GUF	Global Union Federation
GVC	Global Value Chain
HIIK	Heidelberg Institute for International Conflict Research
IADB	InterAmerican Development Bank
ICA	International Coffee Agreement
ICCO	Interchurch Organization for Development Cooperation
ICT	Information and Communications Technology
IDH	Dutch Sustainable Trade Initiative
IEC	International Electrotechnical Commission
IFAD	International Fund for Agricultural Development
IFAT	International Federation for Alternative Trade
IFBWW	International Federation of Building and Wood Workers
IFC	International Finance Corporation
IFTTC	International Fair Trade Towns Committee
ILO	International Labor Organization
ILRF	International Labor Rights Forum
IMF	International Monetary Fund
IMO	Institute for Marketecology (now Fair for Life)
INMECAFE	Mexican National Coffee Institute
IPCC	Intergovernmental Panel on Climate Change
IRIN	Integrated Regional Information Networks
ISEAL	International Social and Environmental Accreditation and Labeling
ISMAM	Indígenas de la Sierra Madre de Motozintla
ISO	International Organization for Standardization
ITGLWF	International Textile, Garment and Leather Workers' Federations
ITUC	International Trade Union Confederation

IUF	International Union of Food, Agricultural, Hotel, Restaurant, Catering, Tobacco and Allied Workers' Associations
KEWWO	Kenya Women Workers Organization
KHRC	Kenya Human Rights Commission
KNCU	Kilimanjaro Native Cooperative Union
KPAWU	Kenya Plantation and Agricultural Workers Union
KTDA	Kenya Tea Development Agency
LFTO	Local Fair Trade Organization
MCC	Mennonite Central Committee
MDG	Millennium Development Goal
MFN	Most Favored Nation
MHN	Max Havelaar Netherlands
MNC	Multinational Corporation
MRV	Measurement/Monitoring, Reporting and Verification
MSC	Marine Stewardship Council
NAATO	North American Alternative Trade Organizations
NAP	Network of Asian Producers
NASFAM	National Smallholder Farmers' Association of Malawi
NGO	Non-Governmental Organization
NI	National (Labeling) Initiative
NSC	National Steering Committee
OCIA	Organic Crop Improvement Association
OECD	Organisation for Economic Co-operation and Development
OPP	Small Producers' Organization (Organización de Pequeños Productores)
P&C	Principles & Criteria
PLA	Plantation Labor Act
PLAAS	Institute for Poverty, Land and Agrarian Studies
PML	Prohibited Materials List
POIG	Palm Oil Innovation Group
RFA	Rainforest Alliance
RSPO	Roundtable on Sustainable Palm Oil
SCSI	Specialty Crop Sustainability Index
SERRV	Sales Exchange for Refugee Rehabilitation and Vocation

SFTF	Scottish Fair Trade Forum
SPO	Small Producer Organization
SPP	Small Producers' Label
STARFA	Santa Rita Farm Workers Association
TBT	Technical Barriers to Trade
TNC	Transnational Corporation
TRAC	Transnational Resource and Action Center
UCIRI	Union of Indigenous Communities of the Region of the Isthmus (Unión de Comunidades Indígenas de la Región del Istmo)
UN	United Nations
UNESCO	United Nations Educational, Scientific and Cultural Organization
UNGC	United Nations Global Compact
UN-NGLS	United Nations Non-Governmental Liaison Service
USDA	United States Department of Agriculture
USLEAP	United States Labor Education in the Americas Project
VSS	Voluntary Sustainability Standard
WAG	Welsh Assembly Government
WFTF	Wales Fair Trade Forum
WFTO	World Fair Trade Organization
WIETA	Wine Industry Ethical Trade Association
WRAC	Workers' Rights Advisory Committee
WTO	World Trade Organization
WWF	World Wide Fund for Nature

PART I

INTRODUCTION: FAIR TRADE

1. Introduction to research on fair trade

Laura T. Raynolds and Elizabeth A. Bennett

INTRODUCTION*

'Fair trade' has emerged over recent decades as a buzzword used by social scientists, socially conscious businesses, international development practitioners, social movement activists and ethically minded consumers. As a concept, fair trade refers to a critique of the historical inequalities inherent in international trade and to a belief that trade can be made more socially just. This notion is increasingly linked to a set of concrete initiatives that challenge global inequalities and create more egalitarian commodity networks, linking marginalized producers in the global South with progressive consumers in the global North. In moving from abstract concept to grounded practice, fair trade works to transform international trade from a vehicle of exploitation to an avenue of empowerment. In the global South, fair trade seeks to enhance wellbeing – by fostering higher prices and wages, stable markets and employment, better work conditions and environmental sustainability – and to bolster individual and collective capacities – by strengthening information exchanges, social service access, opportunities for self-determination and local organizations. In the global North, fair trade seeks to bolster more equitable trade policies, business models and consumption practices by making available a range of goods that are produced under more socially just and environmentally sustainable conditions.

There is now an impressive body of research on fair trade generated by scholars from across the social sciences – sociology, political science, geography, economics and anthropology – as well as business, marketing, policy, international development and other related fields. This Handbook serves as both a synthetic introduction and a guide to the dominant perspectives and concerns in the field. The first of its kind, the volume brings together 43 of the world's foremost fair trade scholars. These scholars use their extensive experience and knowledge to synthesize existing research findings, evaluate key debates and identify the most critical unanswered questions. The Handbook is written for those new to fair trade as well as those well versed in this domain; for scholars interested primarily in theoretical issues and for activists and practitioners focused largely on identifying pragmatic solutions to today's most pressing problems.

This introduction provides a conceptual background to fair trade, laying the groundwork for the rest of the volume. It also identifies the Handbook's structure and logic and how readers can best navigate this collection to identify themes of greatest interest. Following a second, more detailed chapter analyzing fair trade movements and markets, chapters in this volume are grouped according to three dominant research areas: 1) The Fair Trade Movement; 2) The Business of Fair Trade; and 3) Fair Trade and International Development. This introduction highlights the central lines of research in each of these domains, drawing directly on the major contributions of each chapter. It concludes with an assessment of the state of existing research on fair trade and an identification of the most promising directions for future investigation.

THE CONCEPT OF FAIR TRADE

Fair trade is used in common parlance to describe a moral high ground that responds to and critiques conventional trade relations, which for various reasons might be considered 'unfair' trade. This volume focuses more specifically on the notion of fair trade as it is articulated by its major social movement proponents. As defined in 'A Charter of Fair Trade Principles':

> Fair Trade is a trading partnership, based on dialogue, transparency and respect, that seeks greater equity in international trade. It contributes to sustainable development by offering better trading conditions to, and securing the rights of, marginalized producers and workers – especially in the South. Fair Trade Organizations, backed by consumers, are engaged actively in supporting producers, awareness raising and in campaigning for changes in the rules and practice of conventional international trade. (World Fair Trade Organization (WFTO) and Fairtrade International 2009)

According to this Fair Trade Charter, the objective of fair trade is to create 'a world in which justice and sustainable development are at the heart of trade structures and practices so that everyone, through their work, can maintain a decent and dignified livelihood and develop their full human potential'. It presents a strategy for achieving this vision, in five core principles: 1) market access for marginalized producers; 2) sustainable and equitable trading relationships; 3) capacity building and empowerment; 4) consumer awareness raising and advocacy; and 5) fair trade as a 'social contract' between buyers (including final consumers) and producers. In short fair trade is envisioned as a partnership that utilizes trade as a vehicle for promoting progressive change and international development.

Fair trade is allied in its vision and mission with a range of contemporary global social justice and environmental movements. In its critique of neoliberal globalization and advocacy for political and economic justice, fair trade aligns with the human rights, global democracy and trade justice movements (Smith 2008). In its focus on improving social and environmental conditions as well as fostering empowerment and self-determination in the global South, fair trade parallels the alternative development, political ecology, local sovereignty, and women's, peasants', workers' and indigenous rights movements (Evans 2008). Yet fair trade moves beyond many of these contemporary social movements in its efforts to go from vision to practice, seeking to demonstrate through example that more equitable and sustainable relations are possible.

In putting its vision into practice, fair trade joins a growing array of standard-setting and certification systems that establish and promote more rigorous social and environmental conditions in global production networks. These new institutional arrangements are commonly referred to as 'private' or 'voluntary' regulations, as they are not legally mandated, or 'multi-stakeholder initiatives' since they often engage stakeholders beyond the firm in overseeing business practices. Such regulatory systems abound in global manufacturing, where they focus largely on labor issues (O'Rourke 2006), and in agriculture and natural resource sectors, where they focus largely on ecological conditions (Auld 2014). Like other standard-setting and certification systems, fair trade operates largely outside of the legal system and brings together multiple stakeholders, most importantly businesses and non-governmental organizations (Bennett 2014). Yet fair trade distinguishes itself from other initiatives via its breadth, in incorporating both ethical and environmental concerns, and its depth, in regulating both production and trade relations (Raynolds 2000). Fair trade is thus best understood as a system of 'social regulation' that engages diverse social actors and pursues diverse social goals (Raynolds 2012).

This Handbook discusses two major facets of fair trade, distinguished via their spelling.[1] Expressed as two words, 'fair trade' refers to the concept, the movement or products/organizations/businesses promoting the general fair trade vision. This 'fair trade' includes the original direct trade model and practices that were developed first in handicrafts and persist in this and to a lesser extent other commodity areas. However, much of fair trade's recent growth has been through the certification of products by Fairtrade International, a non-profit membership organization which defines fair production and trade standards, establishes auditing procedures and promotes the sale of labeled products. Spelled as one word and capitalized, 'Fairtrade' refers to this specific certification system, as governed by its member organizations: national labeling organizations in countries where Fairtrade products are consumed and producer organizations in countries where Fairtrade products are produced. Certified products currently account for – by far – the majority of fair trade sales, particularly in agriculture and food products.

In addition to Fairtrade International certification there are other influential fair trade labeling systems which are also discussed in this volume. Fair Trade USA – which was until 2011 a member of Fairtrade International – now operates independently, setting standards and certifying products for sale in the United States. A number of chapters discuss this US program, identifying it by its trademarked name 'Fair Trade Certified'. Other fair trade certifications and labels, such as the Institute for Marketecology's 'Fair for Life' and the WFTO's 'Sustainable Fair Trade Management System', are analyzed in this Handbook and are identified using their full program names.

RISING POPULAR AND ACADEMIC INTEREST IN FAIR TRADE

We have over recent decades seen an explosion of interest in fair trade. News reports and opinion pieces related to fair trade are now commonplace in the mainstream print and digital media. Fair trade comes up often in conversations and debates among concerned citizens, producers and social movement activists around the world. While discussions about fair trade were once confined to food cooperatives serving the progressive fringes of society, fair trade is now a topic of conversation among shoppers of all ages in both alternative and mainstream grocery checkout lines. In an effort to capitalize on this interest, companies now reference fair trade (whether they engage these practices seriously or not) to substantiate their business values, rally investor support and foster consumer loyalty. Such claims are not only made by alternative niche market businesses, but also the world's largest retailers and most famous brand corporations.

Where did this interest and engagement in fair trade come from? The contemporary fair trade movement can be traced back to the 1940s, when directly traded handicrafts were first sold out of car trunks.[2] In the decades that followed, volunteers opened fair trade handicraft shops in the United States and Europe, and they allied with Latin American cooperatives to begin selling fairly priced coffee in shops and church basements. This informal economic system was revolutionized in the 1980s and 1990s through the founding of increasingly professional fair trade associations, the harmonization of norms and practices and, most notably, the introduction and promotion of the Fairtrade product certification label in mainstream markets.

Fair trade grew dramatically at the start of the 21st century, with the vast majority of this growth occurring in Fairtrade certified product arenas.[3] Between 1998 and 2004 the number of commodities carrying the Fairtrade label rose from seven to 18; enrollment of certified producer groups rose from 211 to 433; and the volume of certified sales rose from 28 902 to 125 595 metric tons (Raynolds and Long 2007, 25). This impressive growth helps explain how fair trade caught the attention of consumers, producers, activists, businesses and the media; at the same time this broad public enthusiasm helps explain fair trade's impressive growth.

Academic interest in fair trade follows a similar timeline, with a few chapters, articles and books emerging in the 1990s[4] and a surge of research at the turn of the century fueling what is now a vibrant, multidisciplinary and sophisticated body of literature. This Handbook's editors are affiliated with the earliest and still one of the foremost research centers in the field, the Center for Fair and Alternative Trade at Colorado State University in the United States. Handbook authors include many of the scholars who pioneered fair trade studies through grounded, field-based research. They bring to the volume a deep understanding of the history and practice of fair trade and how it has changed over time. Also included are newer researchers who raise novel concerns and bring fresh analytical approaches to the study of fair trade. Drawing on a growing body of empirical data, these researchers together identify and illuminate cutting edge issues, elucidating and contributing to the most current arguments and perspectives in the field of fair trade studies.

HANDBOOK ORGANIZATION AND CONTENTS

Contemporary fair trade research addresses a broad range of questions, draws on disparate theoretical traditions, employs diverse methodologies and is conducted by scholars of various disciplines and from different regions of the world. To capture this diversity, this Handbook brings together over 40 scholars from across the social sciences, including sociology, geography, political science, anthropology and economics, as well as the fields of business, environment and international development. While each scholar brings a distinct perspective to the study of fair trade, Handbook authors share a common commitment to linking theory with praxis. Most authors work in universities and research centers, though some are employed by government agencies or non-profit advocacy organizations. Reflecting the uneven geography of academic scholarship, most authors reside in North America and Europe, although a few are based in the global South and many work extensively in Latin America, Asia and Africa. Since several scholars typically do not publish in English, this volume provides a unique and insightful international perspective.

Handbook authors pursue approaches that range from the highly theoretical to the rigorously empirical. Chapters address key macro-, meso- and micro-level questions, and their answers are informed by both qualitative and quantitative research methods (including commodity network research, content analysis, comparative case studies, formal modeling, historical narrative analysis and participatory action research) and a wide variety of data sources (such as survey responses, interviews, observations, archival documents, popular media, commissioned reports and extant scholarship). To enrich their theoretical insights and empirical relevance, Handbook authors analyze fair trade issues across numerous certified and non-certified commodities, including agro-food products like coffee, tea, cocoa, wine, sugar, flowers, fresh vegetables and honey as well as textiles and other handicrafts. The research compiled here maps the production, trade and consumption relations which characterize and link fair trade in the global North and South, grounding analysis in the experiences of key consuming countries (e.g., the United States, United Kingdom, Italy, France and Switzerland) and major producing countries in Latin America (e.g., Mexico, Nicaragua, Guatemala, Peru and Bolivia), Africa (e.g., Kenya, Tanzania, Ghana, Malawi and South Africa) and Asia (e.g., India and the Philippines).

This Handbook describes and evaluates fair trade's varied dimensions and dynamics. Part I provides an overview of fair trade, beginning with this 'Introduction to research on fair trade' and continuing with a synopsis of fair trade's historical and empirical parameters in Chapter 2, 'Fair trade: Movement and markets' by Laura Raynolds and Nicholas Greenfield. This chapter analyzes fair trade as a movement and market, focusing on the complex and contested nature of dominant institutions, market relations, commodity networks and production conditions. Raynolds and Greenfield demonstrate how fair trade social movement efforts to promote alternative relational and civic values have been repeatedly challenged, but not subsumed, by dominant market forces seeking to advance conventional commercial and industrial interests.

Following the central lines of research in the field, the Handbook's subsequent chapters are organized into three parts. Part II, 'The Fair Trade Movement', examines the varied forces which have historically shaped fair trade activism and organizations. It highlights the complexities, controversies and contradictions that have generated both innovation and fragmentation within the movement. Part III, 'The Business of Fair Trade', examines how the vision of fair trade has been put into practice. Thus, it pays close attention to the dynamics of ethical labeling, the strategies of firms, the role of market forces and shifting consumption patterns. And Part IV, 'Fair Trade and International Development', examines the implications of fair trade for diverse producers and their communities. Typically focusing on a single region, commodity or development objective, each chapter offers a unique perspective on the efficacy of fair trade as a vehicle for development in the global South. Together these sections provide an empirical description of fair trade; explain central theoretical arguments and approaches; outline key ideas, debates and findings; and evaluate the state of existing scholarship. The remainder of this introduction highlights the central concerns and conclusions of each chapter, and draws on them to discuss and comment on the overall state of research on fair trade.

PART II: THE FAIR TRADE MOVEMENT

The chapters in Part II identify and evaluate key dimensions of the fair trade movement in local, national and global arenas. These chapters explain the varied forces that have historically shaped fair trade, including how key groups are organized and governed, and the relationship between fair trade and other social movements and multi-stakeholder initiatives. Discussion focuses on the norms and strategies that define the movement and the debates that divide it. The authors are grounded in the political economy tradition and share a common emphasis on issues of power, yet they apply diverse insights from political science, sociology and geography to illuminate the role of organizational, corporate, labor, consumer, producer and place-based politics in fair trade. As these chapters demonstrate, fair trade is a complex and contradictory social movement located at the nexus between capitalism and its alternatives. In evaluating fair trade's past and future trajectory, this section informs both analysis of and advocacy for the fair trade movement.

Fair Trade in International Political Economy

The early chapters in this section focus on macro-level questions regarding the nature of fair trade in an evolving system of international political economy. Steven Suranovic's chapter, 'The meaning of fair trade', furthers one's understanding of the contested terrain of fair trade by revealing the many distinct ways in which fairness is defined, often in relation to divergent concerns over equality of actions, outcomes or promise keeping. This chapter describes the way fairness is applied in fair trade certification, highlighting the conditions under which labeled products are both consistent and inconsistent with basic fairness principles. In 'Corporate accountability, fair trade and multi-stakeholder regulation', Peter Utting analyzes the changing norms and procedures which characterize new forms of multi-stakeholder regulation, locating Fairtrade certification within the context of other prominent regulatory initiatives, particularly the United Nations Global Compact and the Roundtable on Sustainable Palm Oil. Utting highlights the importance of political economy variables associated with contestation, power relations and participation in explaining regulatory changes and their implications for fostering fair trade and corporate accountability. Elizabeth Bennett's chapter, 'Fairtrade International governance', draws on extensive archival research to examine how Fairtrade International, the Fairtrade certification system's standards-setting body, balances power between producers and other actors in its highest governance bodies. Bennett argues that Fairtrade International's current governance structure is the most democratic and most inclusive of producers in the label's history, but that Fairtrade faces serious challenges due to a prolonged period of excluding producers from governance. Explaining key features in the political economy of fair trade, these chapters reveal the logic of fair trade, the location of fair trade certification within the field of global regulation and the internal politics of Fairtrade International.

The recent dramatic increase in the sourcing of fair trade labeled products from large plantations has spawned research and debates regarding the nature and implications of incorporating wage workers into fair trade. In his chapter on 'Global labor politics and fair trade', Dimitris Stevis identifies major areas of agreement and disagreement between fair trade and labor movements in the recent revision of Fairtrade International's hired labor standards. Arguing that the two movements have found some important common ground, Stevis suggests ways in which this relationship can mature to advance global social dialogue and transnational industrial relations. In a related chapter entitled 'Fairtrade certification, conventions and labor', Lone Riisgaard employs a convention theory lens to analyze Fairtrade labor standards and plantation certification. She identifies the nature and role of industrial and civic conventions in Fairtrade's engagement with hired labor enterprises and explores certification's implications for workers and their organizations, grounding her discussion in field studies of certified flower farms in Ecuador and Kenya. Together these two chapters illuminate the challenges and opportunities for improving the wellbeing and rights of hired workers via fair trade.

Fair Trade in Consumer Countries

The rapid growth of fair trade markets, particularly in Europe and North America, has fueled research on the links between fair trade consumption in the global North and production in the global South, the politics of ethical consumption, programs promoting fair trade purchasing and the potential of new initiatives facilitating fair trade in domestic commodity markets. In their chapter on 'Connections in fair trade food networks', Michael Goodman and Agatha Herman link the history of fair trade marketing in the United Kingdom with the rise of Fairtrade wine production in South Africa. They highlight the tactical practices used to grow and maintain ethical commodity networks, arguing that understanding the ways in which knowledge connections and disconnections are used is central to enhancing the sustainability of fair trade networks. Also focusing on fair trade consumers, Keith Brown's chapter on 'Consumer politics, political consumption and fair trade' analyzes the nature of US fair trade markets and the important history of 'buycotts' in national consumer movements. Situating fair trade within the field of ethical consumption, Brown argues that fair trade's growth has been aided by an ethical turn in markets where social responsibility has become a desirable product attribute. Both chapters reveal the centrality of face-to-face interactions and producer stories in promoting and sustaining fair trade networks.

The final two chapters focus on the national specificities and place-based nature of fair trade movements in the global North. In 'Domestic fair trade in the United States' Sandy Brown and Christy Getz analyze the growing number of initiatives promoting social justice for American farmers and farm workers in domestic commodity networks. They argue that these efforts to 'bring fair trade home' must be understood within the context of US agricultural development, in particular the legacies of agrarianism in shaping farm policy and the central role of marginalized immigrant workers in valorizing the agricultural landscape. Alastair

Smith's chapter, 'Fair trade places', details the rise of campaigns in the United Kingdom to promote fair trade towns, schools and nations, in both discourse and practice. He argues that fair trade places have provided stakeholders in the global North with new arenas within which to contest the nature and purpose of fair trade, but shows how wider power dynamics continue to shape place-based politics and democratization efforts. From different vantage points the two chapters spotlight how Northern initiatives can move beyond individual consumption politics to engage larger communities in promoting trade justice in domestic and international arenas.

PART III: THE BUSINESS OF FAIR TRADE

Part III analyzes the businesses, organizations, systems, relationships and labels that have been developed to put fair trade's goals into practice. These chapters examine the politics of product labeling, weigh the costs and benefits of alternative trade models and evaluate innovations in ethical trade. Several chapters examine fair trade through a business lens, focusing on consumer psychology, ethical branding and the role of labels in capturing markets. These studies often draw on large-scale market research data, compare conventional and alternative trade models or explore innovations in branding. Other chapters draw from geography, sociology and economics to analyze the nature and consequences of varied relationships between fair trade organizations, certification agencies, small businesses and large corporations in major markets in North America and Europe. This section of the Handbook thus elucidates the tradeoffs that key fair trade actors make in selecting strategies for institutionalizing and advancing their objective of making trade fair, and makes arguments about the consequences those strategic choices produce for fair trade markets.

The Organization and Practice of Fair Trade

The first three chapters examine the tensions inherent in trading fairly in a capitalist economy and analyze the cooperatives, businesses, corporations and social enterprises that negotiate these tensions in fair trade production, exporting and marketing. Darryl Reed's chapter, 'Cooperatives, corporations and fair trade', provides an analytic model to explain how cooperatives and corporations both cooperate and compete within fair trade markets, illustrating how the two types of organizations differ in their purposes, values, logics and governance. He argues that while cooperative-led value chains embody fair trade principles and contribute to an endogenous model of development, corporate-dominated value chains promote a corporate-led model of growth which may, but does not necessarily, contribute to poverty alleviation. In his chapter on 'Fair trade and social enterprise', Benjamin Huybrechts shows how an understanding of 'social enterprises' can help reveal the DNA of fair trade organizations and locate these enterprises within a broader organizational taxonomy. Drawing on a study of 57 fair trade social enterprises in four countries, he moves the discussion from what fair trade organizations *do* to what they *are* – innovative social enterprises which link market dynamics with social purpose. Manush McConway and Geoff Moore's chapter, 'Local fair trade organizations and institutional logics', shifts one's focus to fair trade export enterprises in producer countries, examining how these groups manage the competing forces of operating in both fair trade and mainstream markets. Focusing on the case of a craft export enterprise in Peru, they illustrate how a local fair trade organization can successfully respond to and negotiate competing institutional logics. The three chapters thus explain the diverse organizational models and business strategies used by fair trade enterprises, highlighting both important innovations and persistent tensions in global fair trade networks.

Fair Trade Mainstreaming, Certification and Corporate Collaboration

The following three chapters analyze patterns of fair trade mainstreaming, certification and corporate collaboration. These transformations have at once contributed to fair trade's recent market growth and fueled concerns regarding the dilution of standards, reduction in producer benefits, adoption of undemocratic practices and generation of support for corporations with poor human rights records. Ronan Le Velly's chapter, 'Fair trade and mainstreaming', argues that while 'mainstreaming' is commonly used to refer simultaneously to the *aim* of increasing sales, the *means* of utilizing conventional sales channels and the *consequences* of eroding of fair trade principles, it is important not to conflate these related but distinct processes. He studies the 'socio-technical agencements' underlying the sales growth of Artisans du Monde in France (via professionalization) and of Fairtrade International (via the delegation of business activities) to identify the ways in which fair trade goals have been facilitated or endangered. In 'Fair trade certification, performance and practice', Bradley Wilson and Tad Mutersbaugh analyze the fair trade product labeling system, arguing that the embrace of an

ISO-style approach to certification contributes to oft-noted problems in fair trade, including the lack of producer participation in standards-making, the weakness of democratic practices in network activities and the significant burdens placed on producer groups. While certification can foster a disembedding of the solidarity relations that once made fair trade unique, the authors identify practices that may enhance democracy and transparency in fair trade. Complementing the prior chapters, 'Retailers, corporate ethics and fair trade' by Alex Hughes identifies the diverse and evolving pathways of fair trade mainstreaming through corporate grocery retailers. She analyzes the nature and goals of corporate mainstreaming, comparing the adoption of Fairtrade goods by competing UK supermarket own-brand lines, by corporate social-responsibility-oriented top global retailers and by emerging supermarkets in the global South. Collectively these chapters reveal the complex nature of fair trade mainstreaming, pointing to the potential dangers of these processes as well as the possibilities for promoting expanding sales while maintaining fair trade principles.

Fair Trade Markets in the Global North

The final two chapters show how variations in fair trade organizations and patterns of mainstreaming and certification shape major fair trade markets in the global North. In the chapter 'Fairtrade International and the European market', Bob Doherty, Valéry Bezençon and Gaëlle Balineau compare and contrast fair trade market parameters, focusing particularly on Italy, France, Switzerland and the United Kingdom. They demonstrate the critical yet paradoxical contribution of Fairtrade International in developing national markets for Fairtrade labeled products which depend crucially on the marketing strategies of retailers and the structure of their supply chains. April Linton and Claudia Rosty's chapter, 'The US market and Fair Trade Certified', examines the nature of fair trade labeling, certification and mainstreaming in the United States. Drawing on existing scholarship and interviews with fair trade and labor rights advocates, the authors argue that the best strategies for growing fair trade in the United States involve engaging consumers as groups rather than individuals and messaging in a way that connects fair trade issues with larger social justice and sustainability agendas. Studying the world's largest fair trade markets, the two chapters reveal the important role that national context, culture and history play in shaping fair trade organizations and practices.

PART IV: FAIR TRADE AND INTERNATIONAL DEVELOPMENT

Part IV explores the fair trade movement's role and efficacy in promoting sustainable development in the global South. These chapters analyze the local social, cultural, political, economic and environmental implications of fair trade, advancing international development scholarship and providing recommendations for policies and programs to enhance fair trade's impact on the ground. Drawing insights from anthropology, sociology, economics, environmental studies and business fields, the authors reveal fair trade's strengths and weaknesses in bolstering wellbeing and empowerment in diverse communities and countries across Latin America, Africa and Asia. The chapters draw largely on field-based research using participatory, ethnographic and survey methods to illuminate fair trade's organization in key commodities and regions, often using commodity chain analysis to identify local/global connections. Studies unpack fair trade's multidimensional history and diverse operations in order to explain its local development outcomes. The chapters in Part IV reveal how fair trade's grounded impacts vary based on commodity and locality as well as by the nature of producer organizations, production enterprises and export relations. These variations in turn help explain fair trade's differential implications for specific individuals and groups, many of whom are marginalized by inequalities based on race, ethnicity, gender, class, geography and market access.

Fair Trade and its Objectives: Peace, Development, Sustainability and Equality

The first half of Part IV examines fair trade's challenges and opportunities in promoting key international development objectives. The initial chapters explore fair trade's capacity to promote development by addressing three deep-rooted problems: political conflict, underdevelopment and environmental degradation. Eileen Davenport and William Low's chapter, 'Fair trade, peace and development in conflict zones', reinterprets fair trade's evolution, identifying the central role of peacebuilding as a driving force of the early movement and its subsequent marginalization in the mainstreaming of fair trade. The authors argue that the recent introduction of products from conflict and post-conflict zones, such as coffee from the Democratic Republic of the Congo or olive oil from Palestine, marks a re-emergence of an *intentional* focus on peacebuilding as a principal objective, rather than a by-product, of fair trade. In the chapter 'Fair trade and development in African agriculture', Anne Tallontire explores the history of fair trade in African agriculture, highlighting the important role of cooperatives in the engagement of small producers and the rising significance of the Fairtrade hired labor model. She argues that while fair trade has improved local living conditions, colonial-based institutional forces and the current sourcing requirements of retailers and brands limit potential advances in key arenas like infrastructure access and gender equity. Christopher Bacon, Robert Rice and Hannah Maryanski's chapter, 'Fair trade coffee and environmental sustainability in Latin America', analyzes the direct and indirect environmental impacts of Fairtrade certified coffee production in Latin America and the Caribbean. Drawing on surveys, interviews and years of field experience, the authors examine fair trade's implications for biodiversity conservation, pollution reduction and climate change adaptation, finding the results to be mixed and context specific. Taken together these three chapters suggest that fair trade has had some important success in promoting its peacebuilding, social development and environmental sustainability goals and point to concrete ways in which these efforts can be enhanced.

The subsequent three chapters focus on fair trade's capacity to achieve its objective of promoting equality, especially for women and disadvantaged ethnic and racial groups. Each chapter identifies the major challenges facing particular marginalized groups and fair trade's efforts to address them. Sally Smith's chapter, 'Fair trade and women's empowerment', draws on empirical evidence from a range of countries and sectors to demonstrate that there is considerable variation in the extent to which fair trade supports processes of women's empowerment, not least because fair trade impacts are mediated by local contextual conditions. She argues that the new gender strategies being pursued by Fairtrade International and WFTO are conceptually sound, but that implementing these strategies will require significant commitment, leadership and resources. In her chapter on 'Fair trade and indigenous communities in Latin America', Sarah Lyon explores the implications of fair trade for the indigenous groups often depicted in coffee marketing campaigns, drawing on case studies from Mesoamerica, Bolivia and Brazil. Lyon identifies the risks and benefits of strategic essentialisms and identity politics for indigenous coffee farmers and their organizations and concludes that fair trade can foster economic development by helping indigenous communities access and compete in international markets. Jennifer Keahey's chapter, 'Fair trade and racial equity in Africa', pursues a multi-level analysis of Fairtrade certified production which integrates the scholarly literature, organizational interviews and participatory action research with small-scale rooibos tea farmers in South Africa. Keahey finds that while

African organizations pursue innovative approaches to challenging racial inequalities in production and trade, paternalistic benevolence hinders interracial solidarity. She concludes that fair trade's record in promoting racial equity is mixed and that greater producer participation is needed to foster interracial empowerment and ownership. The three chapters thus concur that fair trade has had only partial success in promoting its equity agenda. Chapter authors find that women and non-white populations benefit from fair trade, but argue that increasing the participation of marginalized groups in fair trade governance and practice is necessary to enhance gender, ethnic and racial equity.

Fair Trade for Economically Marginalized Groups

The following set of chapters focus on fair trade's efforts to provide market access, economic opportunity and other benefits to three economically marginalized groups: artisans, small-scale farmers and farm workers. The authors describe how fair trade initiatives have engaged these disadvantaged groups. They also evaluate the success of these efforts and identify how different groups may at times compete for fair trade benefits. Mary Littrell's chapter, 'Fair trade and artisans', examines the experiences and challenges of fair trade artisans in India and Guatemala. She shows how fair trade principles of respect for cultural traditions, including daily lifestyles and artistic production, promote the organizational growth and evolution of local handicraft groups and enhance artisans' cultural identity. Littrell argues that to maintain fair trade's benefits for artisans it is imperative that consumers understand the distinctive nature of fair trade artisan work in an increasingly crowded and confusing ethical marketplace. In 'Fair trade for small farmer cooperatives in Latin America', Marie-Christine Renard analyzes the rise of fair trade labeling from the perspective of small producers and traces recent conflicts between Fairtrade International and the Latin American and Caribbean Network of Small Fair Trade Producers (CLAC). Renard argues that Fairtrade International's emphasis on growing certified markets has privileged corporations over small farmers in fair trade governance. She describes how small producers have responded by launching the new Small Producers Symbol (SPP label), an initiative that aims to reorient fair trade to its original mission and focus on smallholder farmer cooperatives. Rie Makita's chapter, 'Fair trade and plantation workers in Asia', shows how both current and former workers can benefit from Fairtrade, drawing on case studies of a tea plantation in India and a cooperative of former sugarcane plantation workers in the Philippines. She argues that while current workers can use Fairtrade premiums to foster their empowerment if third-party organizations (rather than plantation management) control the premium, former plantation workers can maximize their income by pursuing fair trade production on communal land in conjunction with household livelihood diversification. The three chapters draw on rich empirical data and intensive fieldwork to illustrate how movement- and organizational-level politics play out on the ground and how fair trade can best engage diverse groups of artisans, farmers and workers in the global South.

Fair Trade Impacts

The volume's final chapters analyze fair trade's impacts across commodities and contexts. Valerie Nelson and Adrienne Martin's chapter, 'Fairtrade International's multi-dimensional impacts in Africa', synthesizes the findings of a number of recent field studies on the impacts of Fairtrade on smallholders and hired workers. They find that while certification can generate important benefits, in Africa Fairtrade's record of reducing gender and social inequalities and lifting people out of poverty is mixed, often modest, and highly context specific. Nelson and Martin suggest ways for improving Fairtrade impacts and sustainable trade. 'Quantitative analysis of the impacts of fair trade' by Leonardo Becchetti, Stefano Castriota and Pierluigi Conzo reviews numerous studies of fair trade impacts, analyzing the strength of their methods as well as their statistical findings. The authors argue that rigorous research demonstrates fair trade's benefits in a number of countries, related particularly to fair trade affiliation's impacts on objective measures (like income and food consumption), subjective measures (like life satisfaction and self-esteem) and household issues (like child labor). Both chapters reveal fair trade's important positive impacts yet remind one that these benefits may be less impressive and inclusive than are sometimes assumed and can be undermined by less committed actors.

CONCLUSIONS

The *Handbook of Research on Fair Trade* describes existing challenges and opportunities, informs core debates and raises new questions for the field of fair trade research. While the authors advance scholarship on a broad range of topics, their contributions focus on five key themes: 1) mainstreaming, labeling and the role of conventional actors in fair trade markets; 2) the increasing scale, complexity and diversity of fair trade production; 3) governance, leadership and the balance of power within fair trade and its major organizations; 4) the fair trade movement's relationship to other social and environmental movements and initiatives; and 5) how to bolster fair trade's positive impacts, particularly for extremely marginalized groups. This concluding section summarizes the central arguments and debates within each topic, highlighting major unresolved questions for fair trade researchers and recommendations for fair trade practitioners.

The question of how to theoretically negotiate and practically manage the tension of simultaneously working *within* and *against* the market to achieve social justice aims is an enduring question in fair trade research (see Barratt Brown 1993). Handbook chapters shed new light on this challenge by developing fresh theoretical lenses which merge insights from new approaches, like convention theory, socio-technical analysis and institutional logics, with well-established political economy, organizational and development analytics. Empirically, Handbook chapters show how conventional, profit-oriented actors are increasingly participating in fair trade, either through collaborating with committed fair trade practitioners or by designing their own systems which incorporate select aspects of fair trade. While some authors see this trend as a symptom of fair trade's success in regulating the global economy, others argue that it is indicative of fair washing. Handbook authors agree that fair trade mainstreaming facilitates market growth but disagree about the nature of the related costs and whether the benefits derived from market growth outweigh these costs. Several case studies suggest that fully committed fair trade distributors and producers can negotiate relationships with mainstream actors that channel the benefits of market growth while minimizing the tradeoffs. Further research is needed to understand how and when this type of win-win scenario is possible and whether conventional market actors can bring more to fair trade than expanding markets. The recommendation to committed fair trade practitioners is clear, albeit challenging to implement: successful collaboration with mainstream market actors requires a clear understanding of one another's profit motives and social impact objectives, even if those priorities are not fully shared.

A second common theme addressed by Handbook chapters relates to the increasing scale and complexity of fair trade production. Scholars in this volume describe how fair trade has come to incorporate new types of producer organizations, novel products, lengthier supply chains and additional production locations, generating increasingly complex networks of actors and practices. A more multifaceted and competitive fair trade marketplace is emerging. It's comprised of a proliferating number of ethical labels, a novel set of trading models, a quasi-parallel certification system created by Fair Trade USA's departure from the Fairtrade International umbrella, a set of new domestic (within country) fair trade initiatives and an incipient practice of international South–South fair trade. But a number of critical questions remain. How will this more diverse market affect the fair trade movement and its underlying principles? How will these changes affect the benefits channeled to producers? Fair trade research points to a number of potential negative repercussions from these trends, including discrediting the movement, diluting social and environmental standards, confusing consumers by not differentiating between rigorous and 'light' fair trade, and even jeopardizing the existence of highly committed pioneers. On the other hand, some studies of fair trade suggest that experimentation and innovation may generate novel approaches that harness the strengths of traditional models and mitigate these new challenges. For fair trade practitioners it is a time for creative thinking and fresh approaches. For researchers there is much to learn about the new factors shaping fair trade consumption, trade and production, particularly in rising consumer countries like Mexico, Brazil and South Africa. Whether the current fair trade movement and market are best understood as a terrain of crisis or innovation remains to be seen.

The third major cross-cutting theme addressed by Handbook chapters relates to the challenges of fair trade governance, both within key initiatives and in the larger movement. Scholars in this volume argue that producers' participation in organizational and movement governance is critical and advocate more democratic processes of decision-making and heightened transparency. They raise concerns about the balance of power between different types of stakeholders (e.g., producers versus marketing organizations) and between different types of producer groups (e.g., hired laborers versus small farmers). While fair trade principles promote the incorporation of marginalized producers, research finds that in practice the participation of women, racial and ethnic minorities, and the poorest fair trade communities is often limited. For those involved in fair trade networks, this Handbook points to some of the gaps in democratic practices and some of the promising avenues for fostering participation. This volume also identifies a number of important areas for further research, including how stakeholder participation affects committed fair traders' ability to compete in the crowded 'ethical' market, how different governance patterns influence the content of standards and in what ways increasing producer participation in organizations and in the movement as a whole affects the benefits of fair trade on the ground.

The fourth major issue addressed by the fair trade literature relates to the movement's location among, and relationship to, other global regulatory initiatives, certifications and labeling efforts. On this issue scholars examine how fair trade actors have collaborated or worked independently of solidarity, labor, environmental and food justice movements. Many Handbook authors recommend that fair trade practitioners build stronger alliances with related social movement groups. Given fair trade's growth in large enterprises dependent on hired labor, the relationship between fair trade and international and national unions has become particularly important. As fair trade expands to incorporate new producer groups, scholarship in this area raises the question: fair trade *for whom*? Further research is needed to better understand how fair trade can deliver benefits to different groups and how these benefits compare to those offered by other initiatives. This volume examines fair trade as a form of social enterprise, private regulation and consumption-based political activism. While these studies point to fair trade's similarities with other initiatives, further research is needed to evaluate the ways in which fair trade's advocacy efforts, consumer education and benefits to producers are distinct.

The final theme that emerges frequently in fair trade scholarship relates to the level and type of benefits that fair trade brings to producers, their families and their communities. The research included in this volume shows that fair trade's impacts are variegated, variable and uneven across producer groups and localities. Strategies that generate benefits in some contexts appear not to work as well in others. This is due to differences in prevailing social, economic and political conditions, in commodity and production requirements and in regional development characteristics. Fair trade has fallen short of its goals of pulling people out of poverty, ameliorating entrenched structural inequalities, transforming economies and re-embedding global capitalism. But as studies in this volume demonstrate, fair trade has in some contexts made meaningful contributions to promoting social justice and sustainable development. For researchers the key conclusion is the need to move beyond an overly simplistic dichotomization between fair trade's lofty rhetoric and its more modest impacts, in order to help identify the factors which either facilitate or impede benefit streams. Action-oriented scholars in particular should focus their research on how to improve – as well as measure – fair trade impacts, and how to engage fair trade producers in defining and monitoring success. Handbook authors make a number of recommendations for fair trade policymakers and practitioners to bolster benefit streams, including encouraging livelihood diversification; promoting a living wage for workers as well as farmers; stabilizing contractual relations between buyers and producers; diversifying fair trade practices to accommodate diverse production contexts; and employing and learning from innovative pilot programs.

As this Handbook suggests, academic research on fair trade has a rich history of analyzing and informing the ways in which fair trade principles are put into practice. The editors hope that this volume will advance fair trade as an interdisciplinary and international topic of scholarly inquiry; that it will be a tool for igniting new research on emerging issues as well as perennial debates in the field; and that it will reinforce the links between research and practice. Fair trade research clearly has merit as an intellectual project, but it also can play a critical role in addressing the world's most pressing social, economic, political and environmental problems.

NOTES

* The editors would like to acknowledge and thank Molly Eckman for her substantial assistance in reviewing the entire book manuscript as well as the hard work of the chapter authors and editors at Edward Elgar. This volume has indeed been a collective effort.

1. The terminology follows the Fair Trade Charter, which notes that there are two distinct but complementary fair trade supply channels: 1) 'the integrated supply chain route whereby products are imported and/or distributed by organisations that have fair trade at the core of their mission and activities' and 2) the Fairtrade channel or 'the product certification route whereby products complying with international standards are certified' (World Fair Trade Organization (WFTO) and Fairtrade International 2009).
2. Of course, this was not the first time that social justice-oriented groups appealed to consumers to 'vote with their dollar' (see, for example, Glickman 2009).
3. As Raynolds and Long (2007, 21) document, by the early 2000s certified items had come to account for 88 per cent of total fair trade sales.
4. Particularly prescient was Michael Barratt Brown's (1993) book, entitled *Fair Trade*.

REFERENCES

Auld, Graeme (2014), *Constructing Private Governance: The Rise and Evolution of Forest, Coffee, and Fisheries Certification*, Hartford, CT: Yale University Press.

Barratt Brown, Michael (1993), *Fair Trade*, London: Zed Books.

Bennett, Elizabeth (2014), 'Stakeholder inclusion and power in INGOs: The governance of Fairtrade International', doctoral dissertation, Department of Political Science, Brown University.

Evans, Peter (2008), 'Is an alternative globalization possible?', *Politics and Society*, 36 (2), 271–305.

Glickman, Lawrence (2009), *Buying Power: A History of Consumer Activism in America*, Chicago: University of Chicago Press.

O'Rourke, Dara (2006), 'Multi-stakeholder regulation: Privatizing or socializing global labor standards?', *World Development*, 34 (5), 899–918.

Raynolds, Laura (2000), 'Re-embedding global agriculture: The international organic and fair trade movements', *Agriculture and Human Values*, 17 (3), 297–309.

Raynolds, Laura T. (2012), 'Fair trade: Social regulation in global food markets', *Journal of Rural Studies*, 28 (3), 276–287.

Raynolds, Laura T. and Michael Long (2007), 'Fair/alternative trade: Historical and empirical dimensions', in Laura T. Raynolds, Douglas Murray and John Wilkinson (eds.), *Fair Trade: The Challenges of Transforming Globalization*, New York: Routledge, pp. 15–29.

Smith, Jackie (2008), *Social Movements for Global Democracy*, Baltimore, MD: Johns Hopkins University Press.

World Fair Trade Organization (WFTO) and Fairtrade International (2009), 'A charter of fair trade principles', available at http://fairtrade-advocacy.org/images/Charter_of_Fair_Trade_principles_EN_v1.2.pdf (accessed 26 June 2014).

2. Fair trade: movement and markets

Laura T. Raynolds and Nicholas Greenfield

INTRODUCTION

Fair trade has emerged over recent years as a powerful initiative to socially regulate global markets. This movement seeks to challenge historically unequal international trade relations and promote social justice and environmental sustainability in global production. Fair trade strives to foster the wellbeing and empowerment of producers and workers in the global South through the provision of higher prices, stable market links, better working conditions and community development resources. In the global North fair trade seeks to promote responsible consumption and provide shoppers with alternative, typically certified, socially and environmentally friendly products. Over a million producers and hundreds of millions of consumers participate in these new transnational networks, with annual sales of certified Fairtrade products exceeding US$6 billion (Fairtrade International 2013).

In this chapter we analyze the fair trade movement and market, focusing on the complex and contested nature of fair trade institutions, market relations, commodity networks and production conditions. Our analysis shows how in each of these arenas social movement efforts to promote alternative relational and civic values are repeatedly challenged, but not subsumed, by dominant market forces seeking to advance conventional commercial and industrial interests. We identify major empirical patterns and key tensions in: 1) the shifting ideas, practices and institutions associated with fair trade's recent growth; 2) the growing distribution and consumption of largely certified products in mainstream markets; 3) the decommodification and simultaneous recommodification of a growing array of fair trade products; and 4) the production and export of fair trade products from certified cooperatives and increasingly from large hired labor enterprises. As we conclude, fair trade illuminates the promise and pitfalls in socially regulating global markets, as movement efforts move from social critique to socio-economic construction.

IDEAS, PRACTICES AND INSTITUTIONS

The fair trade movement critiques conventional trade norms, which are defined as 'unfair', and seeks to promote alternative norms of equity, sustainability, trust and partnership in international markets. Key studies apply convention theory (Thévenot 1995) to analyze how fair trade questions the legitimacy of 'industrial' and 'commercial' norms – where items are valued based on price and production efficiency and trade is guided by market competition – and promotes a requalification of economic activity based on 'civic' and 'domestic/relational' norms (Raynolds 2000; 2002; Renard 1999; 2003).[1] Fair trade ideas, practices and institutions link 'civic' conventions based on collective responsibility for global social and ecological wellbeing with personal 'relational' commitments to people and places (Raynolds 2012a). While fair trade's critique is akin to that of other social justice movements, what accounts for this initiative's popularity is its ability to combine visionary goals with practical engagement in creating alternative economic arenas (Raynolds et al. 2007).

By challenging the dominance of abstract economic principles and moving to re-embed economic markets within social relationships (Polanyi 1957), fair trade can be understood as a movement of social protection to resist the destructive impacts of the unfettered market (Jaffee 2007; Raynolds 2000). Infusing commodities with information regarding the people and places involved in production, fair trade seeks to 'humanize' economic transactions and 'shorten the distance' between producers and consumers (Raynolds 2002). Fair trade works to make explicit the conditions under which goods are produced and traded, a strategy similar to other 'values-based labeling' efforts in organic, heritage and geographic origin labeled foods (Barham 2002). Fair trade is allied also with the growing number of certifications in manufacturing and natural resource sectors that strive to improve production conditions through the sale of products carrying social seals and eco-labels (Raynolds 2004).

A key contradiction for fair trade is that it operates 'in and against the market', working through market channels to create new commodity networks for items produced under more favorable social and ecological conditions and simultaneously working against the conventional market forces that create and uphold global inequalities (Raynolds 2000). The ongoing contestation between movement principles and market imperatives has shaped the nature and dynamics of fair trade's institutional development. As outlined below, fair trade ideas and practices have been institutionalized in two key ways: in the older yet now less dominant fair trade organization model and the younger yet rapidly growing Fairtrade certification model.

Non-governmental organizations and faith-based groups focusing on development issues were the first to advance fair trade ideas and practices, creating organizations which purchased handicrafts at favorable prices from associated Southern producers to sell directly to concerned Northern consumers. These fair trade organizations flourished with the rise of international social justice movements in the 1960s and 1970s. Informed by critiques of the role of unequal exchange relations in fueling global poverty, fair trade pioneers created direct trade channels which eliminated middlemen and increased producer returns. Direct trade remains most common in the handicraft sector and is exemplified in the hundreds of Ten Thousand Villages stores found across North America and the numerous world shops located all across Europe. This mission-driven business model was extended to coffee and tea by groups like Equal Exchange in the United States and Cafédirect in the United Kingdom. Fair trade organizations consolidated their norms and practices under the auspices of the World Fair Trade Organization (WFTO), which represents producer groups, importers and retailers selling only fair trade products. As their website states: 'WFTO Members are not just the pioneers of the movement but the innovators of the market', they 'demonstrate a 100% Fair Trade commitment' (WFTO 2013). Fair trade organizations promote relational ties between Southern producers and Northern consumers through direct trade partnerships, personal interactions and extensive information flows as well as civic values through their support for disadvantaged producers, public education and global social justice advocacy (Raynolds 2002; 2012a). Fair trade organizations are deeply mission-driven and devoted to movement principles, yet at the same time they face significant pressure to adopt conventional business practices. To accommodate commercial and market demands, WFTO has over the past decade become more bureaucratic and is currently developing a fair trade guarantee system and product label. Meanwhile mission-driven enterprises have had to make difficult compromises to maintain their economic viability in the face of commercial and market pressures. Sales in this sector have over recent years seen only modest growth (EFTA 2010; Raynolds 2012a).

What is now the dominant fair trade model was established in the late 1980s based on a formal process of certification and labeling for products sold by mainstream retailers. Coordinated by Fairtrade International[2] this system was developed explicitly to get 'Fairtrade into the supermarket where most people do their shopping' (Fairtrade International 2004).

Fairtrade certification uses conventional industrial and market tools to regulate production conditions and signal to consumers the fair trade qualifications of products (Raynolds 2002; 2012a). By translating movement principles into formal bureaucratic institutions and rational rules and by positioning products in mainstream markets, certification has spurred fair trade's commercial growth. Facilitating mainstream market adoption, retailers do not need to adjust their practices in order to sell Fairtrade certified products. Yet Fairtrade International specifies rigorous standards for producers (they must be organized into democratic associations, uphold International Labor Organization standards and promote ecological practices) and for importers (they must buy from certified growers using stable contracts, provide credit and pay guaranteed prices and a social premium).[3] Initially undertaken in-house at no cost to producers, compliance is now overseen by the autonomous FLO-Cert following common fee-based audit procedures. While Fairtrade certification can take credit for fair trade's recent commercial success, its imposition of conventional industrial and market values, practices and institutions clearly threatens the movement's alternative relational and civic conventions (Mutersbaugh 2005; Raynolds 2002; Renard 2003).

The inherent contradictions in fair trade's strategy of working 'in and against the market' are being fueled by Fair Trade USA's recent exodus from the Fairtrade International system. This move reflects a longstanding rift between the market-oriented US labeling agency, Fair Trade USA, and its more movement-oriented European counterparts (Raynolds 2012a). The US labeling agency seeks to increase supplies by certifying: 1) farmers who are not democratically organized; 2) plantations in sectors like coffee which Fairtrade International limits to small producers; and 3) Northern producers (Fair Trade USA 2014). Embracing conventional business logic, Fair Trade USA argues that by growing the market for fair trade products, more producers will benefit. This strategy prioritizes market goals over movement principles and has been widely condemned by Fairtrade International members, by WFTO and its fair trade organization members and by social movement allies. The organizational split threatens to undermine what mission-driven groups call 'Authentic Fair Trade', fragmenting the movement and heightening market competition (Equal Exchange 2012; WFTO 2013).

DISTRIBUTION AND CONSUMPTION

Fair trade's rising popularity is linked to the recent growth of ethical and green consumption. Consumers increasingly use the market as an arena to voice their values, avoiding companies and products associated with negative social and environmental attributes and seeking out those that reflect their value commitments (Micheletti 2003). A large and growing share of people in the global North identify themselves as ethical consumers who take their social and environmental values into account in making purchasing choices. This is particularly true in the agro-food sector, where ethical and ecological commitments converge with food safety and health concerns in fueling the market for fair trade and organic products (Leatherhead Food International 2012; Raynolds 2004). Over half of European and North American consumers believe that their shopping choices can make a positive difference for workers and farmers in poor countries (Fairtrade International and Globespan 2011). Fair trade organizations have promoted ethical consumption through extensive shopper interactions and public education, creating an alternative 'moral economy' (Goodman 2004) which links consumers as 'global citizens' to the fates of distant people and places (Raynolds 2012a). Yet certification has eroded fair trade's relational and civic ties and promoted conventional industrial and commercial norms (Raynolds 2002; Renard 2003) fostering less politicized 'citizen consumers' who vote with their dollars (Johnston 2008). Reflecting the ascendance of certification, 72 per cent of North American and European consumers see third-party certification as the best way to verify social and environmental claims and 57 per cent report a familiarity with the Fairtrade label (Fairtrade International and Globespan 2011).

Fair trade sales are growing across the global North. Accounting for the majority of sales and most of the recent growth, Fairtrade certified agro-food products were valued at US$6.2 billion in 2012 (Fairtrade International 2013). Handicraft sales by fair trade organizations are smaller and have grown more modestly, with total sales by European groups estimated at about US$379 million in 2009/10 (EFTA 2010).[4] As noted in Table 2.1, the United Kingdom has the world's largest market for Fairtrade certified goods, with annual sales of US$2.6 billion. Germany, France and Switzerland also have well developed Fairtrade markets. A wide range of certified Fairtrade products are readily available in European supermarkets, specialty stores, universities and workplaces. Growth has slowed in some parts of Europe, but Fairtrade sales are rising rapidly in many countries, including in Eastern Europe. Fairtrade certified products are not as widely available in North America and many US fair trade organizations prefer not to use the certification label even for coffee, the most commonly certified product. Still, due to its market size, the United States has the second largest national certified market, with earnings valued at US$1.4 billion in 2011. Canada has a fairly well-established and substantial certified market for Fairtrade goods. As a result of rapid growth in recent years, Australia and New Zealand have joined the ranks of major Fairtrade certified product markets.

Table 2.1 Fairtrade International certified sales value in lead countries (US$1 000 000)[a]

	2004	2006	2008	2010	2012
Europe					
UK	256	514	1297	1872	2654
Germany	71	138	313	474	743
France	87	209	376	423	482
Switzerland	169	179	248	306	434
Netherlands	43	51	90	166	259
Sweden	7	20	107	151	249
North America					
USA	267	627	1116	1305	[b]1436
Canada	22	68	190	271	275
Pacific					
Australia/NZ	1	8	27	175	262
Japan	3	5	14	20	100
Total[c]	1034	2039	4351	5728	7985

Notes: [a] Euros are converted to dollars using the US Federal Reserve average annual exchange rate (2004: US$1.24 = 1 Euro; 2006: US$1.26 = 1 Euro; 2008: US$1.47 = 1 Euro; 2010: US$1.33 = 1 Euro; 2012: US$1.29 = 1 Euro).
[b] This figure is for 2011. In 2012 US sales included Fairtrade International certified sales valued at US$74 000 000. Fair Trade USA has not published sales figures for 2012.
[c] Total includes countries not listed on the chart.

Sources: Compiled by the authors using data from Fairtrade International (2006, 2007, 2009, 2011, 2012a, 2013a).

Contrasting the development of US and UK Fairtrade certification reveals the centrality of market and movement tensions in defining national distribution and consumption patterns. In the United States fair trade organizations have worked closely with solidarity groups to support social justice activities and together helped launch the national Fair Trade USA label. Fair trade organizations and activists, particularly student groups, have collaborated to bolster US public understanding of fair trade and the availability of certified products. Yet fair trade organizations and social movement allies have had no role in Fair Trade USA's governance, which over the years has distanced itself from its social movement origins (Raynolds 2007). Fair Trade USA has advanced a market-based strategy of fair trade founded on mainstream corporate sales and consumer choice – as enshrined in their tag line 'every purchase matters'. This mainstreaming strategy has encouraged large corporations with little commitment to fair trade principles to enter and dominate the US market for certified products; it has simultaneously led most mission-driven fair trade organizations to drop the Fair Trade USA label (Jaffee 2012; Raynolds 2009; 2012a).

Fair trade's institutionalization in the United Kingdom has maintained a stronger movement orientation and closer ties among advocacy groups, fair trade organizations and the national label. When fair trade organizations and social movement groups founded the UK labeling organization, the Fairtrade Foundation, they maintained a key role in the group's direction through their shareholder and board of directors positions. These movement ties have shaped the Fairtrade Foundation's strategy for developing the certified market, which includes allying with fair trade organizations and social enterprises as well as mainstream retailers. Rather than focusing only on corporate market acceptance, the Fairtrade Foundation has worked with allied groups to build government support for fair trade and raise public awareness of global social justice concerns in large public forums like the annual 'Fairtrade Fortnight'. The Fairtrade Foundation's success in balancing fair trade movement and market forces is evidenced in the United Kingdom's certified market leadership and in the continued support it receives from mission-driven fair trade organizations and social movement groups (Barrientos and Smith 2007; Raynolds 2009; 2012a).

Fairtrade certified market growth has encouraged corporate involvement, fueling a process of mainstreaming that threatens fair trade's founding principles. As Raynolds (2009) demonstrates there is now a continuum of fair trade vendors ranging from 'market-driven' corporations pursuing mainstream commercial and industrial conventions to 'mission-driven' enterprises that advance alternative relational and civic values. Market-driven corporations, like Procter & Gamble and Nestlé, engage fair trade largely to access lucrative product niches and burnish their brands. These corporations: 1) offer only a small share of Fairtrade products; 2) follow largely conventional business practices; and 3) use certification primarily to enhance traceability in their sourcing arrangements. In contrast mission-driven enterprises, like Equal Exchange and Cafédirect, 1) offer only fair trade items; 2) pursue alternative business models; and 3) pursue partnership goals in certified and non-certified sourcing arrangements.[5] Between these two poles are a growing number of 'quality-driven' firms which: 1) sell a significant share of Fairtrade products; 2) engage fair trade to underpin existing corporate social responsibility commitments; and 3) use certification to strengthen their access to high-quality products. Mainstreaming increases the role of market-driven corporations in fair trade as well as the pressure on other fair trade enterprises to conform to commercial and industrial conventions (Raynolds 2009; 2012a).

DECOMMODIFICATION AND RECOMMODIFICATION

Although the fair trade concept was developed first in the handicraft sector, fair trade's major growth has been in agro-food commodities. Over the past decade there has been a dramatic rise in the range and volume of certified products. Introduced originally in coffee, Fairtrade certification is now available for 300 products,[6] including other early key items like tea, cocoa and sugar; more recently available fresh produce like bananas and other fruits; and a range of products like rice, quinoa, honey, spices and herbs, fruit juices, flowers, wine, cotton, sports balls and gold. In Table 2.2 we outline Fairtrade's growth in major product areas. Fairtrade International has expanded its product range largely in response to mounting demand, allowing supermarkets to move certified products well beyond the coffee aisle and consumers to increase the number of Fairtrade products they can put into their shopping carts (Raynolds et al. 2007).

Analysis of Fairtrade commodity networks reveals a reciprocal process of decommodification and recommodification. Coffee remains the core of the Fairtrade system and accounts for close to half of the value of all certified items (Fairtrade International 2012b). Fairtrade buyer requirements have given certified coffee producers more direct and stable

Table 2.2 Top Fairtrade International labeled commodities by volume (metric tons)

	2004	2006	2008	2010	2012[a]
Bananas	80 640	135 763	299 205	286 598	331 980
Sugar	1960	7159	56 990	126 810	158 986
Coffee	24 222	52 064	65 808	87 576	[b]77 429
Cocoa	4201	7913	10 299	35 179	40 559
Other Fresh Fruit	–	–	26 424	18 396	12 259
Tea	1965	3883	11 467	12 356	11 869
Rice	1384	2985	4685	5048	5623
Honey	1240	1552	2055	2072	1319
Total[c]	126 160	217 628	505 152	601 244	651 900

Notes: [a] This column does not include sales by Fair Trade USA and thus understates total certified product sales.
[b] Although figures for prior years are for roasted coffee, this is for green coffee beans.
[c] Includes other labeled commodities measured by weight (e.g., cotton and quinoa), but not those measured by item or other volume measurements (e.g., flowers, sports balls, fruit juice, wine and beer).

Sources: Compiled by the authors using data from Fairtrade International (2005, 2007, 2009, 2012a, 2013a).

relations with buyers, while minimum price guarantees have provided a partial buffer to the devastating impacts of world commodity price swings. Although Fairtrade standards promote processes of decommodification in trading networks for coffee producers, market engagement fuels recommodification, prioritizing industrial and commercial concerns related to price, quality and volume (Raynolds 2009). The dynamics of decommodification and recommodification are evident also at the market end of the supply chain where over 77 000 tons of Fairtrade certified coffee is consumed in cafés, workplaces, educational institutions and homes (Fairtrade International 2012b). Fairtrade packaging provides shoppers with a visual and informative account of the coffee's origins, unveiling the social and environmental relations that lie behind the product and fostering decommodification (Hudson and Hudson 2003; Raynolds 2000). Yet with rising mainstream market sales, Fairtrade coffee is increasingly purchased for its upscale packaging and certification seal rather than for its underlying civic and relational values, thus reasserting conventional commodity relations (Daviron and Vagneron 2011; Raynolds 2009).

In Fairtrade product arenas beyond coffee, decommodification has proved more difficult and processes of recommodification more vigorous. Bananas are the second most valuable Fairtrade certified product, with annual sales of almost 332 000 tons. Fairtrade banana sales have grown rapidly over the past decade and are now widely available in mainstream markets. In Switzerland more than half of all bananas are Fairtrade certified (Fairtrade International 2013). While fair trade actors in the banana sector have sought to advance decommodification, this is far more difficult than in coffee since fresh fruits require a complex and expensive cool chain to reach the market without spoiling, are often produced and traded by large corporations, and are typically sold without packaging that can be used for consumer education (Raynolds 2007). Cane sugar, another key Fairtrade product, has seen the most rapid volume increases in recent years. Roughly 40 per cent of UK bagged sugar now carries the Fairtrade mark (Fairtrade International 2013). The decommodification of sugar is hampered by the need for industrial-style processing as well as the undifferentiated nature of the consumer product market. As reflected in Table 2.2, other core Fairtrade products like tea and cocoa have also seen rapid growth. Again, although fair trade proponents have worked to promote civic and relational values fostering decommodification, in these sectors extensive processing, complex trading systems and heavy corporate engagement have promoted mainstream industrial and commercial practices and recommodification forces.

Fairtrade International has recently moved beyond the agro-food sector via the certification of products like sports balls and gold. In these new sectors efforts at decommodification have to date proven largely unsuccessful. Sports ball certification has propelled Fairtrade into industrial manufacturing arenas where workers as well as products are highly commodified. In an industry characterized by frequent subcontracting, poor labor conditions and temporary hiring, workers are treated as a variable input valued based on their cost and production efficiency. Human rights groups argue that civic and relational values are largely absent in certified sports balls supply chains, a charge that has led Fairtrade International to review its standards and procedures in this sector (Fairtrade International and International Labor Rights Forum 2010). Fairtrade International has introduced certification in gold in order to improve the conditions of the 15 million artisanal and small-scale miners working in this sector (Fairtrade Gold 2011). Gold certification appears promising since small-scale miners might benefit from many of the same provisions which currently support small-scale farmers.

Unfortunately research suggests that artisanal gold producers often rely on illegal sales since they are unable to compete with large mining corporations in international markets (Hilson and Kamlongera 2012), making it nearly impossible to uphold civic and relations values in the gold commodity network.

In short while the growing array and volume of Fairtrade products opens up opportunities to advance processes of decommodification rooted in the extension of civic and relational values, this promise is not easily realized. Decommodification has been promoted most successfully in traditional fair trade handicraft and coffee sectors through intensive and direct interactions between small-scale producers, fair trade organizations and committed consumers. In coffee, rapidly expanding sales by mainstream corporations and an increasing reliance on product labeling have promoted industrial and commercial values and recommodification forces. In Fairtrade products like bananas, sugar, tea and cocoa which involve more capital intensive, complex and value added production systems, processes of decommodification founded on alternative civic and relational conventions have been challenged even more forcefully by industrial and commercial norms, values and institutions upholding production efficiency and price competition. While both decommodification and recommodification dynamics are evident in major Fairtrade product arenas, in new product arenas like sports balls and gold, Fairtrade appears to have had very limited success in destabilizing traditional commodity relations.

PRODUCTION AND EXPORTS

Fair trade production and exports have grown dramatically in recent years across the global South. This growth has been spurred by burgeoning demand in major markets and by the widespread adoption of neoliberal policies which have increased market competition and fueled a search for new export niches. Southern producers have sought out avenues for differentiating their products according to social or ecological attributes and, where possible, accessing markets sheltered from global commodity price swings. Handicraft producers have seen some expansion in fair trade organization market opportunities. Yet the majority of growth has been for the increasing range of Fairtrade certified products. Reflecting the persistent contradictions of working in and against the market, fair trade seeks to transform production relations working largely within colonial-based circuits of primary product exports from South to North (Raynolds 2012a).

The number of producer enterprises affiliated with Fairtrade International more than doubled between 2004 and 2011, rising from 433 to 991 certified organizations (Fairtrade International 2005; 2012b). There were 1.3 million farmers and workers in 70 countries across Latin America, Africa and Asia involved in the production of Fairtrade certified items in 2012 (Fairtrade International 2013). Latin America is the traditional hub of production and continues to supply most of the world's Fairtrade certified coffee, bananas and sugar and much of its cocoa. As outlined in Table 2.3, over half of Fairtrade International affiliated groups, 538 producer organizations, are located in Latin America and the Caribbean. This region has 355 Fairtrade coffee cooperatives, as well as numerous cocoa and sugar cooperatives. There are also a large number of certified banana and other fresh fruit and juice enterprises, including both small farmer cooperatives and large producers. Africa's participation in Fairtrade has increased sharply in recent years, with the number of Fairtrade International affiliates rising from 78 to 316 between 2004 and 2011 (Fairtrade International 2005; 2012b). Africa is responsible for much of the growth in newly labeled products, with 107 large enterprises supplying certified fruits and juices. The region also has numerous certified coffee cooperatives and tea enterprises, including both large and small producers. Asia has the fewest Fairtrade certified enterprises, which primarily produce tea, sugar and coffee. Fairtrade International has recently begun certifying contract production enterprises, all of which are currently in Asia.

Fairtrade certification was founded in collaboration with small farmers and peasant cooperatives, which still comprise the backbone of production. There are 754 Fairtrade International affiliated small farmer cooperatives: Latin America has 469 small producer organizations with 280 000 members; Africa has 217 producer cooperatives, which are far bigger with over 663 000 members. Small farmer cooperatives provide social and economic representation and services and in some cases also enhance political representation (Raynolds et al. 2004). Fairtrade International's regional association, the Latin American and Caribbean Network of Small Fair Trade Producers (CLAC), is an important advocate for small producers (Bacon 2010).

Fairtrade standards shape the integration of small producers in certified networks and the distribution of benefits. Principles of fairness are advanced most directly within the market via price guarantees which protect marginal producers from bankruptcy when world prices decline (Raynolds et al. 2004). Although Fairtrade International's price-setting position supports traditional North/South inequalities, producers can exert

Table 2.3 Characteristics of Fairtrade International production by region

	Latin America & the Caribbean	Africa & the Middle East	Asia & Oceania
Producer Countries	23	30	13
Total Certified Producer Enterprises	538	316	137
Coffee enterprises[a]	355	87	49
Tea enterprises[a]	1	37	62
Cocoa enterprises[a]	71	75	8
Sugar enterprises[a]	53	36	17
Banana enterprises[a]	130	7	4
Other fresh fruit/juice enterprises[ab]	71	107	36
Small Farmer Coop Enterprises[c]	469	217	68
Small Farm Producers[c]	280 000	663 000	83 000
Hired Labor Enterprises[c]	69	99	45
Hired Laborers[c]	11 400	69 200	88 000
Contract Production Enterprises[c]	0	0	24
Contract Producers[c]	0	0	39 000

Notes: [a] Numbers do not add up to the regional totals because some groups produce other commodities.
[b]Includes fresh fruits (other than bananas) as well as wine grapes, fresh vegetables, dried fruit and fruit juices.
[c]Data are available for 990 enterprises (out of the total 991) audited by February 2012.

Sources: Compiled by the authors using data from Fairtrade International (2012b; 2013a) and FLO-Cert (2013).

significant influence in price negotiations (Bacon 2010). The social premium paid by Fairtrade buyers works beyond the market to support capacity building and community education, health and other programs (Raynolds 2009). Fairtrade standards and audit procedures effectively oversee payments of minimum prices and social premiums, but research finds that they cannot necessarily guarantee trade partnerships (Dolan 2010; Raynolds et al. 2007). While mission-driven buyers go far beyond Fairtrade requirements in promoting relational and civic engagements with producers, providing significant funding, technical support, personal assistance and long-term market commitments, mainstream market-driven buyers largely pursue conventional industrial and market practices, using certification as a supply management tool and their buying power to enforce cost-cutting and supplier competition (Raynolds 2009).

The growing prominence of large hired labor enterprises has recently altered the nature of Fairtrade production. There are 213 large Fairtrade certified enterprises employing 168 600 workers. Almost half of these plantations are in Africa. Although originally envisioned as an initiative for small producers, Fairtrade certification is now available to large and small enterprises in all areas except coffee, cocoa, sugar, honey and cotton. Fairtrade International incorporated hired labor enterprises to increase certified volumes, expand the product offer and extend benefits to hired workers. In tea, bananas, fruits, flowers and juices, certified plantations have come to outnumber and far out produce peasant co-operatives (Raynolds 2012a). CLAC and other small farmer advocates criticize plantation certification, arguing that only peasants need fairer market access. Disagreements over plantation certification have been heightened by Fair Trade USA's recent move to certify large enterprises in all commodities.

Fairtrade International has specific criteria for hired labor enterprises which shape firm participation and worker benefits. These criteria largely affirm industrial guidelines, following International Labor Organization standards related to freedom of association, freedom from discrimination, forced and child labor, occupational health and safety, wages and overtime (Raynolds 2012b). Certification assures that workers receive legally mandated benefits and may raise standards in key areas like worker health and safety, wages, overtime and benefits (Raynolds 2012b; Ruben and Schendel 2008). As in farmer cooperatives, the Fairtrade social premium in large enterprises goes beyond the market in supporting capacity building and education, health and other programs for workers, their families and communities. Fair trade's egalitarian principles may transform workers' situations most fundamentally through enhanced labor representation (Raynolds 2014). Fairtrade International requires that workers be represented in two key organizations: a Joint Body of workers and managers that oversees social premium projects and a Workers' Committee or union that defends workers' interests. In unionized sectors there may be tensions between enterprise-based Fairtrade groups and sector-based unions (Riisgaard 2009), but where unions are absent, worker representation requirements may create avenues for building collective identity and capacity (Raynolds 2012b). Fairtrade International's (2012c) recently announced 'New Workers Rights Strategy' seeks to go beyond an industrial standard approach, bolstering workers' capacity to negotiate their own conditions (Raynolds 2014). While it is too early to know how effective this new approach will be, there is no doubt that extending empowerment benefits designed for peasant producers to hired workers will be challenging.

CONCLUSIONS

In this chapter we outline the historical and empirical parameters of fair trade, laying the groundwork for subsequent more detailed analyses of the initiative's current and future trajectory. We identify four key arenas of ongoing negotiation. In institutional arenas we find that while certification ideas, practices and institutions dominate the market, mission-driven fair trade organizations and social justice allies remain critical in advancing fair trade movement principles. In consumer and market arenas we find that fair trade's rising popularity is tied to growing consumer interest in bettering social and environmental conditions yet is simultaneously fueling the mainstreaming of fair trade and rising power of market-driven corporations in this previously alternative sector. In commodity arenas we find that while fair trade seeks to fuel processes of decommodification by promoting civic and relational values, certification and labeling of products for mainstream markets advances industrial and commercial values, reinforcing a process of recommodification, particularly in commodity networks involving capital intensive and organizationally complex transactions. In production and export arenas we see that fair trade's growth involves a broadening of geographic and enterprise participation, which may widen the potential distribution of benefits yet complicates fair trade's production politics, particularly through the rising participation of large-scale enterprises and hired workers. Fair trade's future market and movement prospects will be shaped via ongoing negotiations in these four intersecting arenas.

NOTES

1. Although convention theory typically refers to 'domestic' relations, we prefer the term 'relational', which in English captures better the idea of personal trust.
2. Fairtrade International was formerly known as Fairtrade Labelling Organizations International (FLO). To avoid confusion we refer to this organization by its current name even when discussing activities prior to its name change.
3. Fairtrade International also specifies commodity-specific standards.
4. The challenges of presenting a coherent picture of the fair trade market are increasing. WFTO does not systematically collect or publish sales data. Fairtrade International does, but the United States will no longer be part of that data collection system.

5. Due in part to the different characters of the national certifiers, Cafédirect carries the UK Fairtrade label while Equal Exchange has dropped the Fair Trade USA label.
6. Fairtrade International (2013, 14) specifies standards for 300 products, but many commodities are grouped, including fresh fruits and vegetables, dried and processed fruits, juices, nuts and oil seeds, grains and composite products.

REFERENCES

Bacon, Christopher (2010), 'Who decides what is fair in fair trade? The agri-environmental governance of standards, access, and price', *Journal of Peasant Studies*, 37 (1), 111–147.

Barham, Elizabeth (2002), 'Towards a theory of values-based labeling', *Agriculture and Human Values*, 19 (4), 349–360.

Barrientos, Stephanie and Sally Smith (2007), 'Mainstreaming fair trade in global production networks: Own brand fruit and chocolate in UK supermarkets', in Laura Raynolds, Douglas Murray and John Wilkinson (eds.), *Fair Trade: The Challenges of Transforming Globalization*, New York: Routledge, pp. 103–122.

Daviron, Benoit and Isabel Vagneron (2011), 'From commoditisation to de-commoditisation … and back again: Discussing the role of sustainability standards for agricultural products', *Development Policy Review*, 29 (1), 91–113.

Dolan, Catherine (2010), 'Virtual moralities: The mainstreaming of Fairtrade in Kenyan tea fields', *Geoforum*, 41 (1), 33–43.

EFTA (European Fair Trade Association) (2010), 'Fair trade facts and figures: A success story for producers and consumers', Maastricht, the Netherlands: EFTA.

Equal Exchange (2012), 'Support the authentic fair trade movement', available at http://www.equalexchange.coop/fair-trade-campaign (accessed 3 March 2012).

Fairtrade Gold (2011), 'Fairtrade and Fairmined gold: Empowering responsible artisanal and small-scale miners', London: Fairtrade International.

Fairtrade International (2004), 'About FLO', available at http://www.fairtrade.net (accessed 3 March 2004).

Fairtrade International (2005), 'Annual report 2004/5: Delivering opportunities', Bonn, Germany: Fairtrade International.

Fairtrade International (2006), 'Annual report 2005/6: Building trust', Bonn, Germany: Fairtrade International.

Fairtrade International (2007), 'Annual report 2006/7: Shaping global partnerships', Bonn, Germany: Fairtrade International.

Fairtrade International (2009), 'Annual report 2008/9: Growing stronger together', Bonn, Germany: Fairtrade International.

Fairtrade International (2011), 'Challenges and opportunities: Supplement to annual review 2010–11', Bonn, Germany: Fairtrade International.

Fairtrade International (2012a), 'Annual report 2011/12: For producers, with producers', Bonn, Germany: Fairtrade International.

Fairtrade International (2012b), 'Monitoring the scope and benefits of Fairtrade: Fourth edition', Bonn, Germany: Fairtrade International.

Fairtrade International (2012c), 'A new workers' rights strategy for Fairtrade', available at http://www.fairtrade.net (accessed 5 January 2013).

Fairtrade International (2013), 'Annual report 2012/13: Unlocking the power', Bonn, Germany: Fairtrade International.

Fairtrade International and Globespan (2011), 'Shopping choices can make a positive difference to farmers and workers in developing countries: Global poll', available at http://www.fairtrade.net/news (accessed 25 October 2011).

Fairtrade International and International Labor Rights Forum (2010), 'FLO commends ILRF for its report on the situation of workers in the sports ball industry', available at http://www.fairtrade.net/news (accessed 5 August 2010).
Fair Trade USA (2014), 'Fair Trade USA', available at http://fairtradeusa.org (accessed 16 October 2014).
FLO-Cert (2013), 'About FLO-Cert', available at http://www.flo-cert.net (accessed 24 January 2014).
Goodman, Michael (2004), 'Reading fair trade: Political ecological imaginary and the moral economy of fair trade foods', *Political Geography*, 23 (7), 891–915.
Hilson, Gavin and Paul Kamlongera (2012), '"Fair trade gold": Prospects for Africa's artisanal miners', in Darryl Reed, Peter Utting and Ananya Mukherjee-Reed (eds.), *Business Regulation and Non-State Actors: Whose Standards? Whose Development?*, New York: Routledge, pp. 277–288.
Hudson, Ian and Mark Hudson (2003), 'Removing the veil? Commodity fetishism, fair trade, and the environment', *Organization and Environment*, 16 (4), 413–430.
Jaffee, Daniel (2007), *Brewing Justice: Fair Trade Coffee, Sustainability, and Survival*, Berkeley, CA: University of California Press.
Jaffee, Daniel (2012), 'Weak coffee: Certification and co-optation in the fair trade movement', *Social Problems*, 59 (1), 94–116.
Johnston, Josée (2008), 'The citizen–consumer hybrid: Ideological tensions and the case of Whole Foods Market', *Theory and Society*, 37 (3), 229–270.
Leatherhead Food International (2012), 'Fairtrade foods – an ethical option for the mainstream?', Surrey, UK: Leatherhead Food International.
Micheletti, Michele (2003), *Political Virtue and Shopping: Individuals, Consumerism, and Collective Action*, New York: Macmillan.
Mutersbaugh, Tad (2005), 'Just-in-space: Certified rural products, labor of quality, and regulatory spaces', *Journal of Rural Studies*, 21 (4), 389–402.
Polanyi, Karl (1957), *The Great Transformation: The Political and Economic Origins of Our Time*, Boston, MA: Beacon Press.
Raynolds, Laura T. (2000), 'Re-embedding global agriculture: The international organic and fair trade movements', *Agriculture and Human Values*, 17 (3), 297–309.
Raynolds, Laura T. (2002), 'Consumer/producer links in fair trade coffee networks', *Sociologia Ruralis*, 42 (4), 404–424.
Raynolds, Laura T. (2004), 'The globalization of organic agro-food networks', *World Development*, 42 (5), 725–743.
Raynolds, Laura T. (2007), 'Fair trade bananas: Broadening the movement and market in the United States', in Laura Raynolds, Douglas Murray and John Wilkinson (eds.), *Fair Trade: The Challenges of Transforming Globalization*, New York: Routledge, pp. 63–82.
Raynolds, Laura T. (2009), 'Mainstreaming fair trade coffee: From partnership to traceability', *World Development*, 37 (6), 1083–1093.
Raynolds, Laura T. (2012a), 'Fair trade: Social regulation in global food markets', *Journal of Rural Studies*, 28 (3), 276–287.
Raynolds, Laura T. (2012b), 'Fair trade flowers: Global certification, environmental sustainability, and labor standards', *Rural Sociology*, 77 (4), 493–519.
Raynolds, Laura T. (2014), 'Fairtrade, certification, and labor: Global and local tensions in improving conditions for agricultural workers', *Agriculture and Human Values*, 31 (3), 499–511.
Raynolds, Laura T., Douglas L. Murray and Peter Taylor (2004), 'Fair trade coffee: Building producer capacity via global networks', *Journal of International Development*, 16 (8), 1109–1121.
Raynolds, Laura T., Douglas L. Murray and John Wilkinson (eds.) (2007), *Fair Trade: The Challenges of Transforming Globalization*, New York: Routledge.

Renard, Marie-Christine (1999), 'The interstices of globalization: The example of fair coffee', *Sociologia Ruralis*, 39 (4), 484–500.

Renard, Marie-Christine (2003), 'Fair trade: Quality, market and conventions', *Journal of Rural Studies*, 19 (1), 87–96.

Riisgaard, Lone (2009), 'Global value chains, labor organization and private social standards: Lessons from East African cut flower industries', *World Development*, 37 (2), 326–340.

Ruben, Ruerd and Lucie van Schendel (2008), 'The impact of fair trade in banana plantations in Ghana', in Ruerd Ruben (ed.), *The Impact of Fair Trade*, Wageningen, the Netherlands: Wageningen Academic Publishers, pp. 137–154.

Thévenot, Laurent (1995), 'Des marchés aux normes', in Gilles Allaire and Robert Boyer (eds.), *Régulation et Conventions dans L'Agriculture et L'Agro-Alimentaire*, Paris: INRA, pp. 33–51.

WFTO (World Fair Trade Organization) (2013), 'About WFTO', available at http://www.wfto.com (accessed 10 December 2013).

PART II

THE FAIR TRADE MOVEMENT

3. The meaning of fair trade

Steven Suranovic[*]

INTRODUCTION

When American politicians discuss international trade on the campaign trail they are likely to use the following popular refrain, 'I am in favor of free trade as long as it is also fair trade'. Politicians are quick to discuss the unfair trading practices of other countries that put American workers at a disadvantage. US corporations usually join in, perhaps because they are the inspiration behind this refrain. Businesses often complain that the practices of foreign companies and foreign governments steal jobs away from American workers and put US businesses at a disadvantage. Allegations usually involve unfairly low wages, lenient environmental and safety standards, child labor and government policies such as subsidies, all of which give foreign firms an advantage in international markets.

The political effectiveness of unfair trade allegations as a rhetorical device is bolstered by several factors. First, virtually everyone supports fairness; no one can reasonably argue that *unfair* policies are acceptable and so there is never opposition to fairness in principle. Second, fairness is a multifaceted concept that can take on different meanings. This implies that a group of people, all in support of fairness, may actually be supporting different notions of fairness simultaneously. Third, most people instinctively and strongly respond to situations they interpret as unfair. For these reasons, if you can convince someone that something is unfair, then you may also convince them to support actions or policies that will protect against or eliminate the unfairness.

In the recent past, living standards and poverty levels have improved significantly around the world. However, many people in the Southern countries, in particular those producing primary commodities, receive very low wages, keeping them in a state of poverty. The multilateral trading system embodied in the World Trade Organization (WTO) promotes liberalization of international trade and investment as one solution. However, the fair trade movement considers current income inequalities to be not only unfair, but also often caused by the current structure of the international trading system.

The rhetorical argument of unfairness is also a key feature in the fair trade movement. The fair trade movement's structure has three main components: '(i) the organization of alternative trading networks; (ii) the marketing of Fair Trade labeled products through licensed conventional traders and retailers; and (iii) the campaign-based promotion of Fair Trade to change both purchasing practices and the rules of conventional trade' (Wilkinson 2007, 219). According to Laura Raynolds, 'Fair Trade represents a critique of historically rooted international trade inequalities and efforts to create more egalitarian commodity networks linking marginalized producers in the global South with progressive consumers in the global North' (Raynolds 2009, 1083). The model gives farmers better prices, long-term trade links, and resources for improving social and environmental outcomes. The model also gives consumers more options to buy products produced at high social standards and campaigns to produce ethically responsible consumers.

For the fair trade labeling system to work, consumers must be persuaded that the trade of coffee, tea, bananas and other commodities under *normal* market circumstances is unfair in some way. Fairtrade International (formerly Fairtrade Labelling Organizations International, or FLO) affixes a label to all commodities that satisfy a set of criteria assuring higher prices and more sustainable production processes among the primary producers. Therefore, if consumers purchase a product with an official fair trade label, they are assured that the outcome and process resulting from their purchase is more fair than conventionally traded products, at least in the eyes of Fairtrade International.

However, fairness can mean different things in different circumstances. Suranovic (2000) suggested that there are seven distinct ways public policy advocates use fairness in discussing trade policy proposals. Each conception of fairness revolves around the concept of equality. However, equality can be applied in several ways: first with respect to actions and processes, and second with respect to final outcomes. These conceptions are considered in turn: first in general terms, second in reference to specific trade situations and finally with respect to labeled fair trade product markets.

FAIRNESS AS EQUALITY OF ACTIONS OR PROCESSES

One application of fairness involves an expectation that people will be treated equally; that individuals will not be discriminated against on the basis of inconsequential characteristics such as gender, race or religion.

For example, if a merchant selling apples charges a white person $1 per apple but charges a black person $1.50 per apple, then blacks will surely be outraged and believe they are being unfairly treated in the market. The same sense of injustice would arise if people of different religions, or ethnicities, or genders were charged a different price for the same product or, even more seriously, if a certain class of person was excluded entirely from participating in a market.

Nonetheless, differential pricing is not always considered unfair. In economics, this practice is referred to as price discrimination, and it can be worthwhile for merchants when they can use it to capture a greater share of the surplus value generated by exchange. For example, wealthier consumers typically are willing to pay more for a good than less wealthy consumers. In this case, a firm would profit more if it could charge the wealthy consumers, who are also less price-sensitive, more than the less wealthy consumers, who are more price-sensitive. This is why retired persons and children receive a discount at movie theaters and also why airline ticket prices will differ for two identical economy class seats if one has a Saturday stay over and the other does not.

In an extreme form of discrimination, even complete exclusion from market participation sometimes occurs and is tolerated. An example of this is the US embargo on trade with Cuba, which prevents all transactions with people of a specific nationality. Clearly, one problem with fairness is that it is not always applied consistently across situations. Whether these actions are considered unfair is subject to interpretation, but certainly a judgment about the fairness of price discrimination depends on the circumstances.

In an application to international trade, equal treatment is incorporated in the form of two non-discrimination principles in the WTO: most favored nation and national treatment. With the most favored nation principle, WTO members agree to offer the most favorable tariff and trade treatment to all other WTO members equally; thus the United States does not charge a higher tariff against China than it does against other WTO members. The national treatment principle requires WTO countries to treat imported products the same way as domestically produced products once the foreign goods have cleared customs. In this way, WTO rules are applied equally and can be interpreted as assuring a fairer outcome in international trade.

Another common use of fairness involves an expectation of reciprocity between individuals. If Tom gives something worth $10 to Sally, then Sally may feel compelled to reciprocate by giving something worth about $10 to Tom. Indeed, all voluntary trades between two individuals involve a reciprocal exchange of two items of approximately the same value (e.g., $2 for one loaf of bread). Since the effect on both sides is positive and approximately equal, we can call this notion of fairness, positive reciprocity.

In an international trade context, a similar quid pro quo occurs in the negotiation of trade liberalization agreements. During negotiations countries offer trade liberalization concessions to partners in exchange for comparable concessions from the other members. For example, one country may offer to lower its tariffs by 20 per cent in a WTO negotiating round if the other countries also lower their tariffs by 20 per cent. Or one country may lower its tariff rates to some degree in exchange for allowances that international intellectual property rights will be enforced. Again, in this case fairness depends on the perception of an equal reciprocal exchange.

Perhaps one of the most frequently applied fairness principles involves an expectation that individuals, or countries, will follow a commonly accepted set of rules. When agents in an economy are perceived to play by different rules, or if the rules seem to be suspended for some, and unequally applied, then others are quick to claim unfairness. Domestically, the rules are the national and state laws a country has incorporated. Internationally, the rules can be treaties or trade agreements. The WTO agreement consists of a set of trade liberalization 'promises' that countries have made to each other and which countries therefore expect to be maintained. When one country does not abide by those promises, other countries typically charge them with unfair trade practices.

Violation of the rules can also inspire another commonly accepted fair response. If someone violates national or state laws and is caught, then the offender will generally be forced to suffer negative consequences, which may include anything from a monetary penalty to incarceration, or even death in some cases. Justice and fairness prevails if the size of the punishment is approximately equal to the harm caused by violating the rule. Since a negative effect is reciprocated with an equal negative response, we can call this negative reciprocity: it is a form of justice. Unfairness, or injustice, arises, however, if the consequence is out of proportion with the harm caused. Thus it may be judged unfair if a murderer gets away with no jail sentence, but it is also unfair if a petty drug dealer gets a lifetime jail sentence. In each case, the penalty is substantially unequal to the damages caused by violating the rules, which thereby generates the perception of unfairness. In an international trade setting, if, after a WTO Dispute Settlement investigation, a country is deemed to have violated its WTO agreement, and if that offending country refuses to correct the problem, then the negatively affected countries are allowed to impose policy changes that will harm the first country by an approximately equal amount; hence, this is an application of negative reciprocity fairness.

At this point it is now possible to illustrate how fairness principles can conflict with each other. Consider again the trade embargo the United States imposes on Cuba. To some observers, the restriction on trade with people of Cuban nationality may seem like unfair discrimination. The people of Cuba, through no fault of their own, must suffer negative consequences by not being allowed to purchase US products. Similarly, US consumers are restricted by law from purchasing Cuban products, such as their world famous Cuban cigars. In contrast, supporters of the policy consider the embargo to be a fair reciprocal response to the harm the Cuban government causes by violating the human rights of its own people. In the first case, the embargo is unfair because of unequal discriminatory treatment. In the second case, the embargo is fair due to an application of negative reciprocity.

The embargo situation is a specific example of a more general phenomenon. Because different conceptions of fairness can be applied to the same situation and because these conceptions often conflict, it is possible to argue that an action is fair with respect to one principle, while unfair with respect to another. Thus, China may argue the United States is unfair because it discriminates by taking many more trade remedy actions against it than against other countries. The United States would argue that these actions are fair because they are following procedures that are allowed under the WTO agreement and thus are adhering to the accepted rules.

FAIRNESS AS EQUALITY OF OUTCOMES

An alternative use of fairness applies a belief in the equality of outcomes. If a person believes that people are all inherently equal in some sense, then it is sometimes difficult to understand why the living standards of people can be so different in the world today. Why do some people earn millions of dollars per year and enjoy the luxuries of expensive homes, autos and vacations, while many others in the world are stuck earning just a dollar a day, or less, and must endure the hardships of poverty and deprivation? Concern about this disparity contributes to the demands for fairness and justice in the form of a more equal distribution of income and wealth.

Many view these disparities in income and wealth around the world as a sign of unfairness and economic injustice. Consequently, there is often support for actions that would effectively reduce that inequality. However, we should ask whether it is valid to describe inequality of outcomes as automatically unfair or unjust and what method of redistribution, if any, is appropriate. For example, is it automatically unfair if CEOs earn extremely high salaries while factory workers in the same company earn only dollars a day? Is it automatically fair to redistribute income from rich to poor via progressive income taxes or by other methods? To illustrate the issue simply, consider the following series of stylized scenarios examining two individuals, Bert and Ernie, who in a series of hypothetical events will experience unequal outcomes.

1. Unequal but not Unfair

In the first scenario, suppose Bert spends all day working to make a table. He collects wood from the local forest; cuts, sands, shapes and nails the lumber together; finally he sands and stains it. He then takes the table to the local market and sells it for $150. With the money he purchases a fabulous meal including steak, lobster, expensive wine and chocolate cake for dessert. Ernie spends the same day lounging around watching television. He has no motivation to make a table and is too tired to go to the market. At the end of the day he finds his cupboards are bare and has nothing but a few leftover stale crackers to eat.

The final outcome in this scenario is clearly unequal. Bert has a fantastic meal to eat, and Ernie has only a few crackers. However, it seems unlikely, given the conditions, that most people would judge this unequal outcome unfair. After all, Bert worked hard all day to produce something valuable enough to sell for $150. His effort seems to warrant the fabulous meal he enjoys at the end of the day. Ernie, on the other hand, did nothing all day. Most would be hard pressed to explain why Ernie 'deserves' to get much more than the stale crackers. Indeed, for both Bert and Ernie, each received approximately what he gave, and so the outcome would appear fair on the basis of reciprocity. Thus, reciprocity fairness can justify the unequal outcome, which we might call 'Unequal, but not Unfair'.

2. Unequal and Unfair

In the second scenario, we will consider some role reversal. Suppose Ernie works hard all day to construct the table, which he then sells at the market and purchases a fabulous meal. Bert behaves as Ernie did before, lounging around all day leaving him with nothing but stale crackers to eat in the evening. However, in a twist of the story, suppose Bert lives next door to Ernie and while passing by in the evening spots the fabulous meal waiting to be eaten, through Ernie's window. While Ernie is occupied on a telephone call, Bert sneaks in and steals the fabulous meal.

In terms of final consumption, the final outcome in this scenario is exactly the same as in the first scenario. Bert has a fantastic meal to eat and Ernie is stuck with a few stale crackers. However, no one is likely to judge this unequal outcome as fair. In terms of reciprocity, this outcome is grossly unfair, since Ernie worked hard all day to produce something valuable enough to sell for $150 but is rewarded in the end only with a few stale crackers. Bert, on the other hand, did nothing all day, and yet by virtue of his thievery was rewarded with a fabulous meal. Additionally, the blatant act of theft, a violation of property rights, easily characterizes this case as unfair. Thus, unfairness due to the lack of reciprocity and an unequal outcome enables us to call this 'Unequal and Unfair'.

3. Unequal and Unfortunate, but not Unfair: Version 1

In the third scenario, we complicate the situation slightly. Bert behaves as in the first scenario, working hard to construct a table, which he then sells at the market and purchases a fabulous meal. Ernie acts as in Scenario 1 as well, lounging around, except in this version, Ernie suffers from a debilitating illness that makes it impossible to wield the tools needed to produce a marketable table. Although Ernie has the motivation and desire to work as hard as Bert does, he is physically unable to do so. If the story plays out as before, because Ernie produces nothing to sell at the market, he must suffer the fate of Scenario 1 and consume nothing but stale crackers at the end of the day.

As in the previous scenarios, the outcome is identically unequal. But is this outcome unfair as well as unequal? Different observers might reach opposite conclusions. As in the first scenario, both Bert and Ernie receive benefits in proportion to their contribution, so in terms of reciprocity the outcome seems fair. However, the fact that Ernie did not produce anything is not his fault, and that seems unfair. On the other hand, the fact that Ernie has nothing is not Bert's fault either, as it clearly was in Scenario 2. One solution may be to deem this outcome 'Unequal and Unfortunate, but not Unfair'.

Is there a solution to fix unfortunate outcomes? There would seem to be two possibilities in this simple scenario. Bert may learn of Ernie's unfortunate circumstance and decide to offer Ernie a part of his meal; perhaps the lobster and half a bottle of wine. In this case, an altruistic and compassionate gesture alleviates the unfortunate suffering. Alternatively, an external entity, like the government, could alleviate the inequality and despair by taxing some of Bert's income and transferring it to Ernie, thereby assuring that both have enough to eat. Both solutions yield the same outcome; however, there is one important distinction. When the government taxes Bert, Bert cannot object. Refusal to pay the taxes may be met with fines, or even arrest (violation of the rules under negative reciprocity fairness). If Bert objects to the transfer and is taxed anyway, he may feel similar to the way Ernie felt in Scenario 2 when his hard earned meal was stolen away. In both cases, and under this interpretation, individuals have some of their own production involuntarily transferred away; in the first case via theft, and in the second case via government taxes.

Now of course, one need not assume, as suggested above, that Bert is necessarily opposed to the government tax and transfer program. Indeed, Bert may feel that the government program is the ideal way to ensure that individuals like Ernie are treated with compassion. Bert may even vote legislators into office that will impose compassionate tax and transfer laws. The key difference now is that the government is merely substituting for what Bert would have done voluntarily. The government becomes a mechanism for compassionate redistribution that is voluntarily accepted by its citizens.

Thus, while transfers are clearly one way to alleviate the unfortunate suffering of someone like Ernie, who cannot produce for himself, whether those transfers are made willingly or unwillingly would seem to be critical in making a judgment about the fairness of the process. Whether via independent giving or via government transfers, if Bert gives what he has produced to Ernie voluntarily, both Bert and Ernie are likely to be satisfied with the process. However, if Bert is taxed involuntarily, Ernie may be grateful, but Bert is likely to feel as if he were robbed.

4. Unequal and Unfortunate, but not Unfair: Version 2

In this scenario, let us assume that Bert behaves again as in scenarios 1 and 3, working hard all day to construct a table which he then sells at the market earning $150, with which he purchases a fabulous meal. Ernie also works hard all day producing a different product that he also takes to the market to sell at the end of the day. Suppose Ernie works every bit as hard as Bert does to produce his good, however, the best price he can get for his product at the market is just $20. With $20 he can afford a basic meal, better than stale crackers, but he cannot afford to eat steak, lobster and wine.

Again, the outcome is unequal but not quite as unequal as in the previous scenarios. Each person did receive something in proportion to the value he created for the market, so the outcome would seem to be fair based on reciprocity. However, if one believes reward, or desert, should be based on effort – a kind of labor theory of value – then the outcome may not be viewed as reciprocally fair since each did not receive something proportional to his effort. Thus, interpretations of unfairness may vary because the measures that are being equalized may differ between two observers.

One might delve deeper and ask whether it is Ernie's fault that he produced a less desirable product. If not his fault, then one may be more inclined to view the outcome as unfair. However, if Ernie simply guessed poorly about what would be desirable in the market, then the outcome seems to be more 'Unfortunate, but not Unfair'.

5. Unfair with Market Access Restrictions

In the final scenario, assume there is a large market for tables and that Bert is just one of many individual producers and sellers of tables. As a result of the competition in the market, imagine that the price of tables is $100 and thus the meal to be purchased by the table producers is good, but not fabulous. Suppose that Ernie learns how to make tables of equal quality as well and decides to enter the market as an additional supplier. With his additional supply the price might fall further to $90. However, suppose Ernie learns that to sell tables in the market he needs to obtain a special license, and those licenses are in limited supply and difficult to obtain. Suppose that Bert and the other table sellers supported the government license system as a way of maintaining jobs and keeping incomes high in the table industry.

Here, the inequality involves the access to the market by different producers. The favored producers ensure that licenses are allocated to themselves. By restricting equal access to the market, the favored producers secure a price premium. This situation would clearly be viewed as unfair to the potential market entrants, as well as to the buyers of tables, who would be able to purchase tables at even lower prices if there were free competition. On the other hand, the original licensed table producers may argue that the system is necessary for quality control; that is, to ensure that only high-quality tables are available for consumers to purchase. Thus, they may claim that the anti-competitive restrictions are necessary and perfectly fair.

These scenarios help us develop a framework for analyzing fairness and equality in several different situations. The next section extends these perspectives to the principles of the fair trade movement in order to better understand what fair trade means, as well as to consider its motives.

FAIRNESS OF FAIR TRADE PRODUCT MARKETS

The fair trade movement includes alternative trade networks, marketing of fair trade labeled products and campaign-based promotions to change current trading behaviors by consumers and conventional trade rules. Fair trade certification began around 1990 with the creation of several alternative trade organizations that directly purchased products from farmers in the global South and marketed them with labels including Max Havelaar, TransFair and the Fairtrade mark. Fairtrade International now encompasses all of these labels under the Fairtrade mark and oversees the Fairtrade system. Principles of this certification include fair prices and direct trade for producers, among others (see Laura Raynolds and Nick Greenfield's chapter in this volume). However, another important aspect of the Fairtrade label is assuring consumers that producers were treated more fairly and that they are making a responsible purchase that will help alleviate poverty. Nonetheless, the fairness principles applied in this situation are not obvious.

Perhaps the most likely motivation for fair trade products are the income inequalities that arise from the very low prices and wages paid to workers who produce the basic commodities. To determine fair prices, Fairtrade International develops agreements with producer organizations, not individuals, and calculates the price minimum 'on the basis of production and broader reproduction costs', among other things (Wilkinson 2007, 222). By raising the price received by low-wage farmers, inequality is diminished somewhat and farmers will earn more and live better. Thus, fair trade products are fairer because they can ensure a higher price is paid to the commodity producers, which will in turn reduce the inequality. However, to determine if low wages and inequality are unfair, as discussed in the scenarios above, it makes sense to evaluate how the inequality arises.

Perhaps the best candidate for unfairness in international commodity markets is the concentration of market power among intermediaries (Nicholls and Opal 2005). The supply chain for fair trade products is often described like an hourglass, in which many producers on one end supply many consumers on the other end, but the product must pass through the hands of a small number of wholesale intermediaries. In the coffee industry, for example, from the early 1990s, four transnational companies – Nestlé, Philip Morris, Sara Lee and Procter & Gamble –

accounted for more than 60 per cent of coffee sales in the major consuming markets. Among the coffee importing companies, five major ones, Neumann Gruppe, Volcafe, ED&F Man, Ecom Agroindustrial and Goldman Sachs controlled 40 per cent of the coffee market (Talbot 2004).

If intermediary import firms can limit free entry by competitors, then they can act with monopsony power, force a lower commodity price and take advantage of poorer farmers. In 2000–2001, coffee growers received only 10.4 per cent of the total income generated by coffee, whereas the value added in the consumer countries was 79.4 per cent (Talbot 2004). With respect to the final consumers, the intermediary processors may use their monopoly power by restricting supply and forcing up the final price. In this way, the intermediaries become richer at the expense of both the farmers and the consumers. Greater competition in the intermediary market would force the final consumer price down and the farmer price up, thereby equalizing to a degree the gain or profit along the supply chain. In this way, competition among intermediaries would raise farm prices and benefit the farmers.

However, if high concentration of firms in the supply chain restricted competition, imposing a minimum price floor for fair trade products would raise the producer price closer to the price they would obtain in a competitive market, that is, a market in which intermediaries could not exercise their monopsony power. The fair trade labeling process could therefore create a non-governmental method of maintaining a minimum wage and would correct for an unfair market outcome (Hayes 2006).

Another bottleneck that prevailed along the supply chain in markets like coffee was government intervention and control by state agencies. These agencies regulated the domestic coffee market by requiring export licenses and setting price supports. Some countries had state marketing boards that had monopoly power on exports of coffee. Although these agencies often provided benefits to farmers in the form of agricultural research and helped to reduce price fluctuations, by virtue of their control of the market, they were also well placed to capture some of the rents arising from regulated markets (Talbot 2004). These rents are monies that can wind up in the hands of the government agencies rather than trickling down to the farmer. Thus, any bottleneck in the supply chain, and the consequent lack of competition, provides a source of rents to those in control of the flow through the bottleneck. Those rents arise by squeezing, some might say exploiting, both the small farmer on one end and the consumer on the other end of the chain. In other words, unfairness arises by restricting free access to the market, much like in the fifth scenario above. However, it is important to recognize that these bottlenecks can be caused both by the concentration of a small number of intermediary firms and by the presence of government agencies that regulate the flow of the product from producer to consumer.

Another source of low prices in commodity markets like coffee could be poor information communicated to the small-scale farmers. Economists often assume that market participants have perfect information including, in this case, knowledge of world market prices. If the small farmer knows the prices received by all other commodity producers, then they are in a better position to bargain, or hold out, for a higher price.

For example, suppose a small-scale coffee producer is willing to accept $1 per pound for coffee while the wholesale firm can make a profit if it can purchase coffee for less than $1.50 per pound. In this case, any deal struck between $1 and $1.50 will generate a surplus that will be split between the two parties. What proportion of the surplus goes to which side will depend on their bargaining capacities, which in turn will depend on the availability of market information. Better information enables farmers to bargain for a greater share of the 50 cent surplus. Thus, the competitive market with perfect information can work more effectively and fairly because the intermediaries cannot fool the small farmers into accepting a low price and thereby claim for themselves a greater share of the surplus value.

If information is not readily available in the rural countryside, then intermediaries can deceive the farmers into accepting a very low price. In this case, the unfairness arises out of a kind of theft by deceptive practices, much like in Scenario 2 above. Fair trade systems that ensure higher prices may thereby generate outcomes that are closer to what would obtain in a system with full information and more balanced bargaining abilities. In addition, the support in fair trade systems for union formation and the establishment of cooperatives offers a mechanism that can ensure a better flow of information to rural farmers.

Coordination problems can also account for low prices obtained by the small-scale farmers. Since products like coffee require planting many years prior to first harvest, the fixed costs in production are high. If many farmers plant coffee because they expect high prices in the future, then higher market supply could push prices much lower than is profitable for the farmers. This kind of situation is typical in most commodity markets and did arise in the coffee market several decades ago. In the late 1980s, coffee prices were relatively high, in part due to an international coffee agreement that artificially restricted trade flows between exporter and importer countries. This allowed surplus rents to be obtained mostly by the intermediary firms and the coffee regulators. After the coffee quotas were suspended in 1989, coffee prices immediately fell and experienced wide swings during the subsequent two decades. New producers, such as Vietnam, began to export a substantial amount of coffee and this contributed to much lower prices in many subsequent years. These conditions make it difficult to predict future prices and also make it extremely difficult for the small-scale farmers who are totally reliant on the coffee market for their livelihood.

In this case, producers misjudge how much others will produce of the commodity and thus make an improper decision about how profitable it will be. Again, the problem is imperfect information. However, in this case it is more difficult to claim the outcome is unfair. The problem arises more out of the inability of numerous commodity producers to coordinate their activities, but not because one group is taking advantage of another. In this way the situation is more like the 'Unequal and Unfortunate, but not Unfair' Version 2 (i.e., Scenario 4) above in which Ernie guesses wrongly about the market and it results in a bad outcome. In a similar way, volatility in commodity prices has unfortunate consequences that might not be deemed unfair. Reductions of volatility can be achieved either by government intervention that ensures consistently high prices for producers, or with a more competitive private insurance market.

CONCLUSION

The analysis in this chapter provides criteria that can be applied to assess whether trading situations are fair or unfair. After evaluating these fairness criteria as they apply in many international trading contexts, we focus on the fairness of the fair trade product markets with labeling systems. However, we do not reach a definitive conclusion with respect to the fairness of the fair trade product markets. Instead, the low prices paid to farmers of primary commodities may be judged either unfair or unfortunate depending on the circumstances that prevail in the commodity market.

Most economists would contend that market outcomes are mostly fair if there is a high degree of competition across the supply chain and if the information needed to make decisions is available to all market participants (Fridell 2007). However, some market participants can take advantage of others if they can limit competition or if they have better information about the market. In this case, economists say that the market is imperfect, or, the market fails. However, simply because prices paid to poor farmers are lower than some observers would like, or even so low as to force incomes below a living wage, that is still not adequate information to ensure that there is monopsony power in the commodity markets, nor is it sufficient to claim that the poorer farmers are being taken advantage of because of inadequate information.

Nonetheless, even if monopsony power is not strong and if information about world market prices is good in the rural farming communities, suppose that some people are simply concerned about the unfortunate circumstances that relegate such a small share of the coffee revenue in the North to the poor small-scale farmers in the South. In this case, the fair trade labeling system enables compassionate consumers in the North to contribute extra money to help out the poorer farmers in the South. The outcome is much like the situations in scenarios 3 and 4 above, in which unfortunate circumstances generates inequality and inspires a compassionate transfer between people (Reinstein and Song 2012). This means that the fair trade system might truly be protecting poor farmers from unfair exploitation by monopsony commodity buyers, or, it may be enabling a compassionate transfer from wealthier commodity users in the North to poorer commodity producers in the South.

In either case, there is one aspect of the fair trade system that should make it less objectionable: the fact that it is a voluntary system. Both primary producers and commodity consumers choose for themselves whether to participate in the fair trade product markets. Even if unfair trade is not actually occurring, the system still acts as a mechanism of income transfer from wealthier to poorer individuals. Economists may contend that this is not the most efficient way to exact transfers from rich to poor; however, this transfer is not made possible because of a coercive tax; instead, the extra premium is paid with the full understanding of its intended purpose, to help support higher wages for poorer farmers in the South. Whether or not a consumer shares the definitions of fairness provided here, that consumer has the intention of contributing to higher incomes for poorer farmers.

There is one circumstance, however, when this voluntary system would fail; that is, if the higher premiums do not reach the final destination and noticeably improve the outcomes for the Southern poor. In this case, the outcome would be a tragic irony because the unfairness would arise from a deceptive fair trade labeling system that promotes itself as providing fair outcomes. Indeed, this is the argument of critics like Sidwell (2008).

For this reason, it is critical to demonstrate that the fair trade labeling system is having a notably positive impact on the livelihoods of poor rural farmers. The research on the issue is mixed, as is to be expected.[1] Two chapters in this volume, that by Leonardo Becchetti, Stefano Castriota and Pierluigi Conzo and that by Valerie Nelson and Adrienne Martin, offer the most recent reviews of the impacts of the fair trade labeling system. The challenge for fair trade labeling, though, especially if its goal is to supplant the free trade system with a fairer alternative, will be to show that fair trade can deliver consistently lower poverty and reduced inequality more effectively than can the conventional free trade system.

NOTES

* Many thanks for support from the Institute for International Economic Policy and for research assistance from Pegi Ylli.

1. Gary (2004) and Bacon (2005) demonstrate mostly positive impacts of fair trade, Beuchelt and Zeller (2011) show mostly negative effects, while the results in Lyon (2011), Sick (2008) and Valkila and Nygren (2010) are more mixed.

REFERENCES

Bacon, Christopher (2005), 'Confronting the coffee crisis: Can fair trade, organic, and specialty coffees reduce small-scale farmer vulnerability in northern Nicaragua?', *World Development*, 33 (3), 497–511.

Beuchelt, Tina D. and Manfred Zeller (2011), 'Profits and poverty: Certification's troubled link for Nicaragua's organic and Fairtrade coffee producers', *Ecological Economics*, 70 (7), 1316–1324.

Fridell, Gavin (2007), *Fair Trade Coffee: The Prospects and Pitfalls of Market-Driven Social Justice*, Toronto: University of Toronto Press, Inc.

Gary, Heather G. (2004), 'Justice is brewing in Guatemala', *U.S. Catholic*, 69 (8), 30–34.

Hayes, Mark (2006), 'On the efficiency of fair trade', *Review of Social Economy*, 64 (4), 447–468.

Lyon, Sarah (2011), *Coffee and Community*, 1st edition, Boulder, CO: University Press of Colorado.

Nicholls, Alex and Charlotte Opal (2005), *Fair Trade: Market-Driven Ethical Consumption*, London: Sage Publications Ltd.

Raynolds, Laura T. (2009), 'Mainstreaming fair trade coffee: From partnership to traceability', *World Development*, 37 (6), 1083–1093.

Reinstein, David and Joon Song (2012), 'Efficient consumer altruism and fair trade products', *Journal of Economics and Management Strategy*, 21 (1), 213–241.

Sick, Deborah (2008), 'Coffee, farming families and fair trade in Costa Rica', *Latin American Research Review*, 43 (3), 193–205.

Sidwell, Marc (2008), 'Unfair trade', Adam Smith Research Trust, ASI (Research), London.

Suranovic, Steven M. (2000), 'A positive analysis of fairness with applications to international trade', *The World Economy*, 23 (3), 283–307.

Talbot, John M. (2004), *Grounds for Agreement: The Political Economy of the Coffee Commodity Chain*, Lanham, MD: Lowman & Littlefield Publishers, Inc.

Valkila, Joni and Anja Nygren (2010), 'Impacts of fair trade certification on coffee farmers, cooperatives, and laborers in Nicaragua', *Agriculture and Human Values*, 27 (3), 321–333.

Wilkinson, John (2007), 'Fair trade: Dynamic and dilemmas of a market oriented global social movement', *Journal of Consumer Policy*, 30 (3), 219–239.

4. Corporate accountability, fair trade and multi-stakeholder regulation

*Peter Utting**

INTRODUCTION

Progressive civil society actors, both historically and today, have played a key role in efforts to tame big business and market forces. But current forms of engagement are quite different to those of the early and mid-20th century when trades unions and faith-based organizations took the lead. This reflects the significant changes that have occurred in the character of civil society, evidenced in: 1) the rise of new social movements such as the anti-sweatshop, fair trade and environmental justice movements; 2) the rapid expansion of 'professional' service delivery non-governmental organizations (NGOs) that depend on government grants, philanthropy and consultancies for their funding; 3) the participation of NGOs in policy dialogues, so-called epistemic communities and public–private partnerships; and 4) new forms of advocacy and policy engagement through networks and multi-stakeholder initiatives. The portfolio of action and institutions that constitute 'civil regulation' (Murphy and Bendell 1997) concerned with environmental, social and governance (ESG) dimensions of business behavior and trade has broadened significantly (Utting 2012b).[1]

One of the most significant developments in recent years relates to the growing importance of NGOs or multi-stakeholder entities as formal regulatory actors. They are assuming regulatory authority, that is, taking on functions – hitherto associated with state institutions – that involve the design, promotion and implementation of standards (Braithwaite 2005). They are not only participating in governmental or inter-governmental processes – for example, designing or revising instruments of international soft law such as the UN Guidelines on Business and Human Rights or the Organisation for Economic Co-operation and Development (OECD) Guidelines for Multinational Enterprises, or participating in the governance structures of institutions such as the United Nations Global Compact (UNGC). They are also taking the lead and assuming direct responsibility for the regulation of business and (fair) trade through various standard-setting and certification initiatives (Abbott and Snidal 2009; Utting 2012a).

Much of the literature within the fields of governance, organizational studies and business management views this new regulatory phenomenon in a positive light: the schemes involved can fill regulatory gaps that have emerged under globalization and the rolling back of certain functions of the state; the field of voluntary initiatives is associated with the ethos of 'continuous improvement' through learning by doing; and multi-stakeholder regulation is part and parcel of civilizing features of modernization and 'good governance' that relate to collaboration, dialogue, transparency and accountability. Indeed, within these literatures is a strong current that suggests that actors are moving from being conflictive interest groups to 'stakeholders' and partners, and that activism centered on confrontation is passé or 'ideological' (SustainAbility 2003; Zadek 2001). From this perspective, trends associated with private governance or multi-stakeholder regulation are part and parcel of a re-emerging model of 'embedded liberalism' that creates and strengthens institutions that can re-embed business and markets in progressive societal values (Ruggie 2003).

A far less sanguine view prevails within various strands of international political economy and critical theory. Such perspectives are concerned that various forms of civil regulation simply help to legitimize efforts to tweak the market liberal paradigm that has prevailed in recent decades (Utting 2013). Such tweaking gives rise to corporate 'greenwash' (Greer and Bruno 1996) or amounts to a savvy repositioning on the part of corporate elites to regain legitimacy and better coordinate global value chains (Sum 2010).

Within this new field of regulation can, indeed, be found quite different approaches. Some sit comfortably within the voluntarist frame of business-friendly corporate social responsibility (CSR). Others conform more to the 'corporate accountability' agenda that places more emphasis on harder forms of regulation and the need to address various blind spots (related to more contentious, often structural, issues) on the CSR agenda (Utting 2012b; see also Alex Hughes's chapter in this volume). The corporate accountability agenda also insists on some sort of penalties for non-compliance and the need for effective redress.

But broad generalizations often overlook the significant changes that can occur through time in the normative orientation and regulatory effectiveness of different multi-stakeholder initiatives. Such variations are often explained with reference to technical, organizational and institutional factors – for example, financial resources, professional expertise, leadership, incentives, path dependence, social and organizational innovation and learning, including 'learning by doing'. But as this chapter emphasizes, it is crucial to factor in political economy variables and contexts related to conflicting interests, discursive struggle, insider and outsider contestation, coalitions, alliances, the balance or reconfiguration of forces within governance structures, and structural opportunities and constraints.

A political economy view of the world leads one to ask whose standards and what notion of development are being promoted, and to better understand why and how the substance of such initiatives is likely to change through time (Reed and Mukherjee-Reed 2012; Utting 2012b). The two sections that follow highlight both the very different regulatory approaches that exist within the contemporary field of business regulation that is being led by NGOs or multi-stakeholder entities and examine the drivers and dynamics of regulatory change within specific initiatives. This analysis centers on the case of the United Nations Global Compact and the Roundtable on Sustainable Palm Oil (RSPO). It then considers briefly some of the implications of this analysis for fair trade. A concluding section reflects on the relevance of political economy analysis for understanding the complex dynamics of institutional change within the new arena of multi-stakeholder regulation.

TRUNCATED REFORM IN THE GLOBAL COMPACT

Since its inception in 2000, issues of credibility have plagued the United Nations Global Compact, which claims to be the world's largest corporate responsibility initiative. Critics of this initiative argue that it does more to enhance the reputation of corporations than to hold them to account. The ten principles related to human rights, labor standards, environmental protection and anti-corruption that the Global Compact promotes tend to be very broad and many companies sign up without significantly modifying their behavior. To address some of these concerns, the Global Compact introduced a procedural reform in 2004, which resulted in 4256 business participants – equivalent to just over half the number of participating companies – being expelled from the initiative by the end of 2013 (UNGC 2014a).

This reform was part of a set of 'Integrity Measures' that aimed to address the Global Compact's image problem. A combination of insider and outsider pressures was instrumental in driving this reform process. The Integrity Measures required participating companies to provide annually a Communication on Progress (COP) in addressing the ten principles. Non-reporting companies were to be named publicly and persistent non-reporters delisted. The Integrity Measures also aimed at controlling the misuse of the Global Compact's name and logo, and they established a complaints mechanism for dealing with allegations of gross abuse of the Global Compact principles by companies.

The initial barrage of civil society criticism of the Global Compact was concerned that this initiative was adding a UN seal of approval for voluntary approaches that were an ineffective substitute for mandatory regulation. It not only lacked teeth and facilitated free-riding, but also allowed for 'bluewashing' whereby global corporations could use their association with the United Nations to project a clean image (TRAC 2000). In response, several high profile activists and civil society and other organizations signed a counter 'Citizens Compact'. Some went on to form the Alliance for a Corporate-Free UN (CorpWatch 2001).

Simultaneously, several prominent NGOs (including Human Rights Watch, Amnesty International and Oxfam International) formally became part of the multi-stakeholder governance structure of the Global Compact, in an effort to reform from within. In 2003, however, their patience ran thin. In a public letter to the UN Deputy Secretary-General, they complained of weak accountability mechanisms and limited evidence of progress, and they called for a series of reforms, including annual reporting by participating companies and effective stakeholder participation in national-level Compacts.

When the Global Compact held its first Global Compact Leaders Summit in New York in 2004, numerous civil society organizations met nearby for the Global Compact Counter Summit. From here they issued the Joint Civil Society Statement on the Global Compact and Corporate Accountability, which accused the Compact of 'reward[ing] rhetoric rather than deeds, and … undermin[ing] our efforts to bring a measure of corporate accountability, rather than purely voluntary responsibility, into the intergovernmental arena' (UN-NGLS 2004). Such criticisms and pressures added to the momentum for reform which other actors were also advocating. Even the consulting firm McKinsey & Company had found that only 9 per cent of participating companies were taking additional actions to improve ESG performance (McKinsey & Company 2004).

From the perspective of corporate accountability, the 2004 reform was not only very partial but it also failed to mark the beginning of a more sustained process of ratcheting-up, as has occurred in several other multi-stakeholder initiatives (see, for example, RSPO below). Although the Global Compact is clearly concerned with the issue of legitimacy and the Board has direct responsibility for safeguarding the scheme's integrity, there have been relatively few substantive measures in this regard. Such safeguards include increasing the number of companies expelled for non-compliance with the reporting requirement from approximately 1000 by mid-2008 to over 4000 by end 2013 (Confino 2012) and introducing a very broad classification of the quality of Communications on Progress.[2]

During the latter half of the decade several of the original civil society actors, networks, forums and campaigns that had criticized the Global Compact withered or redirected their energies elsewhere. Some others emerged, notably Global Compact Critics (Gregoratti 2012), Global Compact Compliance Watch and the End UN Corporate Capture campaign. Launched in the build-up to the Rio+20 conference on sustainable development, this campaign accused the Global Compact of 'merely help[ing] businesses to boost their image and profits, instead of promoting binding obligations that would contribute to changing companies' performance'.[3] A few civil society organizations continued to engage in critical research on the Global Compact and generate evidence regarding corporate influence in the UN system and international development policy,[4] but in keeping with more general trends associated with civil society engagement in research and advocacy, particularly following the 2008 global financial crisis, the resources (human and financial) that critical NGOs and networks had at their disposal tended to decline.

For its part, the Global Compact went from strength to strength in terms of enlisting corporations and other business entities. By the end of 2013, there were 7950 business participants (UNGC 2014a), far in excess of the original goal that had been established of engaging 1000 companies. Indeed, the current target is to double the number of business participants by 2016 (to 16 000) and have 20 000 by 2020 (UNGC 2014b). The Global Compact has achieved a remarkable convening power with leaders of corporations and governments. To raise awareness of and promote the Global Compact's principles and CSR practices, it had established by 2012 an extensive system of Local Networks in 101 countries (UNGC 2013), albeit operating at varying levels of consolidation and multi-stakeholder representation. Moreover, it has enlisted significant support from selected sectors of civil society associated with NGOs and academic institutions. By the end of 2013, some 4119 NGOs, academic institutions and other civil society entities were formally associated with the Global Compact. By the end of 2012, the Global Compact was raising some 12 million dollars a year, mainly from private sector contributions channeled through the non-profit Foundation for the Global Compact, which had been set up in 2006.[5]

The balance of stakeholder forces within this 'multi-stakeholder' initiative is heavily skewed towards business interests and NGOs and academic institutions that generally believe in the power of voluntary initiatives to improve the ESG performance of business. Of the non-business participants there are over 2000 NGOs and 700 academic entities. In recent years considerable effort has gone into enlisting support from business or management schools as a part of the Global Compact's broader strategy to cultivate global learning on corporate responsibility issues. The engagement of this sector of academia has reinforced the management school and organizational studies discourse or theory that has long pervaded the initiative. This is evidenced, for example, in the uptake of terms such as 'corporate sustainability', which is supposed to convey the idea that corporate responsibility is no longer simply about doing good or piecemeal adaptation but seeing ESG practices as fundamental to core or long-term business strategy (UNGC and Accenture 2010).

The number of NGOs and academic entities engaged in the Global Compact contrasts sharply with the approximately 50 labor organizations and the minimal representation of advocacy and grassroots organizations or social movements associated with the global justice movement and alter-globalization perspectives. Representation on the Global Compact Board paints a similar picture. Of the 30 members, 23 represent or are closely associated with business interests, four represent NGOs and two represent labor organizations.[6]

The upshot is an initiative that is long on carrots and short on sticks to shape business behavior. While companies have been held to the reporting requirement, the quality and materiality of reporting leaves much to be desired. The complaints mechanism is 'lite' at best. And the logo policy has taken a bizarre twist a decade after the initial tightening of regulations. In January 2014 a new criterion for use of the logo took effect. Companies are now permitted to use the 'We support the Global Compact' logo if they have donated money to the Global Compact Foundation during the previous 12 months (UNGC 2014b).

The Global Compact remains insistent that it is not a compliance-based initiative but rather one that works on the assumption that public disclosure, leadership commitments and market-based incentives drive performance (Kell 2013). But at a time when even mainstream advocates of voluntary approaches are recognizing the serious limitations of reporting and are emphasizing other instruments of corporate accountability such as verification, grievance procedures and a stronger role for public policy, the Global Compact remains firmly wedded to what is perhaps the bluntest instrument in the portfolio of voluntary action.

Rather than constituting an effective mechanism for corporate accountability, the Global Compact should be seen in relation to broader trends in global governance where business interests, in particular those associated with transnational corporations, have transitioned from being objects of regulation to active subjects in policy framing, standards design and public–private partnerships. The Global Compact acts as an important facilitator in this regard. It has constituted an effective mechanism for providing business with access to United Nations and other policy dialogues and processes (Global Policy Forum 2014). Through networks and forums such as the UN System Private Sector Focal Points, the 100 plus Global Compact Local Networks and Global Compact LEAD (comprising a group of approximately 50 companies regarded by the Compact as leaders in the field of corporate responsibility), it has positioned itself not only as a learning forum but as a key entity within the UN system for facilitating active 'corporate citizenship'.

RATCHETING-UP THE RSPO

A different approach to business regulation has been adopted by a category of multi-stakeholder initiatives concerned with promoting more sustainable patterns of production and consumption of certain primary commodities. This approach has been far more vibrant in terms of the ratcheting-up of standards and procedures, so much so that it now leans more towards the corporate accountability model outlined in the introduction.

Drawing on the experience of the Forest Stewardship Council and the Marine Stewardship Council, established in 1994 and 1997, respectively, the World Wide Fund for Nature (WWF) has established another seven schemes during the past decade that aim to promote more sustainable forms of production of cotton, palm oil, soy, sugarcane, biofuels, farmed salmon and shrimp and beef. These schemes, generally called Roundtables, are part of a broader strategy that emerged in the early 2000s, whereby WWF aimed to spread itself less thinly around the world and concentrate its efforts on protecting a relatively small number of threatened ecosystems (WWF 2012a). In these areas, environmental degradation and risks were partly, if not largely, related to the production of 15 commodities controlled by relatively few agro-food and extractives corporations (WWF 2012b). By enlisting the participation of such corporations and their suppliers in the Roundtables, WWF sought to promote more environmentally friendly production processes and consumption patterns. Such an approach not only made sense in terms of deploying limited resources more effectively but also in view of the limitations of previous approaches to forest conservation centered on creating or strengthening protected areas.

Discourse analysis of the RSPO conducted by Schouten et al. (2012) suggests, however, that only certain discourses on sustainable development frame and inform internal deliberation. These are 'reformist', in the sense of emphasizing the potential for achieving improvements in environmental and social performance of business activities in contexts of growth, corporate control of value chains and large-scale monocultures. So-called radical perspectives tend to be excluded, namely those that highlight fundamental incompatibilities between such economic and production systems and sustainable development, as well as the need for harder regulation of corporate activities. While such perspectives are prominent within deliberative processes outside the RSPO, this research found that initially there is little transmission inwards. Such a situation facilitated internal communication, dialogue and agreement on standards and procedures but had major implications for the issues of scale and quality referred to above. During its start-up phase, the RSPO was less concerned with issues of legitimacy than with 'pragmatism' and harvesting the low-hanging fruit, namely a small number of large companies that sign up and are prepared to take at least some steps to change their production practices (Nikoloyuk 2009).

Nevertheless, concerns (from both within and outside of the initiative) about free-riding, credibility and legitimacy provided impetus for a vibrant ratcheting-up process.

Key changes, which have been examined by several authors,[7] include the following. First, differences over the meaning of sustainability were resolved pragmatically through the development of the RSPO Principles and Criteria (P&C), which were eventually ratified by the RSPO General Assembly in November 2005. Second, following a labor dispute that same year between the International Federation of Building and Wood Workers (IFBWW) and the plantation company, Musim Mas, which held a seat on the RSPO Executive Board, a Code of Conduct was established which, among other things, required growers to meet certain minimum criteria not just in some but in all their holdings. And third, a Grievance Procedure was established and companies were required to report annually on progress (Schouten and Glasbergen 2011). As tensions among producers (concerned with issues of costs and implementation of standards) and NGOs (concerned with issues of verification) heightened in 2006 (Nikoloyuk 2009), attention focused on the establishment of a certification system. In 2007, some three years after its establishment, the

RSPO agreed on rules governing certification and certified palm oil appearing on the market in late 2008.

Early on, the interests of some three million smallholders that produce an estimated 25 per cent of global palm oil (Colchester and Jihan, cited in Pesqueira and Glasbergen 2013) and indigenous peoples were neglected within the RSPO initiative. Insider NGOs such as Oxfam and Sawit Watch raised concerns about the inability of smallholders to meet RSPO criteria. This led to the establishment of the Smallholder Task Force, which has been financially supported by Dutch NGOs and the Dutch government (Pesqueira and Glasbergen 2013). Over time, the neglect of smallholders and indigenous peoples has been partially redressed. The RSPO has referenced international instruments such as Free Prior and Informed Consent, extended the scale of certification from the mill to the farm, adopted the criterion that growers and mills treat smallholders in a transparent and fair manner, and invested funds to assist smallholder organizations, for example, in obtaining certification (Pesqueira and Glasbergen 2013).

Despite constant upward adjustments to standards and procedures, criticism of the RSPO continues. International, Northern and Southern NGOs and NGO networks – whether RSPO members or not – such as Greenpeace, Friends of the Earth, World Rainforest Movement, Forest Peoples Programme and Sawit Watch, have been actively monitoring, appraising and chastising the RSPO. The groups argue that the RSPO provides a platform that legitimizes businesses engaged in greenwashing and sub-standard labor practices and exposes companies that fail to comply with standards. Greenpeace Netherlands, for example, investigated the practices of United Plantations, the first company to be certified under the RSPO standards. Finding problems of deforestation, deep peat conversion, land disputes and illegal practices, this inquiry revealed that a company may certify its plantations in one country while continuing with 'business-as-usual' in another (in this case Malaysia and Indonesia, respectively) (Greenpeace 2008). In another report, Greenpeace exposed the impacts of palm oil production on climate change (Greenpeace 2007).

In 2008, 256 organizations signed the International Declaration against the '"Greenwashing" of Palm Oil by the RSPO', citing ongoing deforestation of tropical forests, adverse impacts on climate change, threat to indigenous peoples, illegal appropriation of land, land tenure conflicts, violation of human rights, increased use of agrochemicals and violation of the right to food and food sovereignty (RSPO 2008). More recently, RSPO members, including the Forest Peoples Programme and Sawit Watch, in collaboration with other NGOs, conducted a critical in-depth appraisal of the situation of indigenous peoples affected by palm oil production. In particular, they aimed to determine whether the RSPO principle of Free Prior Informed Consent was being applied (Colchester and Chao 2013).

As accusations and exposés of greenwashing in relation to palm oil certification grew, subsequent upward adjustments to standards included a stipulation in 2008 that members should produce a time-bound annual plan regarding production or purchase of certified palm oil. Criticisms that some companies were not taking steps to avoid large-scale forest clearance or damage to areas of high conservation value when expanding their operations, led WWF and a palm oil company to propose an extension of RSPO rules, beyond certified areas to new plantings. Formally approved in 2009, RSPO began to implement its 'New Planting Procedure' in January 2010.

As this example shows, certain companies have allied with NGO interests, sometimes at the expense of relations among the business stakeholders. Unilever went so far as to drop one of its largest Indonesian suppliers and blacklisted another in 2010 when it came under pressure from NGOs. Both suppliers were members of RSPO. Unilever and Greenpeace also agreed to work together to lobby for a moratorium on deforestation associated with palm oil production, following an effective campaign by Greenpeace associating the company's Dove brand with rainforest destruction rather than feel-good emotions (Nikoloyuk 2009).

The General Assembly also approved revised P&Cs in 2013. Responding to concerns about ongoing deforestation and the industry's contribution to greenhouse gas (GHG) emissions, producers are now encouraged to plant in low-carbon areas and to report on GHG emissions by 2016. Additional criteria concerning disclosure, labor standards and human rights were also introduced (RSPO 2013). While additional issue areas have been brought into the ambit of the P&C, the proposed voluntary actions (of 'encouraging' and 'reporting') appear weak to environmental groups both inside and outside the initiative (Mongabay 2013).

The RSPO demonstrates clearly the power of sustained contestation and synergistic insider and outside activism and alliances to continually ratchet up standards and procedures, and to ensure that not only environmental but also social and human rights issues get on the agenda. As Glasbergen notes: 'This proactive behavior resulted in a process in which internal and external NGOs shared information and seemed to be able to reinforce each other … This was further strengthened by the formation of more or less formal alliances among Northern and Southern NGOs' (Glasbergen 2013, 359–360).

The process of ratcheting-up within the current format of the RSPO is associated with certain biases and may be encountering definite limits.

Partly reflecting the relative weakness of trade unions within RSPO governance structures, labor issues related to occupational health and safety, wages and workers' protection tend to have been subordinated to environmental and other human rights issues and treated as 'minor violations' (Supiarso 2013).

Even core RSPO stakeholders concerned with environmental issues, notably WWF, are now looking beyond RSPO procedures. Recent revisions to the P&C, while agreed to by the WWF, prompted this NGO to declare that

> because the review failed to accept strong, tough and clear performance standards within the P&Cs on issues like GHGs and pesticides, it is, unfortunately, no longer possible for producers or users of palm oil to ensure that they are acting responsibly simply by producing or using Certified Sustainable Palm Oil (CSPO). Therefore WWF is now asking progressive companies to set and report on particular performance standards within the framework set by the new RSPO P&Cs. (WWF 2013)

To do so, the WWF has joined forces with Greenpeace to form the Palm Oil Innovation Group (POIG) comprising both insider and outsider NGOs and three producer companies. The POIG aims to go beyond the RSPO standards and commitments (Greenpeace 2013a). In November 2013 it established the POIG Charter that encourages innovations, establishes performance standards and addresses additional issues related to environmental responsibility, partnerships with communities and corporate and product integrity (Greenpeace 2013b; POIG 2013). As has occurred in the case of forest management certification, raising the bar can constitute a barrier to entry or prompt businesses to exit and associate themselves with standards and certification schemes seen as more business friendly. In a context in which the supply of certified palm oil far outstrips demand, where producers feel there is little premium for producing certified palm oil (either in terms of price or reputational advantage), there are concerns that producers in Malaysia and Indonesia may opt for a less rigorous approach.

WHICH TRAJECTORY WILL FAIR TRADE FOLLOW?

The above analysis has important implications for fair trade in two key respects. First, as corporations and other conventional for-profit enterprises penetrate and colonize the fair trade market, are standards initiatives conforming more to the corporate accountability or CSR models of multi-stakeholder regulation? Second, how is the configuration and reconfiguration of stakeholder interests within fair trade governance shaping the normative and regulatory trajectory of fair trade? The case of fair trade is dealt with in far more depth in other chapters in this volume. This chapter will simply note certain recent developments that highlight the importance of these questions and political economy analysis.

When the fair trade system was consolidated in 1997 via the formation of what today is Fairtrade International, it was the national labeling organizations that had the significant voice and vote within the organization (Reed 2012). Fairtrade sought to expand the fair trade market not only by increasing demand from ethically oriented consumers, but also by engaging corporations such as Starbucks. The organization subsequently tended to privilege business-friendly policies, such as market access, over more transformative policies associated with agro-ecology and collective action, such as price increases to small producers (Bacon 2010). The real price of Fairtrade coffee declined significantly, losing an estimated 41 per cent of its value between 1988 and 2008 (Bacon 2010) when a readjustment occurred.

Bacon (2010) shows clearly how the process of price readjustment related to the balance of power within Fairtrade governance. The review of the Fairtrade minimum price was initiated by the Latin American and Caribbean Network of Small Fair Trade Producers organization, the CLAC, in 2006. Following consultations with other Fairtrade stakeholders, and revising the proposals downwards following concerns from interests associated with traders and labeling organizations, the proposal was submitted to the Board of Fairtrade International of which the head of CLAC was a member.

With then only one representative on the Board, the bargaining power of producers within this process was very limited. Regarding the composition of the Board, Bacon (2010) also calls attention to the 'voices without votes' or those that are significantly under-represented. These include alternative trade organizations, consumer interest groups, labor unions and development-oriented civil society organizations, as well as those of social justice and food sovereignty activists within the fair trade movement. The balance of power within Fairtrade International was tipped in the direction of national labeling organizations in the global North – the 'companies which pay the licensing fees and sell Fairtrade certified coffee, their boards, foundations, governments, and individuals that make their budgets' (Bacon 2010, 137).

Initially, Fairtrade International's Board rejected the price increase. This prompted more intense lobbying on the part of producers. It also motivated several development-oriented civil society organizations and alternative trade organizations (e.g., Equal Exchange, Cafédirect, Co-operative Coffees) to advocate for the producer-generated proposal. While these allies lobbied Fairtrade International's Board to approve the price increase, the National Labeling Initiatives delayed the process to consult with licensees (Bacon 2010, 131). In 2007 the Board approved a small increase in the price of conventional and organic coffee of 7 and 11 per cent respectively. These adjustments were at the low end of CLAC's proposal for conventional coffee and below its proposal for organic coffee (Bacon 2010).

The (im)balance of power between producers and actors in the North had not only constrained upward adjustments to prices but more generally positioned the growth of market share via alliances with large companies as a strategic priority. The tension between different interests, perceptions and priorities reached a head in 2011, when the US labeling organization, Fair Trade USA (formerly TransFair USA), left Fairtrade International. Fair Trade USA announced unilateral plans to certify large coffee plantations, which was not allowed under Fairtrade International's global standard for coffee (Reed 2012; on CLAC and its activities see also Marie-Christine Renard's chapter in this volume).

The pursuit of different models of development and changes in the governance of Fairtrade underpin these tensions (Reed 2012). Regarding the models, Fair Trade USA favors the scaling up of the Fairtrade niche market by engaging large corporations and agricultural estates, facilitating market access for small producers, and promoting corporate environmental and social responsibility – which targets not only producers but also agricultural workers. It remains to be seen whether Fair Trade USA pursues the corporate accountability route of effective measurement, monitoring, reporting and verification and redress, or whether the lighter touch of CSR will prevail.

Several currents within Fairtrade International, and the larger movement of alternative trade organizations and advocates, promote the original ethos and principles of fair trade, which are centered on fostering solidarity, empowering small producers economically and politically through collective organization and promoting higher standards of agro-ecology. Some Southern producers' organizations recognize the limits of what remains a North–South trading system that locks producers in as suppliers of low-value, largely unprocessed, products (Reed 2012).

Regarding governance, the voice of small producer organizations is increasingly being heard and their vote is carrying ever more weight in Fairtrade International's governance structures, in contrast to the previous situation where the national labeling organizations controlled decision-making.[8] This development did not occur within the governance structure of Fair Trade USA. The change in the balance of social forces within Fairtrade International favored decisions to increase both the Fairtrade floor price and the social premiums that support various local projects (Bacon 2010). Meanwhile, particularly in Latin America, national and regional producer associations have become stronger, are gaining a more robust voice within Fairtrade International, and also reframing the meaning of fair trade. This has involved broadening the focus away from merely considering how to secure premium prices in export markets. Attention has focused on how small-scale producers can capture for themselves the benefits of a growing fair trade market in their own countries and regions. This includes: 1) adding value to their primary products through processing; 2) the need to balance export-oriented commodity production with the principles and practices of 'food sovereignty'; and 3) the need for ongoing political empowerment of producers through self-supporting organization, more effective participation in both policy processes and the governance structures of intermediary organizations, and by building coalitions and alliances. This reflects a very different vision about what development means, as compared to that generally found within both the CSR and corporate accountability agendas (Reed 2012). Indeed, it takes on aspects of what can be called the alter-globalization agenda (Utting 2013).

CONCLUDING REMARKS

The above discussion has sought to highlight some fairly fundamental differences in approach within the new field of private governance or multi-stakeholder regulation that is setting standards related to ESG aspects of business performance and trade. It has also highlighted the relevance of political economy analysis for understanding variations in both regulatory approaches and ongoing processes of normative and procedural reform within multi-stakeholder initiatives.

Illustrative of the CSR approach is the UN Global Compact. It has always claimed to be a business-friendly learning platform rather than a regulatory compliance-based mechanism. Indeed, the potential scope for learning or awareness-raising about CSR seems significant due to the scale of its participant base, global reach, and networking and convening power. But it has been affected by serious problems of free-riding and non-compliance with agreed principles and procedures, which in themselves are often vague or minimalist. Major concerns have also arisen about its positioning as a conduit for corporate influence within policy processes. The RSPO, with its continuous ratcheting-up of standards and efforts to promote more effective measurement, reporting and verification leans more towards the corporate accountability approach, which emphasizes the need for companies to actually prove they are in compliance with agreed standards.

Such variations partly reflect the correlation of interests within the governance structures of these initiatives as well as the extent and trajectory of contestation both internally and externally. In the case of the Global Compact, stakeholder voices and interests calling for corporate accountability tend to be relatively weak within the Compact itself. And, compared to the early 2000s, they appear to have weakened on the outside as well or redirected their attention to other initiatives. In the case of the RSPO, stakeholder representation favors business interests but provides important spaces for critical voices, while contestation on the outside has continued unabated.

Both initiatives are constrained by the way they are nested in broader structures or institutions of market liberalism (Levy and Brown 2012). Such nesting keeps certain issues off the agenda and slows the pace of reform. Such constraints are most obvious in the case of the Global Compact. How far the RSPO can go along the corporate accountability path remains to be seen. The splits that may be appearing within this initiative speak to the very real possibility that market forces and interests favoring a more business-friendly 'CSR' approach will reassert themselves.

Such variations in regulatory approach and the trajectory of reform within standards initiatives have significant implications for a fair trade system that is engaging far more intensively with corporations. A fundamental tension exists between a fair trade model centered on smallholder empowerment, the redistribution of value within value chains and agro-ecology, and a corporate model that must, to some extent, grow and compete by externalizing social and environmental costs. To address this tension the companies involved will have to be seen to be socially and environmentally responsive, pursuing either the CSR or corporate accountability route. But fair trade is also compromising. The trajectory of change will be largely determined by the political economy variables identified above associated with contestation, implicit or explicit alliances of civil society actors and shifting configurations in the balance of power within governance structures. If the corporations engaged in fair trade are to be held accountable, and if fair trade is to uphold its original ideals and objectives, much will depend on the voice, influence and alliance of smallholder interests and ethical consumers seriously committed to a new politics of sustainable consumption and global justice.

NOTES

* The author would like to thank Marie-Adélaïde Matheï for assistance with preparing this chapter.

1. Relatedly, on fair trade and the emergence of social enterprise and social entrepreneurship, see Benjamin Huybrechts's chapter in this volume.
2. See the debate with Georg Kell in Ethical Corporation (2008).
3. See Friends of the Earth International et al. (2012); see also Friends of the Earth International (2012). By 10 June 2012 some 360 civil society organizations had joined the campaign.
4. See, for example, publications by SOMO, Global Policy Forum and others (Pingeot 2014; Theuws and van Huijstee 2013).
5. Of the Global Compact's total income of 16.1 million dollars in 2012, 12.8 was provided by the private sector and 3.3 by governments (see UNGC 2014a and www.globalcompactfoundation.org, accessed 6 February 2014).
6. Data accessed from Global Compact website, 6 February 2014 (UNGC 2014a).
7. See, for example, Glasbergen (2013); Knorringa et al. (2011); Nikoloyuk (2009); Nikoloyuk et al. (2010); Pesqueira and Glasbergen (2013); Schouten (2013).
8. For more on Fairtrade governance issues, see Elizabeth Bennett's chapter in this volume.

REFERENCES

Abbott, Kenneth W. and Duncan Snidal (2009), 'The governance triangle: Regulatory standards institutions and the shadow of the state', in Walter Mattli and Ngaire Woods (eds.), *The Politics of Global Regulation*, Princeton and Oxford: Princeton University Press, pp. 44–88.

Bacon, Christopher (2010), 'Who decides what is fair in fair trade? The agri-environmental governance of standards, access and prices', *Journal of Peasant Studies*, 31 (1), 111–147.

Braithwaite, John (2005), *Neoliberalism or Regulatory Capitalism*, RegNet Occasional Paper No. 5, Canberra: Australian National University.

Colchester, Marcus and Sophie Chao (eds.) (2013), 'Palm oil expansion in South East Asia: Trends and implications for local communities and indigenous peoples', Moreton-in-Marsh, England: Forest Peoples Programme and Bogor, Indonesia: Perkumpulan Sawit Watch, available at http://www.forestpeoples.org/sites/fpp/files/publication/2011/11/oil-palm-expansion-southeast-asia-2011-low-res.pdf (accessed 23 October 2014).

Confino, Joe (2012), 'Cleaning up the Global Compact: Dealing with corporate free riders', *The Guardian*, 26 March, available at http://www.theguardian.com/sustainable-business/ (accessed 6 February 2014).

CorpWatch (2001), 'What is the Alliance for a Corporate-Free UN?', 22 March, available at www.corpwatch.org/article.php?id=617 (accessed 18 April 2011).

Ethical Corporation (2008), 'UN Global Compact – is the Compact raising corporate responsibility standards? Debate between Bart Slob and Georg Kell', 10 May, available at http://www.ethicalcorp.com/content/debate-un-global-compact (accessed 6 February 2014).

Friends of the Earth International (2012), 'Reclaim the UN from corporate capture', Amsterdam: FoEI, available at www.foei.org (accessed 6 February 2014).

Friends of the Earth International, Corporate Europe Observatory, La Via Campesina, Jubilee South/Americas, Peace and Justice in Latin America/SERPAJ-AL, Polaris

Institute, The Council of Canadians, The Transnational Institute, Third World Network, World March of Women (2012), 'Ending corporate capture of the United Nations: Joint Civil Society Statement', available at http://www.foei.org/en/get-involved/take-action/pdfs/statement-un-corpcap-en/view (accessed 10 June 2012).
Glasbergen, Pieter (2013), 'Legitimation of certifying partnerships in the global market place', *Environmental Policy and Governance*, 23 (6), 354–367.
Global Policy Forum (2014), 'Privatizing global governance: Corporate influence at the United Nations', GPF Briefing 1, Berlin: Global Policy Forum, available at https://www.globalpolicy.org/images/pdfs/GPFEurope/GPF__Briefing_1.pdf (accessed 23 October 2014).
Greenpeace (2007), 'How the palm oil industry is cooking the climate', Amsterdam: Greenpeace International, available at http://www.greenpeace.org/international/en/publications (accessed 10 June 2012).
Greenpeace (2008), 'United Plantations certified despite gross violations of RSPO standards', available at http://www.greenpeace.org/usa/Global/usa/report/2008/11/united-plantations-certified-d.pdf (accessed 23 October 2014).
Greenpeace (2013a), 'Certifying destruction', Amsterdam: Greenpeace International, available at http://www.greenpeace.org/international/en/publications/ (accessed 6 February 2014).
Greenpeace (2013b), 'Palm oil companies join NGOs to find palm oil solutions', available at http://www.greenpeace.org/international/Global/international/photos/forests/ (accessed 6 February 2014).
Greenpeace (2013c), 'Certifying destruction', Amsterdam: Greenpeace International, available at http://www.greenpeace.org/international/en/publications/ (accessed 6 February 2014).
Greer, Jed and Kenny Bruno (1996), *Greenwash: The Reality behind Corporative Environmentalism*, Penang, Malaysia: Third World Network.
Gregoratti, Catia (2012), 'The United Nations Global Compact and development', in Darryl Reed, Peter Utting and Ananya Mukherjee-Reed (eds.), *Business Regulation and Non-State Actors: Whose Standards? Whose Development?*, London: Routledge and Geneva: UNRISD, pp. 95–108.
Kell, Georg (2013), '12 years later: Reflections on the growth of the UN Global Compact', *Business and Society*, 52 (1), 31–52.
Knorringa, Peter, Gerdien Meijerink and Greetje Schouten (2011), 'Voluntary governance initiatives and the challenges of inclusion and upscaling', in A.H.J. (Bert) Helmsing and Sietze Vellema (eds.), *Value Chains, Social Inclusion and Economic Development: Contrasting Theories and Realities*, London and New York: Routledge.
Levy, David and Halina Szejnwald Brown (2012), 'The global reporting initiative: Promise and limitations', in Darryl Reed, Peter Utting and Ananya Mukherjee-Reed (eds.), *Business Regulation and Non-State Actors: Whose Standards? Whose Development?*, London: Routledge and Geneva: UNRISD, pp. 109–121.
McKinsey & Company (2004), 'Assessing the Global Compact's impact', available at www.unglobalcompact.org (accessed 7 August 2006).
Mongabay (2013), 'Environmentalists unhappy with new palm oil standard', 25 April, available at http://news.mongabay.com/ (accessed 6 February 2014).
Murphy, David F. and Jem Bendell (1997), 'Partners in time? Business, NGOs and sustainable development', UNRISD Discussion Paper No. 109, available at http://www.unrisd.org/ (accessed 7 August 2006).
Nikoloyuk, Jordan (2009), 'Sustainability partnerships in agro-commodity chains: A model of partnership development in the tea, palm oil and soy sectors', Utrecht, the Netherlands:Utrecht-Nijmegen Programme on Partnerships.

Nikoloyuk, Jordan, Tom Burns and Reiner de Man (2010), 'The promise and limitations of partnered governance: The case of sustainable palm oil', *Corporate Governance*, 10 (1), 59–72.
Pesqueira, Luli and Pieter Glasbergen (2013), 'Playing the politics of scale: Oxfam's intervention in the Roundtable on Sustainable Palm Oil', *Geoforum*, 45, 296–304.
Pingeot, Lou (2014), 'Corporate influence in the post-2015 process', working paper, Global Policy Forum and Brot für die Welt, Germany: Misereor.
POIG (2013), 'Palm Oil Innovations Group Charter', available at http://www.forestpeoples.org/sites/fpp/files/publication/ (accessed 6 February 2014).
Reed, Darryl (2012), 'Fairtrade International (FLO)', in Darryl Reed, Peter Utting and Ananya Mukherjee-Reed (eds.), *Business Regulation and Non-State Actors: Whose Standards? Whose Development?*, London: Routledge and Geneva: UNRISD, pp. 300–314.
Reed, Darryl and Ananya Mukherjee-Reed (2012), 'From non-state regulation to governance? Shifting the site of contestation', in Darryl Reed, Peter Utting and Ananya Mukherjee-Reed (eds.), *Business Regulation and Non-State Actors: Whose Standards? Whose Development?*, London: Routledge and Geneva: UNRISD, pp. 300–314.
RSPO (2008), 'International declaration against the "greenwashing" of palm oil', available at http://www.biofuelwatch.org.uk/docs/17-11-2008-ENGLISH-RSPOInternational-Declaration.pdf (accessed 20 January 2014).
RSPO (2013), 'RSPO P&C: Highlight of changes made', available at http://www.rt11.rspo.org/ckfinder/ (accessed 6 February 2014).
Ruggie, John G. (2003), 'Taking embedded liberalism global: The corporate connection', in David Held and Mathias Koenig-Archibugi (eds.), *Taming Globalization: Frontiers of Governance*, Cambridge: Polity Press, pp. 93–129.
Schouten, Greetje (2013), 'Tabling sustainable commodities through private governance', Utrecht: Mimeo.
Schouten, Greetje and Pieter Glasbergen (2011), 'Creating legitimacy in global private governance: The case of the Roundtable on Sustainable Palm Oil', *Ecological Economics*, 70 (11), 1891–1899.
Schouten, Greetje, Pieter Leroy and Pieter Glasbergen (2012), 'On the deliberative capacity of private multi-stakeholder governance: The Roundtables on responsible soy and sustainable palm oil', paper presented at the 3rd International Symposium on *Cross Sector Social Interactions* (CSSI), 24–25 May 2012, Partnerships Resource Centre, Erasmus University, Rotterdam.
Sum, Ngai-Ling (2010), 'Wal-Martization and CSR-ization in developing countries', in Peter Utting and José Carlos Marques (eds.), *Corporate Social Responsibility and Regulatory Governance: Towards Inclusive Development?*, London: Palgrave and Geneva: UNRISD, pp. 50–76.
Supiarso, Frans (2013), 'Labor auditing in certified palm oil industry', *The Jakarta Post*, 14 November, available at http://m.thejakartapost.com/news/2013/11/14/labor-auditing-certified-palm-oil-industry.html (accessed 15 May 2014).
SustainAbility (2003), *The 21st Century NGO: In the Market for Change*, London: SustainAbility, available at http://www.sustainability.com/library/the-21st-century-ngo#.U2pTSfmSziU (accessed 15 May 2014).
Theuws, Martje and Mariette van Huijstee (2013), 'A comparison of the OECD guidelines, ISO 26000 and the UN Global Compact', Amsterdam: SOMO, available at http://www.somo.nl/dossiers-en/csr/corporate-responsibility-instruments (accessed 15 May 2014).
TRAC (Transnational Resource and Action Center) (2000), 'Tangled up in blue: Corporate partnerships at the United Nations', available at www.corpwatch.org/article (accessed 10 July 2011).
UNGC (2013), 'Global Compact local networks report 2012', avaliable at http://unglobalcompact.org/docs/publications/LN_Report.pdf (accessed 3 May 2014).

UNGC (2014a), 'UN Global Compact bulletin', January, available at http://www.unglobalcompact.org/NewsAndEvents/ (accessed 6 February 2014).
UNGC (2014b), 'United Nations Global Compact strategy 2014–2016', available at http://www.unglobalcompact.org/docs/ (accessed 3 May 2014).
UNGC and Accenture (2010), 'A new era of sustainability: UN Global Compact – Accenture CEO study 2010', available at http://unglobalcompact.org/docs/news_events/ (accessed 3 May 2014).
UN-NGLS (UN Non-Governmental Liaison Service) (2004), 'Joint Civil Society Statement at the Global Compact counter-summit, Church Center, New York, 23 June 2004', *Civil Society Observer*, 1 (3), June–July.
Utting, Peter (2012a), 'Introduction: Multistakeholder regulation from a development perspective', in Darryl Reed, Peter Utting and Ananya Mukherjee-Reed (eds.), *Business Regulation and Non-State Actors: Whose Standards? Whose Development?*, London: Routledge and Geneva: UNRISD, pp. 1–18.
Utting, Peter (2012b), 'Activism, business regulation and development', in Darryl Reed, Peter Utting and Ananya Mukherjee-Reed (eds.), *Business Regulation and Non-State Actors: Whose Standards? Whose Development?*, London: Routledge and Geneva: UNRISD, pp. 38–53.
Utting, Peter (2013), 'Pathways to sustainability in a crisis-ridden world', in Rémi Genevey, Rajandra K. Pachauri and Laurence Tubiana (eds.), *Reducing Inequalities: A Sustainable Development Challenge*, Delhi: Teri Press, pp. 175–190.
WWF (2012a), 'Better production for a living planet', Gland, Switzerland: WWF.
WWF (2012b), 'Green, greener, greenest: Transforming markets', Gland, Switzerland: WWF.
WWF (2013), 'WWF statement on the review of the RSPO Principles & Criteria', available at http://awsassets.panda.org (accessed 6 February 2014).
Zadek, Simon (2001), *The Civil Corporation: The New Economy of Corporate Citizenship*, London: Earthscan.

5. Fairtrade International governance

Elizabeth A. Bennett

INTRODUCTION

Voluntary standards-setting organizations are not neutral entities. They are political constructions in which actors' interests play out and power dynamics shape outcomes. The standards they create are likewise not simple derivatives of scientific evidence or aggregates of professional expertise but instead the products of political negotiation. In private regulatory bodies, as in all political arenas, the good and the awful manage to coexist, and the outcomes are just as subject to manipulation by powerful actors as in any other realm of global politics (Hurrell 2005, 44; Meidinger 2011, 407; Renard and Loconto 2012, 53).

In the late 1990s, as non-state actors began playing an increasingly significant role in the global political economy, a body of literature emerged to discuss the nature and power of private authorities in international affairs (e.g., Cutler, Haufler and Porter 1999; Hall and Biersteker 2002). Scholars argued that private actors had the *potential* to bring public interests – such as sustainability and poverty reduction – and traditionally marginalized voices to the fore of global economic policy-making. They showed how private regulators might provide a counterweight to increasingly powerful multinational corporations or raise social standards in a moment when states were lowering the bar in order to attract foreign direct investment. Yet alongside such optimistic accounts loomed a formidable concern: such (desirable) outcomes depended on private actors' capacities to understand and represent nebulous constituencies with complex and sometimes contradicting objectives. Would private actors be able to create and maintain representative, accountable, transparent systems of governance? Authors in this field continue to suggest that the challenge of developing rigorous systems of democratic participation is a hurdle that voluntary standards-setting organizations have yet to overcome (see Brown 2008; Collingwood 2006; Hammer, Rooney and Warren 2010; Sending and Neumann 2006).

These insights from international relations have encouraged scholars of fair trade to examine how power is balanced among the movement's stakeholders and how fair trade's key institutions play a role in shaping this balance. As Peter Utting argued in the previous chapter of this volume, such variables are key determinants of the extent to which private standards-setting bodies are capable of creating a new politics of sustainable consumption and global justice. This chapter contributes to research on the politics of fair trade governance by examining the movement's foremost institution, Fairtrade International, through a lens of stakeholder participation and representation. The key argument is that formal inclusion (seats and votes) in the highest governance bodies is a necessary but not sufficient condition to ensure that private actors bring traditionally marginalized perspectives to bear in global economic regulation.

Fairtrade labeling stakeholders have a long history of disagreeing about many aspects of fair trade labeling. But since they (generally) feel a harmonized, worldwide label is more effective than a multitude of unique systems, stakeholders seek to develop unified strategies despite their disparate preferences. Particularly contentious issues have included: whether or not to certify hired labor groups; who should pay for third-party auditing; and what percentage of composite products must be Fairtrade certified for the product to bear the seal. Because stakeholders hold very different – and very strong – beliefs about these issues, the institutional rules that balance how each stakeholder is able to influence policy-making are extremely important. The question of how to weigh producers' opinions against the positions of the national labeling initiatives has been a particularly difficult struggle for Fairtrade International.[1] Some fair trade scholars and activists have argued that producers have been largely marginalized by the organization's highest governance bodies and that this arrangement has compromised Fairtrade labeling's ability to deliver on its promises. But in 2011 the organization announced that it would give producers equal ownership over the label. This chapter compares this new iteration of Fairtrade governance with previous arrangements. It answers the questions: How does Fairtrade International include producers of Fairtrade certified products in its governance bodies? And when producers *are* included, to what extent do they reflect and represent the broader producer population?[2] It argues that today's governance structure is the most democratic and representative in the organization's history, even more so than the original Max Havelaar Netherlands label.

The chapter proceeds as follows. First a background section positions this analysis in relation to relevant fair trade studies. Next the data and methods section describes the collection and synthesis of over 17 000 archival documents and more than 100 interviews with Fairtrade leaders and participants. Then an empirical section describes producers' participation in Fairtrade International governance from 1988 to 2014. It is presented in five time periods: label creation (1988–1995); label proliferation (1992–1997); label unification and development (1997–2005); producers as members (2005–2011); and producers as equal owners (2011–2014).[3] The discussion argues that the new structure could be pivotal in shifting Fairtrade outcomes, and it identifies key variables that shape the policy-making process. Some of the policy-making challenges were generated by Fairtrade International's extended period of excluding producers, while others are broadly experienced, enduring problems in governance. The chapter closes with suggestions for future research and by emphasizing the value of including marginalized voices in private regulatory regimes.

BACKGROUND

The politics of Fairtrade International's governance is a frequent topic of scholarly inquiry. The consensus is that its organizational structure is riddled with problems. Among the critiques: it lacks the mechanisms required to facilitate widespread representation (Lyon 2011); its decision-making processes are not democratic (Bacon 2010); the balance of power favors the North over the South (Renard and Perezgrovas 2007); and its bureaucracy does not operate transparently (Johannessen and Wilhite 2010; Mutersbaugh and Lyon 2010). Producer participation is argued to be desirable (Jaffee 2010), though cost and efficiency tradeoffs are acknowledged (e.g., Conroy 2007).[4] Some studies have suggested that producers have recently had less influence over Fairtrade policy decisions than in the early years of labeling (Howard and Jaffee 2013; Marie-Christine Renard's chapter in this volume).

There are several arguments for increasing producer participation in governance. Some arguments emphasize the value of participation as an outcome in itself. Participation can be considered a form of empowerment or a way to promote equality and diversity in global governance (Moore 2004). It can also be considered an appropriate or ethical extension of producers' roles in the past, as producers played a principal role in pioneering the first label in 1988 (Jaffee 2012; Renard and Loconto 2012). Other studies focus on the ways in which producer participation alters outcomes, illustrating how the presence or absence of producers has affected Fairtrade International's policies in specific situations (Bacon 2010). In this volume, Marie-Christine Renard argues that Fairtrade International would have pursued different policies on working with transnational corporations, certifying hired labor groups, increasing fees for certification and creating standards for some new items, had producers been able to participate more fully in governance. Likewise Bradley Wilson and Tad Mutersbaugh (also in this volume) document producers' opposition to Fairtrade International's decision to pursue the ISO (International Organization for Standardization) approach of third-party auditing and certification, suggesting they would have lobbied for an alternative strategy, given the opportunity.[5] And Jaffee (2010) argues that greater producer participation in governance would have prevented Fairtrade International from rigorously pursuing relationships with corporations in order to achieve mainstreaming objectives.

A subset of these arguments stresses that Fairtrade policy outcomes and strategic decisions may not only be *different* because of producer exclusion but actually *against producers' interests*. Bacon (2010) argues that benefits to Fairtrade producers have been diluted, and he argues an eroding Fairtrade minimum price for coffee is an example. Jaffee (2012) argues that producer exclusion has reduced standards for corporations participating in the Fairtrade system. Mutersbaugh and Lyon (2010, 30) argue it has reduced the notion of 'fairness' in fair trade to a minimum price. And Renard (this volume) finds that inadequate producer participation has resulted in low standards for composite products.[6] Collectively, fair trade scholarship argues that low levels of producer participation in strategic decision-making and standard-setting have prevented Fairtrade from 'radically transforming trade relationships into vehicles for social justice' (Lyon 2011, 162).

DATA AND METHODS

This chapter draws on the author's collection of over 17 000 archival documents gathered from ten sources (organizations and individuals) in six countries. The author also interviewed and corresponded with over 100 members of the Fairtrade labeling community including current and former CEOs, board members, executive directors and the staff of Fairtrade International and other relevant organizations and businesses. This chapter cites several specific documents from the archives of Max Havelaar Netherlands and Fairtrade International, interviews with several high-level representatives of Fairtrade International and publicly available documents such as press releases and annual reports. The overall argument, however, reflects insights from the broader set of data.[7]

PRODUCERS IN FAIRTRADE INTERNATIONAL GOVERNANCE (1988–2014)

Each of the following sections describes how producers, as a single stakeholder group, have been included in or excluded from the principal governance bodies in Fairtrade labeling. It also compares the producers *included* in governance with the *broader population* of producers, in terms of commodities produced, countries of origin and type of producer organization. The first two time periods, label creation and label proliferation, overlap by three years (1992–1995) since labels were operating relatively autonomously during that period.

Label Creation (1988–1995)

Max Havelaar Netherlands launched the first fair trade label in 1988 and made major strategic decisions largely independently of other labels for several years before collaborating more closely with other, newer labeling organizations. During this time the Max Havelaar Netherlands board reached decisions on several important, complicated and highly contentious issues, such as how to set a Fairtrade minimum price, the terms of pre-financing, how to incorporate benefits for organic practices, whether to expand to non-coffee products and how to manage relationships with companies engaged in fair washing (MHN 1992d, 1–3; 1995, 5–22).

From 1988 to 1990, producers were on its board of directors, but their representatives were appointed, not elected (MHN 1992b, 1). Beginning in 1990, producer representatives were elected for a term of two years. Any organization of small coffee producers supplying at least 2000 bags of green coffee of 60 kilos during the preceding two years under Max Havelaar's trading conditions was invited to elect three producer representatives to the board (MHN 1992b, 1). The board comprised 13 full voting members and one observer. Of the 13 members, three seats were designated for producers' representatives (MHN 1992e, 6). Representatives for the 1990–1992 term came from cooperatives of smallholder coffee farmers in Zaire, Mexico and Costa Rica (MHN 1992a, 54). In the fall of 1992, coffee was still the only labeled product but cocoa was forthcoming (MHN 1992b, 1, 3). However, in 1995 the governance system was still 'completely based on coffee' (MHN 1995, 21). Max Havelaar divided fair trade producing countries into six regions, with the goal of eliciting a representative or alternate from each: English-speaking Africa, French-speaking Africa, Mexico, Central America, Caribbean and

South America. The 1990–1992 representatives were from cooperatives of smallholder coffee farmers in English-speaking Africa (with an alternate from French-speaking Africa), Mexico (with an alternate from Central America) and the Caribbean (with an alternate from South America) (MHN 1995, 21).

According to Max Havelaar Netherlands (MHN 1992b, 1), there were several reasons for including producers. Logistically, it facilitated communication and increased legitimacy. It was also the 'structural expression' of the organization's principle that the label was 'not launched *for* the producers but mainly *with* them'. The presence of the producers on the board was meant to serve as a 'guarantee that the Max Havelaar Foundation sticks to its roots and purpose' – as a 'democratic instrument to get permanent and fluent feedback on priorities and interests of the producers, depending on changing conditions on the national and international level'. Despite this commitment to inclusion it remained informal – 'the relationship between Max Havelaar and the partner [producer] organization does not have a formal basis, only a personal one … rights and obligations have not been laid down in a formal agreement' (MHN 1992c, 1).

Already in 1992, however, the foundation identified several challenges related to the inclusion of producers on the board and raised doubts about the 'effectiveness and the cost and time efficiency of the producers' representation in the day-to-day practice, due to shortcomings from the producers representatives themselves as well as from the staff and organization of Max Havelaar' (MHN 1992c, 2–3). On the staff side, problems included communicating with many organizations and in more languages, difficulty in providing adequate information to producer board members, the staff's tendency to give more attention to more demanding producer representatives, and the time and organizational resources required to bring representatives to the Netherlands for meetings and send materials to producer representatives in preparation for those meetings. These challenges were attributed to limited institutional capacity and the concerns arising from the organization's motivation to invest as much money as possible in the 'actual promotion of the coffee sales' (MHN 1992b, 2–3).

On the producer side, problems included diversity of interests and circumstances of producer communities, difficulties in communication, organizations reporting that they did not feel adequately represented and informed, representatives growing distant from the coffee farmers, represented organizations gaining advantages over other organizations (allowing them to sell more product) and producer representatives not always being equipped and/or informed to provide a qualified opinion on the issues under discussion at board meetings. As Max Havelaar Netherlands (MHN 1992b, 2) concluded, ‘many producers’ organizations don’t feel themselves effectively represented’.

In 1995 the board discussed how the representation of producers on the board could better reflect their increasing diversity (MHN 1995, 21). Max Havelaar Netherlands had already started labeling cocoa and honey produced by farmer cooperatives and was considering working with the tea and banana plantations other organizations had started labeling as fair trade (MHN 1995, 22).[8] Despite these changes the board continued to include only smallholder coffee farmers. To capture regional diversity, producers continued to elect a representative or deputy from each of six regions: English-speaking Africa, French-speaking Africa, Mexico, Central America, South America and the Caribbean. In sum, although the original fair trade labeling organization always included producers (with a minority vote) on its board, those producers were at first not elected and later on did not capture the diversity of producers within its labeling system (International Coffee Register Committee 1997).

Max Havelaar Netherlands convened the first General Producers’ Assembly in 1990 (MHN 1990). The objective of assemblies, which were then convened every two years, was to provide an opportunity for the board and coffee producer organizations to evaluate the previous two years, discuss the current situation and establish policies on important issues (e.g., price policy, minimum prices, organic) (MHN 1995, 1). At that time coffee was the only labeled product. Although producers developed, debated and voted on policies, the outcomes had to be approved by each initiative’s board. In sum, the Assembly was only authorized to make policy recommendations to boards, and participation and scope were limited to coffee cooperatives.

Label Proliferation (1992–1997)

In June 1992 TransFair International, a coalition of national labeling initiatives, established a new fair trade label called TransFair. By the end of 1994 its membership included six national labeling initiatives, each promoting labeling in a specific country: Austria, Canada, Germany, Italy, Japan and Luxembourg (TransFair International 1994). Simultaneously, several organizations created their own version of the Max Havelaar label, borrowing some ideas from Max Havelaar Netherlands but also working independently. By 1995 there were 12 Max Havelaar and TransFair labeling initiatives, each working in a different country, each with its own board of directors (MHN 1995).

Each of the labeling organizations faced the same strategic questions as the original label: What products and producers should be labeled? How should those producers benefit? And which conventional actors could be good collaborative partners in delivering those benefits? The organizations came to different conclusions. TransFair Germany, for example, almost immediately extended labeling to hired labor groups on tea plantations in India (Eshuis and Harmsen 2003), while other organizations committed to working exclusively with smallholder farmer cooperatives.

As each initiative composed its own board, the balance of stakeholders was not uniform across initiatives (MHN 1995, 10). Aside from Max Havelaar Netherlands (discussed above), TransFair Germany was the only initiative to include producers on its board. Although the organization worked with both hired labor groups in Asia and smallholder coffee cooperatives in Latin America, the seat was always given to a Latin American smallholder coffee producer (International Coffee Register Committee 1997). In sum, at this time, each initiative had authority to develop and pursue its own strategies. It was highly unusual to include producers in the highest bodies of governance (the boards of directors), and as more products and organizational types were added, the initiatives that were including producers did not capture this diversity by adding seats or rotating seats among different producer types.

Label Unification: Fairtrade Labelling Organizations International (FLO) (1997–2005)

Since many of the labeling initiatives shared information and collaborated on specific issues, their leaders formed the 'Trans-Max' working group to examine the potential for an organizational merger. The goal was to streamline activities and save money by consolidating all of the initiatives' individual boards into a single body (FLO 2003, 6). One of the key debates was about the degree to which the initiatives had to be harmonized: Would they all have to label tea from hired labor in India, even if they had previously abstained from working with landless workers? If one initiative wanted to cut a deal with a local brand, did the others have to approve? As it became clear that the initiatives would have to be unified on several issues, the debate turned to how to balance power among them: Should votes be distributed equally among initiatives? Or weighted by Fairtrade volumes sold? (FLO 1997).

Though producers were excluded from these negotiations, the appropriate role for producers in a worldwide system was another topic of (contentious) debate. While some initiatives, such as the Swedish Fair

Trade Association, excluded producers from their governance proposals (Swedish Fair Trade Association 1997), others aimed to elevate the role of producers in governance. In the latter category, Max Havelaar Denmark argued:

> it ought to be 50 per cent producers and 50 per cent labeling organisations in such an international organisation. At the least the producers should have the right to vote. The influence of producers should as a minimum be increased … It is important to include the producers in the debate regarding the international structure … Surely this is crucial if producers are to take a stand on whether they support the international structure. (Max Havelaar Denmark 1997, 1)

In 1997 the national initiatives, without input from producers, launched Fairtrade Labelling Organizations International (FLO) as the worldwide association of all national initiatives. They presented the new organization to producers at the 1997 General Producers' Assembly. The new organizational governance structure comprised three 'organs': the Meeting of Members, the board of directors and a register committee for each product (FLO 1998a). The role of producers was somewhat undecided. As a temporary provision, until an agreement could be reached, producers were given observer status in the Meeting of Members (FLO 1997). The register committees would include producers, but those representatives would be appointed by the Meeting of Members (not selected by producer organizations themselves). No producers sat on the board of directors (FLO 1998a).

According to the 1997 FLO report on the Assembly, the new organization was not well received (FLO 1997, 13). Producers requested FLO make a new proposal regarding the role of farmers within the new structure, to be discussed during regional producers assemblies scheduled for 1998 (FLO 1997, 14). The labeling initiatives' response was mixed. On the one hand, the report expressed understanding of producers' discontent. As it described the situation:

> Producers are right in their complaint that [the creation of FLO] has been a European organization process in which producers were not involved, nor informed about. Among producers it has created a lot of confusion, uncertainty about their role in fair trade and uncertainty about the purpose and weight of an Assembly. They feel left out and without any influence. … most producer representatives feeling that they lost their influence and that the outcome of the Assembly is of no value. (FLO 1997, 13)

The report, however, argued that nothing had changed – FLO simply consolidated all of the individual organizations' boards (all but two of which excluded producers) into a single membership organization (which continued to exclude them). This was justified by arguing that such an arrangement bolstered credibility:

> The initiatives apologize for not having informed the producers before, nor included them in the discussions about the structure of an umbrella organization. Producers, however, have to take into account the fact that the initiatives are social certifiers and like organic certifiers they need independence to build and maintain credibility. (FLO 1997, 13)

The following years were fraught with tension, miscommunication and compromised trust about the role of producers in FLO. 'The producer participation issue' (literally) remained on the agenda for years to come (FLO 1998b, item 1.8.2). Latin American producers lobbied unsuccessfully for a new governance body in which producers, traders and labeling initiatives would come together to take decisions.[9] They were unsuccessful and General Producers' Assembly decisions continued to require approval by the Meeting of Members (FLO 1999a). Raúl Del Aguila, a representative of smallholder coffee farmers in Latin America, recalls his experience as a producer observer in the Meeting of Members:

> The Meeting of Members was for labeling initiatives to discuss how to create a global organization, and some producers were invited to attend as spectators, not as members. I was there … One of the debates was about whether or not to include producers in the Meeting of Members … There was a lot of resistance to this, and it was debated for four years. We [the producers] were not part of this, only spectators. (Del Aguila 2011)

In November 2001, the Meeting of Members created a second board of directors. The existing board of five national labeling initiative representatives was renamed the 'executive board' and expanded to six members. A second, 'extended' board included the executive board members plus four producers and two traders, one alternative and one conventional (FLO 2003). The former maintained authority over overall management and strategy, finances, personnel issues and other elements of FLO's day-to-day functioning. The latter managed and decided on policy and standards issues, appointed the members of key committees and advised the director on standards issues (Zonneveld 2001). The four producers on this board were from Latin America (two), Asia and Africa; three were from cooperatives, one from hired labor; two produced coffee and two produced other products.[10] At that time other major products included cotton, flowers, honey, juices, sugar, rice, sports balls and wine (FLO 2007a).

In sum, producers held four of 11 seats on the board, but the board's authority remained limited, as the Meeting of Members (which excluded producers) was authorized to overrule its decisions (FLO 1999b). During this period of extremely limited producer inclusion, FLO made several pivotal decisions that had deep and enduring impacts on the Fairtrade certification system. The members voted to pursue the ISO-65 inspired strategy of social auditing – sending 'independent' auditors to farms to verify compliance with standards. This decision led to the creation of a new organization, FLO-Cert, to conduct the audits, charging producers a fee to be audited. As noted in the backgrounds section, fair trade studies suggest that a producer-led membership body may not have pursued this strategy.

Producers as Members of FLO (2005–2011)

In 2005 the Meeting of Members dissolved the executive board and made the multi-stakeholder board responsible for all strategic and fiduciary responsibilities. The new board was expanded to include two outside experts – people knowledgeable about fair trade but not representing a specific stakeholder group. Thus, FLO's board composition beginning in 2006 gave producers a percentage of votes unprecedented for a labeling board:[11] five national labeling initiatives, four producer representatives, two traders and two outside experts (FLO Board of Directors 2005, FLO 2007b). Each of the producer networks nominated a candidate or two and the General Assembly approved one from each region plus one additional (FLO 2007b). During this time, FLO pursued the '5-10-15 goals': increasing the number of producers in the Fairtrade system fivefold, delivering ten times the Fairtrade premium and increasing Fairtrade sales tenfold, by 2015 (Cameron 2010, 3).[12] While delivering benefits to a greater number of producers is widely viewed as a good thing, fair trade studies point out that producers already participating in Fairtrade certification may have prioritized maintaining or increasing their own benefits. Renard and Loconto (2012, 57), for example, describe in detail Fairtrade coffee farmers' extensive efforts to increase the minimum price for coffee during this period.

Producer networks are 'associations that Fairtrade Certified Producer Organizations may join if they so wish and which are recognized by Fairtrade International as the representative body of farmers, workers and others belonging to Fairtrade Certified Producer Organizations' (FLO 2007a, 6). Each of the three producer networks – Fairtrade Africa (previously the African Fairtrade Network), the Network of Asian Producers (or 'NAP') and the Coordinadora Latinoamericana y del Caribe de

Comercio Justo (or 'CLAC') – had to be represented, and one network sent a second representative. Each network's suggested representatives had to be approved by a majority of the board and ratified by the General Assembly (FLO 2007b).[13]

In 2006 the national initiatives also expanded the membership body to include producers. The board's Governance Committee argued that this more 'representative and participative governance structure' would demonstrate 'real commitment to the principles of partnership and respect' (FLO Board Governance Taskforce and Executive Staff 2006, 1), and a group of national initiatives, advocating for this shift, said they aimed to demonstrate 'commitment to working with the producers as our equal partners' (TransFair USA, Max Havelaar France, Comercio Justo España, Fairtrade Foundation UK, Comercio Justo Mexico, outgoing FLO president and FLO managing director 2006, 1). Thus, the Meeting of Members was renamed the General Assembly and this new group convened for the first time in May 2007. The General Assembly remained FLO's highest governance body, retaining all of its rights and responsibilities. It was comprised of representatives from 20 national initiatives and three producer networks. Each member had one vote, so producers held three of 20 votes in FLO's highest governance body (FLO 2006).

Producers' participation on the board and in the Assembly represented the interests of producers within their regional networks. However, as the Governance Committee noted, this arrangement did 'not achieve universal representation of Fairtrade-certified producers and workers' (FLO Governance Committee 2006). Palestinian olive oil cooperatives, for example, were excluded because the Middle East was not part of any of the three regions. Hired and contract workers in Latin America were also excluded, as the CLAC was an association of smallholder producer cooperatives – not organized labor. And on the board, the General Assembly always elected a Latin American representative to hold the fourth producer seat.[14] In addition to these issues, the producer networks were not all equally well funded and organized, and each struggled to aggregate the interests of diverse populations within their regions.

Producers as Equal Owners of Fairtrade International (2011–2014)

In January 2011 FLO changed its name to Fairtrade International, dropping the 'Labelling' from the name to acknowledge labeling as a tool for achieving the organization's principal mission but not the mission itself (Kratz 2014).[15] In October it began the process of establishing the organization's current governance structure. Fairtrade International and its US labeling initiative, Fair Trade USA, jointly announced Fair Trade USA's departure from the international Fairtrade system. While the organizations continued to share a mission, they had 'different perspectives' on how to achieve that mission (Fairtrade International and Fair Trade USA 2011). In particular, they could not come to an agreement on the details of how, when, to what extent and with which stakeholders' approval the label should be extended to new producer groups (Fairtrade International 2011a).

Fairtrade International differentiated itself from Fair Trade USA by explaining that its policies were developed in consultation with 'all stakeholders in the system' (Fairtrade International 2011a). It noted: 'We are proud of the increasingly prominent role of producer organizations in our governance and decision-making bodies. Each year Fairtrade aims to engage in more dialogue and become even more consultative' (Fairtrade International 2011b). Subsequently, the General Assembly voted to make producers equal owners of the organization, giving them the same number of votes in the Assembly and seats on the board as the labeling initiatives. In Fairtrade International's words,

> The vote marked a further strengthening of Fairtrade's unique ownership model; networks of certified producer organizations have been co-owners of the system alongside labelling initiatives from consumer countries since 2006. The new shared ownership model means that producers will now have an equal voice in the highest decision-making body of Fairtrade. (Fairtrade International 2011c)

Stakeholders negotiated how to implement this commitment through 2012 and in 2013 the Assembly ratified and began implementing the new constitution. At the June 2014 General Assembly national initiatives were each invited to send a representative and producer networks were invited to send at least four representatives. Each representative voted, and the votes were weighted such that each group (producers and initiatives) had the same number of overall votes. To elect the board, producer networks nominated candidates and the entire General Assembly voted to approve one candidate from each network and one additional board member, based on skills. For the first time, the additional representative came from Africa, not Latin America. The board was comprised of four producers, four national initiatives and two independent experts (who are knowledgeable about fair trade but not responsible for representing the perspective of a particular stakeholder group) (Bretman 2014; Fairtrade International 2013b). Traders are no longer included on the board, which increases the leverage of producer networks over actors in the North.

This arrangement differs from the previous governance structure in that producers and initiatives have equal votes in both governance bodies. Another difference is that all producer countries are included in a producer network. The African network has been expanded to include the Middle East, and the CLAC, at their 2012 assembly in Ecuador, agreed to represent workers on estates. While networks still lack the capacity to foster broad participation and represent diverse interests, the goal is to improve their ability to do so over time (Bretman 2014; Fairtrade International 2013b).

DISCUSSION

Table 5.1 summarizes Fairtrade's shifting balance of power, pointing to how it has included or excluded producers from key governance bodies and the degree to which those included producers reflect the profile of the broader producer population. In the early years of Fairtrade labeling (1988–1997), producers were included on only two of 17 boards of directors. When FLO was established in 1997, producers were completely shut out from the membership assembly and the board of directors. For over a decade they remained largely excluded from these bodies, holding at most 30 per cent of the board seats and 15 per cent of the votes in FLO's membership (in 2005). In 2011[16] producers became, for the first time, equal partners in the governance of Fairtrade International. Today, producers have more formal influence over strategic decisions and policy-making than ever before. They cast half the votes in the General Assembly and hold over a third of the seats on the board of directors (four of 11, equal to national initiatives). Through the producer networks, which can be expanded if new producer countries are added, this organizational structure ensures that all producers – regardless of how they are organized, what they produce or where they live – are represented.

The current governance structure is more democratic than all of the iterations that preceded it, including the original Max Havelaar Netherlands label. Compared to the first label, producers (as a group) now have more seats in governance bodies, and the producers in those seats are more representative of the overall producer population. As the literatures on fair trade and private authority in international affairs argue, formal inclusion in official governance bodies is desirable. The narrative provides evidence for that argument, showing that without official seats at the decision-making table, producers were unable to consistently secure

Table 5.1 The role of producers in Fairtrade International's organizational governance structure (1988–2014)

Governance change and year	Relationships between governance bodies	Producer inclusion in governance bodies	Producers included in governance, compared to population		
			Organization	Product	Region
Label creation (1988–1995)	The board was the highest governance body, though many decisions were made informally.	**Max Havelaar Netherlands board:** producers held 3 of 13 seats.	Small producers – *MHN did not work with hired labor*	Coffee – *MHN also worked with honey and cocoa*	4 Latin America and 2 Africa – *no products from Asia*
		Producers' assemblies: only producer representatives voted.	Small producers – *all coffee from small producers*	Coffee – *exclusively discussed coffee*	Latin America and Africa – *all coffee producing regions*
Label proliferation (1992–1997)	Each initiative's board had full authority over its activities; decisions from producer assemblies ratified by each board.	**Boards of other labeling initiatives:** of 16 initiatives only TransFair Germany, with 1 producer representative.	Small producers– *TransFair Germany initiated hired labor in 1994*	Coffee – *5 other products labeled: tea, cocoa, sugar, honey, bananas*	Latin America – *products also sourced from Asia and Africa*
		Producers' assemblies: only producer representatives voted.	Small producers – *all coffee from small producers*	Coffee – *exclusively discussed coffee*	Latin America and Africa – *all coffee producing regions*
Label unification (1997–2005)	The Meeting of Members is the highest governance body, appointing the board and approving board decisions.	**Meeting of Members:** only national labeling initiatives.	None	None	None
		FLO Board: 0 of 5 seats in 1997; 4 of 12 seats on an extended board in 2002 (initiatives have 6).	3 small producers, 1 hired labor – *contract labor standards still developing*	2 coffee, 1 tea, 1 fruit – *more than a dozen products exist*	2 Latin America, 1 Asia, 1 Africa

Governance change and year	Relationships between governance bodies	Producer inclusion in governance bodies	Producers included in governance, compared to population		
			Organization	Product	Region
Producers as members (2005–2011)	The Meeting of Members becomes the General Assembly. The General Assembly appoints the board.	**General Assembly:** 3 producer networks and 20 national labeling initiatives, each with 1 vote.	Asian and African networks represented all; Latin American only small producers, excluding hired/ contract labor	Wide variety of products represented but network leaders from historically important products	Not all producers included in a network (e.g., Palestinians)
		FLO Board: 4 of 13 seats for producer networks (initiatives have 5). Each network sends 1, plus 1 additional.			1 from each region; additional rep always from Latin America
Producers as equal owners (2011–2014)	The General Assembly appoints the board.	**General Assembly:** 3 producer networks share 50% of the votes.	Each network represents all types of certified producers of all products in its region: Latin America/Caribbean; Asia/Pacific; and Africa/ Middle East		
		FLO Board: 4 of 11 seats for producer networks (initiatives have 4). Each network sends 1, plus 1 additional.	Each network represents all organizational types	Each network represents producers of all products	1 from each region; plus 1 (currently from Africa)

Source: Author's archival research.

positions of influence in the governance structure. That is to say, the informal influence they wielded in the early 1990s did not provide enough leverage to negotiate a place in FLO governance in 1997. This narrative also illustrates how those governance bodies were able to shape Fairtrade strategies and make policy decisions independently of other, informally included, stakeholders.

So what will change now that producers are co-owners of Fairtrade? If scholars are correct in their counterfactual arguments about *what would have happened* had producers been included in formal governance bodies, then we should expect this new structure to increase minimum prices, raise premiums, bolster standards for corporations, improve forward financing and lower certification fees. However, there are a few variables that remain uncertain, and each could be pivotal in determining how the new structure's policy making will unfold. First, to what extent will Fairtrade's bureaucracy implement policies created by the new structure?[17] In the past, Fairtrade's administration at times lacked capacity to fulfill its commitments. For example, it has been unable to review minimum prices according to schedule and has had trouble eliciting feedback when directed to collect input from diverse stakeholders (Fairtrade International Staff 2012). Second, how will producer networks balance original Fairtrade stakeholders and traditionally powerful producer organizations with newcomers or less assertive groups? Currently, the networks are heavily under the influence of producer organizations that have been part of the Fairtrade system since the early years and were pushed out of formal governance in 1997. On the one hand, allowing those groups to maintain their role as leaders in the system would provide some redress for their historic exclusion. On the other hand, continuing to marginalize some producer groups perpetuates the problems generated by exclusive governance. Third, early producer groups (e.g., coffee and cocoa in Latin America and Africa) have inherited a labeling system that scarcely resembles the one they might have created. Will they reshape Fairtrade to reflect the decisions they would have made over the past two decades, or will they move forward in a way that reflects the national initiatives' vision? Finally, to what extent will producer networks be successful in creating systems of communication and interest aggregation so that they can truly represent their diverse constituencies? It is unclear how the networks will afford the requisite investments in bureaucratic infrastructure to work across languages, cultures, countries and economic sectors, reaching out to hundreds of millions of people, many in incredibly remote places.

CONCLUSION

How Fairtrade's new constellation of leaders manages these challenges – some enduring, others newly emerging – will shape Fairtrade's ability to leverage certification as a tool for delivering impacts that are robust, appropriate, timely, efficient and long lasting. Given the elevated role of producer networks in Fairtrade governance, there is a pressing need for research at the producer network level of analysis.[18] An appropriate next step in this agenda would be to pose the questions answered at the international level in this chapter to the regional level: How are producers included in governance bodies? Which producers can and do participate? Research should also focus on how historical practices to coordinate producers at the regional level are being adapted to meet producer networks' increasing responsibilities. What forms of communication and interest aggregation are appropriate for each region's population? To what extent can or should Fairtrade resources be used to engage and represent each of the 1.3 billion certified farmers and farm workers (Fairtrade International 2013a) in global policy decisions? Work in this area should be broadened beyond the categories analyzed here (organization type, product, country) to include whether and how women and minorities are brought into governance.

If private standards-setting bodies such as Fairtrade International are to succeed in bringing traditionally marginalized voices to the fore of global economic governance, they must formally include those groups in their highest governance bodies. Fairtrade International has taken unprecedented steps in this regard. But it must also support the groups that bear the primary responsibility of making inclusive governance work. Producer networks require support to create their own democratic structures of decision-making, representation and accountability. The goal of fostering democracy within a global multi-stakeholder initiative that represents over a billion constituents is as ambitious as making international trade fair; but if private actors are going to represent the populations and interests that public actors forgot, they must strive to do so.

NOTES

1. Fairtrade International is the international, non-governmental organization that sets the standards for the worldwide Fairtrade certification system. It certifies more than 1.3 million farmers and farm workers in more than 70 countries (Fairtrade International 2013a).
2. This chapter is part of a broader project that aims to identify the conditions under which voluntary, ethical standards-setting organizations include or exclude traditionally marginalized groups (e.g., the poor) in their organizational governance structures.
3. While this account focuses narrowly on the role of producers in governance bodies, Bennett (2012) provides details about the governance structure more broadly.

4. This is in contrast to the broader literature on private authority in international affairs, where many scholars question whether and how traditional methods of democratic organization should be applied to the non-state sphere.
5. Though this is sometimes given as the *cause* of producer exclusion as well as the result.
6. Note that not all scholars understand these policy outcomes to be against producers' interests.
7. The author wishes to acknowledge and thank all of these individuals and organizations for their invaluable contributions to this project. Any errors in fact or analysis belong, of course, to the author alone.
8. In 1994 TransFair Germany began certifying tea produced by hired labor groups working on estates (Eshuis and Harmsen 2003).
9. One FLO leader described these efforts as a 'manifesto' asking for an assembly in which 'producers, traders and labellers' could 'meet and take decisions' together, as opposed to producers simply advising labelers (FLO executive leader 1999, 1). As a result, two multi-stakeholder meetings (the FLO Forums) were convened (2001 and 2003) but never given more than advisory status.
10. This is based on a review of all board minutes during this time period. While two of the original board members were replaced in 2004, this did not alter the representation of regions, products and type of producer organization.
11. To review, producers held three of 13 votes on the Max Havelaar Netherlands board and in 2005 were awarded four of 13 seats.
12. Fair trade scholars publishing during that time also noted that growth had become 'a major strategic aim' (Ruben, Fort and Zúñiga-Arias 2009).
13. The organization of producers into regional networks facilitated increased representivity on the board and in the General Assembly as well as other governance bodies, such as the Standards Committee. While the Standards Committee had previously included producers in an ad hoc manor, they could now be more systematic about including one producer from each regional network (Kratz 2014).
14. Based on a review of annual reports, which are publicly available and list producer representatives to the board.
15. Labeling initiatives are now called 'national fair trade organizations' (Kratz 2014), though this chapter continues to use the former name for consistency.
16. 2013 was the year in which the constitution was ratified to reflect this change. The decision to include producers was made in 2011 and the new system was not fully in place until 2014 (Bretman 2014).
17. For more on discrepancies between policy and implementation see Marie-Christine Renard's chapter in this volume. Coscione (2014, 59) also examines the role of informal power in governance.
18. See, for example, Sutton (2013).

REFERENCES

Bacon, Christopher M. (2010), 'Who decides what is fair in fair trade? The agri-environmental governance of standards, access and price', *Journal of Peasant Studies*, 37 (1), 111–147.

Bennett, Elizabeth A. (2012), 'A short history of Fairtrade certification governance', in Janet Dine and Brigitte Granville (eds.), *The Processes and Practices of Fair Trade: Trust, Ethics and Governance*, London: Routledge, pp. 43–78.

Bretman, Ian (2014), strategic advisor to the CAN Alliance of Fairtrade Producer Networks and the former vice-chair of the board of directors of Fairtrade International, interview with Elizabeth Bennett, phone (18 July 2014).

Brown, David L. (2008), *Creating Credibility: Legitimacy and Accountability for Transnational Civil Society*, Sterling, VA: Kumarian Press.

Cameron, Rob (2010), 'Message from CEO Rob Cameron', in *Annual Report: Growing Stronger Together*, Fairtrade International, pp. 2–3, available at http://www.fairtrade.net/fileadmin/user_upload/content/2009/resources/FLO_Annual-Report-2009_komplett_double_web.pdf (accessed 20 June 2014).

Collingwood, Vivien (2006), 'Non-governmental organisations, power and legitimacy in international society', *Review of International Studies*, 32 (3), 439–454.

Conroy, Michael (2007), *Branded! How the 'Certification Revolution' is Transforming Global Corporations*, Gabriola Island, Canada: New Society Publishers.

Coscione, Marco (2014), *In Defense of Small Producers: The Story of CLAC*, Winnipeg, Manitoba, Canada: Fernwood Publishing.

Cutler, Claire, Virginia Haufler and Tony Porter (eds.) (1999), *Private Authority and International Affairs*, Albany, NY: State University of New York.

Del Aguila, Raul (2011), interview with Elizabeth Bennett, Cuzco, Peru (8 December 2011).

Eshuis, Fenny and Jos Harmsen (2003), '15 years of Fairtrade labelled coffee in the Netherlands', report for the Max Havelaar Foundation, Utrecht, the Netherlands.

Fairtrade International (2011a), 'Q & A on Fairtrade International and Fair Trade USA', available at http://www.fairtrade.net/single_view1+M5ea9a970524.html (accessed 3 February 2012).

Fairtrade International (2011b), 'About the mark', available at http://www.fairtrade.net/about_the_mark.html (accessed 5 February 2012).

Fairtrade International (2011c), 'Fairtrade responds to announcement by Fair Trade USA', available at http://www.fairtrade.net/single_view1+M5b3e428e874.html (accessed 30 December 2011).

Fairtrade International (2013a), 'Annual report 2012–2013: Unlocking the power', available at http://fairtrade-maerket.dk/filer/fairtrade-intl-annual-report.pdf (accessed 17 June 2014).

Fairtrade International (2013b), 'Constitution of the association', available at http://www.fairtrade.net/fileadmin/user_upload/content/2009/about_us/Constitution_Fairtrade_International_EN_20131114.pdf (accessed 18 June 2014).

Fairtrade International and Fair Trade USA (2011), 'Joint announcement from Fairtrade International and Fair Trade USA', 15 September 2011, available at http://www.fairtrade.net/single_view1+M5dc4394fdfd.html (accessed 30 December 2011).

Fairtrade International Staff (2012), interviews with Elizabeth Bennett, Bonn, Germany (17 and 20 September 2012).

FLO (Fairtrade Labelling Organizations International) (1997), 'Report of the IV General Assembly of coffee producers of Fairtrade Labelling Organizations FLO International', held 2–6 June 1997 in Tutzing, Germany.

FLO (Fairtrade Labelling Organizations International) (1998a), 'Constitution of the Association, Fairtrade Labelling Organizations International e.V., MoM 7, Version B'.

FLO (Fairtrade Labelling Organizations International) (1998b), 'Minutes of the 5th Meeting of Members of the Fairtrade Labelling Organizations International (FLO)', held 12–13 October 1998 in Bonn, Germany.

FLO (Fairtrade Labelling Organizations International) (1999a), 'Report from the FLO General Producers' Assembly', held 23–27 August 1999 in Mulheim an der Ruhr, Germany.

FLO (Fairtrade Labelling Organizations International) (1999b), 'Minutes from the 6th Meeting of Members of the Fairtrade Labelling Organizations International', held 19–20 April 1999 in Bonn, Germany.
FLO (Fairtrade Labelling Organizations International) (2003), 'Report from the FLO Fairtrade Forum', held 9–12 September 2003 in London.
FLO (Fairtrade Labelling Organizations International) (2006), 'Annual report 2005–2006: Building trust', Fairtrade International, available at http://www.fairtrade.net/fileadmin/user_upload/content/FLO_Annual_Report_01.pdf (accessed 23 June 2014).
FLO (Fairtrade Labelling Organizations International) (2007a), 'Annual report 2006–2007: Shaping global partnerships', available at http://www.fairtrade.net/fileadmin/user_upload/content/FLO_AR_2007.pdf (accessed 23 June 2014).
FLO (Fairtrade Labelling Organizations International) (2007b), 'Constitution of the Association', adopted on 25 May 2007.
FLO (Fairtrade Labelling Organizations International) Board of Directors (2005), 'FLO Outside Board Director: Responsibilities and qualifications', board document, October 2005.
FLO (Fairtrade Labelling Organizations International) Board Governance Taskforce and Executive Staff (2006), 'Resolving Fairtrade Labelling's governance issues: Overview and presentation of the package of documents', background document to the Meeting of Members for decision, 16 May 2006.
FLO (Fairtrade Labelling Organizations International) Executive Leader (1999), Notes on the events of the 1999 General Producers' Assembly, prepared to update board at the 22 September 1999 Board Meeting.
FLO (Fairtrade Labelling Organizations International) Governance Committee (2006), 'Recommendations to the FLO board', document for board approval, 20 March 2006.
Hall, Rodney Bruce and Thomas J. Biersteker (2002), 'The emergence of private authority in the international system', in Rodney Bruce Hall and Thomas J. Biersteker (eds.), *Emergence of Private Authority in Global Governance*, New York: Cambridge University Press, pp. 3–22.
Hammer, Michael, Charlotte Rooney and Shana Warren (2010), 'Addressing accountability in NGO advocacy: Practice, principles, prospects of self-regulation', Briefing Paper 125, One World Trust, London.
Howard, Philip and Daniel Jaffee (2013), 'Tensions between firm size and sustainability goals: Fair trade coffee in the United States', *Sustainability*, 5 (1), 72–89.
Hurrell, Andrew (2005), 'Power, institutions, and the production of inequality', in Michael Barnett and Raymond Duvall (eds.), *Power in Global Governance*, Cambridge: Cambridge University Press, pp. 33–58.
International Coffee Register Committee (1997), fax to Fairtrade Labelling Organizations International, 18 April 1997.
Jaffee, Daniel (2010), 'Fair trade standards, corporate participation, and social movement responses in the United States', *Journal of Business Ethics*, 92 (S2), 267–285.
Jaffee, Daniel (2012), 'Weak coffee: Certification and co-optation in the fair trade movement', *Social Problems*, 59 (1), 94–116.
Johannessen, Silje and Harold Wilhite (2010), 'Who really benefits from Fairtrade? An analysis of value distribution in Fairtrade coffee', *Globalizations*, 7 (4), 525–544.
Kratz, Andreas (2014), correspondence with Elizabeth Bennett, email (15 August 2014).
Lyon, Sarah (2011), *Coffee and Community: Maya Farmers and Fair-Trade Markets*, Boulder, CO: University Press of Colorado.
Max Havelaar Denmark (1997), memo to the national labeling initiatives on April 1997, in preparation for the FLO foundation meeting in Amsterdam.
Meidinger, Errol (2011), 'Forest certification and democracy', *European Journal of Forest Research*, 130 (3), 407–419.

MHN (Max Havelaar Netherlands) (1990), 'Eerste Algemene Producentenvergadering: Stichting Max Havelaar', on the assembly held 13 October 1990.
MHN (Max Havelaar Netherlands) (1992a), 'Report of the second General Producers' Assembly of the Max Havelaar Foundation', on the assembly held 14–15 October 1992 in Amsterdam.
MHN (Max Havelaar Netherlands) (1992b), 'Doc-8: The producers representation in the board of Max Havelaar', in *Report of the Second General Producers' Assembly of the Max Havelaar Foundation*, on the assembly held 14–15 October 1992 in Amsterdam.
MHN (Max Havelaar Netherlands) (1992c), 'Doc-3: The relation between Max Havelaar and the producers organizations in the Max Havelaar Register', in *Report of the Second General Producers' Assembly of the Max Havelaar Foundation*, on the assembly held 14–15 October 1992 in Amsterdam.
MHN (Max Havelaar Netherlands) (1992d), 'Doc-2: Revision of Max-Havelaar price system', in *Report of the Second General Producers' Assembly of the Max Havelaar Foundation*, on the assembly held 14–15 October 1992 in Amsterdam.
MHN (Max Havelaar Netherlands) (1992e), 'List of participants of the second General Producers' Assembly of the Max Havelaar Foundation Holland', in *Report of the Second General Producers' Assembly of the Max Havelaar Foundation*, on the assembly held 14–15 October 1992 in Amsterdam.
MHN (Max Havelaar Netherlands) (1995), 'Max Havelaaer–TransFair–Fairtrade third General Producers' Assembly report', on the assembly held 11–17 June 1995 in Copenhagen.
Moore, Geoff (2004), 'The fair trade movement: Parameters, issues and future research', *Journal of Business Ethics*, 53 (1/2), 73–86.
Mutersbaugh, Tad and Sarah Lyon (2010), 'Transparency and democracy in certified ethical commodity networks', *Geoforum*, 41 (1), 27–32.
Renard, Marie-Christine and Allison Loconto (2012), 'Competing logics in the further standardization of fair trade: ISEAL and the Símbolo de Pequeños Productores', *International Journal of Sociology of Agriculture and Food*, 20 (1), 51–68.
Renard, Marie-Christine and Victor Perezgrovas (2007), 'Fair trade coffee in Mexico: At the center of the debates', in Laura T. Raynolds, Douglas Murray and John Wilkinson (eds.), *Fair Trade: The Challenges of Confronting Globalization*, New York: Routledge, pp. 138–156.
Ruben, Ruerd, Ricardo Fort and Guillermo Zúñiga-Arias (2009), 'Measuring the impact of fair trade on development', *Development in Practice*, 19 (6), 777–788.
Sending, Ole Jacob and Iver B. Neumann (2006), 'Governance to governmentality: Analyzing NGOs, states, and power', *International Studies Quarterly*, 50 (3), 651–672.
Sutton, Shannon (2013), 'Fairtrade governance and producer voices: Stronger or silent?', *Social Enterprise Journal*, 9 (1), 73–87.
Swedish Fair Trade Association (1997), proposal for discussion at the FLO foundation meeting held 20–21 April 1997 in Amsterdam.
TransFair International (1994), 'The year of the seal: Report on the activities of TransFair International during 1994', TransFair International, Schorndorf, Germany.
TransFair USA, Max Havelaar France, Comerio Justo España, Fairtrade Foundation UK, Comercio Justo Mexico, outgoing FLO President and FLO Managing Director (2006), letter to the directors of national initiatives and the FLO board, 30 March 2006.
Zonneveld, Luke (2001), 'FLO's restructuring: Aims, implementation, stakeholder participation', paper for the Fairtrade Forum held in September 2001 in Lingen, Germany, by Luke Zonneveld, FLO Director, September 2001.

6. Global labor politics and fair trade

Dimitris Stevis

INTRODUCTION

During 2014 Fairtrade International adopted its revised Standard for Hired Labor. In this chapter I argue that Fairtrade International and global unions furthered their engagement as a result of this process but that their relationship has not yet reached the level of sustained global social dialogue or institutionalized industrial relations. Significant foundations have been built but important challenges need to be met. In the first part I outline the process that has led to its most recent revision and the scope of the Standard. In the second part I discuss global labor's engagement with Fairtrade International. In the subsequent three parts I discuss, respectively, three core issues: international labor standards, employee organizations and the challenge of regulating the whole production network. These issues are at the heart of the discussions between unions and Fairtrade International. I close with some suggestions for deepening this engagement in the direction of global social dialogue and 'mature industrial relations'.

THE PROCESS AND SCOPE OF THE 2014 FAIRTRADE STANDARD FOR HIRED LABOR

Fairtrade International's predecessors certified a tea plantation as far back as 1994. This commitment eventually led to a comprehensive Standard for Hired Labor. In 2010 the organization decided to review this Standard 'with this fundamental question in mind: *How can Fairtrade best deliver on its mission to empower workers to combat poverty, strengthen their position and take more control of their lives?*' (Fairtrade International 2014b). Central to this goal was the establishment of 'mature systems of industrial relations' (Miller et al. 2011) that center around freedom of association and collective bargaining, a living wage that can be eventually negotiated between management and organized labor, an allocation of the fair trade premium that reflects workers' interests and a workplace organization to manage the premium that is controlled by workers.

In January 2011 Fairtrade International established a Workers' Rights Advisory Committee (WRAC) to ensure that the views of labor unions are better integrated into the review process. That same year the organization hired a Senior Advisor on Workers' Rights and Trade Union Relations. During 2012 Fairtrade launched

> a new progressive Workers' Right Strategy to review the current Hired Labour Standard and look at additional tools beyond the Standard to make trade work better for workers. The new strategy moves Fairtrade beyond the traditional corporate social responsibility model based on standard-setting and auditing, to help build conditions where workers have the tools and ability to negotiate their own work terms and conditions. (Fairtrade International 2014b)

Fairtrade International undertook extensive consultations around the globe involving many of its stakeholders at the production level and also received written feedback from trade unions, non-governmental organizations (NGOs) and others (Fairtrade International 2013). There were some concerns that the timeline for completing the revision hindered adequate participation by some parties, such as local unions, but the WRAC played an important, albeit consultative role in this process. The Standard covers the management of the Fairtrade premium, labor rights and capacity building so that workers can represent themselves, labor conditions, including provisions for moving towards a living wage, and environmental provisions related to the materials used in production (Fairtrade International 2014d; 2014e).

A key addition is the Freedom of Association Protocol, which must be signed by companies 'confirming that they allow workers to associate and submit this protocol to FLO-Cert, the Fairtrade certifying body, before they can be Fairtrade certified' (Fairtrade International 2014c). The Standard also specifies that the right to unionize must be communicated to workers (Fairtrade International 2014a; 2014b; 2014c) and strongly encourages employers to move towards collective bargaining in a deliberate fashion (Fairtrade International 2014d, 3.4; 2014e).

The Standard covers about 170 000 workers in plantations (Fairtrade International 2012) or about 13 per cent of the 1 240 000 farmers and workers in Fairtrade certified production units. Most of the hired labor is in India, Kenya and Sri Lanka (about 119 000), reflecting plantation production in flowers and tea (van der Wal 2008; Gårdman 2008). By contrast hired labor in Latin American countries is in the lower thousands (Fairtrade International 2012, 19). Other products in which hired labor dominates are sports balls (100 per cent), fresh fruit and wine/grapes. The distribution of hired labor reflects certain historical dynamics in the development of fair trade and Fairtrade International (Dickinson 2011).

The number of hired laborers has been increasing but most of the farmers and workers in Fairtrade certified units are still in small producer organizations, the majority of whose members 'must be smallholders who don't depend on hired workers all the time, but run their farm mainly by using their own and their family's labour' (Fairtrade International 2014g). Coffee (580 000) accounts for the largest number of farmers and workers, followed by cocoa (141 800), seed cotton (66 500) and cane sugar (37 200). In none of these products are plantations certified. Recognizing that many workers (about 170 000) are employed in smallholder units, particularly in labor intensive products, the organization decided in late 2013 'to review and improve the Fairtrade model to better reach workers in small producers organizations' (Fairtrade International 2014c; Ostertag et al. 2014).

The Hired Labor Standard covers only workers in producer units and does not apply to workers in the circulation and retail segments of the production network, something that is bound to become a major challenge as mainstreaming grows. That aspect of hired labor has not yet become part of Fairtrade International's standard creation agenda.

FAIR TRADE AND GLOBAL LABOR UNIONS: TOWARDS DEEPER ENGAGEMENT

The revision of the Standard was a response to various concerns expressed by unions and advocacy organizations from around the world (ILRF 2009; USLEAP 2009). While some concerns were raised about the involvement of local and national unions during the revision process, Fairtrade International heard labor's views through various channels such as people on its board or among its staff and through its participation in various initiatives such as the Food and Agriculture Organization's Working Group on Labor Rights in banana production and trade (Food and Agriculture Organization 2014). A more formal path was through union participation in WRAC. In addition to the International Trade Union Confederation (ITUC) and the International Union of Food, Agricultural, Hotel, Restaurant, Catering, Tobacco and Allied Workers' Associations (IUF), the advisory committee also includes a British union, a South African organization of small farmers and farmworkers, the International Labor Rights Forum (ILRF), BananaLink and a number of other organizations. However, while labor is one of Fairtrade International's formal stakeholders, it does not co-govern the organization. Unions have argued that trade union representatives along the production network and the IUF should be included in the decision-making bodies of

Fairtrade International and should be co-responsible for certification (Beaty 2012; Fair World Project 2012).

Global labor organizations fall into two categories: organizations that bring together national intersectoral federations and organizations that bring together national sectoral unions (Stevis and Boswell 2008, Chapter 3). The ITUC is the major intersectoral global union and speaks to broad political and economic issues, such as national and global labor laws and practices. It is for this reason that it joined with IUF, Fairtrade International and the British Trade Union Congress to push the Fijian government to restore democratic and labor rights in the country. The regime's practices against labor rights, in general, and sugar mill workers, in particular, also affected Fairtrade plantation workers in Fiji (Fairtrade International et al. 2012).

Global Union Federations (GUFs) bring together national unions that organize workers in particular sectors. The two GUFs that have been most involved in issues of fair trade and the ethical economy are the IUF and the International Textile, Garment and Leather Workers' Federations (ITGLWF). The IUF represents unions of agricultural workers where most fair trade workers are found, so far, and plays a leading role in WRAC. The first and still a major interface between Fairtrade International and GUFs is in bananas (Raynolds 2007). For much of the 1990s, unions had been seeking to engage the major banana multinationals during a time that bananas emerged as a major fair trade commodity, especially in the United Kingdom. In 2001 the IUF, along with the regional union confederation COLSIBA (Coordinating Body of Latin American Banana and Agro-industrial Unions), and Chiquita signed an International [now called Global] Framework Agreement – agreements between global union organizations and specific multinational companies (see Papadakis 2011). Chiquita had more union members than the other companies and operated in countries that sourced a great deal of fair trade bananas, which were largely produced in plantations. The IUF has since paid attention to the fair trade sector in this and other commodities.

The ITGLWF, an early member of WRAC and now part of IndustriALL, had long paid close attention to the proliferation of codes of conduct in the garment and apparel industry and had argued that Global Framework Agreements (GFAs) were the best route to 'mature industrial relations' at the global level in a sector in which labor intensive production facilitated outsourcing and complex value chains (Kearney and Justice 2005; Miller et al. 2011). The ITGLWF's work on a living wage in the garment sector can be considered as one of the foundations on which Fairtrade International is now building its own living wage strategy (Anker and Anker 2013; Flinterman 2014).

To conclude, the engagement between international labor and Fairtrade International has become more profound over the years, with WRAC playing a regular and active role. The relations have not reached the level of global social dialogue which implies a stronger formal commitment to each other (on social dialogue, see Stevis 2010). From the point of view of unions, such a dialogue can best take place through the inclusion of labor representatives on Fairtrade International's board (along with producers, national Fairtrade organizations and independents), essentially creating a global democratic corporatist arrangement. This would require buy-in by the producers, who now have 50 per cent of the votes in Fairtrade International, something which is both complicated and may well scare some of them away. But it is difficult to see how Fairtrade International can move towards 'mature industrial relations' if labor representatives continue to be relegated to an advisory role and producers are hesitant to allow direct representation by workers at the highest levels. While an advisory role for unions can well-advance labor rights (see Banks 2000 for such an option in the relations between unions and NGOs), a 'mature industrial relations', as far as unions are concerned, requires their participation as representatives of workers at the workplace.

A global social dialogue would require the participation of global union organizations, in this case the IUF, despite their limited resources and authority. There are various reasons for that. First, global union organizations can provide a modicum of cohesion given the dispersed nature of Fairtrade certification. Second, Fairtrade International is promoting global standards for workers, something that requires a global interlocutor representing workers. Third, the production networks to be regulated are global networks, and those networks increasingly include global corporations. Finally, the dispersed workplaces that Fairtrade International seeks to regulate exist within and because of historically global production networks. To put it simply, global social dialogues require global partners.

THE SIGNIFICANCE OF INTERNATIONAL LABOR STANDARDS

As noted, the Standard covers the Internationally Recognized Core Labor Standards (core labor standards) which were enumerated in the 1998 ILO (International Labor Organization) Declaration of Fundamental Principles and Rights at Work. These standards are: 1) freedom of association and the effective recognition of the right to collective bargaining; 2) the elimination of forced or compulsory labor; 3) the elimination of discrimination in respect of employment and occupation; and 4) the abolition of child labor. Each of these standards is based on and clarified by specific ILO Conventions.

There are diverse views about the ILO Declaration. I agree that the Declaration represents a narrowing of labor rules in the direction of liberalism (Standing 2008). Not only does it privilege certain standards over others, but it privileges those standards associated with liberal industrial relations which are largely based on collective agreements between employers and unions, and less those associated with social democratic politics, which include institutionalized industrial relations and are embedded in a social welfare state. Within this context it is important to underscore three things. First, the core labor standards are the result of a strategic compromise within the global union movement and picking and choosing among them will be viewed as an attempt to unravel this compromise. Second, the linkages of these standards to specific Conventions of the ILO are not simply informational. Unions, globally and nationally, are agreed that the authoritative interpreter of core labor standards is the ILO and no one else. Third, unions do prioritize freedom of association and the right to collective bargaining among these standards. In fact they see the formation of independent unions as the best monitoring mechanism and a means to get away from the 'outsourcing of responsibility' that third-party auditing and monitoring implies (Banks 2000; Finnegan 2013).

The concerns of unions over freedom of association and collective bargaining are well founded. Studies have shown that codes of conduct are much more likely to include standards such as non-discrimination, prohibition of child labor and prohibition of forced labor, rather than collective rights (Murray 1998; Wick 2005). The revised Standard includes a protocol on freedom of association that employers have to sign and respect as well as various provisions intended to produce collective bargaining agreements (Fairtrade International 2014d, 3.4). Fairtrade International is fully aware of the gap between freedom of association and the right to collective bargaining and is pushing in the direction of what may be called 'positive neutrality', including training and capacity building so that workers can negotiate. But, while there is strong language on collective bargaining, there is no protocol similar to that on freedom of association (see also Lone Riisgaard's chapter in this volume). However, it seems that one will be developed in accordance in the workers' rights strategy, certainly a positive step.

The emphasis that unions place on freedom of association and collective bargaining is due to the tensions between empowering rights and working conditions, a distinction that is often difficult to convey (see Barrientos and Smith 2007 for one approach; also Banks 2000). A right is a rule that gives workers social recognition and legal standing to pursue their goals, which may include working conditions such as hours of work, health and safety, or wages. However, working conditions can also be put in place by governments or employers choosing the high road or trying to forestall unionization. Working conditions, in short, tend to protect and have often been used to co-opt workers, while rights tend to protect and empower. And, of course, unions are not seeking any rights but, rather, the exercise of collective rights.

For unions the core labor standards provide the floor for standards anywhere in the world. Employers or states cannot violate these standards by claiming that they are following local laws or circumstances, as seems to be the case in Ecuador's cut flowers industry (Lyall 2014; Raynolds 2012). Of course, employers can adopt additional best practices – provided that such practices are not an excuse to dilute core labor standards, especially freedom of association and the right to collective bargaining.

Unions also realize that market-wide health and safety and living wage provisions are important, especially in labor intensive work, both in themselves and because they can provide a fair playing field that prevents downward harmonization (Kearney and Justice 2005; Miller et al. 2011). Such market-wide standards should not wait for unions to be established and, in fact, might facilitate the formation of unions. So, while unions argue that freedom of association and the right to collective bargaining are the best route to a living wage and health and safety conditions, they are not opposed to higher common standards even in the absence of unions. Rather, they want producers, buyers and retailers to engage unions in setting those standards. In the absence of workplace unions these can be national and global union organizations. Thus, Fairtrade International's ambitious living wage agenda and its attention to workplace conditions are consistent with union priorities.

A central concern of unions in this and other cases is the handling of grievances. A strong grievance resolution system should address both violations of working conditions as well as attempts by management to prevent unionization or control workers' organizations. A grievance resolution process that does not address collective rights is likely to become part of human resource management rather than 'mature industrial relations'. Such a grievance system should have its own chapter in order to make it clear that it applies to all practices covered by the Hired Labor Standard (it is currently under Conditions of Employment).

Persistent unfair labor practices as well as workplace arrangements intended to prevent broader unionization should be grounds for decertification.

WORKPLACE EMPLOYEE ORGANIZATIONS

Fairtrade International's Standard for Hired Labor envisions a dual system of workplace organizations – a union (or a workers' organization, in its absence) and the Fairtrade Premium Committee (Premium Committee). Once described I will discuss them in relation to existing models of dual workplace representation, an issue that has become increasingly global as a result of the internationalization of European firms and GFAs (Stevis 2010).

In the absence of a union the workers must democratically elect an independent workers' organization to represent the workers and negotiate with management (Fairtrade International 2014d, 2.1 and 2014e). Recognizing the possibility that management may be unwilling to allow the formation or operations of such an independent organization, the Standard and the associated guidance contain strong language to prevent such practices on the part of management. The Standard envisions that the workers' organization can begin a dialogue with national unions and GUFs and receive information and support from them (Fairtrade International 2014d, 2.1).

The Premium Committee is a workplace organization that is unique to fair trade in its authority and impacts and one that can raise important challenges to unions, as discussed below (Fairtrade International 2104d, 2.1 and 2014f). While the Premium Committee cannot bargain with management, it is responsible for the investing of the fair trade premium to improve the livelihoods for workers and communities. According to the revised Standard, the workers elect the Premium Committee. Union members may be elected to it but there are no guaranteed union seats. The Standard was also revised so that advisors appointed by management do not have a right to a vote and their number must remain significantly smaller than that of workers. This reflects Fairtrade's awareness of the possibility that management can influence the Committee, something that is less likely where independent and active unions are present, such as in northern Colombia (Quesada 2013; but also see Brown 2013). While the tensions identified below are very possible in hired labor situations, they are also possible in small producer organizations to the degree that most of them depend on some hired labor and some of them depend significantly on hired labor (largely seasonal).

There are a number of models of workplace representation (Hogler 2004; Worker Participation.eu 2014). I will discuss three prominent ones, pointing out along the way the implications for Fairtrade International's dual representation system while suggesting the models that, in my view, will deepen the relations between unions and Fairtrade International. The model closest to what is envisioned by the Standard is that used in some Continental European countries and at the level of the European Union, and it provides for representation through a union and a works council. Unions negotiate collective agreements while works councils deal with workplace issues within the parameters of these agreements. Unions can be elected to works councils but they have to compete with independent candidates and, where there are many unions, with each other. That would be a serious problem in countries such as India where the union movement is fragmented and internally contested.

The Standard differs from the above model in two ways that make the Fairtrade International system one of both dual *and* parallel authority. First, the Premium Committee has decision-making powers while almost all works councils are intended to have, at most, implementation powers. Second, the powers and responsibilities of the Premium Committee are outside the negotiating reach of the union while works councils are expected to operate within parameters negotiated by unions. Where that does not happen it leads to conflict between unions and works councils. Individual disagreements can be solved through a dispute resolution process but the structure of the arrangement guarantees continuous friction. If the union cannot control the Premium Committee it will be marginalized by it. Fairtrade recognizes the possibility for friction and requires the Premium Committee to consult with workers' organizations or unions so as not to undermine the bargaining process and their authority.

A second model is a dual but not parallel system, as is the case in Sweden. Here both unions and workplace representation exist by law, but only union members can represent workers and such workplace representation can exist only where unions exist. In such a case there is less distance between the union and workplace representation, even though the two may develop different responsibilities and, often, different dynamics. It is not possible or desirable for Fairtrade International to suspend premium payments until a union is established. In the long term, however, a dual but not parallel system is a route worth exploring and is consistent with Fairtrade International's commitment to mature industrial relations.

The final model discussed here is one that recognizes only unions. In this case workplace organizations, such as Health and Safety Committees, are negotiated between management and unions and controlled by unions. In short, this model is similar to the previous one with the exception that workplace organizations are not prescribed by law but are the product of collective bargaining. In the case of Fairtrade International, unions have argued that the uses of the premium should be negotiated between unions and management within the rules established by Fairtrade.

To summarize, then, the Standard envisions a strong type of dual *and* parallel workplace authority. Many unions around the world, particularly in liberal capitalist countries, are not accustomed to a dual arrangement. Others are familiar with different types of dual systems. A dual system can well provide labor with an institutional presence that management must recognize while giving all employees some voice. However, there have to be clear lines of authority that place unions above workplace organizations which do not deal with collective rights. That is even more necessary when workplace organizations have parallel authority.

THE WHOLE PRODUCTION NETWORK

As mainstreaming and branding have grown, the fair trade economy now includes distribution and retail (Jaffee and Howard 2010; Riisgaard 2008; Riisgaard and Hammer 2011; Stenzel 2013; van der Val 2011). Some of the resulting tensions were highlighted by the Theo Chocolate case in the United States. Theo Chocolate is a company of about 55 employees, with a stated commitment to fair trade and certified by the Institute for Marketecology (IMO), an organization that aims to certify the whole life cycle. Its workers sought to unionize, with the support of a Teamsters' local, sometime after Theo Chocolate got a contract to supply Whole Foods (ILRF 2012). The reasons why these workers sought to unionize are not important. What is relevant here are the reactions by management and the IMO. Management did not facilitate unionization but, instead, hired a labor specialist to educate workers on the pros and cons of unionization. For anyone familiar with US labor politics this is the first step in a union-avoidance strategy. Management claimed that they hired the specific specialist because of his union background and not because they wanted to prevent unionization. Whenever management hires such outside advisors on labor matters, both management and the advisor have to submit certain forms to the Department of Labor. I have concluded, on the basis of those forms, that Theo Chocolate only had to look at the website of the company that the specialist was working with to know that they were hiring a union-avoidance specialist. IMO's response to the ILRF report, moreover, indicates that it does not fully understand the dynamics and sophisticated practices of anti-unionism in the United States (IMO 2013). The Theo case also highlights that managers in the fair trade economy, like those in the rest of the economy, tend to argue that unions are not necessary because workplace conditions are of a high standard and human relations management superior. Such an approach is boosted by the misconception that unions are simply a reaction to abuse rather than an integral part of a regulated and democratic economy (see Lone Riisgaard's chapter in this volume).

The Theo case is not an isolated instance. The Teamsters have also sought to unionize United Natural Foods Incorporated, a Denver-based distributor that specializes in non-conventional foods and products. One of its clients is Whole Foods. Both United Natural Foods Incorporated and Whole Foods are anti-union, not to mention even larger players, such as Walmart, who are also entering the fair trade economy. The point is that under the current path of mainstreaming, large companies with strong anti-union preferences will increasingly set the tone. Fairtrade International and other certifiers do not have enough countervailing power. However, they do have to decide whether and in what ways they will deploy the significant degree of legitimacy that they can confer in the hotly contested market of legitimation providers.

Fairtrade International realizes that it needs to increase its share of the market in order to deliver its benefits to more producers. Labor unions do need to recognize this challenge and support Fairtrade International in the same way that they support unionized firms in non-unionized sectors. However, Fairtrade International will have to decide whether to choose market expanding strategies that are consistent with its core values and its autonomy or whether to compromise them, leading to downgrading along the value chain. Unions, in particular, are not likely to support mainstreaming and branding that compromises core labor rights, does not move towards a living wage and does not attend to occupational health and safety problems.

This is doubly pressing for organizations like Fairtrade International that can be considered part of the collective employer. The more involved a certifier is in organizing and regulating economic activities, the more it can be considered as part of the collective employer. IMO and organizations like it act as service providers. Fairtrade International also provides services. However, the key role of the producers in its decision-making, the detailed standards and the transfer of resources, in the form of the premium, are evidence of more profound relations between the organization and the producers. Even though Fairtrade International has not reached the status of large retailers and companies that license or franchise brands and processes, it does exercise significant authority over (most of) those using its logo. So far, it has focused on producers but, ultimately, it must also address the rest of the production network – a much more serious challenge as far as labor rights go because of the size of the actors involved.

TOWARDS GLOBAL SOCIAL DIALOGUE AND MATURE INDUSTRIAL RELATIONS

A 'global social dialogue' between Fairtrade International and global labor is a worthwhile goal for the near future and a necessary foundation for 'mature industrial relations'. Such a process is particularly pressing because Fairtrade International seeks to regulate global production networks involving some of the least protected workers and where many local and global firms are seeking to take advantage of any economic benefits and legitimacy that Fairtrade International can confer (Jaffee and Howard 2010; Terstappen et al. 2013; Valkila and Nygren 2010; van der Wal 2011; Raynolds forthcoming).

I close by suggesting some elements of a multilevel strategy towards these goals, fully recognizing that the road is particularly hard and that the proof will be more independent and effective unionization in sectors that are not renowned for collective representation. Central to such a strategy would be an upgrading of labor's role in the organization of Fairtrade International itself, especially now that the producers' role has been upgraded. One can imagine an allocation of responsibilities depending on the type of standard being developed or revised.

A second layer would be that any local or national initiatives and policies affecting workers should involve national and global unions, reflecting the globalization of the production networks that are being regulated. Global unions can participate in a process that vets the independence of local and national unions. They can also be parties to any process for the resolution of labor disputes and unfair labor practices. If Fairtrade International signs specific agreements with firms or co-operatives that affect labor rights and standards, national and global unions should be formal participants. Even if such formal arrangements are narrow, participation by global unions legitimates these agreements as well as the global unions themselves – something that is necessary in the absence of strong local and national unions.

A third layer could be the promotion of GFAs for those multinational companies that also operate in fair trade. Fairtrade International could join GUFs in pushing other corporations involved with it, such as Dole, Unilever or Nestlé, to also negotiate GFAs. Fairtrade International does not need to be party to such agreements since most of the sales of these corporations are conventional. It could use the negotiation of a GFA, however, as a criterion for certification. Of course, some of these corporations would not even talk about GFAs, not to mention negotiate with them. But Fairtrade International, and the ISEAL (International Social and Environmental Accreditation and Labeling) Alliance of which it is a member, can and should add their voices in support for such agreements, thus deepening relations with global labor.

There are serious debates about the negotiation, content and implementation of GFAs, as well as about their broader politics (Papadakis 2011; Stevis 2010). However, they are the core response of global union organizations to the onslaught of codes of conduct (Kearney and Justice 2005). GFAs should not be negotiated or accepted if they are weak or intended as sophisticated forms of corporate social responsibility. The best among them, such as the one with Danone, outline a promising strategy towards global industrial relations that cover all the core labor rights and aim to regulate the whole supply chain. In such cases, still a small minority of GFAs, global management formally commits to global social dialogue and industrial relations. To promote these goals management and global union committees meet on a regular basis to solve specific problems as well as advance specific aspects of their transnational industrial relations, ranging from dealing with suppliers to occupational health and safety (for an overview of GFAs see Papadakis 2011).

The Bangladesh Accord on Fire and Building Safety provides an illustration of how these various threads can come together in the direction of creating 'mature industrial relations' (IndustriALL 2013). Specifically, the Accord reflects transnational collaboration among unions and advocates during which GUFs were able to leverage GFAs with specific companies (H&M and Inditex) to move the process forward. The political significance of the Accord is evident by the fact that key US companies have set up the Bangladesh Alliance for Worker Safety (2014). This divergence reflects the relative influence of European and US unions over multinationals from their regions and the deep anti-unionism of US multinationals.

A recent article in the *New York Times* (Greenhouse and Harris 2014) obscures the political significance of these alternatives by focusing on whether one or the other have done more inspections (for a distinction based on process (politics) and outcomes (inspections), see Barrientos and Smith 2007). While effective inspections are central, they are nested within deeper politics. In the case of the Accord, corporations have to recognize and negotiate with labor; in the case of the Alliance, they do not.

Fairtrade International is facing a challenge similar to the Bangladesh case; will the practical be nested within the political or the political within the practical, fully understanding that both are necessary? The Hired Labor Standard, with its emphasis on both rights and standards, shows that Fairtrade International recognizes the significance of politics in dealing with labor. The Standard's legitimacy is not based solely on whether workers will receive a higher premium or women workers treated respectfully by management. Rather, the Standard seeks to move one step further so that the workers can represent themselves and accomplish these goals.

But unions must also recognize and support the political commitments of Fairtrade International, even though the numbers of workers involved is very small. An instrumental approach that is based solely on how many workers are unionized would be shortsighted. There are a number of reasons for that. Cultivating allies that share the same values and may grow in influence and numbers is a proactive strategy. The more unions support Fairtrade as it grows and during periods of crisis, the deeper their longer-term relationship is likely to be. Such a strategy is even more advisable if that ally can play a leading role in the contested arena of private regulation and can help differentiate corporate responsibility from social regulation, an issue very close to labor's priorities (Raynolds 2012; Shamir 2011).

The experiences associated with the revision of the Hired Labor Standard opened a window of opportunity for a more systematic global social dialogue that can lead these two movements beyond temporary alliances and towards a mutual political commitment. Specific institutional arrangements that promote 'mature transnational industrial relations' will be evidence of such a commitment and will contribute to its deepening and effectiveness. Ultimately, the proof of success has to be the empowerment of the most precarious workers in fair trade and not only those workers that are the easiest to organize. Most of these precarious workers may be in the global South but many are in the global North. This is another reason why global union organizations are a necessary component of the transnational industrial relations envisioned by Fairtrade International.

REFERENCES

Anker, Richard and Martha Anker (2013), 'A shared approach to estimating living wages: Short description of the agreed methodology', ISEAL Alliance, available at http://www.isealalliance.org/sites/default/files/Descripton%20of%20Living%20Wage%20Methodology%2020131124.pdf (accessed 2 May 2014).

Bangladesh Alliance for Worker Safety (2014) website, available at http://www.bangladeshworkersafety.org/ (accessed 3 May 2014).

Banks, Andy (2000), 'A labor viewpoint on workplace codes of conduct', *Human Rights Dialogue*, 2 (4), 12–14, available at http://www.carnegiecouncil.org/publications/archive/dialogue/2_04/articles/894.html (accessed August 1, 2014).

Barrientos, Stephanie and Sally Smith (2007), 'Do workers benefit from ethical trade? Assessing codes of labour practice in global production systems', *Third World Quarterly*, 28 (4), 713–729.

Beaty, Tim (2012), 'Fair Trade USA's Draft Farm Workers Standards', available at http://laborrightsblog.typepad.com/international_labor_right/2012/02/fair-trade-usas-draft-farm-workers-standard.html (accessed 1 May 2014).

Brown, Sandy (2013), 'One hundred years of labor control: Violence, militancy, and the Fairtrade banana commodity chain in Colombia', *Environment and Planning A*, 45 (11), 2572–2591.

Dickinson, Rink (2011), 'An analysis of fair trade: Reflections from a co-founder', available at http://www.fairtradecommunity.com/articles/17-fair-trade/674-an-analysis-of-fair-trade-reflections-from-a-co-founder?showall=1 (accessed 2 May 2014).

Fairtrade International (2012), 'Monitoring the scope and benefits of Fairtrade: Fourth edition', available at http://www.fairtrade.net/fileadmin/user_upload/content/2009/resources/2012-Monitoring_report_web.pdf (accessed 27 April 2014).

Fairtrade International (2013), 'Consultation results synopsis: Information to stakeholders on the outcome of the Hired Labour Standard review consultation', available at http://www.fairtrade.net/fileadmin/user_upload/content/2009/standards/documents/generic-standards/2013-10-14_HL_synopsis_FINAL.pdf (accessed 1 May 2014).

Fairtrade International (2014a), 'Workers' rights and trade union relations', available at http://www.fairtrade.net/workers-rights.html (accessed 27 April 2014).

Fairtrade International (2014b), 'A new workers rights strategy for Fairtrade', available at http://www.fairtrade.net/fileadmin/user_upload/content/2009/resources/2012-06-20_Workers_rights.pdf (accessed 27 April 2014).

Fairtrade International (2014c), 'Revised Fairtrade Standard for Hired Labor bolsters support for workers', http://www.fairtrade.net/single-view+M5ec4971ca57.html (accessed April 27, 2014).

Fairtrade International (2014d), 'Fairtrade Standard for Hired Labour', available at http://www.fairtrade.net/fileadmin/user_upload/content/2009/standards/documents/generic-standards/2014-03-14_HL_EN.pdf (accessed 27 April 2014).

Fairtrade International (2014e), 'Explanatory document for the Fairtrade Standard for Hired Labour', available at http://www.fairtrade.net/fileadmin/user_upload/content/2009/standards/documents/generic-standards/2014-03-20_Explan_Doc_HL_EN.pdf (accessed 28 April 2014).

Fairtrade International (2014f), 'Explanatory document for the Fairtrade Premium Committee in hired labour situations', available at http://www.fairtrade.net/fileadmin/user_upload/content/2009/standards/documents/generic-standards/2014-03-31_Ex_Doc_FPC_EN.pdf (accessed 28 April 2014).

Fairtrade International (2014g), 'Standards for small producer organizations', available at http://www.fairtrade.net/small-producer-standards.html (accessed May 16, 2014).

Fairtrade International, International Union of Food Workers, International Trade Union Confederation and Trade Union Congress (2012), 'Joint statement concerning workers' rights in Fiji', available at http://www.ituc-csi.org/IMG/pdf/joint_agreed_fiji_statement_final_21092012.pdf (accessed 28 April 2014).

Fair World Project (2012), 'Civil society letter to FLO regarding representation of workers in Fairtrade system', available at http://fairworldproject.org/in-the-news/civil-society-letter-to-flo-regarding-representation-of-workers-in-the-fairtrade-system/ (accessed 1 May 2014).

Finnegan, Brian (2013), 'Responsibility outsourced: Social audits, workplace certification and twenty years of failure to protect worker rights', available at http://www.aflcio.org/content/download/77061/1902391/CSReport.pdf (accessed 28 April 2014).

Flinterman, Wilbert (2014), 'Journey towards and living wage', available at http://www.fairtrade.net/single-view+M5e839c395a1.html (accessed 2 May 2014).

Food and Agriculture Organization (2014), 'Working group on labour rights (WG3),' available at http://www.fao.org/economic/worldbananaforum/wbf-working-groups/wg03/en/ (accessed 2 May 2014).

Gårdman, Christina (2008), 'Fairtrade and human rights in the Kenyan cut flower industry', Lund University, available at http://lup.lub.lu.se/luur/download?func=downloadFile&recordOId=1315678&fileOId=1316212 (accessed 27 April 2014).

Greenhouse, Steven and Elizabeth Harris (2014), 'Battling for a safer Bangladesh', *New York Times*, electronic edition, available at http://www.nytimes.com/2014/04/22/business/international/battling-for-a-safer-bangladesh.html?_r=0 (accessed 2 May 2014).

Hogler, Raymond (2004), *Employment Relations in the United States: Law, Policy, and Practice*, London: Sage.

IMO (Institute for Marketecology) (2013), 'Public response: ILRF report on Fair for Life and Theo Chocolate', available at http://www.imo.ch/logicio/client/imo/file/news/IMO%20Final%20Response%20ILRF_20130218.pdf (accessed 28 April 2014).

IndustriALL (2013), 'Bangladesh Accord on Fire and Building Safety', available at http://www.industriall-union.org/bangladesh-accord-on-fire-and-building-safety-released (accessed 3 May 2014).

ILRF (International Labor Rights Forum) (2009), 'Letter to TransFair USA regarding fair trade garments pilot project', available at http://digitalcommons.ilr.cornell.edu/cgi/viewcontent.cgi?article=1427&context=globaldocs (accessed 2 May 2014).

ILRF (International Labor Rights Forum) (2012), 'Aiding and abetting: How unaccountable fair trade certifiers are destroying workers' rights', available at http://ethixmerch.com/sites/ethixmerch.com/files/IMO-and-Theo-Chocolate-A-Case%20Study-How-Unaccountable-Fair-Trade-Certifiers-are-Destroying-Workers'-Rights.pdf (accessed 1 May 2014).

Jaffee, Daniel and Philip Howard (2010), 'Corporate cooptation of organic and fair trade standards', *Agriculture and Human Values*, 27 (4), 387–399.

Kearney, Neil and Dwight Justice (2005), 'The new codes of conduct: Some questions and answers for trade unions', in Ingeborg Wick (ed.), *Workers Tool or PR Ploy? A Guide to Codes of International Labour Practice*, 4th revised edition, Bonn and Siegburg: Friedrich Ebert Stiftung and Suedwind Institut fuer Öëkonomie und Öëkumene, pp. 105–127, available at http://library.fes.de/pdf-files/iez/04288.pdf (accessed 28 April 2014).

Lyall, Angus (2014), 'Assessing the impacts of Fairtrade on worker-defined forms of empowerment on Ecuadorian flower plantations', Fairtrade International and Max Havelaar-Foundation, available at http://www.fairtrade.net/fileadmin/user_upload/content/2009/resources/140212-Worker-Empowerment-Ecuador-Flower-Plantations-final.pdf (accessed 27 April 2014).

Miller, Doug, Simon Turner and Tom Grinter (2011), 'Back to the future? A critical reflection on Neil Kearney's mature systems of industrial relations perspective on the

governance of outsourced apparel supply chains', Capturing the Gains, Working Paper 2011/08, available at http://www.capturingthegains.org/pdf/ctg-wp-2011-08.pdf (accessed 28 April 2014).
Murray, Jill (1998), *Corporate Codes of Conduct and Labour Standards*, Geneva: ILO.
Ostertag, Carlos, Oscar Sandoval, Juan Barona and Carolina Mancilla (2014), 'An evaluation of Fairtrade impact on smallholders and workers in the banana sector in northern Colombia', presented by the Corporation for Rural Business Development (CODER) to Max Havelaar Netherlands, available at http://www.fairtrade.net/fileadmin/user_upload/content/2009/resources/140330-Banana-Colombia-Fairtrade-Impact-Study-final.pdf (accessed 27 April 2014).
Papadakis, Konstandinos (ed.) (2011), *Shaping Global Industrial Relations: The Impacts of International Framework Agreements*, Basingstoke, UK: Palgrave Macmillan and ILO.
Quesada, A. and Victor Hugo (2013), 'What can we learn from the banana experience in Colombia?', Bonn: Fairtrade International, available at http://www.fairtrade.net/fileadmin/user_upload/content/2009/resources/201303_Industrial_relations_Colombia_study_final.pdf (accessed 27 April 2014).
Raynolds, Laura (2007), 'Fair trade bananas: Broadening the movement and market in the United States', in Laura Raynolds, Douglas Murray and John Wilkinson (eds.), *Fair Trade: The Challenges of Transforming Globalization*, London and New York: Routledge, pp. 63–82.
Raynolds, Laura (2012), 'Fair trade flowers: Global certification, environmental sustainability, and labor standards', *Rural Sociology*, 77 (4), 493–519.
Raynolds, Laura (forthcoming), 'Fairtrade, certification, and labor: Global and local tensions in improving conditions for agricultural workers', *Agriculture and Human Values*.
Riisgaard, Lone (2008), 'Global value chains, labor organization and private social standards: Lessons from East African cut flower industries', *World Development*, 37 (2), 326–340.
Riisgaard, Lone and Nikolaus Hammer (2011), 'Prospects for labour in global value chains: Labour standards in the cut flower and banana industries', *British Journal of Industrial Relations*, 49 (1), 168–190.
Shamir, Ronen (2011), 'Socially responsible private regulation: World-culture or world-capitalism?', *Law and Society*, 45 (2), 313–336.
Standing, Guy (2008), 'ILO: An agency for globalization?', *Development and Change*, 39 (3), 355–384.
Stenzel, Paulette (2013), 'Mainstreaming fair trade and resulting turmoil: Where should the movement go from here?', *William and Mary Environmental Law and Policy Review*, 37 (2), 617–673.
Stevis, Dimitris (2010), 'International framework agreements and global social dialogue: Parameters and prospects', Employment Sector, Employment Working Paper No. 47, Geneva: International Labour Office.
Stevis, Dimitris and Terry Boswell (2008), *Globalization and Labor: Democratizing Global Governance*, Lanham: Rowman & Littlefield Publishers.
Terstappen, Vincent, Lori Hanson and Darrell McLaughlin (2013), 'Gender, health, labor, and inequities: A review of the fair and alternative trade literature', *Agriculture and Human Values*, 30 (1), 21–39.
USLEAP (United States Labor Education in the Americas Project) (2009), 'Banana unions demand changes with fair trade', available at http://www.usleap.org/banana-unions-demand-changes-fair-trade (accessed 2 May 2014).
Valkila, Joni and Anja Nygren (2010), 'Impacts of fair trade certification on coffee farmers, cooperatives, and laborers in Nicaragua', *Agriculture and Human Values*, 27 (3), 321–333.

Van der Wal, Sanne (2008), 'Sustainability issues in the tea sector: A comparative analysis of six leading tea producing countries', Amsterdam: Centre for Research on Multinational Corporations (SOMO), available at http://somo.nl/publications-en/Publication_2548 (accessed 2 May 2014).

Van der Wal, Sanne (2011), 'Certified Unilever tea: Small cup, big difference?', Amsterdam: Centre for Research in Multinational Corporations (SOMO) and India Committee of the Netherlands (ICN), available at http://somo.nl/publications-en/Publication_3711 (accessed 2 May 2014).

Wick, Ingeborg (ed.) (2005), *Workers Tool or PR Ploy? A Guide to Codes of International Labour Practice*, 4th revised edition, Bonn and Siegburg: Friedrich Ebert Stiftung and Suedwind Institut fuer Öëkonomie und Öëkumene, available at http://library.fes.de/pdf-files/iez/04288.pdf (accessed 28 April 2014).

Worker Participation.eu (2014), 'Map of European industrial relations', available at http://www.worker-participation.eu/National-Industrial-Relations/Map-of-European-Industrial-Relations (accessed 2 May 2014).

7. Fairtrade certification, conventions and labor

Lone Riisgaard

INTRODUCTION

This chapter seeks to broaden our understanding of the potential and limits of Fairtrade certification for improving labor conditions in large-scale agriculture. Although Fairtrade certification was originally designed to support small-scale coffee farmers, it has expanded to include some 20 different commodities, many of which are produced on large plantations using hired labor. In 2012 there were more than 170 000 workers employed on Fairtrade certified plantations producing items such as flowers, tea, fruits and bananas (Fairtrade International 2012). Over the past decade Fairtrade's most rapid growth has been in large agricultural enterprises.[1] This expansion of Fairtrade to hired labor situations has caused significant tensions.

This chapter contributes to the emerging literature on Fairtrade's efforts to incorporate plantations and agricultural workers.[2] More specifically it explores what can be gained from using convention theory to analyze Fairtrade's engagement with hired labor enterprises and its efforts to improve conditions for agricultural workers. Most studies confirm that Fairtrade has brought positive impacts to workers, their households and local communities. Nevertheless, employing a convention theory lens helps us uncover and understand limitations to Fairtrade impacts attributable to the prevalence of particular conventions and the naturalization of specific understandings of what constitutes Fairtrade values. Thus it is argued that Fairtrade, in the implementation of its standards, incorporates more a liberal perception of civic rights than solidarity (which is aimed at greater equality). At the same time it is argued that for labor management systems in large-scale agriculture the stabilization of an industrial convention is a precondition for civic elements to be stabilized, providing there is political pressure for this. Such a stabilization (along with pressure for the civic inflection) can be argued to be promoted by Fairtrade through its focus on stabilizing the contractual relations between buyer and producer. The arguments put forward in this chapter derive mainly from empirical studies of Fairtrade certified flower farms in Ecuador and Kenya.

The chapter starts with a short introduction to convention theory followed by a convention theory analysis of Fairtrade certification's move from small farmer cooperatives to large-scale agriculture and hired labor. This study proceeds to look at labor organizing and finally examines how Fairtrade might help stabilize 'civic' values in hired labor situations.

CONVENTION THEORY: A SHORT INTRODUCTION

Convention theory emerged in France during the 1980s, focusing on issues of inter- and intra-firm coordination and identifying systematic differences between types of coordination. Convention theory saw these differences as reflecting normatively founded systems of collective expectations. It suggested that a number of systematically different normative orientations coordinating markets and firms (conventions or 'orders of worth') had emerged by the mid-19th century and that groups of actors continue to draw on these. Conventions thus express competing rationalities (Boltanski and Thévenot [1991] 2006).

Convention theory has been applied to two areas of economic coordination. The first is the arbitration of product quality (see Daviron 2002 for a summary) while the second is arbitration of the quality of labor (Salais et al. 1986). In both cases the alternative conventions deployed are distinguished and described on the basis of their underlying principles ('modes of evaluation'); the types of information they prescribe as salient ('format of relevant information'); the objects whose qualities they are most interested in verifying ('qualified objects'); the practical questions that they most frequently ask in relation to these objects ('elementary questions'); and their orientations to space and time (the respective relevance of the past, the present and the future). Boltanski and Thévenot ([1991] 2006) strongly emphasize the overlap between economic conventions and political rationalities (within shared 'worlds of legitimate common welfare'). For this reason Gibbon and Riisgaard (2014) argue that it is useful to add distinctions between and descriptions of political orientations to their elaboration.

Different proponents of convention theory elaborate lists of between four and six economic conventions or 'orders of worth' used by actors to justify the legitimacy of different forms of coordination. Four specific conventions are found in almost all these lists, usually referred to as 'domestic', 'industrial', 'market' and 'civic'.[3] The fundamental principles of these conventions are 'tradition', 'efficiency', 'cost' and 'welfare' respectively. The four conventions correspond to different ways of characterizing the common good based on 'market' competition, 'industrial' efficiency, trust and reputation based on customs ('domestic') and 'civic' solidarity aiming at greater equality (Boltanski and Thévenot [1991] 2006). Table 7.1 differentiates these conventions.[4]

Table 7.1 Domestic, industrial, market and civic conventions

	Domestic	Industrial	Market	Civic
Mode of evaluation	Traditional reputation	Technical precision and efficiency	Price, 'value for money'	Benefit to society (and the environment)
Format of relevant information	Exemplary, anecdotal, sometimes oral	Systematic, operational, quantified	Contemporary, practical, demand oriented	Codes, norms, programs, policies
Qualified objects	Patrimony, specific tools and assets	Structures, universal systems, forecasts	Cost units	Associations, negotiations, distributional arrangements
Elementary questions	Can it be trusted?	Is it functional? Can it be scaled-up and stabilized?	Is it economic? What is its equivalent? Are we tied down to it?	Is it just, safe, healthy? How can it be regulated?
Human qualification	Personal acquaintance, experience, seniority	Education/ training (competence)	Price, flexibility	Responsibility, motivation
Time orientation	The past and the (customary) present	The (planned) future, the business cycle	Immediate availability	The deliberative cycle
Space orientation	Proximity, private spaces	A technically predictable universe (Cartesian space)	Compartmentalized, adjustable space	(Homogeneous) public space
Political orientation	Paternalism	Technocratic	Individualistic, contingent	Democratic or corporatist, legalistic

Source: Reproduced from Gibbon and Riisgaard (2014).

CONVENTION THEORY AND THE FAIRTRADE STANDARD

Raynolds (2014), in her ongoing work on Fairtrade, has used the four conventions described above to analyze Fairtrade standards and the changes they have gone through in order to accommodate large-scale producers and agricultural workers. Raynolds aptly demonstrates how a convention theory approach helps identify the compromises inherent in negotiating the place of large-scale producers and agricultural workers in the Fairtrade system.

Convention theory asserts that in most situations, conventions are deployed in hybrid rather than pure forms – what Boltanski and Thévenot ([1991] 2006, 277) call compromises. However, the literature also suggests that some compromises are much more likely than others and that some are unlikely to occur (see also Raynolds 2014; Riisgaard and Gibbon 2014). Compromises between market and industrial conventions are very common and are found in most agro-industrial firms guided by price competition (the market world) and product standardization and efficiency (the industrial world). Fairtrade, however, is also built on civic and domestic conventions, as highlighted by several studies of Fairtrade certified coffee (Raynolds 2002; 2009; Renard 2003; 2005). A widely accepted definition of Fairtrade is as follows:

> Fair Trade is a trading partnership, based on dialogue, transparency and respect, that seeks greater equity in international trade. It contributes to sustainable development by offering better trading conditions to, and securing the rights of, marginalized producers and workers – especially in the South. (World Fair Trade Organization and Fairtrade International 2009)

Raynolds (2014, 279), using a convention perspective, notes that this definition illustrates how Fairtrade seeks to requalify conventional production and trade based on industrial and market conventions (where products and exchange are ruled by efficiency and price competition) with civic values (focusing on human rights and on fostering the general welfare of people and the planet) and domestic values (grounded in personal trust and attachment to people, places and traditions). Although domestic values of interpersonal trust and attachments are typically associated with face-to-face interactions, as Raynolds (2002, 410) argues Fairtrade extends these values to international trade by reconnecting consumers and producers through more direct trade relations and a focus on producer stories accompanying the traded products.

Fairtrade thus aims to temper industrial and market values with domestic and civic ones. The strong focus on domestic values (grounded in personal trust, dialogue and partnership), however, has been challenged by the growth of Fairtrade sales, particularly through mainstream retail outlets. This has bolstered the role of market norms and dominant corporate actors in Fairtrade (Raynolds 2009), challenging the personalized, trust-based trading relations originally promoted by Fairtrade. Market growth has encouraged the formalization of Fairtrade rules and procedures and strengthened industrial conventions (evidenced in the bureaucratic organization and control exercised through standards, audits and certification procedures which regulate production and trade), countering Fairtrade's domestic principles of personal trust (Gibbon and Riisgaard 2014; Le Velly 2007; Mutersbaugh 2002; 2005; Raynolds 2002; 2009; 2014; Renard 2003; 2005).

One can argue that from the start of certified Fairtrade there has been an inherent tension between the compromises made to increase sales and the goal of developing an alternative market (Mukherjee-Reed and Reed 2010). The increase in sales is to a large degree related to Fairtrade moving beyond its original focus on small coffee farmers to incorporate large-scale plantation agriculture (pushed by dominant supermarkets to guarantee large year-round supplies) (Raynolds 2007). Since 1994, when Fairtrade certification was extended to tea and banana plantations, a range of plantation grown products has been incorporated based on the argument that landless laborers, who are often poorer than farmers, should be included to increase the number of beneficiaries of Fairtrade. As noted by Raynolds (2014), the incorporation of new products and large-scale enterprises has been facilitated by Fairtrade's increasingly industrial bureaucratic standards and the fact that Fairtrade International's generic hired labor standards are immediately applicable across commodities.

The certification of large-scale enterprises, facilitated by industrial procedures, thus challenges Fairtrade's domestic ideals of trading relations based on trust and partnerships. In particular, Fairtrade's direct and trust-based trading relations are challenged by the depersonalized nature of industrially produced commodities and by the capital intensive supply chains required for fresh products to be transported effectively without spoilage (Raynolds 2007). As noted by Gibbon and Riisgaard (2014) and Raynolds (2014), Fairtrade, along with other ethical standards, draws explicitly on civic values and qualifications in promoting labor rights. While domestic and industrial values are difficult to fuse, industrial and civic values are much more easily reconciled (as will be discussed later in this chapter, civic and market values are much harder to reconcile).

According to Boltanski and Thévenot ([1991] 2006), compromises between industrial and civic conventions come about mainly as the result of political struggles, with 'workers' rights' as its main expression linking beings from the industrial world (workers) with expectations from the civic world (rights). The latter's institutionalization runs counter to central 'industrial' principles (e.g., the focus on efficiency and increases in productivity) but is nonetheless not uncommon. It seems, furthermore, logical to propose that stability and predictability are prerequisites in both the industrial and civic world, making them relatively compatible (see Table 7.1). This is precisely what happens in Fairtrade organizations which 'draw explicitly on civic values and qualifications in promoting labor rights, echoing what is now a common and powerful narrative that frames workers' rights as human rights' (Raynolds 2014, 5).

In sum, Fairtrade's engagement in the hired labor sector has increased tensions between, on the one hand, traditional market and industrial conventions rooted in price competition, bureaucratic efficiency, product standardization and certification and, on the other hand, alternative domestic conventions rooted in trust, personal ties and partnerships (Raynolds 2014). The incorporation of new products and large-scale enterprises has been facilitated by Fairtrade's increasingly industrial bureaucratic standards and procedures (making Fairtrade International's generic hired labor standards immediately applicable across commodities) since civic and industrial conventions are much easier to reconcile. However, as will be argued in the following section, in the implementation of Fairtrade standards in hired labor situations, some interpretations of civic are favored over others.

IMPLEMENTATION OF FAIRTRADE STANDARDS IN HIRED LABOR SITUATIONS

Different Interpretations of 'Civic'

Although it can be seen that many civic rules are accommodated in Fairtrade (members vote in the General Assembly, gender issues are taken into account, etc.), constituting progress for workers in plantations, Fairtrade standards are based more on the liberal perceptions of civic rights than solidarity (which is aimed at greater equality) (Cheyns 2011; Cheyns and Riisgaard 2014). This means that the main focus is on the individuals to whom rights are given, more than on solidarity – defined as actions aimed at reducing inequalities expressed via organized and solidaristic groupings such as trade unions.

The difference between the two perceptions of civic values is discussed by Thévenot and Lamont (2000), illustrated via the framing of 'civic' ideals in the United States and France respectively:

> A first difference is that in the United States, civic equality is more often primarily framed in terms of citizenship entailing legal rights, whereas in France, it is more frequently expressed in terms of solidarity. A second contrast is that while a market logic and civic equality are intertwined in the American case, civic solidarity is opposed to market inequalities in France. (Thévenot and Lamont 2000, 309)

They note that although the universalistic individualism of the Enlightenment was promoted by the French Revolution, the polity in the French context 'often equates individual interests with egoism and lack of civil solidarity (or the common interests of all citizens)' (Thévenot and Lamont 2000, 309). This conception is foreign to American liberalism, where 'the individual is both the main actor in the market and the entity to which civil rights are given. This is why one can state that in the United States, civic solidarity (defined in legal terms) is compatible with market competition' (Thévenot and Lamont 2000, 309). In the French context, such a strong association between the 'civic' and 'market' principles of evaluation is not present. 'Here, civic legitimacy is more associated with the defense of solidarity defined as action aimed at reducing inequalities' (Thévenot and Lamont 2000, 309).

What is particularly interesting for our discussion of Fairtrade is how these differences might be manifest in the workplace. Thévenot and Lamont (2000, 309), referring to the French interpretation of 'civic', note that:

> This solidarity is also expressed through collective groupings (esp. 'classes') that have been historically construed in the context of the workplace. It is there, in the workplace, that group membership is primarily manifested and where solidaristic policies and movements are developed (and not in the civic/legal realm as in the United States). And in the workplace, individuals are framed as members of a group sharing equal status, as opposed to being framed as independent individuals functioning within the market logic. (Thévenot and Lamont 2000, 309)

Although not employing convention theory, this focus on a particular individualistic interpretation of civic is also noted by Dolan (2008), in what she terms a normalization of western ethical judgments:

> The grammar of rights extended through Fairtrade (rights conceptualized during the seventeenth and eighteenth centuries in Europe and codified in

> various twentieth century covenants, conventions, and declarations), for example, derive from a liberal conception that positions the individual rather than the social, and the right to dignity rather than autonomy, as central in the ethical framework. Indeed the Enlightenment ideal of the autonomous subject, the individual upon whom rights are premised and made meaningful, draws on a notion of personhood that sits uneasily with social formations in more communitarian societies such as are found in Africa. (Dolan 2008, 283)

The specific interpretation of civic which is implemented by Fairtrade can also be illustrated empirically by looking at how they have dealt with or ignored the collective organization of workers in independent trade unions.

FAIRTRADE, LABOR STANDARDS AND TRADE UNIONS

As argued above, the Fairtrade standard incorporates more the liberal perceptions of civic rights than solidarity which is aimed at greater equality. In the implementation of Fairtrade standards in hired labor situations there is a strong focus on individual rights (e.g., as related to the right to a safe workplace, remuneration and working time within stipulated rules, maternity and sick leave, severance pay and medical checks). The standard provisions which can be argued to relate to issues of solidarity include the Fairtrade premium – a mandatory amount above the cost of the goods, the use of which is decided democratically and administered by an elected Joint Body made up of management and a majority of worker representatives, and which can only be used for the social and economic benefit of the workers, their families and communities. Premium use will not be discussed in this chapter, but its potential solidaristic focus is acknowledged, particularly since the premium is not to be given out directly to individual workers in cash or in kind.

The major provisions related to solidarity and equality in the Fairtrade standards are the provisions related to worker organization, particularly the fundamental rights of 'freedom of association' and 'the right to collective bargaining'. As data from Ecuador and Kenya will illustrate, even though they are included in the Fairtrade standard, so far these rights have not been enforced.

A recent study by Riisgaard et al. (2012) compared the impact of Fairtrade standards on six flower plantations in Kenya (2), Tanzania (1) and Ecuador (3) focusing on issues that directly impact workers. The research was commissioned by Fairtrade International and carried out from December 2010 to April 2011. Additional research and feedback sessions were conducted in 2011 and 2012.[5] The following sections are based on findings from this study.

The study finds that Fairtrade contributes to a range of rights and benefits including the following (in general these findings are confirmed by Raynolds 2014):

- Formalization of permanent employment and associated provision of written contracts and legislated entitlements (e.g., social security, annual bonuses and paid leave);
- Improved dialogue and negotiation between management and worker representatives (e.g., through Workers' Committees, trade unions, Joint Bodies, Health and Safety Committees, Gender Committees) and increased leadership and bargaining skills of members of these committees (particularly Workers' Committees, Joint Bodies and trade unions where these exist);
- Empowerment of workers in terms of: 1) improving the possibility for economic mobility via training and premium projects; 2) improving worker organization and representation through committees; and 3) strengthening individual voice and skills of particularly Joint Body members;
- Improved health and safety practices on farms;
- Various premium benefits to workers, their families and surrounding communities.

Fairtrade International standards stipulate that even when a plantation is not unionized, national or international trade unions should be consulted about how to improve collective bargaining. But in the cases studied, this had not occurred. Regional trade union representatives had (except for one case in Kenya) also not been contacted by Fairtrade International inspectors for supplementary information on key issues for workers in the certified plantations. Furthermore, on the plantations which had Workers' Committees but not unions, no plan existed for how to reach independent representation and collective bargaining.

It is the position of Fairtrade International that worker organization is a necessary condition for worker empowerment, and it is a requirement for all Fairtrade certified farms to have either an elected union or a Workers' Committee representing workers to management. One of the main differences between the potential for Workers' Committees versus trade unions for protecting workers' rights is that the latter is backed by a larger network of unions and have a legal position which enable them to evoke larger solidarity networks and to pursue workers' rights violations in the Industrial Court.

An equally important issue is the independence of workers' organizations from management. Problems in this regards were noted on two of the farms studied by Riisgaard et al. (2012): one in Kenya and one in Ecuador. In both cases workers did not feel free to voice concerns and feared that they might lose their jobs if they complained to management. In general one would expect a higher risk of cooptation by farm management with Workers' Committees compared to unions given their different institutional contexts.

Fairtrade and Trade Union Organizing in Ecuador

In Ecuador none of the ten Fairtrade certified flower plantations are unionized.[6] Managements were found to be overtly against active trade unions in the country and worker knowledge about unions was almost non-existent. Furthermore, workers from all three farms stated that representatives of the Labor Ministry had informed them (during Fairtrade stipulated training) that they did not need unions and that unions were inherently harmful (Riisgaard et al. 2012).

It must be acknowledged that labor organizing in Ecuador is a complicated issue. As discussed at some length in Riisgaard et al (2012), enabling trade unions on Fairtrade certified flower plantations in Ecuador is not an easy task. In an interview with the Mayor of Cayambe (Ecuador's largest flower growing area) on 9 April 2011 the Mayor described how plantation owners had closed down plantations as soon as workers had begun to organize. Although he asserted that this practice was no longer as feasible as it once was because of greater government regulations, he affirmed that unions have been stigmatized by workers and owners alike due to the historical link between unions and farm closings (interview conducted by Lyall 2011).

The stigmatization of unions was corroborated by both worker and management interviews. Some of the most common reasons that workers cited for rejecting unionizing as a viable option were corrupt unions and fear of reprisal. The perception of union organizers as corrupt and selfish, seeking their own interests rather than those of the workers, prevailed. This was accompanied by almost no functional knowledge of labor rights, trade unions or collective bargaining. For example, workers responded, 'We don't have information about unions', 'We've never had training on unions', '[unionizing] isn't touched [in training sessions]. I don't know how they function either' (selected worker interviews conducted by Lyall 2011–2012). At the same time, the fear of reprisal from plantation owners and administrators was common, including fear of dismissal and being placed on a black list. For example, workers said 'The old practice is that if [a union] is seen forming, the doors are closed' and 'They said that we can't [unionize] ... It is prohibited for us ... It is harmful for the company' (selected worker interviews conducted by Lyall 2011–2012).

Business representatives often explain the virtual absence of unions in the flower sector with reference to the lack of worker interest. In most cases, however, labor organization is strongly discouraged by management and there is little doubt that freedom of association is actively limited in the sector as a whole. Repression has become commonplace to the point that a representative of EXPOFLORES (the Ecuadorian flower industry association) spoke openly during an interview about the notorious 'black lists' of workers who have tried to organize other workers:

> The idea of a union is rather contentious; the moment that a union is viewed forming, the first thing [management] does is fire them because it is not in [management's] interest; [unions] ask for more than [management] can give ... Sometimes they fire the leaders ... The 'black list' does not exist – it is something sensitive, to have something like that in written form; it happens through phone calls; those [representatives] from Human Resources know each other and they communicate. (Interview conducted by Lyall 2011–2012)

Thus, while not ignoring that the trade union situation in Ecuador is complicated, it seems fair to say that very little effort has been mounted in enforcing freedom of association and collective bargaining on Fairtrade certified plantations in Ecuador.

Fairtrade and Trade Union Organizing in Kenya

In Kenya a different scenario is found. Here many of the Fairtrade certified farms are unionized. However, according to Riisgaard et al. (2012) and Riisgaard and Gibbon (2014),[7] this is mainly due to changes in Kenyan labor law (supporting membership of the existing sector collective bargaining agreement (CBA)) and efforts by Max Havelaar personnel[8] who ran the certification of Fairtrade flowers until 2006 when it was taken over by Fairtrade International in a harmonized and standardized format (see also Riisgaard 2009).

The 2010 flower sector CBA was signed by 57 of around 150 flower operators, including almost all the larger ones. In addition to this, three very large operators are parties to farm-level CBAs. Since 2010 unionization in Kenya has been complemented by de facto public support to so-called closed shops in enterprises that are signatories to national

CBAs. The mechanism in question (the Labor Relations Act of 2007, put into effect three years later) provides that unions who are parties to the sector CBA can require employers who are signatories to collect and remit to them an 'agency fee' from all unionizable – though not necessarily unionized – workers. This means that if a farm has signed the sector CBA then the union can claim the agency fee from all workers of that firm even if there are no union members at all.

Interviews with managers, workers and union branch officials carried out by Riisgaard and Gibbon (2014) all support the view that the combination of widening adoption of private labor standards and adherence to the national CBA, plus the agency fee regulation, have combined to widen local union recognition and promote unionization. A main mechanism at play is that Fairtrade International representatives in Kenya demand that certified farms sign up to the sector CBA (which makes it possible for the union to demand an agency fee from all workers). Also, workers identify union membership with the (likelihood of) improvements in wages in line with CBA determinations, and neutralization of cost of membership as a disincentive to joining – by virtue of this cost being imposed involuntarily on all workers (Riisgaard and Gibbon 2014). As the discussion of Fairtrade and union organizing in Ecuador (not enforced) and in Kenya (enforced only via the requirement to sign up to the sector CBA) illustrates, while Fairtrade score high on promoting the liberal interpretation of civic values (individual rights), they still have quite far to go when it comes to enforcing solidarity aimed at greater equality.

However, changes might be underway that could put more emphasis on a solidarity-based interpretation of civic. The 'New Workers Rights Strategy' for Fairtrade, for example, states that

> Fairtrade's focus should be to help build the conditions whereby workers have the tools and ability to negotiate their own wages and terms of work. … For example, we will ask employers to demonstrate that they accept freedom of association. … Fairtrade liaison officers will have a coordinating role and involve trade unions. (Fairtrade International 2012, 1)

But whether and how this will manifest itself in the forthcoming version of the standard for hired labor situations, and from there to implementation, remains to be seen.

Fairtrade International's specific interpretation of civic is also evident in how certification in practice has not implemented the ideal of a living wage. The study by Riisgaard et al. (2012) found various limitations in terms of the changes made with regards to the aim of achieving living wages on Fairtrade certified plantations. Although Fairtrade International standards require that 'salaries are gradually increased to "living wage" levels' (Fairtrade International 2012), on four out of the six certified plantations visited as part of this study they paid only the minimum wage. Furthermore, in Ecuador – where no trade unions existed – salary negotiations most often did not form part of management–worker negotiations.

Again, a shift towards a more solidarity-based interpretation of civic is arguably underway in Fairtrade International's new labor right strategy which stipulates a move from a requirement of a 'minimum wage' to one of a 'living wage'. This could, if implemented, represent a move to advance Fairtrade's civic commitments toward a new dimension of redistribution, well beyond most current labor standards systems. In sum, however, the specific interpretation of civic which has predominated and arguably still predominates the implementation of Fairtrade in hired labor situations is dominated by the liberal perceptions of civic rights rather than solidarity which is aimed at greater equality, thus illustrating some of the limitations of Fairtrade with regards to labor.

FAIRTRADE AND THE POSSIBILITY OF STABILIZING CIVIC VALUES

A key feature of Fairtrade – one which sets it apart from all other social standards in the sector – is the focus on contract security between producer and buyers. For example, Fairtrade has requirements on the existence and content of contracts and requires buyers to submit a sourcing plan to producers. This section argues, based on data from Kenya (see also Riisgaard and Gibbon 2014), that stabilization of an industrial convention on plantations (which is argued to be a precondition for stabilizing of civic values) along with pressure for the civic inflection can actually be argued to be promoted by Fairtrade, due to the focus on stabilizing the contractual relations between buyer and producer.

Riisgaard and Gibbon's (2014) study of labor management on flower farms in Kenya reveals important insights about the conditions under which civic values can possibly be stabilized in large-scale agriculture. The study finds that an industrial convention of labor management has been stabilized in the dominant part[9] of the Kenyan flower industry since around 2005. Importantly, this industrial convention has been inflected with civic values (although mainly in the liberal interpretation of civic as noted before). For the 'dominant' part of the industry the norm was found to be one of secure employment (including permanent contracts and freedom from arbitrary dismissal); freedom of association; application of nationally negotiated wage rates; improved observance of health and safety standards; provision of maternity leave and special provisions for pregnant and nursing mothers; and restrictions on overtime (see Riisgaard and Gibbon 2014 for more detail). These features are accompanied by scientific planning of work, rule-based payment systems and relatively flat forms of supervision.

This development was driven mainly by the stabilization of a labor-intensive 'medium tech' production system (a system of continuous mass production of largely standardized products) and of output. The latter in turn relates to the stability of demand for Kenyan produce in the main end-market. At the same time, most elements of the labor management system have been inflected in a civic direction. This has generated significant benefits for workers (e.g., by including secure employment, providing maternity leave) but has clear limitations with respect to real wages and effective wage negotiation (i.e., issues of equality and redistribution). The main driver of this inflection was found to be private regulation, supplemented by other factors, but comprehensive enough in its effects for the compromise to be both coherent and stable across a dominant part of the industry. Although it was not possible to study this directly, the civic inflection appears to have been implemented mainly through interactions between non-governmental organization (NGO) pressure and international buyer and industry association demands for compliance with social standards.

As mentioned, the convention theory literature suggests that some compromises (e.g., industrial and civic) are much more likely than others, and that some are unlikely to occur. In the wide-ranging survey by Boltanski and Thévenot ([1991] 2006, 325), *no* examples of compromise between the civic and market conventions are found. While the incompatibility between the market and civic worlds is not explicitly discussed in the literature, Riisgaard and Gibbon (2014) propose that lack of stability and predictability ('sustainability') in the market world makes it difficult to match the two unless there is a strong political imperative to do so, and that even then this would be at the expense of the flexibility demanded by market norms. From this discussion, they argue that while compromises between 'market' and 'industrial' worlds are an imperative of operating a capitalist business, compromises involving the 'civic' world are (unless residual) the result of political imperatives caused by popular struggles. Furthermore, some worlds are more compatible than others. Industrial and civic conventions are compatible to some degree, while market and civic conventions are difficult to reconcile.

Riisgaard and Gibbon (2014) hypothesize that for labor management systems in large-scale agriculture, the prior stabilization of an industrial convention is a precondition for civic elements to be stabilized – providing there is political pressure for this. Not surprisingly, the prior stabilization of an industrial convention, along with political pressure for civic inflections of this system (as found in Kenya cut flowers), is relatively exceptional in large-scale agriculture – even high-value large-scale agriculture. However, such a stabilization (along with pressure for the civic inflection) can actually be argued to be promoted by Fairtrade. The focus on stabilizing the contractual relations between buyer and producer, such that importers must adhere to generic trade standards focusing on contract security, is unique among sustainability standards. This can help address the key precondition for a stabilization of a civic inflection in labor management systems as the stability of demand makes it not just feasible but also desirable to stabilize output and enhance effectivity via an industrial-style labor management system.

Examining the evidence in practice, a study by Riisgaard et al. (2012) found that most farm management noted the stability of markets as the main market related advantage of Fairtrade certification. Management from one farm in Kenya thus relates how to them the key issue is that Fairtrade sales provides a more stable market and that they are able to negotiate prices for a longer time period with buyers of Fairtrade flowers, as compared to other buyers.

According to management, Fairtrade also leads to the stabilization of the workforce. The authors found that greater wellbeing among workers had a positive effect on workforce stability. The turnover on Fairtrade International plantations in Kenya, and in particular in Ecuador, is generally very low. All case study farms were therefore remarkable in the sense that labor stability in comparison with other plantations was very high. On all farms it was found that Fairtrade has contributed to enhanced job security and benefits such as annual leave and maternity leave, due to increased use of permanent contracts.

CONCLUSION

Most studies confirm that Fairtrade has brought positive impacts to workers, their households and local communities. Nevertheless, employing a convention theory lens helps us uncover and understand various limitations to Fairtrade's benefits, resulting from the prevalence of particular conventions and the naturalization of specific understandings of what constitutes Fairtrade values. This chapter has sought to broaden our understanding of the potential and limits of Fairtrade certification for improving labor conditions in large-scale agriculture. Using convention theory and empirical studies of Fairtrade certified flower farms in Ecuador and Kenya, it has made several conclusions.

As Raynolds (2014) argues, Fairtrade's engagement in the hired labor sector has increased tensions between (on the one hand) traditional market and industrial conventions rooted in price competition, bureaucratic efficiency, product standardization and certification and (on the other hand) alternative domestic conventions rooted in trust, personal ties and partnerships. As she argues, the incorporation of new products and large-scale enterprises has been facilitated by Fairtrade's increasingly industrial bureaucratic standards and procedures which make Fairtrade International's generic hired labor standards immediately applicable across commodities.

This chapter asserts that Fairtrade, in the implementation of its standards, incorporates more the liberal perceptions of civic rights than solidarity (which is aimed at greater equality). The specific interpretation of civic which is implemented by Fairtrade is illustrated empirically by looking at the lack of enforcement of the fundamental rights of 'freedom of association' and 'the right to collective bargaining', particularly in Ecuador. The specific interpretation of civic which is implemented by Fairtrade is also evident in how Fairtrade in practice has not implemented the ideal of a living wage.

Finally, research has found that for labor management systems in large-scale agriculture, the stabilization of an industrial convention is a precondition for civic elements to be stabilized, providing there is political pressure for this. The prior stabilization of an industrial convention, along with political pressure for civic inflections of this system (as was found in Kenyan cut flowers), is relatively exceptional in large-scale agriculture. However, such a stabilization (along with pressure for the civic inflection) can be argued to be promoted by Fairtrade. The focus on stabilizing the contractual relations between buyer and producer (importers must adhere to generic trade standards focusing on contract security) are unique among sustainability standards. Thus, apart from pushing for civic labor conventions (albeit mainly in the liberal interpretation of civic), Fairtrade can also help promote the key preconditions for a serious stabilization of such a civic inflection.

NOTES

1. See Laura Raynolds and Nicholas Greenfield's chapter in this volume for an outline of Fairtrade hired labor standards.
2. See chapters in this volume by Dimitris Stevis for more on Fairtrade union relations and Rie Makita for more on Fairtrade's implication for plantation workers in Asia.
3. Boltanski and Thévenot ([1991] 2006), for example, also identify conventions relating to 'inspiration' and 'fame'. These will not be discussed here.
4. Table 7.1 is reproduced from Gibbon and Riisgaard (2014) and draws on Eymard-Duvernay (1989) and Eymard-Duvernay et al. (2005), supplemented by Boltanski and Thévenot ([1991] 2006, 203–212 and 268–272); Storper and Salais (1997) and Salais (2001).
5. Given the size of the sample and the considerable diversity of situations of Fairtrade producers (e.g., per cent of produce sold as Fairtrade, years certified, market outlet, participation in other certification systems), this cannot be taken as a representative sample. Lone Riisgaard was responsible for overall coordination and oversight of the case studies and was also co-researcher on two case studies: Kenya and Ecuador. Angus Lyall carried out the research in Ecuador while Obadia Okinda carried out the fieldwork in Kenya and Tanzania. For each of the plantations, interviews were conducted with a cross section of workers (10–15 workers) and focus groups (2–3 groups of approximately 6–10 workers, each including an all-female group).
6. In 2005 only four of Ecuador's over 400 flower farms had unions (Korovkin and Sanmiguel-Valderrama 2007). According to FENACLE (an Ecuadorian banana workers union), in 2011 this has been reduced to only two farms.
7. These findings are based on fieldwork conducted on 11 (of approximately 170) large-scale cut flower farms in Kenya over a two-month period in mid-2011. The sampling frame was purposively designed to include farms certified to a variety of social and environmental standards (five were Fairtrade certified), as well as some certified to none. The farms in the sample directly accounted for around 20 per cent of national output, and they were fully representative of more than 50 per cent of this output. The research used three main techniques. The first was semi-structured interviews with farm CEOs or managing directors, production managers, human resource managers (where these existed) and chairs or secretaries of Farm Workers' Committees or Joint Bodies and farm-level union branches (where these existed). The second was questionnaire-based surveys of general workers and supervisors. The size of the two samples was 113 and 39 respectively. Third, 17 focus group discussions were organized. For more details see Gibbon and Riisgaard (2014).
8. In Kenya the Max Havelaar Liaison Officer (at the time when Max Havelaar were in charge of the Fairtrade flower producer support) successfully used continuous pressure and dialogue to convince Fairtrade certified to recognize the rights of the workers to farm-level collective bargaining (via the farm union).
9. Representative of more than 50 per cent of export output.

REFERENCES

Boltanski, Luc and Laurent Thévenot ([1991] 2006), *On Justification: Economies of Worth*, translated by Catherine Porter, Princeton, NJ: Princeton University Press.

Cheyns, Emanuelle (2011), 'Multi-stakeholder initiatives for sustainable agriculture: Limits of the "inclusiveness" paradigm', in Stefano Ponte, Peter Gibbons and Jakob

Vestergaard (eds.), *Governing through Standards: Origins, Drivers and Limitations*, Basingstoke, UK and New York: Palgrave MacMillan, pp. 210–235.

Cheyns, Emanuelle and Lone Riisgaard (2014), 'The exercise of power through multi-stakeholder initiatives for sustainable agriculture and its inclusion and exclusion outcomes', *Agriculture and Human Values*, 31 (3), 409–423.

Daviron, Bennoit (2002), 'Small farm production and the standardization of tropical products', *Journal of Agrarian Change*, 2 (2), 162–184.

Dolan, Catherine S. (2008), 'Arbitrating risk through moral values: The case of Kenyan Fairtrade', in Geert De Neve, Peter Luetchford, Jeffrey Pratt and Donald C. Wood (eds.), *Hidden Hands in the Market: Ethnographies of Fair Trade, Ethical Consumption, and Corporate Social Responsibility*, Research in Economic Anthropology, Vol. 28, Bingley, UK: Emerald Group Publishing Limited, pp. 271–296.

Eymard-Duvernay, François (1989), 'Conventions de qualite et formes de coordination', *Revue Economique*, 40 (2), 329–359.

Eymard-Duvernay, François, Olivier Favereau, André Orlean, Robert Salais and Laurent Thévenot (2005), 'Pluralist integration in the economic and social sciences: The economy of conventions', *Post-Autistic Economics Review*, (34), 30 October, 22–40, available at http://paecan.net.PAReview/issue34/Thevenot34.htm (accessed 1 March 2012).

Fairtrade International (2012), 'A new workers rights strategy for Fairtrade', Bonn, Germany: Fairtrade International.

Gibbon, Peter and Lone Riisgaard (2014), 'A new system of labour management in African large-scale agriculture?', *Journal of Agrarian Change*, 14 (1), 94–128.

Korovkin, Tanya and Olga Sanmiguel-Valderrama (2007), 'Labour standards, global markets and non-state initiatives: Colombia's and Ecuador's flower industries in comparative perspective', *Third World Quarterly*, 28 (1), 117–135.

Le Velly, Ronan (2007), 'Is large-scale fair trade possible?', in Edwin Zaccai (ed.), *Sustainable Consumption, Ecology and Fair Trade*, London: Routledge, pp. 201–215.

Lyall, Angus (2011), interview with the Mayor of Cayambe, Ecador (9 April 2011).

Lyall, Angus (2011–2012), interviews with workers, Cayambe, Ecuador (2011–2012).

Mukherjee-Reed, Ananya and Darryl Reed (2010), 'Fair trade and development: What are the implications of mainstreaming?', Universitas Forum, 1 January 2010, available at http://www.universitasforum.org/index.php/ojs/article/view/40 (accessed 21 January 2014).

Mutersbaugh, Tad (2002), 'The number is the beast: A political economy of organic coffee certification and producer unionism', *Environment and Planning A*, 34 (7), 1165–1184.

Mutersbaugh, Tad (2005), 'Just-in-space: Certified rural products, labor of quality, and regulatory spaces', *Journal of Rural Studies*, 21 (4), 389–402.

Raynolds, Laura T. (2002), 'Consumer/producer links in fair trade coffee networks', *Sociologia Ruralis*, 42 (4), 404–424.

Raynolds, Laura T. (2007), 'Fair trade bananas: Broadening the movement and market in the United States', in Laura Raynolds, Douglas Murray and John Wilkinson (eds.), *Fair Trade: The Challenges of Transforming Globalization*, New York: Routledge, pp. 63–82.

Raynolds, Laura T. (2009), 'Mainstreaming fair trade coffee: From partnership to traceability', *World Development*, 37 (6), 1083–1093.

Raynolds, Laura T. (2014), 'Fairtrade, certification, and labor: Global and local tensions in improving conditions for agricultural workers', *Agriculture and Human Values*, 31 (3), 499–511.

Renard, Marie-Christine (2003), 'Fair trade: Quality, market and conventions', *Journal of Rural Studies*, 19 (1), 87–96.

Renard, Marie-Christine (2005), 'Quality certification, regulation and power in fair trade', *Journal of Rural Studies*, 21 (4), 419–431.

Riisgaard, Lone (2009), 'Global value chains, labor organization and private social standards: Lessons from East African cut flower industries', *World Development*, 37 (2), 326–340.

Riisgaard, Lone and Peter Gibbon (2014), 'Labor management on contemporary Kenyan flower farms: The foundations of an industrial–civic compromise', *Journal of Agrarian Change*, 14 (2), 260–285.

Riisgard, Lone, Angus Lyall and Obadia Okinda (2012), 'Assessing the impact of Fairtrade on flower plantations in East Africa and Latin America', Bonn, Germany: Fairtrade International.

Salais, Robert (2001), 'A presentation of the French "economie des conventions": Application to labor issues', *Le Cachan*, 24 (01), 17 March.

Salais, Robert, Laurent Thévenot and Robert Boyer (1986), *Le travail (marches, règles, conventions)*, Paris: Economica.

Storper, Michael and Robert Salais (1997), *Worlds of Production: The Action Frameworks of the Economy*, Cambridge, MA: Harvard University Press.

Thévenot, Laurent and Michèle Lamont (2000), 'Conclusion: Exploring the French and American polity', in Michèle Lamont and Laurent Thévenot (eds.), *Rethinking Comparative Cultural Sociology: Repertoires of Evaluation in France and the United States*, Cambridge: Cambridge University Press, pp. 307–327.

World Fair Trade Organization and Fairtrade International (2009), 'A charter of fair trade principles', Brussels: Fair Trade Advocacy Organization.

8. Connections in fair trade food networks

Michael K. Goodman and Agatha Herman

INTRODUCTION*

Close to two decades ago, Whatmore and Thorne (1997) used fair trade coffee to introduce actor-network theory to the political economy of food and what Evans (2000) called the rise of 'counter-hegemonic globalization'. As well as providing one of the earliest academic descriptions of a fair trade network, they elaborated a '*topological* spatial imagination concerned with tracing points of connection and lines of flow, as opposed to reiterating fixed surfaces and boundaries' (Whatmore and Thorne 1997, 289; original emphasis). Yet, *how* do these connections and flows work? And, importantly, how do they *do* this work as fair trade has moved into the 'everyday' supply chains of supermarkets, corner stores and institutions? In this chapter, we analyze the shifting temporal and spatial *practices* that have given shape to and animate these alternative connections and flows in fair trade's agro-food networks.

The connective practices of fair trade have substantively changed as traditional fair trade products have moved into the commercial mainstream, and new fair trade products, such as wine, have entered the market. Crucially, these connective practices are *tactical* in nature: they have shifted to grow fair trade markets and bring in new goods, but they also facilitate the practical connections across fair trade commodity chain nodes designed to facilitate the flow of these goods from marginalized producers to better-off consumers. But, given that *connections* simultaneously denote *disconnections*, or at least a *lack of* connection, to other networks, we are also concerned with the disconnections that are equally embedded in fair trade's tactical practices and how these too have shifted. The tactical practices of fair trade networks are fundamentally *political* in that they do and say some things over others, make some connections and disconnections over others and create some flows over others. In this chapter, we analyze how fair trade's socio-economic connections and disconnections are communicated to consumers, but also, equally crucially, communicated to the stakeholders who bring fair trade goods to market.

We analyze the tactical practices of fair trade connection through two different but related lenses. The first is that of the shifting marketing practices of fair trade, what Barnett et al. (2005) call the 'practical devices' that bring consumers into fair trade networks. We focus on three key historical 'moments' in the creation of the semiotics and discourses surrounding fair trade goods. These tactical and politicized shifts in the consumer-focused semiotic connections and disconnections of fair trade work up what we, as critique, call fair trade's 'Faustian bargain' (Goodman et al. 2012). In contemporary fair trade markets, the practice of choice is becoming de-politicized and disconnected from the progressive moral economy of the original consumer–producer connections of fair trade networks. There is a trade-off that has supported the growth of the fair trade market and, with this market growth, improved the livelihoods of more fair trade producers than would perhaps otherwise be the case. As mainstreaming in the United Kingdom has proceeded, the figure of the consumer-citizen – what Barnett et al. (2005) refer to as the 'subjects ... of ethical consumption' – actively choosing fair trade goods has been subsumed by the emerging 'corporate-citizen' now supplying fair trade goods as the *only* choice in various product lines.

The second lens highlights the more spatial dimensions of fair trade's tactical practices through a focus on wine networks that have recently flourished in the Western Cape Province of South Africa. Shifting to a more producer-oriented focus, we explore the 'complex lived worlds' (Herman 2010) of fair trade in the ways that Fairtrade regulations have been tactically adopted and adapted on the ground. South Africa is particularly useful in illuminating these temporal and spatial tactics given its dynamic and complex post-apartheid politics. Through the certified Fairtrade wineries of Fairhills and Tukulu, we explore the dynamic interactions between the ethics of Fairtrade and the South African national strategy of Broad-Based Black Economic Empowerment (B-BBEE) that allows a brand to become known in particular, politicized and varying ways throughout its commodity network. More broadly then we critically interrogate the tactical practices by which the deployments of knowledge – and their related impacts and ethics – in fair trade networks have been put in place but have also shifted over time and space in the making of contemporary mainstreamed fair trade markets.

THE SHIFTING CULTURAL POLITICS OF FAIR TRADE: THE CONSEQUENTIAL MOMENTS OF KNOWING AND NOT KNOWING

With respect to food and drink, the visual and textual marketing imaginaries of fair trade have undergone substantial shifts over its history. These shifts have accelerated in the last decade as Fairtrade has rocketed into the mainstream with a market value of over £1.57 billion in the United Kingdom (FTF 2014). These moves have produced equally fluctuating semiotic practices of connection and disconnection that represent the shifting cultural politics of fair trade designed to switch on a consumerist politics of choice *for politics* in the coffee we drink and the chocolate we eat and the bananas we provide to our families. There are a number of critical moments in fair trade's shifting cultural politics which each have a set of tactical practices embedded in their rationales as well as implications for those providing and consuming fair trade goods.

The Originalist Moment of Transparency and Direct, Caring Connections

Early in the widespread commercialization of fair trade, there was a tactical need for it and its products to tell stories about themselves for consumers to come to know the differences and relations of care differentially embedded in fair trade goods. Festooned on product labels such as coffee bags and chocolate bars, in-store/charity-shop marketing materials and advertisements were visual and textual 'thick descriptions' of the producers' lives and livelihoods as written in the smiling faces, laboring bodies, positive words and small, sustainable farms of fair trade farmers. Thus a farmer with the famous Kuapa Kokoo cooperative in Ghana explains that:

> We rely on the money we get from cocoa for everything: for food, clothes, medicines, and school fees. … Kuapa Kokoo pays all its farmers a fair price for their crop, in cash, and on time. I am very happy: since I joined Fair Trade I can afford to send my children to school. (Goodman 2004, 900)

Consumer stories were also common. As the United Kingdom's Fairtrade Foundation related:

> Emily Eavis drinks a lot of coffee. But coffee didn't arouse her passion till she met Fairtrade-registered coffee farmers in the Dominican Republic. 'It was incredibly eye-opening. You arrive here, and you realise that the whole system is completely imbalanced.' … Emily was most struck by 'how simple it could be for consumers in the UK to change things. All we need to do is to be aware of the problem.' (Goodman 2004, 900)

While there is considerable debate about this particular moment in the history of fair trade and its implications (e.g., Le Mare 2007; Marston

2013; Varul 2008; Wright 2004), these testimonials do several crucial things in creating connections in fair trade networks.

First and foremost, this provisioning of knowledge works to encourage and facilitate connectivity between fair trade consumers and producers. Seeing fair trade farmers and hearing their testimonials is a powerful device designed to articulate production-consumption engagements. These connections of care create a 'solidarity in difference': while embedded in the situated cultural, economic, political and power differentials of producers and consumers, fair trade looks to transcend these differences with a move toward a more social justice-like vision of equality in 'the good life' (Smith 1997) for all those involved. Fair trade sought to expand the everyday experiences of care and responsibility to include the 'needs of distant strangers' (Corbridge 1998) through the everyday-ness of eating, drinking and situated commodity production. This spatial dynamics of concern in fair trade networks that works to connect the distant places and spaces of production and consumption offers up a moral economy that is as much discursive, visual and indeed, affective and cognitive, as it is material in the provisioning of the fair trade premium, its minimum prices and more direct trade relations.

Second, this initial marketing moment had a pedagogical function in teaching consumers the difference that the fair trade difference makes. The knowledge regime – or better yet, pedagogical regime – of fair trade networks is the key to educating consumers in the 'what', 'where', 'who', 'why' and 'how' of the practices of fair trade.

Third, fair trade's connections of care and pedagogical regime sought to make its networks semiotically transparent. This works in conjunction with the original material transparency of fair trade networks that made the terms of trade in fair trade supply chains knowable to the public: who is buying from whom, at what price and under what conditions. In this, producers as well as consumers are made to '(re)appear' in the light of marketing materials. Simultaneously, however, a more worrying process was set in motion, namely a pernicious commoditization of people and place. Through these connective stories of fair-trade-led development, a kind of competitive market is created in the need to *have* a marketable livelihood 'story' to sell. The commodification of difference – and indeed care and responsibility for marginalized and poor producers – can make a difference but one that is characterized and confined by the dictates of the market relations – and cultural politics of connection – in which fair trade networks are entangled.

Finally, all of these above processes combine into fair trade's earliest, wide-scale attempts to create new 'subjects of ethical consumption' through the development of the figure of the fair trade consumer-citizen

(Wheeler 2012). This is the self-reflexive figure working to choose fair trade goods over others because of the responsibilized and affective connections they feel to producers put in place by the 'pedagogical transparency' of fair trade labels and its marketing. In this, consumer choice is politicized and embedded with the processes and practices of care and responsibility articulated in fair trade's meaningful semiotic moral economy. In this way, through fair trade, particular forms of global development and – on the part of the consumer – global citizenship are able to be clearly purchased off the supermarket shelf for those fair trade consumer-citizens willing and able to choose fair trade commodities.

The Quality Moment: Branding Care, Virtual Fair Trade Farmers and Institutional Supply Chains

The next tactical phase in the commercialization of fair trade goods was the 'quality' moment whereby there was a move by fair trade businesses and movement NGOs into mainstream supply chains. At the time (circa 2000 to 2006), for some fair trade companies, marketing fair trade goods as quality items began to overtake the previously semiotically front-loaded moral economy embedded in its networks. As a Marketing Manager in the UK fair trade coffee industry put it (Goodman et al. 2012, 214),

> We're not the ethical brand they have on their shelves, we are another brand and sure we're ethical … but we are a brand just like Kellogg's. … So there is definitely the changing focus to premium foods and fair trade second because that is how we see ourselves being, competing under mainstream against the big players, we differentiate on quality and price.

While insisting that 'we are fair trade at our core', he presented one of their newest fair trade lines by arguing that 'it's a great tasting product, and, you know, that's what we are selling it on. It's on quality; it's not on fair trade.' Another interviewee from an organic, fair trade chocolate company put it succinctly: 'I think with [our company], taste is the first thing, and then the fact that it's organic and then the fact its ethical.'

This desire to make fair trade a quality product, much of it led by coffee and chocolate, has had a number of significant and far-reaching effects on the tactical practices by which fair trade is made knowable to consumers. First, across much of the sector, the images and descriptions of farmers and their livelihoods became 'too' ethical and 'fair trade' and thus too closely associated with earlier perceptions of the often poor quality of these goods. When asked about this shift in imagery directly, the same fair trade coffee Marketing Manager put it in no uncertain terms: 'There's not a picture of a smiling farmer on the front and there is a reason for that because that would be very fair trade and very ethical, and you go, "oh look, you know, farming" … but that scares consumers.' The connective and pedagogical transparency of fair trade networks had become a liability in the rapidly mainstreaming spaces of fair trade quality.[1]

Instead, other images of quality – from touristic landscapes, supermarket own-label branding, to images of harvested foods and the tools used in preparing and harvesting them, to stylized fair trade company logos – took over from the previous imaginaries of fair trade goods. Instead, farmers and their livelihoods have gone 'virtual', now being staged on company and fair trade movement websites. Fair trade, in a sense, is being semiotically 're-placed' back into the bodies and places of producing communities as performed through the online forum of the webpages of the likes of the United Kingdom's Cafédirect and Fairtrade Foundation. The 'un-quality' of farmers and their livelihoods has gone virtual, yet in such a way that it does not take away from the sense of product quality that fair trade goods have built up over the last few years. Virtual farmers and their more virtualized livelihoods are 'safe', while more 'real' farmers – at least on the packages of the largest fair trade companies – are not.

Second, as direct connections to farmers and their livelihoods began to disconnect and disappear from marketing materials, the certified Fairtrade logo has become a visual proxy for the relations developed in previous fair trade narratives; this logo has now taken on particularly important meanings in these shifting cultural politics. In the absence of the previous images and voices of farmers, it has now become a branded emblem of trust embodying a pedagogical function – one sees the logo and knows it is about care and development – and taken on fair trade's semiotic connective role – the logo is what connects consumers to poor farmers.

Third, as the growing quality of fair trade networks gained notoriety and visibility, the supply of fair trade goods to and through larger, institutional and corporate supply chains began to accelerate. This was often brokered by fair trade movement activists to have, for example, caterers at university campuses *only* sell Fairtrade coffee (e.g., Wilson and Curnow 2013) and snacks; similar moves, through combined activist work and that of internal buyer decisions, were made by supermarkets (e.g., Sainsbury's) to *only* sell Fairtrade bananas in their stores. In this, the semiotics of connection earlier embedded in fair trade recedes even further into the background as often there is either no or very little indication that what one is buying, drinking and/or eating is fair trade.

To summarize, this quality moment in fair trade networks served to problematically 'muddle up' the semiotic transparency, pedagogical possibilities and knowledge provisioning that was so much a part of its early incarnations. Instead, the Fairtrade logo has taken on the even *more* meaningful mantle of transparency, pedagogy and knowledge and worked to entrench the kind of 'brandification' of care and responsibility in fair trade networks discussed by Lekakis (2012). The pedagogical and connective possibilities of fair trade have now gone virtual, which, by default, requires a different level of intention and a more difficult pathway to the development of the fair trade citizen-consumer who might know about and care directly for the producers of their coffee, chocolate or tea. Even more than this, through the growth of institutional supplies where the semiotics of fair trade are almost completely hidden or simply hang on the Fairtrade logo – creating what Wheeler (2012) calls the 'accidental' fair trade consumer who has no choice *but* to buy fair trade goods – the activist-oriented fair trade consumer-citizen has been replaced quite rapidly with the fair trade 'corporate-citizen' who actively chooses to only supply various fair trade goods. In effect, this removes fair trade's previous politics of choice. As the discussion of the next moment in fair trade's semiotic history highlights, it is through even closer ties to corporate-citizens that fair trade has worked to effectively co-brand itself with some of the most visible and global multinational brands around.

The Co-Branded, Multinational Moment

The most recent shift in fair trade's tactical marketing practices can be encapsulated in its 'multinational' moment as large, previously dismissive corporations have taken up fair trade supplies into existing lines or developed new fair trade lines of goods. Coffee and chocolate have led the way in the United Kingdom, Starbucks and Percol have Fairtrade lines of coffee, while Mars, Cadbury's/Kraft and Nestlé have moved some of their major branded lines to Fairtrade (including Maltesers [Mars], brand-defining Dairy Milk chocolate bar [Cadbury's/Kraft] and globally recognized Kit Kat [Nestlé]).[2] What this means is that, while this has worked to massively expand the fair trade market and its demand, especially in chocolate (Wallop 2009; Wood 2009), fair trade is now in a rather complicated 'co-branding' relationship with the Fairtrade logo sitting side-by-side with the labels of some of the corporations that it originally worked to critique. This is certainly true with Fairtrade's co-branding relationship with Nestlé, one of the most boycotted corporations on the planet, which has some activists crying out for a boycott of fair trade itself or that consumers only buy from '100 per cent' fair trade companies (Baby Milk Action 2011).

The development and entrenchment of this moment not only seems to further muddle fair trade's historical semiotic transparency and connections, it directly and problematically connects fair trade with brands and companies it originally articulated in its oppositional *raison d'être* of support for small, marginalized producers so many years ago. What this has opened up is direct competition by these multinationals for a market that was pioneered by a number of committed, activist brands who now, seemingly, find themselves increasingly contending with the marketing power and wherewithal of newly crowned fair trade multinationals (e.g., Davies et al. 2010, 140; Doherty et al. 2013). This signals to us yet another nail in the coffin of the actively choosing and knowing citizen-consumer given that, for those buying into these particular lines of chocolate, there is no choice but to buy the fair trade version. The fair trade corporate-citizen, in the context of the multinational purveyors of two of their most popular branded lines, is now the key caring and responsible figure constructing fair trade's moral economy.

A Tactical Faustian Bargain: The End of the Fair Trade Consumer-Citizen and Rise of the Fair Trade Corporate-Citizen?

We have traced above in the analysis of fair trade's shifting semiotic marketing moments of tactical connection and disconnection what might be called fair trade's Faustian bargain. The mainstreaming of fair trade through its shift to a quality product and corporate co-branding strategies has come at the 'cost' of substantially reduced connectivity between consumers and producers. The tactical semiotic practices of the deployment of knowledges, connectivities and transparencies that were at the base of fair trade's historical difference – but also, fundamentally, its movement-based, political project – have given way to the equally tactical muddles of the quality-articulating, brandification of fair trade in its logo and the corporate co-branding that make up growing portions of its new networks.

With the rise of Fairtrade-only institutional and corporate supply chains has come the emergence of the fair trade corporate-citizen. The actively choosing consumer-citizen has begun to recede into the background given that the choice for fair trade has been made before consumer choice comes into play. Through the quality and multinational moments in fair trade networks, choice has been actively de-politicized, while farmers' livelihoods have been decommodified and disconnected from the purview of the consumer. The semiotic connections of fair trade have moved into virtual spaces, into the form of the Fairtrade logo/brand and onto the co-branded lines of multinationals, the latter of whom can wield the fair trade brand with relative impunity as they take up the mantle of care and responsibility for some of the world's most vulnerable farmers.

THE COMPLEX LIVED WORLDS OF FAIR TRADE KNOWLEDGES, ETHICS AND CONNECTIONS

So far we have focused on the consumer experience of the connections which fair trade has actively worked to enact (FTF 2005); however, it is clear that how the information, knowledge and network resources are deployed to 'articulate consumption and the consumer through a register of ethics and responsibility' (Clarke et al. 2007, 246) is a complex and dynamic practice. What counts as 'ethical' is neither simple nor uncontested. To complicate matters further, the other stakeholders in these global commodity networks – producers, processors, distributors, importers, exporters and retailers – are also fluid actors, with different and shifting priorities. Therefore, a fair trade commodity needs to adapt how it portrays itself spatially and temporally in order to ensure the enrollment of its stakeholders. Here we focus our attention on the producer end of the network, by exploring Fairtrade wine in the Western Cape Province of South Africa. In this space, Fairtrade interacts with a range of ethical discourses, which allows us to analyze how Fairtrade is practiced and made knowable to producers but also how certain connections and disconnections are directed up the value chain towards the consumer. First, however, we provide a brief background to the South African wine industry.

Fairtrade Wine in South Africa[3]

In the early 2000s, a group of South African wine producers approached Fairtrade International looking to acquire certification for their wines. Fairtrade's external auditing made it attractive because it both enhanced the political credibility and market position of producers (Moseley 2008) and facilitated international market access (Barrientos and Dolan 2006). Fairtrade International was keen to support post-apartheid changes, so certification standards for South African wine grapes were introduced in 2003 (FLO 2006). Since then certification standards have been introduced for Chilean and Argentinean wine grapes but 'the South African wine industry has played a pioneering role in fair-trade wines' (McEwan and Bek 2009b, 260) and wine has become one of South Africa's most important Fairtrade products (FLSA 2012).

Despite the end of apartheid in 1994, the marginalization of the excluded black majority remains (Gray 2006) and the wine industry is no exception. South African agriculture has been grounded in deeply racialized, ingrained and power-laden structures (du Toit 2002) and, despite post-apartheid legislative, social, technological and market changes (du Toit et al. 2008), farmworkers continue to be one of the most socially excluded groups in the country (Brown et al. 2003). The wine industry reflects these trends and remains almost exclusively under white control. This white elite is 'renowned for circumnavigating legislative and voluntary initiatives in order to maintain the status quo' (McEwan and Bek 2009a, 735). Increased international competition and domestic legislation have contributed to the wine industry's restructuring (Ewert and du Toit 2005) and, combined with the increasing downward pressure on prices by retailers (Bek et al. 2007), has meant that investment has been limited. This then is the complex and highly politicized context for Fairtrade in South Africa.

Fairtrade's engagement in South Africa is unique. Given the continuing domination of agriculture by white owner-farmers and plantation-style farms, Fairtrade was, via certification, in danger of 'legitimizing the racial and material legacy of slavery, colonialism and apartheid' (Kruger and du Toit 2006, 203). Fairtrade has therefore adapted to South African specificities through an unprecedented national-level discussion as to what 'fairness' means within this space.[4] B-BBEE is the current national strategy deployed to address South Africa's continuing, racially grounded socio-economic marginalization. Although subject to critiques (see McEwan and Bek 2009a), B-BBEE policies have been incorporated into Fairtrade, making Fairtrade more 'knowable' to local producers by enhancing its relevance and sensitivity and B-BBEE more accountable by tying it into internationally recognized auditing systems.

With a global market worth close to €5 billion (Fairtrade International 2013), it is clear that being certified Fairtrade connects a producer to an established and growing niche market. Combined with the guaranteed price floor and social premium, Fairtrade offers clear market-based, as well as ideological, incentives for producer involvement and through these mechanisms can financially support the implementation of empowerment projects. Despite this, Fairtrade has only limited purchase within South Africa and, with only 16 certified wine grape producers (FLSA 2012), its capacity to enact broad-based socio-economic change is reduced. Indeed, our research suggests that South African wine industry stakeholders tended to position Fairtrade and B-BBEE as separate entities, a move grounded in their recognized area of utility: B-BBEE's national capacity to enact transformation and Fairtrade's international strategic value.[5] B-BBEE's greater domestic relevance and, although it was accepted that there was a place for Fairtrade, the small scale of the latter's operations arguably masks the entangled nature of B-BBEE and Fairtrade to the wider industry. Although Fairtrade may be more widely understood as a commercial strategy within South Africa, we can see variations in how it is practiced through the marketing strategies of two different wine brands.

Adapting to always appeal: ensuring brand survival through tactical (dis)connections in Fairhills

Fairhills emerged out of the long-term supply relationship between Origin Wines (a South African wine sourcing company) and the UK Co-operative Group. The latter wanted to initiate a significant Fairtrade venture that would benefit a whole community as well as acquire a reliable and quality supplier for their own-brand fair trade wine. Origin Wines selected one of its suppliers, the du Toitskloof cooperative cellar in Rawsonville, Western Cape, and Fairtrade accreditation was achieved in 2005. This relationship with an international retailing partner has proved significant for Fairhills, with the Project Manager commenting that 'if it wasn't for them [The Co-op] buying into this project we wouldn't have been in such a developed stage … we've reached in three years' time … what another project would have done probably in ten years.' This progress, combined with the levels of paperwork, capital and effort required to practice Fairtrade, contributed to the Project Manager considering that Fairtrade was more significant to Fairhills than B-BBEE. However, the co-constitutive relationship between Fairtrade and B-BBEE practices was recognized and Fairtrade was felt to have made B-BBEE more credible and operational:

> black empowerment as expressed by Fairtrade and by South African national legislation is two totally different concepts. In South Africa, black empowerment is by ensuring that your business is co-owned by black people or black citizens and basically it's so easy to comply with national legislation … with regards to Fairtrade … is more for us based on empowerment, empowering the lesser fortunate, being the employees on the farms. (Fairhills Project Manager 2008)

This highlights how Fairhills has endeavored to use Fairtrade requirements to enact a broader, more socially responsive form of empowerment than the economic focus of B-BBEE. The Fairhills Association, which consists of the black and colored farmworkers, owns 25 per cent of the

Fairhills brand name. The democratically elected Joint Body chooses how to spend the fair trade social premium, and key project workers, such as the Fairhills Administrator and Crèche Coordinator, are former farmworkers. A craft cooperative and coffee shop have been established to provide alternative employment while day-care centers, school buses, youth, sports and women's clubs and adult education programs have all been initiated to bolster gender equality and education. The Fairhills Association also addresses the social exclusion that resulted from apartheid's restrictions on interaction and movement, and it has used the Fairtrade social premium to build a community center to foster a sense of inclusion and employs a psychologist to build self-esteem, address substance abuse issues and enhance coping strategies among farmworkers. The future goals of the Fairhills project reflect this broader sense of empowerment. They aim to own three production facilities and construct retirement housing and a health center. Although operating within the national B-BBEE agenda of enhancing skills development, ownership and management, these strategies all work towards a more sustainable transfer of power through the social efforts to enhance the farmworkers' capabilities and community capacity.

In Fairhills, Fairtrade enables this broader conceptualization of empowerment to be practiced as it connects to a global market with financial premiums and external auditing, as well as to a more extensive ethical ideology than that which structures B-BBEE. Despite this, B-BBEE remains central as it offers a route for Fairtrade to adopt contextually relevant practices and address the historical and contemporary sensitivities of South Africa. The combination of these imperatives highlights the way in which B-BBEE and Fairtrade have become indispensable within Fairhills. However, the spatial relationality that exists between the different nodes of the Fairhills commodity network means that context is critical in determining how Fairtrade is practiced throughout the network. Despite the essential connections between the two discourses within production spaces, Fairhills is marketed to UK consumers purely on its Fairtrade credentials, which focus on generic statements and, arguably, do not highlight the contextuality of Fairtrade practices:

> Fairhills is one of the largest Fairtrade projects worldwide spanning three countries: South Africa, Argentina and Chile. The Fairhills projects bring life-changing development to the communities by improving working and living conditions, education and health care. Making a better life for all. www.fairhills.co.za. (Fairhills Shiraz Merlot packaging 2011)

The connections of care offered by this label have been distilled into three short sentences, a web address and the Fairtrade label; all the rich, discursive detail to connect the consumer to the impact their purchase has on the producer has gone virtual. Where Fairtrade has been distilled, B-BBEE has disappeared. This disconnect highlights the strategic nature of ethical discourses as the overall durability of Fairhills depends on the micro-level adaptations of its discursive operations. While Fairtrade appeals more to consumers and so has to be foregrounded, Fairhills also depends on maintaining its producer-level credibility and relevance by responding to the national demand for B-BBEE. This tactical adaptability to change throughout the network, in terms of which connections are made visible at different nodes, is essential for Fairhills to appeal to the differing motivations of producers and consumers to engage with Fairtrade specifically in South Africa.

Knowing practices: recognizing the multiple motivations for ethical praxis in Tukulu

Tukulu is a partnership between Distell (a multinational South African producer, marketer and distributor of alcoholic beverages), a community trust and a group of black businessmen. Tukulu combines multiple ethical discourses. It is certified organic, a Biodiversity in Wine Initiative member, accredited by WIETA (the agricultural ethical trade initiative), a 2006 winner of a Farm Health Award and was certified Fairtrade in 2009. The Tukulu case highlights the proliferation of ethical discourses and increasing producer confusion over which to adopt. Although this overlap has increased the economic and time burden on the average producer, Tukulu's connections to the multinational Distell has allowed it to take full advantage of the market opportunities these different ethical frameworks enable.

Adherence to these multiple ethics appeared to be guided more by an economic or political rationale rather than an ethical ideology, with both Fairtrade and organic positioned as critical to establishing international market share. However, they were explicitly understood as separate since the Marketing CEO recognized that 'they mean different things to different people' and it was considered unnecessary to have a wine certified under both codes (Tukulu Marketing CEO 2008). The separation between 'organic' and 'Fairtrade' within Tukulu enables the brand to have broad market appeal without the expense of complying with multiple ethical codes for each wine. Initially, Tukulu placed more emphasis on organic branding but, following Fairtrade certification, the focus shifted as the latter was considered to be useful in accessing the competitive UK market. As the Marketing CEO commented, 'Fairtrade gives you an opportunity in the market, call it sub-category almost', which is essential within the multiple brands, varietals and price points of the UK wine market. Although Distell's BEE Group Manager commented that 'the retailers in the UK are, that's the first question they ask, so it makes business sense … to get a Fairtrade accreditation because it's a license to trade' (Tukulu BEE Group Manager 2008), the Marketing Manager demonstrated a reluctance to market Fairtrade because 'it's quite an ugly label' (Tukulu Marketing Manager 2008), which might detract from the premium positioning of the wine. Fairtrade wine continues to be faced with quality concerns and this hesitation over packaging highlights the potential limitations to being 'too ethical' in the marketplace. In 2008 Fairtrade was considered to have little relevance to the domestic South African market, although this is now changing, and so was seen purely as an international imperative.

The limited practice of ethical consumption within South Africa combined with negative publicity around 'blackwashing' within B-BBEE projects (Iheduru 2004) restricted the market value of Tukulu's B-BBEE credentials. As the Marketing Manager commented, 'we mention it in our brochure but … the perception is that B-BBEE is … just about giving it to people and being a front so we don't push it in the local market'. However, Distell's Head of Farming Operations recognized the potential this could offer in a growing black consumer market: 'There will be a group of people … in South Africa also more sympathetic if you help disadvantaged people especially if you go into the black market and they know that you are doing something behind the scenes to uplift their people.' Despite this recognition of a potential market for B-BBEE within South Africa, the Marketing CEO commented that 'we never really overemphasize or push the empowerment thing as why you must buy the wine' preferring to rely on quality as a more tactical consumer motivator, while trying to avoid the potentially negative quality connotations of being known as an ethical brand.

The market-driven approach to ethical certification adopted by Tukulu highlights the awareness among stakeholders of the potential for different articulations of a discourse. Within Tukulu, these 'scales of knowing' can be seen through the international positioning of Fairtrade and, albeit to an increasingly small extent, organics, while B-BBEE was a route to national credibility but of limited market value. Unlike in Fairhills, Tukulu deployed its multiple ethical discourses relatively independently with limited interaction between them within the production space, which is arguably due to the more corporate motivations underlying their practice. However, the market opportunities they offer are largely based on their ethical nature, which indicates an always present recognition of the other articulations that, for example, Fairtrade may have. How Fairtrade is 'known' at any particular point results from the ways that the motivations to participate are different among various network stakeholders. In fact the micro-scale producer understandings of both Fairtrade and B-BBEE looked to connect to or disconnect from each other as appropriate to ensure continued network and market relevance.

Fairtrade's power to connect its multiple stakeholders is grounded in its capacity to simultaneously balance stability and adaptability: stability to allow for a coherent, tactical message to be disseminated to consumers and a tactical adaptability to appeal to the different motivations of its participants. However, while both Tukulu and Fairhills demonstrated a certain 'knowing' recognition of what appealed at the other scales of their network, even when Fairtrade was 'plugged in' to connect to consumers, it was not monolithic. This 'lead' discourse contained space for local, producer-level understandings grounded in B-BBEE but was ultimately promoted because of its market appeal. Context is clearly critical in governing the practices that shape Fairtrade connections: to consumers it may be a way to support producers in developing spaces, to workers it may represent improvements in living standards and a changed relationship with management while to marketing Fairtrade may be simply an international sales opportunity. It is this capacity to adapt that enables Fairtrade to be made known – and made knowable – to the various stakeholders throughout its networks.

CONCLUSION

In this chapter we have illustrated critical spatial and temporal moments in the shifting cultural politics of fair trade. By tracing its changing marketing strategies as well as how Fairtrade is practiced and used differently among contemporary wine commodity networks, we have shown how Fairtrade is *made known* and *made knowable* to key stakeholders in its networks. These knowledge practices have proved to be both tactical and political – and variable across time and space – with the aim to always appeal to the different and changing motivations of the various stakeholders throughout the networks and so enhance fair trade's mainstream presence.

From both the consumer and the producer sides, the marketing of these originally transparent and direct connections has become muted. The quest for quality and market opportunities is arguably held back by the former connotations of being 'ethical' in terms of product quality and professionalism. Particularly now, fair trade has to negotiate a difficult balance between being *ethical enough* to appeal to, and benefit, producers without being *too ethical* to attract consumers. As the desire to more fully 'normalize' and 'conventionalize' the more established fair trade goods such as coffee and chocolate grows and, if the quality issues surrounding Fairtrade wine persist, we suggest that the Fairtrade logo itself will fade into the marketing background and further accelerate the rise of the 'corporate-citizen' at the expense of the 'citizen-consumer'.

Nevertheless, the adaptability of the fair trade discourse is essential and tactical knowledge connections and disconnections remain central to its successful operation and market success. If fair trade is set to become more virtual and/or 'faded' in its pedagogical transparency, while still enacting its benefits for producers, this strategic capacity and the multiple, complex and differing ways that fair trade can be known, and practice this knowing, is essential to its sustainability – both as a consumer market opportunity and a producer development strategy.

NOTES

* Many thanks to Laura Raynolds and Elizabeth Bennett for help in improving this chapter. Thanks also to Colin Sage and Alexandra Sexton who read earlier versions of this draft and provided insightful comments.

1. See also Sarah Lyon's chapter in this volume.
2. See also Alex Hughes's chapter in this volume.
3. In the following sections we draw on Herman (2010; 2012).
4. See also Jennifer Keahey's chapter in this volume on fair trade and race in South Africa.
5. This discussion is based on three months of fieldwork in the Western Cape, South Africa, in 2008, including 54 interviews with farmworkers, wine industry NGOs, farm owners and other wine stakeholders.

REFERENCES

Baby Milk Action (2011), 'Boycott Fairtrade KitKat – and spread the word about Nestlé's unethical behaviour', available from http://info.babymilkaction.org/nestlefairtrade (accessed 24 June 2014).

Barnett, Clive, Paul Cloke, Nick Clarke and Alice Malpass (2005), 'Consuming ethics: Articulating the subjects and spaces of ethical consumption', *Antipode*, 37 (1), 23–45.

Barrientos, Stephanie and Catherine Dolan (2006), 'Transformation of global food: Opportunities and challenges for fair and ethical trade', in Stephanie Barrientos and Catherine Dolan (eds.), *Ethical Sourcing in the Global Food System*, London: Earthscan, pp. 1–35.

Bek, David, Cheryl McEwan and Karen Bek (2007), 'Ethical trading and socioeconomic transformation: Critical reflections on the South African wine industry', *Environment and Planning A*, 39 (2), 301–319.

Brown, Mercy, Andries du Toit and Levurn Jacobs (2003), 'Behind the label: A workers' audit of the working and living conditions on selected wine farms in the Western Cape', Labour Research Service, Women on Farms Project and the Programme for Land and Agrarian Studies, UWC.

Clarke, Nick, Clive Barnett, Paul Cloke and Alice Malpass (2007), 'Globalising the consumer: Doing politics in an ethical register', *Political Geography*, 26 (3), 231–249.

Corbridge, Stuart (1998), 'Development ethics: Distance, difference, plausibility', *Ethics, Environment, and Place*, 1 (1), 35–54.

Davies, Iain, Bob Doherty and Simon Knox (2010), 'The rise and stall of a fair trade pioneer: The Cafédirect story', *Journal of Business Ethics*, 92 (1), 127–147.

Doherty, Bob, Iain Davies and Sophi Tranchell (2013), 'Where now for fair trade?', *Business History*, 55 (2), 161–189.

du Toit, Andries (2002), 'Globalizing ethics: Social technologies of private regulation and the South African wine industry', *Journal of Agrarian Change*, 2 (3), 356–380.

du Toit, Andries, Sandra Kruger and Stefano Ponte (2008), 'Deracializing exploitation? "Black Economic Empowerment"' in the South African wine industry', *Journal of Agrarian Change*, 8 (1), 6–32.

Evans, Peter (2000), 'Fighting marginalization with transnational networks: Counter-hegemonic globalization', *Contemporary Sociology*, 29 (1), 230–241.

Ewert, Joachim and Andries du Toit (2005), 'A deepening divide in the countryside: Restructuring and rural livelihoods in the South African wine industry', *Journal of Southern African Studies*, 31 (2), 315–332.

Fairhills Project Manager (2008), interview with Agatha Herman, Rawsonville, South Africa (23 May 2008).

Fairtrade International (2013), 'Annual report: Unlocking the power', available at: http://www.fairtrade.net/fileadmin/user_upload/content/2009/resources/2012-13_AnnualReport_FairtradeIntl_web.pdf (accessed 17 March 2014).

FLO (Fairtrade Labelling Organizations International) (2006), 'Wine', available at http://www.fairtrade.net/wine.html (accessed 31 October 2006).

FLSA (Fairtrade Label South Africa) (2012), 'Products', available at http://www.fairtradelabel.org.za/product/wine.1.html (accessed 19 April 2012).

FTF (Fairtrade Foundation) (2005), 'The Fairtrade mark: Core standards and practice behind the five guarantees', available at http://www.fairtrade.org.uk/downloads/pdf/five_guarantees.pdf (accessed 17 August 2007).

FTF (Fairtrade Foundation) (2014), 'Appetite for Fairtrade continues to grow', available at http://www.fairtrade.org.uk/press_office/press_releases_and_statements/february_2014/apetite_for_fairtrade_grows.aspx (accessed 17 March 2014).

Goodman, Michael K. (2004), 'Reading fair trade: Political ecological imaginary and the moral economy of fair trade foods', *Political Geography*, 23 (7), 891–915.

Goodman, David E., Melanie Dupuis and Michael K. Goodman (2012), *Alternative Food Networks: Knowledge, Practice and Politics*, London: Routledge.

Gray, Mel (2006), 'The progress of social development in South Africa', *International Journal of Social Welfare*, 15 (S1), pp.S53–S64.

Herman, Agatha (2010), 'Connecting the complex lived worlds of Fairtrade', *Journal of Environmental Policy and Planning*, 12 (4), 405–422.

Herman, Agatha (2012), 'Tactical ethics: How the discourses of Fairtrade and black economic empowerment change and interact in wine networks from South Africa to the UK', *Geoforum*, 43 (6), 1121–1130.

Iheduru, Okechukwu C. (2004), 'Black economic power and nation-building in post-apartheid South Africa', *Journal of Modern African Studies*, 42 (1), 1–30.

Kruger, Sandra and Andries du Toit (2006), 'Reconstructing fairness: Fair trade conventions and worker empowerment in South African horticulture', in Laura T. Raynolds,

Douglas L. Murray and John Wilkinson (eds.), *Fair Trade: The Challenges of Transforming Globalization*, London: Routledge, pp. 200–220.
Le Mare, Ann (2007), 'Fair trade as narrative: The stories within fair trade', *Narrative Inquiry*, 17 (1), 69–92.
Lekakis, Eleftheria J. (2012), 'Will the fair trade revolution be marketised? Commodification, decommodification and the political intensity of consumer politics', *Culture and Organization*, 18 (5), 345–358.
Marston, Andrea (2013), 'Justice for all? Material and semiotic impacts of fair trade craft certification', *Geoforum*, 44, 162–169.
McEwan, Cheryl and David Bek (2009a), 'Placing ethical trade in context: WIETA and the South African wine industry', *Third World Quarterly*, 30 (4), 723–742.
McEwan, Cheryl and David Bek (2009b), 'The political economy of alternative trade: Social and environmental certification in the South African wine industry', *Journal of Rural Studies*, 25 (3), 255–266.
Moseley, William G. (2008), 'Fair trade wine: South Africa's post-apartheid vineyards and the global economy', *Globalizations*, 5 (2), 291–304.
Smith, David M. (1997), 'Back to the good life: Towards an enlarged conception of social justice', *Environment and Planning D: Society and Space*, 15 (1), 19–35.
Tukulu BEE Group Manager (2008), interview with Agatha Herman, Stellenbosch, South Africa (7 April 2008).
Tukulu Marketing CEO (2008), interview with Agatha Herman, Stellenbosch, South Africa (3 April 2008).
Tukulu Marketing Manager (2008), interview with Agatha Herman, Stellenbosch, South Africa (3 April 2008).
Varul, Matthias Z. (2008), 'Consuming the campesino', *Cultural Studies*, 22 (5), 654–679.
Wallop, Harry (2009), 'Nestle's Kit Kat goes Fairtrade', *The Telegraph*, available at http://www.telegraph.co.uk/foodanddrink/foodanddrinknews/6730155/Nestles-Kit-Kat-goes-Fairtrade.html (accessed 17 March 2014).
Whatmore, Sarah and Lorraine Thorne (1997), 'Nourishing networks: Alternative geographies of food', in David Goodman and Michael Watts (eds.), *Globalising Food: Agrarian Questions and Global Restructuring*, London: Routledge, pp. 287–304.
Wheeler, Kathryn (2012), *Fair Trade and the Citizen-Consumer*, Basingstoke, UK: Palgrave Macmillan.
Wilson, Bradley R. and Joe Curnow (2013), 'Solidarity™: Student activism, affective labor, and the fair trade campaign in the United States', *Antipode*, 45 (3), 565–583.
Wood, Zoe (2009), 'Socially aware chocoholics rejoice as Cadbury's Dairy Milk goes Fairtrade', *The Guardian*, available at http://www.theguardian.com/business/2009/jul/22/cadburys-dairy-milk-fairtrade (accessed 17 March 2014).
Wright, Caroline (2004), 'Consuming lives, consuming landscapes: Interpreting advertisements for Cafédirect coffees', *Journal of International Development*, 16 (5), 665–680.

9. Consumer politics, political consumption and fair trade

Keith Brown

INTRODUCTION

It seems as if Americans are shopping for more causes today than at any point in the nation's history. They can buy cookies to support the Girl Scouts, lemonade and pink-ribbon-endorsed products to fund cancer research, cupcakes for neuroscience research, (RED) products to support AIDS relief and, of course, fair trade products to improve the living conditions of farmers and artisans living in developing countries. Americans are also participating in a wide range of boycotts of products, brands and even places. In recent years, prominent campaigns have been led in the United States against Fox News, Starbucks, Chick-fil-A, Israeli academic institutions, Walmart and Russian Vodkas. It is safe to say that the range of ongoing consumer boycotts in the United States is also at or near an all-time high. Both buycotting (shopping for a cause) and boycotting are examples of political or ethical consumption. This term does not mean that the product is necessarily produced in a socially responsible manner, or that the profits will be directed to a certain cause. It simply implies that the product possesses an attribute that some consumers will view as ethical (Glickman 2009).

In this chapter I will sketch the historical roots of political consumption in the United States and argue that fair trade has been aided by an 'ethical turn' in markets where social responsibility has become a desirable product attribute. I will also highlight the social, psychological and economic factors that are encouraging and limiting growth in markets promoting social responsibility. I conclude this chapter by arguing for more ethnographic research looking at how consumers construct meaning within fair trade markets.

HISTORICAL ROOTS OF FAIR TRADE AND POLITICAL CONSUMPTION

Pick up a wide range of books on fair trade and you will find a similarly wide range of explanations for how fair trade began. Most accounts do not contradict each other; they simply emphasize different causal forces for the growth of fair trade. Many attribute fair trade's origins to the alternative trade organizations arising in post-World War II Europe. Others point to the United States and Edna Ruth Byler's decision in 1946 to begin importing embroidery from impoverished women she met while traveling in Puerto Rico. Byler's mission-driven business continued to grow and is now called Ten Thousand Villages, one of the largest non-profit fair trade organizations in the world (DeCarlo 2007).

Still others argue that the contemporary fair trade movement only came to fruition after the importation of 'solidarity coffee' in the United States and parts of Europe. Ethical entrepreneurs sought to bypass the US embargo against Nicaraguan products and express solidarity with Sandinista coffee farmers (Equal Exchange 2011). This niche market, initially confined to health and cooperative grocery stores, moved into the mainstream during the late 1990s and early 2000s. The growth of fair trade coffee spurred the demand for labeling organizations like Max Havelaar (launched in 1988), Fair Trade USA (founded in 1998, originally called TransFair USA) and Fairtrade International (founded in 1997, originally called Fairtrade Labelling Organizations International) to certify that products are produced under agreed-upon, ethical standards. These certification organizations helped gain legitimacy and awareness for the term fair trade among importers and consumers around the world (Raynolds and Long 2007).

Given the diversity of products that are imported under the term fair trade, it is of little surprise that the official history of fair trade has not coalesced around one narrative. Rather than advocate for one crystalized history of fair trade, we should acknowledge the diverse origins of what we now call fair trade. Moreover, we can learn a lot by looking outside the movement to the historical roots of political consumption in the United States. Doing so reveals lessons lost by current and former political consumers and activists (Glickman 2004; 2009).

Many scholars of political consumption point to the powerful role that consumer boycotts have played throughout history (Cohen 2003). Many cite the boycott of British tea and fabrics prior to the American Revolution and then skip ahead to the lunch counter and bus boycotts during the Civil Rights movement in the United States. These scholars are correct in noting that the modern consumer-rights movement in the United States really began to gain momentum in the 20th century (Cohen 2003; McGovern 2006), but they neglect the first buycott movement that set the foundation for the modern form of political consumption: the free produce movement (Glickman 2004).

The free produce movement was spearheaded largely by Quakers and free black abolitionists. The term 'free' was used to show that products such as clothing, cotton, sugar, shoes and candy were produced without slave labor. The first free produce store was opened by Benjamin Lundy in Baltimore in 1826. One year later, the 'Free Produce Society' was founded in Philadelphia by a small group of radical Quakers (Glickman 2009). By offering alternatives produced with 'free labor', leaders of this movement created the first mainstream 'buycott' in the United States.

There are many similarities between the free produce and fair trade markets. First, retailers in both markets initially struggled to find and sell high-quality products. At first, this was not a major problem because the symbolic significance of their products outweighed product attributes in the minds of entrepreneurs. But over time, free produce retailers expressed concern stating that their sugar occasionally had a 'disagreeable taste and odor' and the rice was 'very poor, dark and dirty' (Glickman 2009). Throughout the 1980s and mid-1990s, fair trade coffee importers faced some struggles in finding high-quality coffee. They also had to deal with consumers' misperception that because the coffee was labeled as fair trade, it was not as good as competing brands. The legacy of this issue remains in fair trade coffee markets as many retailers will emphasize coffee quality over its sustainability attributes (Brown 2013). Another similarity in these movements involves internal friction among supporters. The free produce movement initially received widespread support among abolitionists, but by the late 1840s, many abolitionists distanced themselves from free produce saying that it reduced politics to a form of personal morality (Glickman 2009). In the United States, fair trade is also dealing with friction within the movement among labeling organizations over the best way to support artisans and farmers (Cole and Brown 2014). They also face the challenge of competing with direct traders who feel they do not require an outside organization to show they are trading 'fairly' (Weissman 2008). Both movements have also struggled to convince consumers that their economic support is really going to support their chosen cause. They have struggled to tell authentic and persuasive stories that convey to customers that this is an efficient way to combat slavery and poverty. Along these same lines, both movements had to convince customers that price should not be viewed as a barrier to a worthy cause.

But maybe most importantly, both the free produce and fair trade movements have sought to create solidarity between producers and consumers who likely will never meet each other. The free produce movement's major contribution to 'consumer-dependent' social movements (Goodman 2004), such as fair trade, organic or pink ribbon, is that it encouraged a deeper understanding among consumers about where the products they buy come from and how consumption impacts the living conditions of producers. Within fair trade, those at the center of the movement in the United States have often met producers while traveling to developing countries around the world. Many say these interactions lead to a wholehearted commitment to fair trade (Brown 2013). But many other conscientious consumers have never met face-to-face with fair trade producers and thus need to be convinced, through product narratives, that their money will support producers.

It is clear that many of the current tensions in fair trade and other socially responsible markets were also found in the free produce movement. Consumer activists in the 1820s through 1850s made sharp moral distinctions between supporters and non-supporters of free produce (Glickman 2004; 2009). Abolitionists were clear that non-supporters were, in effect, contributing to slavery. Whereas there is no compelling evidence that the free labor movement played a significant economic role in ending slavery (Glickman 2009), the movement's success rests in its emphasis on consumer citizenship and social responsibility. The free labor movement thus built the cultural foundation for future attempts to create change through shopping.

Americans' desire to seek change at the 'point of purchase' gained significant momentum in the 1930s. Cohen (2003, 31) argues that Americans started to become 'more self-conscious about their identities and interests as consumers'. At this time, a tension between people's roles as citizens and as consumers began to arise. The citizen consumer was responsible for 'safeguarding the general good of the nation, in particular for prodding government to protect the rights, safety, and fair treatment of individual consumers in the private marketplace', whereas the purchasing consumer contributed to society 'more by exercising purchasing power than through asserting themselves politically' (2003, 18–19). The tension between those who believe that all shopping serves as a means of economic development (consumer as purchaser) and those who believe that there is a morally correct way to shop (consumer as citizen) are evident in many markets promoting social responsibility. In many ways, today's consumer-dependent social movements are benefitting from past efforts to infuse social responsibility into everyday purchasing decisions.

ETHICAL TURN

The dramatic growth in sales of fair trade products is largely the result of a transnational effort of farmers, artisans, employees, ethical entrepreneurs and consumers (see Laura Raynolds and Nicholas Greenfield's chapter in this volume for further discussion). This push from *inside* the movement was aided by a number of social, cultural and political forces occurring *outside* the movement that helped grow the broader movement for ethical consumption. I refer to these changes as an 'ethical turn' in markets. In the United States this has roughly occurred since the beginning of the 21st century.

The ethical turn in American markets is characterized by the mainstreaming of socially responsible product attributes. It includes increased efforts to promote corporate social responsibility (King 2006) and attempts to make supply chains more eco-friendly (Dauvergne and Lister 2013). As noted previously, this does not necessarily mean that these products, brands or supply chains are actually ethical, but that they are advertised as such. For instance, we can now buy products that include a 'pink ribbon' that have known carcinogens in them (King 2006).

The debates over which products are truly socially responsible or whether shopping is even the proper means by which to seek social change are also characteristics of this ethical turn. The mainstreaming of social responsibility has led to critiques that some corporations are 'fair-', 'sweat-' or 'green-washing' these movements. Activists levy these charges against corporations that do not appear to be following through with their sustainable claims or that are making only superficial improvements to their products. Others counter that governments have been slow to enact change and that environmental and labor groups need to work with corporations to clean up supply chains (Dauvergne and Lister 2013). They note that claims about the treatment of workers and the environment are now standards by which corporations are competing with each other to appear ethical.

There are many reasons why the ethical turn arose in American markets. Increasing de-industrialization and the loss of smaller family-owned farms are one reason that Americans are becoming attracted to fair trade and other socially conscious products. In the early to mid-20th century, manufacturing provided many secure jobs to the working classes. Rural areas consisted of family-owned farms, and fewer of the factory-farms that now proliferate in the American Midwest (Carr and Kefalas 2009; Shell 2009). If Americans did not work on a farm or in a manufacturing job themselves, they knew many family members and friends who did. But the loss of manufacturing jobs, first to the southern parts of the United States and then to developing countries, has led many Americans to lose knowledge about where the stuff they buy comes from. Similarly, the rise of factory farming resulted in a decline in the number of farmers required to produce the same amount of food. As a result, consumers in the United States are increasingly unaware of who made the products they bought, how the producer benefits from the sale of the object and how the environment is impacted throughout the life course of the object (Kopytoff 1986; Matathia and Salzman 1999). Although this information was relatively easy to obtain when markets were more localized (Shell 2009), it has become a sought-after product attribute in a global economy (Zukin 2004). This has led to a search for 'authentic' stories about how objects are made. This search for authenticity is visible in such diverse markets as outsider art (Fine 2003), blues music (Grazian 2003), country music (Peterson 1997), Community Supported Agriculture (Thompson and Coskuner-Balli 2007), voluntary simplicity (Zavestoski 2002) and even fair trade (Brown 2013).

Increasing awareness about the sustainability of our consumption patterns is probably the most-often-cited explanation for the ethical turn. We can learn about global warming from Al Gore's Oscar-winning documentary *An Inconvenient Truth* (2006), calculate our carbon footprint on a number of different websites or find out about the ill effects of our consumption patterns by reading Annie Leonard's book *The Story of Stuff* (2010). (Her film with the same title has been viewed more than thirty million times online.) Many popular films such as *WALL-E*, *Over the Hedge*, *The Lorax*, *Blood Diamond* and *Avatar* frame overconsumption and sustainability as social problems worthy of our attention.

The increased awareness of sustainability as a social problem has led, somewhat paradoxically, consumers to turn to shopping as a solution. Sales of hybrid cars, halogen and LED lights, pink-ribbon-endorsed products, rain barrels and eco-friendly water bottles are all booming (King 2006; Schor 2010). Shoppers can now find eco-friendly alternatives to conventional automobile oil, home cleaning supplies, cosmetics, lawn-care products and even toothbrushes. Some companies are jumping on the green bandwagon by rebranding their conventional products as eco-friendly, and others have even created their own green standards and certified their own line of products to meet these standards (PR Newswire 2011; Simon 2009).

This growing concern for the environment, whether sincere or simply profit driven, has led to a somewhat unexpected phenomenon: going green has become trendy. Of course, buying products to obtain social status is not a new phenomenon (Veblen 1899). Writing at the end of the

19th century, Thorstein Veblen described how conspicuous consumption is a way the upper-class demonstrates its distinctive status to those below them on the class ladder. More contemporary research suggests that this top-down model of status is not as straightforward as it was in the past. 'Brand communities' now serve as a way of identifying our social and economic status to our peers (Muniz and O'Guinn 2001). We are now members of many brand communities that share common rituals and often share a similar set of cultural beliefs. The success of the Toyota Prius is a prime example of how status within brand communities motivates socially responsible consumption. The Prius outsold many of its comparable hybrid rivals, in part, because of its distinctive design. In focus groups, customers said they wanted an eco-friendly hybrid car, but they also wanted others to know they were driving a hybrid car. Driving a 'green' car, in many communities throughout the United States, became a trendy marker of social status (Griskevicius et al. 2010; Schneider 2004). The distinctive aesthetic design of the Prius confirmed the driver's membership in a seemingly eco-friendly, brand community.

Another stimulus for the ethical turn involves oil. Environmentalists have long cited Americans' dependence on oil as a cause of global warming and as a potential environmental hazard. The 2010 BP oil spill in the Gulf of Mexico reignited the fears of environmentalists, and at least some consumers, who, seeing the spectacle of oil-covered birds in the Gulf of Mexico, started to rethink their own spending habits. (Financial planners selling 'Socially Responsible Investments', who I interviewed, told me that some consumers divested from oil in their retirement portfolios after the Gulf oil spill.) Past research suggests that personal observations can lead to a change in individual attitudes towards issues like global warming (Rabe and Borick 2012). Moreover, the spikes in oil prices over the past ten years, largely due to instability in the Middle East, have increased the number of individuals advocating for cleaner energy. As a result, oil dependency is now viewed as a social problem by a wider segment of Americans than in the past. Those concerned about rising shipping costs or national security issues are aligning themselves with the concerns of environmentalists.

A final but extremely important reason for this ethical turn stems from Americans' loss of faith in the federal government. In the months following the attacks of September 11, 2001, more than 60 per cent of Americans said they 'just about always' or 'most of the time' had trust in the 'government in Washington'. But as the United States entered wars in Afghanistan and Iraq, trust in government began to plunge (PEW Research Center for the People and the Press 2010). By March 2010, following the Great Recession and the bank bailouts and in the midst of high unemployment, only 22 per cent of Americans said they always or mostly trusted the government in Washington, DC (PEW Research Center for the People and the Press 2010). As Americans became increasingly frustrated with their political system, whether because of the wars in Iraq or Afghanistan, the US Supreme Court decision that ended the 2000 election recounts or the constant attacks about governmental corruption from members of the Tea Party, they turned to create change through markets (Brown 2013). Frustrated by the lack of funding for cancer research, they buy a cup of Alex's lemonade; concerned with the deleterious effects of AIDS in Africa, they purchase a (RED) certified t-shirt; tired of seeing impoverished coffee farmers struggling with the aftereffects of the coffee crisis, they organize their morning ritual around a cup of Equal Exchange coffee. They might not be able to elect a politician who shares their same values, but they can feel that they are creating a more socially just world through shopping. (See Michael Goodman and Agatha Herman's chapter in this volume for a related analysis of UK ethical consumption and April Linton and Claudia Rosty's chapter for more on the US market for Fair Trade Certified products).

Whereas all these factors clearly led to the ethical turn in American markets, it is fair to question how these factors influenced both the fair trade market and the purchasing behavior (rather than just attitudes) of individual consumers. Based on my interviews of over a hundred fair trade consumers, activists and store owners along with two years' worth of participant observation within the fair trade movement, I am arguing that fair trade benefits greatly from the positive feelings about social change generated by these other markets. The faddish success of the Livestrong bracelets and the cult-like devotion of Prius owners are infectious. There seems to be a spillover effect from one market (or movement) to another. Seeing that others are shopping responsibly and learning about the funds being raised to support cancer research, AIDS treatments and fair trade farmers, consumers come to believe that shopping can make a difference in the world. This argument is consistent with Gould's theory (1993) that when individuals believe their resources (money, time, etc.) are efficiently going to support their social cause and that others are also supporting that cause, they are more likely to continue to participate in that social movement.

The second question about the link between fair trade attitudes and behavior is more difficult to address. The great majority of research on consumers uses surveys and quantitative methods to assess consumer attitudes. Some of the scholars in this area then infer behavior based on attitudes. Ethnographic research, by contrast, puts the focus on consumer behavior but is usually unable to make generalizations about wider populations. It takes a combination of these approaches, and a rigorous research design, to make the connection between attitudes and behavior. In the United States, two studies examining the connection between attitudes and behavior among ethical consumers are worthy of further discussion.

Kimeldorf et al. (2006) wanted to see if consumer behavior would align with survey research suggesting that a majority of American consumers would pay a higher price for products created in good working conditions. Over a period of months, they altered the price of 'Good Working Condition' sweatsocks and placed the socks next to other products that were not advertised as being produced in this manner. The experiment took place in a working class neighborhood in Michigan. The sample consisted of individuals who are more likely to be price-conscious. The research team then conducted 45 follow-up interviews with consumers who made these purchases to assess their attitudes towards socially responsible consumption. The researchers write:

> Focusing on a store that catered to people with modest means and education, and using a label with which the public was not familiar, our experiment offers a conservative estimate for the extent of conscientious consumption. Despite this conservative bias, we found that, on average, 30 per cent of our customers bought the more expensive [Good Working Conditions] socks. If the results of our in-store interviews are representative, the market for conscientious consumption may extend to a majority of American consumers (28).

Schoolman (2013) also takes an interesting approach to understanding the attitude–behavior gap. Rather than only focusing on individuals who identify as 'ethical consumers' he interviews a random sample of Americans to assess their feelings about shopping for a cause. He finds that when shopping is viewed as an unpleasant experience (crowds, routinized interactions, unsavory marketing techniques), consumers are less encouraged to devote time and energy towards learning about the socially responsible dimensions of products. In essence, the subjective experience of shopping influences whether or not individuals will become ethical consumers.

BARRIERS TO FURTHER GROWTH

Despite the rapid development of fair trade and other socially responsible markets, there are notable barriers to further growth. To start, the empowerment of consumers to enact change through shopping puts a heavy burden on them to possess knowledge about the cultural biographies of the products they buy (Kopytoff 1986). Many are misinformed about their ability to solve social problems such as global warming through shopping (Maniates 2001; Szasz 2007). Others report becoming skeptical and uncertain about the increasing number of shopping decisions they have to make that impact the environment (Connolly and Prothero 2008).

The increased stress about everyday shopping decisions is compounded by the 'certification revolution', where an increasing number of third-party organizations are certifying products and companies as socially responsible (Conroy 2007). The growth of these various types of certifications is often confusing and overwhelming to consumers who do not understand what all the logos mean (Brown 2013; Cole 2014). We often view the growth of certifications as liberating or as a way for us to express our true identities through shopping. But psychologist Barry Schwartz (2004) puts a damper on this optimistic view, arguing that endless choices can lead to anxiety, stress and even depression.

Another barrier to the growth of fair trade is that buying socially responsible products may grant consumers 'license' to shop for other products that are not as altruistic (Mazar and Zhong 2010). Sociologists often refer to this process as 'earmarking' (Zelizer 1997). This occurs when consumers designate some types of products as being appropriate for sustainable shopping (such as food) but not others (such as clothing). I saw evidence of this trend in my own research on fair trade. Melissa's story helps show how earmarking works. I met Melissa while she was shopping at a Ten Thousand Villages retail store in Philadelphia that sells handicrafts from artisans throughout the world. Melissa comes from a working-class background and identifies as a socially conscious consumer who is on a budget:

> I know it's crazy. It's crazy. Going to Walmart allows me to have the money to then spend at Whole Foods. And Whole Foods has really strict policies about the kind of food that they'll sell. … Then when my husband says, 'Oh my God! You spent a dollar for an orange?' I'm like, 'Well, I only spent $5 on a shirt at Walmart.' It's a lot easier to justify why I'm spending money. (Brown 2013, 26–27)

Melissa is acutely aware of the contradictions in her purchasing patterns. She earmarks her money and views socially responsible food as a more important purchase than anti-sweatshop clothing. Whereas many view this type of behavior as an impediment to the growth of socially responsible markets, a number of sociologists reframe this barrier as part of a process of identity formation (Lorenzen 2012; Willis and Schor 2012). They say that consumers are aware of the contradictions in their purchase of ethical goods and are working towards buying more products that align with the person they want to become.

Another threat to more widespread adoption of sustainable consumption patterns is green- or fair-washing by corporations. Green-washing is an attempt by a corporation to position themselves as eco-friendly without necessarily following up with their claims (Micheletti and Follesdal 2007). As it becomes increasingly apparent that consumers are seeking green products, companies have a motive to position themselves as eco-friendly. Whereas consumers can potentially reshape markets by demanding more socially responsible actions from corporations (Simon 2010), corporations can also co-opt the motives of consumers and coerce them into thinking they are buying green or eco-friendly products when that is not necessarily the case (Micheletti and Follesdal 2007).

Many also associate the trend towards increasing individualism as a barrier preventing ethical consumption from achieving its goals (Lyon and Moberg 2010; Szasz 2007). Within this context, many consumer-dependent social movements attempt to solve market-based problems with market-based solutions (Lyon and Moberg 2010). On the one hand, this approach is empowering to consumers who seek to vote with their pocketbooks (Connolly and Prothero 2008). Consumers start to believe they can enact positive changes for the environment by buying organic, fair trade or local produce. On the other hand, these movements for social change are beholden to the rules of the marketplace, which require a profit-driven ethos (Brown 2008; Johnston 2008; Lyon 2011; Lyon and Moberg 2010). Whereas social responsibility is becoming increasingly profitable for corporations (Dauvergne and Lister 2013), there are also times when it conflicts with the need to earn a return on an investment.

Similarly, many ethical shopping initiatives primarily target wealthy, highly educated consumers. If these consumers feel that they can enact real change through shopping, they may not recognize that less-privileged consumers do not possess the same resources (Johnston et al. 2011). Shopping to save the environment may give them false hope that their individual purchases do not require more collective efforts to reduce carbon emissions (Szasz 2007).

'Willful ignorance' also presents an obstacle to the growth of socially responsible markets. Many consumers willfully ignore the environmental and labor implications of shopping for products that will likely conflict with their value system (Ehrich and Irwin 2005; Norgaard 2006; Brown 2009). For instance, Ehrich and Irwin show that even environmentally conscious consumers will refuse to ask questions about product attributes (such as if the wood in a piece of furniture came from a rainforest) when those attributes will likely conflict with their own ideals. Similarly, citizens who benefit financially from the oil industry have been shown to turn a 'blind eye' to social justice initiatives designed to reduce carbon emissions (Norgaard 2006). In my interviews with fair trade consumers, I saw consumers practice willful ignorance often. Adrian, for instance, is a 50 year old social worker who hangs out at a fair trade coffee shop in a Bohemian, Philadelphia neighborhood. She explains, 'I really do try to make socially responsible decisions when I know and when I'm aware. If I'm not aware [then] whatever' (Brown 2013, 102).

Finally, American consumers seem reluctant to discuss the moral implications of shopping. A growing body of research shows that Americans are often reluctant to discuss the ways other people should behave in public domains (Brown 2009; Clydesdale 2007; Eliasoph 1998; Perrin 2007). Whereas Americans like to distinguish themselves from others based on moral criteria (Lamont 1992; 2000), their desire to avoid conflict in everyday interactions (Collins 2004) seems to prevent them from telling others how they should shop (Brown 2009; Johnston et al. 2011). For instance, my research shows that even consumers who care deeply about fair trade coffee are often reluctant to promote fair trade in their everyday interactions. Rather than tell friends and family that they 'need' to buy fair trade because 'it is the right thing to do' and it will help improve the lives of marginalized producers, they emphasize the price, aesthetics, quality or handmade nature of the product. They seek to avoid sounding 'too preachy' and instead focus on the attributes of the product. This does not imply that these consumers do not care about fair trade. In fact, they care greatly, but seek to encourage fair trade consumption by focusing on product attributes instead of moral imperatives. I will provide a few examples to clarify this point.

Nick is a conscientious consumer who learned about fair trade in college while taking a sociology class on globalization. After graduation, Nick landed a job in Center City Philadelphia and began buying his coffee at Cosi, a local chain store. But he was never satisfied with his coffee from Cosi. He knew the coffee was not fair trade, and he feared that the farmers were being exploited. Nick told me it was 'really cool' to learn that Joe Coffee Bar sold fair trade coffee. 'So I didn't know it was fair trade before I came in, but after I did, it was like, "All right. This is awesome". And then, actually, incidentally, that's when I stopped going to Cosi. All of the sudden the Cosi coffee didn't taste any good anymore' (Brown 2013, 84). Although his motivation for continuing to go to Joe Coffee Bar was based on his allegiance to fair trade, Nick partly frames his switch in terms of taste.

Marina is a Ten Thousand Villages customer who is in her late thirties and was born in Bangladesh. I interviewed Marina in her spacious, one-hundred-plus-year-old home in a wealthy Philadelphia neighborhood. She identifies as a progressive person who likes to buy organic and socially responsible food. During the interview, her dog began barking loudly, and this reminded Marina that even the dog's food is organic. Rather than mention the moral, environmental or health implications of buying organic, Marina noted the importance of taste: '[The dog] is the biggest consumer [of organics] in the house because she loves to eat organic dog food. She didn't like it in the beginning, but now, if she has a choice' (Brown 2013, 85). It's hard to imagine Marina's dog ever having the choice between organic and non-organic dog food. But it is important for Marina to tell herself that her dog prefers the taste of organic. The focus on her dog's favorite type of food frames the conversation as an individual preference and avoids emphasizing whether others 'ought to buy' organic food.

A vast range of social, cultural, environmental and economic forces influence whether or not individuals are committed to living a more sustainable lifestyle. Some of these forces are readily apparent to most consumers, whereas others are more covert and, perhaps, more detrimental to consumers' ability to enact change through markets. The sociological perspective seeks to understand these forces and avoids assuming that social change will occur simply through increased knowledge about a social problem or through some inherent desire to act in a more altruistic or sustainable manner.

CONCLUSION: THE SOCIAL CONSTRUCTION OF MORALITY IN MARKETS

One of the most significant contributions of sociologists who study markets is the recognition that goods and brands, and for our purposes we could even add certifications such as fair trade, do not have any inherent meaning (see Bourdieu 1984; Douglas and Isherwood 1979; White 2002). Instead, the meaning of these objects is created through social interactions (Wherry 2008) and in how the meaning of these objects compares to other objects (Bourdieu 1984). Whereas there is a growing body of research on fair trade production and consumption, much of this work neglects to examine the ways consumers construct the meanings of fair trade. Researchers are examining consumer attitudes, the construction of fair trade standards, and retail sales. But few studies take an ethnographic approach that seeks to understand how consumers make sense of fair trade logos or how they talk about fair trade to their friends and family. This bottom-up approach to ethical consumption is warranted because it will help us understand how consumer behaviors differ across cultural contexts. It will also lead to a number of interesting research questions. For instance, is American consumers' reluctance to sound 'too preachy' a barrier to growth in other markets? What are the cultural contexts where consumers feel comfortable telling others how they 'should' shop? How will consumer behavior shape fair trade in emerging markets such as South Korea and Japan? What other cultural forces encourage and limit growth of fair trade across cultures?

REFERENCES

Bourdieu, Pierre (1984), *Distinction*, Cambridge, MA: Harvard University Press.

Brown, Keith (2008), 'Framing a fair trade life: Tensions in the fair trade marketplace', in Daniel Thomas Cook (ed.), *Lived Experiences of Public Consumption*, New York: Palgrave Macmillan, pp. 179–202.

Brown, Keith (2009), 'The social dynamics and durability of moral boundaries', *Sociological Forum*, 24 (4), 854–876.

Brown, Keith (2013), *Buying into Fair Trade: The Culture of Ethical Consumption*, New York: New York University Press.

Carr, Patrick and Maria Kefalas (2009), *Hollowing Out the Middle: The Rural Brain Drain and What it Means for America*, Boston, MA: Beacon Press.

Clydesdale, Tim (2007), *The First Year Out: Understanding American Teens after High School*, Chicago: University of Chicago Press.

Cohen, Lizabeth (2003), *A Consumer's Republic: The Politics of Mass Consumption in Postwar America*, New York: Vintage Books.

Cole, Nicki L. (2014), 'Ethical consumption in the global age: Coffee's promise of a better world', in Nita Mathur (ed.), *Consumer Culture, Modernity and Identity*, London: Sage Publications.

Cole, Nicki L. and Keith Brown (2014), 'The problem with fair trade coffee', *Contexts*, 13 (1), 50–55.

Collins, Randall (2004), *Interaction Ritual Chains*, Princeton, NJ: Princeton University Press.

Connolly, John and Andrea Prothero (2008), 'Green consumption', *Journal of Consumer Culture*, 8 (1), 117–145.

Conroy, Michael (2007), *Branded! How the 'Certification Revolution' is Transforming Global Corporations*, Gabriola Island, BC, Canada: New Society Publishers.

Dauvergne, Peter and Jane Lister (2013), *Eco-Business: A Big-Brand Takeover of Sustainability*, Cambridge, MA: MIT Press.

DeCarlo, Jacqueline (2007), *Fair Trade: Beginner's Guide*, Oxford: Oneworld Publications.

Douglas, Mary and Baron Isherwood (1979), *The World of Goods: Towards an Anthropology of Consumption*, New York: Norton Paperback.

Ehrich, Kristine and Julie Irwin (2005), 'Willful ignorance in the request of product attribute information', *Journal of Marketing Research*, 42 (3), 266–277.

Eliasoph, Nina (1998), *Avoiding Politics: How Americans Produce Apathy in Everyday Life*, New York: Cambridge University Press.

Equal Exchange (2011), 'Our co-op. Our story', http://www.equalexchange.coop/story (accessed 13 June 2011).
Fine, Gary Alan (2003), 'Crafting authenticity: The validation of identity in self-taught art', *Theory and Society*, 32 (2), 153–180.
Glickman, Lawrence (2004), 'Buy for the sake of the slave: Abolitionism and the origins of American consumer activism', *American Quarterly*, 56 (4), 889–912.
Glickman, Lawrence (2009), *Buying Power: A History of Consumer Activism in America*, Chicago: University of Chicago Press.
Goodman, Michael (2004), 'Reading fair trade: Political ecological imaginary and the moral economy of fair trade foods', *Political Geography*, 23 (7), 891–915.
Gould, Roger (1993), 'Collective action and network structure', *American Sociological Review*, 58 (2), 182–196.
Grazian, David (2003), *Blue Chicago: The Search for Authenticity in Urban Blues Clubs*, Chicago: University of Chicago Press.
Griskevicius, Vladas, Joshua Tybur and Bram Van den Bergh (2010), 'Going green to be seen: Status, reputation, and conspicuous conservation', *Journal of Personality and Social Psychology*, 98 (3), 392–404.
Johnston, Josée (2008), 'The citizen-consumer hybrid: Ideological tensions and the case of Whole Foods Market', *Theory and Society*, 37 (3), 229–270.
Johnston, Josée, Michele Szabo and Alexandra Rodney (2011), 'Good food, good people: Understanding the cultural repertoire of ethical eating', *Journal of Consumer Culture*, 11 (3), 293–318.
Kimeldorf, Howard, Rachel Meyer, Monica Prasad and Ian Robinson (2006), 'Consumers with a conscience: Will they pay more?', *Contexts*, 5 (1), 24–29.
King, Samantha (2006), *Pink Ribbons, Inc.*, Minneapolis, MN: University of Minnesota Press.
Kopytoff, Igor (1986), 'The cultural biography of things: Commoditization as process', in Arjun Appadurai (ed.), *The Social Life of Things: Commodities in Cultural Perspective*, Cambridge: Cambridge University Press, pp. 64–91.
Lamont, Michèle (1992), *Money, Morals, and Manners: The Culture of the French and American Upper-Middle Class*, Chicago: University of Chicago Press.
Lamont, Michèle (2000), *The Dignity of Working Men: Morality and the Boundaries of Race, Class, and Immigration*, Cambridge, MA: Harvard University Press.
Lorenzen, Janet (2012), 'Going green: The process of lifestyle change', *Sociological Forum*, 27 (1), 94–116.
Lyon, Sarah (2011), *Coffee and Community: Maya Farmers and Fair-Trade Markets*, Boulder, CO: The University Press of Colorado.
Lyon, Sarah and Mark Moberg (eds.) (2010), *Fair Trade and Social Justice: Global Ethnographies*, New York: New York University Press.
Maniates, Michael F. (2001), 'Individualization: Plant a tree, buy a bike, save the world?', *Global Environmental Politics*, 1 (3), 31–52.
Matathia, Ira and Marian Salzman (1999), *Next: Trends for the Near Future*, New York: Overlook Press.
Mazar, Nina and Chen-Bo Zhong (2010), 'Do green products make us better people?', *Psychological Science*, 21 (4), 494–498.
McGovern, Charles (2006), *Sold American: Consumption and Citizenship, 1890–1945*, Chapel Hill, NC: University of North Carolina Press.
Micheletti, Michele and Andreas Follesdal (2007), 'Shopping for human rights: An introduction to the special issue', *Journal of Consumer Policy*, 30 (3), 167–175.
Muniz, Albert, Jr. and Thomas O'Guinn (2001), 'Brand community', *Journal of Consumer Research*, 27 (4), 412–432.

Norgaard, Kari Marie (2006), 'We don't really want to know: Environmental justice and socially organized denial of global warming in Norway', *Organization and Environment*, 19 (3), 347–370.
Perrin, Andrew (2007), *Citizen Speak: The Democratic Imagination in American Life*, Chicago: University of Chicago Press.
Peterson, Richard (1997), *Creating Country Music: Fabricating Authenticity*, Chicago: University of Chicago Press.
PEW Research Center for the People and the Press (2010), 'Public trust in government: 1958–2010', available at http://www.people-press.org/2010/04/18/public-trust-in-government1958-2010 (accessed 18 January 2012).
PR Newswire (2011), 'SC Johnson settles case involving greenlist labeling', available at http://www.prnewswire.com/news-releases/sc-johnson-settles-cases-involving-greenlist_labeling 125222089.html (accessed 8 February 2012).
Rabe, Barry and Christopher Borick (2012), 'Belief in global warming on the rebound: National survey of American public opinion on climate change', *Issues in Governance Studies*, February, Washington, DC: The Brookings Institution.
Raynolds, Laura and Michael Long (2007), 'Fair/alternative trade: Historical and empirical dimensions', in Laura Raynolds, Douglas Murray and John Wilkinson (eds.), *Fair Trade: The Challenges of Transforming Globalization*, New York: Routledge, pp. 15–32.
Schneider, Greg (2004), 'Toyota's Prius proving to be the hotter ride in hybrids', *Washington Post, Business*, available at www.washingtonpost.com/ac2/wp-dyn/A24832-2004Aug22?language=printer (accessed 17 June 2011).
Schoolman, Ethan (2013), 'How personal is the political? Understanding socially responsible consumption', dissertation, Ann Arbor, MI: University of Michigan.
Schor, Juliet (2010), *Plenitude: The New Economics of True Wealth*, New York: Penguin Press.
Schwartz, Barry (2004), *The Paradox of Choice: Why More Is Less*, New York: HarperCollins.
Shell, Ellen Ruppel (2009), *Cheap: The High Cost of Discount Culture*, New York: Penguin Books.
Simon, Bryant (2009), *Everything but the Coffee: Learning about America from Starbucks*, Berkeley, CA: University of California Press.
Simon, Bryant (2010), 'The rough democracy of buying', available at http://redroom.com/member/bryant-simon/blog/the-rough-democracy-of-buying (accessed 10 January 2012).
Szasz, Andrew (2007), *Shopping Our Way to Safety: How We Changed from Protecting Our Environment to Protecting Ourselves*, Minneapolis, MN: University of Minnesota Press.
Thompson, Craig and Gokcen Coskuner-Balli (2007), 'Countervailing market responses to corporate co-optation and the ideological recruitment of consumption communities', *Journal of Consumer Research*, 34 (2), 135–152.
Veblen, Thorstein (1899), *The Theory of the Leisure Class*, reprinted in (1953), New York: Mentor Book.
Weissman, Michaele (2008), *God in a Cup: The Obsessive Quest for the Perfect Coffee*, Hoboken, NJ: Wiley.
Wherry, Frederick (2008), *Global Markets and Local Crafts: Thailand and Costa Rica Compared*, Baltimore, MD: Johns Hopkins University Press.
White, Harrison (2002), *Markets from Networks: Socioeconomic Models of Production*, Princeton, NJ: Princeton University Press.
Willis, Margaret and Juliet Schor (2012), 'Does changing a light bulb lead to changing the world? Political action and the conscientious consumer', *The ANNALS of the American Academy of Political and Social Science*, 644 (1), 160–190.
Zavestoski, Stephen (2002), 'The social-psychological bases of anticonsumption attitudes', *Psychology and Marketing*, 19 (2), 149–165.

Zelizer, Viviana (1997), *The Social Meaning of Money*, Princeton, NJ: Princeton University Press.
Zukin, Sharon (2004), *Point of Purchase: How Shopping Changed America*, New York: Routledge.

10. Domestic fair trade in the United States

Sandy Brown and Christy Getz

INTRODUCTION

Walmart's February 2014 announcement that it would join McDonald's, Taco Bell and other major food corporations in signing on to the Coalition of Immokalee Workers' (CIW) 'Fair Food Agreement' underscores the growing interest in farm labor issues within the landscape of United States-based agrifood activism. For two decades, the CIW had been organizing in Florida's farm fields and pressuring buyers to support a nominal price premium and Code of Conduct for the tomato workers who are arguably among the most exploited of the nation's agricultural labor force (Marquis 2014). Recently, mainstream media outlets, food bloggers and popular writers have also turned their attention towards the farmworkers who have largely been sidelined within US alternative food movements. At long last it appears that ethical consumers' interest in 'knowing where their food comes from' might move beyond the agrarian idealism of alternative food movements to include the politically and economically marginalized immigrant workforce so central to US agriculture.

Meanwhile, the phenomenal success of international fair trade has prompted calls to 'bring fair trade home' to small-scale farmers and workers within the United States.[1] Yet, despite this flurry of attention, progress has been slow. To date, certification of domestic agriculture remains limited and the question remains as to whether such programs will gain traction within the United States, as they have in international export markets. This disconnect between mounting public interest, on the one hand, and the failure of these initiatives to take hold, on the other, underscores a set of tensions and challenges facing proponents of domestic fair trade. In this chapter we consider the dynamics underpinning this emergent movement and consider how international fair trade might translate within the US context. We argue that this intersection has produced challenges and tensions that both resonate with, and differ from, the international experience. (For further discussion on Fair Trade USA, certification and US market issues, see April Linton and Claudia Rosty's chapter in this volume.) We explore the ways in which fair trade's voluntarist market-based approach and concomitant debates over its appropriate beneficiaries (e.g., small farmers versus large-scale operations and workers) intersect with the legacies of agrarianism and agricultural exceptionalism in shaping US agriculture, food policy and politics. In particular, we highlight the role of immigrant workers in valorizing the US agricultural landscape across virtually all production scales and contexts and the character of United States-based alternative food activism, which has largely accepted dualistic framings of the marginalized small farmer versus industrial agribusiness interests.

Our analysis draws on interviews with farm labor and non-governmental organization (NGO) representatives, farmers, activists and researchers involved in efforts to establish social justice standards for US agriculture (N = 27). In addition we have analyzed publicly available documents from a variety of social certification initiatives aimed at promoting fair trade in the domestic arena, including the Domestic Fair Trade Association (DFTA), the Agricultural Justice Project (AJP), the Food Alliance, the Fair Trade Sustainability Alliance (FairTSA), the Equitable Food Initiative (EFI), Labor Link and Fair Trade USA. Evidence presented in the chapter has also been enriched by over a decade of participation (on the part of both authors) in alternative food movement organizations and in production agriculture. This work has included participation in pilot audits conducted by multiple certification initiatives, conferences and committee meetings sponsored by various certification initiatives and alternative food movement organizations. We also draw on a wide body of literature focused on international fair trade and the political economy of US agriculture and food systems sustainability to develop our conceptual framework for understanding the possibilities and limits of domestic fair trade.

The chapter proceeds as follows: First, we place the movement for domestic fair trade, and domestic social certification more broadly, within the historical and contemporary political economy of US agriculture. We then trace the emergence of a variety of initiatives aimed at promoting fair trade and fair labor standards for domestic production. We focus on formative and ongoing efforts to develop a high-bar approach to fair trade/fair labor, as espoused by the DFTA and the AJP. We also explore the proliferation of social certification initiatives and how this portends a complex, differentiated terrain for proponents of fair trade and fair labor standards. We conclude by highlighting some of the similarities and differences between international and domestic fair trade and suggest the ways in which the US experience may be applicable to domestic fair trade efforts in other Northern countries.

BRINGING FAIR TRADE HOME

The drive to 'bring fair trade's moral charge home' (Jaffee et al. 2004) to the United States has been motivated by a variety of social movement actors and institutions. The marriage of international fair trade's social equity concerns and the organic movement's attention to environmental issues presents an opening for social-justice-oriented food activists to promote a more holistic vision of sustainability within US agriculture. Given the historical and contemporary role of a marginalized immigrant workforce in US agricultural production, domestic fair trade proponents have had to engage with a thorny set of labor questions. In many respects this was the original aspiration of the domestic fair trade movement, to serve as a 'triple-win' for farmers, farmworkers and consumers (author interview: Informant 1 2007).

US-based initiatives have developed to address a wide variety of contexts, from high-bar niche markets to medium and larger-scale operations supplying branded buyers and chain retailers. The NGO and market actors involved in these efforts have had to confront many of the same tensions and challenges facing the international fair trade network. In the international context, these tensions have been well documented. The goal of working 'in and against the market' (Barratt Brown 1993, 156) raises a fundamental question about the potential for market mechanisms to address the deleterious social and environmental consequences inherent in market-based economies. On the one hand, fair trade presents the possibility of re-embedding markets in ethical conventions (Raynolds 2000; Renard 2003). On the other hand, as a voluntary alternative to state-based and multilateral regulation, its potential is constrained by market imperatives of accumulation and competition, which undermine the viability of so-called mission-driven actors attempting to incorporate social justice norms (Fridell 2006; Jaffee 2007; Moberg 2008; Raynolds 2007; 2009; Shreck 2005; Wilkinson 2007).

This problem has gained significant attention in the context of fair trade's rapid market expansion, which has largely been achieved through: 1) an emphasis on certification and labeling, as opposed to direct relationships between producers and buyers; 2) the enrollment of the very transnational corporate food suppliers and retailers associated with unfair trade; and 3) certification of plantation operations that rely more heavily on wage labor than the smallholder producers that the system was originally established to protect. This 'mainstreaming' of fair trade has generated significant debate among activists, NGOs and researchers alike over the appropriate beneficiaries of fair trade (see Ronan Le Velly's chapter in this volume). Historical patterns of uneven development between the global North and South have made the mainstreaming debate particularly salient in the international context. Within the United States, debates have also emerged around questions of production scale and social relations. Framings of the marginalized small farmer versus the corporate agribusiness giant obscure the complex terrain of fair trade production (see Laura Raynolds and Nick Greenfield's chapter in this volume). While these dualistic representations are arguably exaggerated in the international arena, they are even more dubious within the domestic context given highly uneven and differentiated resource and market access.

US Agricultural Exceptionalism: The Legacy of the Jeffersonian Ideal

In this section, we contextualize the historical and current valorization of the small-scale US family farm to identify how the agrarian ideal emerged, how it has shaped policy and how it continues to influence agrifood politics and production relations. The implications of this legacy provide an important referent for considering the possibilities and limits of applying the fair trade model to the US context. Historically, the small-scale farm was widely viewed as the economic backbone of an emerging agrarian society and a large percentage of the population engaged in agricultural production. Thomas Jefferson, one of the nation's founding fathers and third President, was among the most vigorous advocates of agrarian democracy (Boyd 1950). Jefferson's valorization of farmers pivots not only on economic claims but also on political and moral ones, positioning the small-scale farm as *the* national symbol of social and economic justice, democracy and virtue. For over two centuries, this agrarian ideal has played a major role in shaping the national and state policies affecting the agricultural sector, from environmental and labor regulation to public investment in farm subsidies and infrastructure.

Early policies, notably the Homestead Act of 1862 and the National Reclamation Act of 1902, were enacted to put farmland in the hands of small-scale farmers and to make productive improvements that would support family farming (Frampton 1979–1980; Pisani 1984). In the 1930s, New Deal policies explicitly exempted farmworkers from a variety of labor rights and protections. These included exemptions from the National Labor Relations Act of 1935, which granted workers the right to organize into trade unions and bargain collectively with employers, and the Fair Labor Standards Act of 1938, which granted minimum wage and overtime pay and prohibited child labor. Agricultural employers have also been exempted from a variety of occupational health and safety measures, with farms employing fewer than seven workers granted additional exemptions (BAMCO 2011). The rhetoric of agrarianism and resulting US policies demonstrate the ideological traction of 'agricultural exceptionalism' – the notion that agriculture is different from other sectors of the economy. These special protections have been justified on the grounds that small-scale farmers are the bearers of agrarian democracy and also vulnerable due to their reliance on natural forces, the perishability of their product and their disadvantaged position vis-à-vis other industrial actors in ways that small businesses in other sectors are not (Getz et al. 2008; Skogstad 1998).

The underlying philosophy of agricultural exceptionalism also guided the Roosevelt Administration's development of federal farm subsidies during the 1930s Dust Bowl and Depression era. These policies were intended to support small-scale farmers who cultivated their own land and hired workers only as needed to supplement household labor (representing nearly one quarter of the country's population at the time) and to stabilize rural communities (Vogeler 1981). However, numerous loopholes, under-enforcement and blatant fraud thwarted the intent of such policies, which over time ended up privileging large-scale producers, subsidizing land speculators and industrial farmers and undermining and bankrupting many small farms (Vogeler 1981). Concentration of farming operations increased over the next several decades, and not evenly. In addition to seeing a decrease in the number of farms, an increase in the average size of farms and a decline in the percentage of US population residing on farms (from 25 per cent in 1930 to less than 2 per cent today; USDA 2012), the largest farms acquired an increasingly large share of the market. Indeed, by 2007, the top 9 per cent of farms accounted for 77 per cent of farm sales (Hoppe, MacDonald and Korb 2010, 6).

The manner in which federal and state agencies categorize and count farms has, to some extent, obscured this rupture between rhetoric and reality. Today, 98 per cent of all US farms fit the United States Department of Agriculture's (USDA) definition of 'family farms' (Hoppe and Banker 2010, 6), a term whose definition makes no claim about who does the farm work. Additionally, while 88 per cent of US farms are defined as small family farms based on sales of less than US$250 000 per year, over half of these operations are 'residential/lifestyle' and 'retirement' farms that produce little or no income (Hoppe and Banker 2010, 6).

As farm size grew, so did the number of farmworkers needed to provide labor to these farms. Farmers' use of hired labor varies by commodity sector. For example, high-value fruit and vegetable crops require significantly more labor than traditional commodity crops, such as corn and soybeans. Nor is the use of hired labor restricted to large-scale farms. USDA data show that farms of all sizes hire workers, and fully 40 per cent of hired workers are employed on what the USDA classifies as small farms (USDA 2007, 4). Despite the centrality and proliferation of hired workers in the United States, the agricultural sector has maintained its exemption from labor laws. Today, wages and working conditions in US farm fields remain among the worst of all industries, despite moments of heightened farm labor militancy, in particular successful United Farm Worker organizing during the 1960s and 1970s.

Regulatory exemptions, combined with US immigration policy, have produced a politically marginalized workforce and undermined claims to improved rights and protections (Majka and Majka 1982; Schell 2002; Walker 2004). While accurate data on the immigration status of the US farm labor force is unreliable, it is estimated that upwards of 55 per cent of farmworkers are undocumented nationally (US Department of Labor 2001–2002). In California the figure may be closer to 90 per cent in some labor-intensive crops. Increased immigration policing and border militarization have exacerbated these challenges (Mitchell 2007).

Perhaps not surprisingly, recent national and state policy campaigns to improve farm labor conditions have met with fierce resistance not only from conventional agribusiness, but also from sustainable and family-scale agricultural interests. Notable examples include the defeat of: 1) a federal proposal to restrict child labor, which was hailed as a victory for family farmers despite the fact that farm family members would have been exempted (Jamieson 2012); 2) California legislation to extend overtime pay to farmworkers (Associated Press 2012) and to limit stoop labor, despite exemptions for organic farms (Getz et al. 2008); and 3) a New York State proposal to enact comprehensive rights and protections for agricultural workers not covered under federal law (Gray 2013). We attribute these successful efforts to circumvent the labor protections found in other productive sectors to the enduring symbolism of the small family farm as a locus of justice, in the political arena and in the popular imaginary.

US Alternative Food Movements, Agrarianism, Food Localism

Sustainable and alternative agriculture movements in the United States have similarly tapped into the rhetoric of agricultural exceptionalism and the agrarian ideal, widely asserting the importance of small-scale, family and local farming in US society for sustainability and justice in the food system (Allen et al. 2003; Allen and Hinrichs 2008; Guthman 2004).[2] When advocates do address hired labor issues, they tend to do so in polarized terms – contrasting the 'noble' labor of 'family farms' with the 'exploited' labor of 'factory farms' – assuming that small-scale farms either do not hire workers or that their labor relations are somehow inherently more just. This agrarian idealism raises the question: to what extent will protecting small-scale farmers contribute to the goal of ensuring social justice? The answer depends, of course, on what we mean by 'social justice'. We suggest that this approach obscures structural differences between farm employers and farmworkers, assuming that price premiums will trickle down to workers and, potentially, constrain the realm of possibility for public regulation and workers' collective action (Brown and Getz 2008a; Guthman 2007).

DOMESTIC FAIR TRADE AND THE PROLIFERATION OF US-BASED SOCIAL CERTIFICATION

In this section we explore some of the key challenges and tensions facing the multifarious programs that have emerged targeting social criteria for US agricultural production and trade. These include the DFTA, AJP, the Food Alliance, the FairTSA, the EFI, Labor Link and Fair Trade USA. These initiatives differ with respect to their organizational models, stakeholder participation, standard-setting and monitoring processes and strategies for consumer targeting (e.g., individual consumers in alternative outlets versus institutional buyers and chain retailers). They also vary in their explicit reference to the concept of fair trade, as it is understood internationally, as well as their attempts to formally replicate international fair trade standards, in particular through long-term contracts, minimum prices and social premiums. While all of these initiatives operate within the framework of a voluntary, consumption-based system, some have been more deliberate in their attempt to maintain high-bar principles for social equity and sustainability.

The Domestic Fair Trade Association

Nowhere have the tensions of merging the varied visions of international fair trade, sustainable agriculture, farmworker justice and small-scale farming in the United States been more apparent than within the DFTA. The DFTA was established in 2005 with the explicit goal of addressing 'the converging interests of family farmers, farm workers, organic advocates and Fair Trade Organizations in domestic agriculture' (Crowell and Sligh 2006, np). Early members consciously framed their work in opposition, not only to the conventional agrofood system, but also to industrialization and corporatization of both fair trade and organic certification systems (Sligh and Christman 2007). While the intersection of international and domestic alternative food movements has presented new opportunities for promoting a more holistic vision of food system sustainability and accountability, it has also placed the challenges and contradictions associated with these respective models into sharp relief. The tensions highlighted in the DFTA, and expounded on in this section, are largely related to the basic questions of social justice: for whom, by what means and to further what goals?

The DFTA serves as an umbrella for a wide variety of non-profit and market-based entities interested in moving beyond the narrow confines of the USDA's National Organic Program to address broader environmental and social relations of agricultural production and trade (Sligh and Christman 2007). From the outset, leaders explicitly rejected becoming an accreditation or certification body and instead envisioned the organization as a networking, marketing and gatekeeping resource. One of the DFTA's first moves was to develop a 12-point set of foundational criteria addressing a range of issues, including family-scale farming, democratic and participatory control, rights of labor, direct trade, fair and stable pricing, credit access, transparency and accountability and sustainable agriculture (see DFTA website 2014 for more examples). The DFTA has grown to include a variety of alternative food companies and NGOs.[3] In addition, the group's Criteria Committee has developed an elaborate system for vetting domestic social certification programs.

The DFTA's principles, structure and operating procedures reflect commitments to broad-based, inclusionary and democratic stakeholder participation. Membership is based on peer review and recurring self-evaluation vis-à-vis organizational principles, a process borrowed from the North American Fair Trade Federation and the World Fair Trade Organization (formerly the International Federation of Alternative Traders). In addition, members must represent one of the DFTA's stakeholder groups, including: 1) family farmers and farmer cooperatives; 2) farmworker organizations; 3) processors, marketers and intermediary trading organizations; 4) retailers, food cooperatives and farmers' markets; and 5) NGOs and civil society. These constituencies hold equal representation on the steering committee. The group strives to make decisions by consensus and is committed to transparency, accountability and participatory governance (Brown and Getz 2008b).

Yet this discursive construction has been challenged where differing perspectives arise about the translation of broad-based principles into concrete standards. Notable examples include debates over definitions of family-scale farming, whether or not to require organic certification, how to determine fair prices and living wages, and over fair labor practices. We suggest that attempts to simultaneously address farmer and farm-worker interests have made it difficult for the DFTA to reach consensus on a variety of issues. DFTA members' strong focus on family-scale farming implicitly accepts the family farm/industrial agriculture binary that frames labor exploitation as a problem in large-scale farming and small farms as inherently more virtuous. As previously discussed, this focus has obscured the role of immigrant farmworkers at virtually all scales of US agricultural production, at times placing farmers and their representatives at odds with farmworker members.

The Agricultural Justice Project: High-Bar Aspirations, Niche Market Realities

The DFTA's attention to farmworker issues has been bolstered by the participation of the AJP, a US-based certification initiative that was established to promote a holistic vision of sustainability via a comprehensive set of social justice standards for 'fair trade between family-scale farmers and buyers and just working conditions for workers, interns and children on farms' (Henderson et al. 2003). The AJP has spent over a decade developing a comprehensive set of standards to address social justice across the food chain, with extensive input from farmer and farmworker groups. In 2007 the AJP launched a pilot certification and labeling program in conjunction with retail cooperatives in the Upper Midwest. They have subsequently expanded their efforts to enroll farmers and buyers across the United States, including the Northeast, South, Pacific Northwest and California, conducting trainings and pilot audits to develop capacity at the regional level to certify local farms. However, a high-bar approach to labor and trade issues within the voluntary market for standards has made progress slow. Currently, only four farms are AJP certified (AJP 2014).

The AJP has, nevertheless, played a pivotal role in opening up a conversation about labor practices within the DFTA. One AJP leader stated that they are 'involved to influence the programs that are out there and make clear that if labels are going to make claims they have to reflect what workers want and workers participation' (author interview: Informant 2 2006a). Largely at the behest of AJP leadership, the DFTA principle on labor rights includes references to living wages, an independent voice for workers and cooperative workplace structures, in conformance with International Labor Organization (ILO) conventions (Brown and Getz 2008b).

However, while the DFTA may reflect the segment of the US sustainable agriculture community most concerned with social justice, tensions between farmer and farmworker interests have played out in material ways. For example, few farmworker organizations were initially at the table and labor issues were not formally incorporated into early meeting agendas, in contrast to the considerable time spent debating definitions of organic, sustainable and family-scale farming. Farmer representatives have also expressed concerns about the calculation of a living wage and support for workers' collective bargaining rights, asserting their need to maintain control of such determinations. Farmworker groups have responded by demanding the right to determine the scope and shape of their participation in the DFTA and to articulate a strong position on fair labor standards. At the Association's 2007 annual meeting, these groups staged an impromptu walkout. They proceeded to develop a collective statement that the credibility of any domestic fair trade program would hinge on the 'full participation, fair wages, freedom from workplace toxins, and freedom to organize' (Farm Worker Conference for Fair Trade 2007).

Given these significant debates, questions remain about whose interests will be prioritized within the DFTA and the implications for different actors as efforts to promote domestic fair trade progress. While early representation was weighted towards farmers, sustained participation from farmworker organizations suggests that the DFTA will continue to grapple with tensions between the agrarian idealism espoused by alternative food movements and the rights and protections demanded by labor groups. As one farmworker advocate suggested: 'the biggest obstacle is that a lot of the programs and initiatives out there are fairly exclusionary – not intentionally – but they reflect the larger sustainable agriculture movement – some are pro worker, but in a generalized way (author interview: Informant 3 2006b). (For more on labor issues in fair trade, see Dimitris Stevis's chapter in this volume.)

Certifying Fair Food: From High Bar to High Impact?

Meanwhile, other domestic social certification initiatives have also been established, potentially posing a challenge to this high-bar approach. Unlike the DFTA and AJP, these initiatives do not necessarily delineate farm size as a measure of social justice. While this broader focus may produce some openings for improving agricultural working conditions on a broader scale, significant challenges are associated with these efforts. One challenge is the lack of progress in actually certifying farms in the context of a voluntary market-based system in which larger players have, at least thus far, had little incentive to improve wages and working conditions.

Several initiatives are attempting to increase buy-in from larger-scale farming operations and distributors. Among them is the EFI, a certification and labeling program that characterizes itself as 'a unique partnership among businesses and organizations that have come together to develop standards, training processes and a certification to protect farm workers and produce safer, healthier food' (EFI website 2014). Convened by Oxfam America and including many of the major national farmworker organizations,[4] as well as several large-scale food buyers[5] and other NGOs, the EFI has garnered significant resources to develop and market its standards, which were piloted in 2012. EFI reports that it will refine the process through engagement with approximately 40 farms in both the United States and abroad in 2013–2014 and 400 by 2017 (EFI website 2014).

Here again progress appears to be slower than projected. Despite including equity goals and farmworker rights language into its standards, the program has primarily pitched itself as a way for growers to achieve food safety (and other regulatory) compliance; it is through the food safety lens that it has garnered the majority of its media coverage, selling the message that a stable, healthy, well-compensated workforce will be less likely to contaminate the food supply and will, thus, limit growers' liability. That said, the benefits to farmworkers are quite rigorous, including a mandated minimum wage of US$9.05 within the United States and 125 per cent of the prevailing wage outside of the United States. To date, big box chain Costco is the only major retailer to sign on; and the company CEO insists that Costco will not be passing the premium it will pay for the produce to Costco customers because it (food safety) is a 'good business decision' (Weisbaum 2013). The initiative is being piloted with two California farms, which have both been audited and are awaiting certification. The manager of one of these farms noted that its impetus for getting involved in the program is to transform food safety issues they have had 'to good' (Grossman 2013), implying that the real objective for getting involved with EFI was to show consumers that it had a strong food safety footing, not that its labor standards were solid.

Other initiatives include the Food Alliance and the Specialty Crop Sustainability Index (SCSI). The Food Alliance initiative was explicitly developed to support medium-scale farmers in response to the increased polarization of US agriculture between small and large operations and the disappearing middle (Kirschenmann et al. 2008). The Food Alliance does not confer a label or require price premiums, instead opting to promote certified operations with wholesale and retail buyers. While labor practices are included in program standards, operations can conceivably get certified without meeting any of the labor criteria (Brown and Getz 2008a). Larger-scale agribusiness interests established the SCSI, introducing a voluntary set of metrics to support 'people, planet and profit' as a more flexible alternative to certification standards.[6] The SCSI also assembled an impressive list of grower, food business, environmental, public interest and other players, soliciting input from hundreds of diverse stakeholders. However, thus far, established metrics have been limited to water use, energy and soil organic matter, with metrics for biodiversity and ecosystems, greenhouse gas emissions and irrigation efficiency under development. Although the SCSI's proposed labor measures were limited to worker health and safety, it appears that even these narrow issue areas have been abandoned.

Meanwhile, the FairTSA has attempted to enter the market for certification of US production with its own set of standards, modeled on those of international fair trade. FairTSA has framed its domestic initiative as a means of 'protecting small and medium sized farmers; keeping farmers on the land and ensuring continued vitality and viability of rural communities' (FairTSA 2011). However, the standards do not limit farm size in order to qualify for certification. While the group has approached US-based certifiers for collaboration, including the California Certified Organic Farmers, it has thus far not certified any domestic operations (author interview: Informant 4 2012).

A very recent entrant into the farm labor auditing scene, and a non-profit subsidiary of Fair Trade USA, Labor Link aims to increase 'supply chain transparency' regarding working conditions in factories and on farms through the use of mobile phone technology. Like EFI, its focus is both international and domestic and high impact, but unlike EFI, it does not confer a certification or label as part of its social justice monitoring program. Instead it allows either supply chain partners or farm management to select a survey type and participate in creating a set of 10–12 survey questions for farmworkers. Workers can then call a local number at any time during the survey period, anonymously, and answer voice-recorded questions using their telephone keypad. Labor Link will then provide the data as a tool for monitoring and improving working conditions on the farm (Good World Solutions 2014).

Overall we find that the significant differences among these initiatives articulate with broader patterns of market segmentation and dualistic framings of conventional agribusiness versus local, small-scale farming.

On the one hand, high-bar initiatives have focused on rewarding a limited number of smaller-scale, sustainable farmers for current practices within niche markets. The participation of farmworker groups has been critical in making the DFTA more explicit about its position on labor rights and protections and will likely affect future efforts to influence standards. On the other hand, new initiatives have been established targeting institutional buyers and retailers and larger-scale production. In these instances, promoting improved labor practices has also proved difficult, with multi-stakeholder programs continuing to negotiate more flexible standards or metrics in the hopes of attracting conventional agribusiness players. Indeed, this is one of the primary reasons the DFTA formed in the first place, to act as a gatekeeper or, as one Board member suggested, as a 'social justice consumer reporting agency' (cited in Thorn 2009, 81).

CONCLUSION

In many respects, the promise of domestic fair trade lies in its potential to bring together a variety of food justice and sustainability issues and, specifically, to address the labor concerns long sidelined by US alternative food movements. However, the discursive commitments to workers' rights and protections offered by domestic initiatives have yet to be realized in practice. We attribute this to a broader set of tensions associated with market-based certification and labeling, given that supply chain actors must voluntarily commit to participation. We also highlight the particular challenges of translating the fair trade model to the US context. International fair trade was originally established to buffer marginalized farmers from the vagaries of international export markets. In the United States, however, the preoccupation with small-scale family farming has served to obscure the social relations of agricultural production.

On the one hand, emergent initiatives reflect broader patterns of segmentation within US production and trade networks. On the other hand, US agricultural operations *across virtually all scales and contexts* rely on marginalized immigrant workers from Mexico and Central America. Structural differences between farm employers and workers are exacerbated by power asymmetries inscribed through labor, immigration and trade policy. Domestic fair trade proponents, in some sense, invoke a form of farming that does not exist in the US context. While small, resource poor farmers do face challenges related to production costs and market access, they hold a relatively privileged position relative to their purported counterparts in the global South.

Jaffee et al. have argued that US-based fair trade efforts would benefit from engaging with international fair trade actors to address the 'privileged position of farmers as opposed to wage labor' (2004, 171). We suggest that such an engagement must encompass: 1) an acknowledgment of structural differences between farm employers and farmworkers, not simply their overlapping interests; 2) a critical examination of the fundamental role of wage labor across the varying contexts and forms of production encompassed under the rubric of 'family farming'; and 3) the need for certification and labeling to provide a lever for, rather than an alternative to, labor regulation and collective action in the workplace.

NOTES

1. While international fair trade has addressed a broader array of commodities, including handicrafts and apparel, US-focused initiatives have concentrated on agriculture and food sectors.
2. US-based alternative movements have also framed resistance to the conventional food system around environmental and personal health goals (Harrison 2008).
3. Other founders included the fair trade organization and worker-owned cooperative, Equal Exchange, which recently unveiled a new line of products sourced from US-based family farms and cooperatives (Black 2007), representatives from several small fair trade coffee roasters; Dr. Bronners; non-profit organizations representing farmers (Rural Advancement Foundation International-USA, Family Farm Defenders, Red Tomato) and consumers (Organic Consumers Association); organic farmers; retail cooperatives, primarily based in the Upper Midwest region; and a farmworkers' organization (Community to Community Development and El Comité de Apoyo a los Trabajadores Agricolas).
4. Including Farmworker Justice, Farm Labor Organizing Committee, National Farm Worker Ministry, Pineros y Campesinos Unidos del Noroeste and the United Farm Workers, as well as Pesticide Action Network North America.
5. Including Andrew and Williamson Fresh Produce International, Bon Appétit Management Company and Costco Wholesale Corporation.
6. For more information see www.stewardshipindex.org.

REFERENCES

AJP (Agricultural Justice Project) website (2014), 'Current food justice certified farms and businesses', available at http://agriculturaljusticeproject.org/?page_id=20 (accessed 15 January 2014).

Allen, Patricia, Margaret FitzSimmons, Mike Goodman and Keith Warner (2003), 'Shifting plates in the agrifood landscape: The tectonics of alternative agrifood initiatives in California', *Journal of Rural Studies*, 19 (1), 61–75.

Allen, Patricia and Claire Hinrichs (2008), 'Selective patronage and social justice: Local food consumer campaigns in historical context', *Journal of Agricultural and Environmental Ethics*, 21 (4), 329–352.

Associated Press (2012), 'Allen Bill granting farmworkers more overtime pay fails in State Assembly', *Press Democrat*, September 1, 2012, available at http://www.pressdemocrat.com/article/20120901/WIRE/120909998 (accessed 17 October 2012).

BAMCO (Bon Appétit Management Company) (2011), 'Inventory of farmworker issues and protections in the United States', available at http://bamco.com/sustainable-food-service/farmworker-inventory (accessed 12 May 2011).

Barratt Brown, Michael (1993), *Fair Trade: Reform and Realities in the International Trading System*, London: Zed Books.

Black, Jane (2007), 'Fair trade hits home', *Washington Post*, 18 July, available at http://www.washingtonpost.com/wp dyn/content/article/2007/07/17/AR2007071700313.html (accessed 15 March 2014).

Boyd, Julian P. (ed.) (1950), *The Papers of Thomas Jefferson, Volume 8: February 1785 to October 1785*, Princeton, NJ: Princeton University Press.

Brown, Sandy and Christy Getz (2008a), 'Privatizing farm worker justice: Regulating labor through voluntary certification and labeling', *Geoforum*, 39 (3), 1184–1196.

Brown, Sandy and Christy Getz (2008b), 'Toward domestic fair trade: Farm labor, food localism, and the "family scale" farm', *Geojournal*, 73 (1), 11–22.

Crowell, Erbin and Michael Sligh (2006), 'Domestic fair trade: For health, justice and sustainability', *Social Policy*, 37 (1), np.

DFTA (Domestic Fair Trade Association) website (2014), 'Vision, mission, and principles', available at http://www.thedfta.org/about/vision-mission-and-principles/ (accessed 1 May 2014).

EFI (Equitable Food Initiative) website (2014), available at http://www.equitablefood.org (accessed 20 April 2014).

FairTSA (Fair Trade Sustainability Alliance) website (2011), 'Domestic standards for the production of agricultural products and processed foods', available at https://fairtsa.org/index.php?option=com_content&view=article&id=2&Itemid=21 (accessed 3 January 2014).

Farm Worker Conference for Fair Trade (2007), 'Public statement of the farm worker conference for fair trade', Minneapolis MN, 28–29 April 2007, available at http://www.localfairtrade.org/node/114 (accessed 8 August 2007).

Frampton, Mary Louise (1979–1980), 'The enforcement of federal reclamation law in the Westlands water district: A broken promise', *University of California Davis Law Review*, 13 (1), 89–122.

Fridell, Gavin (2006), 'Fair trade and neoliberalism: Assessing emerging perspectives', *Latin American Perspectives*, 33 (6), 8–28.

Getz, Christy, Sandy Brown and Aimee Shreck (2008), 'Class politics and agricultural exceptionalism in California's organic agriculture movement', *Politics and Society*, 36 (4), 478–507.

Good World Solutions (2014) website, 'How Labor Link works', available at http://goodworldsolutions.org/services/how-labor-link-works/ (accessed 25 April 2014).

Gray, Margaret (2013), *Labor and the Locavore: The Making of a Comprehensive Food Ethic*, Berkeley and Los Angeles: University of California Press.

Grossman, Elizabeth (2013), 'From farm to table: A new model for growing food fairly and safely', 6 June 2013, available at http://scienceblogs.com/thepumphandle/2013/06/06/from-farm-to-table-a-new-model-for-growing-food-fairly-and-safely/ (accessed 19 April 2014).

Guthman, Julie (2004), *Agrarian Dreams: The Paradox of Organic Farming in California*, Berkeley, CA: University of California Press.

Guthman, Julie (2007), 'The Polanyian way? Voluntary food labels as neoliberal governance', *Antipode*, 39 (3), 456–478.

Harrison, Jill (2008), 'Lessons learned from pesticide drift: A call to bring production agriculture, farm labor, and social justice back into agrifood research and activism', *Agriculture and Human Values*, 25 (2), 163–167.

Henderson, Elizabeth, Richard Mandelbaum, Oscar Mendieta and Michael Sligh (2003), 'Toward social justice and economic equity in the food system: A call for social stewardship standards in sustainable and organic agriculture', available at www.rafiusa.org/pubs/SocialJustice_final.pdf (accessed 5 April 2007).

Hoppe, Robert A. and David E. Banker (2010), 'Structure and finances of U.S. farms: Family farm report, 2010 edition', EIB-66, US Department of Agriculture, Economic Research Service, July 2010.

Hoppe, Robert A., James M. MacDonald and Penni Korb (2010), 'Small farms in the United States: Persistence under pressure', EIB-63, US Department of Agriculture, Economic Research Service, February 2010.

Informant 1 (2007), interview with Sandy Brown, Santa Cruz, CA (12 April 2007).

Informant 2 (2006a), interview with Sandy Brown and Christy Getz, Berkeley, CA (5 April 2006).

Informant 3 (2006b), interview with Sandy Brown, Santa Cruz, CA (2 April 2006).

Informant 4 (2007), interview with Sandy Brown, Santa Cruz, CA (12 April 2007).

Jaffee, Daniel (2007), *Brewing Justice: Fair Trade Coffee, Sustainability, and Survival*, Berkeley, CA: University of California Press.

Jaffee, Daniel, Jack R. Kloppenburg and Mario B. Monroy (2004), 'Bringing the "moral charge" home: Fair trade within the North and within the South', *Rural Sociology*, 69 (2), 169–196.

Jamieson, Dave (2012), 'Child labor farm rules scrapped by White House under political pressure', *Huffington Post*, 27 April, available at http://www.huffingtonpost.com/2012/04/27/white-house-child-labor-agriculture_n_1458701.html (accessed 17 October 2012).

Kirschenmann, Fred, G.W. Stevenson, Frederick Buttel, Thomas A. Lyson and Mike Duffy (2008), 'Why worry about the agriculture of the middle?', in Thomas A. Lyson, G.W. Stevenson and Rick Welsh (eds.), *Food and the Mid-level Farm: Renewing an Agriculture of the Middle*, Cambridge, MA: MIT Press, pp. 3–22.

Majka, Linda C. and Theo J. Majka (1982), *Farmworkers, Agribusiness, and the State*, Philadelphia, PA: Temple University Press.

Marquis, Susan (2014), 'Rand Corp op ed', available at http://ciw-online.org/ (accessed 15 April 2014).

Mitchell, Don (2007), 'Work, struggle, death, and geographies of justice: The transformation of landscape in and beyond California's Imperial Valley', *Landscape Research*, 32 (5), 559–577.

Moberg, Mark (2008), *Slipping Away: Banana Politics and Fair Trade in the Eastern Caribbean*, New York: Berghahn Books.

Pisani, Donald (1984), *From the Family Farm to Agribusiness: The Irrigation Crusade in California and The West 1950–1981*, Berkeley, CA: University of California Press.

Raynolds, Laura T. (2000), 'Re-embedding global agriculture: The international organic and fair trade movements', *Agriculture and Human Values*, 17 (3), 297–309.

Raynolds, Laura T. (2007), 'Fair trade bananas: Broadening the movement and market in the United States', in Laura T. Raynolds, Douglas L. Murray and John Wilkinson (eds.), *Fair Trade: The Challenges of Transforming Globalization*, London and New York: Routledge, pp. 63–82.

Raynolds, Laura T. (2009), 'Mainstreaming fair trade coffee: From partnership to traceability', *World Development*, 37 (6), 1083–1093.

Renard, Christine M. (2003), 'Fair trade: Quality, market and conventions', *Journal of Rural Studies*, 19 (1), 87–96.

Schell, Greg (2002), 'Farmworker exceptionalism under the law: How the legal system contributes to farmworker poverty and powerlessness', in Charles D. Thompson Jr. and

Melinda F. Wiggins (eds.), *The Human Cost of Food: Farmworkers' Lives, Labor, and Advocacy*, Austin, TX: University of Texas Press, pp. 139–166.

Shreck, Aimee (2005), 'Resistance, redistribution, and power in the fair trade banana initiative', *Agriculture and Human Values*, 22 (1), 17–29.

Skogstad, Grace (1998), 'Ideas, paradigms and institutions: Agricultural exceptionalism in the European Union and the United States', *Governance: An International Journal of Policy and Administration*, 11 (4), 463–490.

Sligh, Michael and Carolyn Christman (2007), *Organic Agriculture and Access to Food*, FAO Inter-Departmental Working Group on Organic Agriculture, Rome: Food and Agriculture Organization of the United Nations.

Thorn, Emily (2009), 'The meaning of markets: How the Domestic Fair Trade Association understands creating social change using market initiatives', MS thesis, Missoula, MT: University of Montana.

USDA (United States Department of Agriculture) (2007), 'Census of agriculture: Farm labor', available at www.agcensus.usda.gov/Publications/2007/Online.../farm_labor.pdf (accessed 13 November 2012).

USDA (2012), 'National Institute of Food and Agriculture: About us', available at http://www.csrees.usda.gov/qlinks/extension.html (accessed 17 October 2012).

US Department of Labor (2001–2002), 'Findings from the National Agricultural Workers Survey (NAWS) 2001–2002: A Demographic and employment profile of United States farm workers', available at http://www.doleta.gov/agworker/report9/toc.cfm (accessed 29 October 2014).

Vogeler, Ingolf (1981), *The Myth of the Family Farm: Agribusiness Dominance of U.S. Agriculture*, Boulder, CO: Westview Press.

Walker, Richard A. (2004), *The Conquest of Bread: 150 Years of Agribusiness in California*, New York: The New Press.

Weisbaum, Herb (2013), '"Culture-changing" initiative to stop food contamination on the farm', 19 August, available at http://www.nbcnews.com/health/health-news/culture-changing-initiative-stop-food-contamination-farm-f6C10855682 (accessed 20 April 2014).

Wilkinson, John (2007), 'Fair trade: Dynamic and dilemmas of a market oriented global social movement', *Journal of Consumer Policy*, 30 (3), 219–239.

11. Fair trade places

Alastair M. Smith

INTRODUCTION

This chapter adopts a phenomenological understanding of 'place', as a distinctive coming together of 'actants' (humans and their identities, geographical spaces and the material world), thereby imbuing a particular space (more or less bounded or diffuse) with an array of intersubjectively constructed meanings (Agnew 2011). Given that place is therefore socially constructed in the critical realist sense (Danermark et al. 2005), the idea of place employed here explicitly accepts the possibility of multiple interpretations and, therefore, the potential for contestations over meanings and identities.

Although the concept of alternative trade, and later fair trade, has been constructed with strong reference to the nature of the practices involved, these have always been embedded in supportive interpretations and senses of place. Fair trade requires the recognition that, far from unfolding within an even plane of empty space, the outcomes of economic interactions are both differentiated by place and contribute to the unique nature thereof. The characteristics of 'producer countries' simultaneously differentiate the outcomes of economic activities while also contributing to the very classification of their associated underlying spaces. Building on these imagined geographies, fair trade is therefore part of a longer and broader tradition to structure trade between places in ways that promote increasing levels of both procedural and distributive justice (Trentmann 2007).

Within the broad geographies of fair trade, more specific places of production have been fundamental to discourses of the movement – and there is a good tradition of scholarship focused on analyzing their associated issues (see, for example, several of the chapters in Part IV of this volume). In contrast, this chapter focuses on formally constituted fair trade places in 'consumer countries' that have specifically focused on: 1) the purchasing and promotion of fair trade goods and 2) wider promotion, awareness raising and activism designed to 'make trade fair'.[1] While this is not to say these activities *necessarily* exist in empirical separation, such conceptual differentiation offers a contribution to understanding the wider fair trade movement. Through focusing on these two elements of fair trade places, on how they have become constructed, reconstructed and therefore are continually operationalized, analysis connects to the wider issue of what the signifier 'fair trade' has come to mean in different empirical contexts.[2]

More specifically, the chapter analyses the development of fair trade places such as towns, schools and nations. The first explicit task here is to provide a history of the emergence of these formalized fair trade places, the account of which is traced to the campaign effort in a small town in Lancashire, in the United Kingdom. However, the major analytical work of the chapter considers how the development of such places has simultaneously interacted with the wider contestation of the fair trade concept.

Situating this focus in its wider intellectual context, many contributors to this book discuss tensions within the fair trade movement, between practices often categorized on a spectrum ranging from the most radical to the most reformist (see chapters in this volume by Laura Raynolds and Nicholas Greenfield; Bob Doherty, Valéry Bezençon and Gaëlle Balineau). Overall, analysis of global fair trade activities suggests that with the mainstreaming of fair trade, it has been the less radical practices that have come to dominate. Moreover, as part of this trend some identify an absolute decline in the activities of dedicated fair trade organizations (FTOs), understood by many to embody the more radical interpretation of fair trade (Doherty, Davies & Tranchell 2013, 181).

In many ways the emergence of fair trade places such as towns, schools and nations has provided consumers with a more organized means of participating in the performance and advocacy of what *they* understand or accept fair trade to require. Bacon (2010) identifies that of all the governance and certification approaches designed to shape international supply chains, it is the constituent networks of fair trade that make it the most democratic; and it is argued here that fair trade places are playing a significant role in contributing to such procedural democracy. In order to make this argument, the chapter undertakes an explicit analysis of how emerging senses of fair trade place have contributed to the contestation of what constitutes legitimate fair trade activity. This emerges as a useful perspective as some previous commentary suggests that place-based campaigning should offer an antidote to the 'diluted notion of individualized "shopping for a better world"' introduced by reformist practices (Low and Davenport 2007, 336). Likewise, some suggest that 'social movement activity by fair trade towns and universities has the ability to create a strong alternative high street in which a limited number of FTOs could maintain their independence' (Doherty, Davies & Tranchell 2013, 181). On the other hand, however, there is concern that fair trade places could reinforce the conventionalization of both discourses and practices (Fisher 2009). Therefore, this chapter presents a first effort to codify a cohesive understanding of the dynamic around fair trade places and, furthermore, outline potential future avenues for both researchers and practitioners working to shape the future of the fair trade movement.

THE EMERGENCE OF FAIR TRADE PLACES: ACCREDITATION AND CONTESTATION

The formal concept of a fair trade place first emerged in the small town of Garstang, in the county of Lancashire, in the United Kingdom. Here the local Oxfam group had been campaigning on issues relating to global poverty and particularly international trade justice (Crowther and Human 2011, 89-90). After the launch of the Fairtrade Mark by the United Kingdom's Fairtrade Foundation in 1994, the promotion of Fairtrade International certified goods also became a prominent element of the group's activities (Garstang Fairtrade 2000–2014). Despite initially limited successes in their campaign, by 2005 the group secured a pledge from 95 per cent of local businesses, all the churches, the local council and all the local schools, that they were committed to sell at least one Fairtrade certified product (Crowther and Human 2011, 90). In order to endorse this achievement, the group requested that the Parish Council recognize this commitment, and the motion was carried in April 2000 following a vote at a public meeting (Garstang Fairtrade 2010–2011).

The development of the world's first formally recognized fair trade place was significant as, to some extent, it moved participants away from a neoliberal model of individual action to instead focus on what could be organized *among* global citizens through group purchasing (Low and Davenport 2007, 344). The achievement of generating widespread community support for Fairtrade, however, was specifically based on embedding the knowledge of this opportunity within the context of place. In 1999 the Oxfam group had participated in an annual fast, held on the theme 'Give it up for Ghana' (Garstang Fairtrade 2000–2014). As part of this activity, the group worked with the local school using the now celebrated Ghanaian cooperative, Kuapa Kokoo, as their example of Fairtrade activity. Moreover, this work was then extended through a project focused on 'Fairtrade and the Slave Trade'. As the steering group themselves identify, drawing on the town's proximity to the neighboring city of Lancaster, previously Britain's fourth largest slave trading port, the promotion of Fairtrade goods could be framed in reference to both historical and contemporary connections between Garstang and Ghana (Garstang Fairtrade 2000–2014). In this way, the fair trade town is seen as 'representing global rather than local belonging and expressing global rather than local responsibility, viewed through the lens of consumption' (Samuel and Emanuel 2012, 191). Here, fair trade places might be understood to respond to Massey's call for 'an adequately progressive sense of place, one which would fit in with the current global-local times and the feelings and relations they give rise to, and which would be useful in what are, after all, political struggles often inevitably based on place' (Massey 1991, 26).

Within the direct embedding of fair trade campaigning in a sense of place, it is important to recognize that the first town emerged not from the Fairtrade Foundation, but from a local group (Alexander and Nicholls 2006, 1247). Right from this early point, the construction of fair trade places was carefully developed in order to encompass participation by actors in a range of key consumption sectors. Importantly, the involvement of government actors has lent an element of state legitimacy to the recognition of fair trade places; as has formal signifiers usually associated with state authority, such as road signs that identify the boundaries of, and formally welcome visitors to, officially demarcated fair trade places.

A final important element to the creation of the world's first fair trade town was the negotiated understanding of what practices should constitute a sense of fair trade place. While the emphasis was largely on Fairtrade certified goods, the Garstang group worked explicitly with mission-driven FTOs, for example in 1995 through participation in the Cafédirect Challenge (Garstang Fairtrade 2000–2014). Also, in addition to drawing on international connections, the fair trade group highlighted relationships with the places of UK agriculture. For this reason, when campaigners held a promotional meal to encourage greater buy-in from local stakeholders, food consisted of both Fairtrade goods and those sourced from local producers (Garstang Fairtrade 2000–2014). This had the direct effect of establishing a connection between local and international social justice and demonstrated the lack of conflict between them (on which Sandy Brown and Christy Getz write more in this volume).

During the campaign to have Garstang recognized as a fair trade place, representatives approached the United Kingdom's Fairtrade Foundation to endorse the status of the town. Initially, the Foundation were reserved about this initiative as they questioned the potential to maintain campaigning in a given place, constantly increase awareness and demand, and also improve the supply of Fairtrade products in a given locality (Samuel 2013, 103). Retrospectively, however, the initiative in Garstang 'inspired the Fairtrade Foundation to develop the Fairtrade Town campaign' (Fairtrade Foundation 2009b). In September 2001 the Fairtrade Foundation launched the 'Fairtrade Town' scheme and in the following November presented Garstang with their accreditation as the very first formally recognized fair trade place (Garstang Fairtrade 2010–2011).

In order to obtain status as a Fairtrade Town in the United Kingdom, the Fairtrade Foundation (Fairtrade Foundation 2009a) has required that:[3]

- The local council passes a resolution supporting Fairtrade and agrees to serve Fairtrade products (for example, in meetings, offices and canteens).
- The area's retailers (shops, supermarkets, newsagents and petrol stations) and catering outlets (cafés, restaurants, pubs) make a range of Fairtrade products readily available.
- Local workplaces and community organizations (places of worship, schools, universities, colleges and other community organizations) support Fairtrade and use Fairtrade products whenever possible. A flagship employer is required for populations over 100 000.
- Media coverage and events raise awareness and understanding of Fairtrade across the community.
- A local Fairtrade Steering Group is convened to ensure the Fairtrade Town campaign continues to develop and gain new support.

As summarized by Harriet Lamb (2008), Executive Director of the Fairtrade Foundation during the launch of the Fairtrade Towns campaign, the development of such a standardized set of 'quality attributes' made it possible for the Fairtrade Foundation to fairly assess, evaluate and certify the claims of any place in relation to their commitment to Fairtrade promotion and consumption. Based on this focus, some have described the Fairtrade Town scheme as a certification for consumption (Fisher 2009), the model for which has also been applied to places of different scales. Although the scheme remains known as Fairtrade Towns, status is also available to villages, cities, islands, boroughs and counties, as well as zones for all other geographical locations not fitting into one of the above categories (Crowther and Human 2011, 93; Fairtrade Foundation 2009a). On this basis, the Fairtrade Town scheme has been hugely successful, and by the early months of 2014, there were 579 accredited Fairtrade Towns in the United Kingdom (Fairtrade Foundation 2014).

In addition to fair trade places defined by the boundaries of state administration, the Fairtrade Foundation has also developed other place-based accreditations. For example, universities and colleges in the United Kingdom have had the opportunity to apply for Fairtrade status since 2003 (Fairtrade Foundation 2011a) and a scheme was introduced for schools in 2007 (Fairtrade Foundation 2011b). The Foundation also offers recognition to places of worship (Fairtrade Foundation 2011c). All these schemes have been based around similar requirements to those of Fairtrade Towns: specifically that a central authority is required to codify a commitment to both purchase Fairtrade goods and support their promotion in the wider sense, including during the United Kingdom's Fairtrade Fortnight (when the Fairtrade Foundation coordinates a nation-wide campaign of promotion, usually themed around the promotion of a given Fairtrade certified product).

Focusing on the centrality of Fairtrade certification, some scholars have primarily analyzed the Fairtrade Towns as a marketing device for Fairtrade goods. Here it is suggested that the development of formally recognize fair trade places represents the third of three marketing approaches. The first approach focused on the Fairtrade *process* to appeal to strongly ethical consumers; a second aimed to widen appeal by highlighting the intrinsic qualities of the fair trade *product itself*; and the third focuses on fair trade *places* and what consumers can do as part of their daily lives (Alexander and Nicholls 2006). In support of this marketing approach, Malpass et al. (2007, 634) argue that campaigns for fair trade places are a different and significant way of practicing ethical purchasing, introducing 'the importance of placed rather than seemingly placeless consumption of fair trade ideas and goods'. For Samuel (2013, 9), Fairtrade Towns have 'shifted existing marketing paradigms, regarding the use and conceptualization of place in the marketing mix' and even move place from being 'last in the line' to being at the center of the marketing strategy.

Taking a wider perspective, Low and Davenport pick up on the coordinated efforts of fair trade places and suggest that they 'hold great promise for expanding sales, shortening the distance between producer and consumer and reinvigorating the message of reforming and transforming international trade relations' (Low and Davenport 2007, 336). (On the changing dynamics of connecting consumers to fair trade producers, see also Eileen Davenport and William Low's chapter in this volume). Other analysis, however, is less optimistic. Fisher (2009, 994) raises the possibility that fair trade places might reinforce reformist and therefore less impactful interpretations of fair trade practices. Although many commentators suggest that such tendencies have been embedded in

Fairtrade International's certification system (Gendron, Bisaillon & Rance 2009), other analysts highlight that impact also depends on the specific type of supply chain governance in operation for any given product (Doherty, Davies & Tranchell 2013; Reed 2009). Based on the first of these interpretations, Smith (2011) points out that linking the concept of fair trade places to the Fairtrade certification system has narrowed the discursive focus to promotion of Fairtrade certified products. This marginalizes other approaches to the fair trade concept and excludes products outside of the (largely food-oriented) Fairtrade International certification system. Others go further to suggest that given the requirements made of local state institutions (requirement number one, see above), the Fairtrade Towns scheme 'compel[s] Local Authorities to serve Fairtrade produce during their meetings and promote Fairtrade produce in their area' (Preuss 2009, 217). Although there is little empirical work that examines the actual activities of Fairtrade places, research in Scotland identifies that practices, particularly with regard to state procurement, do indeed mostly focus on Fairtrade certified goods (Smith 2013b). This therefore reinforces concerns that campaign appeals to the consumers' sense of place are constructing a monopoly market for commodities bearing the Fairtrade Mark: a trend that comes at the expense of both other fair trade practices and authorities (e.g., the WFTO) and other sustainability certification (e.g., Rainforest Alliance) (Mohan 2010, 98). While the value of such prioritization is highly debated vis-à-vis our limited understanding of impact (see Part IV in this volume for a general overview), the barriers to obtaining Fairtrade certification for many producers might be reason enough for reservation over this trend (Smith 2014). In addition, the exclusive focus on consumption arguably constructs fair trade places as accepting of a neoliberal economic model, against which wider and original fair trade activism was attempting to fight. Indeed, Fridell's (2004) research on Fair Trade Universities in the United States highlights the possibility for fair trade status to be used as an 'ethical fig leaf' that obscures the dilution of radical campus politics with growing corporatization.

Having said this, however, there is also evidence that under the right circumstances, fair trade places in the United Kingdom have avoided oversimplifying the construction of fair trade activities. For example, Doherty, Davies and Tranchell (2013, 177) suggest that some Fairtrade Town groups in the United Kingdom have lobbied retailers to stock FTO products and, therefore, have reinforced the existence of more radical fair trade practices. In East Dunbartonshire, Scotland, the involvement of a dedicated FTO and state actors receptive to a wider understanding of fair trade has allowed place-based input into the direct construction of fair trade relationships with the National Smallholder Farmers' Association of Malawi (NASFAM) (Smith 2013b). In addition, there have been educational efforts that go well beyond those usually associated with the marketing of Fairtrade products. This much thicker level of information goes well beyond that embedded in fair trade purchases made in most corporate retail environments and mirrors one of the fundamental functions of dedicated fair trade retailers (Low and Davenport 2007, 337). Moreover, this arguably makes a much greater contribution to developing an outward looking sense of place.

These findings therefore support the recognition that fair trade places open space for multi-directional flows of information between a range of stakeholder organizations (Alexander and Nicholls 2006, 1247). Indeed, it has been suggested that what is important in shaping the nature of fair trade places is the specific communities of practice that constitute them (Smith 2011). Although representatives of the Fairtrade Foundation welcome applicants that go above and beyond the formal requirements, the Foundation places itself in a difficult position by both setting the standards for fair trade places and standing to gain from the activities generated by these. For example, the organization inevitably finds complexities in promoting FTO products over and above others, as this is readily perceived by other licensees as a contradiction to their interests and investments.[4] For this reason, it is pertinent to look towards manifestations of fair trade places in other national and international contexts, and it is to this subject that the next section now turns.

WIDER SENSES OF PLACE: CONTESTING THE NATURE OF SITUATED PRACTICES

Building on the contestation of meaning being played out between the Fairtrade Foundation and activists on the ground in fair trade places, such negotiation can also be identified in the wider international context. This has been embodied in the growth of fair trade places in other countries: in mainland Europe, North America, Asia and more recently New Koforidua in Ghana and Poços de Caldes in Brazil. While different national contexts have drawn on the Fairtrade Foundation's experience, there is a wide range of alternative interpretations about how best to develop the discourses and practices of fair trade places – and not least around the selection of supply chain governance models that communities have accepted and prioritized as part of their place-making activities.

For example, in Australia and New Zealand, the formal recognition of fair trade places is run not by Fairtrade Australia and New Zealand (the Fairtrade International National Labeling Initiative), but by the Fair Trade Association of Australia and New Zealand. This not-for-profit organization self-identifies as the 'peak agency driving the growth of the fair trade movement' (Fair Trade Association Australia and New Zealand 20/03/2014). More specifically, they 'recognize and promote the Fairtrade Mark (managed by Fairtrade Australia and New Zealand), the World Fair Trade Organization, and … [their] own system, Fair Traders of Australia, as credible fair trade systems' (Fair Trade Association Australia and New Zealand 20/03/2014). For this reason, fair trade towns are not just about focusing on Fairtrade certified goods. While the local authority 'should commit to serving Fairtrade Certified™ tea and coffee as the default option', wider commitments should promote fair trade goods, also including handicrafts endorsed by Fair Traders of Australia (FToA) and the World Fair Trade Organization (WFTO) (Fair Trade Association Australia and New Zealand 2013).

In the case of the United States, the administration of fair trade towns remains with Fair Trade USA, despite its departure from the Fairtrade International system in 2011 (Tallontire and Nelson 2013; Wilson and Curnow 2013). However, formal governance of these fair trade places is overseen by a National Steering Committee (NSC) made up of campaigners and stakeholders from across the movement (IFTT 2013). Such an approach is described by the National Coordinator as the 'big tent approach'. Here fair trade places are encouraged to engage with not only Fair Trade USA certified products, but also those certified by Fairtrade America (the newly established National Labeling Initiative of Fairtrade International), the Institute for Marketecology (IMO) Fair for Life certification program and also items sold by members of the Fair Trade Federation.

As was the case with Garstang, the issue of the relationship between fair trade places and local or national agricultural products has remained a pertinent one. In order to recognize this, the schemes in both Belgium and Canada have added a sixth goal of committing to support other forms of sustainable production 'the Committee believes is in the spirit of Fair Trade Towns' (Fair Trade Canada 2012, 8). Having said this, in Canada the campaign literature highlights that 'while you may promote non-certified fair trade products (e.g. from I[nternational] F[ederation of] A[lternative] T[trade][5] or Fair Trade Federation member companies) as part of Goal no. 6 or for general education, all [other] specific targets in this campaign refer to Fairtrade certified products' (Fair Trade Canada 2012, 6).

In response to the internationalization of fair trade places, there have been efforts to develop an International Fair Trade Towns Committee (IFTTC) – currently composed of representatives from Belgium, Germany, Japan, Poland, the United Kingdom and the United States. Taking into account the diversity of international fair trade places, the IFTTC explicitly recognizes the FINE (2001) definition of fair trade, but also the Charter of Fair Trade Principles agreed between the WFTO and Fairtrade International (2009). This is important as among other things, the Charter outlines the validity of both the product certification and the integrated supply chain approach to fair trade practice. This underpinning leads the committee to suggest that while it might be advantageous for new fair trade towns schemes to follow the five goals model (above), 'Any national campaign should include a whole range of fair trade products in particular both Fairtrade certified (and other fair trade certifiers) products if present and also independently recognized fair trade products (for example, from WFTO certified members) when these are present in the national context' (IFTT 2013). Furthermore, it is suggested that national campaigns are facilitated by a number of different national organizations or a coalition (IFTT 2013). This therefore devolves the construction of legitimate fair trade activities to individual countries, and, again, this can be seen to contribute to the formal democratic architecture of the fair trade movement.

On the other side of the power dynamic, despite a previous lack of involvement in fair trade places, the WFTO have moved to redress this. Specifically, connections between those developing fair trade towns in Poland and the WFTO in Europe resulted in the initial development of a relationship. In 2013, therefore, the WFTO passed a motion that encouraged its members to participate in fair trade places and established support for WFTO representation within the IFTTC (WFTO 2013). Only time will tell if this decision has a significant impact on feeding into the democratization of place-based fair trade activities.

BRINGING THE STATE BACK IN? THE ROLE AND POTENTIAL OF FAIR TRADE NATIONS

As identified by Fridell (2010), the fair trade movement of the 1980s was composed of both state and civil society activism for fairer international trade architecture. While local government involvement in fair trade towns has arguably begun the process of reintroducing the state following its wider exit under neoliberalizing forces, the emergence of Fair Trade Nations demands attention as a potential further development.

Here again, the initiative originally emerged from the civil society component of the fair trade movement as an effort to expand place-based campaigning. Following on from gaining recognition for Cardiff as the world's first Fairtrade capital city in 2004, the Wales Fair Trade Forum (WFTF) identified the possibility to work towards similar recognition for the country of Wales as a whole. Mirroring the multi-stakeholder group in Garstang, the WFTF was composed of representatives from a range of organizations. Initially, this included Fair Do's (a dedicated fair trade shop), Tearfund, Oxfam Cymru, Catholic Agency for Overseas Development (CAFOD), Christian Aid and the Co-op Group, and later it expanded to include representatives of Fairtrade Towns from across Wales. Another important change to the group's composition occurred when the Oxfam representative moved to work for the devolved Welsh Assembly Government (WAG).[6] This connected the activists' initiative to the power of the state, initially facilitated by support for the idea from a cross-party selection of Welsh Assembly Members. Simultaneously, members of the WFTF approached the Fairtrade Foundation to help develop a form of national-level recognition. However, the Foundation were again reserved: they felt that recognizing an entire country was 'way beyond our remit' (cited in Smith 2011, 104), and, therefore, the WFTF initiated 'discussions with other organizations in Wales to determine the requirements for the Fair Trade Country' (WFTF 2003, 1). Towards the end of this process, it was agreed that the devolved nation of Scotland would also participate to strengthen the initiative and provide a competitive element – and it was at this time that the conceptual representation of the ideas shifted from a Fair Trade Country to one of a Fair Trade Nation (Fisher 2012).

During initial conversations in Wales it was felt that a fair trade place at the national scale should focus on a threefold agenda of international trade justice, promoting Fairtrade goods and also supporting the consumption of 'locally' and nationally produced food. This again offered the opportunity to use the framing of place to gather a range of interests and highlight connections between them. Early discussion included recognition of a range of fair trade governance systems. It was proposed that a certain number of shops accredited by the British Association of Fair Trade Shops (BAFTS) should be required. Ultimately, however, expecting the establishment of new fair trade infrastructure was rejected and developments focused instead on other criteria that could be assessed quantitatively – as well as promoted within a timeframe to suit the political agenda of the WAG. It was agreed that an independent committee made up of key figures from the fair trade movement would assess the criteria. The committee included representatives from prominent UK alternative trade organizations (ATOs), such as Traidcraft, development organizations and the WFTO, although no one from the Fairtrade Foundation was involved. Following this procedure the first stage criteria were met first by Wales in 2008 and then Scotland in early 2013 (following the convening of a separate Social Audit Committee, of which the author was a participant). The criteria required:

- 100 per cent of counties/local authorities to have active fair trade groups working towards fair trade status;
- 55 per cent of Local Authority areas to have fair trade status, with 10 per cent annual increase in following years;
- 100 per cent of cities to have fair trade status;
- Minimum 55 per cent of towns (based on the Office of National Statistics and General Register Office for Scotland figures of towns with population of 5000 or more) to have active fair trade groups working towards fair trade status;
- 60 per cent of higher education institutions to have active fair trade groups working towards fair trade status;
- a 5 per cent increase each year of the proportion of the population who know about fair trade (initial target of 50 per cent, ultimately to reach 75 per cent);
- 75 per cent of people to buy a fair trade product every year;
- 40 per cent of people to regularly buy fair trade products.

On first reading, it might be assumed that using the signifier 'fair trade' within the Fair Trade Nation criteria implies an open, as opposed to a narrow, approach to defining associated activity. However, while the governments of Scotland and Wales have tended to avoid the use of trademarked signifiers,[7] the requirements of the Fair Trade Nation initiative are still largely focused on Fairtrade certified goods. This is because the majority of criteria are linked to the achievement of certain numbers and percentages of Fairtrade Foundation recognitions for towns and schools and so on. Having said this, however, in addition to the flexibility of the individual schemes (noted above), both Fair Trade Wales and the Scottish Fair Trade Forum (the bodies taking forward the Fair Trade Nation campaigns) promote the discourse of alternative fair trade practices – including those of the WFTO and dedicated FTOs. Furthermore, while the Fairtrade Foundation does provide some limited, although valuable, funding for these coordinating bodies, greater freedom to construct a sense of fair trade place is provided by core financing from the respective devolved governments and other independent sources. For this reason, these national-scale fair trade places are perhaps best understood as localities in which fair trade activity can continue to be shaped and within which future developments could realistically promote more radical interpretations of fair trade principles. After all, as the people of Scotland wait for the greater autonomy promised during their recent referendum on full independence, members of the fair trade movement are no doubt already reformulating what they expect of an increasingly powerful state, already strongly committed to the idea of Fair Trade Nationhood.

CONCLUSION

This chapter has examined the development of formally recognized fair trade places in geographies traditionally associated with fair trade consumer markets. As such, these places are understood as offering a response to an increasingly globalized and economically uneven world. The potential for this emerges from an explicitly more-developed sense of historical and economic positionalities, where activities aiming at addressing perceived international social inequalities are explicitly embedded in collective identity.

Within this broad conceptualization, the chapter has drawn on the socially constructed understanding of place and its associated meaning. Analysis has therefore explicitly considered the multiplicities of interpretation and fundamental contestations identified in current research. More specifically, the chapter has focused on some aspects of how fair trade places offer a further arena for the active contestation over what is legitimately accepted as fair trade activity. Indeed, research in this area must be seen as of genuine significance as it is argued that while fair trade places extend the procedural trappings of democratization of meaning, associated processes will inevitably be shaped by surrounding political economies. For this reason, academic analysis has and should continue to highlight the opportunities for stakeholders to influence fair trade in the future.

Reflecting back, it is suggested that stakeholders of fair trade places have engaged in this dynamic on three planes. First, fair trade places have the opportunity to define the scope and methods of fair exchange through consumption and promotion of certain fair trade models. Here place-based campaigns can influence if fair trade should remain associated only with economic inequality of the international system or if it should also consider its relationship with domestic places of production. Second, and more centrally, fair trade towns, schools and nations can cast a vote proportional to their efforts and resources as to which trade practices, and therefore accreditations, are acceptable in responding to its positionality in the world. Third and finally, fair trade places also have the opportunity to go beyond consumption and re-contextualize themselves in the trade justice movement, raising wider awareness and agitating for structural change.

Starting with the development of the world's first fair trade town in Garstang, the focus has primarily been on overcoming individualized consumption of isolated actors and creating collective purchasing patterns through more intense consumer coordination. As the idea of a fair trade place first emerged, the perceived best vehicle for this was promotion around the Fairtrade Mark, and it was this approach that was adopted by the United Kingdom's Fairtrade Foundation in pioneering formalized place-based campaigns. However, looking at the practices of individual places within this framework resonates with the comment of Lamb (2008, 46), that the intertwining of a certification label and the concept of place 'was a branding-controllers' nightmare and a campaigners' dream come true'. This is because the practices of different fair trade places show a range of willingness to remain within this initial discursive and governance framing. Although some places have met the expectations of status award and little more, others have found their understanding requires the specific championing of dedicated FTOs and wider awareness raising. Although the case study evidence discussed above is insufficient to draw any representative understandings, it nevertheless illustrates the potential of fair trade places to reconnect with more radical practices of the movement. A key finding of existing research is that more radical and proactive efforts are likely to emerge where communities of practice draw on discursive understandings of fair trade that originate from outside the formal Fairtrade Town Campaign.

This potential for diversity is also well illustrated at the international level by other countries that have adopted formal systems of recognition for fair trade places. While some of these have maintained close alignment with the Fairtrade Foundation's initial model, others have explicitly incorporated other fair trade practices and their accreditations, such as that offered by the WFTO and specific national membership bodies. As recommended by the emerging IFTTC, the independent administration of formal recognition for fair trade places then leaves these to make their own choices about how to campaign: a potential development that the Fairtrade Foundation might consider as a means to escape the inherent tensions of efforts to function as both an advocacy and licensing organization.

At the final layer of democratization, the emergence of Wales and then Scotland as claiming Fair Trade Nationhood, offers perhaps the most radical opportunity to bring the state back into the fair trade movement. Indeed, the possibility for increasing devolution in Scotland (and Wales), aligned to the continued claim to operate as a Fair Trade Nation, offers an unprecedented opportunity to embed state activities with the principles of fair trade. However, as has been discussed above, the formal criteria for the self-identification as a Fair Trade Nation have thus far remained strongly associated with the wider UK focus of fair trade place on Fairtrade goods. In this sense, individual places (such as East Dunbartonshire, Scotland), other national fair trade town campaigns (such as New Zealand and Australia) and the leadership of the IFTTC, offer important learning for alternative approaches to fair trade place-making at a variety of scales.

NOTES

1. This classification is drawn from the complementary conceptual constructions of Fridell (2010) and Wilkinson (2007, 223–224).
2. For a more developed ontological discussion see Smith (2013a), and for a discussion of the meaning associated with fair trade see Steven Suranovic's chapter in this volume.
3. It is the intention of the Fairtrade Foundation to alter the requirements of Fairtrade Towns status to a more process-based system, which will mirror changes in producer Fairtrade certification and allow a more self-defined set of benchmarks against which progress is evaluated.
4. Discussions with Fairtrade Foundation representatives over a number of years.
5. IFAT is the previous name of the World Fair Trade Organization (WFTO).
6. The Welsh Assembly Government was the previous title of the now Welsh Government, prior to the more recent stage of further devolution.
7. The tendency to replace the trademarked term of Fairtrade with Fair Trade has been primarily to reduce legal risk previously understood to emerge from the prohibition of preferring specific brands by the European Union Procurement Directives. However, an important reform came in 2014 which explicitly allows the specification of sustainability certification.

REFERENCES

Agnew, John (2011), 'Space and place', in John A. Agnew (ed.), *The SAGE Handbook of Geographical Knowledge*, London: Sage, pp. 316–330.

Alexander, Andrew and Alex Nicholls (2006), 'Rediscovering consumer–producer involvement: A network perspective on fair trade marketing', *European Journal of Marketing*, 40 (11/12), 1236–1253.

Bacon, Christopher M. (2010), 'Who decides what is fair in fair trade? The agri-environmental governance of standards, access, and price', *Journal of Peasant Studies*, 37 (1), 111–147.

Crowther, Bruce and Joe Human (2011), 'The Fairtrade revolution in progress: Campaigning for justice', in John Bowes (ed.), *The Fair Trade Revolution*, London: Pluto Press, pp. 89–106.

Danermark, Berth, Mats Ekstrom, Lisekotte Jakobsen and Jan Ch. Karlsson (2005), *Explaining Society: Critical Realism in the Social Sciences*, London: Routledge.

Doherty, Bob, Iain A. Davies and Sophi Tranchell (2013), 'Where now for fair trade?', *Business History*, 55 (2), 161–189.

Fair Trade Association Australia and New Zealand (2013), 'Fair Trade Communities: Towns guidelines', http://www.fta.org.au/uploads/1/9/7/4/19743811/fair_trade_assoc_communities_towns_guidelines.doc (accessed 20 March 2014).

Fair Trade Association Australia and New Zealand (2014), 'The voice of fair trade', available at http://www.fta.org.au/ (accessed 20 March 2014).

Fair Trade Canada (2012), 'Fair trade towns action guide', available at http://fairtrade.ca/sites/default/files/Fair%20Trade%20Towns%20Action%20Guide%20-%20REVISION%20feb2012.pdf (accessed 20 March 2014).

Fairtrade Foundation (2009a), 'Fairtrade Towns: The five goals', available at http://www.fairtrade.org.uk/get_involved/campaigns/fairtrade_towns/the_5_goals.aspx (accessed 1 May 2011).

Fairtrade Foundation (2009b), 'Two royal honours for Fairtrade pioneers', available at http://www.fairtrade.org.uk/press_office/press_releases_and_statements/january_ 2008/two_royal_honours_for_fairtrade_pioneers.aspx (accessed 13 November 2009).

Fairtrade Foundation (2011a), 'About Fairtrade Universities and Colleges', available at http://www.fairtrade.org.uk/get_involved/campaigns/fairtrade_universities/about_fairtrade_universities.aspx (accessed 28 January 2014).

Fairtrade Foundation (2011b), 'New Fairtrade Schools award FAQs', available at http://www.fairtrade.org.uk/schools/faqs/new_award_faqs.aspx (accessed 28 January 2014).

Fairtrade Foundation (2011c), 'Places of worship', available at http://www.fairtrade.org.uk/get_involved/campaigns/fairtrade_places_of_worship/default.aspx (accessed 28 January 2014).

Fairtrade Foundation (2014), 'Fairtrade Towns', available at http://www.fairtrade.org.uk/get_involved/campaigns/fairtrade_towns/towns_list.aspx (accessed 25 June 2014).

FINE (2001), 'Fair trade definition and principles', available at http://www.fair-trade-hub.com/support-files/fair-trade-definition.pdf (accessed 01 May 2011).

Fisher, Eleanor (2009), 'Policy arena introduction: The policy trajectory of fair trade', *Journal of International Development*, 21 (7), 985–1003.

Fisher, Eleanor (2012), '"The Fair Trade Nation"': Market-oriented development in devolved European regions?', *Human Organization*, 77 (3), 255–267.

Fridell, Gavin (2004), 'The university and the moral imperative of fair trade coffee', *Journal of Academic Ethics*, 2 (1), 141–159.

Fridell, Gavin (2010), 'Fair trade, free trade and the state', *New Political Economy*, 15 (3), 457–470.

Garstang Fairtrade (2000–2014), 'Making Garstang a Fairtrade Town', available at http://www.garstangfairtrade.org.uk/history/index.html (accessed 28 January 2014).

Garstang Fairtrade (2010–2011), 'Making Garstang a Fairtrade Town', available at http://www.garstangfairtrade.org.uk/history/index.html (accessed 31 January 2011).

Gendron, Corinne, Véronique Bisaillon and Ana Rance (2009), 'The institutionalization of fair trade: More than just a degraded form of social action', *Journal of Business Ethics*, 86 (S1), 63–79.

IFTT (International Fair Tade Towns) (2013), 'International fair trade towns guidelines 2013', available at http://www.fairtradetowns.org/resources/reports/international-fair-trade-towns-guidelines-2013/ (accessed 22 January 2014).

Lamb, Harriet (2008), *Fighting the Banana Wars and Other Fairtrade Battles*, London: Rider.

Low, William and Eileen Davenport (2007), 'To boldly go … exploring ethical spaces to re-politicise ethical consumption and fair trade', *Journal of Consumer Behaviour*, 6 (5), 336–348.

Malpass, Alice, Paul Cloke, Clive Barnett and Nick Clarke (2007), 'Fairtrade urbanism? The politics of place beyond place in the Bristol Fairtrade City campaign', *International Journal of Urban and Regional Research*, 31 (3), 633–645.

Massey, Doreen (1991), 'A global sense of place', *Marxism Today*, 38, 24–29.

Mohan, Sushil (2010), *Fair Trade without the Froth*, London: Institute of Economic Affairs.

Preuss, Lutz (2009), 'Addressing sustainable development through public procurement: The case of local government', *Supply Chain Management: An International Journal*, 14 (3), 213–223.

Reed, Darryl (2009), 'What do corporations have to do with fair trade? Positive and normative analysis from a value chain perspective', *Journal of Business Ethics*, 86 (S1), 3–26.

Samuel, Anthony (2013), 'An empirical study of the marketing dynamics of the Fairtrade Towns movement', PhD thesis, Cardiff University, available at http://orca.cf.ac.uk/47570/1/2013%20Samuel%20A%20J.pdf (accessed 25 June 2014).

Samuel, Anthony and Louise Emanuel (2012), 'Fairtrade Towns: Place(ing) responsibility', *International Journal of Urban and Extra Urban Studies*, 2 (2), 191–203.

Smith, Alastair M. (2011), 'Fair trade, public procurement and sustainable development: A case study of Malawian rice in Scotland', PhD thesis, School of Planning and Geography and ESRC Centre for Business Relationships, Sustainability and Society, Cardiff University, available at http://orca.cf.ac.uk/10706/ (accessed June 25, 2014).

Smith, Alastair M. (2013a), 'What does it mean to do fair trade? Ontology, praxis, and the "Fair for Life" certification system', *Social Enterprise Journal*, 9 (1), 53–72.

Smith, Alastair M. (2013b), 'Cross-border innovation in south–north fair trade supply chains: The opportunities and problems of integrating fair trade governance into northern public procurement', in Diego Vazquez Brust, Joseph Sarkis and James Cordeiro (eds.), *Collaboration for Sustainability and Innovation in the Global South: A Role for South-Driven Sustainability?*, London: Springer, pp. 87–105.

Smith, Alastair M. (2014), 'Access to the Fairtrade system: The geography of certification for social justice', *Food Chain*, 4 (1), 49–65.

Tallontire, Anne and Valerie Nelson (2013), 'Fair trade narratives and political dynamics', *Social Enterprise Journal*, 9 (1), 28–52.

Trentmann, F. (2007), 'Before "fair trade": Empire, free trade, and the moral economies of food in the modern world', *Environment and Planning D: Society and Space*, 25 (6), 1079–1102.

WFTF (2003), Minutes of the Wales Fair Trade Forum.

WFTO (2013), 'WFTO resolution on fair trade towns – May 2013', available at http://www.fairtradetowns.org/resources/reports/wfto-resolution-on-fair-trade-towns-may-2013/ (accessed 25 June 2014).

WFTO and Fairtrade International (2009), 'A charter of fair trade principles', available from: http://www.wfto.com/index.php?option=com_content&task=view&id=1082&Itemid=334 (accessed 18 August 2010).

Wilkinson, John (2007), 'Fair trade: Dynamic and dilemmas of a market oriented global social movement', *Journal of Consumer Policy*, 30 (3), 219–239.

Wilson, Bradley R. and Joe Curnow (2013), 'Solidarity™: Student activism, affective labor, and the fair trade campaign in the United States', *Antipode*, 45 (3), 565–583.

PART III

THE BUSINESS OF FAIR TRADE

12. Cooperatives, corporations and fair trade

Darryl Reed

INTRODUCTION

Fair trade is one of the most prominent socio-economic development initiatives of the past several decades. The nature of its contributions to development, however, are contested, with some advocates claiming that it re-embeds the economy back into society, while critics argue that it functions to legitimatize a larger, neoliberal globalization project. What cannot be disputed about fair trade is the fact that it has become an increasingly complex practice over the years. This complexity, along with different normative conceptions of development, helps to account for the radically different evaluations of fair trade.

The premise of this chapter is that a more nuanced analysis of the complex nature of fair trade, especially the relationships between its key economic actors, cooperatives and corporations, can provide better insights into its functioning and its potential for promoting development. In taking up such an analysis, this chapter restricts its scope to the *Fairtrade* network associated with Fairtrade International.[1] Two primary characteristics contribute to the economic complexity in Fairtrade, namely different norms of behavior and the variety of firms involved. For ease of presentation, this chapter abstracts from the wide diversity within Fairtrade by distinguishing two sets of norms (namely, fair trade principles and minimum standards) and two types of firms (namely, cooperatives and corporations). This framework allows for a delineation of different practices within Fairtrade (e.g., by the distinction of different forms of value chains) as well as a systematic analysis of the dynamics of cooperation and competition (which can occur along or across different types of value chains). (For a discussion of the different ways in which trade could be considered 'fair' or 'unfair', see Steven Suranovic's chapter in this volume.)

How such an analysis can account for the varying evaluations of Fairtrade, as well as provide the basis for more effective strategic interventions, is argued in the following manner. First, a short review of the notion of cooperation (and competition) within and among firms is offered. Then a brief account is provided of how Fairtrade changed the previous dynamics of value-based cooperation under alternative trade schemes by introducing an interest-based form of cooperation (involving minimum standards). Next, the utility of value chain analysis for the investigation of cooperation and competition is explained, along with the stakes involved in different patterns of cooperation and competition. The following two sections analyze the dynamics of cooperation and competition in Fairtrade, first within individual value chains and then across different types of value chains, indicating how they align with different models of development.

COMPETITION AND COOPERATION IN BUSINESS

The neoclassical economic tradition elaborates the potential benefits of markets for organizing economic activity. This model explains how, under conditions of perfect competition (ideal markets), goods and services are allocated on the basis of the marginal productivity and the cost of different factors of production. This process effectively drives (economic) profits to zero. Under these circumstances, entrepreneurs are motivated to innovate (by creating new products or new production techniques), so as to gain the short-term profits that innovation allows. The net effect of these dynamics is 'consumer sovereignty', a situation in which consumers enjoy an increasingly wide range of products at low prices. Of course, the conditions of ideal markets (which include large numbers of buyers and sellers, perfect information, zero transaction costs and no negative externalities) never hold true in practice. One result of this situation is that it is often more effective for actors to organize economic activity on the basis of cooperation rather than competition.

Forms and Benefits of Cooperation

Ronald Coase (1937) provides one of the most influential arguments for organizing economic activity on a more collaborative basis. In his account of the firm, he argues that transaction costs often make it more effective to organize economic activity on a non-market basis (e.g., hierarchy). Further developments in business practice and the literature over the years have indicated that there are other alternatives to markets than hierarchical forms of collaboration within firms. Individual firms can cooperate through joint ventures and strategic alliances, for example. Depending upon the forms of cooperation employed, specific benefits can be gained (e.g., access to information, established distribution channels, proprietary technology), whose ultimate contribution is to help firms maximize profits.

In a global economy, different types of cooperation can be employed in different configurations across the length of complex, transnational chains. One of the more insightful accounts of the diversity of approaches to coordinating transnational production is provided by Gereffi et al. (2005), who posit markets and hierarchy as occupying two polar positions as forms of governance of value chains. In between these extremes they identify three other cooperative (or network-based) approaches – modular, relational and captive. They argue that the choice of governance options will be related to three key factors: 1) the complexity of information and knowledge transfer required for transactions; 2) the degree to which information can be codified; and 3) the capabilities of actual and potential suppliers with respect to the transactions required. Again, the specific benefits provided by adapting different forms of networked cooperation will vary according to the forms of cooperation involved, along with other factors, such as the sector, position on the value chain and specific assets of the actors.

Another form of economic cooperation involves the use of non-state regulatory initiatives. The best-known example, the International Organization for Standardization (ISO) created in 1947, has historically been involved in the development of technical standards. More recently, however, firms and other organizations have been establishing new regulatory initiatives that set normative (labor, environmental) standards for business behavior. Insofar as consumers are willing to pay a premium for products or firms that meet such standards, these initiatives create niche 'ethical markets' which potentially provide benefits in the form of higher profit margins (and opportunities for rehabilitating tarnished images).[2]

Interest-Based Cooperation

The different non-market approaches to coordinating activity among firms and along value chains constitute forms of economic cooperation. Such types of cooperation, however, are usually of a particular kind. They are aimed at helping firms achieve their presumed primary goal of maximizing profits. Through 'interest-based' cooperation, actors do not seek a broader social good. If such a result occurs, it is purely an unintended by-product. Nor are they intending to help their partners when they cooperate. While the notion of cooperation implies that all partners must receive some benefit in order to participate, the practice does not necessarily entail an equal (or fair) distribution of benefits.

Rather, each partner tries to seek the maximum benefit for itself. In this regard, there is always a strong element of competition embedded in this approach to cooperation (Gereffi et al. 2005).

While virtually all firms engage in interest-based cooperation, the larger they are and the more diverse their ownership, the more likely they are to engage exclusively in this form of cooperation (Williamson 1970). In smaller firms with more concentrated ownership, it may be possible for decisions to be made, at least occasionally, on a basis other than profit maximization. Dynamics of corporate culture and problems of generating consensus on norms among a diverse ownership group, however, undermine such possibilities in large, widely held corporations (Bowman 1996).

Value-Based Cooperation

In contrast to interest-based cooperation, some types of firms may cooperate on the basis of values. These include not-for-profit enterprises, social entrepreneurs, B Corporations and small proprietors. This chapter concentrates on cooperatives for two reasons. First, cooperatives have played a prominent role in the practice of Fairtrade, especially at the level of production (producer coops) and retail (coop supermarkets). Second, cooperatives are the proto-typical, value-based cooperative organizations in that their commitment to cooperation is institutionalized in ways that do not happen in other business forms (Quarter et al. 2009). First, since the 19th century, cooperatives have subscribed to a common set of cooperative principles. These require, among other things, open membership (i.e., membership is voluntary and equally open to all), democratic control (on the basis of 'one member, one vote'), equitable benefits to members based upon their economic participation, autonomy, a commitment to education, cooperation among cooperatives and concern for the broader community.[3] Second, some cooperative principles are incorporated into cooperative law. These typically include open membership, democratic control and member benefit (Quarter et al. 2009).

COOPERATION AND COMPETITION WITHIN FAIRTRADE

Before the establishment of Fairtrade certification, other types of initiatives connected Southern producers with Northern consumers. In the 1950s and 1960s, 'charity trade', involving the importing of handicrafts made by vulnerable groups (e.g., refugees), arose. The 1970s and 1980s saw the emergence of 'alternative trade' movements (which critiqued the dominant trade system and sought to establish alternative trading relations based upon solidarity) and 'solidarity trade' (which supported governments and movements in the South that were promoting alternative models of development, such as in Tanzania and Nicaragua). What these initiatives had in common was that they were based upon forms of value-based cooperation (Low and Davenport 2006).

The advent of Fairtrade labeling and certification in the late 1980s, which for many marks the transition from alternative trade to Fairtrade, introduced a new dynamic in efforts to link small producers more directly to Northern consumers. While producers favored their value-based, alternative trade relations with Northern cooperative retailers and intermediaries, low levels of demand led them to explore the prospects for distributing their products through conventional retail outlets under more favorable conditions. Certification facilitated this by generating an ethical market based upon interest-based cooperation.

Certification established a system of cooperation in which small producer cooperatives and corporate retailers and intermediaries could better pursue their narrow interests (e.g., developing niche markets which command higher prices) without sharing substantial values. Certification facilitates such interest-based forms of cooperation through the setting of standards and the establishment of monitoring systems that provide assurance to consumers that 'ethical value added' is being generated.

While some cooperative retailers and intermediaries in the North continued to trade directly with small producers, others adopted the new Fairtrade label. In joining the Fairtrade labeling network, Northern cooperatives not only adopted the minimum standards (meant to guide participation of traditional, corporate actors) but also continued to operate on their original value-based norms, or 'fair trade principles'. Several standards-setting organizations and coalitions of fair trade organizations developed their own iterations of these fair trade principles, which typically overlapped to a great extent with the cooperative principles outlined above (Crowell and Reed 2009).[4]

This combination of minimum standards (which initially required sourcing from small producer cooperatives) and Fairtrade principles differentiates Fairtrade from other ethical markets. In most ethical markets there are two areas of competition: the first with actors who are not certified and the second with actors who are also certified. In the former, competition is based on ethical values. In the latter, competition is based upon other product features (e.g., quality, convenience and price).

In Fairtrade, however, the situation is different. Two separate sets of norms – minimum standards and Fairtrade principles – allow for competition within Fairtrade based upon different values. This situation causes confusion about what Fairtrade is (e.g., a practice designed to incorporate more small producers into the existing trade system versus a movement to reform/replace an unjust trade system) and raises questions about what 'fairness' denotes (e.g., paying minimum prices versus equality of opportunity to pursue one's development goals). This situation of actors being held to different sets of norms inevitably raises the question of whether there is 'unfair' competition within the system of Fairtrade. The issue was further complicated when labeling bodies extended the certification of production to include agricultural estates and the use of hired labor. This introduced a new form of competition within Fairtrade – between small producers and large estates – highlighting a practical tension within Fairtrade as a development model (Reed 2012).

VALUE CHAINS AS A TOOL FOR ANALYZING COOPERATION AND COMPETITION

To better understand the dynamics of cooperation and competition within Fairtrade, it is helpful to return to the notion of value chains. While value chain analysis has been used successfully to examine trading relations among conventional, for-profit firms, it needs to be adapted in order to understand Fairtrade dynamics. Specifically, value chain analysis has not adequately captured the dynamics of cooperation and competition in Fairtrade because it does not take into account the role of value-based (or what some might call 'mission-driven') firms, which cooperate on a different basis than investor-owned corporations (Reed 2009). This difference in motivation allows for a qualitatively different form of governance of Fairtrade value chains, one that reflects a value-based form of cooperation.

Distinguishing different forms of value chain within Fairtrade has become especially important due to the increasingly dominant presence of corporate actors. To more easily understand the importance of this task, a model of Fairtrade value chains can be developed using the following simplifying assumptions: 1) there are three levels of activity in the chain (producer, intermediary and retail); 2) which are carried out by either of two types of firms (corporate or cooperative); 3) which employ either interest-based cooperation exclusively (corporations) or a combination of interest-based cooperation (cooperatives interacting with corporations) and value-based cooperation (cooperatives interacting among each other).

On the basis of these assumptions, four types of Fairtrade value chains can be distinguished (see Table 12.1), which will enable a clearer analysis of competition and cooperation within Fairtrade. The first, a wholly cooperative chain (type one), is similar to the alternative trade model, which involves value-based cooperation among producer, intermediary and retail cooperatives. Second, as some cooperative intermediaries embraced the notion of accessing conventional distribution channels (large supermarkets), they created a new variant of the chain (type two) in which they continued their value-based relationships with producers while engaging in interest-based cooperation with commercial retailers. With the entry of large corporate intermediaries, another variant of the value chain would emerge (type three) as they both distributed their products through conventional retailers and sourced from producer cooperatives on the basis of interest-based cooperation (minimum standards). Finally, the introduction of estate production (e.g., in the case of bananas) would lead to another variant of the value chain (type four), in which corporate actors operate at the retail, intermediate and production levels based upon interest-based forms of cooperation (Reed 2009).

Table 12.1 Four variants of the Fairtrade value chain

Type of the value chain	Level of corporate involvement	(Dominant) Form of cooperation
1) Wholly cooperative	None	Value based
2) Cooperative dominated	Retail	Value based
3) Corporate dominated	Retail, intermediary	Interest based
4) Wholly corporate	Retail, intermediary, production	Interest based

WHAT IS AT STAKE IN COOPERATION AND COMPETITION

Before analyzing the dynamics of cooperation and competition within and across Fairtrade value chains, it is important to clarify the stakes involved. There are various particular potential benefits available through participation in Fairtrade, as well as trade-offs and risks involved in pursuing different forms of cooperation and competition. What is ultimately at stake is a competition between rival conceptions of development. Here the two primary paradigms at play are distinguished.

Fairtrade as Cooperative-Based, Endogenous Development

At the heart of the first Fairtrade certification body, Max Havelaar, was an inchoate vision of Fairtrade as a type of endogenous development characterized by broad-based participation in the ownership and control of the local economy (Mukherjee and Reed 2009). One of its founders, Francisco VanderHoff Boersma (2009), has expressed this understanding of development in terms of the need for an 'alternative market' which is characterized by three principles – *collective autonomy, solidarity and justice* – and largely reflects the spirit and practice of alternative trade. Collective autonomy implies that in order to exercise agency, small producers must be organized in cooperatives and apex bodies. It also means that conventional businesses (retailers and intermediaries) cannot be dominant actors, but rather must participate in the alternative market on the basis of principles and guidelines reflecting the collective autonomy of small producers. The principle of solidarity entails producers and consumers being linked through value-based relations of mutual respect and concern (rather than self-interest). This is facilitated by other value-based organizations acting as intermediaries and retailers. The principle of justice requires that small producers be paid the full cost of production, which is what minimum standards were meant to ensure in the face of interest-based corporate participation.

Such a cooperative-based, endogenous development strategy entails growing value-based forms of cooperation along three different axes – the horizontal (to include more small producers), the vertical (to help small producers move up value chains and participate more fairly in the distribution of the value added along the chain) and the transversal (to facilitate cooperation across different sectors to promote a diversified local economy that is locally controlled) (Reed forthcoming).

Fairtrade as Socially Regulated, Corporate-Led Growth

Shortly after the formation of the first certification body, small producers were largely excluded from decision-making processes (see Elizabeth Bennett's and Marie-Christine Renard's chapters in this volume). Although producer organizations would later (re)gain some rights to participate in decision-making, in the interim the certifying bodies made two key decisions that substantially altered the practice of Fairtrade from

VanderHoff Boersma's (2009) vision of an 'alternative market'. First, efforts were undertaken to rapidly grow the market by encouraging more corporate retailers and intermediaries to participate. While small producers generally supported growing the market, at issue were the conditions under which growth should occur. The second, even more controversial decision was to include estate production in Fairtrade. These two decisions gave rise to the dominant position in Fairtrade of the third and fourth forms of value chains described above (Coscione 2014).[5]

These decisions by the labeling bodies had the effect of promoting a different development model. With the introduction of these large corporate value chains into Fairtrade, the goal shifts from one of support for increasing the capacity of small producers (to promote local development) to poverty reduction. Small producers are no longer the prime actors, but rather large corporations become the key players, as they are the ones able to generate the sales of products meeting minimum standards that can lift producers (and workers) out of poverty (Mukherjee and Reed 2009).

COOPERATION AND COMPETITION WITHIN VALUE CHAINS

Within Fairtrade value chains, different dynamics of cooperation and competition operate. These dynamics, discussed further below, can be examined in terms of the primary form of cooperation involved, that is, value based or interest based. As Table 12.1 indicates, the first two Fairtrade value chains – the wholly cooperative and predominantly cooperative – are characterized by value-based cooperation and align more closely with an endogenous model of development. The last two value chains – the predominantly corporate and the wholly corporate – embody interest-based cooperation and promote a corporate-led growth model of development.

Wholly Cooperative Value Chains (Variant One)

Wholly cooperative values chains in Fairtrade largely continue to operate as they did under alternative trade, that is, based entirely upon value-based cooperation (see Manush McConway and Geoff Moore's chapter in this volume). Specifically, intermediaries and retailers are committed to a fairer distribution of value added along the chain (e.g., paying higher than minimum prices, pre-financing), as well as to growing the market (e.g., sourcing exclusively from small producers) and developing local organizational capacity and infrastructure (sharing knowledge, providing additional resources, etc.) (Reed 2009).

With respect to development, this approach to cooperation facilitates the scaling of cooperative practice along three dimensions. First, sourcing exclusively from small producers promotes horizontal growth through the inclusion of more small producers into Fairtrade. Second, the development of organizational capacity through value-based cooperation enables small producers to move up the chain (vertically) and gather more of the value added by engaging in higher levels of processing, developing and marketing their own brands and so on. Third, support for the development of infrastructure and organizational capacity enables producer cooperatives to work across the local economy (transversally), spinning off new businesses and supporting other local cooperatives in ways that promote greater diversity and resilience (Reed forthcoming).

Competition exists in that small producer cooperatives have to compete for the limited demand from cooperative intermediaries and retailers. This situation, however, does not typically result in cost competition among producer organizations. Rather, producer organizations put energy into seeking ways to increase the capacity of organizations and to expand the market. This occurs on a cooperative-to-cooperative basis as well as through national and regional producer cooperative networks (Vander-Hoff Boeresma 2009; Coscione 2014).

Predominantly Cooperative Value Chains (Variant Two)

In cooperative-dominated value chains, value-based cooperation occurs within producer organizations and between producer organizations and cooperative intermediaries. Interest-based cooperation exists between cooperative intermediaries and corporate retailers. The bottom of this chain works in a similar fashion to the wholly cooperative chain, but in the top part retailers have no interest in promoting Fairtrade (except as a niche market) and generally (with some notable exceptions) do not commit to sourcing more than a small percentage of any product line as Fairtrade (Fridell 2009; Barrientos and Smith 2007).

In this chain, cooperative intermediaries, such as Equal Exchange and Planet Bean, still seek to provide support to small producers to enable them to grow along horizontal, vertical and transversal axes but they are limited in their ability to do so by their relationships with the large retailers (Crowell and Reed 2009; Fridell 2009). To the extent that large retailers are able to significantly increase the volume of Fairtrade sales (even if it is only a small percentage of their total sales), this can contribute significantly to horizontal growth of Fairtrade production.

There are fewer possibilities for vertical and transverse growth, however (especially as retailers seek to exert more control over value chains).

In this chain cooperative intermediaries compete to gain access to conventional retail markets (including supplying the 'own brands' of supermarkets). To the degree they do have to compete against each other, cooperative intermediaries try not to engage in cost competition (which comes at the expense of their support for small producers). There are limits to what they can do, however, as increasingly they are also competing with larger conventional intermediaries (Barrientos and Smith 2007; Fridell 2009; Smith 2010).

Predominantly Corporate Value Chains (Variant Three)

In the initial years of Fairtrade, corporations were reluctant to participate. As the market started to grow, corporate retailers and intermediaries did begin to participate, either pushed by pressure from activists or pulled in by the prospect of niche markets. When entering Fairtrade, however, corporations do so with an eye to their own bottom line. This has several basic implications for their practice. First, they typically want to control the value chain, rather than simply buying products from cooperative intermediaries, as this better enables them to control costs and quality. The easiest way to do this is often by trying to keep their existing value chains intact and having their producers become certified. Second, corporate retailers and intermediaries only source as much Fairtrade supply as the market demands. They do not invest in growing the market (e.g., through education, branding) unless they are certain that it will contribute to their profit margins. Similarly, they are reluctant to invest in capacity building of producer organizations unless it directly contributes to their profit margins, such as by ensuring quality, more reliable delivery and so on. Cooperation along this chain is completely interest based. The only value-based cooperation occurs internally within the producer cooperatives themselves (Renard 2010; Smith 2010).

This interest-based form of cooperation has the potential to significantly contribute to horizontal growth of cooperative production as corporate actors have the ability to greatly expand the market. This is only likely to occur, however, in the four Fairtrade markets that do not allow production by large estates (coffee, cocoa, cotton and honey). Moreover, there is virtually no opportunity for producers to move vertically up the chain (by engaging in further processing of their products or developing their own brands), as this would cut into corporate profits. Similarly, an unwillingness of corporations to supply anything but minimum levels of support may result in few resources being available to assist producer cooperatives in extending cooperative relations transversely across local economies.

Within this model there can also be significant competition, especially among small producers. There is some evidence to suggest that corporate actors have tended to favor producer cooperatives that have less experience in Fairtrade, especially producers who are already in their supply chains. One reason is that it may be more costly to establish new supply chains. Another reason is that it may be easier to transfer more of the costs onto newer Fairtrade producer organizations, which are more compliant and do not understand (and are not able to aspire to) the principles of Fairtrade and the broader vision of producer organizations with a longer history of involvement in the fair trade movement (Renard 2010; Smith 2010).

Wholly Corporate Value Chains (Variant Four)

In this final variant of the chain all cooperation is interest based with actors at each level only committing to minimum standards and only engaging in Fairtrade to the degree that it facilitates profit maximization. There is no room for value-based cooperation as none of the firms are value based. With the absence of small producers from this chain, there is little to distinguish this form of Fairtrade from other 'ethical markets' with third-party certification (Reed 2012).

There is still competition in these chains, as intermediaries and retailers may force estates to compete for their market. As many Fairtrade products do not have minimum prices, this can even include cost competition (something that the public does not generally associate with Fairtrade production). Such competition, in principle, should not impact estate workers, to the extent that owners are supposed to respect basic labor rights (health and safety, minimum wage rates, etc.) (Barrientos and Smith 2007).

COMPETITION ACROSS VALUE CHAINS

The presence of different types of chains within Fairtrade means that competition can occur not only along value chains of the same type, but also across different chains. The key difference here is that competition within value chains is typically among the same type of firms (e.g., small producers coops against each other), while competition across chains tends to be among different types of actors, namely cooperative retailers against corporate retailers, cooperative intermediaries against corporate intermediaries and small producer cooperatives against estates.

At issue in this competition are two basic questions. First, there is the concern that such competition may be unfair – either because the rules of Fairtrade under which the different types of firms are competing are unfair or because the actors, routinely functioning as oligopolies, engage in forms of anti-competitive practices to gain advantages in the market. Second, there is the question of how this competition impacts the development aspirations of the actors in question, especially small producers.

Competition between Retailers

With the introduction of corporate retailers into Fairtrade, smaller co-operative retailers (who often acted as intermediaries as well) were concerned that minimum standards would put them at a competitive disadvantage due to their commitment to living up to Fairtrade principles. Practices such as exclusively sourcing Fairtrade products and investing in education implied a higher cost structure. This situation might be surmountable if they could easily distinguish themselves from their corporate competitors, but nothing in the label highlights their commitment (or forces their competitors to be more transparent about their level of participation in Fairtrade) (Barrientos and Smith 2007).

In addition to accusations of a lack of fairness in the rules of Fairtrade, a concern has also arisen about corporate retailers engaging in anti-competitive practices (Fridell 2009; Renard 2005). One example, bait and switch, involves retailers (such as coffee shops) offering a very limited range of Fairtrade products that are not always available and then trying to convince customers to settle for another product (Fridell 2009). Such practices are arguably unfair to cooperative retailers who exclusively source Fairtrade products and small producers, both of whom lose sales through less than transparent business practices.[6]

Another practice is the use of Fairtrade goods, specifically bananas, as cost loss leaders. In the United Kingdom, supermarkets offer Fairtrade bananas at less than their actual cost to lure consumers into the store (on the assumption that they will make up the loss on bananas through other purchases). In addition to the irony inherent in this situation – which contradicts a basic thrust of Fairtrade to educate consumers about the need to pay the full cost of production – there are two issues of fairness here. First, smaller retailers cannot adopt this strategy and therefore will offer Fairtrade goods at higher prices, perhaps resulting in their inability to retain Fairtrade customers. Second, the rapid rise in the demand for

Fairtrade bananas resulting from this practice led to an influx of large estates sourcing bananas. This uncontrolled growth in the market has come to threaten the very existence of small banana producers who cannot compete against estate production (Smith 2010).

The participation of corporate retailers has dramatically increased the availability and sales volume of Fairtrade goods. However, the net benefit to producers is less clear. In the best case scenario, corporate retailers increase the involvement of small producers in Fairtrade (and thereby contribute to an endogenous development model). This would only be expected to occur to a significant extent for producers of the four products only produced by small producers. The impact of corporate retailers is also limited by the small percentage of products they source from Fairtrade producers. These potential impacts, however, are offset by practices that undermine the ability of small producers to move up the value chain and strategies that squeeze smaller cooperative retailers out of the market. In short, without further pressure or restrictions on corporate retailers, their participation in fair trade can be expected to support a corporate-led growth model of development.

The range of tactics to force or induce corporate retailers to behave more fairly is limited. One option mooted has been to encourage retailers themselves to register as Fairtrade traders. The assumption here is that retailers may benefit from increased quality assurance (in niche markets) if they more actively (and fairly) manage their own value chains (Barrientos and Smith 2007). More generally, pressure on retailers must come from either or both of two directions. First, consumers and activists can demand more Fairtrade products, including specific brands with higher ethical value added. The second is competition from the large cooperative supermarkets, which in countries such as the United Kingdom has played an important role in inducing other large retailers to engage in Fairtrade.

Competition between Intermediaries

A similar competitive environment exists at the level of Fairtrade intermediaries, where there are concerns both about the fairness of Fairtrade regulations and about anti-competitive practices. Like cooperative retailers, cooperative intermediaries find themselves at a competitive disadvantage because of the combination of their commitment to higher standards (discussed above), which impact their cost structures, and the failure of the label to signal the difference to consumers between these two practices (Fridell 2009; Renard 2005).

Cooperative intermediaries may also be disadvantaged by the anti-competitive practices of corporate intermediaries and retailers. One behavior involves abuses of the label (including efforts to confuse consumers). Another that can be particularly damaging is the use of slotting fees, whereby retailers charge suppliers to place their goods on supermarket shelves. This practice functions as a barrier to entry to small cooperative firms, while large corporate intermediaries are not only more able to pay such fees, but are also more capable of negotiating around them. The concern is that as larger corporate intermediaries develop their own Fairtrade brands, (unfair) use of their market power (rather than any inherent ethical or quality features of their products) is pushing cooperative intermediaries (who offer more ethical value added) off of large supermarket shelves. As a result, the latter are increasingly forced to survive by accessing cooperative distribution channels exclusively (Renard 2005; Smith 2010).

The increasingly dominant position of corporate intermediaries in Fairtrade mirrors in many respects the presence of corporate retailers. Insofar as they extend the market for goods produced by small producers, this may facilitate endogenous development by increasing participation in Fairtrade among small producers. However, most of their other practices (including their tight control over the supply chain and their predilection to source from estates) and their marginalization of cooperative intermediaries undermine efforts by small producers to pursue endogenous development on the vertical and transversal planes.

A variety of regulatory changes could be undertaken to address concerns about fairness within the label (and support an endogenous development model). These might include minimum purchasing requirements by intermediaries, disclosure regarding the percentage of Fairtrade goods sourced, a distinction within the label to recognize different levels of commitment to sourcing Fairtrade, differential fee structures and stricter control over the label (to cut down on practices designed to deceive customers). The obvious risk in introducing such measures would be their potential to decrease corporate participation (and Fairtrade sales). Other forms of anti-competitive practices (e.g., dumping, establishing barriers to entry) in which corporations regularly engage are even more difficult to address. Some measures could be taken, however, such as regulations to forbid the sale of Fairtrade products below their cost of production.

Competition between Producers

The third area where competition between corporate and cooperative actors occurs is at the level of primary production. The basic regulatory concern is that two types of actors, small producers and large estates, are competing against each other in a situation in which one group is at a distinct disadvantage. Several factors come into play. First, small producers do not enjoy the same economies of scale as large estates. Second, they do not have the same access to capital, which limits their ability to improve their efficiency and quality control. Third, sourcing from small producers involves higher transaction costs and less quality control for intermediaries. The resulting higher costs structures make corporate actors more inclined to work with large estates, which small producers fear could eventually result in their marginalization within (or elimination from) Fairtrade (Coscione 2014). What makes this practice unfair is that the label, originally founded by small producers, does not enable consumers to distinguish between the two forms of production.

In addition to issues of regulation, there are also concerns that estates might be employing anti-competitive practices that unfairly provide them with further advantages. One major issue is whether estates are less likely to produce in more ecologically responsible ways than producer cooperatives (which explicitly adopt a principle of care for the community). While the use of industrial agricultural methods (e.g., mono-cropping, heavy use of herbicides and pesticides) results in huge environmental costs (e.g., soil degradation and contamination, decreased biodiversity), externalizing these costs could unfairly function as a competitive advantage vis-à-vis more responsible producers. While few studies exist on this issue, there is arguably good cause for concern given critiques of the practices of Fairtrade estates and the general concern of corporate efforts to undermine Fairtrade and organic standards (Dolan 2010; Jaffee and Howard 2010).

A variety of steps could be taken in support of small producers and to promote an endogenous development strategy. The most ambitious would be to eliminate, or more stringently regulate, the practice of estate production. Another measure would be to distinguish in the label between goods that are produced by small producers and estates. A related option would be to pair the Fairtrade label with other labels that indicated the nature of production, such as the small producers symbol which is being promoted by producers in Latin American and the Caribbean (see Marie-Christine Renard's chapter in this volume) or the recently developed 'coop logo'.

CONCLUSION

Fairtrade has become a complex practice involving different forms of cooperation and competition within and along various types of value chains. Social science analysis can help us to understand this complexity – often invisible or only partially apparent to many – along with its implications. This chapter has tried to show that enmeshed in the complexity are competing practices of Fairtrade, which entail different values and support different models of development. At issue is the degree to which these competing practices are compatible (i.e., are all the actors satisfied with the trade-offs involved) and stable.

Up to this point Fairtrade International as an organization has not confronted the possibility that its competing practices are not compatible and may not be stable. It has not been willing to subscribe to a particular vision for Fairtrade or to favor one practice over the other. The concern of small producers and cooperative organizations is that unless Fairtrade does take a stronger stand, and one that explicitly favors small producers and value-based cooperation, then the tension in Fairtrade between two competing practices, which remain largely invisible to consumers, will be resolved on the basis of the economic power of corporations and to the detriment of those committed to Fairtrade values. This would result in increasing marginalization or the exit of cooperative organizations.

NOTES

1. In this chapter, the term 'Fairtrade' is used to refer to the Fairtrade network, including both the formal partners, such as the national regulatory initiatives, traders and producer organizations, and other actors that support it, such as non-governmental organizations (NGOs) and social movements.
2. Not only can individual firms gain, but the private sector as a whole might benefit from the existence of ethical markets to the extent that they can help to stave off harder forms of regulation that tend to be more costly (Reed 2012).
3. For the exact formulation of the principles, see http://ica.coop/en/what-co-op/co-operative-identity-values-principles.
4. The Fairtrade principles would become an area of contestation. As a result of efforts by some to induce more corporate participation, for example, a reference to Fairtrade as 'an alternative trading system' was dropped in favor of the notion of a 'partnership' (Reed 2009).
5. The decision to rapidly grow the market by encouraging corporate participation with limited restrictions (e.g., no minimum purchases) and by expanding into new product markets dominated by estate production can be explained by several factors, including: 1) the institutional interests of the Fairtrade labeling bodies, which benefited from the fees generated by the rapid expansion of the market; 2) the rise of competing fair trade labeling bodies, which placed competitive pressure upon Fairtrade; and 3) processes of organizational mimesis which occurred with the growth and professionalization of the Fairtrade labeling bodies; 4) which predisposed them to favor incorporating more producers (and workers) into Fairtrade over maintaining or raising standards (Hutchens 2009; Reed 2012).
6. Another example of anti-competitive behavior is companies opting for more corporate-friendly labels with lower standards (see Reed 2012).

REFERENCES

Barrientos, Stephanie and Sally Smith (2007), 'Mainstreaming fair trade in global production networks: Own brand fruit and chocolate in UK supermarkets', in Laura T. Raynolds, Douglas Murray and John Wilkinson (eds.), *Fair Trade: The Challenges of Transforming Globalization*, London and New York: Routledge, pp. 103–122.

Bowman, Scott (1996), *The Modern Corporation and American Political Thought: Law, Power and Ideology*, University Park, PA: Pennsylvania State University Press.

Coase, Ronald H. (1937), 'The notion of the firm', *Economica*, New Series, 4 (16), 386–405.

Coscione, Marco (2014), *In Defense of Small Producers: The Story of CLAC*, Halifax, NS and Winnipeg, Manitoba: Fernwood Books.

Crowell, Erbin and Darryl Reed (2009), 'Fair trade: A model for international co-operation among co-operatives?', in Darryl Reed and J.J. McMurtry (eds.), *Co-operatives in a Global Economy: The Challenges of Co-operating across Borders*, Cambridge: Cambridge Scholars Publishing, pp. 141–177.

Dolan, Catherine (2010), 'Virtual moralities: The mainstreaming of Fairtrade in Kenyan tea fields', *Geoforum*, 41 (1), 33–43.

Fridell, Gavin (2009), 'The co-operative and the corporation: Competing visions of the future of fair trade', *Journal of Business Ethics*, 86 (S1), 81–95.

Gereffi, Geoffrey, John Humphrey and Timothy Sturgeon (2005), 'The governance of global value chains', *Review of International Political Economy*, 12 (1), 78–104.

Hutchens, Anna (2009), *Changing Business: The Globalization of the Fair Trade Movement*, Cheltenham, UK and Northampton, MA: Edward Elgar.

Jaffee, Daniel and Philip Howard (2010), 'Corporate cooptation of Fairtrade and organic standards', *Agriculture and Human Values*, 27 (4), 387–399.

Low, Will and Eileen Davenport (2006), 'Mainstreaming fair trade: Adoption, assimilation, appropriation', *Journal of Strategic Marketing*, 14 (4), 315–327.

Mukherjee, Ananya and Darryl Reed (2009), 'Fair trade and development: What are the implications of mainstreaming?', *Universitas Forum*, 1 (2), 1–8.

Quarter, Jack, Laurie Mook and Ann Armstrong (2009), *Understanding the Social Economy: A Canadian Perspective*, Toronto: University of Toronto Press.

Reed, Darryl (2009), 'What do corporations have to do with fair trade? Positive and normative analysis from a value chain perspective', *Journal of Business Ethics*, 86 (S1), 3–26.

Reed, Darryl (2012), 'The problematic of non-state regulation', in Darryl Reed, Peter Utting and Ananya Mukherjee-Reed (eds.), *Business Regulation and Non-State Actors: Whose Standards? Whose Development?*, Abingdon, UK and New York: Routledge, pp. 19–37.

Reed, Darryl (forthcoming), 'Scaling the social and solidarity economy: The opportunities and limitations of Fairtrade practice', in Peter Utting (ed.), *Social and Solidarity Economy: Beyond the Fringe?*, London: Zed Books.

Renard, Marie-Christine (2005), 'Quality certification, regulation and power in fair trade', *Journal of Rural Studies*, 21 (4), 419–432.

Renard, Marie-Christine (2010), 'In the name of conservation: C.A.F.E. practices and fair trade in Mexico', *Journal of Business Ethics*, 92 (S2), 287–299.

Smith, Sally (2010), 'For love or money? Fairtrade business models in the UK supermarket sector', *Journal of Business Ethics*, 92 (S2), 257–266.

VanderHoff Boersma, Francisco (2009), 'The urgency and the necessity of a different type of market: The perspective of producers organized within the fair trade market', *Journal of Business Ethics*, 86 (S1), 51–61.

Williamson, Oliver E. (1970), *Corporate Control and Business Behavior: An Inquiry into the Effects of Organization Form on Enterprise Behaviour*, New Jersey: Prentice Hall.

13. Fair trade and social enterprise*

Benjamin Huybrechts

INTRODUCTION

The organizational landscape of fair trade has evolved towards increasing complexity and diversity, even when only taking into account organizations that have a central focus on importing and retailing fairly traded products (Becchetti and Huybrechts 2008; Gendron, Bisaillon and Rance 2009; Huybrechts 2012). Hence, ambiguities may occur when delineating and naming these organizations. Moreover, focusing on 'fair trade' as the defining characteristic of 'fair trade organizations' shifts the attention away from how these organizations are structured and from the many similarities they share with other organizations outside the fair trade sector. This chapter suggests that the notion of 'social enterprise' is useful to capture the DNA of organizations focused on fair trade and to locate them within a broader organizational taxonomy. Without seeking to impose a new term that may not resonate for certain actors or regions, this chapter aims to bring two contributions to fair trade research and practice. First, it is suggested that the social enterprise approach is particularly useful as an analytical tool enabling researchers and other stakeholders to capture the evolution and diversification of organizational models in fair trade. Second, the use of a broader organizational approach that is not specific to the fair trade sector allows for connections with similar organizations in other sectors and brings a shift from considering mainly what the organizations do (fair trade in this case) towards also addressing what they are (innovative social enterprise models combining market dynamics with social purpose). This chapter is structured as follows. First, the concept of social enterprise is introduced and discussed. Second, the evolution of the organizational landscape of fair trade (in the North) is summarized. Finally, fair trade organizations are examined in the light of the social enterprise concept, with illustrations from a study in four European countries (Huybrechts 2010a; 2012).

THE CONCEPT OF SOCIAL ENTERPRISE

The notion of social enterprise first emerged in Italy in the 1990s, embodied by the practitioner's review 'Impresa Sociale', and a few years later in the United Kingdom (Borzaga and Defourny 2001; Defourny and Nyssens 2008b). It rapidly diffused across Europe and the United States with a common basis: in short, developing an economic activity as a tool to pursue a social mission. In other words, social enterprises combine market and social dynamics in the context of a common, 'hybrid' organizational model (Billis 2010; Doherty, Haugh and Lyon 2014; Huybrechts 2012). Beyond this broad acceptance, however, there are diverging interpretations on how this combination should be implemented in terms of organizational structure and practices.

These diverging interpretations are related, to a certain extent, to cultural differences (Defourny and Nyssens 2010; Kerlin 2006). In Europe, social enterprise is generally considered, in the eyes of public authorities, scholars and practitioners, as a market-oriented version of the 'social and solidarity economy', thus referring to non-profits and cooperatives that combine a production activity with a general interest orientation (see for instance Defourny 2001; Defourny and Nyssens 2008b; Thompson 2008). Hence, as will be detailed below, it is generally agreed that giving the primacy to the social mission requires governance forms that put a limit to the distribution of profits to private shareholders and that incorporate diverse stakeholders in the decision-making processes. In the United States, social enterprise is seen as the typical expression of social entrepreneurship, for which any type of business aiming for social impact is considered, regardless of governance forms and profit distribution rules. Here, the focus is laid more on the figure of the social entrepreneur and on the innovative pursuit of social impact, rather than on the organizational model and the types of stakeholders associated to decision-making.

Within the universe of social enterprise conceptualizations, several authors (e.g., Defourny and Nyssens 2010; Kerlin 2013) propose to distinguish three complementary approaches: the two main schools of thought developed in the United States as well as the perspective of EMES, an international research network examining social enterprises, initially in Europe and more recently worldwide.[1]

North American Literature on Social Enterprise and Social Entrepreneurship

Two schools of thought are generally distinguised in the North American literature (Battle Anderson and Dees 2006; Kerlin 2006). The first one focuses on how non-profit organizations have developed 'earned income' strategies to better sustain their social mission in the context of decreasing public and philanthropic support. What Dees and Battle Anderson call the 'Social Enterprise' school has then been extended to any type of business relying on commercial incomes to pursue social aims. What matters here is thus that social enterprises rely on market resources, not whether they emerge from the social or from the business sectors, the boundaries between which are seen as increasingly blurring.

The second school of thought, called the 'Social Innovation' school, focuses on innovation rather than on income generation. Authors related to this school suggest that 'social entrepreneurship needs not to be framed in terms of income. It could be more about outcomes, about social change' (Dees and Battle Anderson 2006, 45). The attention here is not related to exclusive market income (although a significant part of market incomes is welcomed) but rather to underlining the commitment of enlightened social entrepreneurs and their support by foundations and networks (Nicholls 2010b).

These two historical visions have been converging over time, as social enterprise and social entrepreneurship conceptions now tend to embrace all the innovative initiatives that seek to create sustainable social change by blending methods from both the business and the social sectors. Hence, most definitions of social entrepreneurship include three ingredients: social mission, innovation and market orientation (Bacq and Janssen 2011; Huybrechts and Nicholls 2012; Nicholls and Cho 2006). The social component can be defined as 'a context, process and/or set of outputs that might reasonably be considered to be in the public benefit' (Nicholls 2010a, 245). Innovation, as broadly defined by the Austrian economist Joseph Schumpeter, refers to new combinations of goods, services, production processes and organizational forms. Three types of 'social innovation' can thus be distinguished (Gardner, Acharya and Yach 2007; Nicholls 2010a, 247): 'in new product and service development (institutional innovation); in the use of existing goods and services in new – more socially productive – ways (incremental innovation); in reframing normative terms of reference to redefine social problems and suggest new solutions (disruptive innovation).' Finally, market orientation involves a stronger emphasis on competition, performance, rational cost recovery strategies and accountability.

EMES Work on Social Enterprise

For nearly two decades, the scholars of the EMES international research network on social enterprise have examined social enterprises in different sectors and countries across Europe and beyond (Defourny 2001; Nyssens 2006). Social enterprises are defined here as 'not-for-profit private organizations providing goods and services directly related to their explicit aim to benefit the community. They rely on a collective dynamics involving various types of stakeholders in their governing bodies, they place a high value on their autonomy and they bear economic risks linked to their activity' (Defourny and Nyssens 2008b, 5). This approach aims to provide an 'ideal type' that 'can help anyone to locate the position of the observed entities relative to one another and … to establish the boundaries of the set of organizations that he or she will consider as that of social enterprises' (Defourny and Nyssens 2008b, 5).

Common among most social entrepreneurship approaches is thus the centrality of commercial activity as a means to pursue social aims, the diversity of organizational vehicles and the innovative dynamics. However, the EMES approach also differs from other approaches in various ways (Defourny and Nyssens 2008a). First of all, the strong connections with the social and solidarity economy bring the emphasis on explicit rules limiting profit distribution and thus legal forms such as non-profit or cooperative organizations. Unlike other approaches, EMES scholars consider that the primacy of social goals is better guaranteed by formal legal provisions than by the sole appraisal of managers or owners. This limits the eligibility of 'business' forms, few of which adopt such provisions. Another difference is the emphasis on democratic and participatory governance, in line with the principles of the social and solidarity economy. Democracy is generally implemented through the 'one member, one vote' principle (rather than 'one share, one vote') and participation means that different stakeholders concerned by the activity should have a voice (formal or at least informal) in organizational decision-making. Finally, unlike the 'Earned Income' school, EMES relies on empirical work to underline the diversity of resources raised by social enterprises on the market but also through public subsidies, gifts and voluntary work (Campi, Defourny and Grégoire 2006; Defourny and Nyssens 2006). These hybrid resources are seen as a natural corollary to the diverse missions of social enterprises: social, economic, but also in many cases political, in the sense of challenging the broader structures of the economic system.

Fair Trade through the Lens of Social Enterprise

The three approaches offer complementary insights of social enterprise and social entrepreneurship at different levels of analysis: individual (profiles and motivations of social entrepreneurs), process (the dynamics of social innovation and social entrepreneurship) and organizational (the specific features and management of social enterprises). At the individual level, fair trade pioneers have been regularly highlighted as successful and inspiring social entrepeneurs in both academic (Zahra, Gedajlovic, Neubaum and Shulman 2009) and practice-oriented literature (Bornstein 2004; Yunus 2006), featuring leading figures such as Frans van der Hoff (UCIRI), Paul Rice (Fair Trade USA), Tristan Lecomte (Alter Eco, France) and Harriet Lamb (Fairtrade Foundation and now Fairtrade International). At the process level, fair trade is often cited as one of the most emblematic examples of social entrepreneurship (Hervieux 2012; Huybrechts and Nicholls 2012; Nicholls 2010a; Santos 2012) and social innovation (Huybrechts 2013; Mulgan, Tucker, Ali and Sanders 2007; Phills, Deiglmeier and Miller 2008). Finally, at the organizational level, fair trade organizations have been depicted as typical social enterprises (Alter 2006; Doherty 2011; Doherty and Huybrechts 2013; Huybrechts 2012; Huybrechts and Defourny 2008) and case studies of fair trade organizations both South and North have been made using this perspective (Davies, Doherty and Knox 2010; Doherty and Tranchell 2007; Huybrechts 2010b). Given the focus chosen here, the remainder of this chapter will further explore the connections between fair trade and social enterprise at the organizational level.

EVOLUTION OF FAIR TRADE ORGANIZATIONS: FROM ATOs TO SOCIAL ENTERPRISES

The first organizations specifically created from the 1960s to the early 1990s to engage in 'fair' trading relationships with producers in the South called themselves alternative trading organizations (ATOs) (Anderson 2009), 'a name stemming from the early days of fair trade where "fair" seemed too weak a description of the vision that these companies had' (Moore 2004, 76; see also the chapter by Manush McConway and Geoff Moore in this volume). ATOs were relatively uniform in terms of organizational structures and practices, including: non-profit legal forms, massive use of volunteers, retailing through world shops and sympathetic networks (such as church groups), low turnovers and reliance on other funding sources such as gifts and public subsidies.

Pioneer ATOs in Europe, including Traidcraft in the United Kingdom, Artisans du Monde in France and GEPA in Germany, were instrumental in the institutionalization of the movement (Huybrechts and Reed 2010). This included, in parallel: 1) the creation of the International Federation for Alternative Trade (IFAT, now World Fair Trade Organization, WFTO) that gradually also included ATOs from the United States (grouped in the North American Alternative Trade Organizations, or 'NAATO', network) and producer organizations and 2) the emergence of labeling initiatives in different countries (see also the chapter by Bob Doherty, Valéry Bezençon and Gaëlle Balineau in this volume).

The configuration of the fair trade landscape dramatically evolved throughout the 1990s with the development of product-based labeling, the increasing corporate participation and the growth of both sales and public awareness (see also the chapter on mainstreaming by Ronan Le Velly in this volume). Most ATOs adapted themselves to this changing context. Some of them supplied food products to corporate retailers, for instance Oxfam-Wereldwinkels in Belgium, Traidcraft in the United Kingdom or CTM Altromercato in Italy. Some of these organizations in parallel developed their world shop networks, increasing their number and attractivity to consumers. Others joined together to create new companies specifically devoted to selling on mainstream markets, for instance in the United Kingdom with Cafédirect, Divine Chocolate and later Liberation Nuts, all created by a consortium of organizations including Twin Trading, Oxfam GB and Traidcraft.

Hence, the vast majority of ATOs gradually changed their initial organizational structures and practices to deal with market partners (retailers or product transformers), increase the attractivity of their products, manage higher sales volumes and consequently higher volumes bought from producers and increase their accountability. In short, ATOs made commercial activities much more central to their operations. This translated into concrete changes. Most ATOs changed their legal form from non-profit towards cooperative (e.g., CTM Altromercato and other Italian fair traders became 'social cooperatives'), limited company (e.g., new fair trade companies in France and the United Kingdom), a group structure combining non-profit and cooperative forms (e.g., several Belgian fair traders) or non-profit and limited company (e.g., Artisans du Monde in France and Traidcraft in the United Kingdom).

Other ATOs remained as non-profit organizations but subject to commercial company accounting and taxation rules (e.g., Oxfam-Magasins du Monde in Belgium). As commercial departments or sub-structures were created, hiring practices increasingly targeted people with a business training or experience. ATOs conceived more aggressive marketing strategies as well as turnover and profitability targets (including for world shops). Finally, governance structures such as boards of directors and General Assemblies evolved from mainly volunteer-based towards 'multi-stakeholder' including workers, volunteers, partners and business experts as well as consumer and producer representatives

(Huybrechts 2010b; Mason and Doherty 2012; see also Elizabeth Bennett's chapter in this volume).

In parallel, many new entrepreneurs and companies with a '100% fair trade focus' have emerged since the late 1990s, constituting what some have called a 'third wave', after the development of ATOs (first wave) and the rise of labeling (second wave) (Poos 2008). These companies often focus on specific products and/or innovative distribution segments such as B2B (business-to-business), Internet or community marketing. Products can be labeled or not, and the distribution channels can be 'mainstream', 'specialized' or both. These entrepreneurs and small businesses focused on fair trade are traditionally not represented in international fair trade networks but they tend to be much more involved at the local level, in regional or national fair trade networks often connected with other initiatives such as organic foods, local supply chains or integration of low-skilled workers (Özçağlar-Toulouse, Béji-Bécheur, Gateau and Robert-Demontrond 2010).

The commercial evolution of pioneer fair trade organizations as well as the emergence of newcomers have contributed to an overall diversification of products and sales outlets (specialized and/or mainstream) that seems to challenge the traditional 'dual picture' of fair trade based on two distinct distribution strategies: the 'alternative' one, consisting of world shops and volunteer networks, and the mainstream one, consisting of supermarkets and other non-specialized shops (e.g., Moore 2004; Raynolds, Murray and Wilkinson 2007; Renard 2003). The resulting organizational diversity echoes the observation that 'fair trade is translated into chains, structures and organizations that are far more numerous and varied than a simplistic analysis ... restricted solely to labels [and networks] grouped within FINE might suggest' (Gendron, Palma Torres and Bisaillon 2009, 190, author's translation).[2]

Hence, as most organizations became less 'alternative' and as 'alternative trade' only resonated for those pioneers who had identified themselves with this early term, the term 'ATO' became less and less used and was replaced by other terms. The term 'fair trade organizations' is now largely used, among others, by WFTO and Fairtrade International in their annual reports and in their Charter of Fair Trade Principles, where they are defined as 'organizations of which Fair Trade is part of their mission and constitutes the core of their objectives and activities' (WFTO 2009). 'Organizations' is probably the most neutral term to encompass the diversity of actors but other terms are used in the literature such as 'fair trade businesses' (Reed, Thomson, Hussey and LeMay 2010), 'companies' (Davies and Crane 2003) and, increasingly, 'social enterprises' (Doherty 2011; Doherty and Huybrechts 2013; Huybrechts and Defourny 2008).

The purpose here is not to advocate for the use of one or another term, but rather to show that the originality of fair trade organizations as both market players and development actors, and the diversity of forms through which this combination is expressed, fit particularly well into the concept of social enterprise. This is useful in order for fair trade researchers and practitioners to develop an umbrella organizational term enabling to look at who fair trade organizations are (not only what they do) and to build more bridges with similar initatives in other fields. The next section documents in more detail how the different dimensions of social enterprise apply to fair trade organizations.

FAIR TRADE ORGANIZATIONS AS SOCIAL ENTERPRISES

This section reviews a number of connections between the social enterprise approach (at its organizational level of analysis) and the structure and practices of fair trade organizations. To illustrate these connections, data and case examples are provided from a study of 57 fair trade organizations, each belonging to a local or national fair trade network, in Belgium, France, Italy and the United Kingdom (Huybrechts 2010a; 2012). This study examined the organizations' legal forms, governance structures, goals, activities and resources (more details in the original work). Based on these elements, different dimensions of social enterprise can be explored, five of which will be summarized here: 1) combination of commercial activity and social purpose; 2) diversity of organizational vehicles; 3) multi-stakeholder governance models; 4) resource plurality; and 5) societal change.

A Combination of Commercial Activity and Social Purpose

At its heart, fair trade is about using market mechanisms to achieve social change and is thus a natural field for the development of social enterprises. This connection is particularly evident in the United Kingdom as fair trade organizations, together with other initiatives such as work integration enterprises, have fed the conceptualization of social enterprise. Both academics (e.g., Doherty and Tranchell 2007; Nicholls 2006) and practitioners[3] have thus taken fair trade organizations as emblematic examples of social enterprises. More particularly, fair trade social enterprises are, according to Alter's taxonomy of social enterprise 'mission and money' models (Alter 2006), mission-centric and embedded: the social enterprise is not just a device to raise resources to achieve a distinct social mission, but 'the enterprise activities are "embedded" within the organization's operations and social programmes' (212). Nicholls (2010a) suggests that two avenues in fair trade correspond with two types of social enterprise: those that address a social purpose while working within and using the current market institutions and those that try to challenge the configuration of these institutions. This echoes the analyses of fair trade as both 'within and against the market' (Fridell 2003). What may appear as a contradiction is presented by Nicholls (2010a), and others (e.g., Wilkinson 2007), as a strength enabling 'both current exploitation of extant [market] institutions and future reframing of their meaning and functions' (Nicholls 2010a, 247). Logically, the tensions and dilemmas of combining 'market' on the one hand and 'social mission', 'development' or 'solidarity' on the other hand, which are well documented at the social movement level of analysis (Gendron, Bisaillon and Rance 2009; Murray and Raynolds 2007; Nicholls 2010a; Wilkinson 2007), are also observed at the organizational level within fair trade organizations (Audebrand 2012; Davies and Crane 2003) as much as in other 'hybrid' social enterprises (see Doherty, Haugh and Lyon 2014 for a review).

Diverse Organizational Vehicles

The combination of commercial activity and social purpose finds expression in different types of organizational forms. This study of 57 fair trade organizations in four European countries confirmed such a diversity: 28 per cent of the sample were non-profit organizations, 22 per cent were cooperatives or closely related forms (such as the community interest company in the United Kingdom), 26 per cent had a traditional business form that had often adopted statutory rules committing to fair trade and limiting profit distribution, 12 per cent were individual entrepreneurs and another 12 per cent were 'groups' consisting of two or more different forms.[4]

Interestingly, the diversity of structures and practices observed in fair trade organizations echoes the rich diversity of conceptualizations of social enterprise. Indeed, fair trade organizations with a non-profit or cooperative form (see previous chapter on cooperatives in fair trade), a collective dynamic, democratic decision-making and a hybridized resource mix are probably closer to the EMES ideal type, as well as to the 'Social Innovation' school. Conversely, other organizations that rely more strongly on market tools and resources might be better described by the 'earned income' approach. In certain cases of small, entrepreneurial fair trade organizations, a characterization of the distinctive features of the social entrepreneur may be the most useful perspective. It seems clear that each conception may shed light on a particular dimension of fair trade, from the more market-based approaches to those that emphasize the socio-political role of social enterprise, from the broad, 'blurred boundaries' vision to the more narrow situation of social enterprise in the social and solidarity economy, and from the entrepreneur-centred conceptualization to those that emphasize the collective, citizen-based and democratic dynamics.

Multi-stakeholder Governance Models

Although governance issues do not have the same place in all conceptualizations of social enterprise, it seems clear that the involvement of stakeholders at one or another step of decision-making processes is one of the 'key selling points' claimed by social enterprise supporters, more particularly in Europe (Defourny and Nyssens 2010; Huybrechts, Mertens and Rijpens 2014; Spear, Cornforth and Aiken 2009). Interestingly, different patterns of stakeholder involvement can be observed among fair trade organizations that engage with a broad set of stakeholders including producers, customers, workers, businesses, non-governmental organizations (NGOs) and public authorities.

At the most advanced governance level, formal involvement on the board of directors has been practiced by an increasing number of fair trade organizations, some of which have integrated customers and partner organizations in an innovative way (Huybrechts 2010b). The involvement of producers as shareholders and board members is also particularly emblematic and has spread among several organizations such as Cafédirect, Divine Chocolate or Agrofair (Mason and Doherty 2012; see also Elizabeth Bennett's chapter in this volume). Yet, when formal involvement is not possible, for instance because of a very large number of producer partners or because of a lack of financial or organizational capacity, other schemes are possible. Traidcraft in the United Kingdom is one example where advanced dialogue with several stakeholders including procurers has been conducted successfully. Other fair trade organizations regularly connect with producers through mutual invitations to and participation in one another's meetings.

Resource Plurality

Even if fair trade organizations have evolved towards a stronger commercial profile where most of the incomes are generated through the sales of fair trade products, a diversity of resources can be observed when the different types of consumers are distinguished and when non-monetary resources (such as voluntary work) are included. Indeed, many fair trade organizations, even the commercial success stories, are still supported by networks of committed volunteers. Not necessarily 'activists' as in the early days of fair trade, but consumers (De Pelsmacker, Driesen and Rayp 2005; Özçağlar-Toulouse, Shiu and Shaw 2006), employees (Davies and Crane 2003; Diaz Pedregal 2006), investors (Doherty 2011) or social movement partners (Anderson 2009; Davies 2009) whose commitment to fair trade leads them to actively supporting the organization. In certain cases, fair trade organizations also rely on gifts or on public subsidies that are usually dedicated to education and advocacy activities or specific development work with producers.

Finally, it can be argued that consumption and investment by ethically minded individuals is a kind of indirect gift that would be ignored by labeling their contribution as purely 'market based'. Indeed, when consumers accept to pay a higher price for a product or when investors accept to receive a lower return on investment because of the social mission of the fair trade organization, the latter can count on an additional and specific type of resource that deserves attention (Balineau and Dufeu 2010; Becchetti and Huybrechts 2008; De Pelsmacker, Driesen and Rayp 2005).

Societal Change

A last major issue connecting fair trade and social entrerprise is the ambition to act not only to solve particular social problems but to also aim for 'systemic change' (e.g., Bacq and Janssen 2011; Dees 2001). This is one element differentiating fair trade organizations from for-profit companies dealing with some fair trade products, although this ambition may be translated into different practices that do not necessarily take the form of explicit lobbying and advocacy. This study of fair trade organizations in different European countries revealed several patterns, even for individual fair trade entrepreneurs, to contribute to the 'societal change' agenda of the fair trade movement. This contribution took different forms: participation in local and global fair trade networks, involvement in 'fair trade town' campaigns (on this, see the chapter by Alastair Smith in this volume), information on global issues (such as poverty reduction) on the company website or on the entrepreneur's blog, partnerships with advocacy NGOs and so on. A vast majority of interviewed managers and entrepreneurs in this study felt committed to this 'societal change' agenda, even if the types of commitment did vary.

Typically, the smaller and more market-oriented organizations acknowledged that education and advocacy were not their core business (unlike pioneer fair traders) and that they rather saw this as a collective endeavor in which they could modestly participate.

CONCLUSION AND IMPLICATIONS

This chapter's analysis of the connections between fair trade and social enterprise offers two contributions to fair trade research and practice. First, it suggests that social enterprise may be a useful (though not necessarily the only) umbrella notion to name and capture organizations and entrepreneurs totally focused on fair trade. It may indeed help not to refer to only one particular organizational model (such as cooperative) but to encapsulate the sector's organizational diversity in terms of legal forms, governance models and 'generations' (from pioneers to newcomers).

Second, this chapter underlines the nature of the organizations and not only their activities. This is crucial to avoid examining fair trade in a vacuum or as a stand-alone sector whereas its principles and participants in fact share many common features with other movements or sectors populated by organizations using market mechanisms to address societal needs (i.e., social enterprises). Such neighbor initiatives typically include microfinance (in which social enterprises share similar challenges in terms of diversification of participants, 'mainstreaming' and ethical dilemmas – see, for instance, Hudon and Sandberg 2013), but also other fields such as integration of low-skilled workers, renewable energy, recycling, health and education, etc.

While it would be misleading to forget the specific history and challenges of each of these fields, this chapter argues that emphasizing the common features and challenges of social enterprises across these fields is useful in at least four ways. First, several initiatives show the benefits of knowledge and practice exchange across field borders in order to learn from one another's successes and failures. Second, learning to know each other may facilitate inter-organizational collaboration taking advantage of synergies. Third and most importantly, emphasizing the integration of fair trade organizations into a broader social enterprise or social economy movement and identity is particularly useful to increase the size and thus the negotiating power of these types of organizations when communicating and dealing with several stakeholders, such as public authorities, corporations and the general public. Last, in terms of research, the social enterprise approach may help, as other approaches do (e.g., ethical consumption, social movements, development), to locate empirical observations of fair trade against a broader literature, which may help interpret these observations as much as it may be fed by the specific features of fair trade. In these ways, this chapter contributes to the challenging endeavor of building knowledge about fair trade as one of the most exciting socio-economic laboratories of recent decades.

NOTES

* This chapter compiles and elaborates on previous writings including the 2012 Routledge book *Fair Trade Organizations and Social Enterprise: Social Innovation through Hybrid Organization Models* as well as empirical articles examining fair trade social enterprises in Europe. This research has been carried out in the framework of an Interuniversity Attraction Pole funded by the Belgian Science Policy Office under the title 'If not for Profit, for What and How?'

1. EMES is named after its first research program, 'The emergence of social enterprises in Europe' (1996–2000). See more at http://www.emes.net/about-us/who-we-are/#sthash.KaTplKCD.dpuf.
2. FINE is a working group created in 1998 by four fair trade organizations: Fairtrade Labelling Organizations International (now Fairtrade International), the International Fair Trade Association (now the WFTO), the Network of European Worldshops (NEWS!) and the European Fair Trade Association (EFTA). FINE is an acronym of the organizations' names.
3. Examples include numerous collaborations between fair trade organizations and social enterprise networks (for instance, Social Enterprise London) or the examplification of fair trade leaders as social entrepreneurs (for instance, Penny Newman, former CEO of Cafédirect, designated as 'Social Enterprise Ambassador' in 2007).
4. Typically a non-profit and a cooperative (i.e., Miel Maya, Oxfam-Wereldwinkels) or a non-profit and a business (i.e., Artisans du Monde, Traidcraft, Twin, People Tree).

REFERENCES

Alter, Sutia Kim (2006), 'Social enterprise models and their mission and money relationships', in Alex Nicholls (ed.), *Social Entrepreneurship: New Models of Sustainable Social Change*, Oxford: Oxford University Press, pp. 205–232.

Anderson, Matthew (2009), 'NGOs and fair trade: The social movement behind the label', in Nick Crowson, Matthew Hilton and James McKay (eds.), *NGOs in Contemporary Britain: Non-State Actors in Society and Politics since 1945*, Basingstoke, UK: Palgrave Macmillan, pp. 222–241.

Audebrand, Luc K. (2012), 'La gestion quotidienne des tensions dialectiques: Dans l'aire de jeu du commerce équitable', in Marie-France Turcotte and Chantal Hervieux (eds.), *Mettre en marché pour une cause: Enjeux commerciaux et impacts du commerce équitable*, Montréal: Les Presses de l'Université du Québec, pp. 89–102.

Bacq, Sophie and Frank Janssen (2011), 'The multiple faces of social entrepreneurship: A review of definitional issues based on geographical and thematic criteria', *Entrepreneurship and Regional Development: An International Journal*, 23 (5), 373–403.

Balineau, Gaëlle and Ivan Dufeu (2010), 'Are fair trade goods credence goods? A new proposal, with French illustrations', *Journal of Business Ethics*, 92 (S2), 331–345.
Battle Anderson, Beth and J. Gregory Dees (2006), 'Rhetoric, reality, and research: Building a solid foundation for the practice of social entrepreneurship', in Alex Nicholls (ed.), *Social Entrepreneurship: New Models of Sustainable Social Change*, Oxford: Oxford University Press, pp. 144–168.
Becchetti, Leonardo and Benjamin Huybrechts (2008), 'The dynamics of fair trade as a mixed-form market', *Journal of Business Ethics*, 81 (4), 733–750.
Billis, David (2010), *Hybrid Organizations and the Third Sector: Challenges for Practice, Theory and Policy*, New York: Palgrave MacMillan.
Bornstein, David (2004), *How to Change the World: Social Entrepreneurs and the Power of New Ideas*, Oxford: Oxford University Press.
Borzaga, Carlo and Jacques Defourny (2001), *The Emergence of Social Enterprise*, London: Routledge.
Campi, Sara, Jacques Defourny and Olivier Grégoire (2006), 'Work integration social enterprises: Are they multiple-goal and multi-stakeholder organizations?', in Marthe Nyssens (ed.), *Social Enterprise: At the Crossroads of Market, Public Policies and Civil Society*, London: Routledge, pp. 29–49.
Davies, Iain (2009), 'Alliances and networks: Creating success in the UK fair trade market', *Journal of Business Ethics*, 86 (S1), 109–126.
Davies, Iain and Andrew Crane (2003), 'Ethical decision making in fair trade companies', *Journal of Business Ethics*, 45 (1–2), 79–92.
Davies, Iain, Bob Doherty and Simon Knox (2010), 'The rise and stall of a fair trade pioneer: The Cafédirect story', *Journal of Business Ethics*, 92 (1), 127–147.
De Pelsmacker, Patrick, Liesbeth Driesen and Glenn Rayp (2005), 'Do consumers care about ethics? Willingness-to-pay for fair trade coffee', *Journal of Consumer Affairs*, 39 (2), 363–385.
Dees, J. Gregory (2001), 'The meaning of "social entrepreneurship"', paper for the Fuqua School of Business, Duke University, available at http://www.caseatduke.org/documents/dees_sedef.pdf (accessed 26 June 2014).
Dees, J. Gregory and Beth Battle Anderson (2006), 'Framing a theory of social entrepreneurship: Building on two schools of practice and thought', *Research on social entrepreneurship: Understanding and contributing to an emerging field*, Association for Research on Nonprofit Organizations and Voluntary Action (ARNOVA), Indianapolia, IN.
Defourny, Jacques (2001), 'From third sector to social enterprise', in Carlo Borzaga and Jacques Defourny (eds.), *The Emergence of Social Enterprise*, London: Routledge, pp. 1–28.
Defourny, Jacques and Marthe Nyssens (2006), 'Defining social enterprise', in Marthe Nyssens (ed.), *Social Enterprise: At the Crossroads of Market, Public Policies and Civil Society*, London: Routledge, pp. 3–26.
Defourny, Jacques and Marthe Nyssens (2008a), 'Conceptions of social enterprise in Europe and in the United States: A comparative analysis', paper for the 8th ISTR International Conference and 2nd EMES-ISTR European Conference, Barcelona.
Defourny, Jacques and Marthe Nyssens (2008b), 'Social enterprise in Europe: Recent trends and developments', EMES Working Paper, 08 (01).
Defourny, Jacques and Marthe Nyssens (2010), 'Conceptions of social enterprise and social entrepreneurship in Europe and the United States: Convergences and divergences', *Journal of Social Entrepreneurship*, 1 (1), 32–53.
Diaz Pedregal, Virginie (2006), 'Participer au développement du commerce équitable dans les pays du nord: Caractéristiques sociales du personnel des structures de commerce équitable et stratégies de légitimation de la profession', in Xavier Engels, Matthieu Hély, Aurélie Peyrin and Hélène Trouvé (eds.), *De l'intérêt général à l'utilité sociale –*

la reconfiguration de l'action publique entre état, associations et participation citoyenne, Paris: L'Harmattan, pp. 191–204.
Doherty, Bob (2011), 'Resource advantage theory and fair trade social enterprises', *Journal of Strategic Marketing*, 19 (4), 357–380.
Doherty, Bob, Helen Haugh and Fergus Lyon (2014), 'Social enterprises as hybrid organizations: A review and research agenda', *International Journal of Management Reviews*, 16 (4), 417–436.
Doherty, Bob and Benjamin Huybrechts (2013), 'Connecting producers and consumers through fair and sustainable value chains', *Social Enterprise Journal*, 9 (1), 4–20.
Doherty, Bob and Sophi Tranchell (2007), '"Radical mainstreaming" of Fairtrade: The case of The Day Chocolate Company', *Equal Opportunities International*, 26 (7), 693–711.
Fridell, Gavin (2003), 'Fair trade and the international moral economy: Within and against the market', CERLAC Working Paper, available at http://www.yorku.ca/cerlac/documents/Fridell.pdf (accessed 26 June 2014).
Gardner, Charles A., Tara Acharya and Derek Yach (2007), 'Technological and social innovation: A unifying new paradigm for global health', *Health Affairs*, 26 (4), 1052–1061.
Gendron, Corinne, Véronique Bisaillon and Ana Rance (2009), 'The institutionalization of fair trade: More than just a degraded form of social action', *Journal of Business Ethics*, 86 (S1), 63–79.
Gendron, Corinne, Arturo Palma Torres and Véronique Bisaillon (2009), *Quel commerce équitable pour demain? Pour une nouvelle gouvernance des échanges*, Montréal and Paris: Ecosociété and Charles Léopold Mayer.
Hervieux, Chantal (2012), 'Le mouvement du commerce équitable comme exemple d'entrepreneuriat social: Typologie et enjeux stratégiques', in Marie France Turcotte and Chantal Hervieux (eds.), *Mettre en marché pour une cause: Enjeux commerciaux et impacts du commerce équitable*, Montréal: Les Presses de l'Université du Québec, pp. 109–126.
Hudon, Marek and Joakim Sandberg (2013), 'The ethical crisis in microfinance', *Business Ethics Quarterly*, 23 (4), 561–589.
Huybrechts, Benjamin (2010a), 'Fair trade organizations in Belgium: Unity in diversity?', *Journal of Business Ethics*, 92 (S2), 217–240.
Huybrechts, Benjamin (2010b), 'The governance of fair trade social enterprises in Belgium', *Social Enterprise Journal*, 6 (2), 110–124.
Huybrechts, Benjamin (2012), *Fair Trade Organizations and Social Enterprise: Social Innovation through Hybrid Organization Models*, New York: Routledge.
Huybrechts, Benjamin (2013), 'Social enterprise, social innovation and alternative economies: Insights from fair trade and renewable energy', in Hans-Martin Zademach and Sebastian Hillebrand (eds.), *Alternative Economies and Spaces: New Perspectives for a Sustainable Economy*, Bielefeld: Transcript Global Studies, pp. 113–130.
Huybrechts, Benjamin and Jacques Defourny (2008), 'Are fair trade organizations necessarily social enterprises?', *Social Enterprise Journal*, 4 (3), 186–201.
Huybrechts, Benjamin, Sybille Mertens and Julie Rijpens (2014), 'Explaining stakeholder involvement in social enterprise governance through resources and legitimacy', in Jacques Defourny, Lars Hulgard and Victor Pestoff (eds.), *Social Enterprise and the Third Sector: Changing European Landscapes in a Comparative Perspective*, London and New York: Routledge.
Huybrechts, Benjamin and Alex Nicholls (2012), 'Social entrepreneurship: Definitions, drivers and challenges', in Christine K. Volkmann, Kim Oliver Tokarski and Kati Ernst (eds.), *Social Entrepreneurship and Social Business: An Introduction and Discussion with Case Studies*, Wiesbaden, Germany: Springer Gabler, pp. 31–48.

Huybrechts, Benjamin and Darryl Reed (2010), 'Introduction: "Fair trade in different national contexts"', *Journal of Business Ethics*, 92 (S2), 147–150.
Kerlin, Janelle A. (2006), 'Social enterprise in the United States and Europe: Understanding and learning from the differences', *Voluntas: International Journal of Voluntary and Nonprofit Organizations*, 17 (3), 246–262.
Kerlin, Janelle A. (2013), 'Defining social enterprise across different contexts: A conceptual framework based on institutional factors', *Nonprofit and Voluntary Sector Quarterly*, 42 (1), 84–108.
Mason, Chris and Bob Doherty (2012), 'Exploring the governance challenges in fair trade organizations: An empirical study of three fair trade organizations', International Society for Third Sector Research (ISTR) 10th Conference, Istanbul.
Moore, Geoff (2004), 'The fair trade movement: Parameters, issues and future research', *Journal of Business Ethics*, 53 (1–2), 73–86.
Mulgan, Geoff, Simon Tucker, Rushanara Ali and Ben Sanders (2007), 'Social innovation: What it is, why it matters and how it can be accelerated', working paper, Skoll Centre for Social Entrepreneurship, Oxford.
Murray, Douglas L. and Laura T. Raynolds (2007), 'Globalization and its antinomies: Negotiating a fair trade movement', in Laura T. Raynolds, Douglas L. Murray and John Wilkinson (eds.), *Fair Trade: The Challenges of Transforming Globalization*, London: Routledge, pp. 3–14.
Nicholls, Alex (ed.) (2006), *Social Entrepreneurship: New Models of Sustainable Social Change*, Oxford: Oxford University Press.
Nicholls, Alex (2010a), 'Fair trade: Towards an economics of virtue', *Journal of Business Ethics*, 92 (S2), 241–255.
Nicholls, Alex (2010b), 'The legitimacy of social entrepreneurship: Reflexive isomorphism in a pre-paradigmatic field', *Entrepreneurship Theory and Practice*, 34 (4), 611–633.
Nicholls, Alex and Albert Hyunbae Cho (2006), 'Social entrepreneurship: The structuration of a field', in Alex Nicholls (ed.), *Social Entrepreneurship: New Models of Sustainable Change*, Oxford: Oxford University Press, pp. 99–118.
Nyssens, Marthe (ed.) (2006), *Social Enterprise: At the Crossroads of Market, Public Policies and Civil Society*, London: Routledge.
Özçağlar-Toulouse, Nil, Amina Béji-Bécheur, Matthieu Gateau and Philippe Robert-Demontrond (2010), 'Demystifying fair trade in France: The history of an ambiguous project', *Journal of Business Ethics*, 92 (S2), 205–216.
Özçağlar-Toulouse, Nil, Edward Shiu and Deirdre Shaw (2006), 'In search of fair trade: Ethical consumer decision making in France', *International Journal of Consumer Studies*, 30 (5), 502–514.
Phills, James A., Jr., Kriss Deiglmeier and Dale T. Miller (2008), 'Rediscovering social innovation', *Stanford Social Innovation Review*, Fall, 34–43.
Poos, Samuel (2008), *Le commerce équitable en 2008*, Fair Trade Centre – Coopération Technique Belge, Bruxelles.
Raynolds, Laura T., Douglas L. Murray and John Wilkinson (eds.) (2007), *Fair Trade: The Challenges of Transforming Globalization*, London: Routledge.
Reed, Darryl, Bob Thomson, Ian Hussey and Jean-Frédéric LeMay (2010), 'Developing a normatively grounded research agenda for fair trade: Examining the case of Canada', *Journal of Business Ethics*, 92 (S2), 151–179.
Renard, Marie-Christine (2003), 'Fair trade: Quality, market and conventions', *Journal of Rural Studies*, 19 (1), 87–96.
Santos, Filipe M. (2012), 'A positive theory of social entrepreneurship', *Journal of Business Ethics*, 111 (3), 335–351.
Spear, Roger, Chris Cornforth and Mike Aiken (2009), 'The governance challenges of social enterprises: Evidence from a UK empirical study', *Annals of Public and Cooperative Economics*, 80 (2), 247–273.

Thompson, John L. (2008), 'Social enterprise and social entrepreneurship: Where have we reached? A summary of issues and discussion points', *Social Enterprise Journal*, 4 (2), 149–161.
WFTO (2009), 'Annual report 2008', World Fair Trade Organization, Culemborg.
Wilkinson, John (2007), 'Fair trade: Dynamic and dilemmas of a market oriented global social movement', *Journal of Consumer Policy*, 30 (3), 219–239.
Yunus, Muhammad (2006), 'Social business entrepreneurs are the solution', in Alex Nicholls (ed.), *Social Entrepreneurship: New Models of Sustainable Social Change*, Oxford: Oxford University Press, pp. 39–44.
Zahra, Shaker A., Eric Gedajlovic, Donald O. Neubaum and Joel M. Shulman (2009), 'A typology of social entrepreneurs: Motives, search processes and ethical challenges', *Journal of Business Venturing*, 24 (5), 519–532.

14. Local fair trade organizations and institutional logics

Manush McConway and Geoff Moore

INTRODUCTION

The mainstreaming of fair trade from its traditional distribution into conventional channels is a well-known feature of fair trade's development (including in several chapters in this volume). While this is particularly familiar for Fairtrade certified products placed next to competing brands on supermarket shelves – such as coffee and tea – it is also true of fair trade handicraft products. While fair trade has always operated simultaneously 'inside and outside' (Renard 2003, 92) or 'in and against' (Raynolds 2000, 299) the market, mainstreaming has undoubtedly amplified this tension. In particular, mainstreaming presents a dilemma for 'local fair trade organizations' (LFTOs), those fair trade organizations in the global South that purchase and export local products, making them the mediators between local producers and foreign buyers (on the term LFTO, see Hayes 2006). Although considerable research has sought to understand the effects of mainstreaming on fair trade principles, ideology, messaging, distribution systems and producer and buyer relationships, less research has been completed at the level of the LFTO. Thus, little is understood about the effect of mainstreaming on the business practices of LFTOs. This chapter examines how LFTOs manage the dilemma of simultaneously operating in both fair trade and mainstream markets.

This chapter employs the concept of 'institutional logics' to better understand and suggest resolutions to this dilemma. Each institutional order has 'a central logic that guides its organizing principles and provides social actors with vocabularies of motive and a sense of self' (Thornton and Ocasio 2008, 101). The market is one example of an institutional order. However, for LFTOs the market logic presents potentially competing claims with alternative logics, such as the fair trade logic and perhaps also the logic of the producers. This chapter illustrates this tension between institutional logics using a case study of one LFTO. Allpa, a Peruvian handicrafts producer–exporter, was selected because it has been operating in both fair trade and mainstream markets since 1986, and it has clearly confronted contradictions between multiple institutional logics. While other studies have recognized the challenges that producers in the craft industry face when targeting international markets (see, for example, Marston 2013; Page and Slater 2003; Scrase 2003), this is the first to employ institutional logics as a theoretical framework to analyze these challenges.

Recognizing the importance of LFTOs in the success of the fair trade movement (see also Darryl Reed's chapter in this volume), this chapter explores how conventional market, fair trade and local producer logics shape Allpa as an organization, and influence its business strategies, practices and structures, and how Allpa has responded. It concludes that the concept of institutional logics might be applied well beyond the case study organization, and it could be an important analytical tool for understanding LFTOs and fair trade more generally.

THEORETICAL BACKGROUND

Institutional theory takes the main institutional orders to be the market, the corporation (in the business sense), professions, family, religion and the state (Greenwood et al. 2010, 522). Institutional logics are 'the socially constructed, historical patterns of material practices, assumptions, values, beliefs and rules by which individuals produce and reproduce their material subsistence, organize time and space, and provide meaning to their social reality' (Thornton and Ocasio 1999, 804) and so provide 'the basis of taken-for-granted rules guiding behavior' (Reay and Hinings 2009, 629) within organizations. Saz-Carranza and Longo (2012) define the market logic, for example, as having self-interest as the basic norm, with strategies that are aimed at efficient transactions and learning through competition. In contrast, fair trade, with its emphasis on partnership, dialogue and transparency and its focus on sustainable development, clearly has a logic that differs.

The institutional logic literature suggests that when organizations simultaneously work within multiple logics – especially when those logics are in some way incompatible – they face significant tensions (Greenwood et al. 2011). The extent to which these tensions generate problems for the organization depends to some degree on whether the logics at play are specific or ambiguous. As Greenwood et al. note, 'when logics are ambiguous and lack specificity, organizations are provided with relatively more discretion in their efforts to alleviate tensions of complexity ... On the other hand, when conflicting logics are highly specific, organizations face a more problematic level of complexity' (2011, 334).

How, then, do organizations respond to the various institutional logics to which they are subject? Organizational attributes such as structure, ownership, governance and identity are factors that can make an organization more or less sensitive to certain institutional logics. The complexity of organizational structure, for example, has been linked with its experience of institutional complexity (Greenwood and Hinings 1996; Greenwood et al. 2011): 'Organizational structure matters in shaping the organizational experience of complexity and in determining the repertoire of organizational responses available' (Greenwood et al. 2011, 334).

Organizational identity is a further concept that has been developed to explain organizational responses to competing logics. Organizational identity is about membership in a social category or collective identity at the level of the organizational field (Gioia et al. 2010; Lounsbury and Glynn 2001; Ravasi and Schultz 2006). For example, a fair trade organization may identify as a member of the World Fair Trade Organization. Organizational level identity concerns the characteristics of an organization that distinguish it from, or illustrate similarities to, other organizations in the organizational field. Organizational identity guides organizations' prioritization of the expectations placed upon them and shapes their responses to such expectations (Glynn 2008; Sharma 2000). Thus, as Kraatz and Block (2008) note, organizations are not passive recipients of institutional logics, but interpret, translate and in some instances transform them.

Organizational identity plays a significant role in organizations' processes of interpreting institutional logics. Kraatz and Block (2008) propose four different types of organizational responses to competing logics. First is resistance or elimination of tensions by deleting one or more institutionally derived identities. Second is balancing various institutional demands by increasing cooperation among identities. Third, organizations can emerge as institutions in their own right, detaching themselves, at least partly, from their institutional setting. Fourth, organizations can compartmentalize or decouple the logics to which they are subject. These responses, however, are not permanent and may change during the organization's life cycle.

Organizational responses to multiple institutional logics are also related to the interests of those in power (Goodrick and Salancik 1996; Greenwood and Hinings 1996; Greenwood et al. 2011; Lounsbury 2001; Pache and Santos 2010). The ownership and the governance structure determine the logics that will be prioritized or viewed more sympathetically within the organization. Similarly, Heimer (1999) emphasizes that the main actors who have decision-making capacity have more influence than those whose involvement is part-time. For example, the Managing Director of an LFTO would have greater influence than a producer group from which it buys.

The research on organizational responses to conflicting logics suggests various other strategies, structures and practices that organizations adopt to cope with competing institutional demands. Pache and Santos (2010) have developed a model of responses to conflicting demands. They suggest that the nature of demands, plus the internal representation of those demands, determines the way the organization responds. 'Organizations increasingly adopt hybrid forms that draw from and try to integrate sometimes competing logics. An example is the increasing integration of social goals by commercial enterprises and of commercial goals by organizations with a social mission' (Pache and Santos 2010, 471). They distinguish further between the demands that involve conflict at the goal level and demands that are harmonious at the goal level but lead to dispute about the means (functional strategies and processes) required to achieve these goals. They consider functional and process demands to be flexible and negotiable in comparison with goals which are not easily changed or challenged.

Pache and Santos (2013) explore how hybrid organizations, which incorporate competing institutional logics, internally manage the logics that they embody. Their suggestions go against the common proposals in the literature that organizations adopt decoupling or compromising strategies. Instead they found that the organizations selectively coupled intact elements of each logic. They identify a specific hybridization strategy which they refer to as 'Trojan horse', whereby an organization may adopt the behavior of the dominant logic in order to gain acceptance in a given organizational field.

Finally, organizations with better systems of communication may be better equipped to manage conflicting tensions. Saz-Carranza and Longo (2012), in their study of an individual organization, conclude that the participants of public–private joint ventures manage competing institutional logics through good communication and creating mutual learning spaces. In their study of a public–private joint venture, 'communication became the principal tool to overcome tensions caused by sector differences' (Saz-Carranza and Longo 2012, 345). Greenwood et al. (2011) note that most of the research in institutional logics assumes that organizations endorse a single or sustainable response to institutional pressures; however, they also note that responses may be variable across time.

The literature on institutional logics, therefore, argues that organizations whose strategies are guided by multiple and conflicting institutional logics may struggle to respond. Organizations may relieve this tension by adopting hybrid logics, selecting a dominant strategy or building strong systems of communication. It is expected that the tension between market logic and alternative logics will present formidable challenges to LFTOs. The following section introduces the case studied to answer the question: what strategies do LFTOs employ in responding to competing institutional logics?

CASE STUDY

Allpa (Allpa 2014) is a Peruvian craft company which began as a trading organization in 1986. Since then Allpa has been operating in both fair trade and mainstream markets. Allpa's product range is wide, including textiles, ceramics, marquetry and painted glass, Chulucanas ceramics, and silver and costume jewelry. These products are grouped into marketing categories such as personal accessories, house decoration and accessories, jewelry, presents and Christmas decor. The products are sold to both fair trade and mainstream markets in the United States, Switzerland, Germany, the United Kingdom, the Netherlands, Canada, Italy, Austria, Australia and other countries. Allpa only started selling products to the local Peruvian market in 2011. Since average incomes in Peru have increased, their store in the capital Lima is now able to serve the growing middle class. Opening a shop also gave Allpa the opportunity to market products which are less financially viable to export due to their size and cost. While sales fluctuate, over the ten year period from 2004 to 2013 fair trade products represented just over half of Allpa's total sales.

Allpa started as a project initiated by a development non-governmental organization (NGO); both founding directors of Allpa were working in the project as sociologists. The NGO engaged in rural development projects to benefit artisans. The work included assisting artisans in their technical work, empowering them and giving them financial assistance such as loans. The intention of assisting the artisans in their technical work was to improve the quality of the final product. (See Mary Littrell's chapter in this volume for an analysis of related fair trade artisan projects.)

According to Allpa's directors, the NGO continued working and assisting the artisans for several years but soon realized that the quality improvements were not valued by the local market, and no financial gain was being made by the artisans. As a result, the decision was made to start an entrepreneurial project and Allpa was formed to connect the artisans with the market. Thus, exporting to foreign markets became the core idea behind Allpa's existence.

METHODOLOGY, METHODS AND DATA

In order to explore institutional logics and organizational-level responses within a fair trade context, a case study methodology was adopted. Only from an in-depth and longitudinal analysis of a particular case were answers to the research questions (see below) likely to be forthcoming. Fieldwork took place in two phases and involved visits by the first author to Allpa in 2011 and 2013. The first was an exploratory phase with a broad research agenda, trying to become familiar with the business and most importantly exploring the significant influences on the organization. During this phase semi-structured interviews were conducted with Allpa's employees and three producers, organizational archival data was collected and observations recorded. The intention was to examine all the potential influences that the company was subject to and to map them in order to begin to understand the influences on organizational practices and governance. This phase helped to validate the assumption that Allpa is embedded in a complex and potentially competing institutional setting. However, the analysis also left open a series of questions that were used to guide further data gathering and theoretical reflection. It was following this phase of the research that institutional logics was identified as being a suitable theoretical lens and, specifically, the fair trade, mainstream market and local producers' logics to be the most influential for the organization. The inclusion of the local level was also seen to be a novel development of the institutional logics literature, which has tended to assume that such logics are always 'top-down'.

In the second phase the organization was revisited and 29 semi-structured interviews with Allpa's employees, three producer groups and three external Peruvian organizations which work directly with Allpa were conducted. The goal of the interviews was to identify the perceived differences between the previously identified institutional logics, to find out whether these differences had any contradictions and if so what organizational mechanisms there were for coping with them. Among other questions, the respondents were asked to identify the main changes in the organization over time and the reasons behind these changes. The respondents were also asked to describe the identity of Allpa as a company.

The research questions that were addressed were: What has been Allpa's experience of multiple logics and its responses to tensions and contradictions in those logics? How has Allpa's own identity been formed in the process? To explore and answer these questions a grounded theory framework was employed to analyze the data; this approach allowed descriptions of organizational reality to be produced which should be easily recognized by the members of the target organization (Cassell and Symon 2004). Following the usual procedures for such analysis, coding led to themes being identified.

FINDINGS

Allpa's Experience of Multiple Logics

Allpa exists in a complex institutional context. Here, Allpa's experiences of the three major logics which emerged from the research are considered. It is important to note that although fair trade and mainstream market logics are different and potentially contradictory, they both reflect Northern culture and background. The study of the Allpa case suggests that this may vary significantly from the Southern producer logic which represents the local culture.

Size and business practices

One of the fundamental differences among the three logics is the size and practices of the businesses that are represented in fair trade, mainstream and Southern producer organizational fields. Mainstream organizations tend to be large and fair trade businesses are, typically, small to medium sized enterprises, yet fair trade buyer and mainstream organizations in the Allpa case represent large, Northern businesses with specific needs, demands and highly professionalized work practices. In contrast, the handicraft producer businesses supplying Allpa are often small family businesses with informal work practices, old technology and a basic administrative structure. This affects both intra- and extra-organizational relationships and the communications of Allpa with its business partners.

Trading relationships

Allpa sees their trading relationships with fair trade and mainstream markets as being quite different. Fair trade buyers are more understanding of the small size of producers and their corresponding needs, which affect their relationship and commitment with Allpa. This commitment is characterized by long-term relationships, annual visits and regular orders.

Allpa's fair trade clients have placed orders with them for more than 20 years, far longer than their mainstream buyers. This long-term commitment of fair trade buyers allows them to work for many years with the artisans and see them develop and expand. In contrast, mainstream buyers work on a strict contractual basis, are often represented by an agent and deal only with Allpa, not with the producers directly. At the local level, the relationship between Allpa and the producers themselves is more informal and personal, reflecting the size and informality of the business practices identified above.

Goals

A common perception within Allpa is that although the business processes are not dramatically different between fair trade and mainstream buyers, there is a different purpose to their businesses. Employees within Allpa do not distinguish between fair trade and mainstream orders and follow them up with the producers in the same way. However, the employees observe that fair trade buyers tend to do business with them not for the biggest financial gain, but because they have bought before and want to continue the relationship and to support the artisans in order to reduce poverty. As far as the producers are concerned, their main aims are financial stability and sustainability.

Strategic emphasis

The research showed that Allpa's experience of the differences in strategic emphasis is that the mainstream focuses more on product, while fair trade focuses more on their relationship with Allpa and the producers. The product emphasis is demonstrated by mainstream buyers placing large quantity orders on an irregular basis to maximize their own profit. These products tend to be higher value goods or follow fashion trends. Fair trade buyers, however, tend to place small orders on a regular basis for smaller sized items of lower value. Allpa makes larger profits from the mainstream orders, but the fair trade orders provide a regular income which helps to sustain the business in the long term. The strategic emphasis from the producers is, not surprisingly, a combination of both a concern for their products and relationships, together with the associated volumes.

Priorities of the supply chain

One of the main characteristics of the mainstream market is that it is driven by market demands and international competition. One of the main challenges seems to be the fact that the market demands handmade products at mass-produced prices. Many of Allpa's mainstream customers seek products at prices equivalent to Asia, where products can be produced more cheaply due to the difference in minimum wages and the cost of living. The mainstream seems to be guided by price and profit margin, whereas fair trade is driven more by traceability, the story associated with the product, transparency, employment conditions and ensuring fair wages. However, profit from mainstream clients' high-volume orders makes it possible to invest in new technology and to develop the producers' businesses. For the producers themselves, their main priorities are price, volume and the regularity of orders.

Markets and customers

One of the differences between fair trade and mainstream markets in purchasing certain types of products is the end user of the product. Although not necessarily representative of fair trade generally, Allpa believes that in the handcraft market, fair trade has an older clientele (based on the type and style of the products purchased from Allpa), with more conservative tastes compared with the younger demographic of mainstream market clients. There is also a geographic difference; most of Allpa's fair trade buyers are based in Europe, but the mainstream buyers are from the United States.

Pre-financing 50 per cent pre-payment

Fair trade buyers offer 50 per cent pre-payment for their orders, which is vital for Allpa's producers as they normally do not have enough liquidity to proceed with an order without pre-payment to purchase materials. The producers are typically very small businesses with no access to credit, and any credit they can get is very expensive. In contrast, the mainstream does not offer pre-payments; the full price of the order is paid only after the order is shipped.

Mechanisms for Managing Institutional Logics

Communication and organizational structure

Good communication, both internally and externally, seems to be one of the important mechanisms that helps Allpa cope with these different institutional logics. Communicating between fair trade and mainstream buyers and producers can be challenging and Allpa has worked to improve this. In particular, communications between the producers and Allpa is affected by differences in work standards, processes and expectations, for example over durability and uniformity of the products and meeting deadlines. To effectively manage this communication, Allpa has changed the organizational structure at various times and introduced a layer of employees who work directly with artisans to understand their demands and differences. Dedicated staff members regularly visit the producers and monitor production in order to make sure that deadlines are met and products are made according to the specifications and quality required.

The information technology system for communicating order details from buyers to producers has been specifically developed to be appropriate for both, making this work more efficient and productive. Other practices to improve communication include an internal magazine which is circulated among producers and some buyers through the year, producer visits and training. These practices help to bring the world of producers and buyers together, thereby fostering mutual understanding and mitigating tensions raised by multiple logics.

The relationships that Allpa has with producers are very different from the ones they have with the buyers. The business done with the buyers is very professional, based on contracts and negotiation. The word used by many employees to describe the relationships with producers was 'friendship'.

'The clash of two worlds' as one of the employees labeled it, happens within Allpa between different groups of employees. Those that work closely with the producers and those that work more with the buyers seem to clash during meetings as they defend different viewpoints. Resolution is normally through some kind of meeting in the middle. For example, if there is a delay from the artisan which is not necessarily the producer's fault, Allpa understands this, but from the buyer's point of view the responsibility is on Allpa to deliver on time. Interestingly, Allpa's employees see themselves as quite different from the producers as well as their Northern customers. In many interviews the analogy was suggested that Allpa is like a *translator* between the producers and the buyers. Allpa communicates the demands of the buyers to the artisans and educates them about market trends, and it liaises with the buyers to explain any problems affecting production on behalf of the producers.

There is, as noted, a difference in logics and work practices of the artisans and the overseas buyers. These are not only due to the culture, language and mentality but also the operational differences resulting from the differing scales of the businesses. Allpa not only acts as translator between these two 'languages', but also as a guarantor, ensuring the quality and timely shipping of the products.

Organizational flexibility

As illustrated above, there have been major organizational changes over the life of the business and these were examined to understand the reasons behind them. Allpa's leadership sees the company as a live, organic organization and believes that the only way to sustain the business is to be flexible and accommodate changes to respond to market demands. Dealing with the mainstream market, the company has become increasingly more vulnerable to the international economic environment where the market for handmade goods is extremely volatile.

Allpa has made internal changes to remain competitive and proactively take advantage of opportunities. When more opportunities for textile manufacture appeared, for example, Allpa developed more textiles and made internal and external changes as required. Mainstream logics emphasize the best product for the cheapest price. To compete on product quality has become a priority for Allpa. To achieve this goal, the company has been reorganized several times and now uses product-aligned departments which specialize in one type of product and manage all the business processes for these. For example, the textile department receives the order, negotiates the conditions, passes the order to the producers and supervises the process until the order is ready for shipping.

The flexibility of the organization also extends to its product offerings. The mainstream market is becoming more demanding and specific in its requirements. Allpa produces a catalogue of all product lines every year and presents this in various international trade shows. However, according to the Marketing Manager, it is very seldom that a client would choose something from the catalogue without wanting to change the specifications such as color and size. Allpa has been able to accommodate these changes, by providing technological support to the producers. This flexible approach enables them to gain and retain customers.

Efficiency and entrepreneurial thinking

Efficiency and entrepreneurial thinking have been key in facing the mainstream market demands which are rooted in price and product-based logics. It is widely believed throughout the organization that most of the changes that have been made were in order to become more efficient and effective, in order to sell more.

Almost from the beginning of Allpa, an engineer has been hired as a permanent member of staff to solve technological issues both for Allpa internally and for the artisans. There is an awareness that investment is required in order to be fair, particularly to artisans. This requires selling products that are more expensive than those from Asian countries and thus being able to pay better wages and prices to producers. According to the employees, operational changes and improvements have been constant in Allpa in the search for efficiency. Packaging, shipping, quality control and the information technology system are some of the areas where changes have been made, many of them apparently initiated and resolved by the in-house engineer. The constant drive for efficiency has resulted in process redesign, training to improve business processes (e.g., 5S workplace organization and Lean Six Sigma) and the employment of numerous external consultants to help with operational and business planning. However, despite this drive for efficiency, Allpa has decided not to distinguish between orders from mainstream and fair trade buyers, and it makes pre-payment to their producers for both types of order.

Tighter export conditions

From a Southern organization's perspective the Northern fair trade buyers are concerned with paying a fair price for the products. However, the producers interviewed were interested in bigger orders rather than more money per item; bigger orders are what help the producers to make a larger profit. The problem with small orders is that they do not give the producers a chance to grow. To address these issues, Allpa has tightened up its export terms over the last five years such that they now have minimum orders for each line of production. This, however, has resulted in much criticism from the Northern buyers.

How Does Allpa Develop its Own Identity within This Context?

Leadership

The two Managing Directors who form Allpa's leadership are the driving force of Allpa's success and a strong part of its identity. The combination of the vision for the company, the commitment to the artisans and the country, a constant drive for perfection and a thirst for knowledge has not only made the company successful but gained the leaders much respect among the employees, producers and external agencies.

The employees themselves have a lot of national pride, a desire to promote Peruvian crafts representing the country's rich cultural heritage and to save traditions and skills that could otherwise be lost. They have a great deal of respect for the directors of Allpa; the staff look up to them and much of Allpa's success is thought to be due to their leadership.

NGO versus a business

To the question, 'What is Allpa – how would you describe it as an organization?', most of the employees described it as a profit-orientated enterprise, but also as a business that seeks the development and growth of the producers and artisans. The business is seen as a means to the end of sustainable development.

Many times during the interviews employees reinforced the point that Allpa is not an NGO, it is a business seeking a profit. They wished to draw a distinction between Allpa's work and that of many NGOs that have run developmental projects with limited success in helping artisans. When talking about fair trade and its values, most of the employees seemed to think that Allpa had been different from the start; without even having the Fairtrade mark or knowing about fair trade, it had social concerns at the core. As noted above, Allpa started as a developmental project seeking to reach disadvantaged producers; however, they always considered that the only way of actually making a difference in the producers' lives was by increasing sales and enabling financial gains.

Sustainability and investment

The research showed that quality is a concept in Allpa that is strongly related to sustainability, which is part of the organization's key characteristics. When asked to define Allpa's objectives, one of the Managing Directors answered: 'The objective of Allpa is not to export, it is to be in the market in a sustainable way; it means not just today, but yesterday, today and tomorrow. This is the reason for culture of the quality that we have; it's the logic behind the quality.' The organization has been in business for over 25 years, which is a significant achievement in this industry.

The orders from the mainstream clients are a difficult challenge for the artisans. This is due to the high quality and piece-to-piece uniformity standards, strict deadlines and the large order volumes. It is also difficult to meet the 'mass production' price point with a handmade product, and the producer groups have very limited spare resources to cope if there are any problems. Conventional market logic dictates changing providers and finding the ones that meet the price point. However, Allpa tends to work with the producers for the long term and invest in that relationship.

The research shows that the notion of sustainability is strongly linked with Allpa's commitment to the producers and to their investment in their workshops, often via affordable loans. As well as offering pre-financing on orders, Allpa makes considerable financial investments in new technology and machinery to help to lower costs and allow producers to compete internationally. There is also a tolerance of mistakes and delays. There is a perception that mainstream buyers are quick to charge penalties for each point where the company fails to deliver to contract but that fair trade buyers are more tolerant, although they still charge Allpa penalties, and Allpa will, where appropriate, pass these penalties on to producers. One of the Managing Directors thought that a reason why fair trade can be more tolerant is due to their long-term commitment: they have a 'bigger picture' view of the relationship, so they understand why things have gone wrong and how the situation can be corrected. This relationship and commitment is what brings sustainability to the business.

Quality

'We don't want to sell poverty; we want to sell quality' is a quote from one of the Managing Directors that perhaps characterizes Allpa best. The emphasis on quality is an important part of Allpa's identity. This has been demonstrated by the creation of a quality committee on which top management is represented, an in-house quality control unit, and producer training and development. Their emphasis on producer training and development has improved the artisans' approach and therefore the quality of the products they supply to other (non-Allpa) customers. The company managers are happy that there has been an improvement in the overall quality of Peruvian handcrafted exports resulting from this approach.

Design and innovation

Linked to quality, Allpa's identity and success is deeply rooted in the idea of unique product design and innovation. It is believed in the organization that this is the only way to be sustainable in the artisan market. Every year, Allpa's designers produce a new catalogue for every line of products, which is presented in trade shows around the world. Product innovation is at the core of Allpa; as one of the Managing Directors said, the goal of Allpa is 'to transform the artisans into entrepreneurs who are open to innovation'.

DISCUSSION

The case study of Allpa was conducted with the intention of understanding its experience of the differences between fair trade, mainstream and local producer logics and the strategies employed within the organization to deal with the tensions that result. How Allpa's experience of these different logics had shaped its identity as an organization was also of interest.

The research started with an examination of multiple influences on Allpa and identified the most influential as fair trade, mainstream and the local business culture. This was in line with the research of Greenwood et al. (2011) who noted that the majority of studies consider only two logics and recommended that future research should take into account the multiplicity of logics in the given context and be more explicit about the justification of which logics are incorporated into the analysis. They also suggest examining the setting in which more than two competing logics are to be found; to examine the patterns of complexity that confront organizations, arising from the multiplicity of logics to which organizations must respond, and the degree of incompatibility between those logics.

The different logics were reasonably clearly formulated and unambiguous, but it was also noted that they were not always in direct competition with one another. Nonetheless, there was sufficient evidence of difference to indicate that Allpa had to manage its way through the resulting complexity. Allpa combines the competing logics by purposeful selection of various logics among competing alternatives, selectively coupling them as when, for example, it makes pre-payments on all orders and, where appropriate, passes on penalties on both fair trade and mainstream orders. This is in line with Pache and Santos's (2013) work on hybrid organizations. However, in the case of Allpa, communication as a means of overcoming tensions (Saz-Carranza and Longo 2012) was fundamental. The organization often acts as a *translator* of logics, not merely passing the information from the buyers to producers but translating it in both directions into a 'language' more acceptable for the recipient.

Regarding organizational identity, Allpa distinguishes itself from mainstream, fair trade and local producers and positions itself as somewhere in between, as an entity that facilitates dialogue and communication. In this way, it seems as though Allpa emerges as an institution in its own right, detaching itself, at least to some degree, from its institutional setting (Kraatz and Block 2008).

Greenwood et al. (2011) note that although there are some studies describing the differences between the logics and the expression of these differences in organizational practices, there are fewer studies showing the degree to which logics are incompatible. By examining the three logics, seven areas were identified (business size and practices, trading relationships, goals, strategic emphasis, priorities of supply chain, markets and customers, and pre-financing) where the logics were found to have some degree of incompatibility. Although fair trade and mainstream logics are incompatible in some dimensions, in some cases they are also perceived together as Northern world logics which contradict the Southern producers' logics, creating 'the clash of two worlds'.

Organizational attributes such as the leadership determine the organizational experience of institutional complexity and hence the response to it. Allpa's leadership's identity and its rootedness in social ideology makes it more receptive to fair trade logics. This is demonstrated by offering pre-payment for all orders including those for the mainstream, conducting producer training and developing them technically, and the long-term commitment in business relationships. There is therefore a strong link between the role played by Allpa's leadership, their values and beliefs, and the organization's responses to institutional complexity. This also expands one's knowledge of the gap identified in understanding the role of leadership in organizational responses to conflicting institutional logics (Greenwood et al. 2011).

The structure of the organization was found to be linked with the organization's experience of institutional complexity. Allpa's organizational structure has been changed numerous times to accommodate the changes in the market demands from the mainstream and fair trade, to facilitate communication between the buyers, producers and Allpa's employees, and to increase effectiveness. Over time, institutional complexity changes, creating different circumstances and tensions for organizations (Greenwood et al. 2011). Allpa adopts an accommodating strategy, particularly through changes to organizational structure, in handling such fluctuating institutional complexity and tensions. (On organizational structures merging business goals with social objectives see, in this volume, Benjamin Huybrechts's chapter on fair trade and social enterprise.)

CONCLUSION

This study contributes to research on fair trade in two ways. First, it describes the complexity of the institutional environment that LFTOs encounter in working with fair trade and mainstream markets and local producers, and it illustrates how organizations may successfully respond to such complexity. Second, it examines the phenomenon of mainstreaming through a new theoretical lens: institutional logics.

In Allpa's case, the LFTO, while operating under several logics which compete to some extent, has formed its own identity and, most importantly, acts as a translator between the various logics with which it is faced. It has, as a result, largely managed to resolve internally the tensions that the different logics present. The inclusion of the local institutional logic was important to this understanding and is a novel development of the literature.

The concept of institutional logics, conflict and complexity can clearly be applied well beyond the case presented here. As such, it offers an important analytical tool for understanding and developing fair trade in theory and practice. The authors would, therefore, encourage both researchers and fair trade practitioners to draw further on this approach.

REFERENCES

Allpa (2014) website, available at http://www.allpaperu.com (accessed 2 April 2014).

Cassell, Catherine and Gillian Symon (2004), *Essential Guide to Qualitative Methods in Organizational Research*, London: Sage Publications.

Gioia, Dennis A., Kristin N. Price, Aimee L. Hamilton and James B. Thomas (2010), 'Forging an identity: An insider–outsider study of processes involved in the formation of organizational identity', *Administrative Science Quarterly*, 55 (1), 1–46.

Glynn, Mary Ann (2008), 'Beyond constraint: How institutions enable identities', in Royston Greenwood, Christine Oliver, Kerstin Sahlin and Roy Suddaby (eds.), *The Sage Handbook of Organizational Institutionalism*, London: Sage, pp. 413–430.

Goodrick, Elizabeth and Gerald R. Salancik (1996), 'Organizational discretion in responding to institutional practices: Hospitals and caesarean births', *Administrative Science Quarterly*, 41 (1), 1–28.

Greenwood, Royston, Amalia Magán Díaz, Stan Xiao Li and José Céspedes Lorente (2010), 'The multiplicity of institutional logics and the heterogeneity of organizational responses', *Organization Science*, 21 (2), 521–539.

Greenwood, Royston and Bob C.R. Hinings (1996), 'Understanding radical organizational change: Bringing together the old and the new institutionalism', *Academy of Management Review*, 21 (4), 1022–1054.

Greenwood, Royston, Mia Raynard, Farah Kodeih, Evelyn R. Micelotta and Michael Lounsbury (2011), 'Institutional complexity and organizational responses', *The Academy of Management Annals*, 5 (1), 317–371.

Hayes, Mark (2006), 'On the efficiency of fair trade', *Review of Social Economy*, 64 (4), 447–468.

Heimer, Carol A. (1999), 'Competing institutions: Law, medicine, and family in neonatal intensive care', *Law and Society Review*, 33 (1), 17–66.

Kraatz, Mathew S. and Emily S. Block (2008), 'Organizational implications of institutional pluralism', in Royston Greenwood, Christine Oliver, Kerstin Sahlin and Roy Suddaby (eds.), *The Sage Handbook of Organizational Institutionalism*, London: Sage, pp. 243–275.

Lounsbury, Michael (2001), 'Institutional sources of practice variation: Staffing college and university recycling programs', *Administrative Science Quarterly*, 46 (1), 29–56.

Lounsbury, Michael and Mary Ann Glynn (2001), 'Cultural entrepreneurship: Stories, legitimacy, and the acquisition of resources', *Strategic Management Journal*, 22 (6–7), 545–564.

Marston, Andrea (2013), 'Justice for all? Material and semiotic impacts of fair trade craft certification', *Geoforum*, 44, 162–169.

Pache, Anne-Claire and Filipe Santos (2010), 'When worlds collide: The internal dynamics of organizational responses to conflicting institutional demands', *Academy of Management Review*, 35 (3), 455–476.

Pache, Anne-Claire and Filipe Santos (2013), 'Inside the hybrid organization: Selective coupling as a response to competing institutional logics', *Academy of Management Journal*, 56 (4), 972–1001.

Page, Sheila and Rachel Slater (2003), 'Small producer participation in global food systems: Policy opportunities and constraints', *Development Policy Review*, 21 (5–6), 641–654.

Ravasi, David and Majken Schultz (2006), 'Responding to organizational identity threats: Exploring the role of organizational culture', *Academy of Management Journal*, 49 (3), 433–458.

Raynolds, Laura T. (2000), 'Re-embedding global agriculture: The international organic and fair trade movements', *Agriculture and Human Values*, 17 (3), 297–309.

Reay, Trish and Bob C.R. Hinings (2009), 'Managing the rivalry of competing institutional logics', *Organization Studies*, 30 (6), 629–652.

Renard, Marie-Christine (2003), 'Fair trade: Quality, market and conventions', *Journal of Rural Studies*, 19 (1), 87–96.

Saz-Carranza, Angel and Francisco Longo (2012), 'Managing competing institutional logics in public–private joint ventures', *Public Management Review*, 14 (3), 331–357.

Scrase, Timothy J. (2003), 'Precarious production: Globalisation and artisan labour in the Third World', *Third World Quarterly*, 24 (3), 449–461.

Sharma, Sanjay (2000), 'Managerial interpretations and organizational context as predictors of corporate choice of environmental strategy', *Academy of Management Journal*, 43 (4), 681–697.

Thornton, Patricia H. and William Ocasio (1999), 'Institutional logics and the historical contingency of power in organizations: Executive succession in the higher education publishing industry 1958–1990', *American Journal of Sociology*, 10 (3), 801–843.

Thornton, Patricia H. and William Ocasio (2008), 'Institutional logics', in Royston Greenwood, Christine Oliver, Kerstin Sahlin and Roy Suddaby (eds.), *The Sage Handbook of Organizational Institutionalism*, London: Sage, pp. 99–129.

15. Fair trade and mainstreaming

Ronan Le Velly

INTRODUCTION*

The expansion of fair trade sales beyond the radical venues where the movement was born has generated much debate. On the one hand, it has been described as a success. In this way of thinking, sales growth and participation of supermarket chains and transnational firms can be considered levers for generating benefits for producers' organizations and evidence that fair trade is not a form of charity. For instance, Max Havelaar France, the French member of Fairtrade International, displays on its website the growing number of licensed traders and of certified products, the growing value of their sales and the number of certified producers' organizations that export to the French market. It advertises that in 2012, Max Havelaar France's 345 million euros in Fairtrade sales benefited some 400 producers' organizations in the global South (Max Havelaar France 2014). On the other hand, the expansion of fair trade sales into mainstream markets is argued to have compromised the efficacy of fair trade as a tool of ethical consumption and to have degraded the quality of relationships in fair trade supply chains. As we shall see, this kind of accusation has been made by researchers as well as some fair trade promoters. In France, the strategy of Max Havelaar France has been widely criticized by activists and organizations like Minga, which dispute the sale of fair trade products in supermarkets and collaboration with transnational companies like Nestlé. These activists contest the benefits of a strategy that prioritizes the growth of sales, pleading for a 'truly alternative' conception of fair trade that involves conscientious consumers in the construction of fair trade chains with both Southern and local producers (Özçağlar-Toulouse et al. 2010).

In research on fair trade, this issue is commonly associated with the term 'mainstreaming' (Ballet and Carimentrand 2010; Davies, Doherty and Knox 2010; Doherty, Davies and Tranchell 2012; Dolan 2010; Goodman, DuPuis and Goodman 2012; Jaffee 2007; 2010; Low and Davenport 2005; 2007; Raynolds 2009; Raynolds, Murray and Wilkinson 2007; also Bob Doherty, Valéry Bezençon and Gaëlle Balineau's chapter in this volume). But, as is common with catchwords, the mainstreaming of fair trade is rarely – if ever – precisely defined. Usually the term suggests the increasing presence of fair trade products in 'mainstream' distribution channels (i.e., major supermarket, coffeehouse or restaurant chains) and increasing collaboration with 'conventional' actors of production (i.e., large plantations, multinational agribusinesses). It also points to the important growth of fair trade sales. Mainstreaming is then seen as a new phase in the development of fair trade which aims to reach all consumers, not only the most radical ones, by making products available everywhere and by using promotional messages that speak to everyone. Finally, the word 'mainstreaming' stresses the degradations that fair trade faces when its actors and rules become more and more similar to those of 'conventional trade'. Research addresses this issue from different angles: erosion of the Fairtrade standards (Doherty, Davies and Tranchell 2012; Jaffee 2010), depersonalization of the relationship (Ballet and Carimentrand 2010; Dolan 2010), re-fetishization (Goodman, DuPuis and Goodman 2012; also Michael Goodman and Agatha Herman's chapter in this volume), reduction of the political message to a simple invitation to 'shop for a better world' (Low and Davenport 2007), 'clean washing' (Raynolds, Murray and Wilkinson 2007) and competition between companies with unequal commitments to the principles of fair trade (Davies, Doherty and Knox 2010). Even if these tendencies are usually presented as the consequences of mainstreaming, the word 'mainstreaming' on its own seems in that case to include all these degradations. 'Mainstreaming' is then the equivalent for fair trade of what has been called the 'conventionalization' of organic agriculture (Guthman 2004).

This lack of precision may be problematic. It tends to confound in one term the aims (e.g., increasing sales, reaching less radical consumers), the means (e.g., selling in supermarkets, using celebrities in advertising) and the consequences that are contrary to the founding principles of fair trade. It is necessary to analytically distinguish these elements and to study the mechanisms that link them, at least to avoid the implicit assumption that such ends necessarily imply such means and such consequences. It is also necessary to be wary of the binary thinking, also observed in the debates on the conventionalization of organic agriculture (Campbell and Rosin 2011), which identifies only two scenarios, an 'alternative but small' path and a 'big but conventionalized' path, and which assumes a clear partition between the motivations and behaviors of the actors depending on whether they are 'movement oriented' or 'market oriented'. Just like for organic agriculture, this dualistic thinking is inappropriate to understand the dynamics of fair trade (Huybrechts 2010).

In fact, recent studies on mainstreaming have started to avoid dualistic conceptions. They have highlighted successful strategies of 'radical mainstreaming' (Davies, Doherty and Knox 2010; Doherty and Tranchell 2007; Huybrechts 2010; Low and Davenport 2005) and have shown how 'conventional actors' like supermarket chains may have very different behavior towards fair trade (Smith 2010; see also both Bob Doherty, Valéry Bezençon and Gaëlle Balineau's chapter and Alex Hughes's chapter in this volume). Recent studies have also identified some situations that do not fit with the aforementioned binary grammar. For instance, Laura Raynolds described the strategy of 'quality-driven' firms and positioned them on a continuum from alternative to conventional (Raynolds 2009). Yet this representation remains still too simple. Raynolds shows that some companies have built a strategy on a specific 'order of worth' (Boltanski and Thévenot 2006) in which connections to a product's origin and/or gustatory excellence are valued. Such practices in fact escape a continuum of alternative versus conventional trade.

THEORETICAL FRAMEWORK AND ORGANIZATION OF THE CHAPTER

To examine the dynamics of mainstreaming I utilize a theoretical framework drawn from two groups of sociological work on markets. The first one studies what Michel Callon calls the 'socio-technical *agencements*' that constitute and shape actually existing markets (Çalışkan and Callon 2010). This approach puts the stress on the set of people and devices 'whose task is "to *work on the market*", i.e. to construct it, move it, organize it, manage and control it – in short, "agencing" transactions' (Cochoy and Dubuisson-Quellier 2013). This approach is particularly appropriate to grasp the great diversity of functioning that can be observed in fair trade chains. This diversity is linked to the role of the 'market professionals' (Cochoy and Dubuisson-Quellier 2013) who intervene between the producers and the consumers (middlemen in the global North and South, but also designers, marketers, activists, etc.) and the role of the 'market devices' (Muniesa, Millo and Callon 2007) which also contribute to organize the market (standards and labels, shops and supermarkets, advertisings and booklets, etc.) (Dubuisson-Quellier, Lamine and Le Velly 2011). Speaking of 'socio-technical *agencements*' rather than of socio-technical *assemblages* or *arrangements* aims at stressing that markets have an agency, a 'capacity to act' (Çalışkan and Callon 2010). Markets are hybrid collectives that are able to evaluate things, to meet supply and demand, to set prices and to transfer property.

The second approach, inspired by the work of Karl Polanyi (1985), takes into consideration the level of embeddedness of the market. The term 'embeddedness' is extremely equivocal and has been mobilized in the past decades in various and inconsistent ways (Gemici 2008). In this chapter, discussions of disembedding or re-embedding of fair trade refer to the relative strength of the free market regulations, similar to how Fred Block speaks of 'level of marketness' (Block 1990). Three criteria, inspired by the introduction of a Polanyian collection of essays (Bohannan and Dalton 1962), can be proposed to define the level of embeddedness: to what extent 1) are prices the result of a free encounter between supply and demand; 2) does material survival require participation in the market; and 3) are economic decisions guided by market remuneration? Fair trade has frequently been described as an attempt to increase the level of embeddedness, to re-embed the international agrifood chains. But, as the debates on mainstreaming show, the question remains whether this objective is achieved. Fair trade needs to be understood as a range of initiatives with various market socio-technical agencements and uneven levels of embeddedness.

In the first section of this chapter I will focus on the professionalization of the principal French alternative trade organization (ATO), the Artisans du Monde network, which occurred in the 1990s and 2000s.[1] This section will be based on a field study combining observations, archives reading and 40 semi-structured interviews that I conducted between 2002 and 2006. In studying this case I want to move the issue of mainstreaming away from the sole cases of collaboration with 'mainstream' production and/or distribution actors. It is important to consider the more broad transformations of fair trade that are linked to its growth, and the professionalization of Artisans du Monde is a good case for examining this issue. We will see that the modifications of the socio-technical agencements of this network (i.e., formalization of the procedures of selection of producers' organizations, centralization of the import stage, modernization of stores) have produced contrasting effects (i.e., growth in sales, loss of personal contact, higher dependence on market remuneration). The second section will be dedicated to the socio-technical agencements of the Fairtrade system. My aim will be to stress one organizational feature of the Fairtrade system: the delegation of business activities. I will argue that the market devices that have rendered possible this delegation, particularly the standards and the label, have also engendered significant transformations that are the source of a relative disembeddedness of fair trade (i.e., competition increasingly based on prices, purchasing strategies increasingly motivated by market considerations rather than development objectives). Finally, in the third section, I will present some of the recent studies that show how some fair trade organizations resist this tendency towards conventionalization without losing sight of the objective of increased sales.

The argument running through these three sections is that the mainstreaming of fair trade is not a movement where growth inevitably implies degradation. Even if there are many specific instances where these two tendencies are observed together, this finding is not enough to fully understand the dynamics of mainstreaming. The research must detail the reconfigurations of the socio-technical agencements that render possible the growth of fair trade and explain how these reconfigurations facilitate or endanger the realization of its various objectives (inclusion of 'small producers', payment of a 'fair price', etc.). From this perspective, it is possible to highlight the diversity of socio-technical agencements that enable the expansion of sales and to put forward those that are also established in order to maintain a high degree of alternativeness.

THE PROFESSIONALIZATION OF AN ALTERNATIVE TRADE ORGANIZATION

The first Artisans du Monde shop opened in Paris in 1973 and since that date many changes have taken place. I reviewed archives and conducted interviews with fair trade activists to understand the organizational changes that occurred in the 1970s and 1980s. The Artisans du Monde shops maintained direct relations with groups of craftsmen and craftswomen. This was made possible by one person among the producers, typically a doctor or a nun, who established a link with the shop and personally delivered products on his or her occasional visits to France (this was called 'imports in the suitcase'). Sometimes local groups traded products with one another to broaden their range a little, but most of the products were purchased directly. Only a few food products were bought from specialized importers, notably to Swiss and Belgian ATOs. The products were sold in places where people were sympathetic to social causes: outside churches, at conferences about the Third World, in small, poorly situated shops and so on. The clientele believed in the projects supported by their purchases, and many now say that their shopping in such venues was principally driven by sympathy or solidarity with the producers, as opposed to the quality of the products themselves. As one activist told us, Sandinista coffee was 'disgusting' and drinking it was a 'highly militant action!' (Artisans du Monde volunteer 1 2003).

In the early 1990s the Artisans du Monde movement embarked on a series of changes designed to make it more commercially efficient. This orientation reflected the objective of boosting sales in order to support more producers and to raise awareness among a broader public. It also aimed to establish what the movement saw as a more egalitarian relationship with producers. 'Trade, not charity', the volunteers often said, explaining that the consumers – not just the producers – should benefit from the commercial relationship. This desire for professionalization induced profound changes in the socio-technical agencements of the Artisans du Monde's chains. First, shops stopped purchasing directly from producers and began importing through the network's importer, Solidar'Monde. Second, the responsibility of selecting producer groups was delegated to the ten European importer members of the European Fair Trade Association (EFTA). To facilitate producer selection, the importers developed more formalized procedures than in the past (standardized questionnaires, systematic visits) to evaluate producers' economic situations, working conditions and product quality. Third, other market professionals became involved in the fair trade handicraft value chain, working in design, marketing and exporting, for example (Grimes and Milgram 2000). And fourth, at retail level, many Artisans du Monde groups, although not all, have moved their shops to more commercial districts, invested in modernizing them and hired an employee to offer customers more regular business hours and better service.

This centralization and intermediation of imports has generated contrasting feedback. Some Artisans du Monde activists clearly regret the shift and are committed to maintaining at least some direct, personalized links. Many of the volunteers in a group that I observed in a town in western France feel that such relations are vital. For example, this group buys items from a center for physically disabled children in India that was created by a volunteer's uncle. At each meeting this volunteer reads aloud letters recounting life at the center. The letters share information about friends whose lives the group has been following for years, whose successes are reasons for rejoicing (e.g., when the center's children are at the head of their classes in the local school) and whose problems are announced cautiously ('I'm afraid that the news is not good …'). Solidar'Monde tries to facilitate such ties between retailers and producers by sharing information about the producers and providing opportunities for producer representatives to visit France, but these relations are less regular and intense than those facilitated by decentralized import schemes. Despite some activists' discontent with these changes, groups are not planning to return to the old system. Centralized purchasing management enables the network to rely on a larger number of producers' groups, greatly facilitates stock and delivery management and makes the creation of a wide, coordinated and frequently renewed product range possible. In a context where competition between fair trade importers is fierce and selling more is a sign of success, such centralization of importing practices appears to be inevitable.

This brief overview of the changing socio-technical agencements of the Artisans du Monde network enables us to pose the problem in terms of level of embeddedness. It is relevant, echoing Bohannan and Dalton's second criterion (does material survival require participation in the market?), to point out here that shops struggle to finance loan repayments, pay rent in a city center and/or afford employees' wages, on nothing but the profits from their sales. For this reason, the managers of the Artisans du Monde shops whom I met said that if these shops were to survive, the high quality of their products was not only morally desirable but also economically indispensable. The third criterion of Bohannan and Dalton (1962) may then beg the following question: are the financial decisions in Artisans du Monde shops guided by market remuneration? On this point one has to be wary of a clear-cut answer that would not adequately account for the diversity of situations. There is nevertheless agreement on the fact that, today, fair trade importers and retailers cannot disregard the 'commercializable' nature of the products that they select (Le Velly 2007; Littrell and Dickson 1999). For instance, several questions in the assessment questionnaire that EFTA's members used in the beginning of the 2000s were aimed at determining whether the imported goods met European technical standards and consumer tastes (quality approach, innovation, design, etc.) and whether the producers had sufficient production and export capacities.

In view of the above, it is then possible to see a movement of relative disembedding of fair trade in the professionalization of the Artisans du Monde network. The effects of such a movement therefore warrant closer study. For fair trade, the effects of disembedding processes are nuanced. On the one hand, professionalization of Artisans du Monde has enabled it to develop sales beyond a limited circle. Between 1994 and 2004, the average sales of the Artisans du Monde shops have doubled. Since that date, overall sales stagnated but the groups that have undertaken investments to redevelop or to relocate their shops have significantly better results than the others (Fédération Artisans du Monde 2013). On the other hand, the higher quality standards have made it more difficult to work with groups of severely marginalized producers. One volunteer with a long history in the Artisans du Monde movement expresses this tension perfectly:

> [When it comes to] Solidar'Monde, it has to stand on its own two feet; things must be balanced; it is not charity work. And it is true that sometimes we deplored their refusal to work with small co-operatives, with small groups …

> As I objected, 'That is our main reason for being!' Yes, it's wonderful, for example, to import embroidery from Palestine, but if it doesn't sell, whom does it help? What good is it? So, we were truly harassed, we had requests from Palestinian women, it was horrible, truly horrible … We were directly in touch with these Palestinian women, and they wrote us heart-wrenching letters. And then their embroidery didn't sell, because a selling price had to be set, and when it comes to prices, Solidar'Monde is a hard bargainer: if it doesn't sell, they don't take it … Artisans du Monde aims to be more structured. [Silence] In the beginning, Artisans du Monde was like that, somewhat, very strong on relationships, and as it became more structured we lost a little of that. (Artisans du Monde volunteer 2 2003)

THE DELEGATION STRATEGY OF FAIRTRADE INTERNATIONAL

There is no doubt that certification has been the main facilitator of growth in fair trade sales. In this domain, as in many others, standards have been a powerful socio-technical device enabling the extension of market relationships (Giddens 1990). But rather than examining the coordination capacity of standards, I instead highlight a different dimension of this coordination activity: in the case of fair trade, standards have also to be understood as a device for delegating business activities.

The Fairtrade system delegates two types of business activities: selling and importing. In France, Max Havelaar's employees and volunteers are very quick to criticize the way mainstream distribution chains work. However, in a country where, as they systematically point out, the vast majority of consumer goods are sold through such channels, refusing to take part in the mass distribution system would be detrimental to the goal of supporting producers' economic development. In other words, whereas the Artisans du Monde network has fewer than 150 shops across the entire country, by delegating the activity of selling fair trade goods, virtually every resident of France has access to fair trade. The founders of the Max Havelaar Foundation, Nico Roozen and Frans van der Hoff, who developed the first fair trade label, explain that they would have liked to import and process fair trade products for mass distribution themselves but had to give up such ideals because the international solidarity organizations that supported their project lacked the financial means and marketing expertise required to do so (Roozen and van der Hoff 2002). The labeling strategy thus, from its inception, recognized that large-scale business activity had to be delegated to external agents.

There is no doubt that this strategy has been successful in scaling up the size of the fair trade market. In France, the Artisans du Monde network represents 7 million euros of sales while retail sales of Fairtrade certified products reached 346 million euros in 2012. Only 3 per cent of the sales of Fairtrade certified products have been made in fair trade specialized shops like Artisans du Monde (12 per cent if one includes the organic specialized shops like Biocoop or Naturalia) (Max Havelaar France 2013).

However, delegating commercial activities also has controversial effects. First, delegation necessitates the conception of a complex system of standardization and certification to make sure that economic actors are truly making a fair(er) trade. In the case of Fairtrade, it even implied the constitution of two systems, one on standards setting (Fairtrade International) and one on inspection and certification (FLO-Cert), in order to follow the requirements of ISO 65, the international quality norm for certification bodies (see Bradley Wilson and Tad Mutersbaugh's chapter in this volume). These formal systems of standardization and certification have been described as a source of loss of personalization in the fair trade chains (Ballet and Carimentrand 2010; Daviron and Vagneron 2011). Field surveys conducted among producers' organizations report that some of their leaders regret the loss of the more direct relationships they had with ATOs in the beginnings of fair trade (Murray, Raynolds and Taylor 2003; see also Dolan 2010). Other studies point to the culture of surveillance and sanction that has replaced the initial culture of empowerment and partnership (Getz and Shreck 2006; Jaffee 2007). Finally, the complexity and costs of certification, which are primarily incurred by producer groups, constitute a barrier to entry for the smallest producer organizations, especially if they are not sure to export significant volumes at Fairtrade prices (Bacon 2010; Mutersbaugh 2005; Renard and Pérez-Grovas 2007).

Marie-Christine Renard pointed very early on to a second implication of the delegation strategy: 'Paradoxically, while this network was intended to avoid mechanisms for competition, they begin to appear' (Renard 1999, 498). Whereas ATO supply chains are characterized primarily by the establishment of lasting, close relationships with 'partner' organizations, the socio-technical agencements of Fairtrade chains are characterized above all by the constitution of subsets where competitive relationships prevail. Thus, for a producers' organization, being certified proves that it respects certain standards but does not automatically imply that it will find buyers on fair trade conditions. Licensed importers are free to choose the certified organizations with which they work, and Fairtrade International does not influence their choice. Because the supply is generally greater than the demand, the organizations engaged in fair trade are objectively in a competitive situation.

The same applies to licensed companies. For example, in the early 2010s about 20 companies using the Fairtrade mark aimed to sell their coffee in French supermarkets, but such markets only wanted to stock three or four brands of fair trade coffee (see also Smith 2010).

Standardization also plays a role in this process. Reflecting the tensions highlighted by Michel Callon and his colleagues (Callon, Méadel and Rabeharisoa 2002), we could say that on the one hand the socio-technical agencements of the Fairtrade system singularize fair trade products and producers (by distinguishing them from those that are not certified), but that on the other hand they make them comparable (by attributing them with the same qualification, despite different realities). According to Benoit Daviron and Isabelle Vagneron, this second face of standardization has now become dominant. Fairtrade standardization generates, in their words, a process of 're-commoditisation', where the characteristics of the producers are more hidden than unveiled and where the products and producers are made substitutable and placed in head-on competition (Daviron and Vagneron 2011). At the very end of the chain, this veiling effect of standardization particularly concerns consumers who can hardly see what happens 'behind the label'. The basic information that can fit on the packaging of products sold in supermarkets does not enable the consumer to know more about the situation of the producers and the practices of the companies. The consumer may thus consider that every Fairtrade coffee or tea pack is an ethically equivalent offer.

This relative freedom of commercial actors and this relative substitutability of products and producers generate significant tensions. Echoing the Polanyian definition of disembeddedness, forms of competition primarily based on prices can exist. For instance, some producers' organizations agree to waive the pre-financing or to sell the non-fair-trade part of their harvest below the market price, in exchange for a greater volume sold on fair trade conditions. This practice of 'bonded contracts' is a roundabout way of reducing the minimum price. Likewise, with regard to the third criterion of Bohannan and Dalton (1962) (are economic decisions guided by market remuneration?), the substitutable nature of certified products and producers allows for purchasing strategies motivated more by market considerations than by development objectives. As importers are free to choose among organizations of certified producers, most of them prefer the larger structures in the more developed countries (Murray, Raynolds and Taylor 2003; Mutersbaugh 2005). They can also prefer private plantations to farmers' cooperatives. Not all Fairtrade registers propose such a choice, but when they do, as in the case of bananas, competition between plantations and cooperatives generally ends up favoring the former, given their ability to deliver more constant quality and at more regular intervals (Shreck 2002). The pressure by mass retailers on the prices of coffee merchants and other licensed companies also fuels this tendency. And when consumers fail to see that, behind the same label, practices not governed by the standards often differ, they may choose the cheapest fair trade products and thus unwittingly support those licensed companies that are the least committed to the producers' development. The worst case scenario in that perspective would see the most committed companies not withstanding this competition and being forced out of the market by the less committed ones (Doherty, Davies and Tranchell 2012).

These observations show how the standards and rules that organize the Fairtrade system are far from completely controlling the behaviors of traders. Furthermore, because traders are not obligated to participate, many can even threaten to leave if the standards are too high. This threat is made even more credible now that there is a range of competing certification systems. Once again, on this point too, the delegation strategy that founded the Fairtrade system has disputable consequences. The 'dilution' (Jaffee 2010) of the Fairtrade standards has to do with this threat: traders have a power of negotiation in the standards-setting process that exceeds their weight in the governance structures of Fairtrade International. Two convergent ethnographic studies, Bacon (2010) and Reinecke (2010), show how this threat was in everyone's mind during the coffee price debates in 2007–2008. Similarly, the long-standing request to include coffee plantations in the Fairtrade system has clearly been led by actors like Fair Trade USA which believed they could attract more traders with such a change to the standards (Jaffee 2010; Raynolds 2012).

RESISTANCE AND RADICAL MAINSTREAMING

The previous section has reported some of the processes of growth and of conventionalization that are associated with the idea of mainstreaming. These processes have been well documented, but to only focus on them would run the risk of adopting the deterministic and dualistic thinking evoked in the introduction. Recent research on mainstreaming has avoided this pitfall by showing the existence of resistance against these processes and the possibility of socio-technical agencements that combine growth and alternativeness (Davies, Doherty and Knox 2010; Doherty and Tranchell 2007; Huybrechts 2010; Jaffee 2010; Low and Davenport 2007; Raynolds 2009; 2012).

In the United States the mainstreaming has been led by a 'market-oriented' conception of fair trade. Illustrations of this tendency include the lobbying of Fair Trade USA to make standards more accessible and the certification of big coffee companies' minor product lines and of supermarkets' own-brand products (Jaffee 2010; Raynolds 2009; also April Linton and Claudia Rosty's chapter in this volume). But the United States is also, at the same time, a place where other actors try to impose a more 'movement-oriented' conception. Some of these actors are the 'mission-driven companies' that sell only fair trade products yet position themselves in mainstream markets (Raynolds 2009). Equal Exchange is an interesting example, as this cooperative seems to have been able to combine strong business development with a strong commitment to the original values of fair trade, notably with trading practices going well beyond Fairtrade requirements. Public debates on the appropriate strategies of mainstreaming have also been the occasion of mobilization of other actors like ATOs, non-governmental organizations (NGOs) or students groups (Raynolds 2007). Similarly, the departure of Fair Trade USA from Fairtrade International can be interpreted as a consequence of the influence of powerful 'movement-oriented' actors in the governance of the Fairtrade system, who contest Fair Trade USA's proposed changes (Raynolds 2012).

The term 'radical mainstreaming' was used for the first time at the very end of an article critical of current trends of mainstreaming (Low and Davenport 2005). For the authors, these trends should not lead us to plead for isolation from the mainstream, but for the development of ambitious projects that combine significant economic success and political involvement. Among others, they cited the case of The Day Chocolate Company, which has been studied at length (Doherty and Tranchell 2007). The Day Chocolate Company is very much an alternative fair trade project: its range of products is certified by Fairtrade and made from cocoa imported from a farmers' cooperative in Ghana, which also owns a 45 per cent stake in the company. But its strategy is also marked by the choice to compete with other, often less alternative, certified products in the mainstream market. In these conditions, one key factor of their success has been the company's capacity to singularize their chocolates. This has been managed through communication in mainstream media and through specific actions targeting religious, political or activists groups. A second key factor has been the establishment of close collaborations with the Co-op supermarket chain and British ATOs. For instance, Oxfam shops stock the entire range of chocolates sold by Day Chocolate, represent important outlets and provide a useful test market before products are introduced in major supermarket chains like Tesco.

CONCLUSION

Fair trade, perhaps more than any other alternative food system, is characterized by tensions. Since its first formulation by Michael Barratt Brown, the difficulty of being simultaneously 'in and against the market' (Barratt Brown 1993) has been a recurrent finding of fair trade research. This tension is intrinsic to the project of fair trade, but is particularly visible in situations of mainstreaming, where successful commercial development comes with other evolutions contrary to the ambition to establish market socio-technical agencements different from those of the 'conventional market'. Thus the fair trade dilemma seems to be about growing but losing one's soul or remaining small to keep its purity. Mainstreaming is a 'Faustian bargain' which shifts 'fair trade away from its original grounding in transparency, direct producer/consumer relation and global justice' (Goodman, DuPuis and Goodman 2012, 200–201). Various studies, including some presented in the previous sections, have clearly shown that this kind of analysis is not unfounded. The Italian case exposed by Leonardo Becchetti and Marco Costantino tends to confirm this analysis by showing the economic limits of a highly 'movement-oriented' fair trade (Becchetti and Costantino 2010). In a nutshell, there are many empirical reasons to link in the single word 'mainstreaming' the sales growth and the conventionalization of fair trade.

It is nevertheless necessary to consider another kind of analysis that goes further than this finding. It is analytically important to grasp the transformations that lie behind the growth of sales. Studies in economic sociology that stress the socio-technical agencements which constitute and shape actually existing markets are a useful tool for that purpose. The scaling up of fair trade can be explained by studying the work of the market professionals (e.g., designers, marketers, importers, retailers) and the work of market devices (e.g., standards, labels, advertising) that render it possible. Taking this close look also allows us to be mindful of the different strategies of growth of various fair trade organizations. The consequences of growth can then no longer be presumed to fit into a single model of degradation. They have to be carefully observed and analyzed starting from the characterization of the existing socio-technical agencements. The level of (dis)embeddedness in particular is not a direct effect of the level of sales. It is the consequence of the actors' strategies and these strategies are influenced by the market socio-technical agencements in which they develop. Competition on prices, for instance, is a strategy that is rendered possible by the work of standards and labels.

To conclude, I will add that it is also politically important to do this analytical work. Misunderstanding these mechanisms leads the way to a highly deterministic conception of mainstreaming: are there no alternatives to being either 'small and alternative' or being 'big and conventional'? I argue there are other alternatives. If this chapter has shown that we should not be naïve to the risks associated with some strategies of mainstreaming, it also invites us, as researchers and actors, to envisage the diversity of the possible forms of fair trade mainstreaming.

NOTES

* I sincerely thank Elizabeth Bennett and Laura Raynolds for their comments and thoughtful editing.

1. In 2013 Artisans du Monde was composed of 148 local groups, representing around 6000 volunteers whose main activity is to run a shop where fair trade food and craftwork are sold.

REFERENCES

Artisans du Monde volunteer 1 (2003), interview with Ronan Le Velly, Paris (26 March 2003).

Artisans du Monde volunteer 2 (2003), interview with Ronan Le Velly, Nantes (5 February 2003).

Bacon, Christopher M. (2010), 'Who decides what is fair in fair trade? The agri-environmental governance of standards, access, and price', *Journal of Peasant Studies*, 37 (1), 111–147.

Ballet, Jérôme and Aurélie Carimentrand (2010), 'Fair trade and the depersonalization of ethics', *Journal of Business Ethics*, 92 (S2), 317–330.

Barratt Brown, Michael (1993), *Fair Trade: Reform and Realities in the International Trading System*, London: Zed Books.

Becchetti, Leonardo and Marco Costantino (2010), 'Fair trade in Italy: Too much "movement" in the shop?', *Journal of Business Ethics*, 92 (S2), 181–203.

Block, Fred (1990), *Postindustrial Possibilities. A Critique of Economic Discourse*, Berkeley, CA: University of California Press.

Bohannan, Paul and George Dalton (eds.) (1962), *Markets in Africa*, Evanston, IL: Northwestern University Press.

Boltanski, Luc and Laurent Thévenot (2006), *On Justification: Economies of Worth*, Princeton, NJ: Princeton University Press.

Çalışkan, Koray and Michel Callon (2010), 'Economization, Part 2: A research programme for the study of markets', *Economy and Society*, 39 (1), 1–32.

Callon, Michel, Cécile Méadel and Vololona Rabeharisoa (2002), 'The economy of qualities', *Economy and Society*, 31 (2), 194–217.

Campbell, Hugh and Christopher Rosin (2011), 'After the "Organic Industrial Complex": An ontological expedition through commercial organic agriculture in New Zealand', *Journal of Rural Studies*, 27 (4), 350–361.

Cochoy, Franck and Sophie Dubuisson-Quellier (2013), 'The sociology of market work', *Economic Sociology_the European Electronic Newsletter*, 15 (1), 4–11.

Davies, Iain A., Bob Doherty and Simon Knox (2010), 'The rise and stall of a fair trade pioneer: The Cafédirect story', *Journal of Business Ethics*, 92 (1), 127–147.
Daviron, Benoit and Isabelle Vagneron (2011), 'From commoditisation to de-commoditisation … and back again: Discussing the role of sustainability standards for agricultural products', *Development Policy Review*, 29 (1), 91–113.
Doherty, Bob, Iain A. Davies and Sophi Tranchell (2012), 'Where now for fair trade?', *Business History*, 55 (2), 161–189.
Doherty, Bob and Sophi Tranchell (2007), '"Radical mainstreaming" of Fairtrade: The case of The Day Chocolate Company', *Equal Opportunities International*, 26 (7), 693–711.
Dolan, Catherine S. (2010), 'Virtual moralities: The mainstreaming of Fairtrade in Kenyan tea fields', *Geoforum*, 41 (1), 33–43.
Dubuisson-Quellier, Sophie, Claire Lamine and Ronan Le Velly (2011), 'Citizenship and consumption: Mobilisation in alternative food systems in France', *Sociologia Ruralis*, 51 (3), 304–323.
Fédération Artisans du Monde (2013), *Développement réseau 2012*, Paris: Fédération Artisans du Monde.
Gemici, Kurtuluş (2008), 'Karl Polanyi and the antinomies of embeddedness', *Socio-Economic Review*, 6 (1), 5–33.
Getz, Christy and Aimee Shreck (2006), 'What organic and fair trade labels do not tell us: Towards a place-based understanding of certification', *International Journal of Consumer Studies*, 30 (5), 490–501.
Giddens, Anthony (1990), *The Consequences of Modernity*, Palo Alto, CA: Stanford University Press.
Goodman, David, Melanie DuPuis and Michael Goodman (2012), *Alternative Food Networks: Knowledge, Practice and Politics*, London: Routledge.
Grimes, Kimberly M. and Barbara Lynne Milgram (2000), *Artisans and Cooperatives: Developing Alternative Trade for the Global Economy*, Tucson, AZ: University of Arizona Press.
Guthman, Julie (2004), *Agrarian Dreams: The Paradox of Organic Farming in California*, Berkeley, CA: University of California Press.
Huybrechts, Benjamin (2010), 'Fair trade organizations in Belgium: Unity in diversity?', *Journal of Business Ethics*, 92 (S2), 217–240.
Jaffee, Daniel (2007), *Brewing Justice: Fair Trade Coffee, Sustainability and Survival*, Berkeley, CA: University of California Press.
Jaffee, Daniel (2010), 'Fair trade standards, corporate participation, and social movement responses in the United States', *Journal of Business Ethics*, 92 (S2), 267–285.
Le Velly, Ronan (2007), 'Is large-scale fair trade possible?', in Edwin Zaccai (ed.), *Sustainable Consumption, Ecology and Fair Trade*, London: Routledge, pp. 201–215.
Littrell, Mary Ann and Marsha Ann Dickson (1999), *Social Responsibility in the Global Market: Fair Trade of Cultural Products*, Thousand Oaks, CA: Sage.
Low, William and Eileen Davenport (2005), 'Postcards from the edge: Maintaining the "alternative" character of fair trade', *Sustainable Development*, 13 (3), 143–153.
Low, William and Eileen Davenport (2007), 'To boldly go … exploring ethical spaces to re-politicise ethical consumption and fair trade', *Journal of Consumer Behaviour*, 6 (5), 336–348.
Max Havelaar France (2013), *Rapport annuel 2012–2013*, Montreuil, France: Max Havelaar France.
Max Havelaar France (2014), 'Le commerce équitable en chiffres', available at http://www.maxhavelaarfrance.org/le-commerce-equitable/le-commerce-equitable/en-chiffres.html (accessed 1 April 2014).
Muniesa, Fabian, Yuval Millo and Michel Callon (eds.) (2007), *Market Devices*, Oxford: Blackwell Publishers.

Murray, Douglas L., Laura T. Raynolds and Peter Leigh Taylor (2003), *One Cup at a Time: Poverty Alleviation and Fair Trade Coffee in Latin America*, Fort Collins, CO: Fair Trade Research Group, Colorado State University.
Mutersbaugh, Tad (2005), 'Fighting standards with standards: Harmonization, rents, and social accountability in certified agrofood networks', *Environment and Planning A*, 37 (11), 2033–2051.
Özçağlar-Toulouse, Nil, Amina Béji-Bécheur, Matthieu Gateau and Philippe Robert-Demontrond (2010), 'Demystifying fair trade in France: The history of an ambiguous project', *Journal of Business Ethics*, 92 (S2), 205–216.
Polanyi, Karl (1985), *The Great Transformation: The Political and Economic Origins of Our Time*, Boston, MA: Beacon Press.
Raynolds, Laura T. (2007), 'Fair trade bananas: Broadening the movement and market in the United States', in Laura T. Raynolds, Douglas L. Murray and John Wilkinson (eds.), *Fair Trade: The Challenges of Transforming Globalization*, New York: Routledge, pp. 63–82.
Raynolds, Laura T. (2009), 'Mainstreaming fair trade coffee: From partnership to traceability', *World Development*, 37 (6), 1083–1093.
Raynolds, Laura T. (2012), 'Fair trade: Social regulation in global food markets', *Journal of Rural Studies*, 28 (3), 276–287.
Raynolds, Laura T., Douglas L. Murray and John Wilkinson (eds.) (2007), *Fair Trade: The Challenges of Transforming Globalization*, New York: Routledge.
Reinecke, Juliane (2010), 'Beyond a subjective theory of value and towards a "fair price": An organizational perspective on Fairtrade minimum price setting', *Organization*, 17 (5), 563–581.
Renard, Marie-Christine (1999), 'The interstices of globalization: The example of fair coffee', *Sociologia Ruralis*, 39 (4), 484–500.
Renard, Marie-Christine and Victor Pérez-Grovas (2007), 'Fair trade coffee in Mexico: At the center of the debates', in Laura T. Raynolds, Douglas L. Murray and John Wilkinson (eds.), *Fair Trade: The Challenges of Transforming Globalization*, New York: Routledge, pp. 138–156.
Roozen, Nico and Frans van der Hoff (2002), *L'aventure du commerce équitable. Une alternative à la mondialisation par les fondateurs de Max Havelaar*, Paris: JC Lattès.
Shreck, Aimee (2002), 'Just bananas? Fair trade banana production in the Dominican Republic', *International Journal of Sociology of Agriculture and Food*, 10 (2), 13–23.
Smith, Sally (2010), 'For love or money? Fairtrade business models in the UK supermarket sector', *Journal of Business Ethics*, 92 (S2), 257–266.

16. Fair trade certification, performance and practice

Bradley R. Wilson and Tad Mutersbaugh

INTRODUCTION

In this chapter we bring a historical and conceptual perspective to the evolution of product certification through a critical look at the growing 'certified-industrial complex' behind the Fairtrade label (see Gereffi et al. 2001). First, we theorize the political economy of certification within the context of widespread efforts to clean up global supply chains in response to concerns about social, economic and environmental injustice and efforts to foster corporate social responsibility. Second, we briefly describe the rise of fair trade certification, embed it in the broader harmonizing trend of quality certifications and identify important questions that remain to be answered regarding the role of certification in fair trade. Our analysis draws upon the experience of coffee, which due to the relatively lengthy history as a fairly traded commodity provides an excellent standpoint from which to view how commodity chain organization and social practice have been altered by fair trade's shift from a trust-based 'solidarity' network to a standards-based commodity chain subject to ISO (International Organization for Standardization) certification norms.

A key goal will be to signal the paradoxes embedded in the certification process, which, when considered within the broader arena of fair-trade-related activities, may be found to exert its own disciplining effects. In particular, we will discuss the somewhat contradictory process through which *certification as a practice* under certain conditions enhances fair trade outcomes and yet in others contributes to a 'disembedding' of the solidarity relations that once gave fair trade its unique stamp (Wilson 2013). Seen in this manner, fair trade becomes a set of tasks, performances or a labor process and in a sense mirrors the biopoliticized practices of consumer choice identified by Mike Goodman and Agatha Herman's chapter in this volume. Fair trade certification is also, we would like to make clear, a pluralistic process that encompasses a great many fair trade labels that range from NGO-driven labels (e.g., 'small producers' and 'comercio justo') to hybrid labels (such as Naturland) that retain a proprietary set of norms, standards and practices. Although 'Fairtrade certification' under the aegis of Fairtrade International is the most important certification in the global context, it is not always the most important in any particular context given the high degree of balkanization found in market-oriented ethical trade schemes. In addition, as we argue below, certification practices are set by ISO norms, which have played a significant role in driving the shape of fair trade networks.

We also argue that the performance of contemporary certification, harmonized under the ISO rubric along with quality standards that apply to other internationally traded commodities, has contributed to a lack of transparency, participation or coordination throughout the network as a whole and has become a driving force behind a network focus on mainstreaming, legitimization and market growth. As a consequence, we now witness a new trend of internal crisis and balkanization that may hinder the long-term stability of fair trade networks. This process of balkanization may lead to a rethinking of the role and form of the certified-industrial complex and also open up new doors for producer-driven models of verification and marketing that may enhance democracy and transparency at the core of the fair trade movement.

CERTIFICATION AS A GLOBAL PRACTICE

At the outset, we note that one of the difficulties in assessing certification effects lies in the myriad of ways in which it is performed. Although ostensibly undertaken in accordance with transnational ISO norms, in practice there are significant differences in local certification practices that substantially alter the lived experience of certification. First, though, it is useful to think of certification in a wider sense, as a contemporary 'revolution' that can be traced historically to the 1980s when innovative transnational solidarity campaigns based in Europe and the United States reached out to consumers, pressuring retail brands to alter their internal production and purchasing policies (Conroy 2007; see also Laura Raynolds and Nicholas Greenfield's chapter in this volume). Disenchanted with the unresponsiveness of politicians and faltering governmental efforts to protect labor and the environment in an age of state retrenchment, market triumphalism and the globalization of production, nimble social movements in the global North maneuvered into the retail marketplace to air grievances, protect against abuses and call for reform. Campaigns to protect dolphins from tuna fishermen, forest biodiversity from timber harvesters and children from exploitative garment work, carpet-making and infant-formula advertising set off a groundswell of consumer activism in the retail marketplace. Characteristic of these market-oriented campaigns was the use of information networks and media exposés that would 'name and shame' retail brands. As Raynolds and Wilkinson (2007, 42) have argued, the 'cost of the neoliberal dream of transforming market economies into market societies' has not only resulted in the restructuring of global commodity chains, but has also resulted in 'an unimagined expansion of market responsibility and accountability' pursued by civil society groups and organizations.

Even though media and boycott campaigns proved highly successful in raising the ire of consumers to challenge established brands for their business practices at home and abroad, they provided little long-term accountability. Indeed, as scholars note, the use of boycotts and media smear tactics often had unintended consequences, particularly for working communities in the global South, as retail firms sought to 'clean up shop' simply by changing production location (Freidberg 2003). As a consequence, many activists sought global accountability regimes that were geographically extensive and capable of garnering greater 'buy-in' – both in terms of generating economic resources and earning legitimacy in the eyes of consumer coalitions, non-governmental organizations (NGOs) and retail firms (Conroy 2007). Advocates then needed a way to communicate the existence, presence and visibility of these accountability regimes (Barham 2002). Voluntary product labeling filled the void for greater buy-in, bridging the gap between both the demands of consumers to act on their conscience for 'change' and the demands of retailers to maintain their reputation and remain profitable in the face of mounting consumer opposition (Mutersbaugh 2005a, Wilson and Curnow 2013). In other words, voluntary labeling was a means of institutionalizing longer-term accountability to social movements demanding social and environmental change.

As market-oriented ethical product campaigns in the global North shifted to certification in the 1990s, a network of NGOs began to create standards-based accountability structures to certify and monitor compliance with ethical standards (Conroy 2007; Mutersbaugh 2005b). Responding to the regulatory void created by the neoliberal state, the innovation of third-party product certification, codes of conduct and voluntary labeling in the 1990s, NGOs effectively created what Mutersbaugh (2005a, 397) calls 'a public sphere within the private economy' (see also Peter Utting's chapter in this volume). Instead of choosing to protest via boycott, negative advertising or disinvestment, for instance through 'black listing' particular firms or commodities, activists and

NGOs re-channeled resources into promoting firms and products that did meet their moral norms. This shift in movement tactics left an indelible mark on what Brooks (2007, xiii) calls, 'the logic, origins, objectives and consequences of transnational campaigns'. By promoting particular products or retailers that met the criteria of social movement actors, campaigns increasingly adopted the logics of the market they sought to transform (Wilson and Curnow 2013).

FAIR TRADE

The fair trade network is often portrayed as a kind of Polanyian 'counter movement' (Polanyi 1944) that protects society against the dehumanizing impulses of capitalism, particularly the abstract formulation of 'the market' and the self-interested and rationally calculative search for profit as an end unto itself (Fridell 2007; Guthman 2007; Jaffee 2007; Raynolds 2000). For several scholars, fair trade embodies Polanyi's concept in which organic market formations may serve as protective counter-weights against destructive capitalist market logics (cf. Jaffee 2007). Drawing explicitly from Polanyi, Raynolds (2000, 297–298) claims that the fair trade movement challenges those abstract capitalist relations 'that fuel exploitation in the agro-food system', and that fair trade fosters 'the re-embedding of international commodity production and distribution in "equitable social relations"'. Likewise, Jaffee et al. (2004, 170) argue that the fair trade movement has created linkages between consumers and producers that are 'socially embedded' in what Renard (1999, 496) calls 'values of solidarity and fairness' in place of 'the values of the market'.

Central to such claims of social embeddedness has been the notion that solidarity networks fostered by fair trade could help to shorten the conventional supply chain by establishing 'direct' trade with marginalized commodity producers. In this sense, fair trade was believed to collapse social and spatial distances endemic to capitalist modernity (Harvey 1990). Whatmore and Thorne (1997) employed actor-network theory to describe the thickening of socio-economic relationships, claiming that fair trade generates 'nourishing networks' that increase connectivity between Northern consumers and Southern producers. Scholars in geography also frequently reference the ability of fair trade to unveil the commodity fetish that conceals the labor that goes into the production of commodities (Bryant and Goodman 2004; Hudson and Hudson 2003). These conceptualizations of fair trade emphasize both the redemptive qualities of a close geographic connection between consumers and producers of commodities as well as the protective qualities of fair trade as a form of social regulation that resists the otherwise self-regulating market (Guthman 2007).

In recent years, however, fair trade advocates, academics, retailers and development practitioners have questioned the efficacy and politics of existing fair trade certification regimes in translating the noble goals of the movement into the challenging terrain of the marketplace (Wilson 2010; 2013). As fair trade has made greater inroads into the retail mainstream through conventional firms such as Walmart, Nestlé and McDonald's, the image of the fair trade movement as an alternative to capitalist globalization has come under increasing scrutiny (Wilson and Curnow 2013). For some, the presence of fair trade in conventional retail outlets suggests that the ideals embodied within the movement have arrived. Yet for others the efforts by the fair trade movement to court the major retail market players who hold the promise of dramatically increasing the volume of certified fair trade products has inadvertently 'diluted' its alternativeness as a social movement while also generating internal divisions among its supporters (Raynolds and Wilkinson 2007, 43; cf. Fridell 2007; Wilson and Curnow 2013).

These concerns about fair trade in spaces of consumption and production raise critical questions about the politics and practices of certification itself. Challenging earlier claims that the fair trade movement represented a social regulatory *resistance* to conventional market logics, numerous scholars over the past decade have come to suggest that certification economies (Mutersbaugh 2005a), voluntary labels (Guthman 2007), outsourced voluntary regulation and ethical quality conventions (Renard 2005) are reflective of broader changes to agro-food networks in the context of neoliberal globalization that marginalize small-scale producers and workers. Within this context, a combination of changing trade rules, production shifts under post-Fordist regulatory regimes and growing consumer anxiety with respect to food origins, contents and contamination have made product certification and voluntary labeling an important aspect of retail firm strategies for maintaining a green or ethical reputation. As Mutersbaugh (2005a, 398) argues, 'in a general sense, firms share a dependence upon a "green" reputation to sustain profit margins and, with respect to the mechanics of certification, a consequent desire to manage information about quality and avoid the emergence of information that might tarnish that reputation'.

Guthman (2007) theorizes voluntary labeling for fair trade as a sort of 'nice neoliberalization' of social, political and economic processes by devolving responsibilities for social protections from the state to civil society while also enabling new forms of value creation that can be appropriated by capitalist firms (Guthman 2007; see also 2004). Guthman

(2004) and Mutersbaugh (2005a) argue that product certifications and voluntary labels reflect patterns of capitalist accumulation by creating 'rents' via protective barriers to entry that are controlled, not by working communities, but commodity buyers and NGOs. By exploiting the value created by these barriers to entry (created by certifying spaces and communicated through labels), downstream retail firms can garner super-profits from the sale of both the material and semiotic values conveyed in the product (Guthman 2004). McCarthy (2006) has referred to this as the conventionalization thesis, which makes the claim that the rents generated by marked 'alternativeness' will lead 'to some quite mainstream dynamics in aspirationally alternative networks' (McCarthy 2006, 808). Fair trade and other social or ecological labeling initiatives have increasingly become mere quality certifications (Mutersbaugh 2002; Mutersbaugh and Lyon 2010; Raynolds 2004; Raynolds and Wilkinson 2007; Renard 2005).

HISTORY OF FAIR TRADE CERTIFICATION

The idea of selling fair trade products originated as a solidarity initiative and alternative trade network led by NGOs and world shops in Europe and North America (Nicholls and Opal 2005, 142). In the United States, the discourse of fair trade can be traced back to the Mennonite Central Committee, which first began purchasing handicrafts from Puerto Rican artisans in the 1940s. In the United Kingdom, Oxfam played a similar role in selling handicrafts made by Chinese refugees in the 1950s (WFTO 2009). Starting in the 1960s, a range of alternative trade organizations (ATOs) formed in Europe began selling products from Third World artisans. Over the first few decades, ATOs sold exclusively handicrafts. Ideologically, most of these fair trade initiatives rallied around the idea of trade-not-aid, seeking to provide artisans (and later farmers and workers) a premium price for their goods.

Fair trade product certification and voluntary labeling was first established by the Dutch NGO Solidaridad, under the Max Havelaar label in 1988 (Renard 1999). The Max Havelaar label introduced the first standards, certification and labeling scheme for a fairly traded product that provided an audit trail back through the supply chain to the point of production (Renard 1999). The Max Havelaar label was groundbreaking in at least five ways. First, the Max Havelaar label helped extend fair trading to the agro-food sector, as opposed to just handicrafts. Second, the product label made it possible to 'scale up' fair trade sales through conventional retail outlets. The label was specifically designed to certify the symbolic fairness of the product itself and not the firm which sold it. Until then, fairly traded products were sold only inside of the ATO networks and therefore it was the entire enterprise that gave credence to the ethical claims. With the invention of a transferable fair trade label, coffee that was certified by one NGO could be sold in any conventional retail outlet that abided by the standards and agreed to be monitored for compliance. The use of product-specific certification and voluntary labeling as opposed to certifying the ethical business practices of an entire firm (i.e., an ATO), paved the way for fairly traded products to reach mainstream retail channels for the first time.

A third innovation in the Max Havelaar labeling initiative was its concern for paying fair prices and the elaboration of a fair price formula that theoretically reflected costs of production and living standards in producing communities. While fair trade principles sought to improve compensation for disadvantaged artisans, farmers and workers through direct buying relationships, no fair trade initiative to date had attempted to define the parameters of a fair price. The rationale for the creation of a fair price formula for coffee reflected broader international trade concerns. It responded directly to the failure of producer and consumer countries to negotiate an International Coffee Agreement (ICA) in 1987 and mounting concerns that the disappearance of a quota system would lead to overproduction and declining prices. The fourth innovation in the new system was that cooperatives of small-scale producers became the focal point of fair trade exchanges and fair price standards. Frans van der Hoff, who collaborated with Nico Roozen to invent the Max Havelaar label, was a missionary who helped form UCIRI (Unión de Comunidades Indígenas de la Región del Istmo) in Oaxaca, Mexico. UCIRI was arguably the first fair trade certified cooperative in Latin America. Reflecting his work to organize smallholders, the Max Havelaar standards favored farmers organized in cooperatives. Cooperatives were envisioned as hubs for social development initiatives as well as facilitating economies of scale necessary for exporting coffee to fair trade coffee buyers. Max Havelaar standards' emphasis on small-scale farmers and cooperatives would come to distinguish fair trade from all other social and ecological labeling initiatives.

The final innovation was the use of 'certification and labeling' as the mechanism to ensure that the fairly traded commodity met the ideal standards set by Max Havelaar. The goal of product certification for fair trade was to isolate and monitor adherence to specific normative principles by accrediting buyers and sellers, auditing transactions and certifying the chain of custody between qualified producer organizations and licensed importers, roasters and retailers. The labeling and certification approach (to meet overall strategic goals of the fair trade movement) was designed to increase retailer and consumer confidence that normative principles were monitored by an objective third party. Furthermore, voluntary labeling enabled the fair trade movement to extend beyond the network of small-scale retailers and world shops run by the ATOs that pioneered the practice of using fair trade principles in their supply chains. In other words, the fair trade movement obtained credibility for itself by creating a legitimate bureaucratic hierarchy that could 'prove' adherence to the normative standards of the movement. In marrying the fair trade movement to voluntary labeling and certification, these pioneers successfully increased market share and communicated the movement's unique set of values to the public. As we note later, however, this movement legitimacy – rooted in multi-stakeholder standards-making and certification – did not satisfy market actors.

By the mid-1990s, the Max Havelaar label was being used throughout Europe in national labeling initiatives in Belgium, Luxembourg, Germany and Italy. By 1997 the national initiatives employing the Max Havelaar labeling approach formed Fairtrade Labelling Organizations International, later renamed Fairtrade International (Fairtrade International 2008). The creation of Fairtrade International established one uniform agency that could handle the expansion of Fairtrade certified products and the growing number of producer organizations selling Fairtrade certified products around the world. Fairtrade International, as the central governing body for 'Fairtrade', created a 'global standard' for certifying production and processing methods and for measuring fairness in supply chains. It also enabled the agency to branch out beyond coffee into other agro-food commodities such as chocolate, tea, bananas and sugar. Yet, the formation of Fairtrade International as an institution not only represented the formalization of standards-making. It also re-oriented the diverse national initiatives under one umbrella, identifying key campaign brokers around the world that would institutionalize Fairtrade auditing and oversee market growth in all of the major coffee retailing countries.

Organizationally, the restructuring of Fairtrade standards, certification and labeling under Fairtrade International established a clear division of labor between the organization and what were then envisaged as national Fairtrade labeling initiatives. Fairtrade International oversaw 'global' standards-making and the auditing of democratically organized cooperatives through the publication of its international Fairtrade registry. The national Fairtrade labeling initiatives would oversee the development of the Fairtrade movement and market in their own countries. National Fairtrade labeling initiatives, operating under the Fairtrade International rubric, were empowered to grant licenses to firms for the use of the Fairtrade certified label. In return for licenses, firms were to agree to have their contracts audited and pay a licensing fee for label use. Moreover, national labeling initiatives were charged with promoting the Fairtrade certified label in their respective countries.

HARMONIZING FAIR TRADE CERTIFICATIONS

In 2002, Fairtrade International and its network of national labeling initiatives reorganized in conformance with the ISO Guide 65 rubric for certification. Guide 65 sets out a process by which to certify standards compliance (Mutersbaugh 2005a). At a macro level, international certification structures have converged through 'harmonization'. ISO touts a 'strategic alliance' joining ISO to the WTO (World Trade Organization) via the TBT (Technical Barriers to Trade) provision. The TBT, accepted by WTO signatory nations (IEC 2014), is a provision that allows one nation to challenge another's internal trade regulations. This has promoted ISO's role in international trade agreements. For Fairtrade International, adopting ISO certification frameworks allowed it to conform to international trade norms (Fridell 2007, 55). 'Harmonization' across national contexts under the ISO Guide 65 template aids and furthers the trend noted by DeLind (2000, 200) towards the creation of a 'single, manageable dimension' amenable to bureaucratic control and monitoring.

This ISO-induced reorganization has a knock-on effect for fair trade–organic network affiliates, for organizations at each level must reconfigure relations in order to comply with ISO-defined Guide 65 transparency and conflict-of-interest rubrics. Figure 16.1 depicts multi-tiered ISO Guide 65-inspired organizational restructuring. ISO Guide 65 sections 4.2[l] and 4.2[o][1 & 2] require (respectively) that organizations distinguish between certification and non-certification activities, abstain from production and design of products of the type certified and do not engage in consultancy. Effects may be seen in the institutional separation of Fairtrade International from FLO-Cert and corresponding division internal to producer organizations between a 'technical and extension staff' that manages dissemination of standards (produced by Fairtrade International) and 'marketing personnel' that are in turn certified by a third-party certifier that shares information with FLO-Cert.

Figure 16.1 likewise illustrates the separation of information regarding standards from information about compliance. Producers are able to learn

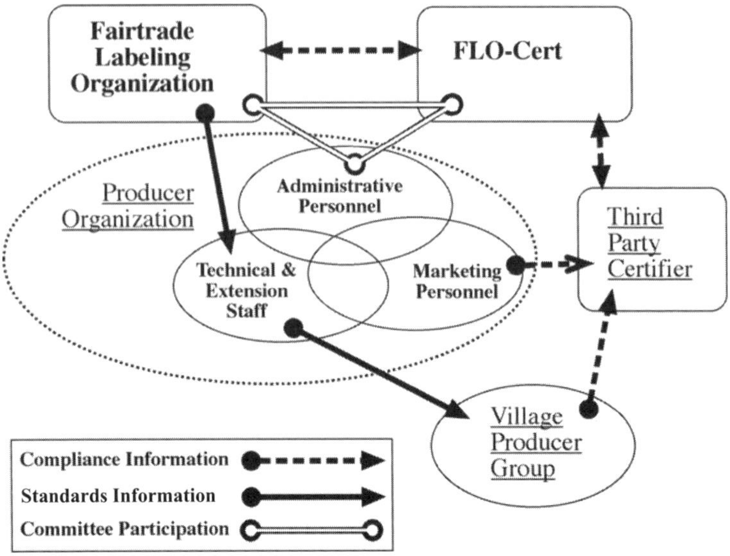

Figure 16.1 Knowledge relations in Fairtrade certification

about Fairtrade International standards via their regional producer organizations (such as Oaxacan producer cooperatives or Nicaraguan cooperatives discussed here) but must turn to FLO-Cert to determine whether they are in substantial compliance with standards (i.e., whether they may trade in Fairtrade markets during a particular annual harvest cycle). Arrows in Figure 16.1 also indicate directionality in the flow of certification information. Producers must provide information requested by certifiers (with respect to standards compliance). Producers may obtain clarification of standards requirements from FLO-Cert, but FLO-Cert is prevented, under ISO Guide 65 norm 4.2 [o][2], from telling producers how they may comply with standards (to gain market access). Farmers must turn to producer organization technical (extension) staff to determine a compliance strategy. In sum, ISO decrees a separation of knowledge-of-standards versus knowledge-of-compliance necessary to certification integrity, transparency and impartiality. This separation, however, fractures the prior integrity of Fairtrade International and affiliated organizations.

Although our principal focus has been to examine how knowledge differences and deficits affect producer solidarity, we note in passing that others in the Fairtrade International/FLO-Cert network are likewise affected. First, ISO norms bar those who have regular, direct contact with producers – namely, certifiers accredited by ISO Cert – from participating in Fairtrade International's policy work. Second, Fairtrade International's personnel generate standards, but institutional separation limits their ability to assess cost impacts of standards on producers. On the one hand, the Fairtrade International/FLO-Cert balkanization leads to a separate calculation of the labor costs required to meet the norms versus the calculation of the costs of attending the certification itself – with the result that the household-level costs of meeting standards are relatively well understood whereas the often severe organizational burdens of attending to inspections and documentation are less well understood (Mutersbaugh 2004). This balkanization represents quite a severe departure from the original 'trust'-based system: prior to the late 1990s, both norms and inspections structures were determined by consensus among network participants and thus the full costs were more easily assessed (see González and Nigh 2005).

This Fairtrade International/FLO-Cert division echoes a similar, prior division in the US organic sector. In the US organic case, organizations such as the Organic Crop Improvement Association (OCIA) and Oregon Tilth initially created a separate certification arm, only to see the original, 'standards design' part of the organization wither away at the expense of the certification group, their standards supplanted by the US Department of Agriculture (USDA) National Organic Program (Gonzalez and Nigh 2005). Although the conditions of fair trade are quite distinct from organic – there is no state-led fair trade program – it is interesting that the Fairtrade International/FLO-Cert division was likewise accompanied by a breakdown in the coherency of the original organization. This certainly raises the question of whether this division and the implementation of ISO-style restrictions on intra-organizational communication was in part responsible for the fragmentation of fair trade organizations. Three important questions remain. First, to what degree did the ISO-induced split in the principal fair trade organization, Fairtrade International, contribute to the broader pattern of balkanization that currently characterizes the fair trade market? Second, how will this split affect the distribution of power, that is to say, who has say-so over standards, practices and rent distributions within the network? And third, will fair trade ever be capable of flourishing in the context of ISO-style certification norms, given the separations imposed by 'conflict-of-interest' norms?

FAIR TRADE CERTIFICATION AS LOCAL PRACTICE

A striking aspect of certification structures is the difference between the global effects and norms ostensibly required to pass ISO Guide 65 norms *versus* the form that certification takes on the ground, whether considered as a task and information structure or as a performance. In this sense, fair trade is understood *not* as philosophy of ethical action, but rather as a double set of performative tasks: 1) those undertaken to comply with norms, such as providing payments and premiums directly to each farmer and 2) those undertaken to *demonstrate* compliance, such as presenting receipts to inspectors in person or documenting social spending activities. As a performance, these activities may detract from (or enhance) farmers' efforts to fight for and attain better conditions of life irrespective of the benefits of a higher income received by farmers. Here we are primarily concerned with this second, demonstration aspect.

As an embodied practice, certification has its greatest effect on this second, demonstration tier, providing an organizational structure and a set of activities that affect local conditions of production and exchange. Thus, our research identifies three certification effects. First, under ISO norms, certification embodies *transparency* by specifying points of inspection, by gathering information about production quantities and prices in folders and reports and by enacting a new set of situated social positions and relations such as encounters between farmers, organizational leaders and farmers that produce information and structure the conditions of fair trade knowledge and indeed of fairness itself. These performances of transparency are substantially shaped by ISO norms, and the associated practices of professional accreditation, which mediate confidentiality and constrain intra-organizational communication (Goodman 2010; Mutersbaugh and Lyon 2010). Second, these performances imply a remaking of the *spatiality* of production. This hidden dimension of certification, as it were, concerns the remaking of the spatialities of communication, of sites (inspections, meetings) of participation, and may have the effect of making public what might otherwise be private – and vice versa – such as information regarding prices, payments and compliance. In this alteration of the transparent, spaces of certification might also provide new venues for questioning practices, obtaining information and building networks (Mutersbaugh 2005a). Third and finally, certification's remaking of social and spatial practices implies significant *labor and monetary cost burdens*. A large downside to certification is the increased costs required to pay for certifications. Payments, broadly considered, include not just the costs to cover inspectors' and label fees, but also the internal, village-level costs required to prepare documents, meet and travel. Although fair trade certifications are relatively inexpensive compared to organic certification (Giovannucci and Villalobos 2007; Pay 2009), fair trade certification nonetheless imposes burdens that may be especially significant for less prosperous farmers. Other hurdles brought by certification include linguistic, educational and cultural ones, as producers may lack the skills necessary to work with documents in, for instance, Spanish, or the patience to learn novel interactional forms (Mutersbaugh 2002).

The restructuring of socio-spatial relations engendered by certification may, under certain conditions, also have a positive effect, as evidenced for example in Mesoamerican fair trade coffee cooperatives. Lyon et al. (2010) identified an increase in women's participation as Fairtrade–organic coffee farmers, from 9 to 29 per cent within one Mexican organization – a number that has risen to 42 per cent during the 2012–2013 harvest cycle according to recent data provided by a Mexican certification organization. Some organizations now have as much as 65 per cent female organic coffee farmers. There are many factors involved in this increase, including men's migration and women's desire to be 'organized' and belong to organizations beyond the community level. Of special note, however, is the role of performing fair trade certifications in Oaxacan communities. During inspections, the inspector has farmers gather in the coffee warehouse to verify whether the payment receipts match up with the registry of sacks sold by the organization. This serves to demonstrate that fair trade participants are knowingly included on the registry and also verifies that the producers did in fact receive the payments to which they are entitled. This process provides an incentive for women to remain as farmers, since they are better able to monitor organizational activity and verify that they are in fact receiving their due. This interaction is particularly linked to the formal demands of fair trade certification and not to organic certification as such, although it is worth noting that the organic's insistence in using certification to tie production to specific parcels plays a role in forcing men to transfer 'farm manager' rights to women rather than, say, sell their coffee through a (male) family relation (Lyon et al. 2010).

This careful tracing to the producer, and the public performance of the linkage between prices and receipts, is not always included in fair trade certification, whether undertaken under the aegis of Fairtrade International or other fair trade certifications such as 'Small Producers' or 'Naturland'. Tea, for instance, encounters difficulties in setting up this sort of direct-to-producer certification practice given the warehouse-oriented repackaging practices found in the tea commodity chain (Dolan

2010). Cotton likewise encounters similar obstacles due to grading and sorting arrangements (Bassett 2010), and handicrafts further difficulties in accounting for issues such as artist quality (Marston 2013). Even in coffee, where the character of the commodity chain facilitates the direct-to-producer checking of registries, the public practices described above do not always occur and may be due in part to pre-ISO certification legacies, such as in the Mexican case where a prominent role was played by Oaxaca's UCIRI and CEPCO (Coordinador Estatal de Productores de Café de Oaxaca) in setting up the contemporary inspections framework.

CONCLUSION

We have argued that certification constitutes an element of fair trade networks that may be analyzed independently, and that it has both negative and positive effects on producers' lives. These effects, however, depend upon the specifics of how certification practices are designed. Under the aegis of ISO-based restructuring, certification as a network-wide practice has been altered such that former communications between producers, buyers, consumers and NGOs within the network are now often precluded by specific ISO rules. These rules, meant to prevent the modification of standards to the benefit of particular players, also have the effect of strictly limiting the channels through which producers – farmers and artisans – are able to challenge specific standards design criteria. Nonetheless, where the style of commodity production and the local network organization permit, certification can be performed in such a manner as to enhance local knowledge access and guarantee producer knowledge regarding conditions of prices and labor.

In concluding we return to the problem of, as Guthman (2007) so aptly put it, 'nice neoliberalism'. In this phrase, Guthman points to the specific problem of moral economy embedded in the commercial framework in which fair trade comes to represent and implicitly champion a shift from social regulation to private forms of regulation. Within this 'neoliberalization' rubric, certification represents the face of private regulation and, to summarize from our above discussion, presents two intractable difficulties. First, when undertaken as an ISO-based practice, certification resorts the social relations of the network to concord with neoliberal principles regarding the elimination of 'barriers to trade', such that producers' engagement in standards design and their say over the broader network structures are significantly reduced, and in consequence farmers have no formal venues through which to seek redress for the socio-spatial effects of certification performance. Second, the protocols of certification – inspections performance, norms compliance – shift the notion of 'fairness' to what the *producer* does and whether the producer herself is able to meet the standards of fairness set out by NGOs and other network actors who are completely inaccessible. To the extent that the performance of fair trade compliance supplants active debates over the notion of fairness itself, either by squeezing out time and energy for social action, or by constituting a neoliberal subjectivity that understands fairness to be an expression of self-regulation and individual responsibility, rather than via collective, solidarity-oriented engagement, fair trade certification is definitely not a 'nice' neoliberalism. Nonetheless, to reprise our opening optimism, our work suggests that a rethinking of fair trade certification practices – coupled with a critical approach to ISO-style norms – may allow us to envision new forms of producer-managed verification or trust-based models that would address some of the embedded strictures on network communication, thereby breathing new life into efforts to democratize fair trade.

REFERENCES

Barham, Elizabeth (2002), 'Towards a theory of values-based labeling', *Agriculture and Human Values*, 19 (4), 349–360.

Bassett, Tom (2010), 'Slim pickings: Fairtrade cotton in West Africa', *Geoforum*, 41 (1), 44–55.

Brooks, Ethel (2007), *Unraveling the Garment industry: Transnational Organizing and Women's Work*, Minneapolis, MN: University of Minnesota Press.

Bryant, Raymond and Michael Goodman (2004), 'Consuming narratives: The political ecology of alternative consumption', *Transactions of the Institute of British Geographers*, New Series, 29 (3), 344–366.

Conroy, Michael (2007), *Branded: How the Certification Revolution is Transforming Global Corporations*, Gabriola Island, Canada: New Society Publishers.

DeLind, Laura (2000), 'Transforming organic agriculture into industrial organic products: Reconsidering national organic standards', *Human Organization*, 59 (2), 198–208.

Dolan, Catherine (2010), 'Virtual moralities: The mainstreaming of Fairtrade in Kenyan tea fields', *Geoforum*, 41 (1), 33–43.

Fairtrade International (2008), 'Frequently asked questions', available at http://www.fairtrade.net (accessed 20 June 2008).

Freidberg, Susanne (2003), 'Cleaning up down South: Supermarkets, ethical trade and African horticulture', *Social and Cultural Geography*, 4 (1), 27–44.

Fridell, Gavin (2007), *Fair Trade Coffee: The Prospects and Pitfalls of Market-Driven Social Justice*, Toronto: University of Toronto Press.

Gereffi, Gary, Garcia-Johnson Ronie and Erika Sasser (2001), 'The NGO-industrial complex', *Foreign Policy*, 125, 56–65.

Giovannucci, Danielle and Andres Villalobos (2007), 'The state of organic coffee: 2007 US update', San Jose, Costa Rica: Sustainable Markets Intelligence Center (CIMS).

González, Alma and Ronald Nigh (2005), 'Smallholder participation and certification of organic farm products in Mexico', *Journal of Rural Studies*, 21 (4), 449–460.
Goodman, Michael (2010), 'The mirror of consumption: Celebritization, developmental consumption and the shifting cultural politics of fair trade', *Geoforum*, 41 (1), 104–116.
Guthman, Julie (2004), 'Back to the land: The paradox of organic food standards', *Environment and Planning A*, 36 (3), 511–528.
Guthman, Julie (2007), 'The Polanyian way?: Voluntary food labels and neoliberal governance', *Antipode*, 39 (3), 456–478.
Harvey, David (1990), *The Condition of Postmodernity*, Oxford and Malden, MA: Wiley-Blackwell.
Hudson, Ian and Mark Hudson (2003), 'Removing the veil? Commodity fetishism, fair trade, and the environment', *Organization and Environment*, 16 (4), 413–430.
IEC (International Electrotechnical Commission) (2014), 'Liaison between WTO and IEC', available at http://www.iec.ch/about/globalreach/partners/international/liaison_iec_wto.htm (accessed 17 October 2014)
Jaffee, Dan (2007), *Brewing Justice: Fair Trade Coffee, Sustainability, and Survival*, Berkeley, CA: University of California Press.
Jaffee, Dan, Jack Kloppenburg and Mario Monroy (2004), 'Bringing the "moral charge" home?: Fair trade within the North and within the South', *Rural Sociology*, 69 (2), 169–196.
Lyon, Sarah, Josefina Aranda Bezaury and Tad Mutersbaugh (2010), 'Gender equity in Fairtrade–organic coffee producer organizations', *Geoforum*, 41 (1), 93–103.
Marston, Andrea (2013), 'Justice for all? Material and semiotic impacts of fair trade craft certification', *Geoforum*, 44, 162–169.
McCarthy, James (2006), 'Rural geography II: Alternative rural economies: The search for alterity in forests, fisheries, food and fair trade', *Progress in Human Geography*, 30 (6), 803–811.
Mutersbaugh, Tad (2002), 'The number is the beast: A political economy of organic-coffee certification and producer unionism', *Environment and Planning A*, 34 (7), 1165–1184.
Mutersbaugh, Tad (2004), 'To serve and to certify: organic coffee, certification services and village cargo service in Mexico', *Environment and Planning D: Society and Space*, 22 (4), 533–552.
Mutersbaugh, Tad (2005a), 'Just-in-space: Certified rural products, labor of quality, and regulatory spaces', *Journal of Rural Studies*, 21 (4), 389–402.
Mutersbaugh, Tad (2005b), 'Fighting standards with standards: Harmonization, rents, and social accountability in certified agrofood networks', *Environment and Planning A*, 37 (11), 2033–2051.
Mutersbaugh, Tad, Dan Klooster, Marie-Christine Renard and Peter Taylor (2005), 'Certifying rural spaces: Quality-certified products and rural governance', *Journal of Rural Studies*, 21 (4), 381–388.
Mutersbaugh, Tad and Sarah Lyon (2010), 'Transparency and democracy in certified ethical commodity networks', *Geoforum*, 40 (1), 27–32.
Nicholls, Alex and Charlotte Opal (2005), *Fair Trade: Market-Driven Ethical Consumption*, London: Sage.
Pay, Ellen (2009), 'The market for organic and fair-trade coffee', study prepared under FAO project GCP/RAF/404/GER: *Increasing Incomes and Food Security of Small Farmers in West and Central Africa through Exports of Organic and Fair-Trade Tropical Products*, Rome: Food and Agriculture Organization.
Polanyi, Karl (1944), *The Great Transformation: The Political and Economic Origins of Our Time*, Boston, MA: Beacon Press.
Raynolds, Laura T. (2000), 'Re-embedding global agriculture: The international organic and fair trade movements', *Agriculture and Human Values*, 17 (3), 297–309.

Raynolds, Laura T. (2004), 'The globalization of organic agro-food networks', *World Development*, 32 (5), 725–743.

Raynolds, Laura T. and John Wilkinson (2007), 'Fair trade in the agriculture and food sector: Analytical dimensions', in Laura T. Raynolds, Douglas Murray and John Wilkinson (eds.), *Fair Trade: The Challenges of Transforming Globalization*, New York: Routledge, pp. 33–48.

Renard, Marie-Christine (1999), 'The interstices of globalization: The example of fair coffee', *Sociologia Ruralis*, 39 (4), 484–500.

Renard, Marie-Christine (2005), 'Quality certification, regulation and power in fair trade', *Journal of Rural Studies*, 21 (4), 419–431.

WFTO (World Fair Trade Organization) (2009), 'What is fair trade?', available at http://www.wfto.com (accessed 3 November 2009).

Whatmore, Sarah and Lorraine Thorne (1997), 'Nourishing networks: Alternative geographies of food', in Richard Peet and Michael Watts (eds.), *Globalizing Food: Agrarian Questions and Global Restructuring*, London: Routledge.

Wilson, Bradley (2010), 'Indebted to fair trade: Coffee and crisis in Nicaragua', Geoforum 41 (1), 84–92.

Wilson, Bradley (2013), 'Delivering the goods: Fair trade, solidarity and the moral economy of the contract', *Human Organization*, 72 (3), 177–187.

Wilson, Bradley and Joe Curnow (2013), 'Solidarity™: Student activism, affective labor, and the fair trade campaign in the United States', *Antipode*, 45(3), 565–583.

17. Retailers, corporate ethics and fair trade

Alex Hughes

INTRODUCTION*

The past few decades since the 1980s have witnessed a 'retail revolution' (Bromley and Thomas 1993; Neilson and Pritchard 2007). This phenomenon has included the expansion of large retail transnational corporations (TNCs), a shift in the balance of power from manufacturers to retailers in supply chains and the development of sophisticated and strongly branded retail store operations in the context of an increasingly consumer-driven and services-led global economy. In the grocery retail sector, brands such as Walmart, Tesco and Carrefour have become key economic actors and household names not only in their home economies of the United States, the United Kingdom and France respectively, but also in countries where they have expanded operations throughout Europe, Latin America, Africa and Asia (Wrigley et al. 2005). This transformation provides the changing commercial context with which Fairtrade has recently engaged.[1] Whereas the 1980s and 1990s for the most part saw the growth of retail corporations and the development of Fairtrade occur quite separately, since the turn of the 21st century their pathways have coincided. From the early 2000s the Fairtrade movement, originally set up in opposition to capitalist business models, began to engage with retail corporations associated with them. This engagement represents a crucial part of the contested and hotly debated process of Fairtrade mainstreaming (see also chapters by Ronan Le Velly, Darryl Reed and Peter Utting in this volume).

Academic debate on Fairtrade's engagement with corporate retailers has incorporated a range of approaches from management science, economic geography, sociology and development studies in order to evaluate the advantages and disadvantages of expanding Fairtrade markets through corporate retail channels. Notions of alterity and its commercialization through retailing and merchandising have been mobilized to capture the tensions, as well as productive relationships, between Fairtrade's moral energies and the profit-maximizing retail strategies they have encountered. Evaluating the governance of Fairtrade supply chains operating through corporate retail buyers, conceptual frameworks of global value chains (GVCs) and global production networks (GPNs) emanating from economic sociology and geography respectively have been adopted. Both of these frameworks, in slightly different ways, identify and explain the role of key actors operating in globally stretched supply chains, locate power and authority in the international provisioning of goods and assess the economic fortunes of those tied into these chains. Research in this area has uncovered the increasing use of market, as well as moral, conventions in the commercialization of Fairtrade supply chains when retail corporations become involved (Raynolds 2009). Moreover, with significance for this chapter, the role of lead (or focal) firms like retailers in influencing the standards and terms of Fairtrade supply chains is illuminated by GVC and GPN approaches (Smith 2010).

This chapter addresses the specific role of corporate retailers in Fairtrade mainstreaming, with the focus mainly upon grocery retail chains. This is because supermarket chains have been at the forefront of engaging with Fairtrade due to the prominence of food and beverages as the core categories for certification. The rising popularity of Fairtrade cotton, however, has increased the participation of clothing retailers (as well as supermarkets). This chapter concentrates on corporate retailers in the grocery sector, predominantly supermarket chains but also mass merchandisers and warehouse clubs, as opposed to fast food chains, restaurants, coffee shops and non-food retailers. First, the chapter outlines the key debates surrounding the corporate mainstreaming of Fairtrade. Second, the chapter considers the part played by Fairtrade in grocery retailers' wider corporate responsibility strategies, which include a broad array of policies on issues such as climate change adaptation, environmental protection, waste management, community engagement, labor standards and consumer health programs. Discussion here draws attention to the pros and cons of Fairtrade's enrollment in discourses and practices of corporate responsibility. Third, using the specific case of the United Kingdom, it situates Fairtrade's encounter with corporate retailers in the wider context of Fairtrade mainstreaming by highlighting the key advantages and disadvantages of Fairtrade products being sourced, marketed and sold by grocery retail corporations. Fourth, the chapter broadens out from the UK case to consider the strategic significance of a set of leading global retailers in the mainstreaming of the movement. These global retailers, many of which have store operations outside their home economies, are increasingly taking their corporate responsibility strategies, including Fairtrade, and exporting them through their overseas operations to host economies. While it remains the case that the Fairtrade movement is centered on markets in Europe, North America and Australasia, reflected in the strategies of these global retailers, the chapter's fifth substantive section progresses to consider a new era of Fairtrade market growth incorporating rising powers and emerging market economies in the global South. Consideration is given to the role of grocery retailers in this fast developing process of Fairtrade market-making with particular reference to the case of South Africa, acknowledged as one of the countries experiencing the most rapid market development for Fairtrade in the world (Fairtrade International 2013).

DEBATE ON THE MAINSTREAMING OF FAIRTRADE

Reed (2009) argues that the corporate mainstreaming of Fairtrade risks diluting the values and rationale of a movement set up originally to empower small producers through trading organizations alternative to those driven by corporate capital. In his argument, 'mainstreaming' is the process of well-known brand name corporations, such as retailers, increasing their participation in both the sale and governance of Fairtrade products. Building on this critique, Doherty et al. (2013, 162) summarize the main advantages and disadvantages of mainstreaming Fairtrade through corporate retail channels as follows. The gains for the Fairtrade movement resulting from corporate retail involvement are seen as: 1) the expansion of Fairtrade markets and sales; 2) the opportunities for knowledge exchange between the Fairtrade movement and supermarkets; 3) raised ethical trading standards in the corporate mainstream; 4) the demonstration of consumer demand for sustainable product ranges; 5) improved consumer awareness of Fairtrade; and 6) the development of Fairtrade brands. The problems presented are: 1) the corporate 'cooption of fair trade'; 2) the compromise, or dilution, of the Fairtrade standard as supermarkets increasingly influence the standard-setting process; 3) damage to the movement when retailers' reputations benefit from carrying Fairtrade ranges, but in some cases with minimal engagement in practice; 4) increased commoditization of Fairtrade; 5) the facilitation of more passive, rather than active, consumer engagement with the Fairtrade movement when shoppers purchase Fairtrade items as part of their larger grocery shopping through mainstream supermarkets.

FAIRTRADE AND GROCERY RETAILERS' CHANGING CORPORATE RESPONSIBILITY STRATEGIES

Fairtrade now forms an integral part of retailers' corporate responsibility strategies. In today's global economy, businesses assume responsibility not only for achieving profitability targets, but also for environmental protection and social groups affected by their activities (Blowfield 2005). Up until the early 1990s the central, and arguably only, responsibility of corporations was doing business, ensuring profitability and maximizing returns to shareholders. Since then, it has become widely accepted that businesses also have social and environmental responsibilities. Corporations are therefore now seen as having some degree of moral agency with respect to various groups and environments influenced by their business strategies and practices including customers, employees, suppliers, communities and natural environments, as well as shareholders.

The articulation of corporate responsibility in the retail sector involves the management of specific reputational and organizational challenges such as relationships with brand manufacturers and own-brand suppliers, complex logistics networks, store image and high staff turnover (Gupta and Pirsch 2008). Retailers' sale of Fairtrade product lines tends to fit in with corporate responsibility strategies for ethical sourcing and social responsibility for communities in economically less-developed countries. Wheeler (2012) observes, for example, the use by supermarkets of Fairtrade Fortnight in order to develop their Fairtrade marketing and sales and, in some cases, to demonstrate their corporate responsibility credentials. Sainsbury's, as one of the United Kingdom's leading supermarkets in terms of support for the movement, exceeded £12 million of sales in Fairtrade products during Fairtrade Fortnight in 2012 and continues to use this annual event to promote its 100 per cent own-brand Fairtrade ranges in categories such as tea, coffee, sugar and bananas (Brooks 2013). The majority of retailers selling Fairtrade goods also communicate their inclusion of Fairtrade product ranges in their annual corporate responsibility and sustainability reports, though the detail provided on the numbers of Fairtrade lines, sales figures and suppliers varies markedly from company to company (Smith 2010).

Over the past decade, Fairtrade, with its original emphasis on social development and economic empowerment, has been challenged in terms of public and political interest by the growing significance of environmental concerns, in particular those connected to climate change. Retailers' corporate responsibility strategies and reports reflect this shift, as increasing attention is paid to policies and projects concerned with waste management, carbon reduction and climate change adaptation. The majority of grocery retailers now report on all aspects of corporate responsibility in a single annual report, including sections on social, environmental and economic sustainability (see for example John Lewis Partnership 2013; Kroger 2013; Sainsbury's 2013; Walmart 2013). In part as a response to this overarching shift, the Fairtrade movement itself now incorporates environmental clauses and risk management requirements into its standards. Moreover, supermarkets' own-brand Fairtrade ranges discussed below are now also combining the Fairtrade mark with other sustainability logos, such as organic (Soil Association) and Rainforest Alliance labels (Smith 2010). The UK supermarket chain, Tesco, for example, retails bananas bearing both organic (Soil Association) and Fairtrade logos. This illustrates the continually evolving strategies employed by retailers towards Fairtrade in the context of changing landscapes of corporate responsibility.

MAINSTREAMING FAIRTRADE THROUGH CORPORATE RETAIL CHANNELS: INSIGHTS FROM THE UK GROCERY SECTOR

The specific processes through which corporate retailers market and source Fairtrade are discussed in more detail now in the context of the United Kingdom. The reason for exploring corporate mainstreaming of Fairtrade through the example of the grocery retail sector in the United Kingdom is that the supermarket industry in this country is often highlighted as one of the most powerful in the world in terms of the concentration of capital into a small number of large chains, with significant implications for the exercise of power in the supply chain and innovation in retailing strategies and formats. Work by Neil Wrigley (2010) has documented the progressive concentration of capital in the sector since the 1950s, enabled by a *laissez-faire* national regulatory environment. This consolidation of market power in UK food retailing gathered pace in the 1980s. While the rank order of these chains and the nature of competition between them have changed since then, the concentration of capital has nonetheless continued to the present (Wrigley 2010). Kantar Worldpanel data shows the following UK grocery market shares in terms of sales for November 2013: Tesco (30.5 per cent), Asda (owned by Walmart) (17.6 per cent), Sainsbury's (16.9 per cent), Morrison's (11.7 per cent), The Co-operative (6.5 per cent), Waitrose (owned by the John Lewis Partnership) (4.6 per cent), Aldi (3.0 per cent), Lidl (2.7 per cent) and Iceland (2.0 per cent) (Butler and Bowers 2013).

Overall, the United Kingdom has witnessed a rapid growth in the sale of Fairtrade products. Sales in 2012 were £1.57 billion, representing a 19 per cent increase on the previous year (Smithers 2013). The main product lines are coffee, tea, cocoa, sugar, honey, bananas, flowers, wine, cotton and fresh fruit (The Co-operative Group 2012). The popularization of

Fairtrade through particular marketing campaigns launched by organizations such as the Fairtrade Foundation (the UK organizational arm of Fairtrade International) is partially responsible for this growth. However, the sale of Fairtrade goods through retail chains, in particular supermarkets, is now another significant contributory factor, fueled in part by the aforementioned consolidation and market power in this sector (Smith 2010).

All leading supermarket chains in the United Kingdom carry Fairtrade product lines, but there is variation between them in terms of the degree to which they have embraced the movement (Smith 2010). The four UK supermarket chains at the forefront of Fairtrade sales and commitment to supporting the movement are the Co-operative, Sainsbury's, Tesco and Waitrose, all of whom publicize information and policy statements on Fairtrade. Moreover, three retail chains – Sainsbury's, the Co-operative Group and Marks & Spencer (formally classified as a grocery retailer) – accounted for around 43 per cent of UK Fairtrade sales in 2006 (Smith 2010). Sainsbury's sees itself as the United Kingdom's (and in fact the world's) largest Fairtrade retailer with over £310 million Fairtrade sales in the financial year ending March 2013, claiming that £1 in every £4 spent on Fairtrade goods in the United Kingdom is through Sainsbury's stores (Sainsbury's 2013). The Co-operative Group reports that it is the leading UK retailer of Fairtrade when the share of sales is viewed in relation to firm size. It had 17.7 per cent share of UK Fairtrade supermarket sales in 2012, amounting to £132 million by value. From the early 2000s, Fairtrade commodities typically stocked by these supermarket chains have been coffee, tea, fresh fruit, packaged fruit juices, chocolate and cereal bars, but have expanded more recently to include clothing (made of Fairtrade cotton), wine and flowers.

Corporate retailers' stocking of alternative trading organizations' (ATOs') Fairtrade products represents one way in which supermarkets have been involved in the mainstreaming of Fairtrade. Another is where leading grocery retailers introduce their *own brands* of Fairtrade products (Elder et al. 2014). Smith and Barrientos (2005) record, for example, that the Co-operative led the way with this strategy by developing own-brand Fairtrade goods in bananas, coffee, tea, fruit, chocolate and drinking chocolate. In 2008 it introduced Fairtrade own-brand hot beverages and sugar, and in 2013 it became the first UK retailer to source all its standard and single-stem roses from a Fairtrade supplier (Smithers 2013). Of its 258 Fairtrade product lines, 159 were own-brand in 2012 (The Co-operative Group 2012). Sainsbury's also developed own-brand Fairtrade ranges in tea, coffee, sugar and bananas by 2009 (Smith 2010), while Waitrose have concentrated on converting their own-brand tea to

100 per cent Fairtrade and promoting own-brand Fairtrade coffee and bananas (Elder et al. 2014; John Lewis Partnership 2013). While not a leading supermarket chain in terms of pushing Fairtrade, Morrison's also has contributed significantly to the growth of Fairtrade sugar sales by converting its own-brand sugar range to Tate & Lyle Fairtrade sugar. Other leading supermarket chains, Asda and Tesco, have own-brand ranges in the traditional commodities such as tea, coffee and fresh fruit (Smithers 2013), as well as Fairtrade cotton garments in the case of Tesco (Tesco 2013).

Smith and Barrientos (2005) and Smith (2006; 2010) address the implications of supermarkets' own-brand Fairtrade lines for supply chain governance. Drawing on GVC analysis, Smith's (2010) research on supply chains for retailers' own-brand Fairtrade products – cocoa and fresh fruit for several different supermarkets – reveals different models of supply chain governance for Fairtrade. In the case of cocoa sourced by the Co-operative Group, close retailer–supplier links, additional trade through ATOs on the part of the producers and an ability to meet the supermarket's demand for high volumes, fosters a sustainable business partnership between producers and the Co-operative Group. The terms of trade here are close to the original objectives of the Fairtrade movement concerning the fair treatment of producers and the elimination of exploitative intermediaries. However, Smith (2006; 2010) highlights how retailer–producer relationships for Fairtrade fruit supply have more in common with conventional buyer–supplier relationships, as costs and risk continue to be pushed down the supply chain in the context of unpredictable retailer demands, perishable products and an emphasis on just-in-time delivery. This contrast is associated with differences in product physicality, the ability of producers to balance business between alternative and mainstream markets and variable retailer commitment to Fairtrade producer groups.

Challenges of working Fairtrade through supermarkets' own-brand ranges are compounded by the fact that these retailers themselves do not have to comply with Fairtrade International standards. Rather, it is the own-brand suppliers who are licensees and bound by Fairtrade stipulations, while supermarkets' buying practices remain unregulated (Barrientos and Smith 2007). In the case of coffee, Elder et al. (2014) observe the growing adoption by large grocery retailers of their own-brand Fairtrade coffee lines, with increasing links made between the quality of the product, its sustainability credentials and the reputation of the brand. In terms of the implications of this shift for the governance of supply chains, they note that the shift in balance of power from the large commercial coffee roasters to the grocery retailers is mirrored in Fairtrade own-brand sourcing chains, as these retailers increasingly cut out the multinational roasters in order to source more directly from local roasters in-country. Moreover, in the coffee sector the same authors cite evidence of supplier switching on the part of grocery retailers sourcing Fairtrade coffee, which goes against the Fairtrade principles of stability in supply relationships. Elder et al. (2014) explain that increasing grocery retailers' own-brand Fairtrade lines in coffee raises the following concerns: 1) the growing marginalization and vulnerability of smallholders in the face of increased supplier switching and retailers' preference for trading with a small number of larger suppliers; 2) the role of retailers in amending the Fairtrade certification system itself, as they appear to be lowering the threshold regarding the proportion of a product line required to be certified Fairtrade in order to display the logo on packaging; and 3) the risk that farmers concentrate investment on meeting retailers' product and technical standards at the expense of the social development programs.

There are also implications of Fairtrade mainstreaming through retailers' own brands for the ethical pioneers who originally developed Fairtrade lines. Within a context in which Fairtrade sales in the United Kingdom are growing – even through the periods of economic recession and austerity following the 2008 financial crisis (Smithers 2013) – supermarket own-brand ranges of Fairtrade have nonetheless put pressure on some of the Fairtrade brands launched by the ATO pioneers. This is illustrated in the case of Traidcraft's sales of Fairtrade goods. Overall sales of Traidcraft-branded Fairtrade goods have fallen recently each year, dropping from £21.7 million in 2008/09 to £15.2 million in 2012/13 (Traidcraft 2013). This situation is linked to recessionary pressure, but also increased competition from corporate brands, including retailers' own-brand Fairtrade lines.

GLOBAL RETAILERS, GLOBAL FAIRTRADE MARKETING?

This section moves beyond the UK context, examining the role of an emerging group of global retailers in Fairtrade mainstreaming. Table 17.1 shows a set of dominant global retailers, defined as the world's leading retail corporations using measures of revenue (Deloitte 2014). While two of these are US retailers solely focused on domestic store networks, the remaining eight are all retail TNCs. The growth of retail TNCs – corporations with store networks created by foreign direct investment

Table 17.1 Top ten global retailers, by revenue, in 2013 and their inclusion of fair trade lines

Rank	Name of company	Country of origin	Dominant Format	2012 retail revenue (US$m)	No. of countries of operation	Presence of Fairtrade/ Fair Trade product ranges
1	Walmart	USA	Hypermarket/ Supercenter/ Superstore	469 162	28	Yes
2	Tesco PLC	UK	Hypermarket/ Supercenter/ Superstore	101 269	13	Yes
3	Costco Wholesale Corporation	USA	Cash & Carry/ Warehouse Club	99 137	9	Yes
4	Carrefour SA	France	Hypermarket/ Supercenter/ Superstore	98 757	31	Yes
5	The Kroger Co.	USA	Supermarket	96 751	1	Yes
6	Schwartz Untemehmens Treuhand KG	Germany	Discount Store	87 236	26	Yes
7	Metro AG	Germany	Cash & Carry/ Warehouse Club	85 832	32	Yes
8	The Home Depot Inc.	USA	Home Improvement	74 754	5	Yes
9	Aldi Einkauf GmbH & Co.	Germany	Discount Store	73 035	17	Yes
10	Target Corporation	USA	Discount Department Store	71 960	1	Yes

Source: Adapted from Deloitte (2014).

(FDI) in countries beyond their home economies – gathered pace significantly from the late 1990s. Fueled by liberalization of retail FDI in emerging markets, an elite group of transnational retailers has emerged within the global economy, including well-known companies such as Walmart, Carrefour, Tesco, Metro and Aldi. Other factors contributing to this phenomenon have been outsourcing, increasing regulatory restrictions in advanced economies and corporate access to low-cost capital during the late 1990s. This elite group is playing a significant role in generating employment, shaping cultures of consumption and orchestrating supply chains on a global scale (Wrigley et al., 2005), which has significant implications for corporate responsibility including the adoption and implementation of Fairtrade in both domestic and overseas store networks.

For some retailers, international expansion through FDI has facilitated their entry into emerging markets and developing countries in Eastern Europe, Asia, Latin America and Africa. With significance for Fairtrade expansion through global retailers, policy-makers, analysts and academics have noted the following key features of globalizing retail: 1) the dominance of food and general merchandising sectors among the elite group of global retailers; and 2) the strong presence in this group of retail corporations with home bases in Western Europe and the United States of America (Coe 2004), where Fairtrade has evolved.

Since the 1990s, media and civil society have paid attention to the global sourcing practices of these high-profile retailers (Hughes et al. 2007). All of them incorporate ethical trade as a key part of their corporate responsibility strategies and include it in their corporate responsibility reporting. Most commonly, global retailers illustrate their support of ethical trade by using codes of conduct to ensure minimum labor standards in their own-brand supply chains. However, communicating commitment to Fairtrade is another indicator of retailers' social responsibility in global supply chains. As Table 17.1 shows, all of the top ten global retailers sell Fairtrade or Fair Trade Certified labeled products including the eight grocery retailers. Within this group, several retailers mention Fairtrade Week/Month as an occasion to advertise and communicate the benefits of ethical sourcing. This engagement with the fair trade movement sits alongside growing endorsement of environmental certification schemes and initiatives, such as the Marine Stewardship Council (MSC) and the Forest Stewardship Council (FSC), and participation in multi-stakeholder initiatives such as the Roundtable on Sustainable Palm Oil.

As in the United Kingdom, the global retailers' commitment to Fairtrade varies considerably. They report a range of Fairtrade products, sales figures, supply chains and Fairtrade institutions with which they engage. This variation has implications for how Fairtrade effectively travels through these corporations and the potential impact it can have on the host as well as domestic markets in which these retailers now trade. Information on the global retailers' Fairtrade policies is sporadic, but the chapter highlights below some key emerging trends that open up questions and areas for further research.

The largest and most globally powerful retailer, the mass merchandiser Walmart, has extensive and detailed corporate responsibility and sustainability policies in light of critical attention to its labor and supply chain practices since the early 1990s (Hughes et al. 2007). However, the main focus of Walmart's ethical sourcing policies is their own-brand supply chains for all food and non-food goods and the corporate codes of conduct and auditing systems implemented to regulate them. Fair trade arguably plays a more marginal role in Walmart's strategy and is centrally focused upon the food and drink products most commonly associated with Fairtrade. A 2012 article by Paul Rice, CEO of Fair Trade USA, nonetheless reports that Walmart is demonstrating corporate leadership in fair trade, in particular with respect to its own-brand Fair Trade Certified (by Fair Trade USA) Sam's Choice and Member's Mark coffees and Sam's Club Fair Trade Certified bell peppers from Mexico (Rice 2012). The company, also through Sam's Club (its warehouse club), introduced own-brand Fair Trade Certified bananas in 2009, showcased during Fair Trade Month that year (Walmart 2009). Although corporate responsibility programs are highlighted for Walmart's overseas store operations, there is no detail formally communicated on Fairtrade product ranges (though it is known that Fairtrade ranges are present in many European stores owned by the company). This leaves a question about the extent to which Walmart is expanding Fairtrade through these overseas markets, or whether in fact it is having minimal impact in this regard.

In terms of the other two US-based grocery retailers in the global top ten, Kroger also reports an expansion in Fair Trade Certified product ranges, focused on coffee, tea and chocolate, throughout its domestic store networks (Kroger 2013). And Costco, like Walmart, has been mainly focused on selling Fair Trade Certified coffee through its own brand, Kirkland Signature, since 2006. Significantly, this product line is developed in practice through Starbucks (Elder et al. 2014; Jaffee and Howard 2011), illustrating the collaborative role sometimes played by other non-retail corporate actors in the mainstreaming process through retailers. Costco, however, does not formally report on whether and how Fairtrade product ranges are included in its overseas stores.

The question of how extensively Fairtrade is being rolled out through overseas store operations is also pertinent to the second largest global retailer, Tesco. One of the most significant and known ways in which this UK-based retailer acts as a conduit for Fairtrade products to reach globalized mass markets, however, is through its sale of manufacturers' brands that have converted some of their product lines to Fairtrade. The most high-profile of these are Cadbury's Dairy Milk and Nestlé Kit Kat chocolate bars (Tesco 2013). However, the implications of this for host economy markets in East Central Europe and Asia would need to be traced in further research.

One of the few global retailers to communicate more clearly its Fairtrade product lines and their pattern of sales through overseas operations is the French-based retailer, Carrefour. Its corporate responsibility report for 2012 highlights that of its 548 Fairtrade certified product lines, 115 of these are own-brand ranges (up from 100 in 2011 and 77 in 2010). Carrefour explains that, '[Fairtrade] products are primarily distributed in five countries, mainly in Europe, where demand is concentrated' (Carrefour 2012, 60). This indicates that Fairtrade markets, shaped in part by global retailers, are still predominantly concentrated in Europe and North America, but they are nonetheless traveling through corporate channels on a supra-national scale. German-based Schwarz Unternehmens Treuhand KG, trading under the name of Lidl, communicates less information about its Fairtrade product lines in its 26 countries of operation but has a strongly branded own-label range, 'Fairglobe', certified by Fairtrade International for sugar, coffee, chocolate, fruit juice and bananas. The other two German-based retailers in the global top ten – the Metro Group and Aldi – also market Fairtrade certified lines but again provide little detail on the pattern of their sales throughout their overseas operations. Metro, however, states in its overview of product ranges that in both Germany and Austria it supports Fairtrade, including the sale of 50 different product lines bearing the Fairtrade International logo covering the categories of coffee, tea, cocoa, chocolate, honey, fruit juices and, in its department stores, cotton and denim trousers. Aldi appears to go a little further in communicating its international corporate social responsibility strategy concerning Fairtrade. The company retails Fairtrade organic bananas, chocolate, coffee, tea and wine, announcing the company's 'international goal … to move to certified sustainable cocoa in all products by the end of 2020, accepting Rainforest Alliance, Fairtrade and UTZ certification' (Aldi 2014). The same report states that Aldi's Australian operations are selling Fairtrade food products and that the ALDI SOUTH group is introducing a corporate responsibility policy, showing growing scope for Fairtrade's expansion through this retailer.

As Kleine (2012) argues in the context of Lidl, a cautionary note should be raised to avoid over-celebratory accounts of these global retailers' engagement with Fairtrade when wider ethical aspects of their businesses, including shop floor labor relations, can be questioned. Jaffee and Howard (2011) also provide a critical note regarding the lack of detail reported by many of these retail corporations concerning Fairtrade, as illustrated above, suggesting that a showcasing of Fairtrade on corporate websites and during Fairtrade Fortnight/Month coupled with a lack of transparency in terms of detailed markets and suppliers, can run the risk of 'fair-washing'. At present, it appears that Fairtrade and Fair Trade Certified goods are mainly concentrated in European and US retailers' domestic markets and their store networks within the advanced capitalist markets in which Fairtrade is already popular. However, the section below suggests that this pattern may be set to change as globalizing middle classes in rising power and emerging market economies are transforming landscapes of consumption, including sustainable forms of consumption, in these contexts.

GROCERY RETAILERS AND EMERGING FAIRTRADE MARKETS IN THE GLOBAL SOUTH

In the wider context of increasing South–South trade, emerging markets and growing middle classes in the global South, Fairtrade International (2011; 2013) reports rising Fairtrade sales in emerging market economies in addition to growth in established markets of Western Europe, North America, Australia and New Zealand. In 2010, the Czech Republic saw 386 per cent growth in Fairtrade sales. In 2012, Estonia's Fairtrade sales rose by 114 per cent, Latvia's by 91 per cent and South Africa's by 220 per cent. In part, this is due to institutional support developing these markets, such as the work of organizations like Fairtrade South Africa. In attempts to match the success in South Africa, Fairtrade Eastern Africa was launched in 2013 to develop markets in Kenya focusing in particular on forging value chains between elite Kenyan consumers in cities like Nairobi and the country's high-profile Fairtrade producers in rural areas. A new Fairtrade marketing organization has also been established in Brazil and similar initiatives are being discussed in Argentina, India, Lebanon and the Philippines (Fairtrade International 2013). In all of these countries, there is an already strong and well-known Fairtrade supply base, implying that a key part of this new trend is a connection made between ethical consumers and producers *within* local and national economies.

In the case of South Africa, which according to Fairtrade International (2011; 2013) is the fastest growing Fairtrade market at present, sales grew from €7 273 254 in 2011 to €22 263 619 in 2012. As highlighted above, Fairtrade South Africa is a key institutional part of this ethical market growth. However, as in Western Europe and the United States of

America, supermarket chains in South Africa are also an important part of market development, as key distribution channels and conduits for Fairtrade marketing and awareness-raising. Naidoo (2011) outlines the structure of grocery retailing in South Africa, showing that the sector is highly concentrated with the five largest chains accounting for 60 per cent of the market. The same author presents estimates from analysts suggesting that ShopRite accounts for 36 per cent of the market, Pick n Pay and Spar each occupy 28 per cent, Woolworths has 8 per cent and is increasing its share rapidly and Walmart entering the market relatively recently has around 2 per cent. Market research on the development of ethical markets in South Africa provides some useful indicators of these retailers' roles in growing Fairtrade sales. This research, conducted by Neilsen for the Belgian Development Agency (2013), acknowledges the rise of Fairtrade sales, in particular in the categories of coffee, chocolate, wine, tea, cotton and food. Sales of imported branded goods carrying the Fairtrade mark, such as Cadbury chocolate, are significant to this growth.

In terms of variation in South African supermarket involvement, the Nielsen survey showed that ShopRite is the least associated with Fairtrade and other ethically labeled goods. Woolworth is the retailer most associated in consumers' minds with sustainable products, connected to the corporation's high-profile corporate sustainability strategy, the 'Good Business Journey'. However, Pick n Pay also announced their formal commitment to Fairtrade in 2010 and have expanded their Fairtrade certified product ranges since then. In the Nielsen survey of 1507 consumers, they found that 7 per cent of the sample was aware of Fairtrade as an organization and 6 per cent were aware of the logo, but when made aware of the organization 22 per cent expressed willingness to purchase Fairtrade products at any price and 26 per cent would purchase them if they matched the price of the cheapest brand. This illustrates potential for further market growth, and it was felt that 'retailers should be doing a great deal more to enable and encourage sales of sustainable products' (Belgian Development Agency 2013, 34).

Fairtrade markets in South Africa are embryonic, but they are growing rapidly and blazing a trail for other rising powers and emerging market economies. Current and future challenges mirror those for Fairtrade in more established markets but additionally include the perceived Eurocentrism of the movement in the minds of consumers in the global South and the potential value, as in Kenya, of connecting Fairtrade consumption more strongly with producer empowerment in these localized contexts.

CONCLUSION

This chapter demonstrates the commercial contexts for Fairtrade mainstreaming through corporate grocery retail channels. The case of the United Kingdom illustrates supermarket chains' varying engagement with Fairtrade, with Sainsbury's and the Co-operative leading the way. The top ten global retailers were then placed in the spotlight to acknowledge that Fairtrade is beginning to travel through the globally stretched store networks of a set of 'big capital' retail chains. While revealing that the core of the Fairtrade movement remains in Western Europe, North America and Australasia, the chapter then evaluated emerging markets for Fairtrade in the global South. The case of South Africa, as one of the fastest-growing Fairtrade markets, demonstrated the growing and potential role for grocery retailers in developing these markets.

There is scope for future research to trace in more detail the ways in which global retailers' promotion and sale of Fairtrade is rolled out in both domestic and overseas store networks. Primary data acquisition and analysis would be useful to quantify and map the precise geographical scale of this roll-out, as publicly available corporate reports contain only limited data. This would capture the extent to which corporate retailers are playing a role in expanding Fairtrade markets and raising consumer awareness of Fairtrade, which are two of the key advantages of mainstreaming identified by Doherty et al. (2013). However, ongoing interview-based and ethnographic research is required, in particular within new and emerging Fairtrade markets, to capture what Smith (2010) sees as the crucial nuances of mainstreaming the movement through corporate grocery retail channels. This is important if one is to understand the processes through which Fairtrade is being mainstreamed by particular retailers in specific places and to evaluate some of the disadvantages, as well as advantages, of mainstreaming associated with the continuing commoditization of Fairtrade. In-depth research into the evolving ways that different retailers adopt the certification system and organize their Fairtrade supply chains, as well as the practices through which consumers purchase and engage with Fairtrade through corporate grocery retailers, are central to advancing knowledge on the pros and cons of what is clearly an ever-expanding and deepening process of mainstreaming through the global economy.

NOTES

* The section on global retailers draws on an Economic and Social Research Council (ESRC) project (RES-172-25-0048) and the author is grateful to research assistance from Catia Gregoratti. The discussion of South African Fairtrade markets is informed by a component of an ESRC project (ES/K005626/1) on which the author is working with Cheryl McEwan and David Bek.

1. The term 'Fairtrade' is used for the most part of the chapter to denote the specific type of fair trade represented by the global certification scheme of the Fairtrade Labelling Organizations International (FLO), now known as Fairtrade International. However, 'Fair Trade Certified' is also used when referring to the certification scheme associated with the US movement, which since the closure of TransFair USA in 2011 has been associated with the newly established Fair Trade USA operating independently from Fairtrade International. Since mid-2012 Fairtrade America has also been established as a new member organization of Fairtrade International, whose certification systems some US firms now use in preference to those of Fair Trade USA (Fairtrade International 2013).

REFERENCES

Aldi (2014), 'Fairtrade', available at https://corporate.aldi.co.uk/en/responsibility/suppliers/fairtrade/ (accessed 07 May 2014).

Barrientos, Stephanie and Sally Smith (2007), 'Mainstreaming fair trade in global production networks: Own brand fruit and chocolate in UK supermarkets', in Laura T. Raynolds, Douglas Murray and John Wilkinson (eds.), *Fair Trade: The Challenges of Transforming Globalization*, London and New York: Routledge, pp. 103–122.

Belgian Development Agency (2013), *Ethical Product Trends in South Africa*, Belgian Development Agency.

Blowfield, Mick (2005), 'Corporate social responsibility: Reinventing the meaning of development', *International Affairs*, 81 (3), 515–534.

Bromley, Rosemary and Colin J. Thomas (1993), 'The retail revolution, the carless shopper and disadvantage', *Transactions of the Institute of British Geographers*, 18 (2), 222–236.

Brooks, Beth (2013), 'Sainsbury looks to boost category sales in Fairtrade Fortnight', *The Grocer*, 2 March 2013.

Butler, Sarah and Simon Bowers (2013), 'Britain's big supermarkets lose ground to cut-price rivals and upmarket grocers', *The Guardian*, 19 November 2013.

Carrefour (2012), '2012 annual activity and responsible commitment report', available at http://www.ecobook.eu/carrefour/2013/ra2012en/index.html (accessed 07 May 2014).

Coe, Neil M. (2004), 'The internationalisation/globalisation of retailing: Towards an economic-geographical research agenda', *Environment and Planning A*, 36 (9), 1571–1594.

Deloitte (2014), 'Global powers of retailing top 250', available at http://www.stores.org/STORES%20Magazine%20January%202014/global-powers-retailing-top-250 (accessed 05 February 2014).

Doherty, Bob, Iain Davies and Sophi Tranchell (2013), 'Where now for fair trade?', *Business History*, 55 (2), 161–189.

Elder, Sara, Jane Lister and Peter Dauvergne (2014), 'Big retail and sustainable coffee: A new development studies research agenda', *Progress in Development Studies*, 14 (1), 77–90.

Fairtrade International (2011), 'Challenge and opportunity: Supplement to annual review 2010–11', available at http://www.fairtrade.net/annual-reports.html (accessed 07 May 2014).

Fairtrade International (2013), 'Unlocking the power: Annual report 2012–13', available at http://www.fairtrade.net/annual-reports.html (accessed 07 May 2014).

Gupta, Shruti and Julie Pirsch (2008), 'The influence of a retailer's corporate social responsibility program on re-conceptualising store image', *Journal of Retailing and Consumer Service*, 15 (16), 516–526.

Hughes, Alex, Neil Wrigley and Martin Buttle (2007), 'Organisational geographies of corporate responsibility: A UK–US comparison of retailers' ethical trading initiatives', *Journal of Economic Geography*, 7 (4), 491–513.

Jaffee, Daniel and Phil Howard (2011), 'Visualizing fair trade coffee', available at https://www.msu.edu/~howardp/coffee.html (accessed 17 February 2014).

John Lewis Partnership (2013), 'John Lewis Partnership sustainability report 2013: Achieving more through collaboration', available at http://www.johnlewispartnership.co.uk/csr/our-progress-and-reports/csr-reports/archived-reports.html (accessed 07 May 2014).

Kleine, Dorothea (2012), 'How fair is fair enough? Negotiating alterity and compromise within the German fair trade movement', in Duncan Fuller, Andrew Jonas and Roger Lee (eds.), *Interrogating Alterity: Alternative Economic and Political Spaces*, Surrey, UK: Ashgate, pp. 113–131.

Kroger (2013), 'Sustainability report', available at http://sustainability.kroger.com/index.html (accessed 07 May 2014).

Naidoo, Sharda (2011), 'Big five fight for food market share', *Mail and Guardian*, 4 November 2011.

Neilson, Jeffrey and Bill Pritchard (2007), 'The final frontier? The global roll-out of the Retail Revolution in India', in D. Burch and G. Lawrence (eds.), *Supermarkets and Agri-Food Supply Chains: Transformations in the Production and Consumption of Foods*, Cheltenham, UK and Northampton, MA: Edward Elgar Publishing, pp. 219–242.

Raynolds, Laura T. (2009), 'Mainstreaming fair trade coffee: From partnership to traceability', *World Development*, 37 (6), 1083–1093.

Reed, Daryl (2009), 'What do corporations have to do with fair trade? Positive and normative analysis from a value chain perspective', *Journal of Business Ethics*, 86 (S1), 3–26.

Rice, Paul (2012), 'How Walmart's support of fair trade is helping farmers live better', available at http://www.walmartgreenroom.com/2012/10/how-walmarts-support-of-fair-trade-is-helping-farmers-live-better/ (accessed 17 February 2014).

Sainsbury's (2013), '20x20 sustainability plan', available at http://www.j-sainsbury.co.uk/responsibility/20x20/ (accessed 07 May 2014).

Smith, Sally (2006), 'Fair Trade Fortnight', *IDS News*, March, available at http://www.ids.ac.uk/ ids/news/SallySmithFairTrade06.html (accessed 11 April 2006).

Smith, Sally (2010), 'For love or money? Fairtrade business models in the UK supermarket sector', *Journal of Business Ethics*, 92 (S2), 257–266.

Smith, Sally and Stephanie Barrientos (2005), 'Fair trade and ethical trade: Are there moves towards convergence?', *Sustainable Development*, 13 (3), 190–198.

Smithers, Rebecca (2013), 'Growing taste for Fairtrade shows it's Britain's cup of tea', *The Guardian*, 2 March 2013.

Tesco (2013), 'Fairtrade: UK position statement', 10 May 2013, available at http://www.tescoplc.com/index.asp?pageid=83 (accessed 17 February 2014).

The Co-operative Group (2012), 'Sustainability report: Building a better society', available at http://www.co-operative.coop/Corporate/sustainability-report-2012/downloads/Co-op-2012_LINKED.pdf (accessed 22 October 2014).

Traidcraft (2013), 'Impact and performance report 2012 – Supporting information', available at http://www.traidcraft.co.uk/about_traidcraft/social_accounts/Supporting+Information (accessed 07 May 2014).
Walmart (2009), 'Sam's Club expands fair trade banana program', available at http://news.walmart.com/news-archive/2009/10/07/sams-club-expands-fair-trade-banana-program (accessed 17 February 2014).
Walmart (2013), 'Global responsibility report', available at http://corporate.walmart.com/microsites/global-responsibility-report-2013/ (accessed 07 May 2014).
Wheeler, Kathryn (2012), '"Change today, choose Fairtrade": Fairtrade Fortnight and the citizen-consumer', *Cultural Studies*, 26 (4), 492–515.
Wrigley, Neil (2010), 'The shifting geographies of UK retailing', in Neil M. Coe and Andrew Jones (eds.), *The Economic Geography of the UK*, London: Sage, pp. 181–195.
Wrigley, Neil, Neil M. Coe and Andrew Currah (2005), 'Globalizing retail: Conceptualizing the distribution-based TNC', *Progress in Human Geography*, 29 (4), 437–457.

18. Fairtrade International and the European market

Bob Doherty, Valéry Bezençon and Gaëlle Balineau

INTRODUCTION

As Raynolds and Greenfield describe in their chapter, Fairtrade International has experienced many changes since its origins. In 1988 the eponymous Dutch non-profit organization Max Havelaar created the first fair trade label with the explicit objective to increase producers' opportunities while mainstreaming fair trade products. Given its success, sister organizations were created in other European countries as well as in the United States. In 1997 the then 17 existing labels grouped themselves into an international foundation based in Bonn, Germany, and called it Fairtrade Labelling Organizations International (FLO, eventually renamed Fairtrade International). Although each national organization first kept its prerogatives (definition of fair trade standards, controls and support to producers), the structure and the governance of the Fairtrade system evolved rapidly, following two main trends. First, a harmonization of Fairtrade principles to create a standardized Fairtrade Certification mark (owned by Fairtrade International). Second, a 'certification revolution' (see Bradley Wilson and Tad Mutersbaugh's chapter in this volume): since 2003, the application of Fairtrade standards is checked by FLO-Cert, a for-profit third-party certification body created for this purpose and still the only one accredited by Fairtrade International. The last change in the Fairtrade system was the recent split between Fairtrade International and Fair Trade USA. The two organizations appear to disagree on the question of contract farming and certifications of large plantations (for more details, see Laura Raynolds and Nicholas Greenfield's chapter in this volume).

This chapter studies the role of Fairtrade International in the development of European fair trade markets. The first part of the chapter shows that Fairtrade International has had a paradoxical double-impact on European markets. More specifically, it explains why a third-party certification system for standardized fair trade goods may have reinforced, as well as eroded, the credibility of fair trade. While the labeling system is uniform across Europe, all European countries show significant differences in terms of per capita consumption of fair trade products. Focusing on four country case studies (Italy, France, Switzerland and the United Kingdom), the second part of the chapter shows how the structure and evolution of global value chains for fair trade products contribute to explain fair trade expansion or stagnation in each national context.

FAIRTRADE INTERNATIONAL AND THE DEVELOPMENT OF THE EUROPEAN FAIR TRADE MARKET: A PARADOXICAL DOUBLE-IMPACT

Direct and Indirect Contributions of Fairtrade to Market Development

Fairtrade International is a major contributor to the economic success of fair trade due to its labeling scheme. Since the introduction of the first Fairtrade label in 1988, the sales of Fairtrade products in Europe grew steadily to reach more than EUR4.2 billion in 2012 (Fairtrade International 2013b). As a comparison, between 2001 and 2009 aggregated fair trade sales from the European Fair Trade Association members (which includes most unlabeled fair trade sales) only grew from EUR150 million to EUR290 million (Boonman et al. 2011). Several factors explain the important role of the label in driving fair trade sales. First the label is the mechanism that scaled up fair trade product distribution in the mainstream. Social enterprise pioneers such as Cafédirect in the United Kingdom began to distribute fair trade products in the mainstream without a label with the campaign support of non-governmental organizations such as Oxfam (Davies, Doherty and Knox 2010). However, the Fairtrade label gave a strong impulse to broaden the mainstream distribution of fair trade products. The Fairtrade label is a brand – third-party labels are specific types of brands (Larceneux, Benoit-Moreau and Renaudin 2012) – and as such, is easier to market than a social movement. It simplifies the consumer meaning of the more complex message conveyed by the movement. In addition, the label standardizes the message across different retailers and thus simplifies consumer understanding of fair trade, albeit in a more shallow manner. This may particularly apply to less-involved consumers who would not seek to understand fair trade otherwise, as shown by Bezençon and Blili (2010) with Swiss consumers. Also, the Fairtrade label benefits from the advantages of recognized brands, such as making the products easily identifiable and memorable (e.g., Keller 1993), as well as improving consumer loyalty (e.g., Kim, Lee and Park 2010).

Retailers have primarily contributed to the promotion of Fairtrade products in three ways: 1) retailers advertise products carrying the label as exemplified by Migros or Coop in Switzerland (Bezençon and Blili 2009), providing a direct contribution to the sales of Fairtrade products; 2) they bring visibility to the brand and in this way Fairtrade International leverages the retailers to build and promote its brand; and 3) through choice editing (i.e., letting Fairtrade be the only option in a given product category), retailers forced the consumption of Fairtrade products – for instance Coop in Switzerland with bananas (Bezençon and Blili 2009).

The Fairtrade label was instrumental in reaching consumer segments beyond the radical fair trade supporters through mainstream distribution (Jones, Comfort and Hillier 2003). Thus the label contributed not only to expanding the fair trade market, but also to diversifying it. The distribution in the mainstream removed a key barrier to reach new consumers: the lack of access to fair trade products (Strong 1997).

The mainstreaming of fair trade through the Fairtrade label has arguably also contributed to advertising the principles and spirit of fair trade outside of its model. This occurs through raising awareness of the fair trade model through well-known brands in Europe (see Table 18.2). In this way the label has created a space for a debate in the media about both ethical issues in trading and consumption. It has also given a space for consumers to 'exercise their beliefs via shopping' (Doherty, Davies and Tranchell 2012, 178). In doing so it created a proof-of-concept for business models with improved social standards in production. Second Fairtrade has contributed to rethinking business relationships and practices. Ingenbleek and Reinders (2013, 471) show that the Fairtrade label was a key factor in creating a sustainable coffee market in the Netherlands: 'Fair Trade did not become the new rule; it became the standard against which others could compare themselves and upon which they could build to develop new standards that would be more feasible in their business models.' Finally, it has inspired similar models in other arenas. The Slow Food movement, for example, started in 1986 in Italy and currently promotes 'a comprehensive approach to food that recognizes the strong connections between plate, planet, people, politics and culture' (Slow Food 2013). Similar to fair trade, Slow Food is rooted in the politicization of food consumption and shares the idea of justice and respect for the producers (Sassatelli and Davolio 2010). Currently, Slow Food is facing a debate about the mainstreaming of the movement as illustrated by the Eataly case. Such debates could benefit from the discussions about and analogy with fair trade (Sebastiani, Montagnini and Dalli 2013).

Fairtrade International: Credibility and European Consumers' Support

The previous section has shown that key characteristics of Fairtrade International, namely standardization, harmonization, third-party certification and mainstreaming, have been successful in: 1) bringing fair trade issues under the spotlight and thus raising demand for more responsible products and 2) increasing fair trade consumption, essentially through the multiplication and mainstreaming of Fairtrade certified products.

Despite large efforts from Fairtrade International to simplify its messages, enforce a credible certification system and communicate on fair trade issues, problems of consumers' trust in fair trade approaches – and in the Fairtrade model in particular – remain important in European countries. Critics and skepticism towards fair trade have increased alongside its popularity (Utting 2009, 128). For Balineau and Dufeu (2010), one explanation lies in the fact that weapons of mass communication and certification developed by Fairtrade International to raise consumer confidence have had a two-sided impact for both fair trade and Fairtrade markets. Indeed, the credibility of a label relies on two conditions. First and foremost, means or 'standards' (Fairtrade price and premium, social standards, etc.) are *effective* to achieve fair trade objectives. Second, standards are *respected.* As regards the second condition, Balineau and Dufeu show that given the third-party certification system implemented by Fairtrade International, the risk of cheating on the system is very low. In fact, European consumers are much more concerned by the first condition: is the Fairtrade model effective to reach fair trade objectives? Other chapters in this volume, such as those by Ronan Le Velly and Bradley Wilson and Tad Mutersbaugh, explain how Fairtrade key characteristics such as harmonization, standardization and the use of certification could have blurred fair trade messages and have a paradoxical double-impact on consumers' confidence: on the one hand, third-party certification reduces the risk of cheating on standards but, on the other hand, standardization weakens the relationship between producers and consumers, which was fair trade's unique contribution. Moreover, instead of a consensus, recognizing that there are several ways to achieve fair trade, tensions have emerged due to mainstreaming (particularly in France, see Ronan Le Velly's chapter in this volume). In a context of competition between many 'responsible-consumption' labels, the 'balkanization' of fair trade approaches (which has recently increased with the split of Fair Trade USA and Fairtrade International) risks to discredit the *whole* sector and hinder the long-term stability of *all* fair trade markets.

Several studies confirm that doubts about fair trade effectiveness are an important obstacle to increasing consumption in European countries. More information and a third-party certification system that should theoretically increase consumers' confidence may in fact have the perverse effects mentioned above (see, for example, Eden, Bear and Walker (2008) for the United Kingdom or De Pelsmacker and Janssens (2007) for Belgium). Moreover, other studies show that doubts are indeed widespread and are an important obstacle to growing consumption. In France (Balineau and Dufeu 2010), large and recurrent polls show that uncertainty about fair trade effectiveness is the second or third reason put forward by consumers to explain why they do not purchase more fair trade goods, just after price and accessibility reasons. In 2008, 78 per cent of interviewed consumers said they were ready to make an effort to 'help countries to develop' but 29 per cent 'do not believe in fair trade'. In the United Kingdom (abbreviated to UK in the rest of this chapter), 'denial of benefit' of fair trade by consumers who think (and say) that fair trade issues are too big to be dealt with at their level also helps to explain why consumers do not buy more fair trade products (Chatzidakis, Hibbert and Smith 2007; see also Keith Brown's chapter in this volume).

While Fairtrade International offers the same model in all European countries, fair trade sales have grown at various rates. The next section relates this to the differentiated structure of value chains.

FAIR TRADE MARKET DEVELOPMENT IN EUROPE

Fair trade has spread globally from the pioneer European markets of Switzerland, Germany and the Netherlands to the other early adopter countries including the UK, Italy, France and Belgium (De Pelsmacker, Driesen and Rayp 2005). More recently, other European states such as the Scandinavian territories and Spain (Loureiro and Lotade 2005) have developed fair trade markets. The market penetration of Fairtrade sales has developed at different rates across national territories and via different value chains. Switzerland records the highest per capita consumption of Fairtrade marked products in Europe at EUR38.6 per capita, the UK third highest with EUR30, France at EUR5.4 and Italy at EUR1.01 per capita (Fairtrade International 2013a).

Despite these national differences, there has been limited analysis comparing fair trade market development across different European countries. This section aims to bridge this gap by comparing the development of fair trade markets in Italy, Switzerland, France and the UK. These four vignettes illustrate several key variations in terms of per capita consumption, value chains utilized and key product categories developed. In order to analyze the contribution of different market value chains in the development of fair trade in specific national contexts, this chapter uses the Global Value Chain (GVC) model developed by Gereffi and Korzeniewicz (1994). The analysis that follows proposes seven distinct fair trade value chains which make up the vast majority of fair trade purchases (see Table 18.1). Value chains one, two and three originated in the social economy, while value chains four through seven were generated through the mainstreaming of fair trade.

Fair Trade Market Development in Italy

The Italian fair trade market is dominated by two competing fair trade value chains: the social economy value chain using the CTM (Cooperazione Terzo Mondo) Altromercato fair trade label (value chain one) and a private supermarket brand using the Fairtrade International label (value chain five). The CTM Altromercato label, which was established in 1988 as a cooperative, displays initially a specialization in handicraft products with partial corporate involvement in the retail sphere. CTM Altromercato is the leading fair trade importer in Italy putting a strong emphasis on educational activity and possesses a supporter base of 6000 volunteers. According to Becchetti and Costantino (2010), CTM Altromercato has maintained its founding principles and these authors argue that there has been a more comprehensive standards development compared to Fairtrade International standards, illustrated by CTM Altromercato's stronger pre-financing arrangements with producers. CTM Altromercato is a leading member of the World Fair Trade Organization, which certifies organizations and not just products. Some authors argue this shows a greater commitment to fair trade (Becchetti and Costantino 2010).

Fair trade in Italy originates from the grass roots movement particularly in Lombardia, Veneto and Trentino-Alto Adige (the Trento area of Italy where CTM Altromercato originated). CTM Altromercato consists of 124 cooperatives representing 300 shops and sells 54 per cent of its product to world shops; but it also sells the remaining 46 per cent of sales to both supermarkets and public procurement customers (CTM Altromercato 2012). CTM Altromercato products can be found in approximately

Table 18.1 Fairtrade value chains

Value chain	Fairtrade value chain	Participants	Features
1	FTO/Social Economy value chain (100% Fairtrade)	FTOs trading with FTOs, e.g., CTM Altromercato trading directly through associated world shops	Strong relationships with producers and even producer equity. Consumer activists buying in this chain.
2	FTO value chain with corporate retail participation	FTO products such as Divine Chocolate are distributed via supermarkets	Strong relationships between FTOs and producers. Retailer purely route of distribution. More convenient for consumers to buy.
3	FTO supplying supermarket own label	FTOs supplying own-label supermarket brand	Strong relationships with FTOs and producers. Some FTOs maintain the intellectual property with reference to producers on packaging.
4	Corporate dominated licensee and retailer	Starbucks Coffee Company is an example	Modular form where corporation has significant control over value chain. Not all corporate products are Fairtrade.
5	Corporate retail dominated but not licensee	Own-label supermarket products sourced from second tier manufacturers such as existing own-brand suppliers	Modular form where supermarket retailer does not have to commit to Fairtrade standards and minimum relationship with producers.
6	Corporate manufacturer as licensee to retailer	Multinational corporation such as Procter & Gamble or Cadbury's converting major brands for general sale	Controlled and dominated by MNCs with limited transparency. Power resides with MNC.
7	Corporations and plantation production	Control of value chain remains the same but with adherence to social premium and Fairtrade price such as large fruit importers Chiquita or Dole	Similar to ethical trade with power very much with the corporation.

Source: Authors' own, adapted from Doherty, Davies and Tranchell (2012, 10–11).

4000 shops throughout Italy. CTM Altromercato's main supermarket customer is leading retailer Esselunga, which has 141 stores mainly in the Northern and Central regions of Italy. CTM Altromercato supply coffee, chocolate and bananas to Esselunga (Euromonitor International 2011).

TransFair Italia was founded in 1994 with the support of both TransFair Germany and CTM Altromercato and in 1997 became part of the Fairtrade International system. However, in 2001 CTM Altromercato removed their support from TransFair Italia after a disagreement on future direction and therefore decided to adopt a different approach to the development of fair trade in the mainstream using primarily value chains one and two. The Fairtrade label recognition in Italy is still low at 28 per cent in comparison to the UK at 96 per cent (Globescan 2011). The main focus for the Fairtrade International label has been gaining distribution in the mainstream retail sector with the Coop Italia retailer, who is the largest food retailer in Italy. The Coop has developed a private own-label Fairtrade brand called Solidal. Solidal's main product categories for Fairtrade sales at Coop Italia are bananas, sugar, chocolate and coffee (Informant 3 2013).

The retail value of Fairtrade marked products in Italy was EUR66 million in 2012, up from EUR58 million in 2011 – a growth of 15 per cent. This gives a per capita consumption of EUR1.01 (EUR1.98 if CTM Altromercato label sales of approximately EUR53 million are added). This growth in Fairtrade International sales is the result of international brands, such as Ben and Jerry's, beginning to source ingredients that are labeled Fairtrade; Carrefour's introduction of a number of private-label Fairtrade products; and growth in specific product categories such as bananas, flowers and composite products. Fairtrade coffee in Italy has not seen the same scale of growth as in countries such as the UK due to the strength of local brands such as Lavazza, which has a very strong Italian identity and do not currently see the Fairtrade label enhancing their current brand.

Both CTM Altromercato and TransFair Italy are part of the AGICES (Association of Italian Fair Trade Organizations), which has 96 members, most of them world shops and Italian importers. AGICES was founded with the approval of the Italian Charter of Criteria for Fair Trade in 1998 and is the association that guarantees adherence to the Charter and is therefore responsible for the running of the Italian Register of Fair Trade Organizations.

Fair Trade in Switzerland

Switzerland shows the highest per capita consumption of Fairtrade labeled products in the world at EUR38.6 (Fairtrade International 2013a). In contrast to Italy, France and the UK, the fair trade story in Switzerland has mainly been driven by Max Havelaar Switzerland, primarily working in partnership with the leading Swiss supermarket retailers (value chain four) in a push strategy towards consumers. Swiss fair trade started with alternative trade organizations such as Claro, but the mainstream supermarket retailers were engaged very early on by Max Havelaar Switzerland. Claro was one of the organizations that set up Max Havelaar Switzerland and is still on the board. However, it has not been involved in the mainstreaming of fair trade. The Swiss fair trade market is dominated by value chain four (see Table 18.1). According to Max Havelaar Switzerland (2012), 84 per cent of the Fairtrade marked sales are represented by the two major retailers: Migros (33 per cent) and the Coop (51 per cent). According to Mahé (2010), by 2006 Switzerland had Fairtrade labeled products in 7000 retail stores, principally Migros and the Coop. In fact only 212 of the fair trade retailers were world shops. Claro is now the main importer of fair trade goods to the world shops in Switzerland.

Food retail in Switzerland is described as a duopoly, with the two large retailers, the Coop and Migros, controlling over 70 per cent of the Swiss grocery market (Euromonitor International 2011). Also, the Swiss Fairtrade market is dominated by high sales in the product categories of flowers/plants and bananas, with respectively 31 and 30 per cent of Swiss total Fairtrade sales in 2010. Fairtrade flowers and plants hold a 50 per cent overall market share in that sector, while bananas have a market share of 54 per cent of the total banana market (Max Havelaar Switzerland 2012). In contrast to the UK, Max Havelaar Switzerland has not been as successful in developing Fair Trade Organization (FTO) brands in product categories such as chocolate and coffee (value chain two). According to a senior manager at Max Havelaar Switzerland, there are two reasons for this: 1) 'the presence of Lindt and Nestlé' and 2) 'we started our mainstream moves with the retailer labels which then makes it difficult to develop FTO brands' (Informant 1 2013). A key theme from the Switzerland case is the focus on key product categories in partnership with retailers.

Fair Trade in France

France is similar to Italy and the UK, both in terms of its population size and gross domestic product. The fair trade movement emerged at a similar time, but the mainstreaming with Fairtrade labeled products commenced approximately ten years later than in the UK, in the form of value chains two and three (see Table 18.1) (Özçağlar-Toulouse, Shiu and Shaw 2006; Poret and Chambolle 2007). In 2013, France sold EUR346 million of labeled Fairtrade products and EUR56 million non-labeled fair trade products (Fairtrade International 2013a). This is nearly three times the sales figures for Italy, but only a fifth of sales in the UK.

In the 1970s, organizations such as Artisans du Monde (established in 1974) began developing the French fair trade market, opening France's first world shops. The FTO Solidar'Monde (founded in 1984) played an important role as a fair trade importer developing supply chains for networks such as Artisans du Monde (Özçağlar-Toulouse et al. 2010). Together, these organizations created an integrated social economy value chain one (see Table 18.1). Max Havelaar France was set up in 1992 with the launch of Fairtrade labeled coffee in partnership with Lobodis. Then in 1997 mainstream retailers in France such as Auchan and Monoprix, working with Alter Eco, started to enter the market with their own Fairtrade private-labeled brands (value chains three, four and five). From 2000 onwards the FTOs in France such as Alter Eco launched their own brands into the mainstream in specific categories such as coffee and chocolate (value chain two). These brands have also focused on being organic with high product quality. By 2012 FTOs resembling value chain two accounted for more than EUR50 million of Fairtrade sales in France, which represents 25–30 per cent of the overall Fairtrade market (Max Havelaar France 2012). This development is in contrast to the UK where brands from the FTOs were the first movers in supermarket distribution and not the supermarket private labels themselves. Public recognition of Fairtrade in France has also increased from 9 to 81 per cent in the past ten years (Globescan 2011). During 2000–2009 fair trade companies such as Alter Eco have also been successful in partnering with organic companies on products such as specialty teas and coffees. Another key development was the launch of Fairtrade cotton in 2005 with new brands of cotton sourced from West Africa.

Another area of Fairtrade growth in the last five years in France has been sales via public sector procurement with companies such as Sodexo. In 2004 the French government introduced a Public Contracts code, which is the consideration of social and environmental issues in public procurement. According to Max Havelaar France, this public sector market could be grown further by the development of the Fairtrade Towns movement in France (Informant 2 2013). However, currently there are only 36 Fairtrade Towns in France in comparison to over 548 in the UK (Fairtrade Towns 2013).

According to Max Havelaar France (2012), currently, Fairtrade sales in France is split 44 per cent via the supermarket/hypermarket channel, with hot beverages having the most significant share of this with 58 per cent, and 56 per cent of sales via both organic specialist retailers and the out-of-home sector (vending, restaurants and hotels, textile partner companies). Still, in France 20 per cent of sales come from the original FTOs. Also, in France there is another more recent fair trade label called Ecocert, which originates initially in organic certification. Ecocert has responded to the demand for products to meet both organic and fair trade certification. Until 2009 Fairtrade grew in France between 15 and 20 per cent each year; however, from 2009 to 2012 the rate has declined to 5–10 per cent (Max Havelaar France 2012). Informant 2 suggests that in 2009 large mainstream supermarkets such as Carrefour launched their own private-label Fairtrade products but at 30–40 per cent lower price than existing Fairtrade products from Alter Eco. According to Informant 2, this created confusion with French consumers and has led to both cannibalization of original pioneer fair trade brands and a lowering of trust in the Fairtrade mark.

In common with Italy there also appears to be a clash between the ideals of fair trade between the radicals and the pragmatists. To bring the movement together and create a spirit of cooperation, the French Fair Trade Platform was founded in 1997 to carry out lobbying and fundraising and to provide leadership to the movement in France. By 2005 French Fair Trade Platform comprised 32 different national organizations.

Fair Trade in the United Kingdom

As in Italy, France and Switzerland, fair trade in the UK began in the 1970s and 1980s with organizations such as Traidcraft, Equal Exchange and Oxfam. Product distribution took place through alternative channels of distribution such as church shop networks and whole food shops. In 1992 the Fairtrade Foundation was established by non-governmental organizations (Moore, Gibbon and Slack 2006).

In the early 1990s FTOs such as Cafédirect, Traidcraft (Geobar) and ethical companies such as Green and Black's pioneered Fairtrade certified products in the UK mainstream supermarket sector. In 1998, Divine Chocolate, another mainstream FTO social enterprise, became the first

UK Fairtrade company to pioneer producer ownership with Kuapa Kokoo Ghanaian farmer's cooperative, having a 45 per cent (initially 33 per cent) share in the company. Then in 2007 Liberation Foods Community Interest Company, a Fairtrade nut company, also launched in the UK, with 42 per cent farmer ownership (Doherty, Davies and Tranchell 2012). The development of FTOs launching brands into the UK mainstream prior to supermarket private/own label is particularly unique to the UK compared to other European territories.

The UK grocery retail market is one of the most concentrated (along with Switzerland) of all the global food retail markets (Euromonitor International 2011). The leading four UK supermarkets account for approximately 70 per cent of all grocery sales in the UK. Furthermore, the UK grocery market exhibits a high market share of 49 per cent for retailer private label (Symphony IRI Group 2011). Therefore during the 1990s the FTOs led growth in the mainstream using value chain two to gain supermarket distribution for their branded products. Ransom (2005) argues that the increased availability of Fairtrade products in the mainstream provides something practical that anyone can do to counteract international trading system injustices. The FTO brands also focused on product quality, with Cafédirect winning five gold great taste awards from the Guild of Food in 2010. Golding (2009) calls this combination of ethical positioning and product quality the dual aspect of fair trade marketing.

It is worth noting here the success of FTOs such as Liberation, Divine and Tropical Wholefoods in supplying private-label products to mainstream retailers. For example, Divine supplies both Starbucks and the Co-operative Retail Group with private-label chocolate. According to Teather (2006), the involvement of major retailers has been key to the growth of Fairtrade in the UK, with the supermarket the Co-operative Retail Group sourcing some of its private-label chocolate line from Divine since 2002 and labeling its full coffee line as Fairtrade certified in 2003. Marks & Spencer (coffee and tea) and Sainsbury's (bananas and own-brand sugar) made similar changes in 2006.

Since 2007 the pace and impact of mainstreaming has increased with multinational corporations (MNCs) such as Starbucks, Tate & Lyle, Nestlé, Cadbury's and Mars Masterfoods entering the UK Fairtrade market. Three of the top five UK chocolate products are now Fairtrade certified. Fairtrade sugar sales now total GBP464 million with 21 per cent growth, recording a 42 per cent share of the UK bagged sugar market (Fairtrade Foundation 2012). Another key category is bananas, with total sales of GBP208 million, 2007 being the key turning point when Sainsbury's supermarkets switched their entire volume of bananas to Fairtrade value chain seven, hence choice editing for consumers.

Analysis of European Country Cases

The country analysis illustrates the differences in fair trade market development between the four selected European countries. Table 18.2 summarizes these differences.

Table 18.2 European Fairtrade market development – country differences

Country	Per capita consumption of Fairtrade marked products in euros*	Fairtrade awareness %	Value chains (VC)	Industry structure	Product categories
Switzerland	38.6	90	Mainly VC 4	Highly concentrated retail & strong national brands – Nestlé	Flowers/ plants bananas
UK	29.65	96	Mainstream first with VC 2 & 3 from FTOs. Now all 1–7 VCs	Concentrated retail structure	Chocolate sugar bananas
France	5.42	61	1–7 but 4–5 VCs before 2 & 3. FTOs have 20% share	Organic an important factor	Hot beverages chocolate
Italy	1.01	28	Mainly 1 & 2 with CTM & now 4, 5, 6 with TransFair Italy	Strong local coffee brands – Lavazza	CTM crafts i-Ice cream ingredients chocolate

Note: * Per capita consumption calculated by dividing Fairtrade marked international sales (Fairtrade International 2013a) by country population.

Source: Authors' synthesis of Globescan (2011), Fairtrade International annual reports (1999–2012) and key informant interviews.

Italy, the UK and France are similar in population size and wealth distribution. Becchetti and Costantino (2010) explain that the Italian market for fair trade started at a very similar time to the UK, following similar roots in religious and alternative trading world shops. However, following the development of Fairtrade International labeling in the 1990s the Italian model continued along this alternative, solidarity-based model using predominantly a social economy value chain (Becchetti and Costantino 2010). In contrast, the UK expanded into other types of value chains, particularly mainstream distribution, in a proactive manner (Davies 2009). The impact on the growth of Fairtrade sales of these decisions is clear. Despite continuing growth in Italy, its fair trade market is only worth EUR119 million: EUR66 million Fairtrade labeled and EUR53 million CTM Altomercato labeled (CTM Altomercato 2012). The UK market sells over EUR1.9 billion in labeled products (Fairtrade International 2013b). Those countries showing both a high per capita consumption and rapid expansion, such as the UK and Switzerland, are also characterized by early mainstreaming via retailers, particularly coops, high awareness of the Fairtrade mark and a focus on specific product categories such as bananas. However, a key difference with the UK is the role played by FTOs, which launched brands into the mainstream before retailers (value chain two). The value chain analysis by country also unveils the importance played by specific value chains in expansion and stagnation of Fairtrade sales and awareness.

Italy, with its two competing labels, appears to have been slower in expanding beyond value chain one, which has led partly to its stagnation in sales growth. Whereas Fairtrade expansion in the UK has utilized all seven value chains, Switzerland has principally expanded through value chain four. Its reliance on two major retailers could be high risk if these retailers decide to change strategy. Another key difference is the role played by different product categories in Fairtrade expansion. This is partly influenced by industry structure and the local institutional context (e.g., presence of strong local brands in both Italy and Switzerland). However, a focus on expanding Fairtrade banana sales in both the UK and Switzerland has been a key factor in early mainstream growth. Max Havelaar France has struggled to follow this banana success.

CONCLUSION

This chapter describes the development of fair trade in Europe, with special attention to the role of Fairtrade International and fair trade labeling. It shows that the expansion of fair trade was contingent upon trade-offs regarding the original ideal of the movement and the new vision carried by Fairtrade International and its labeling scheme. On the one hand, the Fairtrade label may have diluted fair trade standards in Europe. It led to a depersonalization of consumer–producer relations, some tensions in the movement and a shift from an alternative ideal to sustainability standards. Overall the result is that fair trade in Europe has been partly depoliticized to form a trading market. Its transformative ideal has shifted to a pragmatic focus on increasing market transactions. On the other hand, Fairtrade International and the labeling system enabled significant market growth in Europe by reaching out to segments beyond the alternative trade activists. Creating a brand to simplify the fair trade message and partnering with mainstream retailers were two important mechanisms that contributed to reaching those new consumer segments. Furthermore, the impact of Fairtrade extends beyond product sales. It has contributed to raising consumer awareness about ethical issues in trading and inspired new models such as Slow Food.

The second part of this chapter explains the structure of the fair trade markets through four country case studies. Fair trade spread rapidly from pioneer to early adopter countries in Europe, but the development and expansions have followed different routes resulting in a heterogeneous European fair trade market. The value chains' structures differ widely by country, which helps to explain differences in commercial success, as indicated by sales or brand recognition. Early retailer engagement and cooperation or tensions between the different branches of the fair trade movement are important explanatory factors.

Overall, the growth of fair trade driven by Fairtrade International is likely to continue: if in some product categories the penetration of Fairtrade labeled references is stagnating, the development of standards for new product categories should drive growth. Those four case studies also provide contrasting stories on possible developments of fair trade. They may be sources of inspiration for countries with developing fair trade markets that will likely face similar challenges involving trade-offs to make in relation to standardization, dilution, credibility and expansion of fair trade.

REFERENCES

Balineau, Gaëlle and Ivan Dufeu (2010), 'Are fair trade goods credence goods? A new proposal, with French illustrations', *Journal of Business Ethics*, 92 (S2), 331–345.

Becchetti, Leonardo and Marco Costantino (2010), 'Fair trade in Italy: Too much "movement" in the shop?', *Journal of Business Ethics*, 92 (S2), 181–203.

Bezençon, Valéry and Sam Blili (2009), 'Fair trade managerial practices: Strategy, organisation and engagement', *Journal of Business Ethics*, 90 (1), 95–113.
Bezençon, Valéry and Sam Blili (2010), 'Ethical products and consumer involvement: What's new?', *European Journal of Marketing*, 44 (9/10), 1305–1321.
Boonman, Mark, Wendela Huisman, Elmy Sarrucco-Fedorovtsjev and Terya Sarrucco (2011), *Fair Trade Facts and Figures: A Success Story for Producers and Consumers*, Culemborg, the Netherlands: The Dutch Association of Worldshops.
Chatzidakis, Andreas, Sally Hibbert and Andrew P. Smith (2007), 'Why people don't take their concerns about fair trade to the supermarket: The role of neutralisation', *Journal of Business Ethics*, 74 (1), 89–100.
CTM Altromercato (2012), 'Towards the other balance sheet, 2010/2011', Bolzano, Italy: Conzorio CTM Altromercato, available at http://www.altromercato.it/flex/cm/pages/ServeAttachment.php/L/IT/D/e%252F1%252F1%252FD.b996c269ccb73e1649d9/P/BLOB%3AID%3D168 (accessed August 28 2013).
Davies, Iain (2009), 'Alliances and networks: Creating success in the UK fair trade market', *Journal of Business Ethics*, 86 (S1), 109–126.
Davies, Iain A., Bob Doherty and Simon Knox (2010), 'The rise and stall of a fair trade pioneer: The Cafédirect story', *Journal of Business Ethics*, 92 (1), 127–147.
De Pelsmacker, Patrick and Wims Janssens (2007), 'A model for fair trade buying behaviour: The role of perceived quantity and quality of information and of product-specific attitudes', *Journal of Business Ethics*, 75 (4), 361–380.
De Pelsmacker, Patrick, Liesbeth Driesen and Glenn Rayp (2005), 'Do consumers care about ethics? Willingness to pay for fair trade coffee', *Journal of Consumer Affairs*, 39 (2), 363–385.
Doherty, Bob, Iain Davies and Sophi Tranchell (2012), 'Where now for fair trade', *Journal of Business History*, 55 (2), 161–189.
Eden, Sally, Christopher Bear and Gordon Walker (2008), 'Understanding and (dis)trusting food assurance schemes: Consumer confidence and the "knowledge fix"', *Journal of Rural Studies*, 24 (1), 1–14.
Euromonitor International (2011), 'Packaged food: Ethical', London: Euromonitor International.
Fairtrade Foundation (2012), 'Annual report 2011–2012', London: Fairtrade Foundation.
Fairtrade International (2013a), 'For producers with producers: Annual report 2011–2012', Bonn, Germany: Fairtrade International.
Fairtrade International (2013b), 'Unlocking the power: Annual report 2012–2013', Bonn, Germany: Fairtrade International.
Fairtrade Towns (2013), 'About Fairtrade Towns', available at http://www.fairtradetowns.org/about (accessed 27 September 2013).
Gereffi, Gary and Miguel Korzeniewicz (1994), *Commodity Chains and Global Capitalism*, Westport, CT: Praeger.
Globescan (2011), 'Fair trade consumer survey', available at http://www.globescan.com/news-and-analysis/press-releases/press-releases-2011/94-press-releases-2011/145-high-trust-and-global-recognition-makes-fairtrade-an-enabler-of-ethical-consumer-choice.html (accessed 13 November 2013).
Golding, Kirsty (2009), 'Fair trade's dual aspect: The communications challenge of fair trade marketing', *Journal of Macromarketing*, 29 (2), 160–171.
Informant 1 (2013), interview with Bob Doherty, Geneva (17 August 2013).
Informant 2 (2013), interview with Bob Doherty, Paris (13 September 2013).
Informant 3 (2013), interview with Bob Doherty, Milan (15 September 2013).
Ingenbleek, Paul and Machiel Reinders (2013), 'The development of a market for sustainable coffee in the Netherlands: Rethinking the contribution of fair trade',
Jones, Peter, Daphne Comfort and David Hillier (2003), 'Retailing fair trade food products in the UK', *British Food Journal*, 105 (11), 800–810.

Keller, Kevin Lane (1993), 'Conceptualizing, measuring, managing customer-based brand equity', *Journal of Marketing*, 57 (1), 1–22.
Kim, Gwang-Suk, Grace Lee and Kiwan Park (2010), 'A cross-national investigation on how ethical consumers build loyalty toward fair trade brands', *Journal of Business Ethics*, 96 (4), 589–611.
Larceneux, Fabrice, Florence Benoit-Moreau and Valérie Renaudin (2012), 'Why might organic labels fail to influence consumer choices? Marginal labelling and brand equity effects', *Journal of Consumer Policy*, 35 (1), 85–104.
Loureiro, Maria and Justus Lotade (2005), 'Do fair trade and eco-labels in coffee wake-up the consumer conscience?', *Ecological Economics*, 53 (1), 129–138.
Mahé, Thuriane (2010), 'Are stated preferences confirmed by purchasing behaviours? The case of fair trade-certified bananas in Switzerland', *Journal of Business Ethics*, 92 (S2), 301–315.
Max Havelaar France (2012), 'Fairtrade in France annual report', Paris, France: Max Havelaar France.
Max Havelaar Switzerland (2012), 'New product strategy', Switzerland: Max Havelaar Switzerland.
Moore, Geoff, Jane Gibbon and Richard Slack (2006), 'The mainstreaming of fair trade: A macromarketing perspective', *Journal of Strategic Marketing*, 14 (4), 329–352.
Özçağlar-Toulouse, Nil, Amina Béji-Bécheur, Matthieu Gatteau and Philippe Robert-Demontrond (2010), 'Demystifying fair trade in France: The history of an ambiguous project', *Journal of Business Ethics*, 92 (S2), 205–216.
Özçağlar-Toulouse, Nil, Edward Shiu and Deidre Shaw (2006), 'In search of fair trade: Ethical consumer decision making in France', *International Journal of Consumer Studies*, 30 (5), 502–514.
Poret, Sylvaine and Claire Chambolle (2007), 'Fair trade labeling: Inside or outside supermarkets?', *Journal of Agricultural and Food Industrial Organization*, 5 (1), 1184–1193.
Ransom, David (2005), 'Fair trade for sale', *New Internationalist*, April, 34–35.
Sassatelli, Roberta and Federica Davolio (2010), 'Consumption, pleasure and politics: Slow Food and the politico-aesthetic problematization of food', *Journal of Consumer Culture*, 10 (2), 202–232.
Sebastiani, Roberta, Francesca Montagnini and Daniele Dalli (2013), 'Ethical consumption and new business models in the food industry: Evidence from the Eataly case', *Journal of Business Ethics*, 114 (3), 473–488.
Slow Food (2013), 'Slow Food: The history of an idea', available at http://www.slowfood.com/international/7/history (accessed 14 January 2014).
Strong, Carolyn (1997), 'The problems of translating fair trade principles into consumer purchase behaviour', *Marketing Intelligence and Planning*, 15, 32–37.
Symphony IRI Group (2011), 'Retail private label brands in Europe – current and emerging trends', special report, Bracknell, UK: Symphony IRI Group.
Teather, David (2006), 'Big retailers help raise Fairtrade sales by third', *The Guardian Newspaper*, 28 June, 24.
Utting, Karla (2009), 'Assessing the impact of fair trade coffee: Towards an integrative framework', *Journal of Business Ethics*, 86 (S1), 127–149.

19. The US market and Fair Trade Certified

April Linton and Claudia Rosty

INTRODUCTION

Fair trade is a dynamic movement seeking poverty alleviation and empowerment of producers and workers through ethical trading between Northern consumers and Southern producers. The movement is constituted of alternative trading organizations (ATOs), formalized labeling and certification systems and social movement groups supporting fair trade principles (Wilkinson 2007). Each component played an important role in the evolution and expansion of the fair trade movement in the United States. In this chapter we briefly recount its history and address contemporary issues around its practice and growth. How does the United States compare to other markets for fair trade products? What do the differences mean for those who are attempting to grow fair trade in the United States? Can fair trade scale up to supply US markets without diluting its core standards? To address these questions we draw on recent scholarship and interviews with advocates working to promote fair trade and workers' rights in US communities, schools and businesses.

FAIR TRADE IN THE UNITED STATES: A BRIEF HISTORY

Fair trade's US roots trace to small-scale 'alternative' and 'direct' models of international trade. On a 1946 visit to Puerto Rico, a Mennonite Central Committee volunteer met women skilled at creating beautiful lace, but who lived in extreme poverty. She began selling the lace in her home community, delivering the proceeds directly to the artisans. Her work eventually grew to become the fair trade enterprise Ten Thousand Villages (Fair Trade Federation 2014a). At around the same time, a small group of church relief workers established Sales Exchange for Refugee Rehabilitation and Vocation (SERRV) to help refugees in Europe recover from World War II. Today SERRV works with artisans and farmers in 36 countries, providing market access, design, technology and business training (SERRV 2014).

For several decades fair trade in the United States was confined to small-scale buyer–seller relationships mostly involving handicrafts. Then in the late 1970s, American entrepreneurs began to establish fair partnerships with Southern producers. Their network was formally incorporated in 1994 as the Fair Trade Federation, 'a trade association that strengthens and promotes North American organizations fully committed to fair trade' (Fair Trade Federation 2014b). Meanwhile in 1985 the owner of Thanksgiving Coffee Company visited Nicaragua's pro-Sandinista coffee organization, where he learned about the relationship between coffee and revolution. Returning home, this entrepreneur changed his company's slogan to 'Not Just a Cup, but a Just Cup' and donated 50 cents per pound of the Nicaraguan beans he sold to the Sandinistas (Pendergrast 1999, 354). A year later three employees of a New England food coop formed Equal Exchange in order to 'create a process that allows people to reconnect with the people who grow much of the food and with the ecology from which it comes' (quoted in Pendergrast 1999, 355). Equal Exchange was the first US group to specialize in selling fair trade food items. The organizations described above built a small niche for socially conscious consumption in the United States.

In the mid-1990s a more formalized model developed around labeling fair trade coffee; this became a predominant force in US fair trade (Barrientos, Conroy and Jones 2007, 55). While ATOs and labeling institutions are similarly committed to promoting ethical trading and producer empowerment, ATOs have focused on redefining consumer–producer relationships through solidarity networks, whereas labelers of fair trade products such as Fair Trade USA have adopted a strategy grounded on formal standards and third-party oversight, enabling greater market access for producers and products worldwide.

Fair Trade USA

The proliferation of fair trade initiatives and the desire to expand fair trade globally under a unified system led to the 1992 founding of TransFair International to organize fair trade under a single label that could be used across market borders and applied to diverse products (Bennett 2012). TransFair International provided a viable infrastructure for fair trade monitoring, coordination and promotion of national markets under the TransFair logo (Thomson 1995). TransFair USA (now Fair Trade USA) became a member in 1998 when funding from the Ford Foundation enabled Paul Rice to launch the organization. Rice had founded PRODECOOP, a fair trade and organic cooperative representing smallholder coffee farmers in Nicaragua. PRODECOOP's success in capturing European coffee markets introduced Rice to 'the transformative power of fair trade' (Fair Trade USA 2014a). Initially TransFair USA labeled coffee that met the certification criteria established by the Fairtrade Labelling Organizations International (now Fairtrade International). In subsequent years the range of products expanded to include tea, cocoa and other food commodities. While small progressive roasters and ATOs such as Equal Exchange were early TransFair USA licensees, Starbucks' agreement to sell certified coffee in 2000, largely in response to pressure from activist groups, represented a significant expansion of fair trade into the mainstream US specialty coffee sector, within which many other roasters and retailers started to offer Fair Trade Certified coffee (Grodnik and Conroy 2007). These companies' participation resulted in a dramatic increase in fair trade coffee sales.

The success of Fair Trade Certified products in the United States is due to the emergence of a national fair trade labeler and the joint efforts of advocacy non-governmental organizations (NGOs), students and faith-based groups. These fair trade promoters perform complementary functions; some focus on increasing the availability and sales of fair trade products whereas others pursue a transformative agenda that seeks to change 'conventional' trade – to make all trade fair. At times the different emphases and strategies used by fair trade organizations have generated dissent within the movement. In particular the push to mainstream fair trade created new challenges for mission-driven ATOs, who believe that the fair trade movement should remain rooted in cooperative principles and support for small producers as mainstream actors can weaken fair trade's standards and transformative capacity (Barrientos, Conroy and Jones 2007).

The rapid growth of fair trade sales in the United States is mainly attributed to the participation of large retailers such as McDonald's, Costco, Whole Foods, Safeway, Sam's Club, Starbucks and Walmart. Fair Trade USA is at the forefront of the initiative to expand fair trade's reach beyond traditional niche markets in order to extend its benefits to more farmers and farm laborers. Fair Trade USA's focus on building partnerships and alliances with large corporate brands, intention to certify plantations (discussed later in this chapter) and lack of explicit support for 100 per cent fair trade enterprises recently led organizations such as Equal Exchange to abandon the Fair Trade USA label (Raynolds 2012a). Despite these controversies, Fair Trade USA is the leading third-party certifier of fair trade products in the United States and a major player in the movement. The organization's mission is to enable 'sustainable development and community empowerment by cultivating a more equitable global trade model that benefits farmers, workers, consumers, industry and the earth' (Fair Trade USA 2014b).

The United States is the world's second largest market for fair trade products, after the United Kingdom, with annual sales of US$1.25 billion (Raynolds 2012a, 281). The scope and volume of US fair trade imports have grown impressively over time. For example, US imports of Fair Trade Certified coffee increased from 76 059 pounds in 1998 to over 2 million pounds in 1999 to over 163 million pounds in 2012 (Fair Trade USA 2013a). Coffee is still the most important Fair Trade Certified commodity accounting for about 61 per cent of overall Fair Trade USA volume. But over time Fair Trade USA has introduced certified tea, cocoa, sugar, grains, produce, spices, flowers, wine, honey, sports balls, apparel, agave and recently coconut waters and oils to the US market. Fair trade bananas, first imported in 2004, are now the second largest US fair trade commodity (Fair Trade USA 2013a).

In 2012 alone sales of these certified products generated over US$37 million in social premium revenues paid to fair trade producer organizations (Fair Trade USA 2013a). Yet Fair Trade USA's 2012 annual report accurately states that

> fair trade represents only a fraction of the products available to US consumers … the need is much greater. According to the World Bank, more than 2 billion people live on less than two dollars a day. Today's fair trade model reaches only a small percentage of them. Fair trade can and must do more. (Fair Trade USA 2013a)

Fair trade advocates in Switzerland and the United Kingdom have taken a somewhat similar 'must do more' approach, with an emphasis on growing fair trade by increasing access to and sales of fair trade products by making them available in 'mainstream' supermarkets and discount stores. As we will discuss further, this is quite controversial among fair trade stakeholders. Yet mainstreaming holds immense promise in terms of extending the benefits of fair trade. Swiss consumers spend about US$27 a year on Fairtrade certified products, whereas American consumers spend about US$4 (see Bob Doherty, Valéry Bezençon and Gaëlle Balineau's chapter in this volume). If the US figure were to increase by only US$1/year, the social premiums paid to producers that sell in US markets would nearly double.[1]

WHAT DIFFERENTIATES THE US MARKET FOR FAIRLY TRADED PRODUCTS?

In the United States as in other countries, ATOs such as Equal Exchange, faith-oriented groups (e.g., Catholic Relief Services, Lutheran World Relief) and membership-based fair trade groups (e.g., United Students for Fair Trade, Fair Trade Federation) have all contributed to increasing fair trade awareness. These groups have been especially effective at promoting fair trade among conscientious consumers who exercise their political and/or social-justice values by supporting better economic and environmental conditions for farmers and farm workers. Yet despite these efforts, the per capita consumption of fair trade products in the United States is lower than in most European countries (Krier 2007, 19). It seems that there is still sizable potential for further growth in the US market. (For more on consumption in the US market, see Keith Brown's chapter in this volume; on applying fair trade to the US agriculture sector, see Sandy Brown and Christy Getz's chapter in this volume.)

Our interviews with leaders of US-based fair trade and fair labor campaigns focused on two questions: how best to expand fair trade in the US market and what might differentiate US consumers from those in other countries where fair trade has achieved a greater market presence.[2] US activists articulated a common theme: for fair trade to become salient to a majority of consumers, it will require different 'packaging', or 'messaging', than is employed elsewhere. They also concurred that American consumers are less socially conscious than their European counterparts. One interviewee posited that the message 'all people sink or swim together' does not resonate in a society defined by individualized attitudes and behaviors (Interview 1). Another noted, 'In the US, people want to drive SUVs, or buy as much Hershey's as we want. It's about choice, as opposed to impact. The fair trade movement will only get a few people with the impact pitch' (Interview 2).

GROWING FAIR TRADE IN THE US CONTEXT

Despite our interviewees' focus on American individualism, there is evidence that American consumers *do* make value-oriented decisions. Political scientist Shareen Hertel and her colleagues (2009) explored the connection between Americans' attitudes about human rights and their self-reported willingness to pay more for fairly traded goods. They conducted a nationally representative survey of 508 adults,[3] asking questions about freedom from torture, freedom of thought and expression, and the right to a minimum standard of living. Over 60 per cent of respondents said that they considered a guaranteed minimum standard of living to be 'an inviolable human right'. The interviewers asked several questions about willingness to pay more for a sweatshop-free sweater or a pound of Fair Trade Certified coffee. The study's results show a clear association between believing in a right to a minimum standard of living and willingness to pay at least US$1 more for a pound of fair trade coffee. Even among respondents who said they had never seen a fair trade label, 26 per cent expressed willingness to pay more for products that bear it. Hertel and her colleagues (2009, 457) concluded that 'American consumers are more likely to "put their money where their values are" in progressive defense of economic rights than has heretofore been suggested'. While research on how people *claim they would shop* yields far more optimistic results than research on *how consumers actually behave*, this study nonetheless implies that there is untapped market demand for ethically produced goods. In what contexts might Americans' actual purchasing practices reflect values promoting human rights, social justice and/or environmental protection?

An insight comes from management scholar Carolyn Doran (2009). Doran aimed to identify the values most salient to Americans who already buy Fair Trade Certified products by surveying Internet shoppers on the websites of four prominent Fair Trade retailers.[4] Above all, loyal fair trade shoppers were motivated by the principle of universalism, a value set that includes unity with all people and nature. This suggests that commitment to Fair Trade values (as well as products) is related to a more expansive sense of membership – seeing one's connection to people everywhere and to the earth.

Doran's (2009) work highlights the importance of connecting fair trade to a bigger picture. These research findings resonated with the fair trade advocates we interviewed. For example, Billy Linstead-Goldsmith, the National Coordinator of Fair Trade Campaigns, an umbrella group for US efforts to promote fair trade in localities and organizations, explained that because awareness of fair trade is relatively low in the United States, it is important to explicitly connect fair trade with the core values people share with friends, colleagues or congregants and with the broader sustainability landscape (Interview 4).

Fair Trade Campaigns in US Towns and Schools

One way fair trade advocates engage groups of consumers is by establishing and supporting fair trade campaigns in communities. Fair Trade Campaigns provide resources for and recognition to groups of people who seek to make their cities, towns, schools or congregations leaders in sustainability and solidarity and catalysts for global change.[5] This network helps mobilize fair trade consumers and advocates across the United States to increase the availability of fair trade products. Its work is crucial because 'you can't have successful campaigns without the infrastructure to support them' (Interview 4). At the time of this writing there are 208 active campaigns, 59 of which have adopted binding resolutions about fair trade purchasing (Fair Trade Campaigns 2014). Modeled on Fair Trade Towns in Europe (see Alastair Smith's chapter in this volume), US Fair Trade Towns are active communities committed to fair trade principles providing opportunities for 'individuals and groups to join together in a collective movement for change inspired by the notion of consumer power' (Wheeler 2012, 4). As one town organizer explained:

> We keep fair trade in front of people. We send a monthly news brief, recognize new products, new stores. We excite people and educate them by bringing fair trade boutiques to their organizations where they can see the breadth and quality of products available. And we promote businesses that are choosing to offer fair trade products. Education and product availability go hand in hand. Our committees stay engaged by seeing this deepening of fair trade awareness. (Interview 1)

Similarly, fair trade advocates on college and university campuses must achieve a set of goals to gain recognition for their schools' campaigns. The first step is to build a leadership team that includes students, administration and faculty. The team reaches out to campus outlets such as dining halls and bookstores, asking them to offer fair trade products. It promotes education about fair trade via special events and meetings as well as in classrooms. Achieving 'declared' status as a Fair Trade College or University means that a school has passed a resolution that specifically incorporates fair trade into its procurement policies.

In at least one case, campaign leaders were able to bring fair trade under the umbrella of a campus sustainability initiative. Others have framed fair trade as an important part of their school's mission to promote social justice. As one university administrator put it, institutionalizing fair trade on campus means getting people to 'think about how to bring values and price together better'. Students like seeing fair trade on campus, which is good for attracting prospective students (Interview 4).

Asked what keeps an established campus campaign going, faculty and staff working to maintain fair trade procurement practices at colleges and universities talked about education and creating continuity by establishing resources such as sourcing guides, an archive describing successful fair trade events or a list of courses that touch on fair trade. Since students are transient, outreach must be ongoing and systematic. It is especially important for student leaders to cultivate and train their successors (Interview 2). These interviewees also note a need for constant re-evaluation in terms of how a school, through its purchasing power, can promote sustainability and social justice via relations with its suppliers, contractors and workers.

THE PATH AHEAD

Although US fair trade advocates have been active in reaching out to conscientious consumers and creating institutional infrastructure for fair trade practices, only a very small fraction of Americans' coffee, tea, chocolate and other products from the global South are Fair Trade Certified. How best can fair trade scale up to tap into the vast buying power of American consumers, thus increasing returns to producers while maintaining its integrity? To answer this question we must look more closely at the organization, opportunities and difficulties presented by the US fair trade market.

Sociologist Laura Raynolds (2009) distinguishes three types of US businesses: 'mission-driven' companies that actively support and promote all aspects of fair trade, 'quality-driven' buyers for whom fair trade is one strategy to ensure a reliable supply of premium grade produce and 'market-driven' businesses which advance mainstream practices that foster competition between suppliers within buyer dominated value chains. Fair trade relationships with market-driven companies have vastly increased revenues to producers, yet these relationships are often less stable than fair trade partnerships involving mission-driven or quality-driven companies since large corporate buyers are reluctant to enter into long-term contracts or provide pre-financing to producers. Market-driven buyers' environmental and labor practices often do not align with the values of fair trade. For these reasons, within the US fair trade movement there is considerable controversy about the 'mainstreaming' of fair trade.

Some activists see mainstreaming as a pragmatic way to grow fair trade within the current economic model. Others, however, are actively seeking to change that model. The first group attempts to 'penetrate the market and the lifestyle of consumers in order to sell larger quantities of fair products and to strengthen the producer organizations of the South'; the second aims to make all exchanges fair (Renard 2003, 91). Such ideological perspectives and their implications have generated extensive discussions about mainstreaming (e.g., Doherty, Davies and Tranchell

2013; Jaffee 2010; Raynolds 2009), raising two main concerns: large corporations dominate the US fair trade market and these corporations lack a 100 per cent commitment to fair trade.

The United States fair trade market is dominated by Keurig Green Mountain (formerly Green Mountain Coffee Roasters) and Starbucks and includes major multinational corporation plantations (e.g., Dole and Chiquita). This has marginalized the ATOs, many of which are turning away from fair trade labels in favor of alternative schemes. This development has very significant implications for fair trade because there are now licensees with greater power, capital and influence than the certifiers and fair trade organizations put together (Doherty, Davies and Tranchell 2013). Large corporations are also more likely to adopt 'the more convenient elements of fair trade at the expense of its more radical edges' (Doherty, Davies and Tranchell 2013, 163). The lack of 100 per cent commitment to fair trade in the majority of a corporation's sourcing or business arrangements can undermine fair trade certification standards (Raynolds 2009, 1087). For instance, Equal Exchange recommended that Fair Trade USA require that, in order to market fair trade products, at least 5 per cent of large corporations' purchases should align with fair trade standards and principles (Jaffee 2010). However, many of these corporations purchase only 1 per cent of their overall products under fair trade terms. Fair Trade USA 'does not stipulate any particular purchase level to qualify for use of the seal, nor is there a requirement for increases over time; these details are negotiated in private deals with individual firms' (Jaffee 2010, 274).

We recognize the challenges that mainstreaming poses, yet there are also important potential benefits from market growth (Doherty, Davies and Tranchell 2013). Most obviously, more sales create more fair trade social premiums for producers. Further, corporate interest in fair trade indicates that fair trade has succeeded in demonstrating that the market should reward socially just and environmentally sound production. To the extent that the mainstreaming of fair trade leads to changes in corporations' activities, consumer commitment to fair trade becomes less relevant.

Fair Trade USA's Separation from Fairtrade International

In September 2011, Fair Trade USA and Fairtrade International issued a joint statement announcing their separation. Both institutions share the same fair trade principles of ethical trading to empower producers and workers globally and to improve their livelihoods, but they diverge on how to best achieve this mission (Fair Trade USA 2014c). Fair Trade

USA's decision to part ways with Fairtrade International reveals enduring differences between 'the market-oriented US certification agency on the one hand and its more movement-oriented European counterparts and Fairtrade International on the other' (Raynolds 2012a, 285).

Paul Rice (2012), President and CEO of Fair Trade USA, stated that a desire to double fair trade's impact by 2015 was the main reason that Fair Trade USA chose to pursue its own certification procedures. Originally fair trade certification was intended to improve the conditions of small-scale farmer cooperatives that could not compete in the conventional market. However, the need to increase certified commodity volume, variety and to expand fair trade benefits to workers led Fairtrade International to certify estate commodities such as flowers, fresh fruits and vegetables, juices, herbs, prepared fruits and tea while limiting the certification of coffee, cocoa, sugar, honey and nuts to cooperatives since small producers of these commodities have the capacity to supply the necessary certified volume. Fair Trade USA argues that broader certification will extend fair trade's benefits to marginalized hired laborers; whereas Fairtrade International believes estate certification of other commodities will economically disadvantage cooperatives at the heart of fair trade's mission. Fair Trade USA's desire to certify coffee estates and independent smallholders is particularly controversial because coffee is unarguably Fairtrade's most important product.

Committed to a mainstreaming strategy, Fair Trade USA's (2014d) 'fair trade for all' campaign has three ambitious goals: strengthen farming communities via credit, capacity building and development; innovate to make fair trade more inclusive and scalable, with a target of doubling impact by 2015; and ignite consumer demand through education. Fair Trade USA recognizes an alternative certification offered by Scientific Certification Systems that makes it possible for coffee, sugar and cocoa plantations to bear the Fair Trade Certified label in the United States and thus for hired labors to benefit from a system from which they had formerly been excluded. Fair Trade USA still recognizes FLO-Cert certification and continues to work with cooperatives through their Co-op Link programs which seek to help cooperatives improve quality, increase productivity, access capital cost-effectively and become stronger business partners (Fair Trade USA 2014d). While estates and independent smallholders excluded under Fairtrade International certification can now become certified via Fair Trade USA, cooperatives can seek fair trade certification from Fairtrade International *or* Fair Trade USA. Producers can sell to anyone they choose and are free to work with other certifiers such as IMO (Institute for Marketecology, now called Fair for Life) and Rainforest Alliance.

In 2012 Fair Trade USA launched a pilot project to certify independent smallholder coffee farmers and estates that meet high standards of empowerment, economic development, social responsibility and environmental stewardship. Notably most of the pilot participants already have one or more social/environmental certifications besides fair trade (see Table 19.1).

To extend the benefits of fair trade in areas where small producer organizations are not the norm, Fairtrade International also recognizes independent smallholders partnered with intermediary organizations (e.g., an exporter, processor, private enterprise or NGO) that are able and willing to assist them in organizing into autonomous producer organizations that can comply with Fairtrade standards (Fairtrade International 2014a, 4). Currently this certification is only available for producers of Basmati rice and cotton in India, cotton in Pakistan and cocoa in Oceania, but Fair Trade USA is expanding the model to include other independent smallholders, regardless of commodity or geographic location. The difference between independent smallholders and small producers organizations is that the latter own the certification directly, pool their premium income, negotiate collectively with buyers and access preferred training, whereas the former have more flexibility to partner with Fair Trade Certified intermediary organizations that have the same responsibilities of small producer organizations under the certification (Fair Trade USA 2014e, 1).[6] Like Fairtrade International, Fair Trade USA expects independent smallholders to form democratic organizations over time.

Fair Trade USA estate certification expands fair trade benefits across a range of agricultural products as it seeks to promote workers' rights and collective empowerment through democratic organization and leadership capacity. Fair Trade USA requires estates to adhere to national laws or international standards such as International Labor Organization conventions, whichever is highest. In terms of wages, estates must comply with national and local laws, sector regulations and industry averages at a minimum, seeking to continuously improve workers' wages over time (Fair Trade USA 2014f, 2). This certification also benefits workers through a community development premium for worker-driven projects managed by a Fair Trade Committee constituted of democratically elected workers and managers. Managers do not have voting rights but can veto committee decisions if they are illegal or against Fair Trade USA standards. Committee representatives collaborate with workers to plan how the social premium will be invested.

Table 19.1 Fair Trade USA coffee pilots

Name	Location	Fair Trade USA standard	Other certifications	No. of workers/ farmers*	Hectares in production	Use of 1st Fair Trade premium	Notes
Fazenda Nossa Senhora de Fatima	Minas Gerais, Brazil	Farm Worker	Organic, Utz, RFA	110	230	eye and dental care	family-owned farm
Ipanema Agricola	Minas Gerais, Brazil	Farm Worker	RFA, Utz, CAFE Practices	600+1000	3570	healthcare	engaged in many social projects
Fazenda Primavera	Minas Gerais, Brazil	Farm Worker	RFA, Utz, BSCA, Certifica Minas, 4C	200	1032	healthcare	hires independent farmers to supplement their income
Empresas de Nariño	Nariño, Colombia	Independent Smallholder	none	245	260	capacity building	small farmer organization
Hacienda Venecia	Manizales, Colombia	Farm Worker	Utz, Biotropico	30+15+500	161	better living conditions	
Café de Altura de San Ramón	San Ramón, Costa Rica	Independent Smallholder	ISO 14001, Cert. Enviro. Mgmt, Quality Cert., Utz	537	1500	dental care	producer owned and operated
Beneficio Santa Rosa S.A.	Santa Rosa de Copan, Honduras	Independent Smallholder	RFA, 4C	140	1124	teachers, scholarship, school supplies	market access partner for farmers

Mordocofe	Ethiopia (no city listed)	Farm Worker	RFA, Organic	46+300+50	510	cafeteria/ community center, education, grocery store with subsidized prices	family-owned farm
Prodelsur	Junín, Cajamarca, Peru	Independent Smallholder	Utz, CAFE Practices, 4C, RFA	160	712	fertilizers, road improvement, medical, water, education	two regional fair trade committees
Finca La Revancha	La Dalia, Matagalpa Nicaragua	Farm Worker	none	96+500	160	latrines, food assistance for seniors	

Note: * The first number is permanent workers/farmers; the second is temporary/seasonal help; the third is migrant labor.

Source: Fair Trade USA (2013b).

Fair Trade USA standards ensure workers' freedom of association 'to establish or join workers' organizations of their own choosing and to collectively negotiate their working conditions' (Fair Trade USA 2014g, 102). Workers are provided with information about their rights to association and to choose how they want to be represented. However, unlike Fairtrade International (2014b, 20), Fair Trade USA farm worker standards do not mandate collective worker representation. This is important since research on groups certified by Fairtrade International finds that when unions are absent, the existence of workers' committees that represent workers and their interests when negotiating with management can advance workers' collective capacity and rights (Raynolds 2012b).

Critics of 'fair trade for all' argue that, if sales do not increase fast enough, Fair Trade Certified estates could take business away from existing cooperatives. Perhaps Fair Trade USA is 'putting the cart before the horse' by extending certification to more groups before growing demand (Interview 3). It is too soon to adjudicate on this matter because the pilot project is very small. In 2012, only 0.2 per cent of US fair trade coffee imports came from pilot farms, all in Brazil. These purchases represented new business; they did not replace existing cooperative purchases. In fact in 2012 cooperatives exported 18 per cent more fair trade coffee to North America than in 2011 and the number of cooperatives supplying Fair Trade USA's North American partners grew by 23 per cent (Fair Trade USA 2013b).[7]

When farms follow the fair wage and environmental practices that fair trade requires, workers should be able to earn more money and avoid exposure to harmful chemicals. But there are other concerns about making fair trade certification available to estates with hired labor. The Fair Trade USA standard for plantations states that the Fair Trade Committee must reflect the composition of the workforce, including migrant, seasonal workers and other potentially disadvantaged groups. Yet to date very little is known about how these workers benefit in practice from stable prices and social premiums and whether democratic structures of governance will be sidelined if a large proportion of the workforce is temporary.

Keurig Green Mountain, the largest buyer of Fair Trade Certified coffee in the United States since 2011, committed to purchase coffee from Fair Trade USA pilot farms and farmer organizations but not to label this coffee as fair trade until more is known about the pilot's impact. Keurig Green Mountain's Director of Social Advocacy and Supply Chain Community Outreach Rick Peyser commented on the risks of participation in Fair Trade USA's pilot:

> There's a PR risk. There are people who say, 'Why would you even think of supporting estate certification?' But within the company the feeling is that estate workers, especially temporary workers, are among the poorest of the poor. They're often not grounded in their own communities. The housing on the estates is substandard. So if something can be done to improve the lot of workers, that's great. (Interview 6)

Peyser recognizes concerns about benefits for seasonal workers and competition between estates and cooperatives, but he is willing to take a 'wait and see' approach. If Fair Trade Certified does not benefit marginalized workers, we are not going to support it (Interview 6).

Maintaining the Integrity of Fair Trade

Doherty, Davies and Tranchell (2013, 180) offer several valuable recommendations for helping maintain the integrity of fair trade as it grows, including the idea of instituting 'an enhanced fair trade supply agreement where the fair trade standards are pushed further up the value chain to ensure commitment from mainstream actors to the fair trade principles'. This is similar to a responsible sourcing initiative undertaken by mainstream, market-driven brands and manufacturers that are members of the Fair Labor Association (FLA). The problem that 'FLA Principle 8' seeks to address is that brands' just-in-time ordering and last-minute design modifications often contribute to labor and safety violations in factories. Principle 8 sets benchmarks for buyers and suppliers, addressing policy, internal training, accountability, dialogue, and positive incentives for socially responsible production.[8]

FLA's Principle 8 is a modest effort to address the root causes of labor and environmental abuse in factories that produce for global brands. It is grounded in dialogue between buyers and suppliers. As one of its drafters writes, Principle 8 'could even provide a platform for some suppliers and buyers to jointly demonstrate to the industry that working together differently can result in business efficiencies and improvements in labor and environmental issues on the factory floor' (Interview 7).

Could something similar work between mainstream fair trade buyers and estates or farmer organizations? Keurig Green Mountain's Peyser thinks yes, especially in the specialty coffee industry because 'there's a business case for long-term relationships, to assure supply. The industry needs to invest in the future' (Interview 6). Of course, many companies do not want to commit to long-term relationships when the global market is unpredictable. Should this be grounds for exclusion from fair trade value chains? Some would argue yes, that fair trade must maintain a fixed set of standards. Others, such as Fair Trade Campaigns' Linstead-Goldsmith hold that there is no need for 'one size fits all' fair trade. 'A strength of fair trade could be willingness to adapt to meet the needs of producers in different contexts, and fair trade must rely on those producers' participation in evolving the model' (Interview 4).

CONCLUSION

We argue for a nuanced approach to growing fair trade because it is adaptable to producers' actual needs and allows for experimentation and innovation. For example, tropical produce farmers, whose crops grow year round, do not prioritize pre-financing the way coffee farmers do. Perhaps fair trade organizations or an international bank could manage and allocate, as needed, a pre-financing fund seeded with a portion of each buyer's licensing fees. Likewise, if a large producer organization is constantly soliciting new business, it might not be concerned about long-term contracts. It follows that the main imperative for fair trade as it expands is *transparency* – especially in terms of producers' access to information about the fair trade system, buyers and consumers. Without such knowledge, producers cannot make informed decisions about whom to do business with or how best to position themselves in global markets. The first priority of the global fair trade movement should be to create a window through which producers can see buyers at least as well as buyers can see them (Linton 2012).

The fair trade movement continues to grapple with different visions within it, but the differences have not held the movement back as much as one might imagine. The controversies within the fair trade movement are more salient for leaders than for the average consumer (Interview 5). The US case clearly shows the power of fair trade as a conduit via which individuals and institutional actors become aware of international trade issues such as unfair and unsustainable distribution of wealth, environmental degradation and social disruption. At least for some, this awareness is translating into purposeful action. Producers, activists and other stakeholders can contribute to growing fair trade whether they are pursuing immediate economic strategies or longer-term transformational goals.

NOTES

1. This calculation is based on a US population of 318 000 000 (United States Bureau of the Census 2014) and an average fair trade social premium of 10 per cent. In 2012, US sales of fair trade products provided US$37 million in social premiums (Fair Trade USA 2013a).
2. Ten semi-structured interviews, including one via email, were conducted by April Linton during December 2013 and January 2014. Seven of these are directly quoted or cited in this chapter.
3. Responses were weighted based on standard demographics from the US Bureau of the Census' Current Population Survey.
4. Doran's questionnaire employed the Schwartz Value Survey, comprising ten 'value types'.
5. This chapter's first author was a member of Fair Trade Campaigns' steering committee from its inception until January 2014.
6. In the US model intermediary organizations can own the fair trade certification and ensure compliance with fair trade standards, rather than producers through democratic small producer organizations, yet the community development premium is managed by a Fair Trade Committee constituted of elected farmer representatives (Fair Trade USA 2014e).
7. At the time of this writing, data for 2013 was not yet available.
8. The text of Principle 8 as it applies to brands is here: www.fairlabor.org/sites/default/files/fla_principles_of_fair_labor_responsible_sourcing.pdf.

REFERENCES

Barrientos, Stephanie, Michael Conroy and Elaine Jones (2007), 'Northern social movements and fair trade', in Laura T. Raynolds, Douglas L. Murray and John Wilkinson (eds.), *Fair Trade: The Challenges of Transforming Globalization*, London: Routledge, pp. 51–62.

Bennett, Elizabeth A. (2012), 'A short history of Fairtrade certification governance', in Brigitte Granville and Janet Dine (eds.), *The Processes and Practices of Fair Trade: Trust, Ethics and Governance*, London: Routledge, pp. 43–78.

Doherty, Bob, Iain A. Davies and Sophi Tranchell (2013), 'Where now for fair trade?', *Business History*, 55 (2), 161–189.

Doran, Carolyn J. (2009), 'The role of personal values in fair trade consumption', *Journal of Business Ethics*, 84 (4), 549–563.

Fair Trade Campaigns (2014), 'Grow the fair trade movement in your community', available at http://fairtradecampaigns.org/ (accessed 13 February 2014).

Fair Trade Federation (2014a), 'History', available at https://www.fairtradefederation.org/history-of-fair-trade-in-the-united-states/ (accessed 26 January 2014).

Fair Trade Federation (2014b), 'About us', available at http://www.fairtradefederation.org/about-us/ (accessed 26 January 2014).

Fair Trade USA (2013a), '2012 almanac', available at http://fairtradeusa.org/sites/default/files/2012_Fair-Trade-USA_Almanac.pdf (accessed 9 February 2014).

Fair Trade USA (2013b), 'Fair Trade USA coffee innovation program: 2012 results', available at http://fairtradeusa.org/blog/fair-trade-usa-coffee-innovation-program-2012-results (accessed 2 January 2014).

Fair Trade USA (2014a), 'Who we are', available at http://fairtradeusa.org/about-fair-trade-usa/who-we-are (accessed 14 February 2014).

Fair Trade USA (2014b), 'Mission', available at http://fairtradeusa.org/about-fair-trade-usa/mission (accessed 9 February 2014).
Fair Trade USA (2014c), 'Press releases', available at http://fairtradeusa.org/press-room/press_release/fair-trade-usa-resigns-fairtrade-international-flo-membership (accessed 27 April 2014).
Fair Trade USA (2014d), 'Fair trade for all', available at http://fairtradeusa.org/fair_trade_for_all (accessed 25 April 2014).
Fair Trade USA (2014e), 'Independent smallholders standard: Vision, objectives and summary', available at http://fairtradeusa.org/certification/standards/download-center (accessed 8 May 2014).
Fair Trade USA (2014f), 'Farm workers standard: Vision, objectives and summary', available at http://fairtradeusa.org/certification/standards/download-center (accessed 8 May 2014).
Fair Trade USA (2014g), 'Farm workers standard: Guidelines', available at http://fairtradeusa.org/certification/standards/download-center (accessed 6 May 2014).
Fairtrade International (2014a), 'Fairtrade standard for contract production', available at http://www.fairtrade.net/our-standards.html (accessed 27 April 2014).
Fairtrade International (2014b), 'Standards for hired labour', available at http://www.fairtrade.net/our-standards.html (accessed 10 May 2014).
Grodnik, Ann and Michael Conroy (2007), 'Fair trade coffee in the United States: Why companies join the movement', in Laura T. Raynolds, Douglas L. Murray and John Wilkinson (eds.), *Fair Trade: The Challenges of Transforming Globalization*, London: Routledge, pp. 83–102.
Hertel, Shareen, Lyle Scruggs and C. Patrick Heidkamp (2009), 'Human rights and public opinion: From attitudes to actions', *Political Science Quarterly*, 124 (3), 443–459.
Jaffee, Daniel (2010), 'Fair trade standards, corporate participation, and social movement responses in the United States', *Journal of Business Ethics*, 92 (S2), 267–285.
Krier, Jean-Marie (2007), 'Fair trade 2007: New facts and figures from an ongoing success story', available at http://www.european-fair-trade-association.org/efta/Doc/FT-E-2007.pdf (accessed 2 May 2014).
Linton, April (2012), *Fair Trade from the Ground Up: New Markets for Social Justice*, Seattle, WA: University of Washington Press.
Pendergrast, Mark (1999), *Uncommon Grounds: The History of Coffee and How it Transformed Our World*, New York: Basic Books.
Raynolds, Laura (2009), 'Mainstreaming fair trade coffee: From partnership to traceability', *World Development*, 37 (6), 1083–1093.
Raynolds, Laura (2012a), 'Fair trade: Social regulation in global food markets', *Journal of Rural Studies*, 28 (3), 276–287.
Raynolds, Laura (2012b), 'Fair trade flowers: Global certification, environmental sustainability, and labor standards', *Rural Sociology*, 77 (4), 493–519.
Renard, Marie-Christine (2003), 'Fair trade: Quality, markets and conventions', *Journal of Rural Studies*, 19 (1), 87–96.
Rice, Paul (2012), 'Why we parted ways with Fairtrade International', available at http://www.triplepundit.com/2012/01/fair-trade-all-fair-trade-usa-plans-double-impact-2015 (accessed 29 of April 2014).
SERRV (2014), 'About us', available at http://www.serrv.org/category/about-us (accessed 26 January 2014).
Thomson, Bob (1995), 'An unauthorized history of fair trade labels', available at http://www.web.ca/~bthomson/fairtrade/unauthor.html (accessed 7 May 2014).
United States Bureau of the Census (2014), 'Population clock', available at http://census.gov/ (accessed 6 June 2014).
Wheeler, Kathryn (2012), *Fair Trade and the Citizen-Consumer: Shopping for Justice?*, New York: Palgrave Macmillan.

Wilkinson, John (2007), 'Fair trade: Dynamic and dilemmas of a market oriented global social movement', *Journal of Consumer Policy*, 30 (3), 219–239.

INTERVIEWS

1. Joan Harper, Fair Trade Los Angeles and Fair Trade Campaigns, interviewed 13 December 2013.
2. Shannon O'Neill, Fair Trade Campaigns and Director of the Thea Bowman Center for Women at Siena College, interviewed 6 January 2014.
3. David Barnhill, Fair Trade Campaigns and Director of Environmental Studies/Professor of English at University of Wisconsin, Oshkosh, interviewed 23 December 2013.
4. Billy Linstead-Goldsmith, US National Coordinator, Fair Trade Campaigns, interviewed 11 February 2014.
5. Ryan McDonnell, Fair Trade Boston and Fair Trade Campaigns, interviewed 20 December 2013.
6. Rick Peyser, Director of Social Advocacy and Supply Chain Community Outreach, Green Mountain Coffee Roasters, interviewed 16 January 2014.
7. Tammy Rodriguez, FLA Board Member and Director of Corporate Social Responsibility at Esquel Enterprises Ltd., email correspondence 23 January 2014.

PART IV

FAIR TRADE AND INTERNATIONAL DEVELOPMENT

20. Fair trade, peace and development in conflict zones

Eileen Davenport and William Low

INTRODUCTION

Academic discussions of fair trade have traditionally viewed this global social movement through the lenses of international development and globalization as an attempt to address the structural injustice of the prevailing (free) trade system. Fridell (2007, 24) says, 'from a theoretical perspective, the origins of the [fair trade] network's development vision lie in the structuralist, dependency and world systems theories' which argue that the existing gap between core (i.e., rich) and periphery (i.e., poor) countries is maintained, in part, through international trade policies. Murray and Raynolds (2007, 6) agree, suggesting that fair trade, or alternative trade as it was more commonly referred to in its early days, 'is best understood as an emerging response to the negative effects of contemporary globalization, and particularly to the often unjust and inequitable nature of contemporary international trade'.

The fair trade movement, which developed out of an array of approaches to social justice and decolonization, remains multi-faceted, but one of its enduring and to date neglected aspects, we would argue, has been its focus on peacebuilding and the link between peacebuilding and development. However, as we discuss, the concept of peace and peacebuilding within fair trade is contested, as fair trade concepts have embedded both the non-violence of the Historic Peace Churches and the fight for a just peace by the proponents of liberation theology.

In this chapter we propose to do three things. First, we reinterpret the emergence and early evolution of the fair trade movement through the lens of business and peace. Over the last decade 'a highly interdisciplinary field of research has developed to explore the linkages between business and peace' (Oetzel et al. 2012, 352). The social movement we now refer to as fair trade was born (in part) as a response to conflict situations. For example, Oxfam, credited with founding fair trade principles in the United Kingdom, started in 1942 by 'campaigning for food supplies to be sent through an allied naval blockade to starving women and children in enemy-occupied Greece during the Second World War' (Oxfam International n.d., accessed 6 August 2013). These efforts – mirrored by similar organizations discussed below – evolved to sell handcrafts as a means of funding emergency relief for refugee and marginalized groups, a strategy referred to as 'charity trade' (Tallontire 2002). Alternative and fair trade organizations worked with craft and food producers in a wide range of conflict-affected situations throughout the 1960s, 1970s and 1980s through two concurrent strategies referred to as 'development trade' and 'solidarity trade'.

Second, we will argue that working with producers in conflict-affected zones did not fit the mainstreaming of fair trade through the 'labeling supply chain' developed by Fairtrade International from the late 1980s onwards. Labeling commodities such as coffee, tea, bananas, cocoa and sugar and verifying them as produced according to fair trade standards via third-party certification opened the door for the massive growth of fair trade sales, reaching US$7795 billion in 2012 (see Laura Raynolds and Nicholas Greenfield's chapter in this volume). However, as the focus shifted to 'export ready' producers able to guarantee consistent quantities of high-quality product for North American and European mainstream markets, the fair trade supply chain began to favor more stable production environments than had been the case during the early phases of the movement's evolution.

Finally, we highlight a new wave of fair trade organizations intentionally working in conflict-affected and post-conflict regions. Fair trade organizations are pioneering the sourcing of coffee from the Democratic Republic of Congo (DRC), olive oil from Palestine and raisins from Afghanistan (Belgian Development Cooperation 2012), as well as establishing a Fairtrade standard for artisanal gold mining (Fairtrade Canada n.d., accessed 9 August 2013). We argue that fair trade has the foundations (Oetzel et al. 2010) on which to build an *intentional* focus on peace as a principle outcome of the movement's activities rather than as a by-product, and in so doing it contributes to contemporary peace-building efforts.

BUSINESS AND PEACE

The end of the Cold War, symbolically marked by the fall of the Berlin Wall in 1989, was argued to signal a significant shift from an era of conflict and tension between two superpowers to a new era where the principles of liberal democracy would spread to all corners of the globe (Fukiyama 1992). The doctrine of a liberal peace emerged arguing that liberal democracies, which normally are considered to encompass some variant of capitalist market economics, are inherently peaceful and do not engage in armed conflicts with each other. The idea of a liberal peace became, for a time, the dominant paradigm, working in concert with the Washington Consensus, which emphasized market reform and trade liberalization as the route to development. 'The core elements of [liberal peacebuilding] were a focus on democratization and good governance, respect for the rule of law, the promotion and protection of human rights, the growth of civil society and the development of open market economies' (Hoffman 2009, 10). However, the idea of a liberal peace has been strongly criticized: 'One school of thought argues that it was an elite-driven, top-down, outside-in, technocratic and overly formulaic experiment in social engineering that lacked local legitimacy … it is in reality an exercise in power that seeks to subjugate the non-west by creating dependency through chronically weak states' (Hoffman 2009, 10–11).

The debate over the efficacy and even the possibility of a liberal peace could be argued to be an antecedent to the emerging and more explicit focus on the role of business in conflict-affected and post-conflict contexts in the 2000s. Oetzel et al. (2010, 352) suggest that over the last decade 'a highly interdisciplinary field of research has developed to explore the linkages between business and peace, and to explore the argument that ethical business behavior can contribute to peace'. The increased attention on businesses' role in conflict and post-conflict situations is underscored by the rise of regionalized conflict. According to the Heidelberg Institute for International Conflict Research (HIIK), 'the number of conflicts observed per year has risen more or less continuously from 81 in 1945 to 345 in 2008' (Oetzel et al. 2010, 353). Prandi (2012, 18) emphasizes that 'the characteristics of the wars have changed over the past decade, shifting from conflicts between states to internal wars with a higher impact on the civilian population'. These intra-state conflicts result in 'what are called "complex political emergencies" stemming from the proliferation of civil wars; they are characterized by the breakdown of the state and the formal economy, famine, population displacement and food and health crises' (Prandi 2012, 20). By 2015, half of the world's people living on less than US$1.25 a day will be in fragile states.

While poverty has decreased globally since 2000, progress on the first Millennium Development Goal (MDG) is slower in fragile states than in other developing countries. Fragile states are also least likely to meet the rest of the MDGs by 2015 (Letouzé and de Catheu 2012). According to Stewart (2003, 325), 'Countries in conflict frequently show regress rather than progress on the MDG indicators … Besides the direct impact of war in deaths, injuries and flight, conflict undermines the economy and government capacity, and consequently the possibility of achieving the MDGs.' Gates et al. (2012, 1713) also emphasize the impacts of conflict on development: 'Armed conflict often leads to forced migration, refugee flows, capital flight, and the destruction of societies' infrastructure ... Social, political, and economic institutions are indelibly harmed ... War creates a development gap between those countries that have experienced armed conflict and those that have not.' In consequence there has been a significant rethinking on the part of donor organizations about how to engage with fragile and conflict-affected states in terms of development initiatives – recognizing that without a conflict sensitivity 'lens', development initiatives could exacerbate conflict rather than contribute to the achievement of MDGs (e.g., UNESCO 2011).

In the peace studies literature, a distinction is often made between negative peace (the absence of violence) and positive peace (the absence of violence coupled with social justice) (Stephenson 1999). Business can play a central role in the latter to build positive or sustainable peace. A central argument in the peace through commerce literature is the reciprocal nature of the relationship between business and peace (Fort and Schipani 2004). Commerce does not cease during conflicts – trade even continues between warring nations – though often only a limited range of groups and companies with close connections (perhaps ethnic or ideological) to the dominant protagonists benefit economically. Conversely, business in general is likely to flourish in conditions of stability and in the absence of conflict; for example, investment can be done without the added risk from conflict, infrastructure can be maintained and transport is secure. Perhaps most importantly, peace supports the rule of law and enforcement of property rights critical to commercial activity.

In order for business to contribute to peace, the actors must adopt what has been called in humanitarian discourse a 'conflict sensitivity' perspective (Barbolet, et al. n.d., accessed 6 April 2014; Hoffmann 2014). That is, business actors operating in a conflict arena must be aware of the negative and positive impacts their actions can have on the establishment, maintenance and promotion of peace. While not all such actors will contribute to greater peace directly (e.g., facilitate or participate in peace negotiations) the minimum standard of 'do no harm' should be expected of any responsible business. 'Through the "Do No Harm" theory, companies must also be capable of fostering "connectors", that is, elements that lower tension, and minimize "dividers", that is, those that potentially increase the violence within their area of influence' (Prandi and Lozano 2012, 10).

FAIR TRADE'S ROOTS IN PEACE, FAITH AND SOLIDARITY

Fair trade can trace its roots to a broad tradition of alternative approaches to production and consumption (Low and Davenport 2006) including those based on faith, anti-colonialism and social justice. These approaches were not discrete and separate but cross-fertilized and intersected with emerging ideas in complex and changing formations in the ensuing decades.

From the perspective of reinterpreting the evolution and development of fair trade using a peacebuilding lens, it is no coincidence that Oxfam, with its Quaker connection, the Mennonite Central Committee (MCC) through SELFHELP and the Church of the Brethren through SERRV (Sales Exchange for Refugee Rehabilitation and Vocation) were pioneers of the fair trade movement. The three faiths participated in various peace conferences after the First World War and became known as the 'Historic Peace Churches' (Church of the Brethren n.d., accessed 11 August 2013). The MCC website states, 'Christians are called to model Jesus' example of courageous peacemaking, and MCC workers and projects support people making peace across the globe' (MCC n.d., accessed 11 August 2013). The Quaker Peace Testimony (a central principle of Quakerism) dates from 1661 and states: 'We utterly deny all outward wars and strife and fightings with outward weapons, for any end or under any pretence whatsoever. And this is our testimony to the whole world' (Quaker Information Center n.d., accessed 6 August 2013). Brethren believe that 'the church and Christians are called by God to witness to the gospel of peace with such intensity that nations repent and history is changed' (Church of the Brethren n.d., accessed 11 August 2013).

Oxfam, MCC and SERVV are all examples of religiously inspired organizations for which peace was a central tenet of faith in action and which subsequently evolved into international development organizations engaging in alternative trade. These organizations began to use a 'charity trade' model of selling handcrafts and other goods to raise funds for refugee and disaster relief. Oxfam, an acronym for Oxford Committee for Famine Relief, was started in Britain in 1942 by Quakers and other social activists. 'The group campaigned for food supplies to be sent through an allied naval blockade to starving women and children in enemy-occupied Greece during the Second World War' (Oxfam International n.d., accessed 6 August 2013). After the war Oxfam continued its relief work by opening its first second-hand charity shop in 1947 and in the late

1950s started to sell crafts made by Chinese refugees alongside second-hand goods. MCC started SELFHELP Crafts of the World in 1946 to assist Palestinian refugees and marginalized people from Puerto Rico and Haiti (MCC n.d., accessed 21 May 2014). SERRV, established by the Church of the Brethren in 1949, exported locally produced handcrafts (cuckoo clocks from Germany) to fund its refugee relief efforts (SERRV 2013).

A series of parallel developments with explicitly 'political' and 'social justice' rather than religious roots spread alternative trade principles across Europe in the post-Second World War period. The political and social justice elements of the embryonic fair trade movement gave birth to what has been termed 'solidarity trade' (Low and Davenport 2006). Groups within organized labor, leftist political parties and church networks used the sale of coffee and tea (and some crafts) to express solidarity with political struggles – first independence movements in Tanzania and Angola and later, 'liberation' movements in Nicaragua and East Timor, for example.

Two fair trade organizations – one in Scotland and one in Massachusetts both named Equal Exchange (but unrelated) – are interesting examples of solidarity trade. The Scottish Equal Exchange is a worker cooperative founded by three voluntary workers who returned to Edinburgh in 1979 after working on aid projects in various parts of Africa. It began importing instant coffee, dubbed 'Campaign Coffee', from Tanzania in 1981. Its pioneering fair trade work also includes helping to launch Cafédirect in 1991, which has grown into the largest independent coffee brand in the United Kingdom with 10 per cent of the whole bean coffee market, and in 2009 launching the world's first range of organic Fairtrade-certified Palestinian extra virgin olive oils (Equal Exchange 2013). The American Equal Exchange was founded by three friends who met while they worked as managers at a New England food cooperative. It began importing coffee from Nicaragua – Café Nica – in 1986 to 'demonstrate solidarity with the fledgling people's movement and ... challenge US trade policies' (Equal Exchange n.d., accessed 15 April 2014).

The flourishing of the alternative trade networks from the late 1960s and through the 1970s (Littrell and Dickson 1999) also reflected values of communalism and 'counter-culture' that grew out of anti-Vietnam and anti-Cold War peace activism. American support for repressive regimes as part of Cold War geopolitics 'created a basis of sympathy for [progressive popular resistance groups] on the part of the younger generations in Western Europe and the United States during the 1960s and 1970s [and] is one of the reasons why Latin America became one of the first continents to welcome fair trade projects' (Belgian Development Cooperation 2012, 74). Young people's experiences of travel in the 'Third World' led them, on their return home, to marry their 'anti-establishment' views of working outside the mainstream capitalist system with their emerging appreciation of dependency theories of development and under-development.

This led to a flowering of entrepreneurial alternative trade by activists to promote peace and social justice. One such initiative resulted in the founding of Trade Aid in 1972, New Zealand's only fair trade organization, which brought together 'on one side of the table – committed, respected, skilled city business people. On the other side, wide-eyed, idealistic well-travelled revolutionaries, pumped full of liberation theology' (Blundell 1998, 12). Similar experiences emerged from the Peace Corps, established in 1961 following a challenge issued by John F. Kennedy to American university students 'to serve their country and the cause of peace by living and working in the developing world' (Peace Corps 2013). Many Peace Corps volunteers went on to establish alternative trade organizations (ATOs) to support groups they had volunteered with by personally bringing handcrafts home to sell through alternative trade networks (Littrell and Dickson 1999), echoing the actions of the New Zealand founders of Trade Aid half a world away.

The dilemma with using alternative trade to support independence and liberation movements from a peacebuilding perspective is that these movements encompassed both political and armed struggle. However, both forms of struggle could be argued by proponents to be necessary to build a 'just' peace and a 'sustainable' peace. Liberation theology was a key influence in Latin American struggles for social justice in the 1970s and 1980s – a period that was characterized by Marxist insurgencies and civil wars. The message that liberation entailed 'not just spiritual deliverance but emancipation from material oppression and injustice' appealed to the overwhelmingly Catholic populace of the region (Fridell 2007, 215). It would also shape the fair trade movement's next stage of development – mainstreaming – when 'a liberation-theology inspired Jesuit priest from Holland' began working with a small cooperative of indigenous coffee farmers in Oaxaca, Mexico (Bacon 2009, 415).

MAINSTREAMING FAIR TRADE AND THE MARGINALIZATION OF PEACE

Alternative traders experienced a downturn in fortunes during the late 1980s and through the early 1990s (IFAT 1999). As Humphrey (2000, 7) says, growth in the numbers of new ATOs and in the volume of sales of alternatively traded (handcraft) goods slowed as 'fair trade companies lost their "unique selling proposition", or USP, as more companies began to sell similar goods'.

But as sales of handcrafts stagnated, fair trade activists saw the opportunity to increase the sales of tropical food commodities. Food products, such as cane sugar, coffees and teas from Nicaragua, Angola and Tanzania, for example, had played a key role throughout the history of alternative/fair trade, as we have noted in the previous section. However, the breakthrough for fair trade food products came about when Catholic activists, working with indigenous coffee farmers from Oaxaca, Mexico, developed a system that would allow an indigenous cooperative's coffee to be brought to the Netherlands and roasted and sold under the newly developed label 'Max Havelaar' (see Marie-Christine Renard's chapter in this volume).

The creation of the Max Havelaar label was a 'watershed event for fair trade' (Jaffee 2007). Labeling commodities such as coffee, tea, bananas, cocoa and sugar and verifying them as produced according to fair trade standards via third-party certification opened the door to placing these products in supermarkets, thereby greatly increasing consumer access. An international labeling organization, Fairtrade International, was established to create standards for producers who wished to attain and maintain certification, allowing them to use the Fairtrade logo on their products. Labeled commodities, bought on a regular basis by mainstream consumers from conventional retailer outlets such as supermarkets rather than world shops, sparked the growth of fair trade sales, which reached US$7795 billion in 2012 (Laura Raynolds and Nicholas Greenfield's chapter in this volume).

We argue that the success of mainstreaming, despite its early links to liberation theology, led to the marginalization of peacebuilding as one of the driving forces of fair trade. As Goodman (2003) suggests, fair trade took a 'quality turn', emphasizing fairness as a quality of its products to attract a broadly based ethical consumer market. Solidarity and alternative trade consumers became a smaller proportion of the 'market-driven ethical consumption' that increasingly became the visible face of fair trade. Working in conflict zones, we argue, did not fit this modern version of fair trade. The fair trade labeling project, which aimed at getting a much higher volume of products into mainstream distribution channels, and, in particular, retailers in Europe and North America, required both a relatively high degree of market sophistication on the part of producers and a reliable supply chain. Mainstreaming has shifted the focus to 'export ready' and therefore relatively larger producers who are operating in more stable environments compared to the early phases of the fair trade movement's evolution. The demands of a certification system requiring that inspectors audit producers in the field are also not conducive to working in conflict-affected areas.

The 'integrated' supply chain (governed by the World Fair Trade Organization, or WFTO, rather than by Fairtrade International), was much more focused on handcrafts and small volume food products such as spices. The small fair trade organizations established in Europe, North America, Australia and New Zealand through the 1970s and early 1980s, initially focused on very marginal and vulnerable producer groups. The conditions faced by these producers often resulted from conflict situations but poverty not peacebuilding was the primary focus of fair trade at this time. However, as the consumers of the 1990s became more demanding and fair trade's consumer base extended from committed activists buying from a sense of solidarity to mainstream consumers who were at least as concerned with the quality and price of the product as its inherent 'social values', fair trade organizations were forced to make hard buying decisions. It was no longer possible for WFTO members selling through world shops, churches and community organizations to work exclusively with the most vulnerable and marginalized (Low and Davenport 2005). Being more market responsive undercut the capacity of these fair trade organizations to work in conflict-affected areas and thus their unintentional contribution to peace diminished.

(RE-)EMBEDDING PEACEBUILDING AS AN INTENTIONAL TOOL OF FAIR TRADE

Notwithstanding the marginalization of peace in fair trade supply chains, the very nature of working across a range of countries in Latin America, Africa and Asia has meant having to deal with the ongoing consequences of conflict in these regions. For example, coffee has been Colombia's primary source of government revenue since the 1960s resulting in well-established infrastructure to support the world's third largest coffee export market. Fairtrade has certified coffee from 19 Colombian cooperatives since the 1990s, against a backdrop of the US-led 'War on Drugs' and a long-standing Marxist insurgency (Belgian Development Co-operation 2012).

However, in 2009 the Chief Executive of Fairtrade International signaled an intention to increase the organization's focus on sourcing fair trade products from conflict zones. Speaking about bringing Palestinian Fairtrade-certified olive oil to market, she said, 'we hope this will be the first of many more fair trade products coming from the world's conflict zones and least developed countries. If so, it will help to catalyze markets and make a real economic difference to the communities that need it most' (Belgian Development Cooperation 2012, 57). This move is perhaps coincident with an increasing global gaze on conflict-affected and post-conflict zones and a changing approach to the link between peace and the achievement of MDGs in these environments. A focus on fragile situations has become a central concern of the international development and security agenda.

The intention to promote and sustain peace through fair trade is only implicit in the Chief Executive's statement, tracing a possible line between increased incomes and reduced conflict. Tobias et al. (2013, 729) also suggest a relationship between improved livelihoods and reduced conflict using a case study of entrepreneurship in the Rwandan specialty coffee market: 'A specialty coffee farmer earning considerably more money by being involved in specialty coffee production means she probably trusts others somewhat more, in particular the people from formerly antagonistic groups that she encounters on a daily basis while washing, sorting, and selling her coffee beans.' Forrer et al. (2012, 7) make a similar argument stating that 'medium-sized enterprises are windows of opportunity to build stability by connecting different ethnic, social, or religious groups through work'. However, while this perspective may have traction, Berdal and Mousavizadeh (2010, 52) argue that 'the belief that economic activity and cooperation among former adversaries will itself automatically or magically translate into sustainable peace is both naive and ahistorical'. We would echo these arguments and suggest that it is not necessarily just day-to-day casual interaction, or even working in the same organization, that makes the most difference in the perception of 'the other'. Rather, it is the possibility for formerly antagonistic ethnic, factional or religious groups to be involved in intentionally unifying projects or business activities that pay careful attention to the distributional and cultural impacts that can create the difference. For example, Forrer et al. (2012, 4) discuss the peace-promoting potential of projects that facilitate antagonistic groups working together; Cisco Systems is investing US$10 million in projects that intentionally include both Palestinian and Israeli programmers on the same programming teams so that these groups can collaborate both face to face and in cyberspace. The project ensures that all ethnicities are represented in all project roles and does not replicate the dominance of one ethnic group over any other that has been an ongoing source of conflict.

But even the argument that business will lead to more growth and a better standard of living, and so promote peace, must be examined. Forrer et al. (2012) recall the dependency theory viewpoint that business may hamper developing countries' economic growth. This occurs from siphoning wealth from the periphery to the core, which exacerbates the potential for conflict by establishing domestic elites who benefit at the expense of the majority. Thus, we would argue it is the extent to which benefits can be more equally and justly shared that is likely to underline the impact business activity might have on fostering peace. Fair trade approaches these issues through a number of its key characteristics. Fair trade focuses on retaining a greater share of the value chain in the hands of producers through the payment of a 'fair price'; it promotes democratic structures within the producer organizations thus fostering greater participation and potentially empowerment of their members; and it promotes local social development at village or cooperative level to address specific instances of deprivation or inequality. It is through a social premium or dividend from fair trade revenues that fair trade producers can provide community-based medical care, schools, savings plans and the like, and thus tackle the most pressing issues of inequality as determined by the producers themselves.

It is now a widely held opinion by those who support peace and reconstruction processes that the primary burden in building local peace lies with local actors. 'In fact, a strategic approach to peace-building promotes the primacy of local actors' (Belgian Development Cooperation 2012, 4). The fair trade movement is founded on principles that enshrine local control of producer organizations, sustainable use of local resources and, in a number of the more innovative models, the potential for Southern producers to share in the ownership (and thus the profits) of fair trade organizations that sell Southern products in the North. Twin Trading, established over 25 years ago, is an organization that epitomizes the 'new frontier' of fair trade work in conflict zones. Most importantly, Twin has been instrumental in establishing a number of innovative and emancipatory initiatives with its producer partners in the global South. These have included developing the 'Cafédirect' Fairtrade coffee brand in which producers have significant share ownership (and thus share in profits made in the North), helping set up an organization called 'Liberation Foods' in the United Kingdom, which again has a shared producer/wholesaler ownership structure, and in the last five years starting to work in fragile post-conflict situations. Twin states that, 'Post conflict situations present both great need and great opportunity, with potential for high impact, coupled with very significant risks and need for resources' (Fairtrade Foundation 2010). The report on fair trade in conflict zones by the Belgian Development Cooperation (2012, 23) echoes these issues noting that the 'implementation of local production chains in these fragile areas requires anticipating significant costs tied to product market access' – though it adds that these high costs can be offset by the production of high-quality product that commands a premium price. The additional costs to producers who are working in conflict-affected areas are both direct (for example, the losses of vehicles or corruption) and indirect (including road blocks and military controls).

Since 2009 Twin has been working on an initiative to bring coffee produced by SOPACDI (a smallholder coffee producer cooperative), based by Lake Kivu in eastern Democratic Republic of Congo (DRC), to European markets. The eastern lakes area of DRC has been the scene of violent conflicts since the 1990s and became infamous when bodies from the Rwandan genocide were dumped there; the incursion of M23 rebels into the area in late 2012 highlights the fragility of peace in the region. SOPACDI's website says: 'We are over 5600 farmers from different ethnic groups in the Kivu Eastern Democratic Republic of Congo, producing some of the finest coffee in Africa. After years of conflict and civil war, our Fairtrade-certified coffee promotes working together for a better future' (SOPACDI n.d., accessed 4 January 2014). The initiative to bring Lake Kivu coffee from the cooperative into Europe is supported by several key partners, notably a Rwandan coffee cooperative, the UK charity Comic Relief, DFID (Department for International Development) and ICCO (Interchurch Organization for Development Cooperation). There are a number of committed buyers including Finlays (a global horticultural conglomerate) and Sainsbury's (a UK supermarket chain).

The Lake Kivu area of DRC was noted in the past for producing very high-quality, small volume specialty coffee – 'green gold' as it was termed. However, until the first shipment of SOPACDI coffee was imported to the United Kingdom in 2011, none of this specialty coffee had been exported to Europe for over 30 years. Coffee, a traditional export crop, was virtually abandoned across much of North Kivu and DRC's production shrank from 110 000 metric tons in the late 1980s to about 50 000 metric tons in 2009, according to the DRC's national coffee office (IRIN 2013). Since the early 1990s most of the coffee that has been grown in this part of DRC has been smuggled across the lake to Rwanda at night in small boats. This is an incredibly dangerous process as the lake is noted for high waves. Official figures report that a thousand people drown each year, but unofficial figures put the number of people drowned at closer to two thousand (IRIN 2013). Twin has helped SOPACDI to replant coffee trees and improve yields, bean quality and post-harvest processing, enabling its 3500 members to become the first producers in Kivu to achieve organic and Fairtrade certification. This area of South Kivu has been a recruiting ground for armed militias and there is some optimism that coffee production and the income it offers can provide an alternative to life as a militia member. SOPACDI has publicized the job opportunities it has provided to ex-combatants and a number of ex-combatants work at the cooperative's mechanized washing center. The center (which enables coffee berries to be depulped and dried, thus cutting down on waste, assisting product consistency and adding value at source) was paid for by Twin and employs approximately 160 people. Recent interviews conducted by IRIN (Integrated Regional Information Networks, a news agency focusing on humanitarian stories) give some perspectives of former combatants and their views on the future:

> One of the staff at the washing centre, former rebel Habamungu Engavashapa, told IRIN he was happy with civilian life because he was able to spend nights in a house rather than in the forest. Another ex-combatant, Abdul Mahagi, said SOPACDI had trained him as a machinist and given him a contract; he said he was beginning to see a way to organize his life … The main opportunities that coffee co-operatives are likely to provide for ex-combatants in the short term would be to clear land and plant seedlings. (IRIN 2013)

The Twin initiative with SOPACDI provides an example of what has been termed 'local context analysis', which focuses not on externally designed solutions but works with local coping mechanisms and entrepreneurial skills to 'identify local partners and create, in London School of Economics (LSE) professor David Keen's words, "disincentives for violence and positive incentives for peace"' (Berdal and Mousavizadeh 2010, 52–53).

Fair trade offers other interesting recent examples of intentionally bringing together local groups which have experienced long-standing enmity, in order to build peace through business. Peace Oil is a joint effort between the main Israeli and Palestinian fair trade organizations – Sindyanna of Galilee, Green Action and Canaan Fair Trade – which started in 2005, bringing together Jews, Arabs, Druze and Bedouins to produce cooking oil; the oil was certified Fairtrade in 2008. Its vision is to 'build economic interdependence between peoples by creating mutually beneficial business partnerships providing a practical incentive for peace' (Belgian Development Cooperation 2012, 60). Profits from the venture are used to support peace and reconciliation work in the Middle East.

Forrer et al. (2012) suggest that 'international peace could best be sustained by global trade based on long-term relationships of trust and basic integrity'. Here again, we argue that fair trade has a role to play in the prevention of conflict because a foundational principle of fair trade is trust between trading partners and the development of long-term trading relationships (Davenport and Low 2013). This approach is clearly articulated in the WFTO principles, which state that a fair trade organization 'maintains long term relationships based on solidarity, trust and mutual respect that contribute to the promotion and growth of Fair Trade' (WFTO 2013).

CONCLUSIONS

The fair trade movement was conceived and built on a foundation that made promoting peace and ameliorating the effects of conflict central to its mission. Among the movement's founding members, the Mennonite and the Brethren faiths are 'churches known for their work toward peace' (Stenzel 2013, 634), as are the Quakers. The work of other ATOs may have been less explicitly grounded in doctrines of peace compared to their faith-based colleagues, but the ATOs that sprang up during the 1960s and 1970s did share an ethos encompassing a strong current of promoting peaceful change through international development.

The emergence of a more explicitly commercial fair trade system through the 'labeled' supply chain in the late 1980s and early 1990s brought Fairtrade-certified food products onto supermarket shelves but, at the same time, we would argue, unintentionally marginalized the peacebuilding work evident in the earlier movement. Meeting the needs of 'market-driven ethical consumption' required a shift away from the most marginal producers, including those struggling to operate in conflict-affected areas. Supporting peacebuilding processes became a by-product of increased incomes and living standards made possible by growing sales of fair trade products and the social premium payments made by the certification system. This shift carries echoes of the debate over the purpose of business and whether business has a social responsibility beyond making a profit. The 'free market' view (Friedman 1970) holds that businesses' only social responsibility is making a profit because from growth and profit good things will flow. In contrast a communitarian view (Etzioni 1996) and a stakeholder-driven perspective (Handy 2002) believe profit is a by-product (and a facilitator) of pursuing an organization's mission or vision.

Peacebuilding remains part of the mission and vision of the modern fair trade movement. The 'integrated' supply chain, which continues to focus primarily on handcrafts and artisan foods, offers many examples of long-term working relationships with producers in conflict-affected and post-conflict situations to promote sustainable social development. The 'labeled' supply chain is also beginning to work more intentionally in conflict-affected zones. Fair trade holds out much promise as a tool for promoting peace through business but, borrowing from Berdal and Mousavizadeh, 'the challenge lies in identifying [*fair trade's*] appropriate role … in building sustainable peace … through stimulating entrepreneurship, attracting significant investment, facilitating local economic activity and reinforcing incentives for peaceful behavior' (2010, 39).

REFERENCES

Bacon, Christopher (2009), 'Fair trade', in Kenneth A. Reinert, Ramkishen S. Rajan, Amy Joycelyn Glass and Lewis S. Davis (eds.), *The Princeton Encyclopedia of the World Economy,* Vol. 1, Princeton, NJ: Princeton University Press, pp. 412–416.

Barbolet, Adam, Rachel Goldwyn, Hesta Groenewald and Andrew Sherriff (n.d.), *The Utility and Dilemmas of Conflict Sensitivity*, Berlin: Berghof Foundation, available at http://www.berghof-handbook.net/documents/publications (accessed 6 April 2014).

Belgian Development Cooperation (2012), *Fair Trade in War Zones*, Brussels: BTC.

Berdal, Mats and Nader Mousavizadeh (2010), 'Investing for peace: The private sector and the challenges of peacebuilding', *Survival: Global Politics and Strategy*, 52 (2), 37–58.

Blundell, Sally (1998), 'Trade Aid: 25 years of fair trade', Christchurch: Trade Aid Education Unit.

Church of the Brethren (n.d.), 'Peace and justice', available at http://www.brethren.org/peace/ (accessed 11 August 2013).

Davenport, Eileen and William Low (2013), 'From trust to compliance: Accountability in the fair trade movement', *Social Enterprise Journal*, 9 (1), 88–101.

Equal Exchange (2013), 'About', available at http://www.equalexchange.co.uk/about/ (accessed 15 April 2014).

Equal Exchange (n.d.), 'Story', available at http://www.equalexchange.coop/story (accessed 15 April 2014).

Etzioni, Amitai (1996), *The New Golden Rule*, New York: Basic Books.

Fairtrade Canada (n.d), 'Gold', available at http://fairtrade.ca/en/products/gold (accessed 9 August 2013).

Fairtrade Foundation (2010), 'Fair trade in conflict zones', available at www.fairtrade.org.uk/includes/documents (accessed 1 August 2013).

Forrer, John, Timothy Fort and Raymond Gilpin (2012), *How Business Can Foster Peace*, Washington, DC: United States Institute of Peace.

Fort, Timothy L. and Cynthia A. Schipani (2004), *The Role of Business in Fostering Peaceful Societies*, Cambridge: Cambridge University Press.

Fridell, Gavin (2007), *Fair Trade Coffee: The Prospects and Pitfalls of Market-Driven Social Justice*, Toronto: University of Toronto Press.

Friedman, Milton (1970), 'The social responsibility of business is to increase its profits', *New York Times Magazine*, 13 September, 122–124.

Fukiyama, Francis (1992), *The End of History and the Last Man*, New York: Free Press.

Gates, Scott, Havard Hegre, Havard Mikleiv Nygard and Havard Strand (2012), 'Development consequences of armed conflict', *World Development*, 40 (9), 1713–1722.

Goodman, David (2003), 'The quality "turn" and alternative food practices: Reflections and agenda', *Journal of Rural Studies*, 19 (1), 1–7.

Handy, Charles (2002), 'What's a business for?', *Harvard Business Review,* 80 (12), 49–55.
Hoffman, Mark (2009), 'What is left of the "liberal peace"?', *LSE Connect*, Winter, 10–11, available at http://www.lse.ac.uk/alumni/LSEConnect/ (accessed 6 May 2014).
Hoffmann, Anette (2014), 'From "business as usual" to "business for peace"? Unpacking the conflict-sensitivity narrative', CRU Policy Brief No. 28, Den Haag: Clingendael Institute.
Humphrey, Louise (2000), 'Which way to market', Traidcraft Policy Unit Report, Series No. 1, April, London: Traidcraft, available at www.traidcraft.co.uk/ (accessed 30 August 2004).
IRIN (2013), 'Congo-Kinshasa, trading conflict for coffee in DRC', available at www.irinnews.org/report/ (accessed 12 August 2013).
IFAT (International Federation for Alternative Trade) (1999), 'IFAT Milan conference report', Bichester: IFAT.
Jaffee, Daniel (2007), *Brewing Justice: Fair Trade Coffee, Sustainability and Survival*, Berkeley, CA: University of California Press.
Letouzé, Emmanuel and Juana de Catheu (2012), 'Fragile states 2013: Resource flows and trends in a shifting world', Paris: OECD DAC International Network on Conflict and Fragility, available at http://www.oecd.org/dac/ (accessed 10 April 2014).
Littrell, Mary A. and Marsha A. Dickson (1999), *Social Responsibility in the Global Market: Fair Trade of Cultural Products*, Thousand Oaks, CA: Sage.
Low, William and Eileen Davenport (2005), 'Postcards from the edge: Maintaining the "alternative" character of fair trade', *Sustainable Development*, 13 (3), 143–153.
Low, William and Eileen Davenport (2006), 'Mainstreaming fair trade: Adoption, assimilation, appropriation', *Journal of Strategic Marketing*, 14 (4), 315–328.
MCC (n.d.), 'Our story', available at http://www.tenthousandvillages.com/about-history/ (accessed 21 May 2014).
MCC (Mennonite Central Committee) (n.d.), 'Peace', available at http://www.mcc.org/whatwedo/peace (accessed 11 August 2013).
Murray, Douglas L. and Laura T. Raynolds (2007), 'Globalization and its antimones: Negotiating a fair trade movement', in Laura T. Raynolds, Douglas L. Murray and John Wilkinson (eds.), *Fair Trade: The Challenges of Transforming Globalization*, New York: Routledge, pp. 3–14.
Oetzel, Jennifer, Michelle Westermann-Behaylo, Charles Koerber, Timothy Fort and Jorge Rivera (2010), 'Business and peace: Sketching the terrain', *Journal of Business Ethics*, 89 (S4), 351–373.
Oxfam International (n.d.), 'History', available at http://www.oxfam.org/ (accessed 6 August 2013).
Peace Corps (2013), 'History', available at http://www.peacecorps.gov/about/history/decades/1960/ (accessed 10 April 2014).
Prandi, Maria (2012), 'From armed conflicts to peace-building', in Maria Prandi and Josep M. Lozano (eds.), *CSR in Conflict and Post-Conflict Environments: From Risk Management to Value Creation*, Barcelona: School for a Culture of Peace (UAB)/Institute for Social Innovation (ESADE), pp. 17–34.
Prandi, Maria and Josep M. Lozano (eds.) (2012), *CSR in Conflict and Post-Conflict Environments: From Risk Management to Value Creation*, Barcelona: School for a Culture of Peace (UAB)/Institute for Social Innovation (ESADE).
Quaker Information Center (n.d.), 'Friends peace testimony', available at http://www.quakerinfo.org/quakerism/peace (accessed 6 August 2013).
SERRV (2013), 'Our story', available at http://www.serrv.org/category/our-story (accessed 18 May 2014).
SOPACDI (n.d.), 'Home', available at http://sopacdi.com (accessed 4 January 2014).

Stenzel, Paulette L. (2013), 'Mainstreaming fair trade and resulting turmoil: Where should the movement go from here?', *William and Mary Environmental Law and Policy Review*, 37 (2), 617–673.

Stephenson, Carolyn. M. (1999), 'Peace studies: Overview', in Lester R. Kurtz and Jennifer E. Turpin (eds.), *Encyclopedia of Violence, Peace, and Conflict*, Vol. 2, San Diego, CA: Academic Press, pp. 809–821.

Stewart, Frances (2003), 'Conflict and the Millennium Development Goals', *Journal of Human Development*, 4 (3), 325–351.

Tallontire, Anne (2002), 'Partnerships in fair trade: Reflections from a case study of Cafédirect', *Development in Practice*, 10 (2), 166–177.

Tobias, Jutta M., Johanna Mair and Celestina Barbosa-Leiker (2013), 'Toward a theory of transformative entrepreneuring: Poverty reduction and conflict resolution in Rwanda's entrepreneurial coffee sector', *Journal of Business Venturing*, 28 (6), 728–742.

UNESCO (United Nations Educational, Scientific and Cultural Organization) (2011), 'The hidden crisis: Armed conflict and education', Paris: UNESCO Publishing.

WFTO (2013), '10 principles of fair trade', available at http//www.wfto.com (accessed 10 August 2013).

21. Fair trade and development in African agriculture

Anne Tallontire

INTRODUCTION

Fairtrade is increasingly significant in Africa and Africa is increasingly significant for Fairtrade, especially in terms of the numbers of producers and workers who are members of or work for producer organizations certified by Fairtrade International. Over half of the farmers certified according to Fairtrade International standards are in Africa (62 per cent) and nearly half of all workers employed by Fairtrade certified organizations are in Africa (41 per cent) (Fairtrade International 2012, 18). The high numbers of workers in African Fairtrade reflect the significance of the hired labor model for particular commodities that are key to Fairtrade in Africa, particularly flowers (37 500 workers) and wine grapes (4400 workers), but also for tea (where there are proportionately more small-scale farmers involved but the most hired workers globally, at 97 700) (Fairtrade International 2012, 25).[1]

In this chapter I explore the diverse experiences that small-scale producers and workers have in engaging with the Fairtrade system by highlighting the territorial specificity of how Fairtrade is embedded in local contexts across Africa (Loconto and Simbua 2012; Nelson and Martin 2012). I examine cooperatives dating from the colonial period and chart the process of economic and political liberalization over recent decades. I highlight how this has both facilitated fair trade opportunities and presented challenges. I also discuss the experience of the hired labor model, noting its inter-relation with small-scale production in some sectors, and examine how employment on Fairtrade farms affects women.

I focus on traditional tropical beverage export crops which are of fundamental economic importance for many African countries, as well as non-traditional exports such as cut flowers which have been important particularly for the employment of women. My discussion draws largely on the experience of producers in agri-food sectors and associated with Fairtrade International, with particular reference to examples from Ghana and East Africa (including Kenya, Tanzania, Malawi and Uganda). These countries are highly significant in terms of Fairtrade participants (Kenya alone, for example, accounts for 14 per cent of participants in Fairtrade). Furthermore, drawing on examples from East and West Africa helps demonstrate the differing institutional environments in which fair trade is embedded.

Africa has a long history of fair trade with alternative trade organizations (ATOs). There were some instances of 'solidarity' coffee trade, particularly from Tanzania, and exports of honey, but the ATO-led trade was largely craft based and products from African producers tended to be dwarfed in the export market by the volume of merchandise from Latin American and Asian producers. Moreover, African producers did not get involved in Fairtrade labeling until the early 1990s when the Tanzanian cooperatives Kilimanjaro Native Cooperative Union (KNCU) and Kagera Cooperative Union joined the Max Havelaar coffee register and became part of the Cafédirect supplier network. This helps explain why Africa is not featured in the founding narratives of fair trade, especially for food, and perhaps why the voice of African producers has not been as strong as other actors in fair trade debates. Founding narratives in the literature are replete with the language of resistance and struggle against large landowners and the so-called coyotes or private traders, where smallholder-owned cooperatives formed a bulwark of solidarity and collective economic action (Fridell 2007), whereas fair trade in African agriculture has been shaped by different processes and institutions that have received less attention to date in the literature on fair trade.

COOPERATIVES, SMALLHOLDERS AND FAIR TRADE IN AFRICA

The story of fair trade food in Africa is shaped by institutional structures such as the role of farmer organizations, particularly the role of cooperatives, and marketing structures, which in many African countries are part of its colonial legacy, as well as patterns of landholding (including the balance of large-scale commercial and smallholder farming) and social relations related to ethnicity and gender.

In Fairtrade International's small producer model certification takes place at the producer organization level, and in some cases this means working with a secondary cooperative that represents several primary cooperatives which operate at a village or district level. Thus Fairtrade International's impressive statistics on African smallholder participation in fair trade are related to the size of cooperative unions such as KNCU in Tanzania and Kuapa Kokoo in Ghana, which number members in the tens of thousands. The Kuapa Kokoo union had 462 primary societies with a total membership of between 45 000 and 60 000 members across five of the six cocoa growing regions in Ghana, amounting to at least 5 per cent of cocoa growers in the country (Nelson et al. 2013). For reasons of export marketing logistics, but also because of a concern to support the democratic structures of cooperatives as a movement, fair trade has supported African cooperative unions, at times in the face of criticism of unions by those wishing to reinvigorate cooperatives from the bottom up (Redfern and Snedker 2002).

The stories of KNCU and Kuapa Kokoo and the challenges faced by Ugandan coffee cooperatives demonstrate that the small producer model of fair trade in Africa faces some distinct challenges related to the history of farmer organization across the continent, particularly the relatively short experience of operating as member-driven as opposed to government-driven organizations and the dwindling public sector support for agricultural extension (at least until the recent reversal in aid towards agriculture). In many parts of sub-Saharan Africa, European colonists established, and then post-colonial states continued to support, cooperatives as means to promote and collect agricultural production to feed people in the growing urban centers and to generate income from cash crops (Develtere, Pollet and Wanyama 2008).

Different cooperative models can be found in former colonies of Britain, France, Belgium and Portugal but they share some common features in that they were the top-down creations of the state, often closely controlled by the ministry of agriculture and tied up with other public sector agricultural marketing systems. In East Africa, cooperatives became sole agents for the public sector export marketing boards for crops such as cotton and coffee. In the 1970s and 1980s African cooperatives faced a two pronged critique from agrarian socialists who saw them as vehicles of accumulation for relatively wealthy farmers (e.g., Cliffe 1975 with respect to Tanzania) and from neoliberal economists who regarded them as inefficient, bureaucratic and corrupt (Hussi et al. 1993; Lele 1981). In the late 1980s, when Fairtrade labeling was emerging in Latin America based on a farmer-led cooperative model, many African cooperatives were cumbersome, top-heavy organizations unaccustomed to autonomy and active participation in governance by the membership. They were also struggling to survive in the face of World Bank and IMF (International Monetary Fund) pressures on governments to liberalize internal markets.

In East Africa, many cooperatives crumbled as private traders were permitted to purchase key export crops such as coffee directly from the farmers. For example, in Uganda the Banyankole Kweterana Cooperative

Union (BKCU) collapsed in the late 1990s, and the cooperative unions in southern Tanzania were effectively shells by 2001. As agricultural marketing was liberalized in many African countries, farmers who no longer had to sell to the local primary cooperative chose to sell to local traders or agents of multinational trading companies. In other parts of East Africa, however, cooperatives have survived and even thrived in the coffee sector, with fair trade, particularly dedicated fair trade organizations, playing an important role. For example, Fairtrade purchases, while rarely accounting for more than a small percentage of total sales, provided an important lifeline for the KNCU, but more importantly, fair trade partnerships promoted organizational development and enhanced members' technical and marketing skills (Tallontire 1999) and more recently environmental protection (Davies, Doherty and Knox 2010). However, the KNCU struggled to provide inputs on credit, as farmers were often tempted to sell produce to private buyers, threatening the sustainability of the organization.

In Ghana in West Africa, the liberalization of cocoa marketing presented a different challenge: rather than the revival of an established cooperative structure, fair trade actors supported the development of a new cooperative. Structural adjustment policies in the 1990s led to a partial liberalization of cocoa marketing. When non-state cocoa buying operations were permitted in 1993, Kuapa Kokoo was established as the only farmer-owned licensed buying company with assistance from two international non-governmental organizations (NGOs) (SNV in the Netherlands and Twin in the United Kingdom). This new cooperative was certified according to Fairtrade standards in 1995, and in the early 2000s its partnership with the trading arm of Twin enabled the cooperative to be a joint owner and sole supplier to the Divine chocolate brand, produced by a dedicated fair trade company and social enterprise registered in the United Kingdom (Doherty and Tranchell 2005; 2007). This close relationship between Twin and Kuapa Kokoo continues.

Liberalization of crop marketing thus provided more options to farmers as they no longer were restricted to selling to cooperatives, meaning that cooperatives could not always collect sufficient crops to benefit from economies of scale. Some see this as providing a competitive stimulus to enhance the effectiveness of cooperatives, including being more responsive to farmers' needs (Jaffee, Henson and Diaz Rios 2011). From the perspective of processors in the global North, significant concerns were raised about the ability of the liberalized marketing systems in coffee and especially cocoa to mobilize credit and maintain consistent quality as not only were new, inexperienced players buying produce, but also quality control systems in the public sector were eroded. The opposite was true in Ghana, where the Ghana Cocoa Board (known as COCOBOD) has been praised for stemming the cocoa quality decline experienced elsewhere in West Africa (Barrientos et al. 2008; Valerie Nelson and Adrienne Martin's chapter in this volume).

A growth in the number of cooperatives is being reported by movement sources, for example, in Uganda, largely independently of government support (Hartley 2011). A revival is also reported in Kenya in sectors such as dairy and savings and credit (Hannan 2014). These new or revised cooperatives are often at the primary level without the support of the cooperative unions and tertiary, national-level cooperatives that faced criticisms of being too close to the state or overly bureaucratic (Wanyama, Develtere and Pollet 2009). The cooperative sector in Africa has faced a time of dramatic change, through which the fair trade movement (and donors) has supported it by way of organizational capacity building and technical assistance, as well as efforts to enhance local-level democracy. There remain challenges in promoting more active participation in the cooperatives, and the communication channels between cooperative leaders in unions and farmers in primary cooperatives remain weak, with few farmers outside key projects understanding what fair trade is (Coles 2011). Moreover, fair trade has had limited ability to transform more ingrained and structural issues. I turn to this in the next section.

The Operating Environment for Fair Trade

Fair trade in Africa faces a number of structural constraints, particularly for smallholders. Some of these are those related to any kind of trade, notably the hard and soft infrastructure that facilitates trade. A key hard infrastructure challenge is poor transport infrastructure (particularly the dearth of rail links and paved roads), made worse in the case of landlocked countries such as Uganda, Rwanda and Malawi.[2] Other parts of the developing world have remote farmers but in some parts of Africa, for example Malawi, you do not have to be far from the main road to be remote in terms of journey time or access to communication networks (Pound and Phiri 2011). The relative lack of manufacturing industry also creates barriers in terms of access to locally produced inputs. More specifically for cotton, the limited development of an African textile industry, stymied by a lack of technology and also the second hand clothes trade, has in turn constrained the development of African fair trade cotton. Fair trade seed cotton produced in Africa generally is shipped elsewhere to be produced into textiles and ultimately clothing, which increases the final product cost to the consumer, especially compared to India (Nelson and Smith 2011).

There are also challenges related to 'soft infrastructure' that facilitates agricultural trade such as grades and standards. The fair trade movement, both standards organizations and alternative trading companies, has worked hard to enhance the capacity of small producer organizations to produce and market their produce effectively, efficiently and more sustainably, often filling gaps in state provision. However, much of this capacity is embedded in the top echelons of the organizations or in consultants, rather than embedded in producer organizations (Nelson et al. 2013). A recent study highlights a 'critical role' for 'development efforts in supporting continuous improvements to achieve quality and productivity gains, [and] promote smallholder organization' (i.e., to get the basics of trade right) (Jaffee, Henson and Luiz Rios 2011, 145).

Given many of the survival challenges that have faced small producer organizations in Africa, it is perhaps not surprising that some of the capacity development impact of fair trade activities remains with the leadership rather than filtering through to members. This is not to say that members have not benefitted from fair trade – they have, through maintaining market access, better prices and, of course, through the premium investments. However, in many cases fair trade benefits for cooperative members is restricted to the premium investments (such is the case for tea producers in Kenya; see Dolan 2010). Nelson et al. (2013) comment that in Kuapa Kokoo many members were not aware that it was their own Fairtrade sales that generated the premium income that funded projects such as boreholes, upgrades to schools and toilet facilities and food processing equipment, partly because decisions on expenditure are made at the district rather than local level.

On the one hand, some relatively economically secure fair trade groups have been able to use the premium to diversify into more valuable crops or to organize to represent their interests (Fairtrade Africa 2011). On the other hand, for others, like those in the Malawian sugar sector, empowering outcomes may be an unaffordable luxury. In such situations, the central concerns of those engaged in fair trade revolve around sustaining basic needs (Phillips 2010).

Gender

In Africa, social relations shape fair trade impacts at the small producer level, particularly with regard to gender (Smith 2013; see also Sally Smith's chapter in this volume). Membership in small producer organizations across the world, particularly cooperatives, is limited to those who have sufficient volume and consistent quality to sell, who are able to buy shares in the organization and, in many places, who own land. Relatively few women own land in Africa. Under the myriad of customary land tenure systems that prevail across much of Africa, women are more likely to have use rights to land to grow food than to own it themselves and invariably own a lot less land than men: men owned 1.1 to 6.9 times as much land by area as land solely owned by women in several African countries and 99 times as much in Nigeria (Doss et al. 2013). In the mid-1990s in Kilimanjaro, Tanzania, some widows had coffee land but often registered the land in the name of their sons because of cultural pressures (Tallontire 1999), but a decade later there were more female members – up to a fifth of membership noted Sutton (2012). Nevertheless, for the majority of coffee farming households, the proceeds from coffee accrue to the male, even if women do most of the tending of the trees and harvesting.

A corollary of the low female membership in cooperatives is that leadership of export-oriented cooperatives in Africa is, with some significant exceptions, male dominated. Particular efforts have been made to enhance women's involvement in Kuapa Kokoo through a Gender Action Learning project (Twin 2013). Women account for 32 per cent of members according to Twin (2013), with an increasing number of women having taken on elected roles (e.g., as cocoa receivers at the primary societies). Nevertheless, access to land remains a barrier to participation for many women in Kuapa Kokoo's cocoa growing communities (Nelson et al. 2013).

Not all cooperatives involved in fair trade in Africa are huge like Kuapa Kokoo and KNCU, but their stories highlight some of the particular features of fair trade in agricultural products by African small producers: the marketing and infrastructural environment, cooperative support networks and the balance of benefits to men and women. For small farmers, the colonial and post-colonial experience of cooperatives has provided both opportunities and challenges for fair trade in commodities such as coffee, cocoa and tea, especially as internal market liberalization created new competitive forces at the same time as old cooperative support networks eroded. In some of the larger cooperatives, however, the benefits of fair trade participation are not necessarily discernible to all members, as the proportion of sales on a Fairtrade basis is relatively small. This can be the case even when fair trade markets and ATO support have been crucial to their survival, promoting organizational development, technical and market skills and environmental protection.

Smallholder and Commercial Agriculture Links

In African Fairtrade, both smallholder and hired labor models of Fairtrade certification co-exist. This is most evident in Kenyan tea where there are 16 small producer organizations and five hired labor groups certified (Fairtrade International 2012). The evolution of Fairtrade tea in Africa demonstrates how Fairtrade interacts with existing production and trade relations.

The introduction of the hired labor model into tea was motivated by actors in the fair trade movement concerned about the poor quality and low volumes of tea from small producers, but also reflects the complexity of the tea value chain, particularly the central role of the tea processing factory in production and exchange relations. Leaf tea must be processed very quickly after plucking, meaning that the factory acts as a pinch point in the value chain. While there are examples of smallholder groups that have their own factories (e.g., those supported by the Kenya Tea Development Agency), many smallholders are dependent on commercial tea estates for access to processing facilities, and in Malawi smallholder executive committees rely on estates for advice on premium expenditure (Pound and Phiri 2011). The intertwining of small- and large-scale production found in the tea sector is also witnessed in sugar, which is almost exclusively exported by mills and specialist exporters rather than small producers, who tend to sell raw sugar cane to the mills (Fairtrade International 2012).

Case studies of tea plantations, factories and small farmer groups in Tanzania highlight both the diversity of 'ownership arrangements and governance of actors' within the sector and how the 'Fairtrade tea value chain has accommodated' varied forms and scales of production (Loconto and Simbua 2012, 462). Dolan's analysis of Fairtrade tea in Kenya goes further to suggest that, 'With the exception of the social premium there is absolutely no difference between the structures (actors, institutions, regulations and activities) of the conventional tea trade and that of Fairtrade' (2010, 37). Nevertheless, Nelson and Martin's (2013) impact assessment indicates that Kenyan tea experienced the most extensive development benefits from Fairtrade, compared to other cases they examined (largely as a result of improved production practices).

However, the fact that Fairtrade simultaneously supports both hired labor and small producer models in tea, often cheek by jowl, raises challenges for governance and transparency and questions about the most appropriate pathways to empowerment. This is especially true for small producers who often struggle to compete with commercial producers that control production resources, benefit from economies of scale and have more direct access to markets (Dolan 2010; Loconto and Simbua 2012). Moreover, in some sectors, such as tea, small producers may be structurally dependent on larger producers that own and control processing facilities. The competition that smallholder tea producers face from more highly resourced and connected tea plantations was a key motivation for the development of the tea category by Cafédirect; their Fairtrade tea is exclusively from smallholders in Africa and explicitly marketed to the consumer as such.

It has been argued that in some parts of Africa, particularly southern Africa, the hired labor model has greater potential for impact than the small producer model. This is likely to be the case in South Africa where land distribution is skewed due to apartheid, meaning that people in rural areas are more likely to be wage laborers than farmers with their own land, but also for women who, as I note above, for cultural and historical reasons have not had access to their own land. This model is also significant in non-traditional export crops where there may be high barriers to entry related to technology or market knowledge and which also rely to some extent on access to cheap labor. I now move to examine Fairtrade on plantations.

PLANTATIONS, WORKERS AND FAIR TRADE IN AFRICA

The hired labor model of Fairtrade is significant in Africa, for two key reasons. First is the push for certification of plantations (e.g., in tea and flowers) by retailers and manufacturers keen to source Fairtrade products as part of ethical sourcing strategies, often converting existing suppliers to Fairtrade certified sources. Second is the increasing numbers of the rural poor that have no or very little land and are dependent upon income from wage labor, particularly women.

An interesting example to consider with respect to the hired labor mode of Fairtrade in Africa is the cut flower sector, which employs many thousands of workers, many of whom are in low paid and insecure jobs. The Fairtrade labeling system became significant for producers in Kenya partly as a response to vociferous labor rights campaigns in the early 2000s. Labor issues identified on farms included sexual harassment, enforced overtime, poor protection from hazardous chemicals and a sexual division of labor that reinforced gender stereotypes and which denied women many of the benefits of employment (Dolan, Opondo and Smith 2003). While other systems were considered, including a local version of the Ethical Trading Initiative's labor code of practice, Fairtrade was pushed for by UK retailers as it was readily available and suited their reputational needs (see Alex Hughes's chapter in this volume; Tallontire et al. 2011). There are now 27 certified sites in Kenya (with some certified for foliage and ornamentals as well as cut flowers).

Fairtrade tends to be regarded as the benchmark standard for the sector by several leading producers (Nelson, Tallontire and Opondo 2014). Most of the larger farms that are engaged in certification (many have multiple certifications so it is difficult to attribute change to any one standard) have reduced forced overtime and the trend for employing workers on a permanent casual basis has declined. This means that women workers have contracts that enable them to benefit from maternity leave provisions (Women Working Worldwide 2007).

While many of the 'output rights' of workers (working conditions and contracts, Barrientos and Smith 2007) have improved on Fairtrade certified flower farms, wage levels have remained low such that many women workers, often employed in the lowest and least secure jobs, were also involved in income generating projects to supplement wages (Said-Allsopp 2013). Moreover, there is considerable progress to be made with respect to process or empowering rights such as representation and collective bargaining, particularly for women (Nelson, Martin and Ewert 2007).[3] The Kenya Plantation and Agricultural Workers Union (KPAWU) has been criticized as being very weak, with a gulf between the high politics of the general secretary's office and under-resourced regional organizers who rely on public transport to access workers in remote farms (KHRC 2012). Moreover, NGOs have argued that trade unions are not doing their job in representing workers, especially female workers (Nelson, Tallontire and Opondo 2014). The failure of the trade union movement to represent women workers, and allegedly suppress their voice within it, was a motivation for the formation of the Kenya Women Workers Organization (KEWWO), one of the NGOs central to the flower campaign of the early 2000s. However, there have been signs of the union becoming more activated in floriculture, due partly to the influence of Fairtrade, a standard that was accorded the respect trade union leaders denied local NGOs. 'Fairtrade have done a good job. It is because of Fairtrade we have got a CBA [collective bargaining agreement]' with one large firm, a national trade union official told us, relating how the issue was pursued by the Fairtrade auditor despite the management's resistance. He argued that, 'Through pressure with Fairtrade on the labor system' trade union membership was increasing and there was increasing dialogue between trade union officials and Fairtrade auditors (Informant 1 2009).

Fairtrade aims to enhance the representation of women on estates. However, a recent study highlights that even in fairly progressive companies, women's involvement in Fairtrade structures, both on estates and in small farmer organizations, is low. Few women were active in the Joint Bodies set up to decide on the use of the Fairtrade premium, with the outcome that many of the premium expenditures had limited relevance or benefit to women (Said-Allsopp and Tallontire 2014). Fairtrade liaison officers have tried to stimulate more gender aware and balanced Joint Bodies, but this is a very tricky balance to maintain. As a consultant supporting producers explained: 'If you leave it too laissez faire – you can end up with it all men. But you cannot impose it … If you impose it, it will come out that there were "not elections but selections". If you let it go, during the inspection they [Fairtrade auditors] will say that there is not enough women' (Informant 2 2008). Women's ability to perceive themselves as agents of change was limited; regardless of whether they propose ideas for projects that would benefit them during consultation, the projects selected were not those they suggested, nor do they have any idea of how these decisions were reached (ibid.). This study highlights how the benefits that accrue to women as a result of their employment on the flower farms are shaped not only by employment relations, which of course reflect the local regulatory framework, but also household and cultural norms regarding what it is right and proper for men and women to do. These norms are not immutable, and case studies of women workers in the sector demonstrate how some women are using their employment to challenge their husbands and mothers-in-law, but there remain considerable differences in terms of the pathways to empowerment that may be afforded to men and women on fair trade farms (Said-Allsopp 2013).

As discussed above, the hired labor model is also significant in Africa in the tea sector (in Kenya, Malawi, Rwanda and Tanzania) and also wine in South Africa. In tea a gendered division of labor tends to be even more ingrained, with women plucking the tea and men in the factories (Said-Allsopp 2013). For some of the poorest without land or other livelihood assets, wage labor provides the best opportunities, but as those in the fair trade movement are only too aware, those opportunities leave great potential for improving both material outcomes as well as voice.

GOVERNANCE OF FAIR TRADE IN AFRICA

Fairtrade Africa, originally the African Fairtrade Network, was established in 2005 with support and guidance from Fairtrade International.

Fairtrade International was keen to develop mechanisms for enhanced producer voice to link the movement and to enhance producer representation in central Fairtrade International mechanisms.[4] The network states that 'if you are a Fairtrade certified producer in Africa then you are automatically a member of Fairtrade Africa', and as a result it represents a highly diverse group of producers involved in different commodity chains and different types of organization (e.g., from smallholder coffee and cocoa farmers to multinational flower producers) (Fairtrade Africa 2014). A key difference between the African Fairtrade network and that for Central and Latin America is that the latter is explicitly for smallholder organizations whereas the former is more diverse.

This diversity is reflected in the composition of the current board of Fairtrade Africa. It includes a technical director of a horticulture firm in the Middle East, a human resources manager from a multinational tea firm, staff of two development and consultancy organizations, and its leader represents a West African farmers' association (Fairtrade Africa 2013a). Membership, currently across 29 countries, increased from 316 organizations in 2011 to 410 in 2013 (Fairtrade Africa 2013b; Fairtrade International 2012, 95). There are also a number of national networks affiliated to Fairtrade Africa, notably in Kenya and South Africa, where the networks have established their own labeling initiatives. Worker organizations are conspicuous by their absence in this network, with workers represented by their employers in the continental and national networks, though there are links between international trade union bodies and Fairtrade International. The fact that small producers are represented in the same body as hired labor organizations (including some with multinational ownership) in Fairtrade Africa raises some questions about whose voice is heard in this regional network.

A key aspect of Fairtrade Africa's work has been the promotion and support of commodity networks, for example in coffee, cocoa and tea, with new networks being established in cotton, sugar cane and gold. The tea network is made up of producer organizations in Kenya, Tanzania, Rwanda, Malawi and Uganda. Its focus is not only on certification (e.g., preparation for audit visits and sharing information), but also on broader challenges. In July 2011, for example, there were exchange visits on adaptation to climate change and a meeting about carbon credits (Nelson and Martin 2013).

The emerging fair trade networks in Africa are grasping the challenge of linking producers together and to other development processes and local institutions. Fairtrade Africa has faced a number of governance challenges in terms of developing leadership and linking across diverse producers that are spread far apart across the continent. However, it is now starting to develop stronger leadership capacity, separate from the Fairtrade International headquarters in Bonn, with its own voice and identity (see Jennifer Keahey's chapter in this volume).

CONCLUSION

In this chapter I have explored the development of fair trade in Africa with a focus on agriculture. The impacts of fair trade are inevitably gendered: access to land has tended to limit women's participation in small producer organizations and, while women are employed on Fairtrade farms, male employees often accrue a greater share of the benefits. The hired labor model of Fairtrade is particularly significant in Africa where it is often driven by retailers and brands who have made commitments to sustainable sourcing. As I have shown in this chapter, such fair trade businesses often work cheek by jowl with the small producer organization model. This inter-linkage between the large- and small-scale models of Fairtrade is reflected in the Fairtrade Africa network's own governance structure, which seeks to represent both the interests of large- and small-scale producers – a tricky balancing act to maintain, especially as different visions of fair trade are contested. Africa has also been the site of the emergence of innovative business models in fair trade whereby producers share in the financial proceeds from value addition in marketing and branding. Cafédirect has ownership from producers across the world, but there are some examples that are Africa-specific, for example Kuapa Kokoo's stake in The Divine Chocolate Company and also the National Smallholder Farmers' Association of Malawi's involvement in Liberation Nuts.

The discussion of fair trade for African smallholders has focused on how cooperatives, particularly cooperative unions, have shaped the experience of fair trade, as access to Fairtrade markets and generation of benefits depend on the efficient and effective operation of farmers' organizations. Many African cooperatives have a history as quasi-state organizations, are often huge and are only slowly adapting to become member-led. Fair trade in agricultural products was kick-started by ATOs' links with cooperatives, but more recent growth has been facilitated by value chains driven by retailers and specific brands, many of which focus on existing, often large-scale, producers and suppliers. This trend has rapidly expanded the number of farmers and workers participating in fair trade in Africa, even if many workers and smallholders are not necessarily aware of what this means.

NOTES

1. For a discussion of fair trade and hired labor in Asia, see Rie Makita's chapter in this volume.
2. Transport costs from farm gate to the port in Mombasa accounted for 80 per cent of the producer price for Rwandan coffee according to Diop, Brendon and Asarkaya (2005).
3. We can distinguish between those International Labor Organization labor rights that are focused on working conditions and outcomes (e.g., health and safety, working hours) and those that foster worker self-organization and ability to advocate for themselves (process rights such as the right to collective bargaining).
4. World Fair Trade Organization-Africa, formerly Cooperation for Fair Trade in Africa (COFTA) also exists, representing 10 000 artisans and workers in approximately 90 producer organizations from over 20 countries. Members are largely non-food producers, with strengths in crafts.

REFERENCES

Barrientos, Stephanie, Kwadwo Asenso-Okyere, Samuel Asuming-Brempong, Daniel Sarpong, Nana Akua Anyidoho, Raphael Kaplinsky and Jennifer Leavy (2008), 'Mapping sustainable production in Ghanaian cocoa', IDS and University of Ghana Report to Cadbury, London: Cadbury.

Barrientos, Stephanie and Sally Smith (2007), 'Do workers benefit from ethical trade? Assessing codes of labor practice in global production systems', *Third World Quarterly*, 28 (4), 713–729.

Cliffe, Lionel (ed.) (1975), *Rural Cooperation in Tanzania*, Dar es Salaam: Tanzania Publishing House.

Coles, Christopher (2011), 'Kilimanjaro and Oromia Coffee value chain case studies: Producer benefits from fair trade and free market channels', NCCR North–South Dialogue, No. 34, Bern, Switzerland.

Davies, Iain A., Bob Doherty and Simon Knox (2010), 'The rise and stall of a fair trade pioneer: The Cafédirect story', *Journal of Business Ethics*, 92 (1), 127–147.

Develtere, Patrick, Ignace Pollet and Frederick Wanyama (eds.) (2008), 'Cooperating out of poverty: The renaissance of the African cooperative movement', Geneva: ILO/The World Bank Institute.

Diop, Ndiame, Paul Brendon and Yakup Asarkaya (2005), 'Trade costs, export development and poverty in Rwanda', World Bank Policy Research Working Paper 3784, Washington, DC: The World Bank.

Doherty, Bob and Sophi Tranchell (2005), 'New thinking in international trade? A case study of The Day Chocolate Company', *Sustainable Development*, 13 (3), 166–176.

Doherty, Bob and Sophi Tranchell (2007), 'Radical mainstreaming of Fairtrade', *Equal Opportunities International Journal: Special Issue on Culture and Diversity in Marketing*, 26 (7), 693–711.

Dolan, Catherine (2010), 'Virtual moralities: The mainstreaming of Fairtrade in Kenya tea fields', *Geoforum*, 41 (1), 33–43.

Dolan, Catherine, Maggie Opondo and Sally Smith (2003), 'Gender, rights, and participation in the Kenya cut flower industry', NRI Report, Chatham, UK: Natural Resources Institute.

Doss, Cheryl, Chiara Kovarik, Amber Peterman, Agnes Quisumbing and Mara van der Bold (2013), 'Gender inequalities in ownership and control of land in Africa: Myths versus reality', IFPRI Discussion Paper 01308, December 2013.

Fairtrade Africa (2011), 'Report of workshop on impact assessment, Fairtrade Africa convention', ACCRA, 25 November 2011.

Fairtrade Africa (2013a), 'Fairtrade Africa annual review 2012', available at http://www.fairtradeafrica.net/wp-content/uploads/2013/08/ANNUAL-REPORT-ENGLISH.pdf (accessed 26 January 2014).

Fairtrade Africa (2013b), 'African producers set to increase their bargaining power', available at http://www.africafairtradeconvention.net/press-releases/ (accessed 6 January 2014).

Fairtrade Africa (2014), 'FAQs', available at http://www.fairtradeafrica.net/about-fairtrade/frequently-asked-questions/ (accessed 15 May 2014).

Fairtrade International (2012), 'Monitoring the scope and benefits of Fairtrade: Fourth edition', Bonn: Fairtrade International, available at http://www.fairtrade.net (accessed 12 January 2014).

Fridell, Gavin (2007), *Fair Trade Coffee: The Prospects and Pitfalls of Market-Driven Social Justice*, London: University of Toronto Press.

Hannan, Rowshan (2014), 'Good co-operative governance: The elephant in the room with rural poverty reduction', *Journal of International Development*, 26 (5), 701–712.

Hartley, Sally (2011), 'New spaces for a new generation: The rise of cooperatives amongst young people in Africa', Cooperative College Paper 16, Manchester, UK: Cooperative College.

Hussi, Pekka, Josette Murphy, Ole Lindberg and Lyle Brenneman (1993), 'The development of cooperatives and other rural organizations: The role of the World Bank', Vol. 1, World Bank Technical Paper 199, Africa Technical Department Series.

Informant 1 (2009), interview with Anne Tallontire, Nakuru, Kenya (20 July 2009).

Informant 2 (2008), interview with Anne Tallontire, Nairobi, Kenya (9 September 2008).

Jaffee, Steven, Spencer Henson and Luz Diaz Rios (2011), 'Making the grade: Smallholder farmers, emerging standards, and development assistance programs in Africa', available at http://agriskmanagementforum.org/farmd/doc (accessed 10 November 2011).

KHRC (Kenya Human Rights Commission) (2012), '"Wilting in bloom": The irony of women labour rights in the cut-flower sector in Kenya', available at http://www.khrc.or.ke/resources/publications/doc (accessed 30 April 2014).

Lele, Uma (1981), 'Cooperatives and the poor: A comparative perspective', *World Development*, 9 (1), 55–72.

Loconto, Allison and Emmanuel Simbua (2012), 'Making room for smallholder cooperatives in Tanzanian tea production: Can Fairtrade do that?', *Journal of Business Ethics*, 108 (4), 451–465.

Nelson, Valerie and Adrienne Martin (2012), 'Evidence to date and the factors shaping the impact of Fairtrade', *Food Chain*, 2 (1), 42–63.

Nelson, Valerie and Adrienne Martin (2013), 'Final technical report: Assessing the poverty impact of sustainability standards', Report for Department for International Development, Natural Resources Institute, University Of Greenwich, October 2013, available at http://www.nri.org/images/documents/project (accessed 12 January 2014).

Nelson, Valerie, Adrienne Martin and Joachim Ewert (2007), 'The impacts of codes of practice on worker livelihoods: Empirical evidence from the South African wine and Kenyan cut flower industries', *Journal of Corporate Citizenship*, (28), 61–72.

Nelson, Valerie, Kwasi Opoku, Adrienne Martin, John Bugri and Helena Posthumus (2013), 'Assessing the poverty impact of sustainability standards: Fairtrade in Ghanaian cocoa', Natural Resources Institute, available at http://

fairtradekookboek.files.wordpress.com/2013/12/apiss-fairtradeinghanaiancocoa.pdf (accessed 4 July 2014).

Nelson, Valerie and Sally Smith (2011), 'Fairtrade cotton: Assessing impact in Mali, Senegal, Cameroon and India: Synthesis report for Fairtrade Foundation', Natural Resources Institute and Institute of Development Studies, available at http://www.nri.org/projects/fairtradecotton/docs (accessed 30 August 2013).

Nelson, Valerie, Anne Tallontire and Maggie Opondo (2014), 'Transformation or transgression? The development potential of Southern local multi-stakeholder initiatives in the context of retailer power', in Michael Goodman and Colin Sage (eds.), *Food Transgressions: Making Sense of Contemporary Food Politics*, Farnham, Surrey, UK: Ashgate, pp. 15–38.

Phillips, David (2010), 'Fair trade and community empowerment: The case of sugar producers in Malawi', PhD thesis, School of Geography, Politics and Sociology, Newcastle University.

Pound, Barry and Alexander Phiri (2011), 'Taking root: Fairtrade in Malawi: Synthesis report for Fairtrade Foundation', available at http://www.fairtrade.org.uk/includes/documents/cm_docs/ (accessed 14 September 2013).

Redfern, Andy and Paul Snedker (2002), 'Creating market opportunities for small enterprises: Experiences of the fair trade movement', InFocus Programme on Boosting Employment through Small Enterprise Development, Job Creation and Enterprise Department, Geneva: International Labour Office.

Said-Allsopp, Muhaimina (2013), 'Empowerment within global value chains: A study of the dynamics of employment and its impacts on the lives of women employed in Kenyan agricultural export industries', unpublished PhD thesis, School of Earth and Environment, University of Leeds, Leeds, UK.

Said-Allsopp, Muhaimina and Anne Tallontire (2014), 'Enhancing Fairtrade for women workers on plantations: Insights from Kenyan agriculture', *Food Chain*, (4), 66–77.

Smith, Sally (2013), 'Assessing the gender impacts of Fairtrade', *Social Enterprise Journal*, 9 (1), 102–122.

Sutton, Shannon (2012), 'Collaborative governance at Fairtrade Tanzanian co-operatives', Presentation at Co-operative Conference, Université du Québec à Montréal, June 24–27, 2012.

Tallontire, Anne (1999), 'Making trade fair? An examination of the relationship between Cafédirect and a coffee co-operative in Tanzania', unpublished PhD thesis, University of Bradford, UK.

Tallontire, Anne, Maggie Opondo, Valerie Nelson and Adrienne Martin (2011), 'Beyond the vertical? Using value chains and governance as a framework to analyse private standards initiatives in agri-food chains', *Agriculture and Human Values*, 28 (3), 427–441.

Twin (2013), 'Empowering women farmers in agricultural value chains', Twin Trading, available at http://www.twin.org.uk/sites/default/files/images/Empowering%20Women%20Farmers%20in%20Agricultural%20Value%20Chains.pdf (accessed 14 January 2014).

Wanyama, Fredrick O., Patrick Develtere and Ignace Pollet (2009), 'Reinventing the wheel? African cooperatives in a liberalized economic environment', CoopAFRICA Working Paper No. 1, Dar es Salaam: International Labour Office.

Women Working Worldwide (2007), 'Promoting women workers' rights in African horticulture: Overview of research into conditions on horticulture farms in Kenya, Zambia, Tanzania and Uganda', Manchester, UK: Women Working Worldwide.

22. Fair trade coffee and environmental sustainability in Latin America

Christopher M. Bacon, Robert A. Rice and Hannah Maryanski

INTRODUCTION

Certified tropical agricultural products promoting 'environmentally friendly' farming practices form a growing part of mainstream markets and international sustainable development investments (Beddington et al. 2012; Herrero et al. 2010; Raynolds et al. 2007). Certified sustainable coffee accounts for more than 9 per cent of international coffee sales and is projected to increase to 18 per cent by 2015 (COSA 2013). Although detailed farm, household, community and value chain-based research continues, it generally lags behind these changing markets, eco-labels and farming practices.

Researchers often analyze the social impacts of fair trade in producer communities (Bacon 2005) or analyze the environmental performance of organic, Rainforest Alliance and Bird Friendly certifications (Rice 2000). Overall, there is a scarcity of 'methodical environmental assessment' of fair trade (Nelson and Pound 2009), although a few studies include environmental impacts in their broader analysis of sustainable livelihoods, fair trade and organic production in Latin America (e.g., Bacon et al. 2008; COSA 2013; Jaffee 2007; Lyon 2013). This leaves a gap in the research focused on fair trade and environmental sustainability.

In this chapter we analyze the environmental impacts of fair trade coffee in Latin America and the Caribbean. We focus on coffee, since coffee landscapes account for the largest area in Latin America associated with the certification, and 80 per cent of the world's fair trade coffee hails from Latin American farms that average 2.6 hectares (Fairtrade International 2012). We identify three environmental impacts: biodiversity conservation, pollution reduction and climate change adaptation. Smallholders manage much, if not most, of Latin America's biologically diverse shade coffee, and many of them participate in fair trade markets. Fairtrade International's recently revised environmental standards, which include an expanded list of prohibited agrochemicals and price incentives to promote organic production (Fairtrade International 2011a), represent potential direct environmental impacts (Nelson et al. 2010).

In the chapter, we integrate original research, including data gathered from certification agencies, a survey of experts about shade coffee, interviews and informal conversations and a literature review. We build upon a 2013 survey conducted of national and regional experts in Latin America to estimate the percentage change in the area devoted to diverse shade coffee management from 1990 to 2010 (Jha et al. 2014).[1] We also include qualitative data from focus groups, interviews and participant observations. Finally, written consultations with members of Fairtrade International generated information from and links to key documents.

The role of fair trade vis-à-vis coffee has particular environmental salience given the ecological importance of shade coffee (Perfecto et al. 1996) and the threat to biodiversity posed by the possibility of smallholders abandoning this agroforestry crop. Mesoamerican smallholders are frequently associated with the management of these diverse shade grown systems (Rice 2000). Theoretically, fair trade – which emphasizes smallholder market access with stable prices, social development premiums and environmental standards – encourages farm maintenance, soil fertility management and erosion control, thus representing a more sustainable agrifood system. Research also suggests that fair trade's minimum price can partially buffer cooperatives and farmers against commodity coffee price crashes (e.g., Bacon 2005), while shade coffee can reduce on-farm erosion and enable faster recovery following natural hazards, such as hurricanes (Philpott et al. 2008).

The numerous influences on farmers' decisions to adopt environmentally friendly farming practices make it difficult to assess which practices and livelihood outcomes link to fair trade. For the purposes of this chapter, we identify the direct and indirect impacts of participation in fair trade markets and the associated networks that can support international development investments, farmer organizing and more. Direct benefits can be linked to price premiums, changes to certification standards or projects channeled through fair trade networks. Indirect benefits – namely support for democratic smallholder cooperatives, local capacity building (Raynolds et al. 2004) and international development projects funded by non-governmental organizations (NGOs) and coffee companies – are not easily linked to specific standards. Indirect environmental benefits derive from the extent to which fair trade promotes the maintenance of pre-existing sustainable agricultural practices, such as shade coffee, and stimulates the adoption of new ones. Finally, we discuss the persistent challenges of sustainable livelihoods and food security among participating producers, describing several challenges and responses to the impacts of climate change.

DIRECT IMPACTS: FAIRTRADE INTERNATIONAL'S NEW ENVIRONMENTAL STANDARDS[2]

Fairtrade International's environmental standards aim to minimize the risks and negative environmental effects associated with the industrial agriculture model, including, but not limited to, agrochemical pollution, biodiversity loss and increased greenhouse gas emissions. And though much reporting of fair trade organizations includes work on environmental projects, detailed empirical data on the link between Fairtrade certification and reduced environmental damage is minimal.

To become Fairtrade certified a product must undergo auditing and inspection from FLO-Cert, a company owned by Fairtrade International.[3] FLO-Cert certifies Arabica and Robusta coffee production under Small Producer Organization (SPO) standards. The SPO environmental standards for coffee include the required minimum core standards and areas for continued improvement, and they address the following: environmental management, pest management, soil and water, waste, genetically modified organisms (GMOs), biodiversity and energy and greenhouse gas (GHG) emissions (Fairtrade International 2011b, 3.2). The standards also require reporting about biodiversity conservation, buffer zones around water sources and reducing agricultural impacts in areas of high conservation value (as determined by the Forest Stewardship Council) (Fairtrade International 2011b, 3.2). Furthermore, Fairtrade International recognizes and outlines the negative impacts of climate change on agriculture and encourages SPOs to report on carbon sequestration (Fairtrade International 2011b, 3.2.40) and use of renewable energy (Fairtrade International 2011b, 3.2.39).

Fairtrade International's SPO standards for agrochemical use aim to manage pesticide risk. These include the prohibition of aerial spraying and establishing buffer zones around bodies of water and human dwellings (Fairtrade International 2011b, 3.2.39). The Fairtrade Prohibited Materials List (PML) integrates seven international pesticide watch lists and comprises 124 'Red List' (forbidden) agrochemicals and 58 'Amber List' (highly discouraged) agrochemicals (Fairtrade International 2011a). In June 2015, Fairtrade International will release updated lists that may move some Amber List chemicals to the Red List. Several chemicals, namely the organochlorines DDT, hexachlorobenzene, endosulfan and chlordane, are banned, restricted or were voluntarily withdrawn from use in the United States (Center for Disease Control and Prevention 2009), Europe and most Latin American countries (United Nations 2001) as they have pledged to reduce use and production by signing the United Nations Stockholm Convention on Persistent Organic Pollutants. The Stockholm Convention may make Fairtrade International's list redundant for Europe and the Americas, but Fairtrade International's list could reduce organochlorine use in the multiple countries in Africa and Asia that have not signed or ratified the Stockholm Convention. Since the Stockholm Convention is a pledge, regulatory procedures are limited, and it is not an immediate phase-out. For instance, members of the Stockholm Convention added endosulfan to the 'banned' list in 2011 (with some agricultural use exceptions) (United Nations 2011), and it will not be phased out by the US Environmental Protection Agency (EPA) until 2016 (EPA 2010). In developing countries, changes are often slower due to weaker government enforcement. Fairtrade International's PML may also contribute to reduced circulation of organochlorine-tainted products, because some pesticide lists are loosely enforced for imports. Furthermore, unlike many government systems, Fairtrade International's standards require annual farm inspections and audits.

In the case of several non-organochlorines, Fairtrade International's PML introduced additional agrochemical restrictions, suggesting that fair trade has reduced agrochemical use beyond the international lists and treaties. For example, Fairtrade International recently tightened restrictions on paraquat dichloride. The 2007 PML permitted paraquat dichloride under exceptional conditions on tea from India and coffee and sugarcane from Costa Rica (Fairtrade International 2007), but the most recent version banned its use (Fairtrade International 2011a). Additionally, a focus group conducted with Nicaraguan farmers in 2013 identified malathion as one of the most widely used agrochemicals in coffee producing areas (Focus group 2013). Malathion first appears as a restricted chemical on the 2011 Amber List.

More stringent environmental standards likely contribute to fair trade's direct environmental benefits, but producers also face increasing monitoring and compliance costs. Coffee agroforestry systems managed according to agroecological principles can limit, avoid and/or possibly eliminate the use of the synthetic agrochemicals (Harvey et al. 2008; Vaast et al. 2005). While such inputs have led to increased yields for farmers generally, they also increased production costs, pest resistance and damage to human and ecological health. For coffee producers, a diverse mix of shade trees can help control disease and pests (Staver et al. 2001). Research suggests that in place of using chemicals, such as endosulfan, an organochlorine insecticide with neurotoxicity to humans, to control the Coffee Berry Borer (*Hypothenemus hampei*), managed shade cover can enhance the presence of biocontrol agents like fungi and parasitic wasps (Staver et al. 2001). But in some countries (e.g., Guatemala), where the borer has recently been found to affect up to 80 per cent of the farms including those at higher elevations (potentially due to climatic changes), many coffee producers rely on a 1.7 liters/hectare dose of endosulfan in applications timed to fruit development (Anzueto 2014).

CERTIFIED FAIR TRADE AND ORGANIC

Another direct benefit of Fairtrade concerns its promotion of organic agriculture and low input agroforestry systems, such as shade grown coffee (Harvey et al. 2008; Perfecto et al. 1996). In 2011 Fairtrade International revised its pricing standards to include a 50 per cent increase in the organic premium (from \$0.20 to \$0.30 USD per pound) paid for Fairtrade coffee. This change sought 'to account for the higher costs of organic production and provide an incentive to farmers to convert to or maintain organic production' (Fairtrade International 2011c).

Certified organic coffee production contributes to obvious environmental benefits, but the additional impacts attributed to certification are context dependent. Despite both theoretical and empirical research on the productivity benefits and overall sustainability associated with small-scale agriculture (Moguel and Toledo 1999; Vandermeer et al. 2010) – most shade grown coffee in Latin America, as we argue here, qualifies as small scale – published studies linking fair trade to environmental benefits are scarce. Smallholders in Mexico that sold coffee as Fairtrade and Fairtrade/Organic (FTO, meaning that the coffee was certified against both sets of standards) were more likely to practice a range of soil conservation practices compared to their neighbors, a fact that may stem more from being organic than selling into fair trade (Jaffee 2007). Yet, where fair trade coffee is synonymous with organic and shade coffee, 'practices that conserve soil fertility, trap organic matter, increase water filtration, enhance bird and wildlife habitat diversity, fix carbon, and keep acidic coffee pulp and water out of local streams' clearly rank as benefits (Jaffee 2007), an assessment echoed by Fridell (2007). A study comparing conventional and certified organic coffee producers in Costa Rica found that organic producers reported no or significantly lower agrochemical use and were more likely to use environmentally beneficial practices including water collection holes and vegetative barriers to purify water run-off, shade trees, windbreaks and organic fertilizer

(Blackman and Naranjo 2012). Research in El Salvador and Nicaragua suggests similar trends, but also reveals that many organic producers continue to use agrochemicals in the management of their corn and bean plots, while smallholders in Mexico, Guatemala, El Salvador and Nicaragua linked to FTO reported higher farm gate prices for their coffee (Mendez et al. 2010). A recent study in Peru found that organic producers linked to fair trade markets were more likely to increase their use of organic fertilizers (Ruben and Fort 2012).

From 2009 to 2011, the global volume of doubly certified FTO coffee increased by 17 496 metric tons, equivalent to a 46 per cent increase (Fairtrade International 2014). During this same period, the total volume of all exported Fairtrade certified coffee (including FTO) increased by 31 per cent, expanding to 120 316 metric tons in 2011, while the percentage of Fairtrade coffee that is FTO averaged just below 50 per cent (Fairtrade International 2014). The price differential that the Fairtrade system offers for coffee that is also organically certified (FTO), as well as the fact that many international development agencies (e.g., Catholic Relief Services, Lutheran World Relief, Oxfam) work with fair trade cooperatives to implement projects that promote sustainable agriculture and environmental conservation, have combined to rapidly expand certified organic production in many places.

INDIRECT IMPACTS: THE GEOGRAPHY OF SHADE COFFEE PRODUCTION

Prior to addressing Fairtrade coffee's indirect impacts it is important to note several observations about how and why smallholders manage their coffee with a diverse shade cover. Our observations in Latin America coffee growing regions suggest that smallholders generally have more diverse shade trees over their coffee system than producers with large estate holdings (though there are exceptions to these patterns).[4] Many of these small producers belong to cooperatives or associations with varying degrees of organizational capacity, market connections and general linkages to the global coffee network. But they have one thing in common: they are peasant producers.

Peasant coffee producers must carefully make decisions about their small parcel(s) of land. They make their living from the land (sometimes working for others as day laborers) and usually reside on the land, often their only valued resource. Given the limited size of peasant holdings (often less than one or two hectares), and the need for peasants to 'thread the needle' each year, as Berger (1979) puts it – that is, survive year-to-year on the parcel's production and the minimal cash from off-farm labor – these producers are understandably risk-averse regarding land management. Whereas an unshaded coffee crop might lead to higher yields (albeit with costly agrochemical inputs) and more income, few readily devote their entire holding to a single crop. The vagaries of weather, pests and disease and international prices are beyond a farmer's control and can be devastating. Therefore, peasant producers rarely grow open-to-the-sun coffee systems. Rather, these small holders manage coffee within an agroforestry system, cultivating it beneath a canopy of shade trees. This heterogeneous mix of trees provides an array of 'non-coffee' products: firewood, fruits, construction material, home remedies and so on (Rice 2008; 2011). In short, this 'managed biodiversity' creates a heterogeneous farm that can harbor relatively high levels of associated biodiversity (birds, insects, etc.). Most Fairtrade producers in Latin America (Brazil being an exception, due to its dominant open-sun coffee production practices) manage their lands as such.

Coffee, Biodiversity and Ecosystem Services

Beyond the sustainability certifications and specific environmental practices (Pimentel et al. 1992), stakeholders are increasingly interested in the analysis of the range of ecosystem services provided by shade coffee systems, including biodiversity conservation, reduced soil erosion, water conservation, microclimate mitigation, pollination, pest control and more (Jha et al. 2014; Klein et al. 2003; Kellerman et al. 2008; Lin 2007). To what extent does certification influence farmer management systems in ways that enhance the flow of ecosystem services from shade coffee landscapes?

Sun versus Shade and the 'Shade Gradient'

In what is now a familiar characterization of the various management practices in coffee, a gradient ranging from open-sun production to a 'rustic' coffee setting can be described. Moguel and Toledo's (1999) research in Mexico developed this depiction of different coffee-growing systems, offering a gestalt understanding of the range from minimal intervention on the land to an intensified or 'technified' system. This is an effective strategy for characterizing the vegetational complexity that can lead to a host of ecological benefits – including coffee-as-habitat. From the open-sun or scant shade which features a monocultural shade tree pruned to relatively low heights (3–8 meters), the next, slightly more complex, system is the polyculture, which can be either the less diverse commercial polyculture or the more diverse traditional version, and could also be classified as a 'coffee garden'. Planted shade trees figure into these four categories. The final and most forest-like category is the 'rustic' system, where natural forest has been cleared enough to insert the coffee beneath towering forest species – a system normally found in remote areas tended by indigenous populations (Nolasco 1985). In general, as this gradient progresses from the scant shade to the rustic system, the canopy height, tree diversity and structural complexity increase, creating a progressively more forest-like setting.

Given the ecological concept that 'diversity begets stability', the species and structural diversity of the shade coffee systems managed by many fair trade producers stand out in stark contrast to an open-sun farm. The unshaded monoculture promoted so strongly in the 1970s and 1980s in Mexico by the now-defunct INMECAFE and throughout Central America and the Caribbean by the United States Agency for International Development (Rice 1999), while touting increased yields, can claim few, if any, ecological benefits. The open, shadeless system puts coffee plants in direct sunlight, an environment counter to coffee's evolutionary center of origin in the forests of East Africa and a situation that can affect bean growth and quality, as well as the overall physiology of the coffee plant itself (Lin et al. 2008). Moreover, this production strategy requires agrochemical inputs in the form of fertilizers to replace the organic matter/leaf litter/mulch that the shaded system would otherwise provide free of charge, pesticides to check the various insect pests no longer controlled (at least partially) by the agroforest's associated biodiversity and herbicides to control the weeds no longer suppressed by the shade and mulch. These same chemicals must be used cautiously to prevent contamination of waterways and people as well. Furthermore, the typical situation of coffee planted in mountainous regions on broken terrain poses additional problems of soil erosion where shade is not present.

We now focus on the indirect impacts that smallholder systems of shade tree management are likely to have upon the conservation of agricultural biodiversity and ecosystems services. We assume here that smallholders manage most diverse shade, and Figure 22.1 shows the management types of coffee from most of Latin American's leading coffee exporters. Latin America's traditional shade coffee agroecosystems conserve high levels of biodiversity, including many tree, bird and arthropod species. Recent research suggests that although the loss of tree diversity associated with the conversion of shade coffee to sun production systems was lower from 1990 to 2010 than from 1970 to 1990, in many

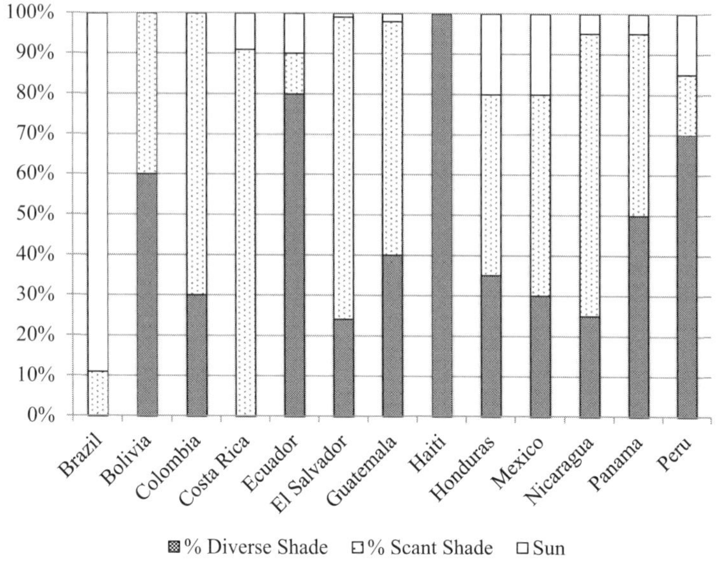

Figure 22.1 Estimated percentage area of shade management regimes, 2010–2012

places this biodiversity declined due to intensification of production practices and the thinning of shade trees (Jha et al. 2014; Perfecto et al 1996).

The geography of fair trade coffee production has shifted during the previous five years (see Figure 22.2), as countries with less shade coffee area, such as Brazil and Colombia, emerged as major Fairtrade coffee suppliers (see Figure 22.1). Of particular note is the rapid growth in the number of organizations in Brazil. In 2010, experts estimated that only about 10 per cent of Brazilian coffee had some type of shade cover. However, production has also expanded rapidly in Peru, in which a high percentage of coffee lands are managed under a diverse shade canopy. These sourcing changes could have significant implications for biodiversity and ecosystem service benefits associated with the Fairtrade international system, particularly if more Fairtrade coffee is sourced from coffee growing countries and regions with less shade.

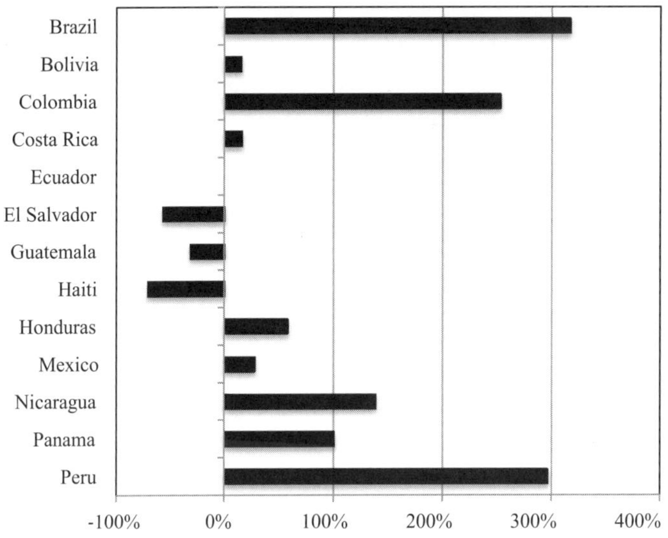

Source: FLO-Cert (2014).

Figure 22.2 Percentage change in certified Fairtrade producer organizations, 2005–2013

CLIMATE CHANGE, FARMER LIVELIHOODS AND FOOD SECURITY ISSUES

One interesting aspect of an agroforestry system like shade coffee is the general buffering effects it has on a number of climatic and/or weather phenomena. Meteorological models concerned with climate change have predicted that the Central American and Caribbean region will experience a drying trend over the next several decades (Neelin et al. 2006). A shade canopy in an agroforestry system like coffee shows the ability to maintain the ambient temperature of the system within a more narrow range, keeping the environment warmer at night and cooler during the day. As shade cover decreases, the fluctuations in temperature, humidity, moisture availability and solar radiation during the course of the day are greater (Lin 2007), an important consideration in the face of a predicted drying trend. The benefits of shade are directly related to the mitigation of variability in microclimate and soil moisture in coffee systems (Lin 2007).

Central America and the Caribbean fall within the western Atlantic's region of high hurricane activity, events that can wreak havoc on agricultural areas, with high winds and heavy rainfall. A diverse shade canopy, characteristic of many Fairtrade producers, has been reported anecdotally by two cooperatives (RR communication) after Hurricane Stan crossed the isthmus in October 2005 to have protected those coffee farms from the extensive flooding and landslides experienced by farms with little or no shade. Research after this event concluded that vegetation complexity (like diverse shade coffee systems) tends to protect the land from hurricane-induced landslide events (Philpott et al. 2008). Agroforestry systems have been identified as having great potential in mitigating climate change due to the carbon fixed in the soil and biomass of the trees they contain (Lal 2004; Verchot et al. 2007). A Mexican coffee study comparing various shade levels' ability to sequester carbon found that a polycultural system's biomass fixes 16 metric tons of carbon per hectare on average compared to a monocultural shade's 4.5 tons per hectare. A diverse rustic system fixes more than 42 tons per hectare (Dávalos Sotelo et al. 2008).

To the extent that Fairtrade producers have a diverse, closed canopy production system, we should connect this to the ever-changing climate. At least for Central America, a general drying trend is predicted. Shade would help mitigate that somewhat. Also, even though this drying trend is predicted, a trend towards more late-season hurricanes of greater intensity is also predicted – the same months in which coffee berries are almost ready or are ready for harvest. High winds would be dampened at ground level, thus protecting the harvest more than in unshaded systems. These weather patterns will likely combine to impact agriculture – testing not only cash crops like coffee, but subsistence crops as well.

Aside from the inherent environmental benefits associated with these shaded systems that many fair trade coffee producers in Latin America manage, the larger fair trade network recently started to coordinate several responses to climate change. Fairtrade International currently includes 'climate change adaptation' as one of its targeted goals in aiding producers, with mitigation efforts that address deforestation, water use and shade management. The German grocery chain Lidl and the UK-based Twin Trading recently helped to train lead farmers (or promoters) in the Sonomoro Cooperative in Pangoa, Peru, in risk assessment. Identifying reforestation as a major challenge for the region, Lidl arranged to plant one tree for every package of Fairglobe coffee sold, pledging to plant a minimum of 40 000 native trees (Fairtrade International 2013). In another tree-planting effort to counteract deforestation and fix carbon, the United Kingdom's Cafédirect worked with

6600 coffee farmers of the Central Piurana de Cafetaleros cooperative (Cepicafe) in northern Peru. For every ton of carbon sequestered in this reforestation scheme, Cepicafe banks a carbon credit. These credits can then be traded on the global market – to firms like coffee roasters, for example – in order to benefit the producer community (Siegle 2012).

The 2014 Intergovernmental Panel on Climate Change reports that coffee regions do and will have temperature and rainfall changes affecting the coffee sector throughout Central and South America (IPCC 2014). Where drought conditions currently hold, or are expected, water scarcity and quality becomes a central issue for coffee processing, an activity historically quite wasteful and polluting of surface water sources (Schroth et al. 2009). In Nicaragua's department of Estelí, climate experts predict future declines in rainfall and rising temperatures. The PRODECOOP cooperative union has already implemented several adaptations, including the installation of efficient wet processing mills and filtration systems to clean the smaller quantities of water run-off. Similar projects and water filtration pits have been installed to reduce the run-off from nutrient rich water in projects worldwide (Trade Aid 2012).

Farmer food insecurity is a fundamental challenge to the goals of fair trade coffee and other sustainable coffee certification programs (Bacon et al. 2008) and climate change will exacerbate this challenge among participating producers dependent upon rain fed agriculture. In the mid-2000s, marketing campaigns from coffee certification organizations often implied that certified farmers were experiencing considerably improved livelihoods (including food security) due to their participation in fair trade markets (Goodman 2004). The field research conducted at this time showed several livelihood and organizational benefits (Jaffee 2007), but it identified potential limits and trade-offs (Raynolds et al. 2007) and generally found limited evidence for the elimination of poverty among affiliated producers, including those linked to sustainable markets (Ruben and Fort 2012). Another study started with the lived experiences of producer communities and then traced changing livelihoods and power dynamics through time, documenting patterns of household differentiation and diversification in response to multiple forces, opportunities and hazards (Fraser et al. 2014).

CONCLUSIONS

Fair trade is associated with several understudied, significant and generally beneficial environmental impacts. Direct impacts derived from specific environmental standards include restricted agrochemicals use, the recent 50 per cent price premium increase for FTO coffee and the promotion of certified organic agriculture. However, these changes will likely generate additional labor requirements as farmers and coops often scramble to complete reports that document compliance with new regulations (Presa 2013). The indirect benefits of shade grown fair trade coffee include the conservation of biodiversity – both managed (trees) and associated (birds, insects, etc.) – as well as a broad set of ecosystem services, such as water conservation, nutrient cycling, erosion control, pollination and pest control. Recognition that smallholders manage much of Latin America's diverse shade canopy in coffee – and that such shade can provide a host of environmental benefits – is long overdue.

The geographical shift in the fair trade coffee supply is particularly concerning because the fastest-growing supply regions include countries with minimal diverse shade management, such as Colombia and Brazil. Fair trade initially emerged as a relationship linking solidarity-based traders with organized Mesoamerican smallholders who used agroforestry systems to grow coffee beneath a diverse shade canopy. The environmental implications of fair trade production's shifting geographies and exports deserve more attention from researchers. We also should note that even within small producers who manage a diverse shade over their coffee, there undoubtedly exists a range of diversity, both in species composition and structurally. If fair trade standards were to consider incentives for greater environmental benefits, one suggestion would be to create distinct categories for shade management. Finally, research tackling the impact of fair trade producers' projects is sorely needed. We firmly believe that positive benefits are associated with smallholder agroforestry production and links to fair trade networks. Although there are also negative impacts common to most coffee production systems (e.g., water contamination), additional research, extension, incentives and institutional reforms could prevent pollution, maximize environmental benefits and help deliver on the elusive promise of cultivating fair and sustainable coffee.

NOTES

1. Rice and Bacon consulted coffee and agricultural experts from the top 20 coffee producing countries. Surveys were sent in English and Spanish and phone or Skype calls were often used as a follow-up. The experts included members of national institutes and coffee associations (e.g., the Colombian Coffee Federation), staff from agricultural ministries in coffee producing countries, certification agencies and academics. Experts were selected based on their knowledge of coffee and sustainability

issues in specific countries, their reputation as credible sources within the Specialty Coffee Association of America and the existing professional networks of research teams.

2. Given its international scope and depth of experience, we have focused our standards analysis on Fairtrade International's certification system. The systems operated by the Institute for Marketecology's Fair for Life and under development by Fair Trade USA are an important subject for future research.
3. For more on the organization of certification see the following chapters in this volume: Bradley Wilson and Tad Mutersbaugh; Laura Raynolds and Nicholas Greenfield; and Elizabeth Bennett.
4. These are personal observations based on frequent travel and ongoing research conducted by Rice and Bacon in Latin America coffee growing regions during the past 20 years.

REFERENCES

Anzueto, Francisco (2014), Director of Research at Guatemala's *Asociación Nacional del Café* (Anacafé), interview with Robert Rice (6 February 2014).

Bacon, Christopher M. (2005), 'Confronting the coffee crisis: Can fair trade, organic, and specialty coffees reduce small-scale farmer vulnerability in Nicaragua?', *World Development*, 33 (3), 497–511.

Bacon, Christopher M., Ernesto Mendez and Jonathan A. Fox (2008), 'Cultivating sustainable coffee: Persistent paradoxes', in Christopher Bacon, Ernesto Mendez, Stephen R. Gliessman, David Goodman and Jonathan A. Fox (eds.), *Confronting the Coffee Crisis: Fair Trade, Sustainable Livelihoods and Ecosystems in Mexico and Central America*, Cambridge, MA: MIT Press, pp. 337–372.

Beddington, John, Mohammed Asaduzzaman, Megan Clark, Adrian Fernández, Marion Guillou, Molly Jahn, Lin Erda, Tekalign Mamo, Nguyen Van Bo, Carlos A. Nobre, Robert Scholes, Rita Sharma, Judi Wakhungu (2012), 'Achieving food security in the face of climate change: Final report from the Commission on Sustainable Agriculture and Climate Change', CGIAR Research Program on Climate Change, Agriculture and Food Security (CCAFS), Copenhagen, Denmark, available at www.ccafs.cgiar.org/commission (accessed 4 July 2014).

Berger, John (1979), *Pig Earth*, New York: Vintage Books.

Blackman, Allen and Maria A. Naranjo (2012), 'Does eco-certification have environmental benefits? Organic coffee in Costa Rica', *Ecological Economics*, 83, 58–66.

Center for Disease Control and Prevention (2009), 'Fourth national report on human exposure to environmental chemicals', available at http://www.cdc.gov/exposurereport/pdf/FourthReport.pdf (accessed 13 February 2014).

COSA (Committee on Sustainability Assessment) (2013), 'The COSA measuring sustainability report: Coffee and cocoa in 12 countries', Philadelphia, PA: The Committee on Sustainability Assessment.

Dávalos Sotelo, Raymundo, Maria Rodrigues Morato and Enrique Martinez Pinillos-Cueto (2008), 'Almacenamiento de carbon', in Robert H. Manson, Vincente Hernandez-Ortiz, Sonia Gallina and Klaus Mehltreter (eds.), *Agroecosistemas Cafetaleros de Veracruz: Biodiveridad, Manejo y Conservacion*, Mexico: Instituto de Ecologia A.C., pp. 223–234.

EPA (Environmental Protection Agency) (2010), 'Endosulfan phase-out', available at http://www.epa.gov/oppsrrd1/reregistration/endosulfan/endosulfan-agreement.html (accessed 4 July 2014).

Fairtrade International (2007), 'FLO Prohibited Materials List', available at http://www.fairtrade.net/fileadmin/user_upload/contentFLO_Prohibited_Materials_List_March_2007_EN.pdf (accessed 12 February 2014).

Fairtrade International (2011a), 'Prohibited Materials List', available at http://www.fairtrade.net.fileadmin/user_upload/content/2012-01-10_PML_Red_and_Amber.pdf (accessed 29 December 2013).

Fairtrade International (2011b), 'Fairtrade standard for small producer organizations', available at http://www.fairtrade.net/fileadmin/user_upload/content/2009/standards/documents2012-07-11_SPO_EN.pdf (accessed 29 December 2013).

Fairtrade International (2011c), 'Revised Fairtrade prices and trade standards for coffee: Main changes, March 15th, 2011', available at http://www.fairtrade.net/fileadmin/user_upload/content2009/standards/documents/150311_EN_MainChanges_coffee.pdf (accessed 16 April 2014).

Fairtrade International (2012), 'Monitoring the scope and benefits of fair trade', available at http://www.fairtrade.net/fileadmin/user_upload/content/2009/resources/2012Monitoring_report_web.pdf (accessed 23 April 2014).

Fairtrade International (2013), 'Climate change adaptation takes root in Peru', available at http:/www.fairtrade.net/single-view+M59e722954e5.html (accessed 16 April 2014).

Fairtrade International (2014), personal communication and data file from Miyako Takahashi, Business Analysis Manager, Department of Monitoring, Evaluation and Planning, Bonn, Germany (23 April 2014).

FLO-Cert (2014), 'List of certified operators', available at http://www.flo-cert.net/flo-cert29.html (accessed 15 January 2014).

Focus group (2013), smallholder coffee farmers with Christopher Bacon, Estelí, Nicaragua (5 July 2013).

Fraser, James, Eleanor Fisher and Alberto Arce (2014), 'Reframing "crisis" in fair trade coffee production: Trajectories of agrarian change in Nicaragua', *Journal of Agrarian Change*, 14 (1), 52–73.

Fridell, Gavin (2007), *Fair Trade Coffee: The Prospects and Pitfalls of Market-Driven Social Justice*, Toronto, Canada: University of Toronto Press.

Goodman, Michael K. (2004), 'Reading fair trade: Political ecological imaginary and the moral economy of fair trade foods', *Political Geography*, 23 (7), 891–915.

Harvey, Celia A., Oliver Komar, Robin Chazdon, Bruce G. Ferguson, Bryan Finegan, Daniel M. Griffith, Miguel Martínez-Ramos, Helda Morales, Ronald Nigh, Lorena Soto-Pinto, Michiel van Breugel and Mark Wishnie (2008), 'Integrating agricultural landscapes with biodiversity conservation in the Mesoamerican hotspot', *Conservation Biology*, 22 (1), 8–15.

Herrero, Mario, Philip K. Thornton, An M. Notenbaert, Stanley Wood, Siwa Msangi, H.A. Freeman, Deborah Bossio, John Dixon, Michael Peters, Jeaneatte van de Steeg, John Lynam, Pingali Parthasarathy Rao, Susan Macmillan, Bruno Gerard, John McDermott, Carlos Seré and Mark Rosegrant (2010), 'Smart investments in sustainable food production: Revisiting mixed crop-livestock systems', *Science*, 327 (5967), 882–885.

IPCC (Intergovernmental Panel on Climate Change) (2014), 'IPCC WGII AR5 Chapter 27: Central and South America', available at http://ipcc-wg2.govAR5/images/uploads/WGIIAR5-Chap27_FGDall.pdf (accessed 11 April 2014).

Jaffee, Daniel (2007), *Brewing Justice: Fair Trade Coffee, Sustainability, and Survival*, Berkeley, CA: University of California Press.

Jha, Shalane, Christopher M. Bacon, Stacy M. Philpott, Robert A. Rice, Ernesto V. Mendez and Peter Läderach (2014), 'Shade coffee: Update on a disappearing refuge for biodiversity', *BioScience*, 64 (5), 416–428.

Kellerman, Jherime, Matthew D. Johnson, Amy M. Stercho and Steven C. Hackett (2008), 'Ecological and economic services provided by birds on Jamaican Blue Mountain coffee farms', *Conservation Biology*, 22 (5), 1177–1185.
Klein, Alexandra-Maria, Ingolf Steffan-Dewenter and Teja Tscharntke (2003), 'Pollination of Coffea canephora in relation to local and regional agroforestry management', *Journal of Applied Ecology*, 40 (5), 837–845.
Lal, Rattan (2004), 'Soil carbon sequestration impacts on global climate change and food security', *Science*, 304 (5677), 1623–1627.
Lin, Brenda B. (2007), 'Agroforestry management as an adaptive strategy against potential microclimate extremes in coffee agriculture', *Agricultural and Forest Meteorology*, 144 (1–2), 85–94.
Lin, Brenda B., Ivette Perfecto and John Vandermeer (2008), 'Synergies between agricultural intensification and climate change could create surprising vulnerabilities for crops', *BioScience*, 58 (9), 847–854.
Lyon, Sarah (2013), *Coffee and Community*, Boulder, CO: University of Colorado Press.
Mendez, V. Ernesto, Christopher M. Bacon, Meryl Olson, Seth Petchers, Doribel Herrador, Cecilia Carranza, Laura Trujillo, Carlos Guadarrama-Zugasti, Antonio Cordon and Angel Mendoza (2010), 'Effects of fair trade and organic certifications on small-scale coffee farmer households in Central America and Mexico', *Renewable Agriculture and Food Systems*, 25 (3), 236–251.
Moguel, Patricia and Victor M. Toledo (1999), 'Biodiversity conservation in traditional coffee systems of Mexico', *Conservation Biology*, 13 (1), 11–21.
Neelin, J. David, Matthias Münnich, Hui Su, Joyce E. Meyerson and Christopher E. Holloway (2006), 'Tropical drying trends in global warming models and observations', *Proceedings of the National Academy of Sciences*, 103 (16), 6110–6115.
Nelson, Valerie, John Morton, Tim Chancellor, Peter Burt and Barry Pound (2010), 'Climate change, agricultural adaptation and Fairtrade: Identifying the challenges and opportunities', Natural Resources Institute, University of Greenwich.
Nelson, Valerie and Barry Pound (2009), 'The last ten years: A comprehensive review of the literature on the impact of Fairtrade', Natural Resources Institute, University of Greenwich.
Nolasco, Margarita (1985), *Café y Sociedad en México*, Mexico City, Mexico: Centro de Ecodesarrollo.
Perfecto, Ivette, Robert A. Rice, Russ Greenberg and M.E. VanderVoort (1996), 'Shade coffee: A disappearing refuge for biodiversity', *BioScience*, 46 (8), 598–608.
Philpott, Stacy M., Brenda B. Lin, Shalane Jha and Shannon J. Brines (2008), 'A multiscale assessment of hurricane impacts on agricultural landscapes based on land use and topographic features', *Agriculture, Ecosystem and Environment*, 128 (1–2), 12–20.
Pimentel, David, H. Acquay, M. Biltonen, P. Rice, M. Silva, J. Nelson, V. Lipner, S. Giordano, A. Horowitz, and M. D'Amore (1992), 'Environmental and economic costs of pesticide use', *BioScience*, 42 (10), 750–760.
Presa, Merling (2013), General Manager of PRODECOOP, interview with Christopher Bacon, Estelí, Nicaragua, (16 December 2013).
Raynolds, Laura T., Doug Murray and Andrew Heller (2007), 'Regulating sustainability in the coffee sector: A comparative analysis of third-party environmental and social certification initiatives', *Agriculture and Human Values*, 24 (2), 147–163.
Raynolds, Laura T., Doug Murray and Peter Leigh Taylor (2004), 'Fair trade coffee: Building producer capacity via global networks', *Journal of International Development*, 16 (8), 1109–1121.
Rice, Robert (1999), 'A place unbecoming: The coffee farm of northern Latin America', *Geographical Review*, 89 (4), 554–579.

Rice, Robert A. (2000), 'Noble goals and challenging terrain: Organic and fair trade coffee movements in the global marketplace', *Journal of Agricultural and Environmental Ethics*, 14 (1), 39–66.
Rice, Robert A. (2008), 'Agricultural intensification within agroforestry: The case of coffee and wood products', *Agriculture, Ecosystems and Environment*, 128 (4), 212–218.
Rice, Robert A. (2011), 'Fruits from shade trees in coffee: How important are they?', *Agroforest Systems*, 83 (1), 41–49.
Rice, Robert A. and Christopher M. Bacon (2013), 'Survey of coffee experts', data from a survey of coffee experts conducted by Robert Rice and Christopher Bacon.
Ruben, Ruerd and Ricardo Fort (2012), 'The impact of fair trade certification for coffee farmers in Peru', *World Development*, 40 (3), 570–582.
Schroth, Gotz, Peter Laderach, Jan Dempewolf, Stacy Philpott, Jeremy Haggar, Hallie Eakin, Teresa Castillejos, Jaime Garcia Moreno, Lorena Soto Pinto, Ricardo Hernandez, Anton Eitzinger and Julian Villegas-Ramirez (2009), 'Towards a climate change adaptation strategy for coffee communities and ecosystems in the Sierra Madre de Chiapas, Mexico', *Mitigation and Adaptation Strategies for Global Change*, 14 (7), 605–625.
Siegle, Lucy (2012), 'Peru's coffee growers turn carbon traders to save their farms from climate change', *The Observer*, 12 May 2012, available at http://www.theguardian.com/environment-2012/may/13/peru-coffee-climate-change-carbon-trading (accessed 13 April 2014).
Staver, Charles, Falguna Guharay, D. Monterroso and Reinhold G. Muschler (2001), 'Designing pest-suppressive multistrata perennial crop systems: Shade-grown coffee in Central America', *Agroforestry Systems*, 53 (2), 151–170.
Trade Aid (2012), 'Pick of the crop: The climate issue', available at https://www.tradeaid.org.nz/reports/0389479001330288864.pdf (accessed 15 April 2014).
United Nations (2001), 'Stockholm Convention on Persistent Organic Pollutants', available at https://treaties.un.org/pages/ViewDetails.aspx?src=TREATY&mtdsg_no=XXVII-15&chapter=27&lang=en (accessed 13 February 2014).
United Nations (2011), 'The new POPs under the Stockholm Convention', available at http://chm.pops.int/TheConvention/ThePOPs/TheNewPOPs/tabid/2511/Default.aspx (accessed May 2014).
Vaast, Phillipe, John Beer, Celia Harvey and J.M. Harmand (2005), 'Environmental services of coffee agroforestry systems in Central America: A promising potential to improve the livelihoods of coffee farmers' communities', paper presented at Integrated Management of Environmental Services in Human-Dominated Tropical Landscapes, CATIE, Costa Rica. http://web.catie.ac.cr/CATIE/CONFERENCIA%20WALLACE_ES2/documentos/35.pdf (accessed 17 April 2014).
Vandermeer, John, Ivette Perfecto and Richard Levins (2010), 'The agroecological matrix as alternative to the land-sparing/agriculture intensification model', *Proceedings of the National Academy of Sciences*, 107 (13), 5786–5791.
Verchot, Louis V., Meine Van Noordwijk, Serigne Kandji, Tom Tomich, Chin Ong, Alain Albrecht, Jens Mackensen, Cynthia Bantilan, K.V. Anupama and Cheryl Palm (2007), 'Climate change: Linking adaptation and mitigation through agroforestry', *Mitigation and Adaptation Strategies for Global Change*, 12 (5), 901–918.

23. Fair trade and women's empowerment

Sally Smith

INTRODUCTION

Gender equality and women's empowerment are considered core development objectives in their own right, as part of a just and equitable society grounded in respect for human rights. They are also recognized as instrumental for achieving other development objectives, including economic growth and food security, improved health and an end to the intergenerational transmission of poverty – the so-called smart economics argument advanced by the World Bank (World Bank 2006 and 2011). Formal commitment of the international community to gender equality dates back to the United Nations (UN) Convention on the Elimination of All Forms of Discrimination against Women which came into force in 1981, reinforced by the 'Platform for Action' adopted at the Fourth World Conference on Women in Beijing (1995), which required the UN and its signatory states to mainstream gender issues across all policy processes. The UN's inclusion of the goal to 'promote gender equality and empower women' as one of its eight Millennium Development Goals in 2000 has since galvanized attention and, importantly, directed resources towards gender-focused interventions and policy implementation.

The nature and implications of gender inequality in agriculture has received particular attention in recent years. An estimated 70 per cent of the world's very poor live in rural areas and the majority are dependent on agriculture-based livelihoods (IFAD 2010). Improved productivity and participation in commercialized agriculture are seen as key drivers of poverty reduction. But progress is constrained by a 'gender gap' in access to resources and opportunities, with women generally having more limited access to agricultural assets, inputs, services and (quality) employment than men (FAO 2011). According to the UN Food and Agriculture Organization (FAO), closing the gender gap in agriculture would bring significant development gains, including reducing the number of hungry people in the world by 12–17 per cent.

A spotlight has also been shined on gender issues in the textile and apparel industries, which have burgeoned in many developing countries since the 1980s. Women typically represent a high percentage of the workforce in these industries, and this employment can provide them with an important source of income, autonomy and self-regard. However, they are often employed in precarious, low paid forms of work and subjected to exploitative and undignified working conditions. In such cases their work may offer little in the way of empowerment or an escape from poverty (Kabeer et al. 2013; Standing 1989).

In this environment of increased awareness and action around gender, many within and outside the fair trade movement have become interested in fair trade's contribution to gender equality and women's empowerment. Until relatively recently the gendered dimensions of goals and strategies in fair trade remained largely unexplored in the fair trade movement, with the implicit assumption that access to fairer trading opportunities would benefit (and empower) both men and women. While World Fair Trade Organization (WFTO) 'Principles of Fair Trade' include 'a commitment to nondiscrimination, gender equity and women's economic empowerment and freedom of association',[1] reference to gender in the Fairtrade certification system has been mainly in relation to non-discrimination, in both small producer organization membership and hired labor employment. A growing body of research suggests that in general women derive less benefit than men from participation in agriculture-based fair trade due to gender inequalities underlying the production and trade of farmed goods, although there are marked differences from one context to the next (Le Mare 2008; Nelson and Pound 2009; Smith 2013). This appears to be less often the case for artisan-based fair trade, where women tend to have higher levels of involvement, including as members of women-only organizations, and are often specifically targeted for support by fair trade organizations (Jones, Smith and Wills 2011; Le Mare 2012). Where women's participation is high, and in other situations where women are recognized as producers in their own right and gender inequalities are being tackled head on, fair trade has been associated with significant economic and social benefits for women, including improved income, assets, skills, confidence, status and influence (Jones, Smith and Wills 2011; Le Mare 2012; Smith 2013). However, even positive examples in the literature tend to suggest limitations in the extent to which women are empowered through their experiences with fair trade (Hutchens 2010; Le Mare 2012).

Increasing knowledge of the variability in outcomes for women has led both Fairtrade International and the WFTO to take a more proactive stance on gender. In 2010 Fairtrade International established a multi-stakeholder working group tasked with developing a gender strategy for the Fairtrade system. Fairtrade International's board of directors unanimously approved the resulting strategy in 2012.[2] Similarly, a Gender Working Group was formed by WFTO members in 2011 and the gender strategy subsequently produced was approved at the Annual General Meeting in 2013.[3]

This chapter draws on findings from empirical research in various countries and sectors to analyze the role of fair trade in facilitating women's empowerment, focusing primarily on fair trade in agriculture. The analysis is based on an understanding of women's empowerment as both an individual and collective process, with economic, social and political dimensions. It concludes with some reflections on the approach being taken by Fairtrade International and WFTO in their gender strategies, assessing the extent to which they respond to the experiences of women in fair trade to date and the multiple and complex challenges involved.

CONCEPTUALIZING GENDER EQUALITY AND WOMEN'S EMPOWERMENT

Gender equality is a relatively straightforward concept, with the UN Women's definition being fairly typical:

> Gender equality refers to the equal rights, responsibilities and opportunities of women and men and girls and boys. Equality does not mean that women and men will become the same but that women's and men's rights, responsibilities and opportunities will not depend on whether they are born male or female. Gender equality implies that the interests, needs and priorities of both women and men are taken into consideration, recognizing the diversity of different groups of women and men.[4]

Relevant here is the distinction often made between women's strategic interests and their practical needs (Molyneux 1985; Moser 1989). Strategic interests relate to challenging the structural basis of women's subordinate position in society, such as eliminating the gender division of labor, reducing the domestic burden of care work, removing institutionalized forms of discrimination, assuring sexual and reproductive rights and achieving political equality. Practical needs are the immediate, concrete needs of women based on their individual circumstances, including the gender division of labor in their households and gender biases in their access to resources and income-generating opportunities. Addressing women's practical needs may alleviate their experience of gender inequality and reduce inequity at a local level, but it will not fundamentally change the status of women in their society.

This distinction is useful when thinking about women's empowerment. There is considerable variation in the way women's empowerment is understood and interpreted in the development community. From a feminist perspective this is no accident, as the more political interpretations based around a reconfiguration of power structures have often been avoided by bilateral and multilateral agencies in the global North (Eyben, Kabeer and Cornwall 2008). When feminists and women's organizations first used the term in the 1970s, it explicitly referred to 'a transformation of economic, social and political structures at national and international levels' (Bisnath and Elson n.d., cited in Mosedale 2005, 247). By the 1990s it had been mainstreamed into development language largely as a call for women to have more access to and control of resources, with little reference to more collective visions of societal change (Batliwala 2010; Mosedale 2005).

Feminist development scholars have produced frameworks for conceptualizing and measuring women's empowerment, helping to expand mainstream understanding of the concept. In one such framework women's empowerment is defined as 'the process by which those who have been denied the ability to make strategic life choices acquire such an ability' (Kabeer 1999, 435). This process is dependent on three indivisible elements: access to resources (material, human, social), an ability to define one's goals and act on them (agency) and the extent of achievement realized. Understanding empowerment as a process rather than an end state is important; it signals a spectrum of achievement from the personal, including addressing practical needs, to the collective, working with others to achieve more widespread change. Another way of conceptualizing this is by looking at different kinds of power which can be acquired: power *within* (sense of self-esteem and self-worth), power *to* (capabilities to achieve) and power *with* (collective action to achieve more than is possible for an individual alone) (Mosedale 2005).

The concept of empowerment is integral to fair trade. Responding to unequal relations of power in conventional trade was the impetus for its development, although with mainstreaming the focus has shifted from creating alternative trading networks to better equipping small producers and workers to derive benefits from existing market structures. According to the Charter of Fair Trade Principles, the fair trade movement believes that 'the marginalized and disadvantaged can develop the capacity to take more control over their work and their lives if they are better organized, resourced and supported, and can secure access to mainstream markets under fair trading conditions'.[5] There is therefore an implicit aim to restructure power relations within markets and supply chains, primarily through building the capacities of small producers and their organizations to trade on fair terms and strengthening workers' bargaining position with employers, as well as through campaigning to change the rules and practices of conventional trade.[6]

As stated earlier, there has historically been little explicit focus on exploring and addressing unequal power relations between men and women in fair trade. However, this does not mean that fair trade has not made a contribution in this area, through its broader approach to supporting empowerment among small producers and workers which emphasizes organizational development (power *with*) and access to resources and opportunities (power *to*), and its commitment to the principle of non-discrimination, including specific reference to gender inequality (power *to*). The purpose of this chapter is to understand better when and how fair trade supports the process of women's empowerment in practice, drawing on empirical evidence from a range of contexts.

FAIR TRADE'S CONTRIBUTION TO WOMEN'S EMPOWERMENT

Most research on fair trade has not interrogated gender impacts deeply, but there are a number of studies which provide useful insights in three particularly relevant areas: recognizing and rewarding women's contribution to fair trade production; enabling collective action and giving women a voice; and addressing women's practical and strategic needs. Each area is explored in turn below.

Recognizing and Rewarding Women's Contribution to Fair Trade Production

Women constitute approximately one quarter of all registered small producers and workers in certified Fairtrade (Fairtrade International 2012).[7] The percentage is higher for hired labor situations, where women make up around 47 per cent of workers, compared to small producer organizations (SPOs), where only around 20 per cent of members are women. The figures also vary by sector and region: on banana plantations, for instance, women constitute 14 per cent of workers, compared to 52 per cent for tea plantations, while in coffee only 14 per cent of certified SPO members are women, compared to 75 per cent in oil seeds and oleaginous fruit. Women's participation in SPOs is higher in Latin America and the Caribbean (22 per cent) and Africa and the Middle East

(20 per cent) than in Asia and Oceania (13 per cent), while for hired labor it is the reverse, being highest in Asia and Oceania (56 per cent) and lowest in Latin America and the Caribbean (22 per cent).

This variation can be sourced to a range of contextual factors, including gender norms and attitudes towards women's work, opportunities for employment in other sectors (for men and women), levels of migration, gender patterns of ownership of land and tendencies for particular crops to be deemed either 'male' or 'female' crops. It is not possible to generalize about 'women in fair trade' as if they form a homogeneous group, with differences based not only on geographical location but also on a woman's individual circumstances (age, marital status, education, wealth, etc.). However, what is clear from research is that for small producers, SPO membership figures often do not paint an accurate picture of women's actual contribution to production. That is, in many instances women are heavily involved in the production of fair trade crops but are not members of associated SPOs (Blowfield and Dolan 2010; Dilley 2011; Imhoff and Lee 2007; Lyon, Bezaury and Mutersbaugh 2010; Nelson and Smith 2011; Opondo 2009). Studies show that women often perform labor-intensive tasks and those which are critical to the quality of final products, such as weeding, harvesting and post-harvest processing, while men (in male-headed households) typically take responsibility for taking goods to market (as well as other tasks). This has implications for the impact of fair trade, as it often means men have more decision-making power over the income earned and distribution of other benefits, with women's contribution potentially not sufficiently recognized or rewarded. In such a situation, fair trade can be said to reinforce pre-existing gender inequalities, rather than counter them.

Some studies have shown that fair trade *can* help challenge pre-existing inequalities, under certain conditions. One such study showed that the requirement in the Fairtrade cotton standard[8] that women be paid directly for the cotton they produce contributed to increased recognition of women's right to earn an income from their labor on cotton in West Africa (Senegal, Mali and Cameroon) (Nelson and Smith 2011). This, along with other factors, resulted in an increase in the cotton farmed by women and in the income they earned on their own account. Other contributory factors were: the proactive stance of buyers and support organizations in sensitizing communities and ensuring enforcement of the Fairtrade standard; high market prices for cotton at the time, which were an incentive to all farmers to grow more cotton; and the introduction of organic practices which eliminated the need to apply agrochemicals and made cotton production more attractive and affordable for women. Some women reported that the increase in own-account income had given them greater decision-making power in their households (an indicator of empowerment), although others said men still retained ultimate control of all household income. In contrast the positive effects were not found in the case study in Gujarat, India, as most women did not have access to land to farm their own cotton, instead only working alongside male relatives. This demonstrates the importance of context for fair trade impact, with a single strategy leading to different outcomes depending on the context, including at the level of individual women.

Research in the Nicaraguan coffee sector provides further insights into how fair trade can interact with local contextual processes to support women's empowerment, including increased recognition and reward for their labor. In the case of Nicaragua, these processes date back to the Sandinista revolution in the 1960s and 1970s, during which women played a prominent role in fighting for social and agrarian change, with an estimated 30 per cent of combat forces being women (Bacon 2010). A relatively strong women's movement emerged from that period, and during the subsequent years of Sandinista government (1979–1990) women gained important rights and recognition, including acknowledgement of their importance to Nicaraguan society and economy (Bacon 2010; Dilley 2011). Women's contribution to agricultural production was also recognized, with land titles granted to both men and women as part of agricultural reform.

Meanwhile, in the coffee sector the Sandinista government encouraged the formation of cooperative organizations. Women were active participants in coffee cooperatives, albeit still as a minority of total membership and under-represented in management (Bacon 2010). State intervention limited the extent to which cooperatives developed as viable independent businesses, and when the Sandinistas lost power to a right-leaning government in 1990, a withdrawal of state support led to the collapse of most coffee cooperatives. Those that survived were the stronger organizations, in terms of ability to organize and to expand their enterprises, but also leadership and vision. In this context, and in the years of the 'coffee crisis' which followed, the emerging fair trade market provided vital opportunities for these coffee cooperatives to grow as businesses while also progressing their socio-political agendas (Bacon 2010; Dilley 2011; Hoskyns, Hoskyns and Butler 2012).

For some this included an explicit interest in continuing the progress made in improving the situation of women. Coffee cooperatives such as SOPPEXCCA and PRODECOOP, both in Nicaragua, have led the way with strong (female) leadership and strategic intent in relation to women's empowerment and holistic approaches for achieving it. SOPPEXCCA has around 600 members, one third being women (Dilley 2011). It has assisted women to become active cooperative members, helping them cultivate their own coffee and access loans and land, as well as holding workshops with men, women and youth on key gender issues such as gender equity in the household, women's sexual and reproductive rights and gender-based violence (Dilley 2011). A recent innovation has been to incorporate the cost of women's unpaid work into calculations of coffee prices, with the resulting premium used for improving the situation of temporary women workers at the cooperative's processing plant, who are considered to be the most disadvantaged (Hoskyns, Hoskyns and Butler 2012). As a result of these actions, women members of SOPPEXCCA report increased self-confidence, self-esteem and status within the household, cooperative and community, in addition to the economic benefits of increased income, assets and skills (Dilley 2011).

Likewise, PRODECOOP, a secondary-level cooperative uniting 39 primary societies and around 2400 members, adopted a gender policy in 2008 that identified a range of practical and strategic actions for the achievement of greater gender equality (Jones, Smith and Wills 2011). These include gender sensitization in communities, health and education services and preventative action against gender-based violence, as well as income generating activities and access to credit for women. The empowerment effect for women is summed up in the following quote from a member of PRODECOOP:

> To be able to recognize that I am an important woman, with rights and that I can decide for myself in my life. Now I control the work in my home and it's me who decides whether to get involved in the projects that the cooperative offers. Also, now that I'm organized I feel safer and more confident, I have been able to see the place that [the cooperative] gives to women. (Jones, Smith and Wills 2011, 32)

The role of fair trade in contributing to this empowerment is indirect – it helps the cooperatives access higher value markets, protects them from price volatility and delivers a premium for collective investments, all of which help build the economic foundations necessary for fulfillment of their strategic objectives, including those around gender. This helps to explain why, even in a relatively conducive national context, the contribution of fair trade cooperatives to women's empowerment is far from uniform. Reflecting on gendered empowerment processes in three different Nicaraguan coffee cooperatives, one author concluded that 'historical cooperative organizing practices and government policy intersect with participation in Fair Trade networks in different combinations that can either enhance or inhibit individual and collective empowerment' (Bacon 2010, 50). Differential outcomes are linked to the fact that fair trade does not systematically challenge the status quo of pre-existing gender relations in producer organizations, with no provision for ensuring women are able to become members and can access the full benefits of membership.[9] This is explored in more detail below.

Enabling Collective Action and Giving Women a Voice

Under-representation of women in agriculture-based fair trade producer organizations, relative to their contribution to production, is a widely reported phenomenon, with women also less likely to be found in positions of leadership or management (Blowfield and Dolan 2010; Fridell 2007; Le Mare 2008; Lyon, Bezaury and Mutersbaugh 2010; Nelson and Pound 2009; Opondo 2009; Ronchi 2002; Smith 2010). There are various reasons for this, all of which reflect structures of gender inequality (Smith 2013):

- Becoming a member of an agricultural cooperative often requires ownership of land, which automatically excludes large numbers of women due to gender bias in land ownership and inheritance systems.
- Most cooperatives only permit one member per household; in male-headed households it is typically the senior man who is the member, even where women do most of the agricultural work.
- Women's burden of domestic work often limits their ability to participate in producer organizations, in terms of the time it would require and the timing of meetings.
- In some parts of the world, social, cultural and religious beliefs and practices constrain women's mobility and participation in public and mixed sex spaces. When women do attend meetings, social norms may make it difficult for them to speak freely in front of men.
- Lower levels of education among rural women, particularly older generations, make them less likely to take up leadership positions than men. Language ability (linked to education) can also be an inhibiting factor in multi-lingual settings.

In what could be described a 'vicious circle', the male bias of agricultural cooperatives and concomitant lack of gender-aware policies and services itself acts as a disincentive to women to participate, as they do not see the organization acting in their interests. Women are likely to choose to devote the limited time they have to, or prefer to make sacrifices for, organizations in which they feel more welcome and through which they feel more represented (Lyon 2008). This becomes clear when women's participation in artisan-based fair trade is looked at: that women often form the majority of such organizations (Hutchens 2010; Jones, Smith and Wills 2011; Le Mare 2012) demonstrates that constraints to active participation in producer organizations are not insurmountable.

Research with women artisans and farmers in seven countries (Kenya, Uganda, Tanzania, Nepal, India, Nicaragua and Mexico) found that women experience numerous benefits from participation in producer organizations linked to fair trade (Jones, Smith and Wills 2011). Economic benefits include economies of scale, improved knowledge and skills, and access to inputs, services and markets, while social benefits include increased self-confidence and self-esteem, a sense of solidarity with others and material and emotional support in times of difficulty. In addition to a higher standard of living, many women reported changes which represent significant shifts in gender relations and women's status in their households and communities. Although evidence of women organizing for change beyond their immediate environs is limited, they have clearly gained access to *resources* (material, human, social), demonstrate increased *agency* and are experiencing *achievements* which they are proud of and which are reinforcing effects on resources and agency. The resulting empowerment is summed up by Josefina Oliva, a member of the Ya Munts'i Behña cooperative in Mexico:

> Before [the group formed] women didn't have value or power to decide things, because of the fear that one had. Women weren't worth anything, they should just stay at home, cleaning or looking after children. I think that it's something really important that in the group one can learn … how to value [ourselves as] women. (Jones, Smith and Wills 2011, 30)

In this study of seven countries, 12 of the 16 enterprises studied are women-only organizations, and the rest are proactive in promoting gender equality. Many have received substantial external support since inception, including from fair trade organizations. Reported benefits associated with fair trade are wide-ranging, including organizational and skills development, technical and financial support, market linkages, price premiums, improved working conditions, and opportunities to network and build alliances.

Mary Littrell's chapter in this volume reports similar findings on the impact of fair trade for artisans in India and Guatemala. In other contexts, especially in agriculture-based fair trade, research suggests women are less likely to benefit to this extent because of their limited participation in producer organizations. However, research in various sectors and countries indicates fair trade standards and principles *can* enhance women's involvement in producer organizations through: strengthening organizational and administrative processes and practices, including making them more democratic and transparent (Pound and Quintana Guadarrama 2008); encouraging representation of women in committees and management and women's participation in training (Riisgaard et al. 2009); and creating space for democratic discussion and decision-making (Sen n.d.). As described previously, fair trade can also have an indirect impact by providing support for producer organizations which take unilateral action to increase women's membership. A good example is PRODECOOP in Nicaragua, which has removed the requirement that members own land to make it easier for women to become members (Jones, Smith and Wills 2011).

The available evidence suggests that in hired labor situations fair trade can also enhance representation of women in trade unions, workers committees and Fairtrade Premium Committees (Charman 2010; Pound and Phiri 2009; Smith 2010). Women report favorably on these new opportunities, although they also talk about the constraints they continue to face which parallel those of women small producers: lack of education, skills and confidence to take on leadership roles; burden of domestic work; and social and cultural norms limiting active participation (Smith 2010). In general, for both workers and small producers there are questions about how far increased representation has taken women in terms of their influence over decision-making and the extent to which their practical and strategic needs are being met (Fridell 2007; Hutchens 2010; Imhoff and Lee 2007; Lyon 2008; Nelson and Smith 2011; Sen n.d.; and, in this volume, chapters by Mary Littrell and Valerie Nelson and Adrienne Martin).

Addressing Women's Practical and Strategic Needs

The evidence presented thus far suggests fair trade may help women meet their practical needs, and to a certain extent their strategic needs, through providing support and favorable trading conditions to organizations with a focus on women's empowerment. However, in the Fairtrade certification system there is a more direct route through which women's needs may be met: the Fairtrade premium. The premium is used for economic, social and environmental purposes, based on collective, democratic decision-making around priority needs.[10] There are many examples of premium use which could reduce the amount of hours spent on unpaid care work in small producer and worker households, which would free up women's time to focus on other activities such as paid work, education and training, and organizational life. These include investments in access to water, healthcare, childcare facilities and transport, as well as communal food processing equipment (e.g., mills for grinding corn, maize and other staples) and household domestic goods (e.g., stoves, water storage, fridges). Other examples of premium use that may particularly benefit women include adult literacy classes and street lighting (for security).

Fairtrade-certified organizations earned on average €82 000 in premium funds in 2010–11, equating to around €56 per small producer or worker (Fairtrade International 2012). The way expenditure is currently categorized does not make it possible to identify the percentage invested in addressing women's practical and strategic needs.[11] Less than 1 per cent was spent on investments specifically categorized as 'gender equity' (such as women's income generation projects and gender training), but SPOs invested 10 per cent in community development and health, rising to 21 per cent for hired labor organizations, and other categories of expenditure may also be particularly relevant for women (e.g., education, direct financial support). Research has documented sporadic use of the premium in the areas mentioned above (e.g. CEval 2012; Charman 2010; Nelson and Smith 2011; Pound and Quintana Guadarrama 2011; Smith 2010). A few studies have examined the connection between allocation of funds and gender outcomes, such as impacts on women's burden of work. For example, the electrification of a village in Malawi has resulted in private owners installing hammer mills, which have reduced the time women dedicate to getting maize milled as they previously had to walk 5 kilometers (Pound and Phiri 2010). Another example is an Indian tea plantation in which the fair trade premium has funded gas cylinders and pressure cookers for workers' households, resulting in men spending less time collecting firewood and women less time cooking, meaning both have more leisure time (CEval 2012). On fruit and wine farms in South Africa premium-funded community crèches have allowed women to more easily engage in on-farm employment and other income-generating activities (Charman 2010). Fairtrade status has also enabled farms to leverage further funds from donors and buyers for others projects with a gender impact, including training emphasizing women's rights. This 'honeypot' effect has been reported elsewhere (CEval 2012; Nelson and Pound 2009) and may be an important channel for gender impacts.

Some research suggests the premium may do little to advance women's economic empowerment if premium-funded projects focus on non-income generating activities, such as health and subsistence farming, rather than directly supporting women to improve their income streams (Lyon 2008). Even when used for women's income generation, this can be problematic if projects are not well conceived and funded (ibid; Imhoff and Lee 2007) or if women are unable to participate due to their heavy burden of work (CEval 2012). The latter is potentially a fundamental limitation for fair trade impact on gender equality, with research suggesting fair trade typically has little impact on the division of labor in households, with women continuing to perform the majority of unpaid care work on top of productive activities. Although premium-funded projects may reduce the time women spend on unpaid work, further progress towards gender equality requires a more equitable allocation of all forms of work between men and women.

THE FUTURE OF GENDER AND WOMEN'S EMPOWERMENT IN FAIR TRADE

To summarize, the available evidence suggests that there is considerable variation in the extent to which fair trade supports processes of women's empowerment, not least because the effects of fair trade are mediated by local contextual conditions. A key determinant is the positioning of producer organizations in relation to participation of women and commitment to gender equality, which is in turn influenced by historically based social and political processes and the gendered nature of local economies. In some cases this means fair trade is having a significant effect in helping women to access income, status and influence, but in others it is replicating and reinforcing pre-existing gender-based structures of inequality. Until relatively recently fair trade has not explicitly set out to address gender biases in local institutional arrangements, beyond advocating for democratic processes and non-discrimination. Although some fair trade organizations have targeted women for support, particularly in handicrafts, this has often been done with a welfare rather than rights-based approach (Hutchens 2010; Jones, Smith and Wills 2011).

Over the last decade the situation has changed. An increased focus on gender in the wider development community has penetrated the fair trade movement at all levels, including among producer organizations. In their new gender strategies both Fairtrade International and WFTO recognize the need for a fundamental shift in how fair trade approaches gender equality and women's empowerment. Crucially, both emphasize that a context-driven, bottom-up approach is required, with regional networks of Fairtrade producers and WFTO members taking the lead on developing action plans which respond to localized gender contexts, rather than prescribing a universal course of action from the center. Fairtrade International specifically rejects using the Fairtrade standards as a tool (for instance, by incorporating quotas for women's membership and representation), on the basis that imposing gender equality on producer organizations from the outside is neither effective nor sustainable. Instead it seeks to facilitate analysis and understanding of the gendered context and impacts of fair trade production and trade, including through exchange of good practice between producer organizations, and build capacity to respond at the local level. WFTO also recognizes the need for increased gender analysis and capacity, as well as an improved institutional policy framework with greater representation of women in governance and a stronger advocacy strategy.

The research evidence supports the approach being taken by Fairtrade International and WFTO, as it demonstrates that most progress is made in supporting women's empowerment when producer organizations have the capacity and leadership to drive change in their specific gender contexts. As such, the underlying principles of both gender strategies are sound. However, the evidence also suggests that fair trade principles and standards related to democratic organization and non-discrimination are important for establishing the responsibilities of producer organizations. The absence of a clear policy framework on gender equality and women's empowerment in Fairtrade International is therefore potentially a weakness, and more could be done to incentivize and reward good practice among producer organizations in both Fairtrade and WFTO networks. Furthermore, the scale of the task cannot be overstated and progress is likely to be slow unless significant resources (human, financial) are invested in implementation. With many competing demands on internal resources, it will be critical that leaders within the fair trade movement give this area of work priority and that external funders provide earmarked funding for it. Current interest in gender and agriculture among donors and the private sector should help, both in terms of accessing resources and maintaining pressure on the fair trade movement to 'do better'. Indeed, Fairtrade International has recently secured funding to begin implementing activities outlined in its gender strategy in 2014, and the coming years will provide opportunities to reflect on what has been achieved and how effective the strategy is in practice. In the meantime a burgeoning body of research on fair trade will expand understanding of fair trade's contribution to women's empowerment in different contexts and under different trading arrangements, including innovative marketing by fair trade organizations seeking to connect consumers directly with women producers.[12]

NOTES

1. WFTO's '10 Principles of Fair Trade' can be found on their website at http://www.wfto.com.
2. The author was involved in the Gender Working Group as an external expert. Knowledge of Fairtrade International's gender strategy referred to in this chapter is derived from that experience, as the strategy is not currently publicly available.
3. As stated in the conference report from the 12th WFTO Biennial Global Conference, 26–28 May 2013, Rio de Janeiro, Brazil, available at http://www.wfto.com (accessed 10 February 2014). WFTO's gender strategy was shared with the author but is not currently publicly available.
4. As stated on UN Women's website, http://www.unwomen.org/ (accessed 10 February 2014).
5. A Charter of Fair Trade Principles (2009, 6). The Charter was agreed between Fairtrade International and WFTO in 2009, and is available at http://fairtrade-advocacy.org/images/Charter_of_Fair_Trade_principles_EN_v1.2.pdf (accessed 10 February 2014).
6. As outlined in the new Workers Rights Strategy for Fairtrade and revised Fairtrade Standard for Hired Labour, both available at http://www.fairtrade.net/hired-labour-standards.html, accessed 15 February 2014.
7. Figures on the number of girls involved in WFTO-linked fair trade are not available.
8. This is not part of the Generic Fairtrade Standards for Small Producer Organizations; rather, it is an additional requirement in the product-specific standards for cotton and is unique to this product.
9. For a related discussion on the limitations of fair trade for tackling pre-existing gender inequalities, see Valerie Nelson and Adrienne Martin's chapter on fair trade outcomes in Africa in this volume.
10. See Fairtrade International's website for details: http://www.fairtrade.net/.
11. Fairtrade International is currently developing a new monitoring system which will allow better categorization of premium expenditure, including for gender-related investments.
12. Examples include Equal Exchange's 'Grown By Women' coffee brand (see http://www.equalexchange.co.uk/grown-by-women/) and the women producer-owned 'Café Feminino' brand (see http://homepage-cafe.com/cafefemenino.html).

REFERENCES

Bacon, Christopher (2010), 'A spot of coffee in crisis: Nicaraguan smallholder cooperatives, fair trade networks, and gendered empowerment', *Latin American Perspectives*, 37 (2), 50–71.

Batliwala, Srilatha (2010), 'Taking the power out of empowerment – an experiential account', in Andrea Cornwall and Deborah Eade (eds.), *Deconstructing Development Discourse: Buzzwords and Fuzzwords*, Oxford: Practical Action Publishing in association with Oxfam GB, pp. 111–122.

Blowfield, Michael and Catherine Dolan (2010), 'Fairtrade facts and fancies: What Kenyan Fairtrade tea tells us about business' role as a development agent', *Journal of Business Ethics*, 93 (S2), 143–162.

CEval (2012), 'Assessing the impact of Fairtrade on poverty reduction through rural development', Final Report, Fairtrade Impact Study, Germany: Center for Evaluation (CEval), Saarland University.

Charman, Andrew (2010), 'Impact study of Fairtrade in South Africa: Synthesis report', unpublished independent research commissioned by the Fairtrade Foundation, Cape Town, South Africa: Sustainable Livelihoods Consultants.

Dilley, Catherine (2011), 'Women and fair trade coffee production in Nicaragua', *Malaysia Journal of Society and Space*, 7 (1), 74–84.

Eyben, Rosalind, Naila Kabeer and Andrea Cornwall (2008), 'Conceptualizing empowerment and the implications for pro poor growth', a paper for the DAC Poverty Network, Sussex, UK: Institute of Development Studies.

Fairtrade International (2012), 'Monitoring the scope and benefits of Fairtrade: Fourth edition', Bonn, Germany: Fairtrade International.

FAO (2011), *The State of Food and Agriculture 2010–11: Women in Agriculture – Closing the Gender Gap for Development*, Rome: Food and Agriculture Organization.

Fridell, Gavin (2007), *Fair Trade Coffee: The Prospects and Pitfalls of Market-Driven Social Justice*, Canada: University of Toronto Press, Inc.

Hoskyns, Catherine, Nicholas Hoskyns and Felicity Butler (2012), 'Pricing fair trade products to include unpaid labour and empower women – the example of Nicaraguan sesame and coffee cooperatives', *Oñati Socio-Legal Series*, 2 (2), 24–35.

Hutchens, Anna (2010), 'Empowering women through Fair Trade? Lessons from Asia', *Third World Quarterly*, 31 (3), 449–467.

IFAD (International Fund for Agricultural Development) (2010), 'Rural poverty report 2011: New realities, new challenges: New opportunities for tomorrow's generation', Rome: IFAD.

Imhoff, Sandra and Andrew Lee (2007), 'Assessing the potential of fair trade for poverty reduction and conflict prevention: A case study of Bolivian coffee producers', Switzerland: University of Basel.

Jones, Elaine, Sally Smith and Carol Wills (2011), 'Trading our way up: Women organizing for fair trade', Cambridge, MA: Women in Informal Employment Globalizing and Organizing (WIEGO).

Kabeer, Naila (1999), 'Resources, agency, achievement: Reflections on the measurement of women's empowerment', *Development and Change*, 30 (3), 435–464.

Kabeer, Naila with Ragui Assaad, Akosua Darkwah, Simeen Mahmud, Hania Sholkamy, Sakiba Tasneem and Dzodzi Tsikata, and with statistical support by Munshi Sulaiman (2013), 'Paid work, women's empowerment and inclusive growth: transforming the structures of constraint', New York: UN Women.

Le Mare, Ann (2008), 'The impact of Fair Trade on social and economic development: A review of the literature', *Geography Compass*, 2 (6), 1922–1942.

Le Mare, Ann (2012), 'Southern fair trade enterprises as agents of empowerment', *Gender and Development*, 20 (1), 95–109.

Lyon, Sarah (2008), 'We want to be equal to them: Fair-trade coffee certification and gender equity within organizations', *Human Organization*, 67 (3), 258–268.

Lyon, Sarah, Josefina Aranda Bezaury and Tad Mutersbaugh (2010), 'Gender equity in fairtrade–organic coffee producer organisations: Cases from Mesoamerica', *Geoforum*, 41 (1), 93–103.

Molyneux, Maxine (1985), 'Mobilization without emancipation? Women's interests, the state, and revolution in Nicaragua', *Feminist Studies*, 11 (2), 227–254.

Mosedale, Sarah (2005), 'Assessing women's empowerment: Towards a conceptual framework', *Journal of International Development*, 17 (2), 243–257.

Moser, Caroline (1989), 'Gender planning in the Third World: Meeting practical and strategic gender needs', *World Development*, 17 (11), 1799–1825.

Nelson, Valerie and Barry Pound (2009), 'The last ten years: A comprehensive review of the literature on the impact of Fairtrade', London: Fairtrade Foundation.

Nelson, Valerie and Sally Smith (2011), 'Fairtrade cotton: Assessing impact in Mali, Senegal, Cameroon and India', Chatham, UK: Natural Resources Institute, University of Greenwich.

Opondo, Margaret (2009), 'A gender value chain analysis of coffee farmer cooperative societies in Nyeri, Kenya', unpublished study commissioned by SMS and HIVOS, Kenya: University of Nairobi.

Pound, Barry and Eduardo Quintana Guadarrama (2008), 'Development of a participatory impact monitoring system for the Belize Sugar Cane Farmers Association', unpublished report commissioned by the Fairtrade Foundation, Chatham, UK: Natural Resources Institute, University of Greenwich.

Pound, Barry and Eduardo Quintana Guadarrama (2011), 'Second impact monitoring study of the Belize Sugar Cane Farmers Association', unpublished report commissioned by the Fairtrade Foundation, Chatham, UK: Natural Resources Institute, University of Greenwich.

Pound, Barry and Alexander Phiri (2009), 'Longitudinal impact assessment study of Fairtrade certified tea producers and workers in Malawi', unpublished study commissioned by the Fairtrade Foundation, Chatham, UK: Natural Resources Institute, University of Greenwich.

Pound, Barry and Alexander Phiri (2010), 'Longitudinal impact assessment of Fairtrade groundnut producers in Malawi', unpublished study commissioned by the Fairtrade Foundation, Chatham, UK: Natural Resources Institute, University of Greenwich.

Riisgaard, Lone, George Michuki, Peter Gibbon and Simon Bolwig with Nynne Warring and Louise Lund Rantz (2009), 'The performance of voluntary standard schemes from the perspective of small producers in East Africa', Copenhagen: Danish Institute for International Studies.

Ronchi, Lorraine (2002), 'The impact of fair trade on producers and their organisations: A case study with Coocafe in Costa Rica', PRUS Working Paper, 11, Sussex, UK: Poverty Research Unit at Sussex University.

Sen, Debarati (n.d.), 'Fair trade organic tea production and women's political futures in Darjeeling, India', PhD research summary, available at http://digitalcommons.macalester.edu/cgi/viewcontent.cgi?article=1730&context=himalaya&sei-redir=1#search=%22sen+fair+trade+tea+darjeeling%22 (accessed 4 July 2014).

Smith, Sally (2010), 'Fairtrade bananas: A global assessment of impact', Sussex, UK: Institute of Development Studies.

Smith, Sally (2013), 'Assessing the gender impacts of Fairtrade', *Social Enterprise Journal*, 9 (1), 102–122.

Standing, Guy (1989), 'Global feminization through flexible labour', *World Development*, 17 (7), 1077–1095.

World Bank (2006), 'Gender equality as smart economics: A World Bank Group gender action plan – fiscal years 2007–10', Washington, DC: The World Bank.

World Bank (2011), 'World development report 2012: Gender equality and development', Washington, DC: The International Bank for Reconstruction and Development and The World Bank.

24. Fair trade and indigenous communities in Latin America

Sarah Lyon

INTRODUCTION

> Yuri works hard to maintain the indigenous cultural and agricultural knowledge of her people. Fair Trade helps make that a reality. By taking part in a system that provides key market access, financial training, and the ability to invest in things like education, healthcare, food security and clean water, the farmers and workers of Fondo Paez are able to participate in vibrant global trade while simultaneously strengthening their own cultural heritage. (Fair Trade USA 2011)

In terms of romantic imaginings, global capitalism and indigeneity are seemingly placed at opposite ends of a vast continuum. Yet, indigenous people are highly heterogeneous in their opinions, goals and practices. As noted in the Fair Trade USA public relations statement above, some indigenous communities are in fact thriving within today's global economy through their participation in fair trade networks. This is in spite of the fact that few, if any, of the fair trade certification standards established by international organizations such as Fairtrade International explicitly address indigenous rights or issues specific to indigenous peoples.[1] This chapter explores the impact of fair trade on indigenous communities across Latin America. The bulk of the existing research on this topic has focused on the significant number of successful fair trade coffee cooperatives found in Mesoamerican indigenous communities. However, case studies from Bolivia and Brazil are also included for comparative purposes.

The Latin America agricultural sector includes an estimated 65 million small farmers, the majority of whom are indigenous people belonging to more than 600 different groups (Toledo et al. 2010). Across Latin America indigenous communities suffer poverty rates much higher than their mestizo counterparts and continue to endure the lingering effects of centuries of colonialism, institutional racism and inequality. Therefore, fair trade can play a vital economic development role in many indigenous communities by helping them to access and compete in international markets. Researchers have found in many cases that fair trade's emphasis on participatory democracy through producer unions is a natural fit for indigenous communities with historical traditions of mutual aid and reciprocity. However, it is certainly not universally true that all indigenous communities reap significant benefits from fair trade participation. Therefore, this chapter also explores some of the circumstances resulting in more mixed outcomes. Finally, the fair trade movement has long relied on the images of producers to sell products. Indigeneity is often integral to such marketing campaigns. The chapter ends with a discussion of the risks and benefits of these strategic essentialisms and the politics that such practices generate for indigenous farmer organizations.

INDIGENOUS LATIN AMERICA

Defining Who Is Indigenous

Latin America's indigenous population is estimated at 51 million people, though there is some divergence depending on measurement methods. However, there is significant diversity in how these indigenous populations are concentrated: Bolivia and Guatemala have indigenous national majorities and there are majority concentrations in southern Mexico and highland and Amazonian Ecuador and Peru (Van Cott 2010). While indigenous people comprise only 11 per cent of the region's entire population, because they constitute majorities in several Latin American countries, they are in some instances a relatively powerful force in both national and international politics. Measurement is difficult because there is no universal definition of indigenous peoples. The United Nation's system has developed an understanding of this term that is based on several factors: self-identification; historical continuity with precolonial societies; strong links to territories and surrounding natural resources and economic or political systems; distinct language, culture and beliefs; and the fact that they form non-dominant groups of society who work to maintain and reproduce themselves as distinctive peoples and communities (United Nations n.d.). This rather fluid definition results from the fact that indigeneity emerges from larger social fields of difference and sameness. It acquires its meaning not from some essential properties of its own, but instead through its relation to what it is not: indigenous cultural practices, institutions and politics become such in articulation with what is not considered indigenous in the particular social formations where they exist (De la Cadena and Starn 2007, 4). Thus, indigenous identity should be thought of as a historically contingent process; a series of encounters and set of relationships rather than a fixed, static state of being.

The plight of Latin America's indigenous peoples under colonialism was documented as early as the 16th century by the Dominican Friar Bartolomé de las Casas who argued against their oppression and enslavement at the Spanish court (Stavenhagen 2013, 46). In colonial and post-colonial Latin America indigenous populations were long seen as a 'problem' by members of the political elite in their quest for economic modernization. For example, in spite of (or perhaps because of) their dependence on indigenous labor, Guatemala's elite coffee plantation owners consistently depicted the nation's Maya population as a barrier to economic modernization, stereotyping them as lazy, stupid, dirty and drunken (Handy 1984; McCreery 1995). Despite formal citizenship, across the region indigenous peoples have frequently been treated as second-class citizens and these circumstances have contributed to the dire economic conditions facing many indigenous Latin Americans today.

Poverty and Economic Development

Globally, the population of 370 million indigenous people constitutes only 5 per cent of the world's population but makes up 15 per cent of the world's poor and one-third of the world's extremely poor rural people (United Nations 2009). Latin America's income distribution is the most unequal in the world due to a highly unequal distribution of education and land combined with a rapidly expanding labor force, which together depress earnings for unskilled labor (Morley 2001). A World Bank study on indigenous people and poverty in the region concluded that poverty among Latin America's indigenous population is pervasive and severe (Hall and Patrinos 2006) and a similar study by the Inter-American Development Bank (IADB) observed that being poor and indigenous were synonymous in Latin America (IADB 2006).[2] According to the International Labor Organization (ILO), indigenous workers in Latin America make on average about half of what non-indigenous workers earn, and between 25 and 50 per cent of this income gap is due to discrimination and non-observable characteristics, such as quality of schooling (2007, 27).

Hall and Patrinos (2012) provide six principal explanations for why indigenous people suffer disproportionately higher rates of poverty: 1) spatial disadvantages and geographic characteristics ('remoteness' and lack of access to basic infrastructure); 2) human capital disadvantages, such as a lack of education and poor health; 3) asset-based shortcomings and poverty traps; 4) social exclusion and discrimination; 5) cultural and behavioral characteristics, such as the inability to speak the dominant language; and 6) institutional party dependence such that inequality is structurally reproduced via historically determined social and political relationships, exploitation and opportunity hoarding by elites. Historically, academics studying indigenous movements have privileged cultural and identity differences between groups rather than their similarities, focusing more on cultural demands than claims associated with social class and socioeconomic mobility. Consequently, one could add to the above list a seventh explanation: the fact that groups traditionally labeled indigenous and those in the process of reindigenization[3] are often encouraged to use a language based on cultural identity rather than economic rights and social justice in order to be heard (Novo 2013). In contrast, one of the strengths of fair trade as an economic development strategy is the fact that it provides training, market access and financial resources to help indigenous communities in the region to combat several of these distinct challenges.

POVERTY ALLEVIATION THROUGH FAIR TRADE IN INDIGENOUS COMMUNITIES

Mexican Coffee Cooperatives and Economic Development

This section explores how fair trade first emerged in Latin America from efforts to better link indigenous coffee producers to international markets. Mexico, the world's largest organic coffee producer (Hernandez and Ford 2010), has over 200 000 small coffee producers who occupy 770 000 hectares[4] (Martinez-Torres 2006). (On environmental issues in coffee production in Latin America, see Christopher Bacon, Robert Rice and Hannah Maryanski's chapter in this volume.) Histories of the fair trade movement often date its origins to the post-World War II era when alternative trade organizations started importing artisan products into Europe and North America. However, the contemporary certification-based fair trade market for agricultural commodities in fact has its very roots in Mexico's indigenous communities. In 1983 the members of 17 indigenous peasant communities in the Mexican state of Oaxaca formed the Union of Indigenous Communities of the Region of the Isthmus (UCIRI) in an attempt to address the fact that they were not receiving fair prices for their coffee. In 1988 they submitted a proposal to Solidaridad, a Dutch development organization, which resulted in the formation of Max Havelaar, the first fair trade certifying body (VanderHoff Boersma

2009). Simultaneously, in 1985 the Catholic Church's local cooperative commission held a seminar with Maya coffee growers in Chiapas, Mexico, to reflect on problems and seek possible solutions, resulting in the formation of the Indígenas de la Sierra Madre de Motozintla (ISMAM) cooperative. Similar efforts were also occurring in neighboring Guatemala where the 1970s witnessed an explosion of cooperative organizing in highland Maya communities (Handy 1984). In 1990 the Group of Fourteen, an alliance of small coffee producer organizations in Guatemala, formed and began to export fair trade coffee to the Dutch market through Max Havelaar (Lyon 2011).

Throughout the 1970s and 1980s a number of grassroots small-scale agriculture, credit and artisan cooperatives were formed across Latin America. Many of these were influenced by the Catholic Church's liberation theology and ideas about social justice inspired by the participatory action and mutual support structure of ecclesiastical base communities (Vásquez-León 2010) which encouraged campesinos to analyze and address the root causes of their poverty through collective effort. In working with their partners in consuming countries, the Mexican and Guatemalan coffee cooperatives offered an alternative vision for creating a just society 'in which markets provide a means for meeting human needs rather than defining the essence of what it is to be human' (VanderHoff Boersma 2009). This ethic clearly influenced the ultimate goals and practices of the emergent certification-based fair trade movement. As the section below explores, the fair trade democratic organizing principles resonated with indigenous traditions of mutual assistance and participatory democracy.

Fair Trade, Indigeneity and Social Capital

The long-term success of these fair trade coffee associations is in part due to the fact that their cooperative relations emerged within a cultural context that prioritized collaboration. Many indigenous communities in Latin America relied on autonomous forms of political and social organization under the shadow of the colonial and post-colonial state. This tradition, which continues in the present, contributed to the maintenance of local governance structures and practices of mutual assistance such as the Mesoamerican *cargo* system and communal work in the form of Mexican *tequios* or Andean *mingas*. These processes also contributed to the formation of social capital, which is defined as traditional community values and socioeconomic structures. Social capital can include collective control and sustainable management of natural resources; reciprocal and mutually supportive work systems; strong social organization and high levels of communal responsibility; and a deep respect for the knowledge of community elders (Hall and Patrinos 2012, 7). These are cultural assets found in many Mesoamerican indigenous communities and in the case of fair trade coffee markets they played an important role in the formation of cooperative economic organizations and the strategies they employed to diversify their livelihoods.

The Mesoamerican *cargo* system and 'associative corporations'

In many indigenous villages the coffee associations use a system of *cargos*, or unpaid service work performed by community members, to accomplish required tasks and maintain institutional governance (cf. Lyon 2011; Mutersbaugh 2004). Community participation in the *cargo* system has long been a central component of Maya social structure across Mesoamerica and today it articulates with the requirements for participation in transnational coffee markets. Historically, the *cargo* system consisted of civil-religious hierarchies in which male community members alternated between ranked positions in religious brotherhoods and the civil government (with critical behind-the-scenes support from their wives). Although marked differences exist between the historical *cargo* system and its current manifestations, the behavioral ideal of communalism rooted in service continues to structure expectations and reinforce community values within many Maya villages.

While these early indigenous fair trade coffee cooperatives used their existing social capital and community traditions to build a foundation for success, one should not mistake them as remnants of a timeless, pre-capitalist Maya existence. To the contrary, in important early research on ISMAM, Nigh (1997) described the coffee cooperative as an 'associative corporation' or a hybrid organizational structure, one that combined aspects of traditional Maya community democracy and the characteristics of a modern capitalist corporation. He explained how these collective organizations were based on traditional indigenous concepts of reciprocity and communitarian democracy yet had clearly defined administrative structures and business-like financial controls. In later research Martinez-Torres (2006) found that the emergence of the new pan-indigenous identity in Chiapas helped to further solidify solidarity and a sense of common purpose within coffee organizations. In turn, the social capital that indigenous cooperative members had accumulated in their organizations and networks played a critical role in helping them to survive the reconfiguration of the global coffee market and the 1989 collapse of Mexico's National Coffee Institute (INMECAFE). Therefore, while fair trade helped these indigenous coffee producers to access international markets, their success depended in large part on their own cultural traditions and existing forms of social capital within their communities.

Fair Trade and Grassroots Development in Bolivia

Beyond Mesoamerica there are other successful stories of fair trade development in indigenous communities and for comparative purposes it is useful to highlight the work being done in Bolivia. In 1994 Bolivia's Law of Popular Participation transferred 20 per cent of the national budget to the country's 311 municipalities and mandated grassroots participation in local planning and budgetary oversight (Kohl 2003). This law laid the groundwork for the development of fair trade in Bolivia because it necessitated the creation of Grassroots Territorial Organizations which, well organized and accessible, became ready recipients of aid-based business development initiatives. Stenn explains that until 2005 Bolivian fair trade existed solely within the context of foreign fair trade initiatives but in 2009 *comercio justo*, or fair trade, was introduced as a legal part of the new Bolivian constitution. In Bolivia fair trade resonates with *Suma Qamaña*, or the Aymara notion of 'wellbeing', a constitutionally mandated Andean concept of socioeconomic organization where people engage in the local community to collectively meet one another's needs (Stenn 2013, 104).

Organizational capacity building through fair trade

While Stenn is referring primarily to artisan associations, there are also examples of indigenous Bolivian farmers who have successfully participated in fair trade commodity markets, notably for coffee and quinoa. For example, Imhoff and Lee (2007) found that Bolivian fair trade coffee producers are gaining broader knowledge of production processes, mainly because they are now involved at later stages of processing and even export. The fair trade cooperatives provide members with training on coffee markets, organic production, environmental issues, administrative tasks and financial management. In essence, fair trade market participation is helping to strengthen their organizational capacity in addition to providing economic development opportunities.

Organizational capacity building is a long-term process of assessing and responding to internal strengths and weaknesses and external challenges and opportunities. It includes creating space for individuals within cooperatives to exercise and build on their existing knowledge and skills.[5] Combined, these features enhance organizations' abilities to perform activities that are central to their vision and mission (Lyon 2013). This capacity building speaks to the fact that fair trade's benefits for indigenous communities extend far beyond economic improvements. In Mexico, VanderHoff Boersma (2009) found that fair trade coffee market participation increased producers' sense of self-worth, leading to increased capacity building in the economic and social realms. Importantly, it also fostered empowerment in the political realm since members now have much more confidence in dealing with different levels of government.

Fair Trade and Human Rights in Guatemala

The above cases clearly speak to the ability of fair trade to contribute to economic development in indigenous communities. However, there is more to fair trade than market access and poverty alleviation. For example, in this volume Sally Smith explores fair trade's contributions to women's empowerment and Jennifer Keahey analyzes fair trade's mixed record in addressing racial inequalities in South Africa. Similarly, in relation to Latin America's indigenous communities it is important to note that fair trade can work to promote and protect human rights. This is accomplished via two primary channels: First, as previously discussed, the fair trade certification system requires producer groups to be democratic, transparent and accountable, which reinforces indigenous traditions of participatory democracy and mutual aid. Second, the relationships formed between producer groups and international market actors, such as coffee roasters or importers, help to promote and protect the secure organizational space that is necessary for cooperation and producer initiated community development. The freedom to organize and respect for cultural practices, both supported by fair trade, are key components of human rights compliance and are critically important in countries such as Guatemala with its history of violent repression, structural inequality and cultural discrimination against indigenous populations and community organizers.

The rapid expansion of the agricultural cooperative movement in 1970s Guatemala coincided with the increasing violence of the nation's civil war, and individuals who participated in successful community projects and development organizations consistently faced accusations that they were engaging in subversive or guerrilla activities (Sanford 2003). Close to 200 000 people were murdered during Guatemala's civil war, 83 per cent of whom were Maya who died at the hands of the Guatemalan military (CEH 1999). In the aftermath of the war, many Maya villages were understandably plagued by ongoing fear and mistrust, which served to constrain community organizing and development efforts. In researching a coffee cooperative in a Guatemalan Maya community (Lyon 2007) this author found that fair trade market participation enabled the organization to build valuable long-term partnerships with coffee roasters and importers, such as Green Mountain Coffee Roasters. Through these partnerships the cooperative gained access to information and resources that enabled it to improve coffee quality and better navigate the transnational market. However, just as importantly, these relationships forged through the fair trade market provided the cooperative with access to international arenas outside the scope of the nation-state's power and consequently relatively free from discrimination. This helped bolster the self-confidence of the Maya coffee farmers and provided them with a secure organizational space in which they were able to initiate community development projects, such as trash collection services and a tourism project, without fear of violence or oppression. (For more on fair trade, peace and conflict, see Eileen Davenport and William Low's chapter in this volume.)

Income Security amid Market Volatility

While the organizational support these exchange partners offered was critical, the cooperative's community development efforts could not be sustained without the higher and more stable prices that fair trade coffee producers earn. The guaranteed minimum price (currently US$1.60/pound) is a critical component of fair trade certification, especially for commodities with volatile markets such as coffee. In recent years international coffee prices have ranged from a 30-year low of 45 cents per pound in October 2001 to a 36-year high of three dollars per pound in April 2011 (Fairtrade International 2014) and back to a five-year low of a little over a dollar per pound in November 2013 (Almeida 2013). At the time of writing, in April 2014, the price had again risen to over two dollars per pound as a result of the Brazilian drought (Neate 2014). This extreme price volatility makes it exceedingly difficult for small coffee producers to plan for future household and production related expenses and means that they may be less willing to invest in expensive quality improvements that might help them capture a higher market price. Throughout these market reversals, the Guatemalan cooperative members have consistently earned the guaranteed minimum price (or the market price, whichever is higher), enabling them to continue repaying their debts, maintain their standard of living, retain their landholdings and pay for their children's education. According to Fairtrade International, fair trade prices act as a safety net for vulnerable smallholders, ensuring that they can continue to secure their livelihoods through coffee production (2014). The United Nations (UN) defines the right to development as an inalienable human right and asserts that human beings have an individual and collective responsibility for development (United Nations 1986). Participation in fair trade markets helps indigenous producers to collectively take responsibility for their own community development in locally appropriate political, social and economic forms (Lyon 2007).

FAIR TRADE'S MIXED OUTCOMES IN INDIGENOUS COMMUNITIES

As detailed, researchers have found in many cases that fair trade market participation has enabled indigenous communities to prosper economically while continuing to maintain cultural traditions. However, this is certainly not universally true. In some cases fair trade fails to bring significant economic benefits to participating indigenous communities. Latin America's indigenous communities are highly diverse, ranging from the highland Maya corporate communities with their long traditions of small-scale agricultural production to tribal Amazonian populations who live primarily through hunting, gathering and swidden (slash and burn) horticulture. Consequently, indigenous experiences in the fair trade market are as varied as their cultures. While fair trade has enabled many indigenous communities to capitalize upon their existing social capital in order to thrive in the transnational marketplace, other communities have experienced more mixed results. It is important to highlight some of the problems they have encountered so that the fair trade movement can better strategize about how to best meet the needs of diverse populations.

The Asuriní, AmazonCoop and The Body Shop

The experiences of the Brazilian Asuriní tribe represent an instance in which a Latin American indigenous population failed to reap sustained benefits from fair trade market participation. AmazonCoop, an organization serving approximately 2000 indigenous people living in 14 villages and representing eight tribes in a very remote part of Brazil, was founded in 1989 with the assistance of a FUNAI (National Indian Foundation) administrator (Burke 2010). The organization cultivated a market with The Body Shop for its harvested nuts. The company, an ethical trading pioneer since its founding in 1976, used the nuts in its bath and body care products.

In a study of AmazonCoop's fair trade market participation, Burke found that the partnership with The Body Shop provided significant material benefits to indigenous Brazilian nut harvesters. Interviewed members of the Asuriní tribe were unanimous that the cooperative had improved their lives by providing access to money and goods in exchange for Brazil nuts. However, the partnership also made the indigenous people more vulnerable and more dependent on outsiders, failed to include them as informed participants in their own development and perpetuated discriminatory distinctions among them (Burke 2010, 32).

Learning from AmazonCoop's mistakes

One of the key limitations AmazonCoop faced was its organizational structure which was top-heavy with decision-making authority concentrated outside of indigenous villages and, in some cases, outside of Brazil (Burke 2010, 45). There was a lack of cooperative education and genuine participation and decision-making. Consequently, cooperative members were not empowered to undertake their own self-development through the cooperative. At the same time that the organizational structure discouraged indigenous participation, the cooperative relied on identity politics and romanticized indigenous symbolism to generate income (Burke 2010, 32). While links with government agencies and international organizations facilitated access to new markets, resources and allies, The Body Shop products mythologized the indigenous producers as pristine, exotic and fragile, perpetuating a history that falsely denied their participation in over 400 years of trans-Atlantic political-economic activities (Burke 2010, 47).

This example illustrates the danger associated with imposing development strategies on indigenous communities. As opposed to the indigenous coffee producers discussed earlier, who eagerly sought out and even helped create fair trade markets, AmazonCoop did not adequately tailor the fair trade model to the distinct Amazonian context and failed to capitalize upon the existing strengths of the indigenous communities it served. Furthermore, the organization did not anticipate the fact that participation in this international market would create problematic new needs and reduce interest in traditional customs among these relatively isolated communities. Therefore, in this particular instance, while fair trade brought material benefits to the participating indigenous communities, it did not help to promote or protect cultural traditions and indigenous identity in any substantial way.

Fair Trade Quinoa

Like the case of the Asuriní and AmazonCoop, the growth in fair trade quinoa markets has resulted in mixed outcomes for Andean indigenous communities. There is a marked diversity in the organization of the commodity's production and marketing strategies and fair trade exists alongside both conventional markets and competing certifications, such as Designation of Origin (DO). Significantly, even within fair trade there is a high variability of quinoa market initiatives and it is therefore difficult to make generalizations about impacts (Cáceres et al. 2007). The case of the Lipeño *quinueros*, outlined below, demonstrates the limitations of a one-size-fits-all approach to fair trade and it serves as an important reminder that beyond the politics of competing certification regimes rests a highly diverse fair trade movement. (For more on fair trade politics see Elizabeth Bennett's chapter in this volume.)

Quinoa market growth

Quinoa, an indigenous, protein-packed grain grown in one of Bolivia's more isolated regions, has successfully populated international markets. Bolivia's quinoa export market grew 26 per cent between 2011 and 2012 in a trade worth more than US$800 million (the majority is exported to the United States) (Stocker 2013). The United Nations even named 2013 'The Year of Quinoa'. Yet, unlike other fair trade crops, such as coffee and cocoa, quinoa is not a traditional export product. Of the 70 000 quinoa producers in Bolivia's northern Altiplano, 80 per cent are farmers with limited economic resources practicing small-scale subsistence agriculture who use between 70 and 85 per cent of their crop for household consumption (Cáceres et al. 2007). Therefore, this market success story is accompanied by growing fears that the grain, an indigenous staple, will become too expensive and scarce for consumers closer to home. In response to the numerous media reports raising these concerns over the past two years, the founder of Alter Eco wrote that 'it's OK to eat (fair trade certified) quinoa' (Rollet 2013). Alter Eco has been working with fair trade quinoa producer organizations, such as the National Association of Quinoa Producers (ANAPQUI), in the Bolivian Altiplano since 2002 and Rollet argues that access to fair trade markets has helped farmers to invest in quality and productivity, increase household incomes, diversify livelihoods, improve access to schooling and diversify their diets. However, in contrast Ofstehage (2012) found that fair trade offered little real change for indigenous quinoa farmers due to the relatively low minimum guaranteed price (currently US$2250/metric ton).

Quinoa production in Los Lípez, Bolivia

Ofstehage worked with farmers in the Los Lípez region of the Southern Altiplano who have formed the Mancomunidad de la Gran Tierra de Los Lípez, a regional governance organization with a central focus on the quinoa business. Mancomunidad works to differentiate the region's farmers from the mass of Bolivian *quinueros* (quinoa growers) on the basis of non-mechanized farming and Lipeño farmer identity. People in Lípez maintain that their quinoa has unique mythological origins (having been given to the people by the god Nusta Juira), different needs as a crop and distinct farming traditions (Ofstehage 2011). The Mancomunidad was granted a DO for 'quinoa real de Lípez' in 2009, a DO understood by local *quinueros* in San Agustín in terms of identity and ownership: social labor, cultural know-how and personal sacrifices are all materialized in their quinoa. Because cooperatives aggregate local quinoa production and sell it to the national fair trade quinoa cooperative, ANAPQUI, the fair trade market was viewed by the indigenous farmers as a loss of their quinoa's important identity because at the cooperative level it was combined with that grown by other producers across the region.

In San Agustín, quinoa farmers actively work to create new market channels, rather than simply embracing fair trade networks, since this offers them a measure of control in the market while enriching their work and trade and expressing broad moral visions of the community and nation (Ofstehage 2012, 442). What is particularly unique about the quinoa case is that it is a product grown primarily by indigenous farmers that has experienced exponential market growth over a relatively short period of time. Consequently, *quinueros* have rapidly mobilized their values and interests through the marketplace. Ofstehage maintains that the farmers use their fluid market channels to frame and reframe fair trade and solidarity in different ways, rather than simply adopting the definitions provided by the international certifiers and ANAPQUI.

This is not necessarily an example of how fair trade has 'failed' these quinoa farmers. On the contrary, it represents the development of an indigenous and locally meaningful concept of fair trade. Even when selling their quinoa outside of fair trade channels, these farmers have adopted many of the core principles of fair trade (fair and stable prices, links between producers and consumers, democratic governance and opportunities for economically disadvantaged producers). These values are becoming endogenous to the emerging regional economy constructed by farmers, cooperatives, intermediaries and activists (Ofstehage 2012, 446). The case of the Lipeño *quinueros* demonstrates the limitations of a narrowly defined vision and one-size-fits-all approach to fair trade and it serves as an important reminder that beyond the politics of competing certification regimes lies a fair trade movement that is much more than a simple and singular market.

Fair Trade's Strategic Essentialisms

As several of the above cases have alluded, fair trade products have a seemingly innate tendency towards romanticized marketing imagery. In contrast to most consumer goods, fair trade products are inherently linked with the remote regions where they were produced, making distant landscapes an integral part of fair trade packaging and marketing (Wright 2004). This type of imagery can be employed by indigenous producers as a form of strategic essentialism, or a form of self-presentation. Strategic essentialisms sometimes take the form of self-commodification, or a set of beliefs and practices in which an individual chooses to construct a marketable identity product while striving to avoid alienating him or herself (Bunten 2008).

There are many successful examples across Latin America where indigenous groups have harnessed the romantic imagery which fuels fair trade market growth for their own advantage. For example, the members of the ISMAM coffee cooperative, detailed above, have used an evocation of a past harmony with nature as cultural capital in the global market (Hernández Castillo and Nigh 1998) while coffee grower organizations across Chiapas have successfully used their identity as a 'marketing hook' in the world market (Martinez-Torres 2006, 76). The case of the Bolivian quinoa producers, discussed above, could also be understood as an attempt by farmers to ensure that their identities, skills and cultural meanings inhere to their product in a meaningful way, something they were forced to accomplish outside fair trade channels which, in this case, celebrate generic indigenous Bolivian farmers. Varul (2008) demonstrates how the romanticization of commodified agricultural and artisanal producers is integral to fair trade's market strategy and the crafting of authenticity. He shows how in fair trade Third World citizens are imagined as suffering, simple and benevolent, and that such depictions have implications for equity. He argues that fair trade is about what is *perceived* to be simple manual labor power that *seems* to be relatively easy to calculate; however, this rendering erases the skills involved in farming, processing and marketing fair trade products (cf. Adams and Raisborough 2011).

Taking advantage of strategic essentialism

As demonstrated in the case of AmazonCoop, when strategic essentialisms are deployed outside the control of indigenous peoples themselves it can result in the reification of harmful and inaccurate stereotypes. Therefore, in order to use strategic essentialisms to their advantage, it is clear that indigenous groups must carefully work to maintain control over their market representations and work to translate these into lasting economic relationships. For example, among some indigenous coffee producers in Guatemala, essentialized portrayals of Maya identity have become a central component of market success (Lyon 2011). However, cooperative members have worked to remain active agents in the construction and presentation of their identity like other Latin American indigenous people who embrace the use of strategically essentialized representations of cultural authenticity to facilitate tourism and artisan sales rather than political or cultural goals (cf. Little 2004; Stephen 2005; Zorn 2004). In this case the relationship between market success and Maya identity is dialogical. While indigenous identity certainly provides a market advantage, participation in the fair trade market and a cooperative that combines cultural norms of reciprocity and contemporary business practices contributes to the preservation and promotion of local cultural traditions. At the same time, fair trade market participation provides international validation of Maya cultural traditions, historically denigrated within the Guatemalan nation-state (Lyon 2011).

Burke (2010) outlines two clear steps that indigenous producers can take to ensure that strategic essentialisms work to their advantage: first, they should use the power and publicity gained through essentialism to frame issues in political-economic dynamics rather than cultural frames and, second, they should work to institutionalize the partnerships created through strategic essentialisms so that they are likely to endure. Fair trade organizations also have a responsibility to ensure that marketing materials employing images and descriptions of indigenous producers are culturally appropriate and approved by the people themselves prior to circulation. This will hopefully ensure that harmful stereotypes are not reproduced and that existing strategic essentialisms work to the advantage rather than detriment of indigenous communities.

CONCLUSION

The United Nations named 2005–2015 the Second International Decade of the World's Indigenous People with the hope of promoting five main objectives: 1) including indigenous peoples in the design and implementation of laws, policies, resources and projects; 2) promoting full and effective participation of indigenous peoples in decisions affecting their lives and customs; 3) redefining development policies around ideas of equity and cultural appropriateness; 4) adopting targeted policies for the development of indigenous peoples; and 5) developing strong monitoring mechanisms and enhancing accountability (United Nations

2004). Unfortunately, although important progress has been made in the political arena (e.g., the 2007 passing of the UN Declaration on the Rights of Indigenous People), indigenous people around the world still suffer from the consequences of disproportionately high poverty rates as detailed at the start of this chapter. Consequently, while the official decade is soon coming to a close, critical work remains to be completed, especially within the arena of economic development.

Fair trade has been proven to be an avenue for culturally appropriate economic development in indigenous communities in Latin America. One goal of this chapter is to explicitly recognize the important role that the fair trade movement has played in improving economic circumstances, building organizational capacity and protecting human rights among indigenous producers. However, the fair trade movement needs to work diligently to solidify and extend these efforts in the years to come in order to ensure sustained positive impact in indigenous communities. In further developing fair trade market opportunities for indigenous producers, it is critical that they are included in the design and implementation of projects and the decision making that affects their lives and cultural traditions. As part of this process communities should be given an opportunity to cultivate and maintain indigenous forms of fair trade alongside formal certification regimes where appropriate. Fair trade retailers, producers and advocates also must work to ensure that the movement's strategic deployment of essentialized images of producers, especially indigenous ones, works to their advantage rather than reinforces harmful cultural stereotypes. Under these circumstances fair trade will undoubtedly continue to alleviate poverty through culturally appropriate forms of economic development among indigenous producers in Latin America and beyond.

NOTES

1. Fairtrade International does require companies to respect the rights of indigenous peoples and their standards are grounded on ILO Convention C169 (Indigenous and Tribal Peoples Convention) (Fairtrade International 2013).
2. According to the United Nations Development Program's 2010 Regional Human Development Report on inequality, rates of extreme poverty (living on less than a dollar/day) are twice as high among the region's indigenous peoples (Freeman 2012).
3. Reindigenization is a process of reasserting indigenous identity and cultural practices that existed prior to processes of colonization.
4. Close to two million acres.
5. This definition builds on the United Nations Development Program's description of community capacity building (United Nations 2006).

REFERENCES

Adams, Matthew and Jayne Raisborough (2011), 'Encountering the Fairtrade farmer: Solidarity, stereotypes and the self-control ethos', *Papers on Social Representations*, 20 (8), 1–21.

Almeida, Isis (2013), 'Coffee falls to five-year low on growing supplies; cocoa climbs', available at http://www.bloomberg.com/news/2013-11-05/coffee-falls-to-five-year-low-on-growing-supplies-cocoa-climbs.html (accessed 14 April 2014).

Bunten, Alexis C. (2008), 'Sharing culture or selling out? Developing the commodified persona in the heritage industry', *American Ethnologist*, 35 (3), 380–395.

Burke, Brian J. (2010), 'Cooperatives for "fair globalization"? Indigenous people, cooperatives, and corporate social responsibility in the Brazilian Amazon', *Latin American Perspectives*, 37 (6), 30–54.

Cáceres, Zina, Aurélie Carimentrand and John Wilkinson (2007), 'Fair trade and quinoa from the southern Bolivian Altiplano', in Laura T. Raynolds, Douglas Murray and John Wilkinson (eds.), *Fair Trade: The Challenges of Transforming Globalization*, New York: Routledge, pp. 180–199.

CEH (1999), '*Guatemala*: *Memoria del silencio*: *Conclusions and recommendations*', Guatemala City: Comision para el Esclarecimiento Historico, United Nations.

De la Cadena, Marisol and Orin Starn (2007), 'Introduction to indigenous experience today', in Marisol De la Cadena and Orin Starn (eds.), *Indigenous Experience Today*, New York: Berg, pp. 1–32.

Fair Trade USA (2011), 'Fair trade empowers indigenous communities', available at http://fairtradeusa.org/blog/fair-trade-empowers-indigenous-communities# (accessed 21 October 2014).

Fairtrade International (2013), 'Standards document', available at http://www.fairtrade.net/fileadmin/user_upload/content/2009/standards/documents/2013_05_06_EN_FT_HL_DRAFT_standard.pdf (accessed 23 January 2014).

Fairtrade International (2014), 'Coffee', available at http://www.fairtrade.net/coffee.html (accessed 14 April 2014).

Freeman, Ethan (2012), 'Poverty rates strikingly high among indigenous populations', available at http://www.ipsnews.net/2012/06/poverty-rates-strikingly-high-among-indigenous-populations/ (accessed 24 January 2014).

Hall, Gillette and Harry Anthony Patrinos (2006), *Indigenous Peoples, Poverty and Human Development in Latin America*: 1994–2004, London: Palgrave Macmillan.

Hall, Gillette H. and Harry Patrinos (2012), *Indigenous Peoples, Poverty, and Development*, New York: Cambridge University Press.

Handy, Jim (1984), *Gift of the Devil: A History of Guatemala*, Boston, MA: South End Press.

Hernandez, Gabriel and Mark Ford (2010), 'Mexico corners the market on organic coffee production', available at http://gain.fas.usda.gov/Recent%20GAIN%20Publications/Coffee%20Annual_Mexico%20City_Mexico_5-24-2010.pdf (accessed 14 April 2014).

Hernández Castillo, Rosalva and Ronald Nigh (1998), 'Global processes and local identity among Mayan coffee growers in Chiapas Mexico', *American Anthropologist*, 100 (1), 136–147.

IADB (2006), 'Operational policy on indigenous peoples and strategy for indigenous development', available at http://publications.iadb.org/handle/11319/2631 (accessed 21 October 2014).

Imhoff, Sandra and Andrew Lee (2007), 'Assessing the potential of fair trade for poverty reduction and conflict prevention: A case study of Bolivian coffee producers', available at http://www.swisspeace.ch/fileadmin/user_upload/Media/Topics/Further_Topics/Business_and_Peace/

Imhof_Sandra_Assessing_the_Potential_of_Fair_Trade_for_Poverty_Reduction_and_Conflict_Prevention.pdf (accessed 23 December 2013).

International Labour Organization (ILO) (2007), 'Equality at work: Tackling the challenges', Global Report under the follow-up to the ILO Declaration on Fundamental Principles and Rights at Work, Report of the Director General, International Labour Conference 96th Session, Geneva: ILO.

Kohl, Benjamin (2003), 'Democratizing decentralization in Bolivia: The Law of Popular Participation', *Journal of Planning Education and Research*, 23 (2), 153–164.

Little, Walter (2004), *Mayas in the Marketplace: Tourism, Globalization and Cultural Identity*, Austin, TX: University of Texas Press.

Lyon, Sarah (2007), 'Fair trade coffee and human rights in Guatemala', *Journal of Consumer Policy*, 30 (3), 241–261.

Lyon, Sarah (2011), *Coffee and Community: Maya Farmers and Fair Trade Markets*, Boulder, CO: University Press of Colorado.

Lyon, Sarah (2013), 'Coffee tourism and community development in Guatemala', *Human Organization*, 72 (3), 188–198.

Martinez-Torres, Maria Elena (2006), *Organic Coffee: Sustainable Development by Mayan Farmers*, Columbus, OH: Ohio University Press.

McCreery, David (1995), 'Wage labor, free labor, and vagrancy laws: The transition to capitalism in Guatemala, 1920–1945', in William Roseberry, Lowell Gudmundson and Mario Samper Kutschbach (eds.), *Coffee, Society and Power in Latin America*, Baltimore, MD: Johns Hopkins University Press, pp. 206–231.

Morley, Samuel (2001), *The Income Distribution Problem in Latin America*, Santiago de Chile: CEPAL.

Mutersbaugh, Tad (2004), 'Serve and certify: Paradoxes of service work in organic-coffee certification', *Environment and Planning: Society and Space*, 22 (4), 533–552.

Neate, Rupert (2014), 'Drought in Brazil drives the price of coffee beans to a record high', available at http://www.theguardian.com/world/2014/apr/10/drought-brazil coffee-beans-prices (accessed 11 April 2014).

Nigh, Ronald (1997), 'Organic agriculture and globalization: A Maya associative corporation in Chiapas, Mexico', *Human Organization*, 56 (4), 427–436.

Novo, Carmen Martinez (2013), 'Why are indigenous organizations declining in Latin America', in Ann T. Jordan and Douglas Caulkins (eds.), *A Companion to Organizational Anthropology*, New York: Blackwell Publishing, pp. 471–492.

Ofstehage, Andrew (2011), 'Nusta Juira's gift of quinoa: Peasants, trademarks, and intermediaries in the transformation of a Bolivian commodity economy', *Anthropology of Work Review*, 32 (2), 103–114.

Ofstehage, Andrew (2012), 'The construction of an alternative quinoa economy: Balancing solidarity, household needs, and profit in San Agustín, Bolivia', *Agriculture and Human Values*, 29 (4), 441–454.

Rollet, Edouard (2013), 'It's OK to eat (Fair Trade Certified) quinoa', available at http://fairtradeusa.org/blog/it-s-ok-eat-fair-trade-certified-quinoa (accessed 14 April 2014).

Sanford, Victoria (2003), *Buried Secrets: Truth and Human Rights in Guatemala*, New York: Palgrave Macmillan.

Stavenhagen, Rodolfo (2013), *The Emergence of Indigenous Peoples*, New York: Springer.

Stenn, Tamara L. (2013), *The Cultural and Political Intersection of Fair Trade and Justice: Managing a Global Industry*, New York: Palgrave Macmillan.

Stephen, Lynne (2005), *Zapotec Women: Gender, Class and Ethnicity in Globalized Oaxaca*, Durham, NC: Duke University Press.

Stocker, Ed (2013), 'Quinoa: Good for you – bad for Bolivians', *The Independent*, 26 June 2013, available at http://www.independent.co.uk/life-style/food-and-drink/features/quinoa-good-for-you–bad-for-bolivians-8675455.html (accessed 30 January 2014).

Toledo, V.M., E. Boege and N. Barrera-Basols (2010), 'The biocultural heritage of Mexico: An overview', *Landscape*, 3, 6–10.

United Nations (1986), 'Declaration on the right to development', available at http://www.un.org/documents/ga/res/41/a41r128.htm (accessed 12 April 2014).

United Nations (2004), 'Second international decade of the world's indigenous people', available at http://undesadspd.org/IndigenousPeoples/SecondDecade.aspx (accessed 31 January 2014).

United Nations (2006), 'Definition of basic concepts and terminologies in governance and public administration', Committee of Experts on Public Administration, available at http://unpan1.un.org/intradoc/ (accessed 14 April 2014).

United Nations (2009), 'State of the world's indigenous peoples', available at, http://www.un.org/esa/socdev/unpfii/documents/SOWIP_web.pdf (accessed 13 December 2013).

United Nations (n.d.), 'Indigenous people, indigenous voices fact sheet', available at http://www.un.org/esa/socdev/unpfii/documents/5session_factsheet1.pdf (accessed 23 January 2014).

Van Cott, Donna Lee (2010), 'Indigenous peoples' politics in Latin America', *Annual Review of Political Science*, 13, 385–405.

VanderHoff Boersma, Francisco (2009), 'The urgency and necessity of a different type of market: The perspective of producers organized within the fair trade market', *Journal of Business Ethics*, 86 (S1), 51–61.

Varul, Matthew Zick (2008), 'Consuming the campesino: Fair trade marketing between recognition and romantic commodification', *Cultural Studies*, 22 (5), 654–679.

Vásquez-León, Marcela (2010), 'Walking the tightrope: Latin American agricultural cooperatives and small-farmer participation in global markets', *Latin American Perspectives*, 37 (6), 3–11.

Wright, Caroline (2004), 'Consuming lives, consuming landscapes: Interpreting advertisements for Cafédirect coffees', *Journal of International Development*, 16 (5), 665–680.

Zorn, Elayne (2004), *Weaving a Future: Tourism, Cloth and Culture on an Andean Island*, Iowa City: University of Iowa Press.

25. Fair trade and racial equity in Africa

Jennifer Keahey

INTRODUCTION*

> If by integration you understand a breakthrough into white society by blacks, an assimilation and acceptance of blacks into an already established set of norms and code of behavior set up by and maintained by whites, then YES I am against it. I am against the superior-inferior white-black stratification that makes the white a perpetual teacher and the black a perpetual pupil (and a poor one at that) … If on the other hand by integration you mean there shall be free participation by all members of a society, catering for the full expression of the self in a freely changing society as determined by the will of the people, then I am with you. (Biko 1978, 24)

Do Fairtrade markets offer an avenue for free participation in which all members, regardless of their race, ethnicity or creed can directly influence the rules of exchange; or are producers of color largely relegated to the status of perpetual pupil as they struggle to learn about and comply with a certification system over which they have little control? Using Biko's concerns about integration as a framework for examining the racial dimensions of Fairtrade participation, in this chapter I clarify how certification is both reinforcing and transcending longstanding disparities. Providing evidence from the African continent[1] I argue that while Fairtrade is not immune from the savage inequities found in the global economy, certified markets offer a viable space for building interracial solidarity as African networks tackle the racial hierarchy in production and trade.

African Fairtraders are addressing racial imbalances in two important ways. First, continental actors are developing African markets in order to transcend the colonial division of labor that has limited African industry to a model of primary production for Northern consumption. Having launched domestic markets in South Africa and Kenya, groups are establishing intra-continental exchanges that will enable African consumers to purchase certified items manufactured in multiple African nations (Fairtrade Africa 2013; Fairtrade International 2013a). Second, South African certifiers have incorporated broad-based black economic empowerment (BEE) protocols into national hired-labor standards in order to reduce racial inequalities on farms. This move requires South African estates to comply with governmental BEE legislation in addition to international Fairtrade requirements (Kruger and du Toit 2007). While Fairtrade standards prohibit racial discrimination on farms (Fairtrade International 2007), BEE requirements stipulate the gradual transfer of skills, management and ownership to people of color who were forcibly excluded from land and markets during the apartheid era (Department of Trade and Industry 2009).

These developments suggest the potential for the fair trade movement to challenge racial disparities wrought by slavery, apartheid and colonialism, but certified markets are generating mixed outcomes (Raynolds and Keahey 2014). Anne Tallontire's chapter in this volume argues that African fair trade is failing to deliver on its empowerment agenda despite 'islands of good practice'. Likewise, the chapter by Valerie Nelson and Adrienne Martin discusses how the benefits of participation are not substantial enough to reduce poverty. Product certification supports members in the form of minimum pricing guarantees and social premiums for community development (Raynolds, Murray and Wilkinson 2007), but producers must assume the cost of regulatory compliance and there is evidence that Fairtrade's least-advantaged members are being compelled to submit to a regulatory system that they do not understand and cannot influence (Daviron and Vagneron 2011). Moreover, research on Africa is uncovering how certification processes replicate racial hierarchies in cases where white experts dictate the terms of compliance to poor people of color (Dolan 2010). I posit that these issues derive from the movement's differing approaches to producer engagement as discussed in the section below.

BENEVOLENCE VERSUS SOLIDARITY TRADE

Gendron and colleagues (2009, 65) state that multiple social movements converged to generate a strategy of 'benevolence trade' that later became known as fair trade. This analytical strategy helps the authors clarify the trajectory of movement institutionalization, shedding light into the conflict between the fair trade's commercial and radical poles. Yet the absorption of fair trade's diverse roots – which included political solidarity movements – under the general moniker of benevolence trade obscures differing movement approaches in relation to praxis. Benevolence trade implies a system that is set up and maintained by elite actors in a spirit of charitable generosity whereas solidarity trade invokes the language of mutual interest and collective action. By distinguishing between benevolence and solidarity activism, scholars may uncover the hidden assumptions driving fair trade's commercial and developmental activities in order to examine critical equity dimensions such as race, gender and social class.

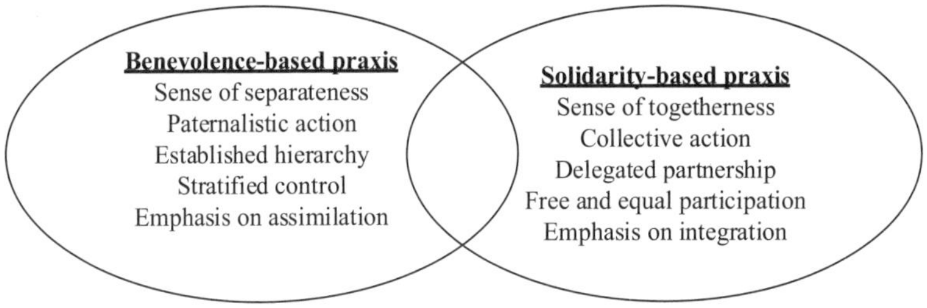

Figure 25.1 Distinguishing between benevolence and solidarity activism

In practice the distinction between benevolence and solidarity activism is often blurred; thus Figure 25.1 presents these as ideal types. Whereby hard paternalism involves the blatant control of one over another as in the slave–master relationship, soft paternalism is less overtly oppressive and may be embedded in benevolence-based approaches where established hierarchies inform engagement. Soft forms of paternalism occur when dominant actors attempt to influence the choices of subordinates in order to improve their situations (Boluk 2011); and libertarian paternalism can represent an equitable division of labor where one party agrees to be assisted by another for the benefit of both (Thaler and Sunstein 2003). However, when profound inequalities are present, such forms of paternalism are marked by subtle expressions of power that replicate underlying assumptions of superiority and inferiority.

With its lack of emphasis on equal ownership, benevolence activism may promote a culture of assimilation, replicating racial divisions. Yet solidarity activists are using certification as a platform to achieve more significant political transformations and fair trade coalitions and networks are increasingly diverse. If fair trade's failure is that its participatory language is not always translated into praxis (Gendron, Bisaillon and Rance 2009), its opportunity lies in the movement's ability to open space for transnational dialogue and collaborative actions (Del Felice 2012). To foster the expansion of solidarity-based exchanges, networks must welcome a reflexive examination of the racial dimensions impacting engagement.

THE POLITICAL ECONOMY OF AFRICAN TRADE

The colonial division of labor lies at the root of Africa's historical inability to profit from global markets and it continues to inform African production today. Regions throughout the global South became producers for Northern markets during an era of European ascendance, but the colonial division of labor has persisted in African economic structures more so than in other parts of the world. This is primarily due to: 1) the fractured nature of African colonization; 2) the small size of many newly independent nation states that conformed to colonial rather than cultural boundaries; and 3) the post-colonial transfer of power to local elites whose wealth depended upon maintaining exports to their former colonizers (Barratt Brown 2007).

African globalization has not been marked by a process of integration. Rather it is characterized by 'highly selective and spatially encapsulated forms of global connection combined with widespread disconnection and exclusion' (Ferguson 2006, 14). The rise of voluntary standards and certifications are helping African businesses increase their product value, but these transformations appear to be benefiting powerful firms at the expense of marginalized groups (Gibbon and Ponte 2005). Indeed most African producers remain trapped in a cycle of low-value production (Barratt Brown 2007).

South Africa's political economy differs from that of the broader continent due to its distinct pattern of colonial settlement, but there are racial parallels. By the early 20th century South Africa had become a self-governing union with a settled white population that collaborated in excluding people of color from lands, markets and rights (Thompson 2001). When the Afrikaner National Party came into power in 1948 it instituted a system of apartheid that mandated white supremacy, and this racist system of governance persisted into the 1990s when it collapsed due to protracted political and economic crises (Feinstein 2005).

The apartheid-era government effectively maintained the colonial division of labor by removing black and colored (mixed-race) South Africans to homelands where they would serve as a base of cheap laborers for white development (Thompson 2001). While the post-apartheid government has invested in infrastructure and services for its formerly disenfranchised citizens, more than half of South Africans live in poverty and stark racial disparities remain. White South Africans have traditionally controlled over 90 per cent of the nation's land and post-apartheid efforts at land reform have failed to deliver demonstrable changes, forcing most agriculturalists of color to remain in positions of servitude (Ntsebeza and Hall 2007).

South African inequities are paralleled in the exploitive trading relations that continue to shape broader African experiences with globalization. In this context fair trade seeks to address disparities by promoting trading relations that ensure a better deal for member producers. In the following section I detail the innovative strategies that Fairtraders are developing to reduce the racial hierarchy in African production and trade.

AFRICAN FAIRTRADE

Southern groups have played a pivotal role in forming the fair trade movement (Low and Davenport 2005) and continue to shape global praxis (Kruger and du Toit 2007; Wilkinson and Mascarenhas 2007). Having achieved rapid growth in production to become Fairtrade's second-largest producer region,[2] Africa is increasingly central to global movement functioning (Fairtrade Africa 2011; Raynolds and Keahey 2009).

Despite active Southern involvement, Fairtrade's certification system is replicating a sense of racial separateness that stems from structural inequalities. As certifiers codify ethical modes of production for market gain, they may inadvertently lock producers into a system of surveillance that fetishizes their involvement (Fridell 2007). Fairtrade advertising bears a stark resemblance to colonial-era market campaigns that presented exotic and smiling subjects in order to normalize a system of racial hierarchy by attesting to 'the ethical and moral nature of the product' (Ramamurthy 2012, 1471). Certain forms of Fairtrade producer engagement likewise reinforce a sense of racial hierarchy: research on Kenya finds that white overseers are informing black tea pickers what they must do in order to justify the morality of Fairtrade (Dolan 2010). In the following two sub-sections I discuss how African organizations are working to address racial disparities and clarify the challenges involved in transforming inequitable systems of praxis.

Pan-African Solidarity

Fairtrade Africa was established in 2005 to generate continental growth, and one of its first moves was to develop a joint Africa plan in conjunction with Fairtrade International. As part of this process the organization has supported producer-initiated efforts to institute standards for indigenous items such as marula and baobab oils (Fairtrade International 2011). Fairtrade Africa also communicates regional debates to global entities and seeks culturally grounded solutions for local concerns.

Fairtrade Africa states that it is in a unique position to influence policy, and that capacity building should include grassroots political training to ensure that certification operates as a 'development approach' instead of as a 'policing approach'.[3] In 2013 it became the first Southern entity to assume regional control over Fairtrade producer services, a governance function traditionally managed from Fairtrade International's headquarters in Bonn, Germany (Fairtrade International 2013a). The organization has expanded its regional networks to develop more effective support mechanisms for its growing producer base. Moreover, Fairtrade Africa views its producer members as market entrepreneurs rather than as development beneficiaries, and the organization is working to ensure a client-based approach to support.[4]

With its regional networks now functioning, Fairtrade Africa is prioritizing pan-African commerce by convening Fairtrade actors who are interested in shortening the value chain via the formation of direct trading linkages between African nations. According to its 2010 Executive Director, Fairtrade operatives 'must shift ideologically from thinking of the West as consumers and [Africans] as producers'.[5] This entails Africanizing fair trade by restructuring colonial trade patterns that dictate international trade agreements and inform Africa's industrial infrastructure.

Continental activism tends to ignore the topic of race in favor of a business-oriented discourse that emphasizes pan-African leadership and unity. Yet leaders are working to liberate Africa's position in the global economy, and as Fairtrade Africa assumes control over producer services, its client-based approach may help reduce the prevalence of paternalistic interventions. Further research is necessary to determine the efficacy of these changes, but the impact of African networks is growing. As I discuss in the following section, South African operatives have pioneered Fairtrade racial equity protocols that represent 'an unprecedented, and to date unrepeated national level negotiation of "fairness"' (Herman 2012, 1124).

South Africa's Empowerment Alliance

In South Africa the racial hierarchy in production has generated a system of farm paternalism whereby impoverished laborers of color work for a white elite who maintain control of the land and resources (du Toit 1993; 2005). To address racial imbalances on South African farms, local stakeholders have worked with Fairtrade International to integrate national-level BEE regulations within Fairtrade's hired-labor standards (Kruger and du Toit 2007). Although BEE is a matter of national law, the post-apartheid government is unable to effectively monitor compliance and firms often fail to meet BEE codes. With its well-developed auditing system, Fairtrade engages the partnership to ameliorate compliance issues on its certified estates (Richey and Ponte 2011).

The alliance has benefited multiple groups. White farm owners profit from their commitment to racial equity via access to lucrative certified markets and government grants for leadership and skills training (Linton 2012). Farmworkers are able to invest in development projects for their communities as well as secure knowledge, skills and, in some cases, farm shares (Jari, Snowball and Fraser 2013); and the alliance has engendered laudable successes in South Africa's wine sector, where some estates are now black owned (Herman 2012). Finally, Fairtrade governance has benefited from the alliance as well. Without the integration of BEE, South African Fairtraders would have legitimated the racial exploitation occurring on South African farms, damaging movement credibility (Kruger and du Toit 2007).

Fairtrade certifiers note that BEE protocols are difficult to meet as estates must demonstrate steps towards black ownership.[6] In many cases the alliance is failing to shift ownership and managerial responsibility to people of color (Fairtrade Foundation 2010). As BEE promotes an individualized model of self-improvement, it enriches a few without addressing the structural conditions that leave most people of color in positions of servitude (du Toit, Kruger and Ponte 2008). In this sense BEE fails to achieve meaningful change, while exacerbating racial tensions. Whereas supporters view BEE as an opportunity for people of color to gain equitable footing in white-dominated industries, detractors view it as a zero-sum game that empowers blacks by taking from whites. As one informant explains, 'people think it is about buying whites out of business. For us it is about blacks buying into business.'[7]

It must be remembered that egregious labor violations – including modern forms of slavery – are occurring within global production networks (Van den Anker 2004). Fairtrade certification is failing to address the root causes of poverty and underdevelopment in Africa, but membership does make a difference to the lives of individual producers (Manokha 2004). In South Africa, farmworkers continue to face highly exploitative production practices (Smith 2011), and in this context membership has helped laborers secure better conditions. Moreover, South African Fairtraders have achieved modest successes in relation to black ownership, and the BEE alliance provides a 'broader conceptualization of empowerment than does Fairtrade alone' (Herman 2012, 1129). Perhaps South Africa's most significant contribution to the global movement lies in its willingness to grapple with the question of race and to incorporate protocols that challenge systemic white privilege.

There is one group that may not be profiting from Fairtrade's empowerment alliance: small-scale producers. BEE protocols are designed to support farmworkers on large estates rather than producers on small farms. Yet South African farmers of color are establishing their own enterprises by renting or buying small plots of land, forming into cooperatives and seeking smallholder certification (Jari, Snowball and Fraser 2013; Raynolds and Ngcwangu 2010). Although these cooperatives are owned and operated by people of color, neither Fairtrade nor governmental operatives have problematized BEE in the context of small-scale production. In the following section I employ the case of rooibos tea to examine the impact of Fairtrade on small-scale producers of color, arguing that certification processes and practices are replicating numerous structural disparities, diminishing the potential for interracial collaboration and broad-based solidarity.

THE CASE OF SOUTH AFRICAN ROOIBOS TEA

South Africa's post-apartheid government denotes farmers of color as emerging in recognition of their ongoing exclusion from land and markets (Cousins 2010). Despite 18 years of redistributive land reform policies only 8 per cent of commercial farmland has been transferred to people of color, making it difficult for these populations to enter agricultural markets (Aliber and Cousins 2013). Nevertheless, colored[8] rooibos farmers have become South Africa's first small-scale producers to join the Fairtrade system (Raynolds and Ngcwangu 2010).

In addition to critical land shortages, this population faces a series of structural inequalities that make it challenging to profit from Fairtrade membership, including: 1) an atmosphere of unproductive competition due to the entry of large white-owned estates into certified rooibos markets; 2) the bifurcated regulatory distinction between hired-labor and smallholder production which may segregate producers of color into less profitable modes of production; and 3) insufficient levels of support, often delivered in the form of top-down interventions that perpetuate a culture of soft paternalism.

First, the decision of Fairtrade International to implement hired-labor standards for rooibos has negatively impacted cooperatives. The demand for certified tea is approximately 300 tons and total cooperative production approximates 250 tons per annum.[9] Had Fairtrade International restricted the rooibos exchange to cooperative-based production as small-scale farmers anticipated, it would have achieved production and market balance. Instead, newly certified estates flooded Fairtrade markets with cheap tea, and this glut led to the collapse of South Africa's largest cooperative, which had been expanding production in order to meet estimated demand.[10] With few buyers specifically seeking cooperative tea, small-scale groups that previously collaborated with one another to grow Fairtrade markets were compelled to compete for buyers.[11]

Second, some emerging rooibos farmers would like to engage Fairtrade membership as a commercialization vector and feel constrained by the regulatory distinction between Fairtrade International's hired-labor and smallholder standards. Certifiers are willing to support such goals by working with larger-scale farmers who wish to certify under hired-labor protocols.[12] However, most emerging farmers lack the land and resources to establish themselves as independent estates under Fairtrade's hired-labor standards. The Fairtrade system may not be able to resolve the complex structural barriers preventing emerging producers from commercializing in the same way as their white peers have done, but its dual-standard system may inadvertently exacerbate racial divisions, particularly in cases such as rooibos, where standards exist for both groups.

Although Fairtrade International's dual-standard system is race neutral in design, in practice it serves to segregate white farmers from producers of color despite their membership in the same movement. Some small-scale producers believe certification locks people of color into dependent production roles, either as estate-based farmworkers or as cooperative-based producers. These respondents note with some bitterness that white farmers are able to enter the Fairtrade system as independent estates with sufficient land and resources to dominate certified markets.[13] Rooibos cooperatives thereby struggle to surmount the challenges of having to operate in a bifurcated system where hired-labor estates are not required to operate cooperatively with the broader production base.

Third, participation does not guarantee a change in racial relations when small-scale producers lack technical skills and confidence (Linton 2012). Both Fairtrade regulations and global markets are complex, and producers require access to long-term and broad-based training if they are to succeed (Moseley 2008; Raynolds and Keahey 2014). Small-scale rooibos farmers have received insufficient levels of support, often in the form of singular training sessions with varying numbers of attendees. Many are disenchanted with the development process, feeling that they represent mere 'numbers' to be counted by external experts who are not interested in listening to their concerns.[14]

Cooperatives have a long history in South Africa, but the apartheid state controlled cooperative functioning and restricted membership to whites. The post-apartheid government views cooperatives as an important vector of empowerment, but paternalistic interventions and severe disparities are preventing the emergence of a racially integrated cooperative movement (Williams 2013). Moreover, cooperatives of color offer Fairtraders a critical opportunity for supporting the advancement of racial equity in South African trade, but efforts to problematize BEE in the context of small-scale producers remain nascent (Raynolds and Ngcwangu 2010). South African Fairtrade may address the problematic cooperative–estate distinction by investigating avenues for interracial collaboration and deepening their commitment to cooperative empowerment.

Small-scale producers are neither powerless nor passive. Emerging rooibos farmers have remained active in Fairtrade markets and continue to seek relations with reliable buyers. Fairtrade goes farther than conventional systems in that it addresses historical inequalities in trade via pricing guarantees and avenues for political inclusion (Herman 2012; Williams 2013). Indeed benevolence activism is not always problematic, particularly as the line between benevolence and solidarity is often unclear. Yet while acts of kindness may lead to positive outcomes, small-scale rooibos farmers are not interested in charity. They want fair payment for their hard work and access to business partners who are willing to invest in information sharing and mutual growth.[15] In some ways solidarity-based efforts are already occurring: African Fairtraders are working with rooibos cooperative members to build lobbying skills for policy negotiations (Fairtrade Africa 2012). In the next section I explore how solidarity activists may improve support mechanisms in ways that unite different groups operating within a given product chain.

THE PATH TO GREATER RACIAL EQUITY

Fairtrade International (2013b) supports African efforts to build racial equity in trade, but the certification system remains riddled with a series of contradictions. It employs language that invokes universal themes of rights, empowerment and justice, but it imposes a costly system of surveillance upon its least-advantaged members (Daviron and Vagneron 2011; Dolan 2010). Its identity is one of trading partnership (FINE 2003), but it replicates a sense of colonial hierarchy (Barratt Brown

2007; Trentman 2007). Moreover, Fairtrade's producer support systems remain underdeveloped and often rely on a paternalistic development infrastructure that views producers as beneficiaries to be counted rather than as clients with something to offer. The core issue is that Fairtrade's certification system has been designed to hold impoverished members more accountable than elite participants. Similarly to BEE, Fairtrade runs the risk of burying inequalities under a pleasant discourse of empowerment and fairness (du Toit, Kruger and Ponte 2008).

Fairtrade necessarily operates within the inequitable landscape of global exchange, and within this challenging terrain it has achieved positive outcomes. The movement's common charter of principles offers a blueprint for building greater equity in production and trade (WFTO and Fairtrade International 2009); and the charter espouses a series of important organizing principles, including: 1) freedom of association; 2) equal opportunity; 3) capacity building and empowerment; and 4) transparent and accountable management (WFTO and Fairtrade International 2009). The movement's emphasis on democratic engagement is critical as participatory democracy is increasingly viewed as fundamental to human development (Habib 2008). Certification networks may employ fair trade's charter to expand services in ways that support the entry of Fairtrade's least-advantaged members into positions of partnership and leadership.

As Eileen Davenport and William Low illustrate in their chapter in this volume, the fair trade movement provides the foundations for building peace in regions where groups have been locked in conflict. Fairtrade organizations may do this by incorporating formal peace and reconciliation protocols into fair trade praxis and by investing in participatory networking projects that bring historically segregated groups together to share information, build solidarity and pursue collaborative opportunities. Yet participatory projects are only as inclusive as practitioners are prepared to be and incomplete efforts can generate a 'tyranny' of participation (Cooke and Kothari 2001, 4).

Figure 25.2 provides a framework for differentiating between genuine forms of participation that are marked by cooperation and empowerment and the more tyrannical forms of pseudo-participation where manipulative domestication and paternalistic consultation occur. The analytical distinction between false and genuine forms of participation is straightforward, but similarly to benevolence and solidarity activism, it can be difficult to separate the two forms in practice. Solidarity activists may more effectively harness Fairtrade markets by instituting participatory networking protocols that drive the creation of more equitable commercial partnerships, but stakeholders must commit to frank dialogue,

Citizen Control →	Empowerment →	Genuine Participation
Partnership *(delegated power)*	Cooperation	
Consultation (placation) →	Assistencialism *(paternalism)* →	Pseudo-participation
Informing *(manipulation)*	Domestication	

Source: Michener (1998) adapted from Deshler and Sock (1985).

Figure 25.2 Participation typology

self-reflection and reflexive action if they are to achieve genuine levels of participation (MacIntyre 2008; Mohan 2001).

CONCLUSION

African Fairtrade networks are working to transcend the colonial division of labor in a variety of ways. These include investing in pan-African exchanges and working to ensure the delivery of client-based services that promote political participation. Yet structural conditions are leaving Fairtrade's small-scale farmers in positions of extreme vulnerability. Not only are outcomes mixed, certification practices may be generating a culture of passive assimilation rather than one of active participation. If Fairtrade networks are to address Biko's (1978) concerns regarding white-dominated racial integration, these must promote a praxis of interracial solidarity. In this chapter I have drawn from participatory action fieldwork with South African rooibos farmers to address some of the racial challenges facing African groups and to offer suggestions for developing more inclusive strategies for producer engagement. While the focus has been on Africa, insights from this chapter may have relevance for other Fairtrade regions where members are struggling to transform hierarchies in production and trade.

NOTES

* South African fieldwork was graciously funded by a 2010 Horticulture Collaborative Research Support Program (HortCRSP) grant. I am indebted to various project partners and stakeholders, including the Center for Fair and Alternative Trade (CFAT), the Institute for Poverty, Land and Agrarian Studies (PLAAS), Sandra

Kruger & Associates and an outstanding team of community-based farmer leaders. While the information presented in this chapter engages their contributions, I alone am responsible for any errors, omissions or incompleteness of understanding.

1. The original findings presented in this chapter derive from participatory action fieldwork in South Africa's small-scale rooibos tea sector.
2. Certified African producer groups increased by 43 per cent between 2007 and 2010 alone (Fairtrade Africa 2011).
3. Information provided by Fairtrade Africa's Executive Director during a panel discussion with Jennifer Keahey at Fair Trade South Africa's annual general meeting, Cape Town (28 October 2010).
4. Regional Manager of Fairtrade Africa's Southern African Trade Network, interview with Jennifer Keahey, Cape Town (22 November 2010).
5. Stated by Fairtrade Africa's Executive Director at the Fair Trade South Africa annual general meeting (28 October 2010).
6. Regional Manager of FLO-Cert Africa and the Middle East, interview with Jennifer Keahey, Cape Town (10 November 2010). This organization serves as the regional inspection and certification body for Fairtrade certified products.
7. General Secretary of Bawsi Agricultural Workers Union of South Africa, interview with Jennifer Keahey, Paarl, South Africa (24 November 2010).
8. The world's supply of rooibos is entirely produced in South Africa's Western Cape where the agricultural population primarily consists of white farm owners, colored laborers and a growing group of emerging colored farmers.
9. Technical Manager of Rooibos Limited, interview with Jennifer Keahey, Clanwilliam, South Africa (16 November 2010). Rooibos Limited is South Africa's largest rooibos processing firm.
10. Informant from Wupperthal Small Farmers Cooperative Management, interview with Jennifer Keahey, Wupperthal, South Africa (30 September 2010). This cooperative was liquidated in early 2011 after protracted conflict deriving from the organization's inability to pay its members the prices it had promised.
11. From Rooibos Limited interview.
12. From FLO-Cert interview.
13. Rooibos Farmer Leader, interview with Jennifer Keahey, Elim, South Africa (19 October 2010).
14. This sentiment was commonly expressed during fieldwork with small-scale rooibos farmers in August, September and October of 2010.
15. This attitude was likewise commonly stated by the small-scale rooibos farmers participating in this project.

REFERENCES

Aliber, Michael and Ben Cousins (2013), 'Livelihoods after land reform in South Africa', *Journal of Agrarian Change*, 13 (1), 140–165.

Barratt Brown, Michael (2007), '"Fair trade" with Africa', *Review of African Political Economy*, 34 (112), 267–277.

Biko, Steve (1978), *I Write What I Like*, San Francisco: Harper & Row.

Boluk, Karla (2011), 'Revealing the discourses: White entrepreneurial motivation in black South Africa', *Tourism Planning and Development*, 8 (2), 199–213.

Cooke, Bill and Uma Kothari (2001), *Participation: The New Tyranny?*, London: Zed Books Ltd.

Cousins, Ben (2010), 'What is a "smallholder"? Class-analytic perspectives on small-scale farming and agrarian reform in South Africa', PLAAS Working Paper 16, Bellville, South Africa.
Daviron, Benoit and Isabelle Vagneron (2011), 'From commoditisation to de-commoditisation … and back again: Discussing the role of sustainability standards for agricultural products', *Development Policy Review*, 29 (1), 91–113.
Del Felice, Celina (2012), 'Transnational activism and free trade: Exploring the emancipatory potentials of global civil society', *Voluntas: International Journal of Voluntary and Nonprofit Organizations*, 23 (2), 302–327.
Department of Trade and Industry (2009), 'Codes of good practice on broad based black economic empowerment', *Government Gazette*, (32305), 3–30.
Deshler, D. and D. Sock (1985), 'Community development participation: A concept review of the international literature', International League for Social Commitment in Adult Education, Ljungskile, Sweden.
Dolan, Catherine (2010), 'Virtual moralities: The mainstreaming of Fairtrade in Kenyan tea fields', *Geoforum*, 41 (1), 33–43.
du Toit, Andries (1993), 'The micro-politics of paternalism: The discourses of management and resistance on South African fruit and wine farms', *Journal of Southern African Studies*, 19 (2), 314–336.
du Toit, Andries (2005), 'Chronic and structural poverty in South Africa: Challenges for action and research', University of the Western Cape, Bellville, South Africa.
du Toit Andries, Sandra Kruger and Stefano Ponte (2008), 'Deracializing exploitation? "Black economic empowerment" in the South African wine industry', *Journal of Agrarian Change*, 8 (1), 6–32.
Fairtrade Africa (2011), 'Fairtrade growth facts and figures: Growth in producers in Africa', available at http://www.fairtradeafrica.net/market-info/ (accessed 7 November 2011).
Fairtrade Africa (2012), 'Producers learn how to raise their voices', *Fair Post Africa*, (8), 2.
Fairtrade Africa (2013), 'African markets: Where are the markets', available at http://www.fairtradeafrica.net/markets-in-africa/where-are-the-markets/ (accessed 3 October 2013).
Fairtrade Foundation (2010), 'Impacts of Fairtrade in South Africa', London, UK.
Fairtrade International (2007), 'FLO training manual 2.0: Introduction to the Generic Fairtrade Standards for Hired Labour', Bonn, Germany.
Fairtrade International (2011), 'Challenge and opportunity: Annual review 2010–11', Bonn, Germany.
Fairtrade International (2013a), 'Unlocking the power: Annual report 2012–13', Bonn, Germany.
Fairtrade International (2013b), 'Impact areas', available at http://www.fairtrade.net/impact_areas0.html (accessed 26 April 2014).
Feinstein, Charles (2005), *An Economic History of South Africa*, Cambridge: Cambridge University Press.
Ferguson, James (2006), *Global Shadows: Africa in the Neoliberal World Order*, Durham, NC: Duke University Press.
FINE (2003), 'What is FINE?', available at http://www.rafiusa.org/programs/Bangkok (accesssed 17 May 2006).
Fridell, Gavin (2007), 'Fair-trade coffee and commodity fetishism: The limits of market-driven social justice', *Historical Materialism*, 15, 79–104.
Gendron, Corrine, Véronique Bisaillon and Ana Isabel Otero Rance (2009), 'The institutionalization of fair trade: More than just a degraded form of social action', *Journal of Business Ethics*, 86 (S1), 63–79.

Gibbon, Peter and Stephano Ponte (2005), *Trading Down: Africa, Value Chains, and the Global Economy*, Philadelphia: Temple University Press.

Habib, Adam (2008), 'South Africa: Conceptualising a politics of human-oriented development', *Social Dynamics*, 34 (1), 46–61.

Herman, Agatha (2012), 'Tactical ethics: How the discourses of Fairtrade and black economic empowerment change and interact in wine networks from South Africa to the UK', *Geoforum*, 43 (6), 1121–1130.

Jari, Bridget, Jeanette Snowball and Gavin Fraser (2013), 'Is Fairtrade on commercial farms justifiable? Its impact on commercial and small-scale producers in South Africa', *Agrekon*, 52 (4), 66–88.

Kruger, Sandra and Andries du Toit (2007), 'Reconstructing fairness: Fair trade conventions and worker empowerment in South African horticulture', in Laura T. Raynolds, Douglas L. Murray and John Wilkinson (eds.), *Fair Trade: The Challenges of Transforming Globalization*, London: Routledge, pp. 200–219.

Linton, April (2012), 'Growing fair trade in South Africa', *Globalizations*, 9 (5), 725–740.

Low, William and Eileen Davenport (2005), 'Postcards from the edge: Maintaining the "alternative" character of fair trade', *Sustainable Development*, 13 (3), 143–153.

MacIntyre, Alice (2008), *Participatory Action Research*, Thousand Oaks, CA: Sage Publications.

Manokha, Ivan (2004), 'Modern slavery and fair trade products: Buy one and set someone free', in Christien van den Anker (ed.), *The Political Economy of New Slavery*, Basingstoke, UK: Palgrave Macmillan, pp. 217–234.

Michener, Victoria (1998), 'The participatory approach: Contradiction and co-optation in Burkina Faso', *World Development*, 26 (12), 2105–2118.

Mohan, Giles (2001), 'Beyond participation: Strategies for deeper empowerment', in Bill Cooke and Uma Kothari (eds.), *Participation: The New Tyranny?*, London: Zed Books Ltd., pp. 152–167.

Moseley, William (2008), 'Fair trade wine: South Africa's post-apartheid vineyards and the global economy', *Globalizations*, 5 (2), 291–304.

Ntsebeza, Lungisile and Ruth Hall (2007), *The Land Question in South Africa: The Challenge of Transformation and Redistribution*, Cape Town: HSRC Press.

Ramamurthy, Anandi (2012), 'Absences and silences: The representation of the tea picker in colonial and fair trade advertising', *Visual Culture in Britain*, 13 (3), 367–381.

Raynolds, Laura T. and Jennifer Keahey (2009), 'Fair trade, gender, and the environment in Africa', in Kevin Gallagher (ed.), *The Elgar Handbook on Trade and Environment*, Cheltenham, UK and Northampton, MA: Edward Elgar.

Raynolds, Laura T. and Jennifer Keahey (2014), 'Fair trade: Social justice and production alternatives', in Martin Parker, George Cheney, Valérie Fournier and Chris Land (eds.), *The Routledge Companion to Alternative Organization*, New York: Routledge, pp. 165–181.

Raynolds, Laura T., Douglas L. Murray and John Wilkinson (2007), *Fair Trade: The Challenges of Transforming Globalization*, New York: Routledge.

Raynolds, Laura T. and Siphelo Ngcwangu (2010), 'Fair trade rooibos tea: Connecting South African producers and American consumer markets', *Geoforum*, 41 (1), 74–83.

Richey, Lisa Ann and Stefano Ponte (2011), *Brand Aid: Shopping Well to Save the World*, Minneapolis, MN: University of Minnesota Press.

Smith, David (2011), 'South African wine industry rooted in human misery, says report', available at http://www.guardian.co.uk/world/2011/aug/23/south-african-wine-industry-misery (accessed 22 August 2011).

Thaler, Richard H. and Cass R. Sunstein (2003), 'Libertarian paternalism', *American Economic Review*, 93 (2), 175–179.

Thompson, Leonard (2001), *A History of South Africa*, New Haven, CT: Yale University Press.

Trentman, Frank (2007), 'Before "fair trade": Empire, free trade, and the moral economies of food in the modern world', *Environment and Planning D: Society and Space*, 25 (6), 1079–1102.
van den Anker, Christien (2004), *The Political Economy of New Slavery*, Basingstoke, UK: Palgrave Macmillan.
WFTO (World Fair Trade Organization) and Fairtrade International (2009), 'A charter of fair trade principles', available at http://fairtrade-advocacy.org/images/Charter_of_Fair_Trade_principles_EN_v1.2.pdf (accessed 26 April 2014).
Wilkinson, John and Gilberto Mascarenhas (2007), 'The making of the fair trade movement in the South: The Brazilian case', in Laura T. Raynolds, Douglas L. Murray and John Wilkinson (eds.), *Fair Trade: The Challenges of Transforming Globalization*, New York: Routledge, pp. 157–179.
Williams, Michelle (2013), 'Alternative production and consumption relations?: Fair trade, the state, and cooperatives in the global South', *Journal of Contemporary African Studies*, 31 (1), 1–17.

26. Fair trade and artisans

Mary A. Littrell

INTRODUCTION

'Our hands are our future' conveys artisans' hopes to secure sustainable markets for their handcrafts. When asked what they needed most, artisans respond, 'more work so we can give our children a better life'. Together these statements express artisans' dreams and apprehension as they enter a global marketplace where their handmade products must compete with inexpensive manufactured goods.

Artisans draw on their technical expertise, aesthetic norms and design languages to create objects of great beauty and practical use – textiles, ceramics, baskets, wood items and metal ware. In this chapter I examine how artisans' cultural heritage fares under the *artisan sector* of the fair trade model. Maureen Liebl and Tirthankar Roy (2004, 67), long-time participants in craft development, concluded that no traditional craft skill can survive unless it has a viable market. Does the fair trade market offer hope to artisans for generating sustainable income and for reaching their social goals in a world of globalization?

In the first section, I describe the context in which fair trade artisans work and explain the challenges they face. In the second section, I present two case studies that illuminate how fair trade artisan groups are tackling these challenges and achieving desired trade and socio-economic benefits. One case offers insight into how a 28-year-old fair trade organization flexibly evolved into a high-impact enterprise, while working within the cultural context of artisans' daily lives. The other case profiles a newer artisan group whose members are focused on retaining cultural artistic traditions as they engage in new product development for the global market. In the final section I assess certification issues for the fair trade artisan sector.

In this chapter I employ the UNESCO (United Nations Educational, Scientific and Cultural Organization) definition of artisan products as 'those produced by artisans, either completely by hand, or with the help of hand tools or even mechanical means, as long as the direct manual contribution of the artisan remains the substantial component of the finished product' (UNESCO/ITC Symposium 1997). The term craft skills refers to 'living links to the past and a means of preserving cultural meaning into the future' (Finger and Schuler 2004, 7).

SOCIO-ECONOMIC CONTEXT AND CHALLENGES FOR ARTISANS

Both within and outside fair trade, artisans face challenges due to a variety of global conditions. Often living on society's economic fringe, artisans want to support their families and enhance their quality of life through increased sales. The international market presents rapidly changing and often elusive demand from wholesale buyers and retail customers. As artisans form enterprises, they experiment with culturally viable approaches for leveraging their skills to attract new markets. Because of these complex challenges, questions arise as to whether product adaptation for market appeal will erode or vitalize centuries-old traditions?

Social-Economic Reality of Daily Life

For the majority of the world's artisans, living in poverty is a daily reality. Artisans face unrelenting competition as their handmade products disappear to cheaper, machine-produced alternatives. In Guatemala, women now carry well water in plastic containers rather than in ceramic jugs; young adults in India choose jeans and t-shirts over their mothers' saris; Peruvian villagers sleep under light synthetic blankets rather than heavy hand-woven textiles of the past. Artisans' sales in the local economy have evaporated. Entering new markets offers a glimmer of hope for income generation to meet daily needs (Liebl and Roy 2004, 67–70). Yet few know where or how to start.

Although artisans are highly skilled in their craft, poor education and illiteracy block new market access. Women's participation as artisans is further hindered by heavy household responsibilities. For example, fair trade artisans working for the international producer and retailer Market-Place: Handwork of India must intersperse their five to six hours of artisan work among eleven hours a day devoted to household tasks (Littrell and Dickson 2010, 80). Home-based work is an imperative lifestyle condition for these women who must stay at home because of religious, in-law and spousal restrictions (Eversole 2006, 946; Littrell and Frater 2013, 383; Stenn 2013, 143). Within a context of extreme poverty, few social services exist for ameliorating chronic illness, malnutrition, family conflict, mental stress and illiteracy. Yet, when these problems are addressed, artisans bolster their strength and abilities to engage with other artisans in collectively seeking market access.

Enterprise Management and Sustainability

For those artisans who join business enterprises, finding solutions for managerial challenges occurs on a daily basis. The exacting demands of the global market require establishing strict quality control, increasing efficiencies, expanding productivity for timely delivery of large orders, initiating technical innovations, acquiring working capital for raw materials and infrastructure improvements, negotiating organizational factionalism and fostering leadership. Only when organizations begin acquiring steady orders can members start to plan for their family's welfare, such as paying biannual school fees, buying medicines for chronic illness and making household improvements. Long-time fair traders assess that, more than paying fair wages, 'the greatest poverty reduction comes from sustaining long-term trading relationships' (Layton 2004, 91).

Global Market Trends

Global market trends paint a picture of divergent consumer demand. At one end of the export spectrum, low- to mid-range goods cater to customers who shop with a discount-focused mindset. To fulfill these large volume orders, artisans submerge individual creativity in order to mass-produce ceramics, jewelry and housewares to the exacting specifications from wholesale buyers. Some artisan development practitioners lament the homogeneity brought on by globalization. Others point out that high-volume orders from retailers such as Macy's, Walmart and Crate & Barrel provide earnings for artisans who might not otherwise have work within their villages (Vencatachellum 2013, 12). While large mainstream retailers talk about ethical sourcing in their promotions, members of the fair trade movement question whether the retailers will continue to push for bare bones pricing and shorter lead times endemic to their business practices, actions that stand to negatively impact artisans (Keahey, Littrell and Murray 2011).

In contrast to the lower-end market, an expanding group of consumers value the artistic creativity in higher-end, individualistic pieces. These consumers balance their desires for unique products with questions about the social impact of their purchases. Customers ask who made a ceramic vase, what were they paid, what was the production facility like, how does the production affect the environment (Vencatachellum 2013, 12).

Purchasing culturally linked handcrafts addresses consumers' motivation to create pleasing and creative aesthetic experiences in their lives, enhance a self-identity and connect with artisans and their cultures (Littrell and Dickson 1999, 53; Nicholls and Opal 2005, 166; Padilla 2013, 105). These divergent market segments contribute to opportunities for artisans' market entry at a range of price points.

Adaptation and Change

To enter the global market calls for adaptation and change in artisan practices and products (Nicholls and Opal 2005, 169–172). The topic spawns intense debate among craft development planners (Littrell and Frater 2013). Some fear that product development may lead to such drastic change that a craft tradition is no longer recognizable. Camilla Padilla counters that in the 21st century, 'folk art, as a living art, adapts in tandem with the cultures that create it. Through change, many timeless traditions are sustained, particularly in the face of obstacles that would otherwise lead to their extinction' (2013, 73–74). Questions about how crafts will change and who will control the change for new markets fuel the debate.

One part of the debate centers on the role of outside designers in new product development. Judy Frater, who co-founded Kala Raksha Trust in India and has worked with artisans for over 20 years, believes that when artists execute designs provided to them by outside designers, they are relegated to the role of menial workers and are not empowered (Littrell and Frater 2013, 378–380). Other development practitioners counter that outside assistance is not bad, especially in cases where sustained, collaborative relationships form among outsiders and artisans as they adapt the size, function or design of what were often utilitarian objects to suit new uses (Waterman, 2014). Padilla summarizes,

> It's a brave new world for folk artists striving to balance the cultural and the commercial, the local and the global. At least initially, few artists find success in going it alone. The best outcomes often result from partnerships between artists and cultural connectors – individuals, buyers and sellers, support organizations and philanthropists, local and global governments. These partners embrace collaboration and innovation to create nonprofit or for-profit enterprises that market the singular skills and knowledge of folk artists and the historic role of their handmade traditions. (2013, 99–100)

FAIR TRADE CASE STUDIES

Both the Fair Trade Federation (FTF) and the World Fair Trade Organization (WFTO) highlight protection of cultural traditions as integral to their guiding principles. FTF states that their members 'respect the development of products, practices, and organizational models based on indigenous traditions and techniques to sustain cultures and revitalize traditions. Members balance market needs with producers' cultural heritage' (Fair Trade Federation 2014). In a similar manner, the WFTO 'promotes and protects the cultural identity and traditional skills of small producers as reflected in their craft designs, food products and other related services' (World Fair Trade Organization 2014). (For more on fair trade and indigeneity, see Sarah Lyon's chapter in this volume.)

Two fair trade case studies offer examples of how organizations operationalize these principles of respect for cultural lifestyles and aesthetic traditions at grassroots levels. The cases illustrate that high-impact fair trade efforts are 'raising women's organizations in a holistic way, so that they are not only educated, healthy, or able to run a micro-financed enterprise, but that she [*sic*] can effectively navigate the way in the socio-cultural environment in which she functions' (Handy et al. 2006, 130). The cases also demonstrate how organizations with generational activities support members to progressively widen their perceptions and abilities to impact others within and beyond the group (Korten 1987, 147). Finally, each case illustrates how attention to cultural context, in one case to daily lifestyles and in the other to long-standing patterns of production and aesthetics, have strengthened and enhanced artisans' cultural identity.[1]

MarketPlace: Handwork of India

Mumbai slums are home to the central office, workshops and homes of the over 450 artisans of MarketPlace: Handwork of India.[2] Founders Pushpika Freitas and Lalita Monteiro grew up in a home where their mother modeled assistance to others through her ground-breaking social work in the slums. Originating in the mid-1980s with a few women who came to their home seeking work, the initial patchwork-quilting project evolved into MarketPlace's contemporary Western-style products with two distinguishing hallmarks. Women do not join MarketPlace steeped in Indian textile traditions learned at the hands of family master artisans. Rather, MarketPlace leaders train the women in the requisite sewing, embroidery and printing skills. All apparel and interior products incorporate base fabrics of hand-dyed, printed or woven fabrics. Each product is embellished with striking, hand-embroidered points of interest. MarketPlace products are 'India inspired' but not rooted in the textile traditions of a singular geographic region of India. MarketPlace textiles are sold exclusively outside of India through specialty and fair trade retail stores, a mail-order catalog and the Internet, all managed through their Chicago (US) office.

From the beginning, MarketPlace fostered a workplace that meshed culturally with the women's daily activities and addressed their evolving socio-economic needs. Desperate poverty, chronic family illness and goals for educating their children drove the women's search for work. Before joining MarketPlace, few women were contributing to household incomes. Following marriage, most women had migrated from across India to Mumbai, where they lived under their mothers-in-law's domination in ten- by ten-foot, one-room homes in the slums. Formal schooling was limited, as was experience in expressing opinions or taking initiative. Household responsibilities permeated the women's days. For the 30 per cent of Muslim women at MarketPlace, leaving home was allowed only if the workplace protected their privacy from males. Being able to complete at least some of the work at home was essential.

MarketPlace's integrated goals of income generation through fair wages and social development of artisan members guided organizational planning. Over time, the means to achieve goals evolved as women acquired business and entrepreneurial skills, grew in self-worth and gained confidence for making critical family decisions and confronting social inequities.

In MarketPlace's first years, women gathered at a single workshop for fabric cutting, embroidery, sewing, quality control and shipping. The central workshop served many important functions – establishing systems for production management, learning about cash flow, instilling standards for quality control and acquiring an organizational identity. However, by the 1990s MarketPlace became top-heavy with supervisors who directed the work of others.

MarketPlace founders recognized the need to change if they were to adhere to their mission of helping *all* women hone business skills, make sound personal decisions and become leaders. A new organizational structure evolved that offered greater opportunity for grassroots leadership through group decision-making. In 2000 MarketPlace decentralized into seven smaller production workshops in several slums across Mumbai. Younger or unmarried women who were free to leave their homes for longer periods of time went to the workshops to assemble garments on sewing machines housed at the workplaces. Women with busy families walked to the workshops several times a week to gather products, attend training and participate in workshop meetings. Returning home, they fit embroidery in among their other household tasks.

MarketPlace has often called in outside industry experts with India experience and expertise for collaborative training programs. Each of the workshops sent representatives to the central office for instruction. In an interactive learning environment, artisans practiced and applied what they were learning. They then returned as 'teacher trainers' for their workshop members. Littrell and Frater assessed, 'For the artisans, their evolving business and decision-making skills emerged as new cultural property. Women who previously rarely left their homes now project an identity as business leaders producing fashion for the global fashion market' (2013, 386–387).

As MarketPlace organized social programming for capacity building, they listened closely to the artisans for topics of concern. MarketPlace artisans brought life experiences from multiple ethnicities, religions and castes to weekly workshop meetings. Women initially discussed nutrition, parenting, health and ways to speak up at home and in public. As the artisans gained self-confidence, their needs evolved into discussion of legal issues surrounding women's rights, property tenure and domestic violence.

In addition to artisan-generated discussions, each workshop took on a project that contributed to their family and community wellbeing. Through these social action ventures women confronted the lack of trash removal in their slums, rallied against corrupt rationing of foodstuffs and presented street plays about HIV. The Armann Club for children of MarketPlace members augmented their mothers' capacity building through after school discussions of youth concerns, community projects and recreation. Armann Club members learned to question age-old prejudices and to hold high expectations for their futures. The youth also started Saturday morning karate classes for developing skills to defend themselves from violence in the slums.

As a fair trade organization, MarketPlace focused on the holistic development of their members in their decentralized workshops, where attention to individual needs was possible. MarketPlace impacts illustrate the interactive nature of a comprehensive mission as measured by Chambers' economic, social and psychological indicators of wellbeing (1997, 9). MarketPlace artisans contribute significantly to their households, averaging 40 per cent of the household income. Artisans have been able to cement floors and repair ceilings in their homes, enroll children in English-medium schools and purchase a television for family entertainment. Yet, apparel production varies seasonally because of Western fashion cycles and fluctuating demand from US customers. Artisans are left with bursts of work followed by several idle weeks at a time. Spreading resources across to the next pay period is difficult to achieve. Artisans' plea for additional work remains a constant.

With their MarketPlace work, women have acquired skills that carry over into their lives outside the workshops. For many women, going outside the slum, riding a bus or train, sourcing sewing supplies around Mumbai and using a telephone were first-time occurrences, as was voicing one's opinions in group settings. When asked if their work at MarketPlace translated into positive regard from others, artisans cited greater respect from husbands (70 per cent), in-laws (63 per cent), children (88 per cent) and neighbors (83 per cent). Respect translated into a central role in household decision-making concerning number of children, choice of a husband for daughters and daughters' marriage age.

Women commented that before joining MarketPlace their lives were lonely and stressful. They had little idea that other women shared their hardships or were suffering from mental and physical abuse. Women described their MarketPlace workshops as psychological refuges where 'I feel free to talk about anything with the other women'. As the women became active in workshop discussions and in social action projects they supported each other and brainstormed strategies for change.[3]

MarketPlace exemplifies the fair trade model of collaboration as opposed to top-down direction. Pushpika Freitas, founder and President, reflected,

> For me, the essence of MarketPlace is that it is not a program or a plan, but a way of thinking and attitudes and beliefs. It is the belief that these women can accomplish a great deal if given the chance. I spend much of my time in India asking women what they think and want. We are partners, and they know we listen and work with them. It is really the women who are involved in deciding programs, and then crafting them with a little help. We are the listeners. (Freitas 2014)

Clearly, MarketPlace exemplifies how a fair trade organization can evolve into a high-impact organization that addresses artisans' economic and social livelihood. MarketPlace grew in a manner that generatively met fair trade artisans' needs as they progressed from bedrock economic welfare to broader household decision-making and advocacy for others in their slums. Throughout their evolution, MarketPlace honored local cultural patterns for integrating work with household responsibilities while also expanding women's horizons as economic contributors and community leaders. The next case study also focuses on cultural patterns, but this example of artistic traditions illustrates how production and design can be modified while retaining a distinct cultural identity for the artisans and their products.

Maya Women's Rug Hooking Cooperative of Guatemala

The Maya Women's Rug Hooking Cooperative of Guatemala originated from the confluence of a natural disaster and the desperate need for income among fair trade artisans.[4] In 2005 Hurricane Stan brought ravaging landslides to villages around Lake Atitlán. Buildings stood buried in mud up to their roofs. Weavers lost their looms, their sole source for generating income. Over 400 people were dead or missing, while thousands remained homeless.

To the north, in the Guatemalan highlands, fair trade weavers and embroiderers found sales declining for their product lines of bags, belts and wall hangings. Demand waned in a saturated market. Given the artisans' desperate need to support their impoverished families, the weavers were keen for new product development.

Serendipitously, Mary Anne Wise, an accomplished rug designer from rural Wisconsin in the United States, traveled to Guatemala during the 2006 national crisis. Mary Anne, observing the artisans' desperation, wondered if the weavers might be interested in learning to produce high-quality, one-of-a-kind rugs that she believed would sell in the international market. She reasoned that the work would be compatible with the women's lives. Rug hooking was portable and equipment was inexpensive. In addition the necessary raw material for cutting fabric strips to hook in the rugs was readily available at the used clothing *pacas* – small clothing shops selling inexpensive used clothing shipped into Guatemala from the United States.

By introducing rug hooking in a weaving culture, Mary Anne and the artisans were charting new territory in organizational advancement. Fair trade development projects commonly focus on indigenous technology and aesthetics in tandem. In this case the group would be learning a new technique to which they would apply their long-honed cultural aesthetics. Making rugs was not a foreign concept to the weavers due to their cultural practice of making *alfombra*s, elaborate street rugs created from colored sawdust, flower petals, pine needles, sand and rice for Holy Week events.

In response to the opportunity to learn a new income-generating skill, 30 women arrived for Mary Anne's first classes in 2009. In the early classes, the students sat nearly immobilized when handed pencils and paper for designing. Like many artisans around the world, the women were not skilled at looking closely at what was around them and then transposing their everyday material environment into potential rug designs. What ensued was a series of activities for developing observation skills. Together the students walked around their classroom and in the village discussing how designs could evolve from rock patterns on stone walls or shapes on an iron gate. During market visits, they picked up old textiles and practiced showing each other how to isolate a single geometric or figurative motif. In a visit to the *Museo Ixchel*, the national textile museum in Guatemala City, the artisans began to internalize Mary Anne's aim: 'The museum will help you see how the world values your textile heritage. If you see it with your own eyes and feel it in your heart, it will be easier for you to communicate in your rugs.' Slowly the women began to see that design ideas were everywhere around them in the Guatemalan highlands and in their dazzling woven attire. They could begin to 'see the familiar' in ways they had not seen before. One artist described,

> In each design my culture and my identity come alive. There are many events in my life, in my family and community that I am able to incorporate into my rugs. I see ideas for rugs everywhere. In color, we represent the colors of Guatemala, in design we use the symbols from our native land, such as volcanoes that we represent by a diamond, or the sun which we represent by a circle surrounded by triangles.

As their technical and design skills improved, the students' interest in rug hooking intensified. When asked what they liked about rug hooking, the students replied that creating something original was creative and fun. Rug hooking contrasted with the repetitive weaving to precise specifications that was demanded in their other fair trade work.

However, as the classes progressed, the women worried whether their rugs would sell. Several had been asked by family members, 'Who is going to buy something made from old clothes?' Many of the women were traveling three to four hours by bus to attend the classes. They wondered if their investment of time and energy away from their families would be rewarded.

To test the market, a small outside grant supported three of the artisans to travel to Minnesota and Wisconsin for a lecture, trunk show and exhibition. The women experienced, first-hand, that customers were attracted to the rugs which echoed the striking motifs of their Guatemalan clothing. Shoppers valued one-of-a-kind textiles with an artisan story. The artisans also learned that upcycling, or re-use, of old clothes from the *pacas* to their rugs was a selling point to 'green' and 'sustainability' consumers. That they sold all 80 rugs they brought on the trip convinced the novice rug hookers of Mary Anne's market savvy. Upon returning to

Guatemala, the travelers' stories helped quell their fellow artisans' anxiety about the potential for generating income from rug hooking.

Based on her prior knowledge of both successful and failed artisan development projects, Mary Anne believed that for the project to become sustainable, she as an outside designer must no longer be essential to its operation. She became intrigued with the idea of working with a handful of the most talented students to develop a curriculum for them to become *design teachers* for other women in their communities. When the artisans could act as teacher-mentors to other women, more artisans could acquire sustainable income opportunities without dependence on Mary Anne's external design direction. The second stage of classes, a teacher-training design school, would support project sustainability and allow Mary Anne to exit the project.

As Mary Anne had done in the initial classes, she continued to expand her teaching pedagogy to fit her students' needs. For example, she learned from her students that a good teacher 'makes your heart feel like a glass of water – so full' and a bad teacher 'makes you feel small' and 'doesn't pay attention to you'. Keeping the students' perceptions in mind, Mary Anne taught the students how to critique each other's work in ways that learners could hear and feel encouraged. Critique sessions proved difficult for women living in a culture where they were discouraged from voicing an opinion in public settings.

During the four-week, teacher-training course, the artisans not only expanded their own rug-making skills but also contemplated how they would teach others. One important strategy involved learning to be more efficient when shopping at the *pacas* for raw materials for their rugs. Formerly, the women would quickly grab what they liked from the 5-foot-high rag piles without considering the fabric's use or quality. Instead, the students learned to take small drawings of their rug designs with them to the *pacas* and to carefully select appropriate fabric colors to execute their designs and to assess the clothing as raw material for producing quality rugs. After new strategies were learned, each student 'practice taught' one of the other teachers-to-be. To complete their training, each teacher-in-training brought several women from her village who were not involved in rug hooking to the final class. In the final session, the student teachers applied what they had learned to 14 aspiring rug hookers.

Across the five years from 2009 to 2014, the women closely adhered to fair trade practices of paying fair wages, collaborating on design and production decisions, conserving resources, protecting cultural identity and developing leadership. For the women who initially took advantage of the product development opportunity, sales from their rugs have surpassed their two previous revenue sources – fair trade sales of woven belts, bags and placemats and weaving *huipiles* for women in their communities who no longer wove. Markets include tourists in Guatemala, a specialty retail store, an online website and an international folk art market in the United States. The newly formed rug hooking cooperative has expanded from the original seven teachers to over 50 rug hookers in six villages.

The artistry of integrating vibrant motifs from their Maya textile tradition with a new textile technology has encouraged the Guatemalan women to move their aesthetic traditions in new directions, thus keeping the traditions vital and alive. When asked about weaving now that they possessed rug hooking skills for generating enhanced income, the women insisted that they would not give up their centuries-old weaving tradition. Weaving their own clothing retains its cultural importance for projecting a Maya identity and for use during festivals and special occasions. Yet by adding rug hooking to their textile repertoire, the women are significantly expanding their potential for enhanced livelihood.

The teacher-training program offers an approach for fair trade organizations that are concerned about overreliance on outside designers. Outsiders may have little knowledge of indigenous aesthetics and patterns of life for integrating artisanal work with household responsibilities. At the Maya Women's Rug Hooking Cooperative of Guatemala, women with little formal education and who would never have imagined themselves as teachers are now leaders in helping their artisan students interpret Maya design aesthetics within their villages.

Each of the two case studies highlights how artisans are increasing their income and strengthening their cultural identity as leaders by having the opportunity to work within an organizational environment undergirded by FTF and WFTO principles of respect for artisans' lifestyles and artistic traditions. In each case organizational leaders have listened closely to the artisans' needs and developed workplaces and teaching strategies that encourage individual growth and greater self-confidence, along with establishing a place in the global market.

Critical Decisions for Fair Trade Performance

While each fair trade enterprise follows practices unique to its cultural context, several critical decisions permeate both groups in describing their fair trade performance. Commonalities that hold potential for cross-cultural application include:

- Production that complements the artisans' heavy household responsibilities by incorporating some home-based work.
- Evolution of production in flexible ways, including decentralizing a large organization into smaller groups for more inclusive leadership development or introducing a new technology of rug hooking in a weaving culture.
- Collaboration for product development with outside designers who were familiar with the international market. Through collaboration artisans learn to assume design responsibilities.
- Product development that emerged from textile traditions while making adaptations that move the traditions in new directions for the global market.
- Mentoring skill development for speaking up in groups; for design, production and personal decision-making; and for entrepreneurial leadership within and outside the group.
- Offering safe environments for sharing of daily hardships and family concerns.
- Encouraging artisans to assume more complex tasks as their skills and self-confidence expand.
- Training artisans to assume teaching roles for new production processes and for design as a strategy for avoiding overreliance on outsiders and for creating organizational sustainability.

CERTIFICATION FOR THE FAIR TRADE ARTISAN SECTOR

Certification is standard for many fair trade agricultural commodities; however, certification in the artisan sector is far less common. The artisan sector presents unique challenges for certification as described by Tony Hall (2011): 'Certification of hand-crafts under a single inflexible commodity standard is impossible due to the large number of craft product types (50,000+) and their dizzying array of source materials. Unlike homogeneous commodity cash and food crops like coffee, sugar and cacao, no finished craft or producing community are alike.' Despite these challenges, leaders in the artisan sector believe that working towards certification is critical as consumers increasingly ask questions about fair wages, exploitation of children and the environment footprint. Bob Chase, long-time CEO of SERVV (Sales Exchange for Refugee Rehabilitation and Vocation), argues the position:

> The reality is that as interest in fair trade grows, consumers will require and deserve third party verification of fair trade claims. Some continue to say that it is not possible to establish measurable standards for handmade products. Others feel that requiring home based artisans to be paid a fair hourly wage will price their products out of the market. And some feel that the systems necessary to assure compliance to a certification system will leave poor producers and small importers at a disadvantage in competing with much larger organizations. These are the same arguments which have been made consistently to oppose minimum wage laws and fair labor standards in our own country. Developing meaningful certification systems will require ingenuity and creativity and there will be costs involved in adopting and adhering to a certification system. But these costs should be seen as an investment in insuring the integrity and sustainability of the fair trade marketplace. (Geffner 2012, 17–18)

Within the artisan sector, two major organizational certification programs are available through the FTF and the WFTO. Fair trade is defined by a range of principles related to wages, working conditions, child protection, capacity building, environmental resources, cultural identity, business transparency and commitment to sustained trading partnerships. Use of the FTF or WFTO label implies that the organizations' operations and management have been third-party certified for all fair trade principles.

In addition, the WFTO is currently investing in a trial system for craft product certification, monitoring and labeling. Rudi Dalvai, President of WFTO, notes that artisan producer groups in the global South are particularly keen to have certification. Wholesale buyers have indicated to the artisans that the label will open up new markets for their products (Geffner 2012). Dalvai believes that wholesale buyers may have planted false expectations for growth without the artisans also understanding the buyers' stringent expectations for quality, timely delivery and 'right' prices.

Two other endorsement programs focus on definitions or guidelines that parallel some but not all the FTF or WFTO principles. The All India Artisans and Craftworkers Welfare Association's (AIACA) Craftmark label denotes genuine Indian handmade products and assists Indian artisans to meet minimum standards for production (AIACA 2010). A 2012 study showed that artisans' sales increased by 30 per cent when they earned the right to use the Craftmark label (West Elm 2014). The new Alliance for Artisan Enterprise, formed in 2012 under the auspices of the US State Department and hosted by the Aspen Institute, has established a working group for developing a 'handmade' label as well.

The working group believes such a label is necessary for artisans to validate and demand higher prices for their products in the global market.[5]

Still, other businesses are using terminology in their promotional materials that mirrors fair trade principles but without identifying a form of third-party verification. For example, Fair Indigo, a company with clothing and handcraft product lines, uses the phrase fair trade in describing their operating practices. In addition their catalog and website are scattered with photos of artisans, their work and stories of impacts from their work with Fair Indigo. As part of the Clinton Global Initiative Commitment to Action, West Elm has committed US$35 million paid directly to artisans through 2015 for their 'Handcrafted' lines of household furnishings (West Elm 2013). Customers to the website can watch numerous YouTube video clips where artisans discuss how they are preserving traditions, gaining self-confidence, becoming leaders and working under healthier conditions through their West Elm collaborations. These videos are intended to validate West Elm's commitment to artisans and their artisan-centered practices.

Each of these approaches – third-party fair trade certification, handmade verification or employing fair trade terminology – along with other concepts such as 'organic', 'green' or 'sustainable', addresses ethical issues which consumers are raising in their marketplace decisions. Renee Bowers, FTF Executive Director assesses, however, that with the proliferation of fair trade and other ethical claims, it is becoming increasingly difficult to say 'fair trade' and have people know what that means, both inside and outside the fair trade movement.[6]

At the beginning of this chapter I asked the question: does the fair trade market offer hope to artisans for generating sustainable income and for reaching their social goals in a world of globalization? Based on the evidence, I answer in the affirmative. Fair trade has led the way in proactively putting artisans first in their decision-making since the mid-1950s. By interacting with artisans at the grassroots, they have had on-the-ground access to learning about artisans' daily challenges in a cultural context, to understanding their rich artistic traditions for production and design and to developing collaborative programs that meet artisans' needs. The two case studies in the chapter exemplify fair trade organizations with vision, flexibility and creativity.

In the early 21st century, fair trade organizations no longer have the only corner on carrying out business in an ethical and sustainable manner. What distinguishes fair trade is its commitment to a comprehensive set of parameters for defining 100 per cent fair trade among fair trade producers and vendors. This inclusive approach contrasts with the singular ethical factors upon which other organizations often concentrate. Consumers are currently confused about the meaning of fair trade. Most immediately, it seems imperative that for market growth, fair trade organizations should campaign to distinguish clearly their comprehensive business practices. A campaign would help consumers understand the wide-ranging and interrelated components of what ethical business practice can be. In a climate where artisans' and consumers' sensibilities are closely aligned (Padilla 2013, 105), fair trade has the opportunity to attract consumers towards inclusive ethical decisions for purchasing artisan products.

NOTES

1. For assessment of an additional case study focused on Peruvian handcrafts, see the chapter by Manush McConway and Geoff Moore in this volume.
2. Field research with MarketPlace: Handwork of India was conducted in Mumbai, India, across two years from 2001 and 2003 and funded by the Earthwatch Institute. Along with interviews with 161 artisans, additional sources of data included photo-documentation and participant observation in multiple activities. The complete socio-economic audit, including research methodology, is described in *Artisans and Fair Trade: Crafting Development* (Littrell and Dickson 2010).
3. For additional discussion of issues related to women's empowerment in fair trade, by contrast in fair trade agriculture, see the chapter by Sally Smith in this volume.
4. The author has documented the evolution of the Maya Women's Rug Hooking Cooperative of Guatemala since their inception, including field research with the artisans in September 2011 and June 2012 and through ongoing communication with Mary Anne Wise following each of the design workshops with the artisans.
5. Information about the incipient 'handmade' working group (HAND/EYE Magazine, ByHand Consulting, Aid to Artisans and West Elm) was provided in an interview between the author and Karen Gibbs, founding member of the Alliance for Artisan Enterprise.
6. This assessment was provided in an interview between myself and Renee Bowers, Executive Director of the Fair Trade Federation, on 17 January 2014.

REFERENCES

All India Artisans and Craftworkers Welfare Association (AIACA) (2010), 'Our mission', available at http://www.aiacaonlineorg/aboutus-mission.asp?links=ab2 (accessed 10 January 2014).

Chambers, Robert (1997), *Whose Reality Counts? Putting the First Last*, London: Intermediate Technology.

Eversole, Robyn (2006), 'Crafting development in Bolivia', *Journal of International Development*, 18 (7), 945–955.

Fair Trade Federation (FTF) (2014), 'Fair Trade Federation principles', available at http://www.fairtradefederation.org/fair-trade-federation-principles (accessed 10 January 2014).

Finger, J. Michael and Philip Schuler (eds.) (2004), *Poor People's Knowledge: Promoting Intellectual Property in Developing Countries*, Washington, DC: The World Bank.

Freitas, Pushpika (2014), 'Our mission', available at www.marketplaceindia.com/category/172 (accessed 24 October 2014).

Geffner, Dana (2012), 'Challenges of certification for fair trade crafts: Part 2', *For a Better World*, (4), 17–18, available at http://fairworldproject.org/voices-of-fair-trade/the-challenges-of-certification-for-fair-trade-crafts-part 2/ (accessed 12 January 2014).

Hall, Tony (2011), 'The challenges of certification for fair trade crafts', *For a Better World*, (3), 17–18, available at http://fairworldproject.org/voices-of-fair-trade/the-challenges-of-certification-for-fair-trade-crafts/ (accessed 12 January 2014).

Handy, Femida, Meenaz Kassam, Suzanne Feeney and Ranade Bhagyashree (2006), *Grassroots NGOs by Women for Women*, New Delhi: Sage Publications.

Keahey, Jennifer A., Mary A. Littrell and Douglas L. Murray (2011), 'Business with a mission: The ongoing role of Ten Thousand Villages within the fair trade movement', in Alain Epp Weaver (ed.), *A Table of Sharing*, Telford, PA: Cascadia Publishing House, pp. 265–283.

Korten, David C. (1987), 'Third generation NGO strategies: A key to people-centered development', *World Development*, 15 (Suppl.), 145–159.

Layton, Ron (2004), 'Enhancing intellectual property exports through fair trade', in Michael J. Finger and Philip Schuler (eds.), *Poor People's Knowledge: Promoting Intellectual Property in Developing Countries*, Washington, DC: The World Bank, pp. 75–93.

Liebl, Maureen and Tirthankar Roy (2004), 'Handmade in India: Traditional craft skills in a changing world', in Michael J. Finger and Philip Schuler (eds.), *Poor People's Knowledge: Promoting Intellectual Property in Developing Countries*, Washington, DC: The World Bank, pp. 53–73.

Littrell, Mary A. and Marsha A. Dickson (1999), *Social Responsibility in the Global Market: Fair Trade of Cultural Products*, Thousand Oaks, CA: Sage Publications.

Littrell, Mary A. and Marsha A. Dickson (2010), *Artisans and Fair Trade: Crafting Development*, Sterling, VA: Kumarian Press.

Littrell, Mary A. and Judy Frater (2013), 'Artisan enterprise, cultural property, and the global market', in Sandy Black, Amy de la Haye, Joanne Entwistle, Agnés Rocamora, Regina A. Root and Helen Thomas (eds.), *The Handbook of Fashion Studies*, London: Bloomsbury, pp. 371–390.

Nicholls, Alex and Charlotte Opal (2005), *Fair Trade: Market-Driven Ethical Consumption*, London: Sage Publications.

Padilla, Carmella (2013), *The Work of Art: Folk Artists in the 21st Century*, Santa Fe, NM: International Folk Art Alliance Media.

Stenn, Tamara L. (2013), *The Cultural and Political Intersection of Fair Trade and Justice: Managing a Global Industry*, New York: Palgrave Macmillan.

UNESCO/ITC Symposium (1997), 'Building confidence: Crafts for development', available at http://portal.unesco.org/culture/en/ev.phpURL_ID=35418&URL_DO=DO_TOPIC&URL_SECTION=201.html (accessed 13 January 2014).

Vencatachellum, Indrasen (2013), 'Introduction', in Carmella Padilla, *The Work of Art: Folk Artists in the 21st Century*, Santa Fe, NM: International Folk Art Alliance Media, pp. 11–13.

Waterman, Annie (2014), 'Design counselor: Helping artisans become more self-sufficient through better design', available at http://handeyemagazine.com/content/design-counselor (accessed 23 January 2014).

West Elm (2013), 'Letter from Brooklyn: West Elm's 2013 Clinton Global Initiative Commitment to Action', available at http://blog.westelm.com/2013/09/26/west-elm-cgi/ (accessed 20 January 2014).

West Elm (2014), 'Craftmark Indian artisans connecting craft communities with mainstream markets', available at http://www.westelm.com/pages/handcrafted/maker-handmark.htm (accessed 20 January 2014).
World Fair Trade Organization (WFTO) (2014), '10 principles of fair trade', available at http://www.wfto.com/index.php?option=com_content&task=view&id=2&Itemid=14 (accessed 10 January 2014).

27. Fair trade for small farmer cooperatives in Latin America

*Marie-Christine Renard**

INTRODUCTION

Labeled fair trade was born as Max Havelaar in 1988 at the request of Mexican coffee producers to a Dutch non-governmental organization (NGO).[1] Twenty-five years later, Latin America continues to lead the fair trade movement as measured by the volume of its products circulating in commercial fair trade networks, the number of small producers involved and the dynamism of supporting organizations. Coffee maintains its position as the chief fair trade product. However, the founders of this initiative and this story's protagonists no longer identify themselves with the fair trade movement. Instead they seek to reclaim fair trade's founding principles through a system under their own control: the Small Producers' Label (SPP).[2] This chapter will discuss this history and the relationship between small Latin American and Caribbean producers and Fairtrade International, the primary fair trade organization (formerly known as Fairtrade Labelling Organizations International). This is a story of how actors in the global South insist on not being treated solely as beneficiaries of fair trade but rather as full and equal partners (Wilkinson and Mascarenhas 2007). It illustrates how actors articulate diverging definitions of what fair trade should be and examines the rivalry for its legitimate definition (Renard 2005; Renard and Loconto 2013). For Latin American producers' organizations, fair trade should be a means for development – a tool for their own empowerment and survival in the global market. Thus they critique fair trade's current commercial orientation in which sales volumes have become the most important consideration and 'growth has become an end in itself' (CLAC 2010). Latin American producers' opposition has focused on the strategic decisions informed by this commercial orientation regarding who to accept within the system and who to certify. These decisions threaten their accomplishments and, by doing so, their existence as producers.

A WIDENING GAP BETWEEN FAIRTRADE INTERNATIONAL AND SMALL PRODUCERS

The distance and differences between Fairtrade governance bodies and the producers of fair trade products emerged in 1997 when Fairtrade International was established as a centralized organization. Up until then National Initiatives (NIs) in the global North (e.g., Max Havelaar Netherlands, TransFair Germany) had carried out the administrative activities, regulation and relationships with producer cooperatives. The employees of these initiatives came from civil society and alternative trade activism. Thus, they maintained personal and trusting relationships with producer cooperative administrators with whom they had long been collaborating. After all, together they had built the network of fair trade. With the expansion of fair trade to other countries and its growth to include more products, the initiatives decided to centralize their activities through Fairtrade International headquartered in Bonn, Germany. Fairtrade International created a professionalized bureaucracy whose employees were unfamiliar to producers.

Until 1999 only NIs were members of Fairtrade International's core governance body; six NIs made up the administrative committee with producers only attending as observers (Coscione 2012; Renard and Pérezgrovas 2007; Renard 2010a). The staff of these NIs gradually shifted from individuals who shared the fair trade labeling founders' vision of fair trade and connection to Third World advocacy, to individuals with backgrounds in business. This change partially occurred due to requests from producers themselves who wanted NIs to increase sales in their respective countries.[3] However, the inclusion of new organizations also influenced this shift. TransFair USA quickly became the largest NI with the highest volume of certified products after joining Fairtrade International in 1999. It became blatantly clear to producers that Fairtrade and the NIs no longer prioritized developing and empowering producers' organizations but rather increasing sales volumes and revenues. Fairtrade International representatives justified this shift by arguing that larger sales benefited a greater number of small producers (statement by Paul Rice, CEO of TransFair USA in, among others, Jaffee 2007, 207). Producers answered that the volumes of sales could not be reached at any cost and that among the changes that they could not accept were the certifications to plantations and transnational corporations. These have been two of the most conflictive developments in the relationship between producers and Fairtrade International (Renard and Pérezgrovas 2007).

THE CONTROVERSY OVER CERTIFYING PLANTATIONS

Small producers developed fair trade for small producers. Plantations entered the system in 1995 when European NIs, specifically TransFair Germany and Max Havelaar Switzerland, decided to sell tea with the fair trade label despite Latin American producers' and Max Havelaar Netherlands' opposition (Renard 1999).[4] In the beginning of the fair trade movement, NIs could only purchase from plantations when purchasing products rarely cultivated by small producers. However, certified plantations have grown rapidly in the system, especially in Africa and Asia, and have come to include goods that small producers offer, such as bananas (Barrientos et al. 2007).

Growth of plantation certification corresponds with the increase in demand from supermarket chains and corporations that have chosen to participate in this dynamic niche market. These new markets require large volumes of homogeneous products and thus prefer to enter into commercial contracts with a single owner of large-scale agricultural enterprise rather than the administration of a cooperative. Small producers criticize the unequal competition they face from plantations due to economies of scale, especially since they have not been able to sell all their products in the fair trade market and many small producers continue to be excluded from the system (CLAC 2004). Proponents of plantation certification have argued that it could help raise labor standards for plantation workers who are often the poorest and most marginal populations in rural regions. Producers have three counterarguments. First they point out that certification does not guarantee improved conditions for workers as the primary benefactor is the plantation owner. Second they argue that there are other mechanisms for the protection of workers' rights under the International Labor Organization, while for small producers no such mechanism exists. Third they contend that plantations represent a model of worker exploitation and land usurpation that has a dark history in Latin America (CLAC 2004).

Small producers' opposition succeeded in prohibiting Fairtrade certification of plantations producing four products: coffee, cacao, cotton and honey. However, this prohibition expires in 2015 (Fairtrade International 2013). At that time the Fairtrade International Board will discuss the issue once again. Considering Fairtrade International's recent decisions – as will be seen below – it is probable that they will choose to extend certification to plantations producing these products. This poses a great risk for small producers.

CERTIFYING CORPORATIONS?

Fairtrade International's certification of transnational corporate buyers is another cause for small producers' concern. Corporations' fair trade purchases account for only a small percentage of their entire product lines and leads to 'fair washing'. Corporations engaged in this type of behavior compete against businesses that only purchase fair trade products and take advantage of the investments made by fair trade pioneers (Jaffee 2010; Reed 2009; Renard 2005). The most negative consequence is that corporations' purchasing power (the volumes they handle) allow them to incentivize the dilution of norms and standards (Jaffee and Howard 2010; Reed 2009). Although the Fairtrade International label is differentiated from other 'fair' labels by its minimum price, the dilution of standards can be observed here as well: despite producer protests, the minimum price for coffee remained constant until 2007 even though it had depreciated by 39 per cent in real terms (Bacon et al. 2006). Similarly, Fairtrade International delayed three years to update the minimum price for cacao from US$1750 per ton to US$2000. In this case, Fairtrade International simply raised the minimum price to the market price (Eberhart 2013) and has considered the possibility of lowering the price to previous levels once again and replacing it with an investment fund. When sugar producers asked for an increase in the Fairtrade minimum sugar price, the price guarantee disappeared entirely (interview with the president of the CLAC sugar network, Coscione 2012). Some have suggested directing the social premium, currently freely used by cooperatives, to a production improvement fund, which is a strategy used by African cacao corporations to ensure product quality (Coscione 2012, 245; Eberhart 2013). The increasing influence of corporations has also led to the growth of plantations in the Fairtrade system due to their demand for a constant and homogeneous supply. Sainsbury's and Waitrose chains' decision to exclusively purchase Fairtrade bananas in 2005 has meant the incorporation of many banana plantations in the Dominican Republic and Colombia (Eberhart 2013). Today, banana plantations produce 30 per cent of the total volume of Fairtrade bananas.

CONTRACTED AGRICULTURE: ANOTHER TROJAN HORSE

Corporations also entered the Fairtrade system as traders (exporters) through the contracted production model, a decision made against the wishes of the CLAC (Latin American and Caribbean Network of Small Fair Trade Producers; CLAC 2010; Coscione 2012, 97). The case of coffee in Mexico offers a concrete example of the consequences of the adoption of this model. FLO-Cert, Fairtrade International's certification organization, has certified corporations that now wage commercial war on cooperatives in coffee-producing regions. The case of United Agroindustries of Mexico (AMSA),[5] a subsidiary of Ecom Trading group dedicated to the commodities business, offers an example. AMSA is currently the largest coffee purchaser and exporter in Mexico.[6] Its coffee division is one of the largest in the coffee market and thus has branches in the principal coffee producing countries. Aside from controlling the majority of conventional coffee, AMSA has likewise entered the quality coffee market including organic and 'sustainable' labeled coffees. It buys these types of coffee for roasting corporations, including Rainforest Alliance certified coffee for Kraft Jacobs Suchard.[7] In Ixhuatlán, Veracruz, AMSA has partnered to provide Nestlé with a special coffee for the production of Nespresso (Larroa 2010). In the region of Jaltenango, Chiapas, Starbucks has declared AMSA as its preferred supplier for its coffee, produced following the corporation's CAFÉ Practices (Renard 2010b). AMSA has brought to Mexico the Union Control certifier that provides all existing certifications including Fairtrade certification for coffee.

Leaders of Coopcafé, the coordinating group of Chiapas and Oaxaca coffee-cultivator cooperatives, assert that AMSA's purchasing power allows it to pay cash for small producers' coffee sold outside their cooperatives.[8] Small producers accept the transaction in order to obtain money immediately. In effect, the cooperatives have to sell off part of their harvest in order to compensate their members, delaying the final payment. In this way AMSA has been able to undermine the cooperatives by stealing their members. AMSA has roped coffee farmers into providing it with coffee and has created false producers' organizations using credit, programs and public subsidies (Renard 2012). Some of this coffee passes FLO-Cert inspections and thereby allows AMSA to sell it as Fairtrade, competing with the coffee of authentic small farmers' organizations. When trainers from Costa Rica's office provided FLO-Cert training workshops regarding the Fairtrade certification process in Chiapas in October 2013, the majority of participants were employees at AMSA's coffee collection centers in southeastern Mexico. Representatives from the aforementioned fictitious organizations also attended and small producers identified them as purchasers (*coyotes*) servicing AMSA. The workshop consisted of a description of criteria and procedures for certification following a procedural logic (how things ought to be done), with scarce mention of the values and principles of fair trade.[9]

The 2010 CLAC Fourth General Assembly's declaration rejected both the certification of transnational corporations and plantations as well as contracted production, 'considering that this mechanism of certifying unorganized producers as Fairtrade comes into conflict with the FLO strategic framework that states the *raison d'être* of this system as strengthening and developing small producers' organizations' (Coscione 2012, 97). Fair trade was born to create spaces for small producers in a market dominated by transnational oligopolies, enabling them to survive the vicissitudes of the market (Jaffee 2007; Renard 1999). Today, corporations have occupied these spaces with the authorization of FLO-Cert, which has essentially 'let the fox into the henhouse'.

THE SEPARATION OF STANDARDS-SETTING AND CERTIFICATION BODIES

In 2003 Fairtrade International instituted an important change: they created FLO-Cert, an independent and professionalized organization responsible for regulating the certification process. Fairtrade International hoped to gain consumer credibility through this measure by adopting a third-party certification and ISO 65 accreditation. Producers agreed to this change to ensure reliable verification despite the fact that the change would introduce fees for a previously free certification. Nevertheless, the certification process and its costs have been another source of conflict between producers and Fairtrade International. Despite reaching a consensus on a payment system in September 2003, two months later, in a meeting where no producers were present, Fairtrade International decided to institute a different system. The new system uses production volume quotas that punish the largest cooperatives. Tensions ran so high that the CLAC decided not to pay FLO-Cert. Fairtrade International threatened to suspend their registry, to which the CLAC responded that they would instead work directly with their buyers. In order to remedy the conflict, the groups entered into a provisional agreement in 2004 (Renard and Pérezgrovas 2007). In addition to increasing the costs for cooperatives, the professionalization of FLO-Cert has meant more complicated bureaucratic processes with increasing criteria and required documentation.[10] In Mexico producers managed to lower the certification costs with the accreditation of Certimex, a Mexican certifier founded in the 1990s, for small organic coffee farmer organizations that do not deal in US dollars. Certimex obtained ISO 65 accreditation before FLO-Cert. Fairtrade

International stopped recognizing Certimex as a certifier, demanding that it finance its own accreditation and pay to use Fairtrade International's database. Certimex could not agree to these demands due to their inordinate costs.[11]

Fairtrade certification has become an extremely technical process carried out by people without any investment in the fair trade movement who do not differentiate in their certification of corporations and cooperatives. Fair trade scholarship has emphasized how professionalization of certification processes and the creation of professional agencies result in the disempowerment of those who initially created the regulatory systems (Jaffee 2012; Renard 2010a; Renard and Loconto 2013). In a few years, fair trade transitioned from a relationship based on negotiation and consensus between Northern and Southern actors to the control of the North over Southern activities (Yepez and Mormont 2006).[12]

WINNING VOTES BUT NOT POWER

Pressure from producers, primarily from Latin America, has resulted in the gradual expansion of seats in Fairtrade International's Board of Directors. In 1997 producers did not have any votes. In 1999 they won two seats, one for Latin America and one for Africa. In 2001 the Board expanded to include four producer representatives (two for Latin America and one for Africa and Asia respectively) and two purchaser representatives (one commercial and one alternative trade organization). In 2005 the Board reduced NI representation by five and added three 'independent' representatives or consumer representatives (Renard and Pérezgrovas 2007). Still, the voice of small producers remained a minority and their vote was on many occasions isolated.[13]

Many Fairtrade International administrators made decisions without the preferences of producers' organizations or even against their wishes. Producers' organizations have seen themselves marginalized from procedures determining membership registry, label users and regulations, and from trading decisions dominated by NIs and commissions made up of Northern personnel. For instance, in 2009 Fairtrade International adopted regulations for fair trade gold (from Peru) despite opposition from the CLAC and its Asian and African counterparts. In a statement, the CLAC explains its opposition. They argue that mining should not be certified due to ecological reasons, like soil erosion and water contamination, and the social costs of mining, like the working conditions of miners, the use of child labor and the threat to subsistence agriculture. These ecological and social considerations go against CLAC principles

(CLAC 2009; Coscione 2012, 107). They end their statement with the following words:

> Fair trade is of utmost importance to our producers, our collective effort created it to offer an alternative ruled by democracy and participation, by respect for the environment and human beings, by solidarity, equity, and transparency. We understand gold as a threat to these values. The benefits are small compared to the threats posed to the system and our producers' lives. The CLAC does not follow the FLO's decision, given that *we cannot accept that the market controls the fair trade market.* (CLAC 2009, emphasis added)

SMALL PRODUCER EMPOWERMENT: THE CLAC AND THE SPP

The marginalization of small producers in Fairtrade International's decision-making convinced them to organize themselves in order to better defend their interests. The Latin American Coordinator of coffee farmers has existed since 1996. In its Fifth Regional Assembly in Oaxaca, Mexico, in August 2004, participants decided to form the Latin American and Caribbean Network of Small Fair Trade Producers (CLAC).[14] It achieved legal status with the approval of its statutes in 2005 in El Salvador, where its headquarters are located (Coscione 2012; Renard and Pérezgrovas 2007). The CLAC is organized by product networks and by country (National Coordinators). There are networks for coffee, cacao, bananas, sugar, honey, fruit juices, fresh fruit and quinoa. Membership also includes producers of medicinal herbs and dried fruits. More than 300 organizations in 21 countries comprise the CLAC. The General Assembly meets every two years, serving as the primary decision-making mechanism. Thirteen representatives compose the Board of Directors. No country can have more than two representatives on the Board of Directors.

The CLAC also serves another purpose: better coordinating producers in order to handle purchasers who do not respect the conditions of fair trade. Years after the establishment of fair trade cooperatives, this problem continues to affect many of the cooperatives. In the CLAC's Fifth Assembly in 2012 and the Second Fair Trade Andean Meeting in 2013, cooperatives raised numerous complaints against those purchasers who tie their agreement to purchase at Fairtrade prices with purchases at conventional prices or who do not honor the payment of the social premium.[15] When cooperatives from one country refuse this treatment, these purchasers simply find in other countries cooperatives that are willing to accept these terms. Thus an important role for the CLAC and the National Fair Trade Coordinators is to avoid this through co-ordination.

In 2006 in Chiapas, Mexico, the CLAC went even further and released its own label, the Small Producers' Label (SPP). This initiative seeks to return to the original principles of fair trade – in other words, placing producer economic and social development at the center of the strategy. The SPP is an initiative by and for small producers under their own control.[16] The SPP does not endorse any qualification: it is not a label indicating fairness, sustainability or ethics. These concepts can have criteria subject to controversy and competition. Instead, SPP presents itself as the symbol of small producers.[17] Its founders have developed a registry and certification system that avoids the pitfalls they critiqued in Fairtrade International's system. The General Regulation contains the SPP certification criteria, which bases itself on the Declaration of Principles and Values. All participants seeking certification must sign the Ethics Code, which binds them to behave according to the values of inclusion, sustainability, solidarity, respect, transparency, liberty, equity, diversity, congruence, local economy, responsibility, justice, integrity, confidentiality, honesty, quality, protection of children from labor and professionalism.[18] This code anchors the possibility of Objection Procedure, which allows members to raise objections about the certification of producers' organizations or businesses according to conflicts with the SPP Ethics Code. This offers a guarantee against the corporations that producer countries questioned due to their unethical practices (FUNDEPPO 2013). Moreover, the regulation demands:

> The minimum requirement for a business wishing to use the SPP in (some) of its products: it must trade at least 5% of its total volume according to SPP criteria, with a long-term commitment to reach at least 25%. This is exactly to avoid that large businesses take advantage of our label with relatively minimal efforts and reap large benefits in terms of image. (FUNDEPPO 2013)

The Foundation of Organized Small Producers administers the initiative, with FUNDEPPO as the regulatory mechanism that is headquartered in Mexico. At the end of March 2014, 58 organizations used the SPP certification (increasing from 17 in 2012 and 53 in 2013) that group more than 67 000 producers of which 20 are Mexican coffee cooperatives (FUNDEPPO 2014a). It has agreements with 18 purchaser businesses in the United States (5), Canada (4), France (4), Mexico (1), Honduras (1), Colombia (1), Germany (1) and Ecuador (1) (FUNDEPPO 2014b). Equal Exchange's participation was significant because Equal Exchange is a pioneering US fair trade alternative trade organization. It terminated support for the Fairtrade International system in 2004 due to a disagreement with TransFair USA's orientation (Jaffee 2010). SPP works with seven certifier agencies, including Certimex, MAYACERT Biolatina and IMO Control Latinoamérica. It offers higher prices than Fairtrade International.[19]

Since 2012, Fairtrade International has raised questions about the relationship between SPP and the CLAC that created it, as described in the following section. In particular, Fairtrade International has questioned whether the CLAC, a member of Fairtrade International, can or should support another label, especially one whose very existence is an implicit criticism of its model.

FAIRTRADE INTERNATIONAL, FAIR TRADE USA AND THE CLAC IN LABELING GOVERNANCE

TransFair USA's exit from the Fairtrade International system in 2011 had consequences not only for producers but also for Fairtrade governance. TransFair USA, renamed as Fair Trade USA, was the NI with the highest product volumes and thereby a significant contributor to Fairtrade International through fee payments. Its exit has meant a market loss for certain organizations[20] and coffee cooperatives fear displacement by plantations following the implementation of Fair Trade USA's 'Fair Trade for All' model. It likewise signaled Fairtrade International's loss of hegemony in fair trade (Ballet et al. 2012). This hegemony has been called into question by SPP's existence and other 'sustainable' initiatives related to corporations like Utz and Rainforest Alliance that compete for fair trade market consumers (Fridell et al. 2008). Fairtrade International responded by strengthening ties with producer networks and ceding to demands for power sharing. In 2011, Fairtrade International offered producers 50 per cent of the General Assembly votes and 50 per cent of the positions on the Board of Directors as well as allowing CLAC to administer the Liaison Officers of Fairtrade International in Latin American countries. Nevertheless, Fairtrade International added a new article in the statutes prohibiting members from supporting or promoting another label, unless agreed upon with the Board, in clear reference to the SPP. That is to say, at the same time it offered co-ownership of the initiative, Fairtrade International demanded that the CLAC abandon SPP or submit it as a 'sub-label' of Fairtrade.

At the beginning of 2014 it is still not clear how Fairtrade International will distribute producer votes. Their representation is divided according to the three producing regions: the CLAC for Latin America, the Network of Asian Producers for Asia and Fair Trade Africa. The CLAC is the only organization that exclusively represents small producers, considering that the Asian and African networks include many plantations.[21] If votes were distributed equally among the networks, CLAC would receive 16.6 per cent of the votes despite having larger sales volumes in the system.

There have already been changes in the relationship between the CLAC and the SPP. In the CLAC's Fifth Assembly in Quito, Ecuador, in November 2013, participants discussed the quandary that Fairtrade International statutes presented to CLAC. On the one hand there are the years of disagreement and effort that SPP represents; on the other hand, the fact that sales in the Fairtrade International system decouples the incipient SPP sales. Given this situation the CLAC member organizations have adopted the following agreements:

- Approve the new Fairtrade International Constitution and adopt the terms with criticism (Accord 2).
- Give the property rights of SPP to Latin American civil society and organize a committee to make the transition in a single year (Accord 1).

In April 2014 a joint statement from the CLAC and FUNDEPPO enumerated the following agreements reached by the Assembly:

- The Small Producers' Organization (OPP)[22] certified SPP will be the new proprietors of FUNDEPPO (Accord 1).
- The CLAC cedes legal rights to the SPP and FUNDEPPO brands completely and definitively (Accord 2).
- The OPP certified SPP will be shareholding partners of FUNDEPPO's General Assembly with voice and vote … (Accord 3).
- The CLAC accompanies the FUNDEPPO in its search for funding for itself and the SPP in order to achieve sustainability (Accord 7). (CLAC–FUNDEPPO 2014)

In other words, the CLAC did not abandon the SPP but instead is leaving SPP certified organizations with greater label autonomy. It also shows that, while still defending its point of view, the CLAC takes seriously co-ownership of Fairtrade International.

In February 2014, through statutes and in a temporary capacity, the CLAC's president was appointed president of Fairtrade International's Board of Directors. This has strengthened the perception that CLAC and small producers are empowered within Fairtrade International. Despite this important position, celebrated extensively on Fairtrade International's website, changes in governance do not necessarily change decision-making processes. Fairtrade International has shown resistance in delegating some of its power, particularly in changing these decision-making processes, which are very centralized in the organization's bureaucracy.[23] In 2004, for example, reports from the producer representatives in the Board of Directors emphasize that Fairtrade International personnel have not implemented some Board decisions (Coscione 2012, 79).

Fairtrade International is still very far from taking into account small producers' points of view. Fairtrade International's November 2013 adoption of a new model, the Fairtrade Sourcing Programs (FSP) for cacao, sugar and cotton – three products that cannot be sourced from plantations until 2015 – clearly shows this. The model stipulates that a product like chocolate will be required to only have a single one of its ingredients certified instead of the maximum possible (current policy).[24] That is to say, Fairtrade International diminished the criteria in order to attract corporations and increase sales with mass consumer products. Such products will use a logo only slightly different than the current one, ensuring that most consumers will not notice a difference. The CLAC rejected this proposal, arguing that it will foster, among other things:

- Consumer confusion regarding the alternative 'Fairtrade' label, weakening the message of the Fairtrade label, something that affects all Fairtrade products in the market.
- Unfair competition between two models and two labels, considering that interested companies in the FSP have significant capital to promote the new label (CLAC 2013).

The CLAC was the only member that voted against the proposal. Fairtrade International's CEO has already announced an agreement with Mars and another eight companies that will lead to an increase of cacao sales by 14 per cent in 2014.[25] This is to say that while Fairtrade International announces greater participation for small producers in its organization, its actions reveal a predominant market logic that will likely lead to new tensions among the organizations of the CLAC and Fairtrade International. Having accepted the co-ownership of Fairtrade International with criticisms, Latin American producers decided to continue fighting for the respect of their values without abandoning the 'other path', the SPP. They fear that Fairtrade International will continue to adapt regulations to the wishes of corporations, and in 2015 this will include extending certification to plantations for the products currently reserved for small producers.

CONCLUSION

Fair trade has undergone many changes in the past years, including the questioning of Fairtrade International's hegemony from a variety of fronts, from small producers, Fair Trade USA and other initiatives related to corporations. Actors have been moving and redefining the very conceptualization of what constitutes 'fair'. Given the proliferation of labels and standards, concepts like ethics, social justice and fairness have become ambiguous and are subject to constant renegotiation (Reinecke et al. 2012). Conflicts arise concerning their definitions and the hegemony and legitimacy of varied regulations and standards (Renard and Loconto 2013).

Through this process of redefinition, Latin American small producers have organized the CLAC, with their product networks and their National Coordinators playing an essential role. The CLAC aimed to address small producers' marginalization in decision-making in an initiative founded by and for small producers. Subsequently, they have attempted to reclaim the values of empowerment and development for their organizations and avoid the 'free rider' strategies employed by businesses. Small producers seek to build a network with the collaboration of companies that have a commitment to their principles and values. Fair trade finds itself, and not for the first time, at a crossroads: although it has improved the inclusion of small producers in the market and has helped them survive, these accomplishments are constantly eroded and threatened while corporations 'colonize' fair trade's criteria and organizations (Morgan et al. 2006). In the fight for who will define fair trade and who will be its primary actors and benefactors, this is a critical moment.

NOTES

* Many thanks to Sean Luna McAdams for his assistance in translating this chapter from Spanish to English.

1. Its own protagonists have told this story (Roozen and van der Hoff 2002).
2. Símbolo de los Pequeños Productores.
3. Interview with the first CLAC president in Coscione (2012).
4. Interview with Victor Pérezgrovas, representative of Latin American producers in Fairtrade International's Board of Directors in 2006.
5. Agroindustria Mexicana S.A.
6. Interview with coffee purchasers in the State Coffee Council in Chiapas in 2010; there are no official data on volumes purchased by various corporations.
7. Interview in the Union Control agency office in Jaltenango, Chiapas, in 2010.
8. Interviews conducted over the course of more than ten years with producers' organizations' administrators and advisors, principally in Chiapas but also in Oaxaca (Mexico). See also Renard (1999) and Renard and Pérezgrovas (2007).

9. Participants often asked if the minimum price really was an obligatory regulation; the instructor, ex-employee of the Chiquita company, seemed surprised when the author commented about the conflicts between producers and AMSA and ignored that certain producers' organizations were in fact created by AMSA. AMSA employees informed that since it was granted a single certification for the whole company, storage centers were not inspected and only the three dry mills were inspected. The documents are processed in the central office, which does not allow for producer verification. (Data collected by author in a training workshop.)
10. There were 150 criteria for certifying producers and 70 for marketers (workshop of FLO-Cert, for producers and marketers (Tuxtla Gutiérrez, Mexico, October 2013).
11. Interview with Certimex, November 2010.
12. See Bradley Wilson and Tad Mutersbaugh's chapter in this volume for more on Fairtrade certification practices.
13. In the voting procedures, the CLAC's vote was often isolated, with African representatives afraid to oppose Fairtrade International and Asian representatives clearly defending plantation interests (interview with Victor Pérezgrovas 2006 and 2014, producer representative in the Fairtrade International Board of Directors and CLAC president 2004–2006; see also Coscione 2012, 63).
14. Coordinadora Latinoamericana y del Caribe de Pequeños Productores de Comercio Justo.For more information about the CLAC, see http://clac-comerciojusto.org.
15. Meeting attended by author in Cuzco, Peru, in November 2012.
16. One of FUNDEPPO's mottos is 'the SPP is not speaking for the small producers; WE ARE the small producers' (FUNDEPPO 2014b).
17. Small producers' organizations is defined as organizations whose membership consists of at least 85 per cent of farmers that have less than 15 productive hectares or less than one greenhouse hectare or 500 bee hives. Fifteen per cent of members can have up to twice these limits, but these exceptions are going to be revised (FUNDEPPO 2014b).
18. More information about the SPP is available at its website www.tusimbolo.org. See also Renard and Loconto (2013).
19. The price for SPP certified coffee (by pound) is US$1.60 sustainable minimum + $.20 SPP incentive + $.40 organic premium. The price of Fairtrade coffee is $1.40 guaranteed minimum + $.20 social premium + $.30 organic premium.
20. For example, after TransFair USA's exit, coffee purchasers no longer supply from Peru and organizations like CENFROCAFÉ have lost 50 per cent of their fair trade sales (data collected at the Second Fair Trade Andean Meeting, Cuzco, in November 2013).
21. Statements made by Merling Preza, third CLAC president (Coscione 2012, 80). Remarks collected by the author at the Fifth CLAC Assembly, Quito, Ecuador, in November 2012.
22. Organizaciones de Pequeños Productores.
23. Statements made by Raúl del Águila, second CLAC president (Coscione in 2012, 80). Statements made by Marike de Peña, fourth CLAC president and new president of Fairtrade International's Board of Directors (Coscione 2012, 111). Remarks collected by the author at the Fifth CLAC Assembly, Quito, Ecuador, in November 2012.
24. 'Rather than focusing on all the ingredients for one final product, Fairtrade Sourcing Programs means companies can now make big commitments to use Fairtrade cocoa, sugar or cotton across product ranges or even their whole business. It offers companies an alternative way to work with the Fairtrade label' (Fairtrade International 2014).
25. FSPs are part of Fairtrade International's global three-year strategy 'Unlocking the Power of the Many' which seeks to dramatically increase Fairtrade's impact for

farmers and workers. As Harriet Lamb, CEO of Fairtrade International, noted, 'We're delighted to have so many businesses already on board – and you can be sure there's more to come!' (Fairtrade International 2013).

REFERENCES

Bacon, Christopher, CAFENICA and CLAC (2006), 'Estudio de costos y propuesta de precios para sostener el café, las familias productoras y organizaciones certificadas por el Comercio Justo en América Latina y el Caribe', CLAC.

Ballet, Jérôme, Marie-Christine Renard and Aurélie Carimentrand (2012), 'Le commerce équitable Sud–Sud et l'émergence des labels locaux', *Mondes en Développement*, 160 (4), 75–84.

Barrientos, Stephanie, Michael E. Conroy and Elaine Jones (2007), 'Northern social movement and fair trade', in Laura T. Raynolds, Douglas Murray and John Wilkinson (eds.), *Fair Trade: The Challenge of Transforming Globalization*, New York: Routledge, pp. 51–62.

CLAC (2004), 'Private plantations and FLO's future', unpublished document to be discussed by the Fairtrade International Meeting of Members and FLO Board.

CLAC (2009), 'Pronunciamiento ante FLO sobre la no certificación de oro', internal memo sent to author and FLO.

CLAC (2010), 'Declaración de la IV Asamblea General de la CLAC en relación a la participación de grandes plantaciones y la producción por contrato en el Sistema de Comercio Justo', San Pedro Sula, Honduras: CLAC.

CLAC (2013), 'Carta de respuesta de la CLAC a Fairtrade International', September.

CLAC–FUNDEPPO (2014), 'Comunicado sobre el Símbolo de Pequeños Productores', 27 March, Lima, Peru.

Coscione, Marco (2012), 'La CLAC y la defensa del pequeño productor', editorial, Funglode (Fundación Global Democracia y Desarrollo) and CLAC.

Eberhart, Nicolas (2013), 'Cambio de escala para el comercio justo: riesgos y limitaciones', paper from the Second Fair Trade Andean Meeting, Cuzco, Peru.

Fairtrade International (2013), 'Unlocking the power of the many: Fairtrade International's 2013–15 strategic framework', available at http://www.fairtrade.net/fileadmin/user_upload/content/2009/about_us/documents/EN_Unlocking_the_power_of_the_many_strategic_framework_final.pdf (accessed 19 May 2014).

Fairtrade International (2014) website, available at www.fairtrade.net (accessed 22 February 2014).

Fridell, Mara, Ian Hudson and Mark Hudson (2008), 'With friends like these: The corporate response to fair trade coffee', *Review of Radical Political Economics*, 40 (1), 8–34.

FUNDEPPO (2013), 'Opinión SPP-FUNDEPPO con respeto a la participación de empresas multinacionales en el Comercio Justo internacional', internal memo.

FUNDEPPO (2014a), 'Lista de organizaciones de pequeños productores certificadas', internal memo.

FUNDEPPO (2014b), 'Small Producers' Symbol', presentation at the Specialty Coffee Association of America Event, Seattle, Washington, April 2014.

Jaffee, Daniel (2007), *Brewing Justice: Fair Trade Coffee, Sustainability and Survival*, Oakland, CA: University of California Press.

Jaffee, Daniel (2010), 'Fair trade standards, corporate participation, and social movement responses in the United States', *Journal of Business Ethics*, 92 (S2), 267–285.

Jaffee, Daniel (2012), 'Weak coffee: Certification and co-optation in the fair trade movement', *Social Problems*, 59 (1), 94–116.

Jaffee, Daniel and Philip H. Howard (2010), 'Corporate cooptation of organic and fair trade standards', *Agriculture and Human Values*, 27 (4), 387–399.
Larroa, Rosa María (2010), 'Ixhuatlán del café frente al poder transnacional', *La Jornada del Campo*, 29, 13 February.
Morgan, Kevin, Terry Marsden and Jonathan Murdoch (2006), *Worlds of Food: Place, Power and Provenance in the Food Chain*, Oxford: Oxford University Press.
Reed, Darryl (2009), 'What do corporations have to do with fair trade? Positive and normative analysis from a value chain perspective', *Journal of Business Ethics*, 86 (S1), 3–26.
Reinecke, Juliane, Stephan Manning and Olivier von Hagen (2012), 'The emergence of a standards market: Multiplicity of sustainability standards in the global coffee industry', *Organization Studies*, 33 (5–6), 791–814.
Renard, Marie-Christine (1999), *Los intersticios de la globalización: Un label (Max Havelaar) para los pequeños productores de café*, Mexico City: Center of Mexican and Central American Studies.
Renard, Marie-Christine (2005), 'Quality certification, regulation and power in fair trade', *Journal of Rural Studies*, 21 (4), 419–431.
Renard, Marie-Christine (2010a), 'Régulation et gouvernance du Commerce Equitable: une analyse stratégique des évolutions récentes', in Marie-France Turcotte and Chantal Hervieu (eds.), *Mettre en marché pour une cause*, Montréal: Presses de l'Université de Québec, pp. 27–39.
Renard, Marie-Christine (2010b), 'In the name of conservation: CAFE practices and fair trade in Mexico', *Journal of Business Ethics*, 92 (S2), 287–299.
Renard, Marie-Christine (2012), 'Los retos de la valorización de un café de "origen": el caso de la Reserva del Triunfo de Chiapas', in Gerardo Torres Salcido and Rosa María Larroa Torres (eds.), *Sistemas agroalimentarios Localizados: Identidad territorial, construcción de capital social e instituciones*, Centrode Investigaciones Interdisciplinarias en Ciencias y Humanidades, Facultad de Ciencias Pollíticas y Sociales Uiversidad Nacional Autónoma de Mexico y Juan Pablos Editores, pp. 117–133.
Renard, Marie-Christine and Allison Loconto (2013), 'Competing logics in the further standardization of fair trade: ISEAL and the Símbolo de Pequeños Productores', *International Journal of Sociology of Agriculture and Food*, 20 (1), 51–68.
Renard, Marie-Christine and Víctor Pérezgrovas (2007), 'Fair trade coffee in Mexico: At the centre of the debate', in Laura T. Raynolds, Douglas Murray and John Wilkinson (eds.), *Fair Trade: The Challenge of Transforming Globalization*, New York: Routledge, pp. 138–156.
Roozen, Nico and Frans van der Hoff (2002), *La aventura del Comercio Justo*, Atajo Ediciones.
Wilkinson, John and Gilberto Mascarenhas (2007), 'Southern social movements and fair trade', in Laura T. Raynolds, Douglas Murray and John Wilkinson (eds.), *Fair Trade: The Challenge of Transforming Globalization*, New York: Routledge, pp. 125–137.
Yepez, Isabel and Marc Mormont (2006), *Le commerce équitable face aux nouveaux défis commerciaux: Evolution des dynamiques d'acteurs*, Brussels: Politique Scientifique Nationale.

28. Fair trade and plantation workers in Asia

Rie Makita

INTRODUCTION

In the agricultural sector of the global South, Fairtrade certification has aimed to benefit both *landed* small farmers through their cooperatives and *landless* workers through the plantations for which they work. Existing studies suggest that whereas Fairtrade has improved social conditions and collective capacity for workers in Latin America and Africa (e.g., Raynolds 2012; Valerie Nelson and Adrienne Martin's chapter in this volume), Fairtrade has not helped workers in the hierarchical structure of tea plantations in India (Besky 2014). Conceding the limitations of Fairtrade in Asian plantations, in this chapter I argue that workers can turn such limitations to their own advantage and substantially benefit from Fairtrade within two different contexts in Asia.[1]

Some hired laborers in Asia make their living within the plantation system, while others seek opportunities in alternative contexts. To illustrate how Fairtrade certification can work for both groups, I draw on two case studies (Makita 2012; under review): 1) a tea plantation in India and 2) a cooperative of former sugarcane plantation workers in the Philippines. The first examines how current tea plantation workers take advantage of the invisibility of Fairtrade under the important patron–client power relations between plantation management and workers. The second evaluates how the former sugarcane plantation workers incorporate Fairtrade into their total livelihood strategies under a land reform program, especially by making certification-supported farming compatible with other livelihoods.

CURRENT TEA PLANTATION WORKERS IN INDIA

Historical Background

Tea plantations in India are a legacy of the British colonial administration. In the 1830s, workers were recruited from different tribal areas, many of which were afflicted by famine. The objective of such a form of worker recruitment was to retain a captive labor force at low wages without developing a free labor market. Planters preferred to recruit families rather than single workers, not only to fetter male workers, but also to ensure labor force reproduction. Females were also preferred as workers because of their sensitive fingertips suitable for tea plucking and lower inclination to unionize. Once migrant laborers reached the plantations, they were bound by contract and other coercive measures to serve for specific periods. Planters were able to arrest laborers who absconded without a warrant and imprison those who refused to work. Thus, plantation work was sometimes described as 'unfree' or 'bonded' labor. After India gained independence, departing British planters were replaced by a new cadre of Indian management, which took the form of small individual family-owned plantations, large Indian-owned corporations or multinational corporations (Behal and Mohapatra 1992; Chakrabarti and Sarkar 2005; Chatterjee 2001; Dasgupta 1992; Sharma and Das 2009).

The 1951 Plantation Labour Act (PLA) was a landmark in the welfare of plantation workers. This prohibited employers' inhumane behavior towards employees and exhaustively regulated the working and living conditions of workers, including their entitlements concerning housing, sanitation, drinking water, medical facilities, canteens, crèches and primary schools. To date, however, there are very few tea plantations where all PLA provisions have been fully implemented (Sharma and Das 2009; Singh et al. 2006). Thus, the safe working conditions required by Fairtrade are by no means redundant in the contemporary era.

There is a distinct hierarchy in the plantation system, that is, the class structure of employees. The vertical hierarchy broadly comprises four categories: 1) management, including plantation managers, assistant managers and factory managers; 2) staff, including all white-collar employees in senior supervisory positions; 3) sub-staff, including all other subordinate employees in supervisory positions; and 4) rank-and-file workers engaged in either field or factory operations. In the typical management style of plantations, orders issued from the top are relayed through this structure, which serves to maintain and widen social distance between management and workers as well as between the upper and lower ranks of employees (Chakrabarti and Sarkar 2005).

Analytical Framework: Patron–Client Relations inside the Plantation System

Fairtrade applied to the plantation sector aims to benefit fixed-wage workers through standards to ensure better working conditions and

Fairtrade premiums used for worker communities (Fairtrade International 2009). When workers stay in the plantation sector, worker benefits are shaped by how plantation management offers workers an enabling environment, which is greatly influenced by traditional patron–client relations between the management and workers. The patron–client relationship is defined as:

> A special case of dyadic (two-person) ties involving a largely instrumental friendship in which an individual of higher socioeconomic status (patron) uses his own influence and resources to provide protection or benefits, or both, for a person of lower status (client) who, for his part, reciprocates by offering general support and assistance, including personal services, to the patron. (Scott 1972a, 92)

In this chapter I discuss the strength or weakness of this reciprocal patron–client relationship, focusing on the degree of compliance rather than affectivity and coercion. The patron grants favors to gain compliance from the client in matters crucial to patronal interests; the patron must also comply, to some extent, with client preferences and needs. 'The higher the degree of compliance, the stronger the relationship' (Carney 1989, 45).

The interactions of Fairtrade with patron–client relations are analyzed as the influence of patron–client relations on workers' perceptions of Fairtrade from two perspectives: 1) the influences that existing power relations have on shaping workers' perceptions and 2) whether certification helps strengthen or weaken the relations. In other words, workers' perceptions are interpreted as the consequence of the long-established power relations on the one hand and as the impact of Fairtrade on the relations on the other.

The Case: A Tea Estate in Darjeeling

Workers' perceptions of Fairtrade were observed in a tea estate in one of the major tea-producing areas of the world: Darjeeling, India. The Sonapahar tea estate (pseudonym) was selected for study for three reasons. First, it was one of the first estates in India to acquire both organic and Fairtrade certifications. At the time of my fieldwork in 2009, it had been exporting to Fairtrade markets for 15 years. Fairtrade was therefore expected to have affected the estate workers more fully here than in other certified tea estates. Sixty to 80 per cent of exports from Sonapahar went to the fair trade market. Second, while most Fairtrade-certified estates belonged to large-scale companies, Sonapahar was one of a few family-owned independent plantations; it therefore seemed more suitable for the direct observation of patron–client relations between management and workers. In May 2009, 555 permanent workers of Nepali origin worked and lived with their families on 670 hectares, including tea gardens, factories and nine worker settlement communities. Third, Sonapahar was one of nine Darjeeling tea plantations that allowed a non-governmental organization (NGO) called the Community Health Advancement Initiative (CHAI) to assist worker communities in the fields of health care, small-scale infrastructure and income generation. In Sonapahar, the CHAI project started in 2005 and plantation management agreed to spend part of the Fairtrade premiums on it.

Data collection focused on worker households living in one community that was close to both the factory compound and the highway connecting two major Darjeeling cities. Community residents were therefore expected to have access to more information than those in remote communities, implying that if this focus group did not have any knowledge about Fairtrade, neither did the average worker. Primary data were collected from all 62 households in the community through semi-structured interviews. The most positive answer from each household was taken as the perception of the entire household. If at least one member had some knowledge, the household was regarded as having knowledge; only when none of the adult members of a household had any knowledge, was the household counted as having no knowledge.

Typical patron–client relationships were evident on the Sonapahar estate. I noted all five of the patron-to-client flows identified by Scott (1972b, 9): 1) basic means of subsistence; 2) subsistence crisis insurance; 3) protection; 4) brokerage and influence; and 5) collective patron services. The management provided all estate workers with steady employment, land for living and other basic services in compliance with the PLA. Even in the years of poor harvests, the company guaranteed the same levels of wages and services by absorbing losses. It also provided loans or grants in the case of sickness or accident to workers' families. After monsoon damage, the management negotiated with the local government and outside supporters for the repair of workers' houses and common facilities. Fairtrade certification can be interpreted as an example of the 'brokerage' function; the management of Sonapahar used its power and influence, at least partly, 'to extract rewards from the outside for the benefit of [its] clients' (Scott 1972b, 9) by accessing Fairtrade markets. Finally, in cooperation with the management of other estates, the Sonapahar management promoted organic cultivation in the entire Darjeeling tea sector; such promotional activities led to the economic security of plantation workers in the district. By contrast, the flow of goods and services from clients to patrons was, as Scott (1972b,

9) conceded, 'hard to characterize since, as his patron's "man", a client generally [lent] his labor and talents to the patron's designs, whatever they may be'. Estate workers were employed at the same wage rate not only for tea cultivation but also for personal domestic services in the houses of the owner and managers.

The livelihood of Sonapahar workers was heterogeneous. While 55 of the 62 households in the focus community contained at least one permanent estate worker, in the remaining households (11 per cent), none of the family members worked on the estate as a permanent or temporary worker; nevertheless, they were allowed to continue to live inside Sonapahar because their deceased parents or grandparents had been permanent workers. Although the majority of the 55 households relied primarily on wages from the estate, non-estate income exceeded estate income in ten households. Between the management and those families that did not rely on estate work, there still existed a certain level of reciprocity, albeit lower than that observed between the management and those reliant on estate work. In brief, the increasing mobility to non-plantation work has generated economic disparities among worker households that were equally poor when they or their ancestors arrived on the estate. At present, clients can be divided into two groups: those who do and do not need to rely heavily on the patron.

Interactions of Fairtrade with Patron–Client Relations

Invisibility as a consequence of existing power relations

While none of the people living in the focus community, apart from one office worker, knew the concepts of Fairtrade certification, the term 'Joint Body' was more familiar to some people. I therefore asked people in Sonapahar about activities of the Joint Body, which Fairtrade International (2009) defines as a group of *elected* worker representatives organized to use Fairtrade premiums democratically. Even those who knew something about the Joint Body knew nothing about its financial sources. They guessed that it was financed by the management or donations from foreign well-wishers. Although 24 families (39 per cent) recognized a few members of the Joint Body, they merely had opportunities to see them attending a meeting at the head office. I did not come across anyone on the estate who had actually participated in the selection process of Joint Body members. Although reports from the estate office list a variety of projects in which Fairtrade premiums were invested in recent years, only microcredit, which was suspended in 2000, was significantly identified as an activity of the Joint Body (see Table 28.1). These facts suggest that rank-and-file workers have barely been informed about Fairtrade premiums, which make up an extra budget for workers' welfare as well as a return from the sales of tea – the fruits of their hard work.

Table 28.1 Worker households' perceptions of benefits from the Joint Body's activities

Benefits	No. of households
Received no benefits	22
Received*	40
Microcredit from the Joint Body	(15)
Microcredit from the estate	(19)
Cash grant from the Joint Body	(1)
Cash grant from the estate	(8)
Materials from the estate (for bio-gas)	(1)
Temporary employment from the estate	(1)
Training (medical) from the Joint Body	(1)
Total	62

Note: * Some families referred to more than one kind of benefit.

Source: Makita (2012, 98).

All of the people the focus community recognized as Joint Body members came from the staff or sub-staff; no workers from the lowest category of the hierarchy were included in the Joint Body. Two members confessed to me as follows:

> Invited by a neighbor, I happened to attend a meeting. It was a meeting of the Joint Body. Then, I was also appointed as a member on the spot. (Female paramedic in the health center)

> I was asked by the previous chief manager to attend a meeting of the Joint Body only once. I am just a reserve member, not an official member. (Male chief field supervisor)

These quotes suggest that the current Joint Body members were not elected by workers but appointed by the management. My interviews with the appointed members further revealed that they were indebted to the management in various ways; some had been given special training opportunities, while others had been promoted to good positions more quickly than their peers. Therefore, to maintain good personal relationships with the management, the members spared the minimum time and effort for duties such as attending meetings arranged for visitors and replying to questions from Fairtrade inspectors.

There were some reasons why Fairtrade was largely invisible to the workers. The chief manager conceded that it was actually difficult for uneducated workers to understand the system of Fairtrade premiums and manage the funds. He also noted that some active trade union members were attempting to use the Joint Body to pursue their union's objectives:

> Some trade union members asked me to choose them as members of the Joint Body. We [the management] refused their offer because the Joint Body should be a non-political organization. The trade union members got angry and instigated workers who had received microcredit from Fairtrade premiums to default on their repayments.

This was the reason why the popular microcredit program was suspended (Table 28.1). There had been tensions between the management and the trade union seeking wage rises. The management feared that the trade union might empower itself by organizing workers under the name of the Joint Body and by funding its anti-management activities with Fairtrade premiums. Although the management accepted the premiums for the benefit of workers, the degree of benefit had to be within the management's tolerable limits. They never allowed the Joint Body to destroy the hierarchical system on the estate. As a consequence, the management avoided informing workers about Fairtrade and made a substantial number of decisions on how to use premiums.

The impact of Fairtrade certification on existing relations

Even without knowledge of the Joint Body, many worker households enjoyed substantial benefits from Fairtrade premiums as extra services or welfare assistance other than those stipulated by the PLA (Table 28.1). The invisibility of Fairtrade led them to believe that such assistance resulted from the management's generosity. Although the premiums were used not only for such assistance to individuals but also for the operation of community facilities such as a library and a crèche, the workers had few opportunities to become aware of the facts. Workers who had received special assistance from the management showed gratitude towards them; in other words, the workers perceived that the degree of patron compliance had increased. The workers were required to work harder in response to the patron's new compliance level. Because of the invisibility of Fairtrade on the estate, the premiums simply worked as an increase in the patronage of the management towards specific individuals.

The Role of Fairtrade Certification for Current Plantation Workers

In contrast to the invisibility of Fairtrade, the community development project of an NGO, CHAI – funded partly from the Fairtrade premiums – was familiar to worker communities: 58 out of 62 households (93 per cent) in the focus community had some knowledge of the NGO project. The CHAI staff initially held a number of meetings with community members and helped them discuss and identify ways to improve their lives. In the focus community, people decided to build latrines for those households without one, using materials provided by CHAI. Regardless of the fact that their period of participation was relatively short – from 2005 to 2008 – community members were impressed by their experience of participatory community development. This was because they had been accustomed to asking the management for help, but instead, here they were able to solve their problems themselves for the first time. The workers' perceptions of the CHAI project were not influenced by the existing power relations, but simply by their own participation.

Community beneficiaries never knew that a significant portion of CHAI project funding came from Fairtrade premiums because they did not know about Fairtrade itself. The invisibility of Fairtrade, which led the workers to regard cash grants and employment funded by the Fairtrade premiums as a sign of the management's generosity, simply led them to believe that the CHAI project was a gift from the NGO. As long as the real picture concerning Fairtrade remained hidden, the management was unable to reveal their investment of the premiums in the CHAI project. Ironically, the invisibility of Fairtrade enabled workers, free from existing power relations, to take action by themselves for the benefit of their own communities.

In this case, the intervention of CHAI, an organization not affiliated with the tea estate, was required for the worker communities to achieve a development goal using the premium. It was impossible for the Joint Body to play the role played by CHAI under the hierarchical plantation system, where top-down and not bottom-up communication prevailed. The lowest category of workers could not ask questions of the staff or sub-staff who constituted the Joint Body; likewise, the staff could not ask questions of their managers. Only a third-party body such as CHAI could communicate effectively with all the different strata of the hierarchy. The intervention of a third party in the operation of Fairtrade premiums opens up a promising opportunity to make Fairtrade substantially *visible* in such a hierarchical plantation society.

FORMER SUGARCANE PLANTATION WORKERS IN THE PHILIPPINES

Historical Background

The Philippines is well known for its strong association between rural poverty and inequality of land ownership. Although several land reform programs to redress this have been attempted since the 1930s, significant inequality in land distribution still existed in 1988, when the government launched the Comprehensive Agrarian Reform Program (CARP). Under CARP, large private landowners were expected to sell their land to the government or directly to peasants, who could buy land with a government-supported loan repaid over a 30-year period. Whereas earlier land reform programs were primarily limited to rice and corn fields, CARP extended for the first time the opportunity to own farmland to landless sugarcane plantation workers (Asia Development Bank 2005; Billing 1993; Diprose and McGregor 2009; Reyes 2002).

Although CARP is seen as quite successful, it has not been easy for sugarcane plantation workers to acquire farmland. Sugarcane has long played an important role in the Philippine economy. In the face of plantation owners' strong resistance, the government assigned a low priority to the redistribution of sugarcane lands. Even after acquiring land, recipients tended to cultivate sugarcane by themselves without any training, credit or marketing assistance. Although the state and labor unions promoted the formation of cooperatives for land reform beneficiaries, most cooperatives failed, compelling many to lease their land to planters or entrepreneurs and work as hired wage laborers, on their own land (Billing 1993; Reyes 2002; Rutten 2010; World Bank 2009).

To improve land reform outcomes, some NGOs have worked to facilitate the transfer of land from plantation owners to landless workers as well as to develop farms on redistributed lands (Borras and Franco 2007). As detailed later, one such local NGO has been supporting associations of former plantation workers with Fairtrade certification on the island of Negros. The island is composed of two provinces, Occidental and Oriental, and is characterized by the most inequitable distribution of land in the Philippines. When CARP began, more than half of the available agricultural lowlands were under sugarcane monoculture on large estates, producing about two-thirds of the country's total crop (Diprose and McGregor 2009).

Analytical Framework: Livelihood Diversification by Land Reform Beneficiaries

When plantation workers are given the opportunity to become independent farmers under a land reform program, they must maximize profit from their livelihoods in both farm and non-farm sectors to pay land acquisition fees. For Fairtrade certification to contribute to former plantation workers' farming, Fairtrade-supported farming must be compatible with former plantation workers' other income-generating activities.

This case study was designed to explore this issue, drawing on the concept of livelihood diversification. Livelihood diversification is interpreted as 'the process by which rural households construct an increasingly diverse portfolio of activities and assets in order to survive and to improve their standard of living' (Ellis 2000, 15). Diversification has usually been analyzed from two contrasting motivations: survival or accumulation (Hart 1994) or necessity or choice (Ellis 1998). In general, poor people's diversification aims at 'coping with temporary adversity', whereas wealthier actors invest in 'diversification for accumulation and reinvestment' (Scoones 1998, 9). As I argue elsewhere (Makita 2007, 68), 'if actual livelihood diversification is an outcome of balancing the two types, there should be a shifting process from diversification for coping with temporary adversity to diversification for accumulation and reinvestment'. My past research in rural Bangladesh identified three phases of livelihood diversification: for survival (Phase 1), from survival to accumulation (Phase 2) and for accumulation (Phase 3). This concept of three-phase livelihood diversification can be used to interpret how former plantation workers incorporate Fairtrade-supported farming into their households' livelihood strategies.

The Case: A Cooperative of Sugarcane Producers in Negros Occidental

The NGO Alter Trade Foundation Inc. (ATFI) provides technical assistance and production loans for associations of former plantation workers in the province of Negros Occidental, and its associated company, Alter Trade Corporation (ATC), purchases association sugarcane and exports traditional brown *muscovado* sugar to Fairtrade and other ethical markets in Europe and Northeast Asia. Unlike many cooperatives that were formed by individual land reform beneficiaries but eventually disbanded, those under the auspices of ATFI and ATC have continued to cultivate sugarcane collectively to maintain the economies of scale in former plantations.

Of the 14 former workers' associations supported by ATFI, data collection focused on the oldest and closest to the province's capital city.[2] The association called STARFA (Santa Rita Farm Workers Association) was organized in 1994 and officially registered as a cooperative in 2007.[3] The membership increased from 60 to 73 households without any of the original group having left the association (as at August 2011). Semi-structured interviews were carried out with 54 members, and supplementary interviews were conducted with the staff of ATC and ATFI and some non-member residents. STARFA has leased 20 hectares of sugarcane fields from a plantation owner since 1994. Although the members are scheduled to take *collective* ownership of the 20 hectares, they have not yet received an official land ownership certificate. Until they receive a certificate, they must continue to pay the lease fee to the plantation owner. Many members of the cooperative also expect to obtain an *individual* ownership certificate for other plots of farmland separate from the communal land. When STARFA gained the communal 20 hectares for its 60 members, the land was too small for all members to rely on it as their main income source. Therefore, those who could afford to lease individually have been waiting for both collective and individual ownership certificates.

Assistance provided by the Alter Trade Group for STARFA began in 1995. ATFI guided the associations to add organic value to their sugarcane production. STARFA and the other associations were certified as organic in 1995 and as Fairtrade in 2004, and their organic sugar has been exported through ATC since 1995.

The former plantation workers accepted organic practices easily in contrast to small farmers or landowners who usually hesitate to switch from conventional to organic farming for fear of appreciable decreases in productivity (Eyhorn 2007, 141–144). When association members were plantation workers, they all used chemical fertilizers and pesticides, but they did not pay attention to yields on the plantations. Only after land was distributed to them, did they begin sugarcane cultivation as farm managers. Although there may have been a decrease in yields from the same plots of land, association members could not compare the productivity of conventional farming on the plantations and organic farming on their own communal land. They simply appreciated the opportunity to export to Northern organic markets.

Coexistence of Certification-Supported Farming with Other Livelihoods

Limited tangible benefits from certification

Although organic and Fairtrade certifications enabled STARFA to access export markets, their direct monetary impact is not large. The cooperative sells about 40 per cent of its total production to ATC. Owing to financial constraints (detailed later), ATC's purchase prices are kept at the level of local conventional market prices. While lacking organic price premiums, the cooperative has benefited from Fairtrade's minimum price guarantees and premiums. They used part of the premiums to produce organic fertilizers using buffalo dung and other locally available manures. The production of organic fertilizers brought the dual benefits of cheaper production costs compared with purchasing chemical fertilizers and an additional income stream generated through the sale of organic fertilizers to outside farms. While these profit-oriented indicators point to limited success, the outcome in terms of overall livelihood strategies is more significant.

Livelihood diversification practiced by cooperative members

When STARFA was organized, most of the original members were landless plantation workers of near equal economic status; however, over time a clear economic disparity has emerged. Although the change from plantation worker to joint farm owner was an advance in livelihood, members felt it insufficient to escape poverty. Currently, only six member households (8 per cent) rely on the cooperative's collectively operated land as their primary income source. Thirty members (41 per cent) lease up to 3 hectares of farmland in addition to the communal land.[4] For them, sugarcane production on their individual land is the largest income source. Although they sell sugarcane from their individual land to local markets, they also practice organic farming individually, expecting to sell to ATC in the future. The primary income source of the remaining members who live in the village is no longer on-farm activities: they depend more on non-farm jobs, working as drivers, security guards and shop managers, or on remittances from abroad or the capital city. Fifteen members (20 per cent) and their families chose to migrate permanently out of the original village, abandoning agricultural life. All these members, including non-resident members, keep up their membership as a secondary or tertiary income source. In sum, the majority of members do not seem to attach much importance to income from certification-supported farming through the cooperative.

Why does certification-supported farming coexist with members' other diversified livelihoods? Many members understand that no other cash crop is presently more lucrative than sugarcane and that small-scale sugarcane monoculture does not have a bright future. The ATC staff confessed to me that they were confronted with two difficulties in expanding their organic Fairtrade sugar exports. The first difficulty, namely, the limited capacity of ATC's milling factory, may be solved if they are sufficiently financed. However, a solution to the second problem seems to be out of their control: organic sugar from other major sugar-producing countries such as Brazil is increasingly competing with ATC's products.[5] Even in ethical markets, ATC cannot compete with larger producers that can offer lower prices. Consequently, it is difficult for ATC to buy more produce from STARFA and the other associations at a higher price and for each association to accept more members. This is why the cooperative's members have attempted to diversify their livelihoods while taking advantage of certification-supported sugarcane production. They will continue with the current method of sugarcane production as long as they gain a profit and other fringe benefits from the cooperative. Yet they need both certification-supported farming and diversified activities.

How can the current situation of the cooperative members' livelihood diversification be interpreted using the three-phase framework? Regarding the nature of livelihood diversification, there is a clear difference between the six members who depend on the cooperative as their primary income source and the others who have access to individual farmland and non-farm opportunities. For those six households, both the member and the member's family attempt to find as much work as possible in the cooperative and to complement their income from the cooperative by engaging in activities requiring no capital, such as charcoal burning. The six members can be regarded as being still in Phase 1 of livelihood diversification: they must diversify income-generating activities for survival. Although it is impossible to classify the remaining members clearly into either Phase 2 or Phase 3 of livelihood diversification, at least two members have steadily increased their families' income sources and continue to reinvest part of their income in the existing diversified economic activities on a larger scale than others. Their livelihood diversification can be interpreted as falling into Phase 3: for accumulation. They are fortunate in having not only their individual access to farmland but also other assets such as rice paddy fields inherited from their fathers or personal networks for access to jobs overseas. Whereas all members of the cooperative have equally benefited from certification-supported farming, the determinants of the current level of livelihood diversification derive from factors other than the effect of certification.

The Role of Fairtrade Certification for Former Plantation Workers

Fairtrade certification has contributed to the members' livelihood strategies by allowing them to diversify their livelihoods in conjunction with certification-supported farming. My research identified two mechanisms through which certification-supported farming is made compatible with members' diversification.

The first mechanism is the cooperative system, which is designed to benefit all members in the different phases of livelihood diversification. Benefits from the cooperative that members perceived correspond with the phase of livelihood diversification the members have reached (Table 28.2). The cooperative plays a particularly crucial role for the survival of the six member families in the first phase of livelihood diversification. Priority is given to these poorer members in the allocation of work opportunities inside the cooperative as well as in the distribution of fringe benefits such as bonuses for workers and scholarships for members' children. In other words, certification-supported farming has helped such cooperative-dependent members diversify their livelihoods for survival *inside* the cooperative.

Although the majority of members (except for those in Phase 1) share the perception that the communal land no longer yields significant income, they have kept up their membership not only to gain land ownership but also to use dividends and microcredit from the cooperative's revenue. Eligible members interviewed all make use of microcredit for a variety of purposes, including diversified economic activities *outside* the cooperative such as running grocery stores and individual farming – typical of the livelihood portfolio falling into Phases 2 and 3 of livelihood diversification. It is highly likely that profits from certification-supported farming have worked as a stable basis for some members' diversification into higher-value activities, namely, for the transition from survival to accumulation and for accumulation.

The second mechanism is collective farming on communal land that has been maintained in parallel with members' individual activities, both farming and non-farming. Each member's way of becoming involved in collective farming depends on the phase of livelihood diversification his or her household has reached. Members in Phase 1 (for survival) are most intensely involved in collective farming. Those in Phase 2 (for the transition from survival to accumulation) divide their own and their

Table 28.2 Benefits of the cooperative perceived by STARFA members

Livelihood diversification	Benefits
Phase 1: For survival	– Dividends from the cooperative – Wages for physical work on the communal land – Microcredit – Priority in the allocation of additional work – Priority in scholarships for members' children
Phase 2: For the transition from survival to accumulation	– Dividends from the cooperative – Wages for physical work on the communal land* – Microcredit – Production loans for individual land
Phase 3: For accumulation	– Dividends from the cooperative – Microcredit – Production loans for individual land (confined to members who operate farmland individually)

Note: * The shorter work period makes the Phase 2 members' annual income from wages lower than that of the Phase 1 members.

Source: Makita (under review).

family's workload between farming on the communal land, farming on individual land and non-farm activities, in consideration of seasonal work demands for each livelihood. For members practicing livelihood portfolios classified as falling into Phase 3 (for accumulation), farming on both communal and individual plots is sustained by the Phase 1 members and non-member workers employed from outside. In the case of this cooperative, collective farming has enabled all members to diversify their livelihoods.

Even if the direct impact of Fairtrade certification is not large, Fairtrade can help former plantation workers by making certification-supported farming compatible with their diversified activities. The operation of communal land with Fairtrade certification seems to be an effective form of assistance to land reform beneficiaries who are in the different phases of diversification.

CONCLUSION

In this chapter I have illustrated how plantation workers can substantially benefit from Fairtrade certification in two Asian contexts. The first case study in India revealed that current plantation workers had unknowingly used Fairtrade premiums. Although the invisibility of Fairtrade reinforced the existing patron–client relations between management and workers, when the operation of the premiums was transferred from the management to a third-party body, the same invisibility hid management patronage and contributed to the empowerment of workers. This case suggests that Fairtrade International should contract administration of premiums to an intermediary organization as a prerequisite for certification. As the second case study in the Philippines reveals, Fairtrade certification can be applied to cooperatives of former plantation workers who are struggling to be landowning farmers. During the long process of pursuing land ownership, they attempt to maximize their income through livelihood diversification, in addition to farming on their promised land. Therefore, certification should be used not only to give added value to their farming, but also to allow them to make farming compatible with their individual livelihood diversification at different phases. Fairtrade organic double certification may be effective particularly for land reform beneficiaries who can readily accept organic practices.

NOTES

1. For more on Fairtrade plantation standards see Laura Raynolds and Nicholas Greenfield's chapter and Lone Riisgaard's chapter in this volume.
2. This location allows us to observe more diversity in livelihoods than the other associations.
3. Although it is currently registered under another name, the abbreviation of its original name, Santa Rita Farm Workers Association, is still used.
4. An individual certificate is, in principle, limited to a maximum of 3 hectares per person under CARP (World Bank 2009, 22).
5. The Philippines accounts for only 1 per cent of world sugar production (FAO 2010).

REFERENCES

Asia Development Bank (2005), *Poverty in the Philippines: Income, Assets and Access*, Manila, Philippines: ADB.

Behal, Rana P. and Prabhu P. Mohapatra (1992), 'Tea and money versus human life: The rise and fall of the indenture systems in the Assam tea plantations 1840–1980', *Journal of Peasant Studies*, 19 (3&4), 142–172.

Besky, Sarah (2014), *The Darjeeling Distinction: Labor and Justice on Fair-Trade Tea Plantations in India*, Berkeley and Los Angeles: University of California Press.

Billing, Michael S. (1993), 'Syrup in the wheels of progress: The inefficient organization of the Philippine sugar industry', *Journal of Southeast Asian Studies*, 24 (1), 122–147.

Borras, Saturnino M., Jr. and Jennifer C. Franco (2007), *The National Campaign for Land Reform in the Philippines*, Brighton, UK: Institute of Development Studies.

Carney, Christopher P. (1989), 'International patron–client relationships: A conceptual framework', *Studies in Comparative International Development*, 24 (2), 42–55.

Chakrabarti, A.M. and K. Sarkar (2005), *Productivity and Labour Welfare: A Study in Tea Gardens*, Kolkata, India: State Labour Institute, Government of West Bengal.

Chatterjee, Piya (2001), *A Time for Tea: Women, Labor and Post/Colonial Politics on an Indian Plantation*, Chapel Hill, NC: Duke University Press.

Dasgupta, Ranajit (1992), 'Plantation labour in colonial India', *Journal of Peasant Studies*, 19 (3&4), 173–196.

Diprose, Gradon and Andrew McGregor (2009), 'Dissolving the sugar fields: Land reform and resistance identities in the Philippines', *Singapore Journal of Tropical Geography*, 30 (1), 52–69.

Ellis, Frank (1998), 'Household strategies and rural livelihood diversification', *Journal of Development Studies*, 35 (1), 1–38.

Ellis, Frank (2000), *Rural Livelihoods and Diversity in Developing Countries*, Oxford: Oxford University Press.

Eyhorn, Frank (2007), *Organic Farming for Sustainable Livelihoods in Developing Countries? The Case of Cotton in India*, Zurich, Switzerland: Vdf Hochschulverlag AG.

Fairtrade International (2009), 'Why Fairtrade is unique', available at http://www.fairtrade.net/why_fairtrade_is_unique.html (accessed 25 August 2009).

FAO (Food and Agriculture Organization of the United Nations) (2010), *FAO Statistical Yearbook 2010*, Rome: FAO.

Hart, Gillian (1994), 'The dynamics of diversification in an Asian rice region', in Bruce Koppel, John Hawkins and William James (eds.), *Development or Deterioration? Work in Rural Asia*, Boulder, CO: L. Rienner Publishers, pp. 47–71.

Makita, Rie (2007), *Livelihood Diversification and Landlessness in Rural Bangladesh*, Dhaka, Bangladesh: University Press Limited.

Makita, Rie (2012), 'Fair trade certification: The case of tea plantation workers in India', *Development Policy Review*, 30 (1), 87–107.

Makita, Rie (under review), 'Livelihood diversification with certification-supported farming: The case of land reform beneficiaries in the Philippines'.

Raynolds, Laura T. (2012), 'Fair trade flowers: Global certification, environmental sustainability, and labor standards', *Rural Sociology*, 77 (4), 493–519.

Reyes, Celia M. (2002), 'Impact of agrarian reform on poverty', Discussion Paper Series No. 2002-02, Manila, Philippines: Philippine Institute for Development Studies.

Rutten, Rosanne (2010), 'Who shall benefit? Conflicts among the landless poor in a Philippine agrarian reform programme', *Asian Journal of Social Science*, 38 (2), 204–219.

Scoones, Ian (1998), 'Sustainable Rural Livelihoods: A Framework for Analysis', IDS Working Paper 72, Brighton, UK: Institute of Development Studies.

Scott, James C. (1972a), 'Patron–client politics and political change in Southeast Asia', *American Political Science Review*, 66 (1), 91–113.

Scott, James C. (1972b), 'The erosion of patron–client bonds and social change in rural Southeast Asia', *Journal of Asian Studies*, 32 (1), 5–37.

Sharma, K.R. and T.C. Das (2009), *Globalization and Plantation Workers in North-East India*, Delhi, India: Kalpaz Publications.

Singh, S.N., A. Narain and P. Kumar (2006), *Socio-economic and Political Problems of Tea Garden Workers*, New Delhi, India: Mittal Publications.

World Bank (2009), *Land Reform, Rural Development and Poverty in the Philippines: Revising the Agenda*, Pasig City, Philippines: The World Bank.

29. Fairtrade International's multi-dimensional impacts in Africa

Valerie Nelson and Adrienne Martin

INTRODUCTION*

In this chapter we use emerging empirical evidence on the impact of Fairtrade, drawing on studies by the authors and other researchers. Combined, these studies provide a much stronger evidence base than has been previously available. We have extracted the findings on Fairtrade International impact in Africa from multi-region studies. We consider primarily the impacts for producers and workers, but also the implications at an organizational level. We identify the key factors which determine Fairtrade's impact in different contexts. We argue that the evidence shows that there are many positive benefits generated by Fairtrade, but there are questions arising from a development perspective and a need for new Fairtrade strategies and innovation.

Impact Literature

Until recently there has been little evidence on Fairtrade's impact in Africa. A meta-review found comparatively few studies focusing on regions beyond Latin America, commodities other than coffee, and some issues were neglected (e.g., gender and social difference, hired labor issues) (Nelson and Pound 2009). The relative efficacy of Fairtrade vis-à-vis other sustainability standards was not addressed and the studies had limited comparability and rigor. A series of studies has been published on Fairtrade impact since 2010, making a stronger evidence base including recent studies commissioned by Fairtrade organizations[1] and donors.[2] We analyze the findings of these studies after briefly discussing methodological challenges and issues.

The Fairtrade commissioned studies are largely qualitative in nature and thus generally lack quantitative measurement of impacts and statistically controlled comparisons.[3] This does not mean they are not valuable, since they provide rich insights into *if* and *how* Fairtrade is making a difference. They have helped to advance methodologies and rigor is continually improving (see Nelson and Martin 2014). Quasi-experimental designs are increasingly difficult to implement. This is because certification is expanding in many industries, limiting opportunities for constructing counterfactual comparisons (i.e., comparing between certified and non-certified groups). Mixed designs and combined methods are desirable, especially for first generation policy-oriented studies funded by donors. But these are more challenging for institutions and researchers working under resource constraints (e.g., on standard system funded studies) (Nelson and Martin 2014). (On fair trade impacts, see also Leonardo Becchetti, Stefano Castriota and Pierluigi Conzo's chapter in this volume.)

Few of the earlier studies in this field assessed the overall ability of Fairtrade to have an impact on poverty. Fairtrade should be judged realistically in terms of its own stated goals: sustainable livelihoods, making trade fair and empowerment. Agricultural development has to respond to increasingly urgent and inter-linked challenges such as climate change mitigation and adaptation, tackling inequality and generating green economic growth, achieving global food security and reducing environmental degradation. (For more on fair trade and environmental sustainability, see Christopher Bacon, Robert Rice and Hannah Maryanski's chapter in this volume.) We explore Fairtrade International's impact in Africa in the light of how far it can respond to these challenges. This is a policy question for many donors and governments, who seek to understand whether Fairtrade is an effective policy option and how it compares to other complementary or alternative interventions.

In this chapter we first summarize the findings on the multidimensional impacts of Fairtrade International in Africa, drawing on several new, in-depth impact studies. We then highlight several issues that have been somewhat neglected previously, including gender and hired labor on smallholder farms. Next we identify the key factors which influence the outcomes and impacts of Fairtrade, such as contextual conditions, interventions from other programs and projects, specificities of the commodity itself and associated value chains and the inherent characteristics of the sustainability standard itself. We conclude by discussing some of the future strategies for Fairtrade to improve their impact.

MULTI-DIMENSIONAL FAIRTRADE IMPACTS IN AFRICA

Smallholder Impacts

Fairtrade has a range of economic and institutional mechanisms for achieving its intended impacts. It operates along the value chain through its trader standards and engages primarily with farmers and workers via their organizations through producer standards, support and networking. Fairtrade International has other strategies: advocacy, growing markets and raising consumer awareness. There is, however, little study of how effectively this is done and this is not a focus of our study.

Early impact studies highlighted the positive benefits of Fairtrade. A meta-review found studies of variable quality and concluded that despite many positive benefits, these fall short of lifting producers and workers out of poverty. Reaching more disadvantaged groups is difficult for Fairtrade because of the assets needed to participate in export trade (Nelson and Pound 2009). In a more recent in-depth study we have found that while Fairtrade and other sustainability standards often bring social, economic and environmental benefits to individual producers and strengthen their organizations, this is not always the case. Impacts are variable and poverty reduction has been fairly modest (Nelson and Martin 2013).

In the Kenyan smallholder sector we found substantial positive impacts resulting from a scaling up of certifications (both Fairtrade and others sustainability certifications) and investments by external agencies. We found that both certified and non-certified smallholders have seen positive benefits. The certified groups achieved an overall higher level on major indicators. However, the newly involved organizations showed a more rapid rate of improvement over the study period (Nelson and Martin 2013). Spillover effects in Kenya were common because of the organization-wide influence of the overall policies of the Kenya Tea Development Agency (KTDA), the management agency for smallholder tea companies in Kenya. Staff also circulate between the member companies, sharing information and practice relating to certifications. The commitment of major buyers to buying only certified teas and major investments by donor and private sector actors have driven this rapid uptake of standards in the industry, encouraging more systemic levels of change.

Recent research finds that the impacts of Fairtrade and other standards on incomes are mixed. Certified East African coffee farmers receive only marginally more income than their non-certified counterparts. Although they tend to achieve better yields and product quality and they obtain better prices with certification, these benefits are not sufficient to tackle poverty among certified farmers and they lack sufficient incentives to make long-term investments (Hoebink et al. 2014). No significant differences in income were found in our Ghanaian cocoa case: all farmers (certified and non-certified) had seen increased household income and income from cocoa due to rising cocoa prices, but farmers also faced rising food and input costs. The non-certified producers perceived a larger decrease in income than the certified farmers, so the latter are still better off, but the differences are modest and all farmers reported a significant decline in their ability to cover basic needs. No statistical differences emerged in relation to household asset building. These outcomes are unsurprising given that Ghanaian cocoa prices are set nationally. Many Fairtrade competitors are private companies who have greater access to capital and offer similar incentives to farmers. Until recently Fairtrade sales have been limited. However, there was a significant difference in how farmers perceived change in market access, safer use of pesticides, access to training, health services and the environment, with Fairtrade farmers being more positive than their counterparts (Nelson and Martin 2013).

In Kenya, tea smallholder farmers said they had gained income benefits from improved tea yields and quality as a result of Fairtrade and Rainforest Alliance certifications. Although certified farmers had a higher annual income from tea, they also had a higher average acreage under tea. A significantly greater improvement between 2010 and 2012 was perceived by the farmers who were *not* certified in 2010, compared to earlier certified farmers, since many of the latter had already perceived improvements in their income in the two years prior to 2010, while the former were benefitting from improvements introduced as part of their earlier certification (Nelson and Martin 2013).

Fairtrade has improved the socio-economic situation of farmers and workers in two African cases by providing more stable market prices and greater security to farmers, allowing for money saving (Klier and Possinger 2012). Community benefits were realized through Fairtrade premium investments in education and health in the Kenyan flower case, but were not realized in Ghanaian cocoa (Klier and Possinger 2012). Our research found significant internal challenges within the Ghanaian cocoa farmers union, limited benefits being realized by smallholders and increasing competition from other more agile producer organizations (Nelson and Martin, 2013).

While Fairtrade seeks to engage disadvantaged smallholders, marginal smallholders are less able to participate in Fairtrade due to their limited access to land and other assets. In the Ghanaian cocoa study, no significant differences were found between the certified and non-certified farmers in terms of farm sizes and wealth, but they are both widely seen as being better off than non-cocoa farmers. In Kenya the smallholders that are shareholders in the smallholder tea companies, and which in turn are managed by the tea management agency (KTDA), are widely considered to be better off than other smallholder farmers in other sectors (non-tea) (Nelson and Martin 2013). Fairtrade tends to reach groups who already have sufficient assets to participate in export trade, although Fairtrade is still more likely to reach poorer groups than the more mainstream standards, such as Utz Certified (Hoebink et al. 2014). Standards can also be complementary: producer organization is needed before the generation of welfare benefits for individual members occurs, thus Fairtrade could *precede* other standards, supporting organizational development, and then other standards could provide further support so producer organizations can achieve dynamic competitive advantage (Hoebink et al. 2014).

The relative reliance on a particular crop for household income varies. In some regions there is competition from other cash crops or livelihood activities and Fairtrade has less traction than in zones where farmers are highly reliant on the focal crop. Fairtrade had led to an expansion of land under coffee in East Africa with smallholders becoming *overly* reliant on coffee in one study (Hoebink et al. 2014). Fairtrade had encouraged coffee specialization, yet, in comparison, non-certified farmers were investing in other crops, livestock and non-farm employment and accruing greater wealth and income diversification, especially in Kenya (Hoebink et al. 2014).

The proportion of sales on Fairtrade terms also influences the difference Fairtrade can make to an organization. In the Kenya coffee case, farmers reported that only a quarter to one-third of their total income comes from coffee, and less than a third of the coffee sold is certified (either as Fairtrade or Utz). Thus only about a tenth of farmers' incomes are generated from sales of certified coffee at the certified price (Hoebink et al. 2014). The cocoa producer organization in our study had struggled with single digit percentages of total sales on Fairtrade terms for many years (Nelson and Martin 2013).

Many sustainability standards, including Fairtrade, improve farmers' access to training (Nelson and Martin 2013; Hoebink et al. 2014). In both studies certified farmers, including Fairtrade farmers, are generally fairly satisfied with the technical assistance provided by their cooperatives. The

Kenyan tea case indicates the value of best practice approaches to farmer training and extension, for example through the use of farmer field school and lead farmer approaches. But improved access to training does not automatically mean higher yields, quality and longer-term welfare effects. Fairtrade farmers had not achieved higher yields in the East African coffee cases (Hoebink et al. 2014), although these are more marginal groups.

Fairtrade can create price uplift for farmers when world market prices are low *and* where producer organizations are efficient and motivated to improve member returns. The safety net is important to many farmers but is less visible to smallholders when world market prices are high, as was the case in our cocoa and tea cases (Nelson and Martin 2013). In Kenyan coffee one study found that prices paid to Fairtrade farmers were lower than for Utz producers, but were overall better than for non-certified farmers even where coffee was not sold as Fairtrade certified. However, price impacts on total (gross) incomes were deemed 'modest and fairly limited' for both Fairtrade and Utz certifications (Hoebink et al. 2014).

Fairtrade seeks to work along the entire value chain to create impact. In the Ghanaian cocoa case the support of the alternative trade organization has enabled the farmer-owned organization in Ghana to achieve part-ownership of a chocolate company in the United Kingdom. This is a concrete example of upgrading in the value chain and limited economic benefits are accruing to the producer organization in dividend payments and improved knowledge among managers of end markets. But there are frequently limited impacts on value chain relations. In a multi-country cotton study, the actors and the nature of the value chain relationships had not significantly changed as a result of Fairtrade interventions (Nelson and Smith 2011). Price remains a key factor shaping sourcing decisions, and this places West and Central Africa Fairtrade lint at a disadvantage compared to Indian lint. The lack of a well-developed textile sector in West and Central Africa compared to India's structured, vertically integrated sector is a further disadvantage for the region's producers. With an increase in Fairtrade registered operators, there remains little difference between the Fairtrade and conventional value chains (Nelson and Smith 2011). Similarly, Hoebink et al. (2014) found that in their African coffee cases, farmers could not increase their bargaining power and capture more than 6 to 8 per cent of the retail price in end markets for certified coffees partly as a result of over-certification. Fairtrade International is implementing new sourcing strategies for cocoa and cotton. This may increase overall sales to some extent, but ultimately other changes in trader standards may be needed.

Issues of dependency also arise for smallholders, but particularly in our studies for outgrowers, who are linked to a particular estate. Pound (2013) studied three Malawian certified tea organizations and for two smallholder outgrower groups he found modest living standards improvements and organizational strengthening, but also concerns about over-reliance on the estate to which they are each linked. However, one group has plans to develop their own processing facility and so may escape this dependence (Pound 2013).

The Fairtrade premiums generated in different industries and for different commodities vary. All of the sugar produced by a Fairtrade smallholder association in Malawi is sold to a single sugar mill and all of the sugar sold by the estate and smallholder outgrowers is on Fairtrade terms. While the outgrowers face risks of over-dependency, they are benefitting from *significant* premium funds (Euros 682 076 in 2011). The standard of living of members has improved since 2009 compared to non-members who do not grow sugar cane and lack access to irrigated land, indicating positive Fairtrade impacts (Pound 2013).

Malawi groundnut farmers have benefitted from Fairtrade, developing better agricultural practices and reducing their dependence on tobacco cultivation, but the impacts are modest in scale compared to the development challenges faced (Pound 2013). There are also significant challenges relating to aflotoxins and achieving the required quality specifications for export trade, meaning that Fairtrade markets are challenging for them. The Fairtrade minimum price has to be raised as it is low compared to production costs, and premiums need to be increased for this commodity as sales are low (Pound 2013). A new agri-processing facility could lead to increased production and interest from farmers, generating greater impacts, but higher local prices have led to changes in purchasing practices by the main buyer, which were deemed unsatisfactory in terms of cash flow, transparency and the lack of price incentives (Pound 2013).

Collaborative programs involving combinations of donors, companies, non-governmental organizations (NGOs) and standards are increasingly being undertaken in efforts to scale up these impacts. There have been few impact assessments of these public–private partnerships, but independent studies of the Dutch Sustainable Trade Initiative (IDH), which covers cocoa, cotton and tea and which has invested in each sector in a *range of activities* including supporting sustainability certification, found significant impacts for farmers, transformations in markets and major improvements in farm productivity and ecological sustainability (IDH 2013). The IDH concludes that the collaborative programs have leveraged significant private sector investment (particularly in cocoa in farm development and cocoa premiums), but additional investments are needed to tackle more complex issues such as gender and child labor. Thus, even where there is major accompanying investment from donors and the private sector, some areas are still not being addressed – areas of central importance to poverty impact. There are also political economy issues in terms of value chain governance and power which are not fully addressed by the IDH studies.

Impacts for Hired Labor on Plantations

Fairtrade faces particular challenges in the hired labor sector. Klier and Possinger (2012) found that Fairtrade monitoring has ensured that Kenyan flower companies comply with international regulations and national legislation, and working conditions are better on certified compared to non-certified farms. A qualitative Malawi tea study (Pound 2013) finds that an effective Joint Body is respected by workers and management and has improved relations between the two groups. Food security for workers' families has improved, as well as workers' working conditions. However, wages were said by workers to be inadequate, although they exceed the national minimum wage. Workers on plantations need to receive a living wage – something which is not yet being required or achieved by Fairtrade or other sustainability standards, and which should not be introduced at the expense of jobs. Kenyan tea estate workers reported in 2010 that the stricter leaf quality standards required by certification had reduced the number of kilograms of green leaf which they could pluck per day and this has affected their incomes, but the higher sales prices earned due to the higher quality green leaf influenced the collective bargaining agreement (CBA) negotiations and the subsequently agreed plucking and wage rate increases (Nelson and Martin 2013). This study found no improvements in promotion opportunities for workers.

Recognizing some of these challenges, Fairtrade has developed a new hired labor strategy which includes clearer linkages to strong trade unions, promotion of social dialogue along the value chain, living wages and freedom of association (see Lone Riisgaard's chapter in this volume). Changes have been made in Fairtrade rules on premium decision-making in the Joint Body, with management having only an advisory role rather than voting rights and rules being more flexible so that workers can decide to spend it to supplement their wages rather than restricting investments to collective projects alone.

NEGLECTED ISSUES: GENDER, RURAL DIFFERENTIATION AND RURAL TRANSITIONS

Gender and intersecting social differences mediate Fairtrade impact, but have been relatively neglected by previous Fairtrade and impact studies (Nelson and Martin 2013; Nelson and Pound 2009). Available data are scarce and largely descriptive (Ruben 2008). Gender inequality is widespread, but relations and norms vary with context. Women tend to have less control over export crop income and there are barriers to women's participation in Fairtrade (Nelson and Pound 2009). There has been limited representation by women in terms of producer organization membership and in official positions, and in terms of the poor quality of women's participation in meetings and decision-making (Nelson and Pound 2009). In a meta-review there were just a few positive examples of organizations taking serious steps to tackle gender inequality (e.g., by reserving places on the elected board for female members) and these all stemmed from Latin America (see also Sally Smith's chapter in this volume).

Isolated examples also exist in the new evidence on impact, but overall the gender impact of Fairtrade in Africa is clearly very limited. For example, by 2013 the Ghanaian coffee cooperative had made some improvements in terms of women's representation by retaining positions on primary society committees, and until recently they had a female leader, but this has not translated into wider economic or political empowerment for women (Nelson and Martin 2013). Hoebink et al. (2014) also find limited membership of women in certified organizations. Membership in many cooperatives is linked to the holding of land title (e.g., KTDA rules for Kenyan tea smallholder members requires land title), and this tends to exclude women (Nelson and Martin 2013). There are fewer opportunities for women to participate in Fairtrade premium decision-making (Klier and Possinger 2012). It is not easy to tackle entrenched gender norms and structural barriers, but *action* is needed, particularly in getting women into management positions.

There are multiple pathways by which Fairtrade could support women smallholders and worker empowerment. While increasing the awareness and commitment among producer and estate leaders is critical, Fairtrade needs greater capacity to reach producers in the private domain. Women need to be accepted as full members of cooperatives and included on the board. In Ethiopia and Kenya, for example, women had more influence where they achieved independent membership of the coffee cooperatives and achieved ownership of land, trees and education (Hoebink et al.

2014). In Kenyan tea, women smallholders have benefitted from Fairtrade funded construction of collection centers closer to their homes, saving them time and energy (Nelson and Martin 2013). But female outgrowers in the west of the Rift Valley had no knowledge of Fairtrade certification and do not attend outgrower meetings, which are held at inappropriate times. However, Said-Allsopp and Tallontire (2014) found that gender committees established as part of Kenya Flower Council codes had been much more effective than the Fairtrade Joint Bodies.

Shifting entrenched attitudes towards gender requires not only training or technical inputs, but a process of experiential, personal and peer learning by female *and* male farmers and workers, so that they are encouraged to question their ideas of what are possible gender roles and norms. Role models and cross-cultural learning are both relevant to show people that gender norms are constructed and so can change. Fairtrade is well placed to innovate and would do well to collaborate with other sustainability standards facing similar challenges.

Gender inequality is just one facet of rural differentiation and intersects with other forms of discrimination and disadvantage associated with age, ethnicity, wealth and so on. One of the new impact studies finds that Fairtrade tends to reach more marginal groups than other standards (Hoebink et al. 2014). These groups are still relatively poor, but are more advantaged than others in the same rural economy, such as farmers without land or assets to participate in export agriculture.

There is widespread use of hired laborers on cocoa farms in Ghana. Cooperative managers have identified a few positive steps (i.e., training on health and safety for some hired laborers), but otherwise there have been no major changes to their working conditions or wages. Caretaker farmers are not able to join the producer organization as members, as they are not cocoa farm landowners, and thus they are excluded from many Fairtrade benefits (Nelson and Martin 2013). In Kenyan tea, smallholders employ hired laborers to pluck tea. Mostly they are drawn from poorer neighboring households who supplement their own tea farm incomes, although some have more distant origins. Certification by Fairtrade and Rainforest Alliance has led to some minor improvements say the laborers. They have better accommodation, provision of lunch, water and toilet facilities, fair and regular payment. On a dual certified farm, the pluckers interviewed knew about both standards, had received training from the host farmers on plucking, maintained plucking tables, educated their children and managed their wages, and some had participated in field days supported by the standards. However, at another Fairtrade certified farm, pluckers were not aware of the standards and rarely talked to their employers, but had heard that Fairtrade had funded the construction of concrete sorting tables, water tanks and the electrification at the collection centers (Nelson and Martin 2013).

Beyond these positive examples there are few changes occurring for hired laborers on smallholder farms. There are vastly differing situations for hired laborers depending upon the overall starting points for the smallholders themselves in terms of their land holdings, assets and incomes. If Fairtrade is to increase its poverty impact across rural societies, new Fairtrade strategies are needed to reach these groups.

FACTORS INFLUENCING IMPACT

What does the new impact evidence tell us about the factors which shape impact? Answering this question will help to inform future Fairtrade strategies, especially if these are more tailored by region, although this requires that Fairtrade be more flexible.

Fairtrade has inherent sources of complexity, including multiple impact pathways, variable implementation and non-linear impact trajectories (much can happen in the early phases in preparing for certification). Starting points vary in contextual conditions and baseline indicators (e.g., education levels of members, size of farm holdings, age of trees, knowledge of sustainable agricultural production practices, type and nature of gender relations, history of cooperatives within a country) (Nelson and Martin 2012).

Given the diverse factors determining Fairtrade impact (see Nelson and Martin 2012), we have grouped them into four main areas: 1) contextual conditions; 2) interventions from other programs and projects; 3) the specificities of the commodity itself and the value chains and markets through which it is traded; and 4) the inherent characteristics of the sustainability standard (see Figure 29.1; Nelson and Martin 2013). In this section we explore these four types of factors and provide illustrations from the new empirical evidence.

Many of these factors are at work in shaping Fairtrade impacts in the Kenyan tea sector. The existing organizational policies and regulations of the umbrella KTDA shape the practices of *all* the member companies and the policies are being influenced by certification processes so there are spillover effects (Nelson and Martin 2013). There has been rapid expansion of Rainforest Alliance certification across the sector, resulting from buyer pressure (e.g., the Unilever sourcing pledge) and the uptake of multiple certifications by producer groups and estates, as well as investments of a range of organizations, notably the IDH. Jointly, these investments and initiatives are creating momentum across the industry

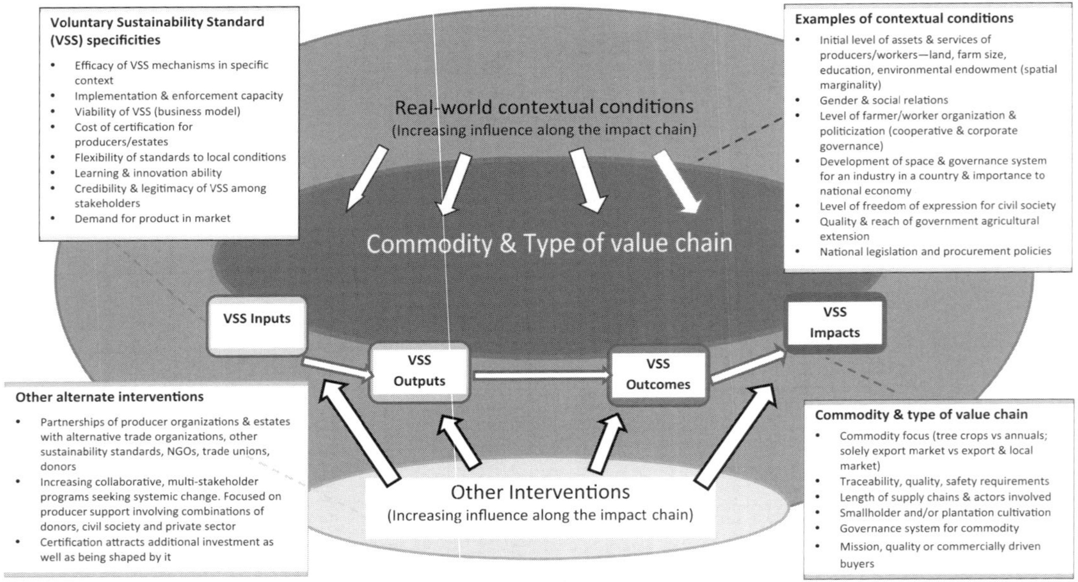

Figure 29.1 *Factors determining outcomes and impacts for voluntary sustainability standards such as Fairtrade*

and may amplify the effects of Fairtrade and vice versa. Contextual factors constraining Fairtrade impact in Kenyan tea include the lack of monitoring and enforcement of (relatively comprehensive) national environmental protection, employment and basic rights legislation plus the prevailing social inequalities in rural societies. The high market price of made tea at the time of the study had an effect, as did the increasing costs of living and production. An increasingly unpredictable climate, land fragmentation and disinterest of youth in tea farming are contextual trends (Nelson and Martin 2013).

The Ghanaian cocoa sector is a joint governance system (Ton et al. 2008) and this limits Fairtrade's traction. The state is fairly active and global buyers are relatively passive compared to other countries. Following partial liberalization, a Ghanaian government cocoa body controls external marketing and quality and sets cocoa prices for producers, which have been consistently above the Fairtrade minimum price during our study. The traction of Fairtrade is less strong and the impacts less visible to producers in such a context compared to neighboring Côte d'Ivoire, where there is full privatization.

Producer Organization Governance and Leadership

Good organizational governance and effective leadership are important if Fairtrade organizations are to be strong and realize benefits for workers and smallholders (Nelson and Martin 2012). This is the supply side of producer organization governance. On the demand side of governance are individual members' understanding of value chains, markets and Fairtrade, including their rights and responsibilities (see Figure 29.2). This understanding is often missing at the farmer level (Nelson and Martin 2013). In other, words there is a lack of political literacy among smallholders and workers to hold their organizations to account. Behavior change at the cooperative or intra-household level are both less likely where cooperative trust and loyalty are weak (Klier and Possinger 2012). This is shaped by members' views of the effectiveness and motivations of organizational leadership at different levels.

The history of a farmer organization and its degree of federation can make a difference in terms of its business and management skills, organizational ethos and ability to develop new markets and build democratic processes (see also Anne Tallontire's chapter in this volume). The large cotton producer organizations in West Africa are federated and well established, but are somewhat top-down in nature (Nelson and Smith 2011). The Ghanaian cocoa cooperative was established in the early 1990s with the support of Fairtrade as the only farmer-owned cooperative

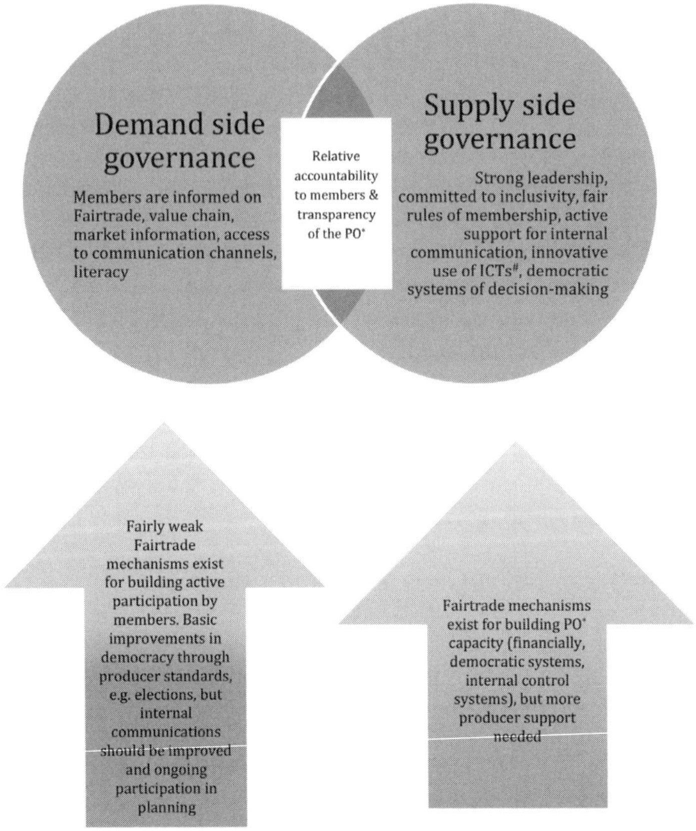

Notes: *producer organization; # information communications technology.

Figure 29.2 Producer organization governance and Fairtrade

that holds a license to buy cocoa. It is competing against large multinationals that benefit from economies of scale and many professional staff. In contrast the cooperative union has expanded across many regions of Ghana, involving 60 000 plus farmers, in order to buy sufficient quantities of cocoa, but struggles in terms of organizational capacity, providing services to members and in having sufficient influence over the buying company (Nelson and Martin 2012). Most cooperatives require capacity strengthening in terms of their business management skills and need to be pushed to improve their overall levels of efficiency.

Corporate Governance and Leadership

The style of management, ownership structure and personality of estate managers influence attitudes towards corporate responsibility and how an estate will respond to market signals (Nelson and Martin 2012). Many of the certified agrifood commodities have been produced on these estates since the colonial era. Practices within often isolated settings can be somewhat entrenched, with current workers being the latest in many generations to have lived and worked on a particular estate in a paternalistic system (Nelson and Martin 2012). Gaining management buy-in for ethical codes and standards is critical, otherwise tit-for-tat changes may be instituted to save on costs, rather than to drive up performance (Nelson, Martin and Ewert 2007).

Relations with External Agencies, Government and Sustainability Standards

Fairtrade may not be the only external body to engage with producer organizations and companies. Sometimes Fairtrade certification attracts other agencies to support a producer organization or estate, but on other occasions such support is not attributable specifically to Fairtrade.

In a cotton study in the Malian case, more positive impacts were found where the producer organization primary societies had been supported by an external international NGO, especially because the overall federation is somewhat top-down in approach (Nelson and Smith 2011). In Malawian tea, the smallholder organizations studied have received significant support from the estates they are linked to and new entrants would require this kind of assistance to participate in Fairtrade (Pound and Phiri 2011). There are many instances of Fairtrade cooperatives receiving support from alternative trade organizations that support fair trade for farmers.

Interdependencies also exist between Fairtrade and other sustainability standards. Increasingly, producer organizations are stacking up multiple certifications to widen their market access, a practice now common in Kenyan tea, for example (Nelson and Martin 2013). Fairtrade premium funds have been used to enable a producer organization to achieve other certifications (particularly organic). Relations with local government vary, but have rarely been strong. Sometimes Fairtrade premium funding is invested in infrastructure that could also be considered the responsibility of the state (e.g., provision of boreholes in Ghana by the cocoa producer union).

While the Fairtrade system has its own producer support services, liaison officers have to reach multiple producer organizations, often in different countries. Therefore the level of support they can provide is limited and more investment is needed or new mechanisms found for more direct engagement given the scale of the capacity gap. Producer support services are currently being moved to regional producer networks, opening up the possibility for more tailored approaches in each region, but this is untested as yet and resources are necessarily limited in an intervention that is based on trade rather than aid. Fairtrade has placed insufficient attention in the past on the importance of sustainable agricultural practices and improving productivity and quality for members, but since 2011 it requires producer organizations to discuss the investment of 25 per cent of the Fairtrade premium in productivity and quality with members. However, collaborative programs with external agencies are likely to be needed to achieve a significant poverty impact given the capacity gap. Fairtrade should also improve its support for producers, particularly business service and leadership capacity building, where there are clusters of producer organizations in a locale.

Environmental Entitlements and Spatial Marginality

Power relations determine individuals' and communities' access to resources. Spatial marginality means that more remote groups often need more support to link to value chains. Interestingly, for coffee cooperatives in Kenya, Uganda and Ethiopia, certification brought the *highest* returns in more remote areas, because competition from other commodities and livelihood options is less intense than in less remote commercialized areas (Hoebink et al. 2014). Understanding how environmental entitlements vary between social groups and spatially may be relevant for future Fairtrade strategies aimed at scaling up impact.

Certified Markets, Value Chain Relations, Industry Development and Governance

The value chain relationships, the size of certified markets and the level of development and governance of an industry in different countries all influence Fairtrade impact. The size of the market is important. More Fairtrade sales improve producer organization viability and generate more premium funds. A Fairtrade Malawi sugar outgrower group has achieved a significant rise in Fairtrade sales and premium monies benefitting members and communities (Pound 2013).

Buyers may pressure suppliers to adopt certifications, but this pressure is not necessarily even and can vary between buyers and their specific markets. In Kenya, tea buyers have been adding pressure for their estates to become certified and for the estates' outgrowers to comply. This is because buyers want the outgrowers' tea, which is needed to sustain the made tea flavor and to manage reputational risk. The dual certified estate managers complained about the lack of demand for Fairtrade certified made tea among buyers during periods of high prices (Nelson and Martin 2013). In some markets sustainability standards are now a pre-requisite for market access and so are not really voluntary. Value chain power relations vary depending upon the type of value chain and who is calling the shots. There are dependency risks for smallholder and outgrower groups relying on particular estates; there are similar risks for producer groups with just one major buyer. Ghanaian cocoa farmers are benefitting from new sourcing contracts from a big chocolate company, but there are risks if this company decides to buy more cocoa from new Fairtrade certified Ghanaian producer groups.

The level of establishment of an industry – its infrastructure and markets – influences whether there are relatively high volumes of production already being traded and thus how quickly sustainability standards can spread and the scale at which they can generate premiums and so on. Malawi sugar cane producers receive premiums far outweighing those for groundnut producers (Pound 2013).

More work is needed to map – for each sector and country – the initial conditions that shape Fairtrade impacts. Research is also needed to evaluate strategies for scaling up, taking into account the potential future scenarios for livelihood and industry trajectories in a locale (Nelson and Martin 2013). The International Finance Corporation is leading such a process of analysis (see IFC 2013), but it is unclear to what extent power relations will be central to this analysis.

CONCLUSIONS

Fairtrade has diverse strategies and these are implemented in more than 60 countries worldwide. This inevitably means that there are complex impact pathways and impacts in multiple dimensions. Specifically, focusing on Africa our review of the evidence, including recent studies and new data, indicates mixed findings and impacts that are highly context specific. Although there are positive impacts, there is also clear room for improvement. The evidence points to some limitations in terms of the extent of Fairtrade impact vis-à-vis the scale of rural development challenges. This is not to denigrate the pioneering role and positive impacts of Fairtrade to date. Fairtrade has played an important role in raising the profile and in shaping the overall agenda on sustainable development in international export trade. Fairtrade should reflect upon its theory of change and identify particular mechanisms which require strengthening, in particular its mechanisms for engaging with producers and strengthening their capacity, particularly in terms of leadership, business management and efficiencies and engaging members as active participants in the organization. Complementary measures will also be needed to achieve the rural transformations required to respond to global development challenges. These measures should move beyond the farm or estate level, to landscape-, sub-regional- or territorial-scale interventions.

Our analysis indicates that Fairtrade's benefits for women and marginalized social groups in Africa is limited. Women, and wage laborers or caretaker farmers on smallholders' farms, do not benefit adequately and there is a risk that existing inequalities could even be exacerbated.

Market fluctuations, capacity gaps and the requirement of functioning linkages along the chain make trade interventions for smallholders *inherently* challenging. But when these interventions succeed they generate positive outcomes over time without reliance on donors. On balance it is better to be in a certified organization than not for workers and smallholders in Africa. But scaling out is needed to reach more producers overall and scaling up and down the rural spectrum to reach different segments of society. Both Fairtrade International and the standards-setting membership organization ISEAL (International Social and Environmental Accreditation and Labeling) are currently investigating strategies for scaling up, including the development of more achievable steps, which could achieve recognition, prior to full certification (ISEAL 2011). Likewise, ensuring equitable outcomes is a persistent challenge for such interventions.

In conclusion, we address the question of how voluntary sustainability standards can be improved as policy tools for responding to rural development challenges. First, internal changes in their strategies are needed for sustainability standards to respond to more diverse segments of rural society. The very poorest households often have insufficient assets to participate in export (and national) value chains, which are quite risky. These groups may need basic social protection measures, land reform and investment if they are to step up the rural poverty ladder and realistically be supported by sustainability standards. If standards can expand their market penetration, be less costly and complex, cooperate more with each other in delivery of producer support and engage with local stakeholders more then this should enable them to reach more disadvantaged smallholders and workers. Strategies are needed to improve the livelihoods of those without assets at all (i.e., the landless and hired laborers) perhaps through a more stepped approach. Fairtrade is already pushing for change on living wages and should continue to do so as a way of increasing their impact on plantations. More radical changes should also be considered, though, such as more regionalized standards owned by the producer networks, participatory guarantee systems, tightening the requirements in the trader standards and guaranteeing relatively fair prices for individuals – not just export prices. Fairtrade has an important role to play both in smallholder development and in generating rural employment. It has to retain market credibility and sales. It is easier to do so if it can communicate a positive narrative of market growth and expansion, but demonstration of impact is also a critical element.

Second, the relationships needed to tackle rural development challenges in a particular locale require greater attention. What kind of brokerage role can standards play or where can they support others, beyond engaging with individual producer organizations or individual farmers? Fairtrade should not be considered glorious isolation, but in the wider context of a dynamic sustainable trade and standards landscape, sub-region or territory. By focusing pilots on destinations with multiple organizations, there are opportunities for action between cooperatives or workers groups.

The trajectories of livelihood dynamics and rural economies in specific localities or territories have not been addressed by sustainability standards given the standardization inherent in global approaches to certification and their single commodity focus. The dynamics of a specific rural economy need to be understood, as well as the potential future scenarios in terms of individual farmers' livelihood choices, likely industry development and alternative options. In some commodities the business case for participation for smallholders is becoming less clear as other commodities become more attractive (e.g., competition between cocoa and rubber in Ghana). There are limits to the scale of producer support that sustainable trade schemes can currently provide and so cooperation between certified organizations (and wider stakeholders) on the ground is important – they can compete in the market.

A first step is realizing that a wider horizontal vision beyond individual farms and communities is helpful, in combination with the vertical value chain view. Being ready to play a brokerage role where necessary could help to lever investment in producer support, but also help producers and workers to claim their rights and better service provision and so on.

Second, the potential of collaborative programs involving combinations of donors, the private sector, standards and NGOs requires attention. Focusing on export commodity sectors they seek to scale up impact, often with investment in productivity and quality, access to inputs and credit, and agricultural extension. They may help to unlock the potential of voluntary standards, by providing the more intensive accompaniment that many smallholder organizations need to be effective. However, much greater scrutiny is needed of their effectiveness and power implications. For example, there are risks that such programs continue to promote the interests of the large multinationals, concentrating power further in their hands.

Third, voluntary sustainability standards should try to return to being more than standards. As well as risk assurance and auditing, they need to be generators of innovation and reclaim their origins as movements. Rather than engaging with the broader public as consumers only, the standards should seek to engage with the public as citizens, who could be mobilized in pursuit of advocacy and action on trade justice or environmental conservation.

The potential of the Fairtrade regional producer networks in Africa is highly significant as they facilitate producer voice and representation, as the networks are now part of the governance structure of the overall organization. National networks are also emerging (e.g., in South Africa). This producer networking, and the role of producers in governance, is unique to Fairtrade among voluntary sustainability standards. While still fairly young, more evidence will be needed in future that these networks can deliver – in different parts of the world – on both political and economic empowerment goals *in practice*. The question of who they represent is also pertinent when considering rural differentiation. Who is representing smallholders who have insufficient assets to participate in export value chains but may be engaging in domestic and local trading?

Fourth, analysis of the discursive space occupied by sustainability standards in development and agricultural trade should be both recognized as an area of impact and scrutinized in terms of what alternative approaches may be being excluded from consideration. The standards bodies have played quite a dominant role in framing sustainability issues and appropriate responses. Yet other types of interventions and initiatives *could* be more effective in practice and indeed other approaches are already being tried. Within the field of standards, the more established standards and labels in agriculture are not only competing, but also being challenged by newer social labels. Beyond standards, large retailers and manufacturers are increasingly using sustainability standards as a pre-competitive tool, more for risk assurance than market differentiation, and some are developing their own initiatives instead, such as the Waitrose Foundation (Sustainability 2011). Donors are also directing funding to public–private partnership programs, market-based mechanisms and other private sector-led development. These may involve sustainability standards, but they have less prominence than before. Few of these latter approaches have been evaluated to date, and they may also show mixed results if the same scrutiny is placed upon them as the other standards.

All sustainability standards will need to be scaled up and their impact deepened, by identifying mechanisms to reach more smallholders and seeking to reach those with fewer or no assets but who participate in the chain (hired laborers on smallholder farms), and by empowering women smallholders and workers.

Fairtrade and other sustainability standards *cannot* be expected to tackle rural poverty on their own – the structural challenges that exist and the scale of development challenges in many regions are simply too great. The standards are also not yet achieving more than 50 per cent of sales being certified and so have room still to grow and achieve synergies. But there do need to be significant *changes* in strategies, partnerships and levels of intervention to bolster impact and retain crediblity. This is not easy in a large, multi-stakeholder system such as Fairtrade International, but the standards need to make these changes if they are to remain relevant.

NOTES

* In this chapter we draw upon research funded by the UK Department for International Development on the poverty impact of sustainability standards, but in no way represents their opinions. The African research was undertaken by us and by Tanya Stathers and Charity Gathuthi.

1. Fairtrade commissioned studies include: 1) a Natural Resources Institute led impact monitoring study on sugar, tea and groundnuts in Malawi (Pound 2013); 2) a Max Havelaar funded study covering six commodities including Ghanaian cocoa and Kenyan flowers (Klier and Possinger 2012); 3) a four country qualitative study on cotton covering Cameroon, Mali, Senegal and India (Nelson and Smith 2011); and 4) a global banana study including a Ghanaian cocoa case (Smith 2010).
2. 1) An impact evaluation covering multiple countries, diverse enterprises from different sectors (producer organization, outgrowers and estates), several standard systems (primarily Fairtrade and Rainforest Alliance) and two commodities across four countries (Nelson and Martin 2013) and 2) a study assessing the impact of coffee certification on smallholder cooperatives in Kenya and Uganda and a study in Ethiopia in 2011 covering Fairtrade and Utz certification (Hoebink et al. 2014).
3. The Klier and Possinger (2012) study does include control groups, but there is no use of advanced statistical techniques to tackle potential selection bias.

REFERENCES

Hoebink, Paul, Ruerd Ruben, Willem Elbers and Bart van Rijsbergen (2014), 'The impact of coffee certification on smallholder farmers in Kenya, Uganda, and Ethiopia', Centre for International Development Issues Nijmegen (CIDIN), Radboud University Nijmegen, the Netherlands for Solidaridad, available at http://www.ru.nl/cidin/research/new-solidaridad/ (accessed 24 February 2014).

IDH (Sustainable Trade Initiative) (2013), 'Impact studies: Sustainable market transformation in action', available at http://eudevdays.eu/sites/default/files/Impactboek%202013.pdf (accessed 10 May 2014).

International Finance Corporation (IFC) (2013), 'Building a roadmap to sustainability in agro-commodity production', available at http://www.aidenvironment.org/news/building-a-roadmap-to-sustainability-in-agro-commo (accessed 24 February 2014).

ISEAL (2011), 'Stepwise approaches as a strategy for scaling up: Background report', April 2011, available at http://www.isealalliance.org/sites/default/files/Stepwise_Approaches_Background_Report_April2011.pdf (accessed 19 June 2014).

Klier, Sara and Sonja Possinger (2012), 'Final report Fairtrade impact study: Assessing the impact of Fairtrade on poverty reduction through rural development', Transfair Germany and Max Havelaar Foundation.

Nelson, Valerie, Adrienne Martin and Joachim Ewert (2007), 'The impacts of codes of practice on worker livelihoods: Empirical evidence from the South African wine and Kenyan cut flower industries', *Journal of Corporate Citizenship*, (28), December, 61–72.

Nelson, Valerie and Adrienne Martin (2012), 'The impact of Fairtrade: Evidence, shaping factors and future pathways', *Food Chain*, 2 (1), 43–63.

Nelson, Valerie and Adrienne Martin (2013), 'Final technical report: Assessing the poverty impact of sustainability standards', report for the UK Department of International Development, Chatham, UK: Natural Resources Institute, University of Greenwich, available at http://www.nri.org/programmes/equitable-and-sustainable-trade/publications (accessed 24 February 2014).

Nelson, Valerie and Adrienne Martin (2014), 'Rigour, utility and politics in Fairtrade impact assessment', *Food Chain*, 4 (1), 14–33.

Nelson, Valerie and Barry Pound (2009), 'The last ten years: A comprehensive assessment of the impact of Fairtrade', Chatham, UK: Natural Resources Institute, University of Greenwich.

Nelson, Valerie and Sally Smith (2011), 'Fairtrade cotton: Assessing impact in Mali, Senegal, Cameroon and India: Main report', Report for the Fairtrade Foundation and Max Havelaar France, Chatham, UK: Natural Resources Institute, University of Greenwich, available at http://www.nri.org/programmes/equitable-and-sustainable-trade/publications (accessed 24 February 2014).

Pound, Barry (2013), 'Branching out: Fairtrade in Malawi: Monitoring the impact of Fairtrade on five certified organizations: Phase two of a longitudinal study', for University of Greenwich, Fairtrade Africa, Fairtrade International, Malawi Fairtrade Network, Fairtrade Foundation, available at http://www.nri.org/images/Programmes/EquitableTrade/2013-04-Malawi-Fairtrade-Impact-FinalLR.pdf (accessed 20 May 2014).

Pound, Barry and Alex Phiri (2011), 'Taking root: Fairtrade in Malawi: A synthesis report', Chatham, UK: Natural Resources Institute, University of Greenwich, available at http://www.nri.org/images/Programmes/EquitableTrade/ft_malawi_synthesis_study_taking_root.pdf (accessed 19 June 2014).

Ruben, Ruerd (ed.) (2008), *The Impact of Fair Trade*, Wageningen, the Netherlands: Wageningen Academic Publishers.

Said-Allsopp, M. and Anne Tallontire (2014), 'Enhancing Fairtrade for women workers on plantations: Insights from Kenyan agriculture', *Food Chain*, 4 (1), 66–77.
Smith, Sally (2010), 'Fairtrade bananas: A global assessment of impact', Final Report: April 2010, Institute of Development Studies, University of Sussex, UK.
Sustainability (2011), 'Signed, sealed … delivered? Beyond certifications and labels', available at http://www.sustainability.com/library/signed-sealed-delivered-1#.UwuUO4nivIU (accessed 24 February 2014).
Ton, Giels, Geoffrey Hagelaar, Anna Laven and Sietze Vellema (2008), 'Chain governance, sector policies and economic sustainability in cocoa', Markets, Chains and Sustainable Development Strategy and Policy Paper, No. 12, Wageningen, Netherlands: Stichting DLO, available at http://www.boci.wur.nl/UK/Publications/ (accessed 20 May 2014).

30. Quantitative analysis of the impacts of fair trade

Leonardo Becchetti, Stefano Castriota and Pierluigi Conzo

INTRODUCTION

Fair trade is not only one of the most well-known bottom-up welfare responses to globalization, but also a leader in bringing questions about the role of business in society to the fore of public consciousness. Profit maximizing companies operating in domestic markets were reconciled with social optimum by the authority and action of domestic institutions. Global integration of money, labor and product markets altered this equilibrium since companies could immediately start to operate in a global scenario while rules and institutions remained domestic, thereby creating an imbalance of power between the two forces. The bottom-up action of socially and environmentally concerned citizens has helped restore this equilibrium, rewarding companies that avoid a race to the bottom in social and environmental criteria through fair trade and related initiatives.

Fair trade is a multifaceted complex phenomenon. It sells a bundle combining traditional commodities with socially and environmentally responsible value chain features and educational content (Becchetti and Huybrechts 2008). Two of the most important and interesting effects of fair trade are: 1) the impact on producers' wellbeing on the supply side and 2) the contagion effect of fair trade commodities on traditional profit maximizing sellers on the demand side. The latter is made possible by the behavior of socially responsible consumers who vote with their wallets and are willing to pay a premium for the 'ethical content' of fair trade products. The goal of our contribution is to quantitatively assess these two types of fair trade impact.

On the supply side the main question is whether Fairtrade certified products deserve responsible consumers' premium by meeting the promise to improve the wellbeing of primary producers. Impact studies have tried to answer this question. Fairtrade impact studies are something more complex than just analyzing trends of wellbeing indicators after fair trade is introduced. The first best counterfactual experiment is impossible to achieve since we cannot compare affiliated farmer performance under Fairtrade adoption and what would have happened to them without it. The second best alternative of a randomized experiment is also beyond reach in almost all cases. The problem with Fairtrade is that we want to analyze the effects of a 'treatment' that already exists (i.e., the impact of a partnership which has been at work for years or even decades). This makes it impossible to randomize ex-ante local participation in the Fairtrade 'treatment group' and to a control group of non-Fairtrade affiliated, the latter having ex-ante characteristics not different from those of the treatment group. The third best is to create ex-post conditions as close as possible to those of randomized experiments.

As we will document, impact studies have tried to achieve this 'third best' goal with various approaches including propensity score matching, instrumental variable approaches, retrospective data and control for pre-affiliation trends. What emerges from this literature is a quite reliable set of general results concerning the impact of affiliation on several objective (revenues, productivity, child labor, health) and subjective (life satisfaction, self-esteem) performance indicators. Empirical evidence documents that affiliation years generally produce a significant positive impact on producers' revenues (Becchetti and Castriota 2008; Becchetti, Conzo and Gianfreda 2012; Becchetti and Costantino 2006) when they are compared with corresponding changes in the control group of non-affiliated producers living in the same areas. The issue is whether this is the effect of the price premium or, as well, a result of an improvement of productivity. Effects on productivity are not so clear-cut since it seems its increase is partially compensated by higher volumes which bring down productivity again in equilibrium. In essence, productivity gains in the Fairtrade value chain push farmers to dedicate more hours to cultivation of Fairtrade products and less to secondary work. Since marginal productivity is decreasing, the extra hours worked reduce it and this leads to more worked hours but to a productivity which is not dissimilar from that in non-Fairtrade value chains (Becchetti, Conzo and Gianfreda 2012).

An interesting case is that of the impact on child labor. According to the well-known 'luxury axiom', benevolent parents send their children to school whenever they exceed a minimum income threshold below which child schooling is a luxury they cannot afford (Basu and Van 1998). Fairtrade does not explicitly ban child labor in small farm production (while it does in plantations) but aims to tackle it by improving those conditions (parental income and their vulnerability to income shocks) that are well-known deterrents to school drop-out. The Fairtrade affiliation effect has been proved to be positive and significant when farmers are brought above the luxury axiom threshold while not significant when this is not the case (Becchetti et al. 2011; Becchetti, Castriota and Michetti 2013; Becchetti, Conzo and Gianfreda 2012).

Another dimension on which Fairtrade produces significant impact is on the consumer side and in final product markets. In this respect Fairtrade is probably the most well-known example of how bottom-up action by concerned consumers who vote with their wallets triggers a new form of competition between companies which start 'retailing public goods' (Besley and Ghatak 2007).[1] A theoretical literature has modeled this emerging form of competition with horizontal or vertical differentiation duopolies where a not-for-profit entrant produces a good which incorporates socially and environmentally sustainable features for which consumers are willing to pay. The not-for-profit entrant conquers part of the market share of the profit maximizing incumbent. The optimal reaction of the latter is to compete in prices but also, under reasonable parametric conditions, in social and environmental responsibility with partial imitation. More specifically, partial 'ethical' imitation is pushed up to a point where the marginal benefit arising from reconquering the most sensitive consumers is compensated by the marginal cost of reducing the profit margin due to the partial adoption of Fairtrade practices.

These theoretical models replicate important stylized facts of competition between Fairtrade pioneers and imitating incumbents on consumer markets.[2] Several large players have, in fact, adopted partial imitation strategies after Fairtrade entries and have introduced Fairtrade criteria on a limited range of their products. The most notable examples are Nestlé and Starbucks, which started selling Fairtrade coffee, and Tesco and Sainsbury's, which converted to Fairtrade 100 per cent of bananas sold in their UK supermarkets. This move triggered further contagion and imitation with one of the main world players, Chiquita, introducing an original own standard (Rainforest Alliance) which closely resembles that of Fairtrade. Based on these summary considerations, in the following two sections we examine the impact of Fairtrade on local producers and the opportunities and threats facing producers and traders.

THE IMPACT OF FAIRTRADE ON LOCAL PRODUCERS

Quantitative Approaches and Main Concerns

Analyses of Fairtrade's impact on producers typically compares a treatment group (Fairtrade producers) with a control group (traditional producers) on the basis of the changes in income, productivity, health, child schooling and so on. In this way the impact of affiliation to Fairtrade is compared with a counterfactual scenario controlling for possible changes in the outcome variable that would have occurred if Fairtrade projects were not implemented. This approach allows the researcher to interpret the relationship between affiliation to Fairtrade and the outcome variable in a causal way from the first to the second since – apart from Fairtrade affiliation – no other observable/unobservable factors ('confounders') affect the outcome variable. However, this comparison can often lead to biased estimates because of endogeneity and selection issues. First, individuals tend to self-select into Fairtrade affiliation – and/or local Fairtrade affiliated producer organizations select their members – on the basis of unobservable factors (for instance, their intrinsic ability, motivation and trustworthiness) which are often correlated also with the outcome variable. Hence the impact of Fairtrade affiliation on income is overestimated when selection is not properly taken into account. Second, since most Fairtrade projects worldwide have already been set up, it is difficult to run counterfactual analyses, so that the search for a proper control group (i.e., a control group mostly similar to the treatment one) often becomes a search for the Holy Grail.

A possible solution to the first problem is the implementation of randomized control trials which – by randomizing the treatment assignment (i.e., the Fairtrade affiliation in our case) – may reduce the bias caused by selection and ensure high comparability between the treatment and control group (Duflo, Glennerster and Kremer 2008). Consequently, the observed changes in the outcome variable (before and after the treatment assignment) are not driven by unobservable confounding factors and therefore can be causally attributed to Fairtrade affiliation. However, randomization is very costly and often it does not lead to superior and endogeneity-free estimates for many practical problems (see Deaton 2009). In addition, randomization is not always free of ethical concerns mainly related to the opportunity of assisting some producers instead of others as well as to the consequent social conflicts which are likely to emerge among producers in treatment and control groups. More importantly, in many contexts Fairtrade programs are already at work and ex-ante randomization is not viable.

These contexts are suitable, instead, for quasi-experimental impact analyses which use a combination of experimental methods (i.e., a comparison of treatment and control groups) with econometric tools (i.e., instrumental variables, propensity score matching, retrospective panel data, affiliation length analysis for the treatment sample, etc.) to address endogeneity issues and potential heterogeneity between Fairtrade affiliated and non-Fairtrade affiliated producers.[3] Since, to our knowledge, there are no empirical studies on fair trade in which randomized control trials are implemented, we describe the outcomes of Fairtrade impact evaluations based on quasi-experimental data. (See also Valerie Nelson and Adrienne Martin's chapter in this volume for mixed method studies of Fairtrade's impact in Africa.)

The Impact of Fairtrade on Economic Wellbeing

Becchetti and Costantino (2006) analyze the impact of Fairtrade on monetary and non-monetary measures of wellbeing. The authors compare Fairtrade and non-Fairtrade affiliated Kenyan farmers using a treatment regression model to control for selection into the local cooperative (Mehru Herbs). They find that Fairtrade directly contributes to the improvement of wellbeing since, relative to those not affiliated to Fairtrade, treatment group farmers spend more money for household food and show a lower probability of infant mortality. Consistently with these findings, using a panel dataset on 157 mills operating in Costa Rica, Ronchi (2006) identifies also a positive impact of Fairtrade and vertical integration on market power of affiliated producers.

Ruben, Fort and Zúñiga-Arias (2009) find the opposite in their study of the direct (income, livelihoods, welfare) and indirect (credit access, capital stocks, investments and risk preferences) effect of Fairtrade on 13 cooperatives and 700 coffee and banana producers in Peru and Costa Rica. The authors use propensity score matching to correct for self-selection of Fairtrade affiliated farmers[4] and show that Fairtrade and non-Fairtrade farmers do not significantly differ in terms of income and perceptions of past and future welfare improvements. According to the authors, the lack of a direct Fairtrade effect is the result of: 1) a substitution effect (i.e., Fairtrade farmers neglect other income-generating activities); 2) the higher costs associated with Fairtrade production; and 3) the redistribution of Fairtrade premium to a wider community. Fairtrade affiliation is shown to have a significant and positive (indirect) effect on credit access, attitudes to risks and willingness to invest, use of organic inputs, higher prices or higher producers' bargaining power also for non-Fairtrade products sold in neighboring regions and the general community wellbeing through the redistribution of the Fairtrade premium.

The Impact of Fairtrade on Price Differentials

There is a long-standing belief Fairtrade's principal benefits to producers were generated by the guaranteed minimum price. Becchetti and

Costantino (2006) show that Kenyan Fairtrade farmers are more satisfied with the price obtained than their non-Fairtrade counterparts, while positive Fairtrade price differentials (i.e., a higher price received by Fairtrade producers than the price obtained by conventional ones) have been found by Bacon (2005) among Nicaraguan small farmers, Utting (2009) among members of Nicaraguan coffee cooperatives and Gitter et al. (2012) in coffee production in Mexico. On the other hand, De Janvry, McIntosh and Sadoulet (2010) analyze the premiums paid by Fairtrade importers to a large cooperative in Central America. Using several methodologies and controls for product quality the authors find that the estimated premium is generally below that suggested by Fairtrade International. Ruben (2012) uses propensity score matching on a sample of coffee growers in Peru and finds no statistically significant differences in price received by Fairtrade versus that received by conventional producers. This is not surprising since the study was carried out in 2007, a year when the conventional market price was close to – or even higher than – the Fairtrade minimum. Since the market prices for conventional and Fairtrade products have been fairly close over recent years, benefits derived from the provision of a price premium to affiliated producers seem to weaken.

This finding is understated since the mentioned studies do not take into account the certification costs implied by the Fairtrade certification. With data on a representative sample of Mexican coffee growers, Weber (2011) finds a significant price premium for Fairtrade-organic producers and a gross income gain of 5 per cent of total household income. However, since the gain is net of the cooperative participation but not of Fairtrade certification costs, the authors conclude that 'price premiums alone have a limited potential to increase household returns from growing coffee'.

A limitation of these approaches is that the measure of the price premium is often cross-sectional while the benefit of Fairtrade price has to be evaluated in an inter-temporal perspective. More specifically, the real benefit provided by Fairtrade price policies is the insurance of an implicit floor which prevents prices from falling below a 'decent price' threshold. This produces countercyclical Fairtrade price premiums, which are significant in times of conventional market price lows, while disappearing in times of conventional market price highs. This is consistent with the evidence of no significant difference between the two prices in times of a high conventional market price found by Ruben (2012).

The Impact of Fairtrade on Productivity and Price Stabilization

Studies on the impact of Fairtrade on productivity provide mixed results. A field study on Fairtrade and organic rice in Thailand by Becchetti et al. (2011) shows that per capita income from agriculture is positively affected by organic farming and Fairtrade affiliation years. The authors exploit the different timing in the decision to affiliate to Fairtrade and to receive the organic certification to disentangle the effect of each on per capita income. Results from the Davidson and McKinnon test (1993)[5] show that the Fairtrade affiliation effect prevails on the organic farming one. However, consistently with Ruben, Fort and Zúñiga-Arias (2009), the income effect does not translate into higher productivity because of the concurrent increase in hours worked. Conversely, Becchetti and Castriota (2008) show evidence of a positive and significant impact of affiliation to Fairtrade on productivity of Chilean honey producers. Correcting for the heterogeneity between the treatment and control group through a treatment regression model and propensity score matching, the authors explain the superior productivity of the Fairtrade affiliated producers in terms of the indirect benefits they receive from exploiting the economies of scale that derive from participation in the Fairtrade cooperative activities.

The presence of a positive price premium is not, however, a necessary condition for Fairtrade to be useful. In fact, De Janvry, McIntosh and Sadoulet (2010) suggest that demand-driven over-certification and the consequent competitive pressures in Fairtrade open-access markets lower the rents associated with Fairtrade price premiums. However, the Fairtrade floor price can serve as an insurance mechanism if the prices of Fairtrade and/or organic goods are more stable than those of conventional goods. This implies that risk averse growers who are willing to pay to have stable prices/revenues would also accept potentially negative net premiums. According to this scenario, affiliation to Fairtrade can be used as an alternative mechanism to cope with crises with respect to other (more damaging) solutions like pulling children out of school to avoid expenses, migrating, increasing borrowing, substituting crops and decreasing inputs (Bacon 2005).

Evidence of Fairtrade price stabilization is provided by Calo and Wise (2005), who compare conventional and niche market coffee prices from 1998 to 2005 and find that the Fairtrade market guaranteed floor prices stabilize producers' returns with respect to market price. For this reason, Fairtrade price stabilization has a positive effect on farmers' perceived income (and, more generally) life vulnerability. For example, Bacon's findings from a 2001 field survey in northern Nicaragua show that conventional farmers are four times more likely to perceive a risk of losing the title to their land because of low coffee prices than Fairtrade members (2005).

The Impact of Fairtrade on Health, Social Capital and Child Labor

Indirect positive effects on objective wellbeing have been found with respect to health status, child labor and social capital. Exploiting the same Kenyan dataset used by Becchetti and Costantino (2006), Becchetti and Gianfreda (2008) investigate the impact of Fairtrade affiliation years on farmers' health status, controlling for selection bias with a two-stage selection model. Results document that an additional year of affiliation reduces by 1.8 per cent the probability of declaring more than 15 days lost because of illness. With respect to the positive effect of the Fairtrade affiliation length on health, Arnould, Plastina and Ball (2009) compare Fairtrade and non-Fairtrade coffee producers in Nicaragua, Peru and Guatemala in terms of reported illnesses. They do not find significant effects of Fairtrade affiliation status on a synthetic index of health conditions; however, in their estimates senior Fairtrade members (i.e., participants with at least six years in the Fairtrade affiliation) enjoy better health and are more able to receive medical treatment than short-term Fairtrade participants.

To study the impact of Fairtrade on child labor, Becchetti, Castriota and Michetti (2013) collect field data in a Chilean Fairtrade honey cooperative and, with a 'backcast panel' approach, reconstruct dynamic data from a unique cross-sectional survey. Each producer is asked to recall the number of his/her offspring, their age, the number of schooling years for each of them, the age at which each child started school and the schooling episodes of exits and re-entries (if any).[6] The authors build a yearly based panel (from 1987 to 2007) on households' schooling decisions and regress them on Fairtrade participation in fixed effect estimates, controlling also for reverse causality and endogeneity through a Generalized Method of Moments approach. The empirical evidence shows a positive and significant impact of Fairtrade affiliation years on the household schooling decision. The authors argue this is because of the higher income of affiliated producers vis-à-vis the control sample and/or the large cooperative's attention towards child schooling.

In an analogous retrospective impact analysis of organic rice producers in Thailand, Becchetti, Conzo and Gianfreda (2012) find that the probability of school enrolment is positively affected by Fairtrade affiliation years, especially in large households. Results are robust to a 3SLS (three stage least squares) estimation controlling for endogeneity in producers' choice with respect to: 1) entry to/exit from the local cooperative; 2) adoption of organic/conventional farming techniques; and 3) exploitation/non-exploitation of the Fairtrade channel. Similar results are found by Becchetti et al. (2011) in two Peruvian districts with Fairtrade handicraft-based projects where Fairtrade affiliation significantly contributes to schooling of children decision, especially when they are in the 14–18 age cohort. Consistently with the luxury axiom hypothesis, this effect is more pronounced in the district where the standards of living are higher.

In the same vein, Gitter et al. (2012) study the determinants of schooling decisions in the rural areas of the Oaxaca and Chiapas in Mexico. The authors analyze a household's decision of how to allocate an adolescent's time between schooling and coffee production using data on 845 farmers surveyed between 2005 and 2006 and stratified by Fairtrade-organic/non Fairtrade-non organic production and by migration history. Using fixed-effects and instrumental variable models the authors show that households' participation in a Fairtrade-organic cooperative contributes to a 0.7 year increase in female schooling, while results for males have an indeterminate effect. Conversely, Arnould, Plastina and Ball (2009) do not find direct effects of Fairtrade on children's educational attainment in a sample of coffee farmers in Nicaragua, Peru and Guatemala.[7] However, by estimating the joint impact of Fairtrade affiliation on child schooling and income with a two-equations system, they find that – consistently with the luxury axiom hypothesis – Fairtrade has only indirect (positive) effects on child education. In other words, the higher performance in terms of child schooling of Fairtrade members seems to be driven by the higher income Fairtrade members receive in comparison with non-Fairtrade ones.

Summarizing, empirical evidence seems to support the idea that Fairtrade may realize the goal of reducing child labor indirectly by breaking the vicious circle between the substitution axiom (child labor reduces adult wages) and luxury axioms (parents send children to school if their income is above a given threshold), as described by Basu and Van (1998). Because Fairtrade increases household income due to price premium and price stability effects, the consequent reduction of child labor in the area due to the higher income generates a positive effect on adult wages in the area. Higher wages, in turn, reinforce the Fairtrade income effect, pushing such wages farther from the luxury axiom threshold.

Fairtrade is shown to affect positively also the social capital of affiliated farmers in Kenya and, in particular, participation in elections and trust in trade unions, political parties and the government (Becchetti and Michetti 2008). Similarly, Elder, Zerriffi and Le Billon (2012) study Fairtrade's impact on social capital (measured as farmer trust and participation) using 2009 survey data from Rwandan coffee producers and controlling for membership in a cooperative organization. Regression results provide little support to the hypothesis that cooperative organization and Fairtrade certification are associated with social capital (none of them are statistically linked to perceived trust among community members), while there is a positive correlation between Fairtrade/ cooperative membership and farmers' perception of increased participation in decision-making. This last result is in line with Bassett (2010) and Utting's (2009) evidence on the positive effect of Fairtrade on women's participation in producer cooperatives.

The Impact of Fairtrade on Life Satisfaction

Some empirical evidence suggests that Fairtrade also affects subjective wellbeing. Becchetti, Costantino and Portale (2007) investigate the nexus between Fairtrade affiliation and life satisfaction of Peruvian producers and find both a direct (i.e., through Fairtrade cooperative membership) and indirect (i.e., through income) positive effect of the former on the latter, with the income effect becoming less important when living standards improve. The effect of the Fairtrade affiliation in the performance equation is purged of the effect of self-selection into cooperative membership through the estimation of a selection equation. The findings are consistent with the assumption of diminishing marginal returns of income on happiness. Fairtrade's positive impact on monetary and non-monetary wellbeing are partially in line with Bacon's impact assessment of small-scale farmer livelihoods in Nicaragua during the 1997 to 2001 coffee crisis. Bacon shows that participation in organic and Fairtrade coffee networks reduces farmers' livelihood vulnerability,[8] while the higher income received by Fairtrade producers through the price premium does not compensate the negative impact of other factors on quality of life indicators.

Before continuing, a note of caution: most articles showing positive effects of Fairtrade affiliation on wellbeing are based on field studies of farmers' cooperatives. This approach somewhat overestimates Fairtrade benefits since cooperatives redistribute profits among members. In this respect, a broad analysis including also private firms – that is, large second-level hired-labor companies acting as intermediaries between local (first-level) cooperatives and foreign importers – would be welcome additions to the current literature.

OPPORTUNITIES AND THREATS FOR PRODUCERS AND TRADERS

Pioneers and New Entrants

While rising demand for Fairtrade products is good news, it also elicits the participation of companies who aim to earn a profit or improve their image. These new entrants could have direct and indirect negative consequences on incumbent Fairtrade participants, such as increased competition in more profitable sectors and impact on the fair trade movement's reputation.

The debate about Fairtrade competition on final product markets has typically been developed on the theoretical framework of mixed oligopoly models with horizontal and vertical differentiation. Such models, originally created to analyze competition between private profit maximizing and state owned enterprises, have been extended to new forms of competition. The advantage of these models is that they may be easily adapted to the new form of competition object of our inquiry. When we reinterpret the consumer segment in terms of ethical preferences instead of geographical distance and assume heterogeneity of tastes we have a horizontal differentiation model of competition between a Fairtrade incumbent and a profit maximizing new entrant. If, on the contrary, we assume that socially and environmentally responsible product features are unanimously considered a quality improvement by all consumers, we fall into vertical differentiation models originally devised to study competition between technological innovators (Becchetti and Solferino 2011).

These simple models provide a rich theoretical framework which helps us to understand some important elements of Fairtrade competition on the final product market. They outline conditions under which partial imitation is the optimal response of a profit maximizing incumbent thereby providing evidence of the contagious effect of Fairtrade and socially responsible consumers who vote with their wallets. They also document the original feature of a duopoly, which may potentially produce more wellbeing for primary producers than a domestic benevolent planner maximizing consumers' welfare. Beyond the model's features this implies that imperfect competition between the Fairtrade value chain and traditional profit maximizing producers plays a subsidiary role partially compensating for the lack of a global benevolent planner (or global rules and institutions) that takes into account producer and consumer wellbeing.

New Entrants' Unfair Competition

Findings from this theoretical literature leave some crucial issues open to further discussion. A first threat concerns the fact that newcomers, especially large multinationals, enter the market with a clear profit target. When doing so they obviously focus on the goods that provide the higher returns, such as specialty food items, and avoid handicrafts. Incumbent fair trade importers typically use profits generated by food to cover the losses generated by handicrafts, in an effort to balance financial sustainability and social mission. In the long run this sort of 'unfair competition' by new entrants who trade only the lucrative items can force the incumbents to abandon the sale of unprofitable goods, which are often produced in very poor communities. In other words, newcomers tend to buy from those who are already empowered and require less support while abandoning producers in more difficult markets.

Building and Maintaining a Collective Reputation

Turning to the second problem, many of the theoretical models discussed above assume perfect information of consumers in the final product market. Quite to the contrary, one of the main problems of Fairtrade is that the socially and environmentally responsible features of these products are not an 'experience good' (i.e., a product feature for which asymmetric information may be progressively bridged with repeated consumption habits by consumers). In the presence of imperfect (asymmetric) information where buyers are not fully aware of the product quality, reputation and certification are key tools for increasing consumer confidence. Even though Fairtrade producers and traders actively work to build a reputation at the individual level, they do not work in isolation and reputation ends up being a sort of public good. A shared brand/certification can reduce information asymmetries, especially for small producers, when individual agents fail to establish a reputation on a stand-alone basis. Tirole (1996) models collective reputation as an aggregate of individual reputations. Reputation is history-dependent: after episodes of bad behavior, either the group is stuck in a 'bad-reputation trap' or it takes several periods to re-establish consumers' trust. In such a context the risk of members' misbehavior decreases if sustained with the threat of exclusion from the group.

Up to a certain point the growth in the number of Fairtrade producers/traders increases the buyer base which, combined with word-of-mouth phenomena, improves their visibility. However, as outlined by Kandori (1992), when members have to sustain a common rule but operate in a context where agents care only about their own interests, a higher number of community members implies less effective social norms. Similarly, in their theoretical model of collective reputation, Fishman et al. (2008) conclude that, in absence of perfect monitoring, members have an incentive to invest in the group reputation, but also an incentive to shirk on quality investments (free ride). This is especially true when the group size increases, since the benefits overcome the costs. In an empirical analysis of the Italian wine market, Castriota and Delmastro (2011) confirm these intuitions and find that the effect of group size on the collective reputation is inverse U-shaped: in the beginning reputation increases, but after a peak it starts a declining pattern.

When applying these concepts to the Fairtrade market it is natural to consider this sudden increase in the number of players (especially those profit-maximizers) as a threat. This is even more so if we consider that the controls on the local producers aimed at verifying the respect of Fairtrade criteria are carried out by the importers/partners, which generates a clear conflict of interest. The problem is most serious when inspections refer to big suppliers able to provide a large selection of products of good quality at reasonable prices due to their economies of scale. In this case the high switching costs connected with the search of a new supplier (Porter 1979) can reduce the probability of a negative evaluation even though they are weighted by the risk of loss of reputation for Fairtrade importers. Since the process of collective reputation building is asymmetric – that is, it takes a lot of time and effort to create reputation, but it is very easy and fast to destroy it – the most challenging and interesting frontier for the future is how the asymmetric information problem will be solved with different information intermediaries which operate in this sector to solve the problem (labels, standards, ethical rating agencies, etc.). A stimulating question on this issue is how technological innovations, such as cell phone apps capable of reading q-bars, will affect competition in this field. It is reasonable to anticipate that such technologies will reduce consumers' asymmetric information on ethical quality standards and further boost market growth.

Butler et al. (2013) present experimental evidence that providing an entrant with a non-zero reputation improves efficiency in trades (i.e., lower prices) and fosters investments in high-quality production. The first effect may be driven by the higher competition and complexity in the market, whereas the latter derives from the incentive for everybody in investing in reputation formation. This result can be applied to the Fairtrade market if the Fairtrade certification is accompanied by an initial endowment of 'reputation points' that can be extended or reduced according to firms/producers' behavior in the market (i.e., according to their compliance with standards). This point-based approach replicates the reputational feedback systems common in many online vendor platforms, such as Amazon or eBay.

CONCLUSIONS

Fair trade played a pioneering role in demonstrating how the bottom-up pressure of socially responsible consumers voting with their wallets can have profound effects at both ends of the value chain. The success of this idea paved the way for myriad imitation practices. Social and environmental responsibility is now an established factor of competition, consistent with the declared (and to a lesser extent demonstrated) willingness of conscious consumers to pay for ethical products. The success of Fairtrade ideas is paradoxically challenging the survival of their inventors and pioneers due to the proliferation of competitors and imitators (see Ronan Le Velly's chapter in this volume for a more detailed analysis on Fairtrade and mainstreaming).

On the product side the challenge of Fairtrade remains that of documenting whether and how Fairtrade produces significant changes in affiliated farmers' livelihoods. The literature has shown that affiliation years generally produce a significant positive effect on members' productivity, revenues, health and life satisfaction. Furthermore, when farmers are brought above the luxury axiom threshold the education level of the children of Fairtrade affiliated members increases. In this respect a principal benefit – which needs to be further explored – is the impact of long-term stable relationships with importers on subjective and objective wellbeing indicators.

On the consumer side the main challenge is how pioneers, which originated Fairtrade and are the more sincere promoters of its social goals, may differentiate from partial imitation of profit maximizing competitors. As has been widely shown, large multinationals may easily introduce in their product range some ethical products mimicking exactly Fairtrade characteristics and may even adopt social dumping strategies by selling those products at lower price as a form of marketing expenditure in their corporate social responsibility. The main competitive response of original Fairtrade pioneers is therefore that of communicating their difference in terms of 100 per cent dedicated activity. From a dynamic point of view, the tighter competition in social and environmental responsibility triggered by Fairtrade should be viewed as an important stimulus to the overall movement.

NOTES

1. See Arora and Gangopadyhay (1995) and Bagnoli and Watts (2003).
2. The EU Commission acknowledges this contagion effect in a communication to the European Parliament when it declares that 'Fairtrade has played a pioneering role in illuminating issues of responsibility and solidarity, which has impacted other operators and prompted the emergence of other sustainability regimes. Trade-related private sustainability initiatives use various social or environmental auditing standards, which have grown in number and market share' (EU Commission 2009).
3. See Imbens and Wooldridge (2009) for a detailed description of quasi-experimental methods for policy evaluation.
4. The propensity score matching consists in matching couples of treatment and control producers which are similar in terms of selected socio-demographic variables and estimating the average treatment effect of the treated in order to retrieve an unbiased measure of the specific contribution of Fairtrade affiliation on the outcome variable (for details on this approach see, among others, Dehejia and Wahba 2002).
5. In Becchetti et al. (2011), the Davidson–McKinnon (1993) approach is used to test which of the non-nested 'competing models', including either organic certification or Fairtrade affiliation years as key explanatory variables, perform best. This test is based on a comparison of two models by checking whether the predicted values from the specification with only one of the two key regressors may capture part of the variability when added to the specification in which only the other key variable is used (for further details on this method see, among others, Becchetti et al. 2011).
6. The validity of such an approach hinges on the quality of the memory effort and thus on the extent of the measurement error; both of them are plausibly lower when events are easy to recall (e.g., children's age and schooling) than when events are more complicated and require a huge memory effort (e.g., past levels of income).
7. The authors, however, do not control for non-random assignment of Fairtrade affiliation.
8. Vulnerability is measured as the perceived risk of losing the land title due to low coffee prices.

REFERENCES

Arnould, Eric J., Alejandro Plastina and Dwayne Ball (2009), 'Does Fairtrade deliver on its core value proposition? Effects on income, educational attainment, and health in three countries', *Journal of Public Policy and Marketing*, 28 (2), 186–201.

Arora, Seema and Shubhashis Gangopadyhay (1995), 'Towards a theoretical model of voluntary overcompliance', *Journal of Economic Behavior and Organization*, 28 (3), 289–309.

Bacon, Christopher (2005), 'Confronting the coffee crisis: Can Fairtrade, organic, and specialty coffees reduce small-scale farmer vulnerability in northern Nicaragua?', *World Development*, 33 (3), 497–511.

Bagnoli, Mark and Susan Watts (2003), 'Selling to socially responsible consumers: Competition and the private provision of public goods', *Journal of Economics and Management Strategy*, 12 (3), 419–445.

Bassett, Thomas J. (2010), 'Slim pickings: Fairtrade cotton in West Africa', *Geoforum*, 41 (1), 44–55.

Basu, Kaushik and Pham Hang Van (1998), 'The economics of child labor', *American Economic Review*, 88 (3), 412–427.

Becchetti, Leonardo and Stefano Castriota (2008), 'Is Fairtrade honey sweeter? An empirical analysis on the effect of affiliation on productivity', ECINEQ Working Papers No. 104, available at http://www.ecineq.org/milano/WP/ECINEQ2008-104.pdf (accessed 11 May 2014).

Becchetti, Leonardo, Stefano Castriota and Melania Michetti (2013), 'The effect of fair trade affiliation on child schooling: Evidence from a sample of Chilean honey producers', *Applied Economics*, 45 (25), 3552–3563.

Becchetti, Leonardo, Pierluigi Conzo and Giuseppina Gianfreda (2012), 'Market access, organic farming and productivity: The effects of Fairtrade affiliation on Thai farmer producer groups', *Australian Journal of Agricultural and Resource Economics*, 56 (1), 117–140.

Becchetti, Leonardo, Pierluigi Conzo, Fabio Pisani and Elisa Portale (2011), 'Does Fairtrade help to avoid poverty traps? The effect of Fairtrade on producers' income and schooling decisions', *Rivista Italiana degli Economisti*, 16 (2), 281–318.

Becchetti, Leonardo and Marco Costantino (2006), 'Fairtrade on marginalised producers: An impact analysis on Kenyan farmers', *World Development*, 36 (5), 823–842.

Becchetti, Leonardo, Marco Costantino and Elisa Portale (2007), 'Human capital, externalities and tourism: Three unexplored sides of the impact of Fairtrade affiliation on primary producers', CEIS Working Paper No. 262.

Becchetti, Leonardo and Giuseppina Gianfreda (2008), 'When consumption heals producers: The effect of Fairtrade on marginalised producers' health and productivity', ECINEQ Working Paper No. 86, available at http://www.ecineq.org/milano/WP/ECINEQ2008-86.pdf (accessed 11 May 2014).

Becchetti, Leonardo and Benjamin Huybrechts (2008), 'The dynamics of Fairtrade as a mixed-form market', *Journal of Business Ethics*, 81 (4), 733–750.

Becchetti, Leonardo and Melania Michetti (2008), 'When consumption creates social capital: Creating room for manoeuver for pro-poor policies', ECINEQ Working Paper No. 88, available at http://www.ecineq.org/milano/WP/ECINEQ2008-88.pdf (accessed 11 May 2014).

Becchetti, Leonardo and Nazaria Solferino (2011), 'What to do in globalised economies if global governance is missing? The vicarious role of competition in social responsibility', *International Review of Economics*, 58 (2), 185–211.

Besley, Timothy and Maitreesh Ghatak (2007), 'Retailing public goods: The economics of corporate social responsibility', *Journal of Public Economics*, 91 (9), 1645–1663.

Butler, Jeffrey V., Enrica Carbone, Pierluigi Conzo and Giancarlo Spagnolo (2013), 'Reputation and entry in procurement', CEPR Discussion Paper No. DP9651, available at http://papers.ssrn.com/sol3/papers.cfm?abstract_id=2326515 (accessed 11 May 2014).

Calo, Muriel and Timothy A. Wise (2005), 'Revaluing peasant coffee production: Organic and Fairtrade markets in Mexico', Medford, MA: Global Development and Environment Institute.

Castriota, Stefano and Marco Delmastro (2011), 'Inside the black box of collective reputation', working paper, available at http://econpapers.repec.org/paper/piawpaper/89_2f2011.htm (accessed 11 May 2014).

Davidson, Russell and James G. McKinnon (1993), *Estimation and Inference in Econometrics*, Oxford: Oxford University Press.

Deaton, Angus S. (2009), 'Instruments of development: Randomization in the tropics, and the search for the elusive keys to economic development', NBER Working Papers No. 14690, available at http://www.nber.org/papers/w14690 (accessed 11 May 2014).

Dehejia, Rajeev H. and Sadek Wahba (2002), 'Propensity score-matching methods for nonexperimental causal studies', *Review of Economics and Statistics*, 84 (1), 151–161.

De Janvry, Alain, Craig McIntosh and Elisabeth Sadoulet (2010), 'Fairtrade and free entry: Generating benefits in a disequilibrium market', working paper, available at https://www.aae.wisc.edu/events/papers/DeptSem/2010/mcintosh.03.01.pdf (accessed 11 May 2014).
Duflo, Esther, Rachel Glennerster and Michael Kremer (2008), 'Using randomization in development economics research: A toolkit', in Thomas Schultz and John Strauss (eds.), *Handbook of Development Economics*, Vol. 4, Amsterdam and New York: North Holland, pp. 3895–3962.
Elder, Sara D., Hisham Zerriffi and Philippe Le Billon (2012), 'Effects of Fairtrade certification on social capital: The case of Rwandan coffee producers', *World Development*, 40 (11), 2355–2367.
EU Commission (2009), 'Contributing to sustainable development: The role of fair trade and non-governmental trade-related sustainability assurance schemes', Communication from the Commission to the Council, the European Parliament and the European Economic and Social Committee, COM(2009) 215, Brussels, 5 May 2009.
Fishman, Arthur, Israel Finkelshtain, Avi Simhon and Nira Yacouel (2008), 'The economics of collective brands', Discussion Paper 14.08, The Hebrew University of Jerusalem, available at http://departments.agri.huji.ac.il/economics/en/publications/discussion_papers/2008/simhon-collective.pdf (accessed 11 May 2014).
Gitter, Seth R., Jeremy G. Weber, Bradford L. Barham, Mercedes Callenes and Jessa M. Lewis (2012), 'Fair trade-organic coffee cooperatives, migration, and secondary schooling in Southern Mexico', *Journal of Development Studies*, 48 (3), 445–463.
Imbens, Guido M. and Jeffrey M. Wooldridge (2009), 'Recent developments in the econometrics of program evaluation', *Journal of Economic Literature*, 47 (1), 5–86.
Kandori, Michihiro (1992), 'Social norms and community enforcement', *Review of Economic Studies*, 59 (1), 63–80.
Porter, Michael (1979), 'How competitive forces shape strategy', *Harvard Business Review*, 57 (2), 137–145.
Ronchi, Loraine (2006), 'Fairtrade and market failures in agricultural commodity markets', World Bank Policy Research Working Paper No. 4011, available at http://elibrary.worldbank.org/doi/book/10.1596/1813-9450-4011 (accessed 11 May 2014).
Ruben, Ruerd (2012), 'The impact of Fairtrade certification on coffee farmers in Peru', *World Development*, 40 (3), 570–582.
Ruben, Ruerd, Ricardo Fort and Guillermo Zúñiga-Arias (2009), 'Measuring the impact of Fairtrade on development', *Development in Practice*, 19 (6), 777–788.
Tirole, Jean (1996), 'A theory of collective reputations (with applications to the persistence of corruption and to firm quality)', *Review of Economic Studies*, 63 (1), 1–22.
Utting, Karla (2009), 'Assessing the impact of Fairtrade coffee: Towards an integrative framework', *Journal of Business Ethics*, 86 (S1), 127–149.
Weber, Jeremy G. (2011), 'How much more do growers receive for fair trade-organic coffee?', *Food Policy*, 36 (5), 678–685.

Index